# Tasmania

## Lyn McGaurr

## LONELY PLANET PUBLICATIONS
Melbourne • Oakland • London • Paris

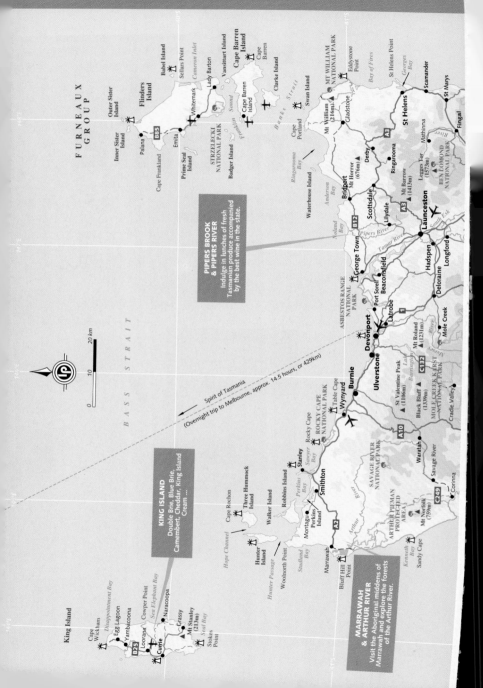

**King Island**

Cape Wickham
Disappointment Bay
Egg Lagoon
Yambacoona
Cowper Point
Sea Elephant Bay
Naracoopa
Loorana
Currie
Mt Stanley (213m)
Grassy
Stokes Point
Seal Bay
B25

**KING ISLAND**
Double Brie, Blue Brie, Camembert, Cheddar, King Island Cream ...

BASS STRAIT

Spirit of Tasmania
(Overnight trip to Melbourne, approx. 14.5 hours, or 429km)

0  10  20 km

**MARRAWAH & ARTHUR RIVER**
Visit the Aboriginal middens of Marrawah and explore the forests of the Arthur River.

Cape Rochon
Three Hummock Island
Hunter Island
Walker Island
Robbins Island
Perkins Island
Montagu
Perkins Bay
Studland Bay
Hope Channel
Hunter Passage
Woolnorth Point
Marrawah
Bluff Hill Point
Arthur River
A2
ARTHUR PIEMAN PROTECTED AREA
Mt Norfolk (759m)
Kenneth Bay
Sandy Cape
C249
Corinna
Savage River
SAVAGE RIVER NATIONAL PARK
Waratah
A10
Stanley
Smithton
Rocky Cape
Newpier Bay
ROCKY CAPE NATIONAL PARK
Table Cape
Wynyard
Burnie
Ulverstone
St Valentine Peak (1106m)
Black Bluff (1339m)
Cradle Valley
MOLE CREEK KARST NATIONAL PARK
C132
Mt Roland (1231m)
Mole Creek
Devonport
ASBESTOS RANGE NATIONAL PARK
Port Sorel
Latrobe
Deloraine
Longford
Hadspen
Beaconsfield
George Town
B12
Pipers River
Tamar River
Launceston
A3
Mt Barrow (1413m)
Legges Tor (1573m)
BEN LOMOND NATIONAL PARK
Lilydale
Scottsdale
Bridport
Mt Horror (674m)
Derby
Ringarooma
Anderson Bay
Ringarooma Bay
Mt William (216m)
MT WILLIAM NATIONAL PARK
Gladstone
Eddystone Point
Bay of Fires
St Helens
St Helens Point
Georges Bay
Scamander
St Marys
Mathinna
Fingal
Esk River
South Esk
Mersey River
Noland Bay

**PIPERS BROOK & PIPERS RIVER**
Indulge in lunches of fresh Tasmanian produce accompanied by the best wine in the state.

FURNEAUX GROUP

Cape Wickham
Outer Sister Island
Inner Sister Island
Palana
Emita
Cape Frankland
Prime Seal Island
B85
Flinders Island
Whitemark
Babel Island
Sellars Point
Cameron Inlet
Lady Barton
Vansittart Island
STRZELECKI NATIONAL PARK
Badger Island
Franklin Sound
Cape Barren Island
Cape Barren
Clarke Island
Banks Strait
Swan Island
Cape Portland
Waterhouse Island
Anderson Bay

**THE OVERLAND TRACK**
Australia's most famous bushwalk has serene glacial lakes and windswept plains.

**STRAHAN**
Enjoy river cruises and scenic flights in this charming seaside town.

**SALAMANCA PLACE**
These 1830s sandstone dockside warehouses are brimming with cafes, arts and crafts shops and restaurants and are host to the lively Salamanca Market.

**FREYCINET PENINSULA**
With beautiful views of Wineglass Bay, the peninsula offers some of the best ocean kayaking and abseiling in the state.

**Elevation**
1500m
1000m
500m
200m
0m

DOUGLAS APSLEY NATIONAL PARK
FREYCINET NATIONAL PARK
Bicheno
Friendly Beaches
Coles Bay
Schouten Island
Moulting Lagoon
Great Oyster Bay
Mercury Passage
Cape Boullanger
MARIA ISLAND NATIONAL PARK
Cape Peron
Blackman Bay
Pirates Bay
Forestier Peninsula
TASMAN NATIONAL PARK
Tasman Peninsula
Cape Pillar
Tasman Island

Campbell Town
Swansea
Lake Leake
Ross
River
Macquarie
Poatina
Millers Bluff (1210m)
Mt Franklin (1102m)
Oatlands
Lake Sorell
Lake Crescent
Melton Mowbray
Triabunna
A3
Sorell
A9
Lauderdale
Port Arthur

Breona
Miena
Lake Echo
Woods Lake
Bothwell
Table Mountain (1095m)
Black Bluff (773m)
Hamilton
Westerway
New Norfolk
Bridgewater
HOBART
Kettering
Alonnah
Bruny Island
SOUTH BRUNY NATIONAL PARK
Tasman Head
Adventure Bay
Storm Bay
B68
A6
D'Entrecasteaux Channel

Rosebery
Cradle Mountain (1545m)
WALLS OF JERUSALEM NATIONAL PARK
CRADLE MOUNTAIN-LAKE ST CLAIR NATIONAL PARK
Lake Mackintosh
Lake St Clair
Mt Olympus (1449m)
Derwent Bridge
A10
Tarraleah
Bradys Lake
MT FIELD NATIONAL PARK
Mt Field West (1439m)
Strathgordon
B61
Huonville
Geeveston
Hartz Peak (1255m)
Federation Peak (1224m)
HARTZ MOUNTAINS NATIONAL PARK
Southport
New River Lagoon
South East Cape

Zeehan
Mt Sedgwick (1114m)
Queenstown
Strahan
Mt Sorell (1144m)
Macquarie Harbour
Cape Sorell
FRANKLIN-GORDON WILD RIVERS NATIONAL PARK
Lake Burbury
Lake King William
Lake Gordon
Lake Pedder
SOUTHWEST NATIONAL PARK
Mt Rugby (771m)
Bathurst Harbour
Maatsuyker Group
Prion Bay
Trial Harbour
Point Hibbs
High Rocky Point
Low Rocky Point
Elliott Bay
Wreck Bay
South West Cape
Port Davey
Hilliard Head

TASMAN SEA
To Macquarie Island (1500km)
SOUTHERN OCEAN

**Tasmania**
**2nd edition** – August 1999
**First published** – September 1996

**Published by**
**Lonely Planet Publications Pty Ltd**  ABN 36 005 607 983
90 Maribyrnong St, Footscray, Victoria 3011, Australia

**Lonely Planet Offices**
**Australia** Locked Bag 1, Footscray, Victoria 3011
**USA** 150 Linden St, Oakland, CA 94607
**UK** 10a Spring Place, London NW5 3BH
**France** 1 rue du Dahomey, 75011 Paris

**Photographs**
All of the images in this guide are available for licensing from
Lonely Planet Images.
email: lpi@lonelyplanet.com.au
Web site: www.lonelyplanetimages.com

**Front cover photograph**
King crab sunbathing on Boat Harbour Beach, North-West Tasmania
(photograph by John Hay)

ISBN 0 86442 727 1

Printed by The Bookmaker International Ltd
Printed in China

Although the authors
and Lonely Planet try
to make the informa-
tion as accurate as
possible, we accept
no responsibility for
any loss, injury or
inconvenience sus-
tained by anyone
using this book.

# Contents – Text

## THE NORTH                                                      226

## THE NORTH-WEST                                                 259

## THE WEST                                                       280

## MT FIELD & THE SOUTH-WEST                                      308

## THE ISLANDS                                                    317

## INDEX                                                          332

## MAP LEGEND                                                back page

## METRIC CONVERSION                                 inside back cover

# Contents – Maps

# MAP INDEX

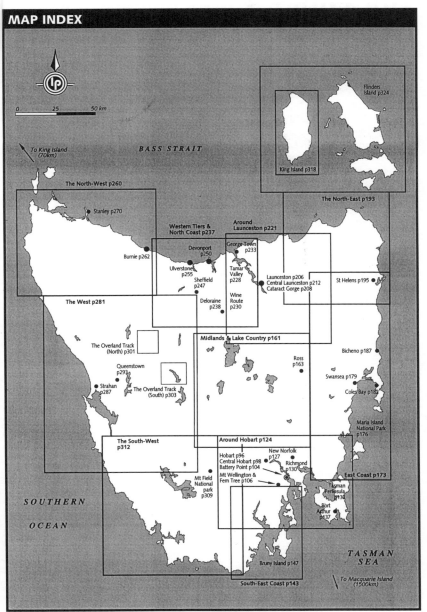

0    25    50 km

# The Author

## Lyn McGaurr

Before joining Lonely Planet as an in-house editor in 1988, Lyn worked as a current affairs TV researcher and trainee reporter at the ABC in Hobart, as a sub-editor on a national magazine in Melbourne and as a research assistant and information officer for the Commonwealth government. In 1997, she spent a fascinating six months at the Antarctic CRC in Hobart, before returning to editing in 1998 and taking on the update of the *Tasmania* guide. Lyn has lived in Hobart on two occasions, for a total of 11 years, and has worked as a freelance editor for Lonely Planet since the birth of her first child in 1990. She has three children.

## From the Author

Many thanks to Hugh Sibly for walking the Overland Track in perfect weather for this edition. Thanks also to Kathy Chisholm for accompanying him and proving that a 32-year-old mother of two with no previous overnight bushwalking experience can walk the track in four days and still have the energy to write about the toilets. And finally, thanks to Lonely Planet author Graeme Cornwallis, who walked the track independently a few weeks later in dreadful weather, thereby confirming that conditions are unpredictable, even in high summer. Graeme spent longer on the track than Hugh and Kathy, and so had some useful information to offer about side trips and socialising. (But the thing he really wanted to talk about was the mud!)

Staff at visitors' centres around the state and hosts at innumerable hotels, hostels and B&Bs provided invaluable information. Others without whom this edition would not have been possible are Jayne Balmer and Nigel Ricketts at the Parks & Wildlife Service, Ashley Fuller at the Resource, Planning & Development Commission, the guys at the Bicheno visitors' centre, the staff at the Hobart visitors' centre, David Machin at the YHA office in Hobart and Kathy Van Dullemen at the Cradle Mountain visitors' centre.

Finally, those to whom I am especially indebted are Jeanette and Darcy McGaurr, for everything; Kathy Chisholm again, this time for her good sense; Ted McDonald for his home brew; Martin Ross for the cafés; Nathaniel Lee Bindoff, for the yarns and the boats (from ice breakers to nesting dinghies); Ruth and David Hardy, for their Canadian clarity; and, at Lonely Planet, editor Martine Lleonart, senior editor Mary Neighbour and author Tom Smallman, for all their kindness, advice and support.

# This Book

The 1st edition of this book was written by John and Monica Chapman. This 2nd edition was updated by Lyn McGaurr.

## From the Publisher

This edition of *Tasmania* was produced in Lonely Planet's Melbourne office. Martine Lleonart coordinated the editing with assistance from Sally O'Brien, Kristin Odijk and Errol Hunt, who assisted with proofreading. Pablo Gastar coordinated the mapping and design with assistance from Jenny Jones and Kusnandar. The illustrations were drawn by Martin Harris, and Jamieson Gross designed the cover. Mary Neighbour, Jane Hart and Glenn Beanland provided advice and assistance and Tim Uden helped with layout.

## Thanks

Many thanks to the travellers who used the last edition and wrote to us with helpful hints, useful advice and interesting anecdotes:

Tina & Rasi, Karen & David Berton, Johan G Borchert, James Boyce, Tasha Bray, Jeff Broadhurst, Kate van den Broek, Ann Brown, Mark Bruce, Lynda Burek, W J Carter, J Chan, Amy Chan, John Chaplin, Michael Chittick, Michael & Patricia Clarke, Len Cook, Vicki Cowles, Michael Cummins, Richard Denham, Leonhard Dietze, Laurie Dillon, Marjilke van Duin, Jim Duncan, Hannah Dunleavy, Susie Dunlop, Jerry & Carolyn Farmer, Serge Ferrier, Claudia Frosch, Tony Gerber, David Greilach, Mardi Grimshaw, Dennis Gullan, Nick Hardy, Andrew Hazel, Gabi Hilgner, Theresa Hill, Susan Hood, Jan Hyde, Greg James, Paul Keen, Alistair Kelly, Alexandra King, Richard & Suzy Lenne, S Lenne, Kathryn Lockrey, Margery Maconacky, Nigel Marsden, Alan & Shirley Martin, Karen McIvor, Erica V Merritt, Lorraine Miloro, Christine Moran, Laura Murphy, Marcus Ogden, L Paynes, Jane Penton, Brian Rawding, Dirk Reiser, Stuart Reynolds, William Richards, Hans Rolfsmeier, Rita & Erik Ronning, T Schamm, Brad Shade, Desmona Sheridan, Caroline Smith, Egbert Stams, Joel Stettner, Julie Taylor, Joe Varrasso, Rudiger Voberg, Stan Walerczyk, Fiona Wallace, Fran Wells, Anna Wilde, Vikki Williams, D & P Williams, Petra Wink, A Wright, Ben Wright, Cheryl Wright.

# Foreword

## ABOUT LONELY PLANET GUIDEBOOKS

The story begins with a classic travel adventure: Tony and Maureen Wheeler's 1972 journey across Europe and Asia to Australia. Useful information about the overland trail did not exist at that time, so Tony and Maureen published the first Lonely Planet guidebook to meet a growing need.

From a kitchen table, then from a tiny office in Melbourne (Australia), Lonely Planet has become the largest independent travel publisher in the world, an international company with offices in Melbourne, Oakland (USA), London (UK) and Paris (France).

Today Lonely Planet guidebooks cover the globe. There is an ever-growing list of books and there's information in a variety of forms and media. Some things haven't changed. The main aim is still to help make it possible for adventurous travellers to get out there – to explore and better understand the world.

At Lonely Planet we believe travellers can make a positive contribution to the countries they visit – if they respect their host communities and spend their money wisely. Since 1986 a percentage of the income from each book has been donated to aid projects and human rights campaigns.

**Updates** Lonely Planet thoroughly updates each guidebook as often as possible. This usually means there are around two years between editions, although for more unusual or more stable destinations the gap can be longer. Check the imprint page (following the colour map at the beginning of the book) for publication dates.

Between editions up-to-date information is available in two free newsletters – the paper *Planet Talk* and email *Comet* (to subscribe, contact any Lonely Planet office) – and on our Web site at www.lonelyplanet.com. The *Upgrades* section of the Web site covers a number of important and volatile destinations and is regularly updated by Lonely Planet authors. *Scoop* covers news and current affairs relevant to travellers. And, lastly, the *Thorn Tree* bulletin board and *Postcards* section of the site carry unverified, but fascinating, reports from travellers.

**Correspondence** The process of creating new editions begins with the letters, postcards and emails received from travellers. This correspondence often includes suggestions, criticisms and comments about the current editions. Interesting excerpts are immediately passed on via newsletters and the Web site, and everything goes to our authors to be verified when they're researching on the road. We're keen to get more feedback from organisations or individuals who represent communities visited by travellers.

Lonely Planet gathers information for everyone who's curious about the planet – and especially for those who explore it first-hand. Through guidebooks, phrasebooks, activity guides, maps, literature, newsletters, image library, TV series and Web site we act as an information exchange for a worldwide community of travellers.

**Research** Authors aim to gather sufficient practical information to enable travellers to make informed choices and to make the mechanics of a journey run smoothly. They also research historical and cultural background to help enrich the travel experience and allow travellers to understand and respond appropriately to cultural and environmental issues.

Authors don't stay in every hotel because that would mean spending a couple of months in each medium-sized city and, no, they don't eat at every restaurant because that would mean stretching belts beyond capacity. They do visit hotels and restaurants to check standards and prices, but feedback based on readers' direct experiences can be very helpful.

Many of our authors work undercover, others aren't so secretive. None of them accept freebies in exchange for positive write-ups. And none of our guidebooks contain any advertising.

**Production** Authors submit their raw manuscripts and maps to offices in Australia, USA, UK or France. Editors and cartographers – all experienced travellers themselves – then begin the process of assembling the pieces. When the book finally hits the shops, some things are already out of date, we start getting feedback from readers and the process begins again ...

## WARNING & REQUEST

Things change – prices go up, schedules change, good places go bad and bad places go bankrupt – nothing stays the same. So, if you find things better or worse, recently opened or long since closed, please tell us and help make the next edition even more accurate and useful. We genuinely value all the feedback we receive. A well travelled team that reads and acknowledges every letter, postcard and email and ensures that every morsel of information finds its way to the appropriate authors, editors and cartographers for verification.

Everyone who writes to us will find their name in the next edition of the appropriate guidebook. They will also receive the latest issue of *Planet Talk*, our quarterly printed newsletter, or *Comet*, our monthly email newsletter. Subscriptions to both newsletters are free. The very best contributions will be rewarded with a free guidebook.

Excerpts from your correspondence may appear in new editions of Lonely Planet guidebooks, the Lonely Planet Web site, *Planet Talk* or *Comet*, so please let us know if you *don't* want your letter published or your name acknowledged.

Send all correspondence to the Lonely Planet office closest to you:

**Australia:** Locked Bag 1, Footscray, Victoria 3011
**USA:** 150 Linden St, Oakland, CA 94607
**UK:** 10A Spring Place, London NW5 3BH
**France:** 1 rue du Dahomey, 75011 Paris

Or email us at: talk2us@lonelyplanet.com.au

**For news, views and updates see our Web site: www.lonelyplanet.com**

## HOW TO USE A LONELY PLANET GUIDEBOOK

The best way to use a Lonely Planet guidebook is any way you choose. At Lonely Planet we believe the most memorable travel experiences are often those that are unexpected, and the finest discoveries are those you make yourself. Guidebooks are not intended to be used as if they provide a detailed set of infallible instructions!

**Contents** All Lonely Planet guidebooks follow roughly the same format. The Facts about the Destination chapters or sections give background information ranging from history to weather. Facts for the Visitor gives practical information on issues like visas and health. Getting There & Away gives a brief starting point for researching travel to and from the destination. Getting Around gives an overview of the transport options when you arrive.

The peculiar demands of each destination determine how subsequent chapters are broken up, but some things remain constant. We always start with background, then proceed to sights, places to stay, places to eat, entertainment, getting there and away, and getting around information – in that order.

**Heading Hierarchy** Lonely Planet headings are used in a strict hierarchical structure that can be visualised as a set of Russian dolls. Each heading (and its following text) is encompassed by any preceding heading that is higher on the hierarchical ladder.

**Entry Points** We do not assume guidebooks will be read from beginning to end, but that people will dip into them. The traditional entry points are the list of contents and the index. In addition, however, some books have a complete list of maps and an index map illustrating map coverage.

There may also be a colour map that shows highlights. These highlights are dealt with in greater detail in the Facts for the Visitor chapter, along with planning questions and suggested itineraries. Each chapter covering a geographical region usually begins with a locator map and another list of highlights. Once you find something of interest in a list of highlights, turn to the index.

**Maps** Maps play a crucial role in Lonely Planet guidebooks and include a huge amount of information. A legend is printed on the back page. We seek to have complete consistency between maps and text, and to have every important place in the text captured on a map. Map key numbers usually start in the top left corner.

Although inclusion in a guidebook usually implies a recommendation we cannot list every good place. Exclusion does not necessarily imply criticism. In fact there are a number of reasons why we might exclude a place – sometimes it is simply inappropriate to encourage an influx of travellers.

# Introduction

Tasmania is Australia's smallest state, and the only island state. Usually referred to by Australians as 'Tassie', it is a place of great contrasts – of wild ocean beaches and thick rainforests, rugged mountain ranges and delicate alpine moorlands.

The state was originally known as Van Diemen's Land, and became notorious as a British penal colony during the mid-19th century. Reminders of its convict heritage can be seen in the ruins of the penal settlement at Port Arthur, the many convict-built bridges, and the beautifully preserved Georgian sandstone buildings in more than 20 historic towns.

Tasmania's pristine wilderness areas are also known worldwide. The battles for the conservation of wilderness areas and wild rivers have attracted international attention and many visitors come to see these beautiful areas. About one quarter of Tasmania is contained in national parks, and most of this – about 20% of the state – has World Heritage status.

The beaches on the east coast of Tasmania offer a diversity of water sports. In the north, there are wineries, patchwork hillsides and magnificent coastal scenery (especially around Stanley and Table Cape). Over in the west, the lunar landscape of Queenstown provides a stark contrast to the tall rainforests of the Gordon River. Also in the west is the world-famous Cradle Mountain, and walks (even short ones) in this area are a must.

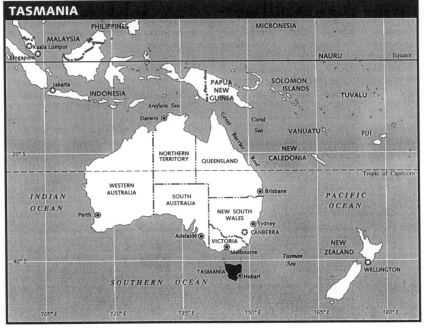

Hobart, Tasmania's capital, has historic buildings, a lively market and a magnificent waterfront. The Tasman Peninsula has spectacular sea cliffs, which tower some 300m above the ocean. South of Hobart, in the Huon Valley, are some culinary surprises: good food at reasonable prices in an area not often discovered by visitors. Farther south are beaches and more rugged coastline.

Tasmania has something for everyone.

# Facts about Tasmania

## HISTORY
### Aboriginal People

Since European settlement, the story of Australia's Aborigines has been an unhappy one, and nowhere has it been more tragic than in Tasmania. Here the Aborigines were removed so quickly that almost nothing of their history, culture or language was recorded. Slowly, however, pieces of their history are being discovered in various caves and other sites around the state. Among these finds are early rock paintings in caves, carvings on rocky outcrops, middens that are the remains of meals, and quarries where stone tools were created.

Tasmania was settled by Aborigines at least 40,000 years ago, when they probably migrated across the land bridge that joined Tasmania to the rest of Australia. The sea level was much lower then, and the Tasmanian climate was much drier and colder. The Aborigines at that stage seem to have settled the western side of the state, where extensive grasslands supported the animals they hunted. The eastern half of the state was probably too barren and dry for settlement.

When the last ice age ended and the glaciers retreated, sea levels rose, and between 12,000 and 10,000 years ago, Tasmania became separated from mainland Australia. From that time on, the culture of the Tasmanian Aborigines diverged from that of their mainland counterparts. While the mainland people developed more specialised tools for hunting, such as boomerangs and spear-throwing holders, the Tasmanian people continued to use simpler tools, such as ordinary spears, wooden waddies and stones.

As the climate changed, the vegetation in the western half of the state altered, enabling tall forests to become established, while in the east rainfall increased and extensive grasslands developed. Most of the Aborigines abandoned their caves and shelters and followed the animals they hunted to the more open eastern side of the state. Those who did remain in the west lived primarily on the coast.

Tasmanian Aborigines lived by hunting, fishing and gathering, and sheltered in bark lean-tos. Despite the island's cold weather, they went naked apart from a coating of grease and charcoal. Their society was based on sharing and exchange. It is estimated that there were between 5000 and 10,000 Aborigines in Tasmania when white people arrived.

Europeans began settling Tasmania in 1803. Finding the land fertile, they soon started fencing it to make farms, preferring the same areas as the Aborigines. In such circumstances, conflict was inevitable, and by the 1820s killing on both sides had escalated to such an extent that the period became known as the Black War. The Aborigines speared shepherds and their stock and, in turn, were hunted and shot. Europeans abducted Aboriginal children to use as forced labour, raped and tortured Aboriginal women, gave poisoned flour to friendly tribes, and lay steel traps in the bush.

In 1828 martial law was proclaimed by Lieutenant-Governor Arthur in the island's central districts, giving soldiers the right to arrest or shoot on sight any Aboriginal person found in an area of European settlement. Finally, in 1830, in an attempt to flush out all Aborigines and corner them on the Tasman Peninsula, a human chain of approximately 2000 people, known as the Black Line, was formed by settlers, convicts and troopers, and this moved for three weeks through the settled areas of the state. Ultimately unsuccessful (only two Aborigines were captured) it disturbed the Aborigines so much that soon afterwards many gave themselves up.

At about the time of the Black Line, Lieutenant-Governor Arthur gave missionary George Robinson permission to run an expedition to 'conciliate' the remaining

Aborigines. During the next three years, Robinson travelled over most of the state and collected virtually all the Aborigines in mainland Tasmania, taking them to a succession of settlements in the Furneaux Islands. Although he believed in using peaceful means to encourage the Aborigines to join him, in his later journeys he resorted to force to capture the western Aborigines, whose society was still relatively intact. It was his belief that his actions were ultimately in the best interests of these people, yet even as he was mounting his final expeditions, Europeans were virtually abandoning the west coast, and historian Lyndall Ryan argues in *The Aboriginal Tasmanians* that 'the western Aborigines would probably have survived if Robinson had not captured them'.

Some historians argue that the Aborigines who had been captured or had surrendered were placated and enticed to the Furneaux Islands by a verbal treaty that they believed promised them sanctuary and the trusteeship of land. Instead, upon their arrival they were subjected to European attempts to 'civilise' and 'Christianise' them and made to work for the government. After enduring a number of moves, they were finally settled at Wybalenna on Flinders Island, where at last they briefly enjoyed a reasonable standard of living. All too soon, however, they came to be regarded as mere pensioners, to be supported as cheaply as possible. With nothing to do but exist, most of them died of despair, homesickness, poor food or respiratory disease.

In 1846 the few who remained petitioned Queen Victoria complaining of their treatment. The following year, they were transferred to mainland Tasmania. Of the 135 who had been sent to Flinders Island, only 47 survived to make the journey to Oyster Cove south of Hobart. Yet even here they continued to be neglected. Provided with inadequate rations and restricted to such an extent that they could not follow their traditional way of life, the entire population of Aborigines at Oyster Cove perished within 32 years.

Until quite recently, it was widely accepted that Truganini, the last of the Oyster Cove

## Truganini

Truganini was one of the last surviving full-blooded Tasmanian Aboriginals. She was born on Bruny Island in 1812 as a daughter of Mangana, the chief of the Nuenanne tribe. She left her island home to travel with GA Robinson on his mission to round up the remaining Aboriginal people and twice saved his life. Robinson was one of the few Europeans who tried to befriend the Aboriginal people and had lived with them on Bruny Island. The remainder of Truganini's life was spent on Flinders Island and then at Oyster Cove, near Hobart.

Truganini died on 8 May 1876, and with her went the last opportunity for Europeans to receive eyewitness accounts about the life of her people. For many years her skeleton was displayed as a public exhibit in Hobart. One hundred years after her death, her wishes were granted when her ashes were finally scattered in the channel beside her beloved Bruny Island.

GOVERNOR DAVEY'S
PROCLAMATION
TO THE ABORIGINES
1816.

This document reads: 'Why Massa Gubernor', said Black Jack — 'You Proflamation all gammon' 'How blackfellow read him eh? He no learn him read book' 'Read that then' said the Governor, pointing to a picture.

group, was also the last full-blooded Tasmanian Aboriginal person. It is claimed that there is now evidence, however, that she may have been outlived by two other full-blooded Tasmanian Aboriginal women taken separately to Kangaroo Island in South Australia.

**Furneaux Islands** European sealers had been working in Bass Strait since 1798, and although they occasionally raided tribes along the coast, on the whole their contact with the Aborigines was based on trade. Aboriginal women were traded or stolen in raids, and many sealers settled on the Bass Strait islands with these women and raised families. Many other women were kidnapped, raped and murdered.

By 1850 a new Aboriginal community, with a lifestyle based mainly on European ways, had emerged in the Furneaux Group of islands, saving the Tasmanian Aborigines from total extinction. Most of these people lived on Cape Barren Island and were initially treated as slaves. They survived as peasant farmers, however, and soon came to be regarded with some respect by their white Australian neighbours.

The 20th century brought new technology to farming, and white Australians on the islands began to prosper. Islanders of Aboriginal descent, however, generally did not share in this wealth, and the economic inequality that resulted led to the communities growing apart. As a consequence, islanders of Aboriginal descent now align themselves more closely with the wider Australian Aboriginal community, with whom they feel they share similar inequities.

**Today** Today, Aborigines throughout Australia are claiming rights to land and compensation for past injustices, and the Tasmanian group is no exception. Increasing awareness of the plight of Aborigines by white Australia has resulted in the recognition of native title to land, and in 1995 the Tasmanian government returned 12 sites, including Oyster Cove, to the Tasmanian Aboriginal community. There is, however, still much to be reconciled.

## European Discovery
The first European to see Tasmania was the famous Dutch navigator Abel Tasman, who arrived in 1642 and called it Van Diemen's Land, after the governor of the Dutch East Indies. Between 1770 and 1790, Tasmania was sighted and visited by a series of famous European sailors, including captains Tobias Furneaux, James Cook and William Bligh. They all visited Adventure Bay on Bruny Island and believed it to be part of the Australian mainland rather than an island off Van Diemen's Land. In 1792 Admiral Bruni D'Entrecasteaux explored the

Abel Tasman

south-eastern coastline more thoroughly, mapping and naming many of its features. Most major landmarks still bear names from this expedition.

European contact with the Tasmanian coast became more frequent after the soldiers and convicts of the First Fleet settled at Sydney Cove in 1788, mainly because ships heading to the colony of New South Wales (NSW) from the west had to sail around the island.

In 1798 Lieutenant Matthew Flinders circumnavigated Van Diemen's Land and proved that it was an island. He named the rough stretch of sea between the island and the mainland Bass Strait, after George Bass, the ship's surgeon. The discovery of Bass Strait shortened the journey to Sydney from India or the Cape of Good Hope by a week.

## Founding of Hobart

In the late 1790s, Governor King of NSW decided to establish a second settlement in Australia, south of Sydney Cove. Port Phillip Bay in Victoria was initially considered, but this proposal was rejected due to a lack of water on the Mornington Peninsula; so, in 1803, Risdon Cove in Tasmania was chosen for settlement. One year later, the settlement was moved to the present site of Hobart. The threat of other nations gaining a foothold by starting settlements prompted more expansion, and later in 1804 the first settlement on the Tamar River was established, at George Town.

## Convicts

Although convicts were sent out with the first settlers, penal colonies were not built until later, when free settlers demanded to be separated from convicts. The initial penal colony was established in 1822 in as far away and inhospitable a place as possible, Macquarie Harbour. The actual site was on the small Sarah Island and the prisoners who were sent there were those who had committed further crimes after their arrival in Australia. Their punishment was hard, manual labour, cutting down Huon pines in the rainforest. It is believed that so dreadful were the conditions here that some prisoners actually murdered in cold blood in order to be sent to Hobart for trial and execution.

The number of prisoners being sent to Van Diemen's Land increased, and in 1825 – the year the island was constituted a colony independent of NSW – another penal settlement was established, on Maria Island. Here prisoners were treated more humanely. In 1830, a third penal colony was established, this time at Port Arthur. Shortly after its construction, the other two penal colonies

Hand cuffs and leg fetters were commonly used during the convict era.

were closed – Maria Island in 1832 and Macquarie Harbour in 1833.

The site of each of these colonies had been chosen because it was naturally escape-proof. Punishments meted out to convicts at Port Arthur included weeks of solitary confinement, sometimes in total darkness and silence, while the worst of prisoners were sent to work in the coal mines of nearby Saltwater River, where they were housed in miserably damp underground cells.

In 1840, convict transportation to NSW ceased, resulting in an increase in the number of people being sent to Van Diemen's Land and leading to a peak of 5329 new arrivals in 1842. In 1844 control of the Norfolk Island penal settlement was transferred from NSW to Van Diemen's Land, and by 1848 the colony was the only place in the British Empire to which convicts were still being transported.

Much opposition to the transportation of convicts came from free settlers, and in 1850 they formed the Anti-Transportation League to lobby for change. The last convicts transported to the colony arrived in 1853.

Van Diemen's Land had been the most feared destination for British prisoners for more than three decades. During those years, a total of 74,000 convicts had been transported to the island. The majority of them had served out their sentences and settled in the colony, yet so terrible was its reputation that in 1856, the year it achieved responsible self-government, it changed its name to Tasmania in an attempt to divorce itself once and for all from the horrors of its past.

## Exploration & Expansion

After Hobart and George Town were established, they attracted new settlers, resulting in demand for more land. Initially the spread was along the southern coast towards Port Arthur (Richmond and Sorell), along the east coast and around the Launceston area. By 1807 an overland route from Hobart to Launceston had been discovered. The earliest buildings were rough timber huts, but as towns developed, settlers with stone masonry skills arrived. Stone was readily available, and many of the early stone buildings have survived.

The big unknown was the rugged hinterland, where difficult, mountainous country barred the way. The first Europeans to cross the island were escapees from Macquarie Harbour; many escaped but only a few survived the journey across to Hobart Town. A significant early explorer was George Robinson, who in 1830 set out on his historic journey to placate and capture the Aborigines and so became the first European to walk across much of the state.

In 1828 George Frankland was appointed surveyor-general of Tasmania. He was determined to map the entire state and, during the 1830s, sent many surveyors out on epic journeys, often accompanying them. By 1845, when Frankland died, most of the state was roughly mapped and known.

Building roads across the mountainous west was difficult, and many were surveyed across all sorts of difficult country before being abandoned. Finally, in 1932, the Lyell Hwy from Hobart to Queenstown was opened, linking the west coast to Hobart.

## Mining

In the 1870s gold was discovered near the Tamar River and tin was found in the northeast. These discoveries prompted rushes, with prospectors coming from around the world. In the north-east a number of Chinese miners arrived and brought their culture with them. Mining was a tough and dangerous way of life and most people did not make a fortune. The story of Tasmania's mines is similar to the stories of those elsewhere in Australia. Individual prospectors grabbed the rich, easily found surface deposits. Once these were gone, the miners formed companies and larger groups to mine the deeper deposits until eventually these either ran out or became unprofitable to work. Remains of the mine workings at Derby and Beaconsfield can still be seen today.

Once it was realised that there was mineral wealth to be found, prospectors randomly explored most of the state. On the west coast, discoveries of large deposits of silver and lead resulted in a boom in the 1880s and an associated rush at Zeehan. In fact, so rich in minerals was the area that it ultimately supported mines significant enough to create the towns of Rosebery, Tullah and Queenstown. Exploitation, however, generally went unchecked, and by the 1920s copper mining at Queenstown had gashed holes in the hills that surrounded it, while logging, pollution, fires and heavy rain had stripped the terrain of its vegetation and topsoil. Only over the past few decades has the environment begun to repair itself.

The rich belt of land from Queenstown through to the northern coast is still being mined in several places, but this is now being done with more regard for the environment, and the effects of these operations are less visible than in the past. Undoubtedly new finds will continue in this mineral-rich belt, and mining will continue to be an important industry to Tasmania. In 1998 for example, companies were investigating the feasibility of mining magnesite at two sites in the north-west. If the mines go ahead, Tasmania will become the largest producer in the world of this metal which, refined into magnesium, is being used in rapidly increasing quantities by the car industry in the production of lighter, more economical vehicles.

## Conservation Issues

Tasmania is renowned worldwide for its pristine wilderness. In the late 1960s and early 1970s, the efforts of bushwalkers and conservationists to stop Lake Pedder in the south-west from being flooded for the purposes of electricity production resulted in the formation of what is believed to be the first Green political party in the world. Although that campaign was ultimately unsuccessful, the lessons learnt during the fight were crucial in enabling a new generation of activists to plan and execute a vastly more sophisticated campaign a decade later that saved the Franklin River – one of the finest wild rivers in the world – from being flooded for similar purposes.

(For more information on these events, see the South-West chapter.)

More recently, a successful campaign in the late 1980s to prevent the construction of a new pulp mill in the north-west saw the formation of a party of Green independents led by Bob Brown and the election of five of its members to parliament. Greens held the balance of power in the Tasmanian parliament from 1989 to 1998.

### Dr Bob Brown

Bob Brown is undoubtedly the most famous figure in the conservation movement in the country. A qualified doctor, he became interested in conservation after rafting down the Franklin River in 1976. This experience changed him into a strong advocate for the wilderness. Together with friends, he made films about the Franklin and soon became a public figure.

He became the Wilderness Society's director and a leading figure in the battle to save the Franklin River. During the 1970s he stood for parliament, but was not successful. At the height of the Franklin River Blockade in 1983 he was arrested and imprisoned for protesting. In a strange turn of fate he went directly from jail to parliament because, with the resignation of Green independent Dr Norm Saunders, the seat passed to the runner-up at the previous election, who was Bob Brown.

Once he was in the state parliament he became a strong but solitary voice as an independent. He eventually formed his own political party and by 1989 his Green Independents held five of the 35 seats in parliament and had become a significant political force. After many years in the state parliament, Bob followed his mentor, Dr Norm Saunders, and stood for Federal Parliament. He just made it, winning his seat by only a handful of votes, and joined the other green independents (who weren't members of Bob's Green Party) in the Upper House of Parliament.

## GEOGRAPHY

Tasmania is the smallest of Australia's states and the only one that is an island. It's about 240km south of Victoria, across the stormy and treacherous Bass Strait. To its east is the Tasman Sea, which separates Australia and New Zealand, while to its west and south is the Southern Ocean, which separates Australia and Antarctica. It is 296km from north to south and 315km from east to west. Including its lesser islands, it has an area of 68,049 sq km.

Although its highest mountain, Mt Ossa, is only 1617m (about 5300 feet) high, much of the interior is extremely rugged. One indication of the dearth of flat land on the island is the proximity of the centres of its two largest cities, Hobart and Launceston, to extremely steep hills. The only large, relatively flat area is the broad, undulating plain extending from Launceston south towards Hobart.

The coast is beautiful, with charming coves and beaches, shallow bays and broad estuaries, the result of river valleys being flooded by rising sea levels after the last ice age. By contrast, the Central Plateau, which was covered by a single ice sheet during the last ice age, is a bleak, harsh environment unsuitable for farming; Australia's deepest natural freshwater lake, Lake St Clair, is on this plateau.

Most of the western half of the state is a maze of mountain ranges and ridges that bear signs of recent glaciation. The climate there is inhospitable, the annual rainfall is a discouraging 3m or more, and for much of the year raging seas batter the coast. Yet for decades, the cliffs, lakes, rainforests and wild rivers of that magnificent region have been among Tasmania's greatest attractions, drawing walkers, adventurers and photographers from around the world (see World Heritage Area in the 'Flora, Fauna, National Parks & Reserves' special section).

## CLIMATE

Australia's seasons are the opposite of those of the northern hemisphere: here, midsummer is in January and midwinter in July.

Tasmania is in the path of the Roaring Forties, a notorious band of wind that encircles the world and produces very changeable weather. Not surprisingly, therefore, the west and south-west are subject to strong winds and heavy rain. Nevertheless, because the state is small and an island, it enjoys a maritime climate, which means that it is rarely extremely cold or extremely hot.

The prevailing airflow is westerly, creating a rain shadow that results in the west receiving much more rain than the east: while the annual rainfall in the west is 3m or more, the east receives only about 1m. The east coast is nearly always warmer and milder than anywhere else in the state, and the Bureau of Meteorology in Tasmania (quaintly classified as the Tasmania *and*

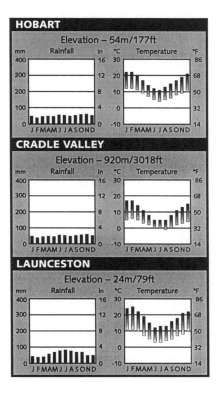

*Antarctica* Regional Office (our italics), much to the chagrin of some tourist operators, who despair at the impression of the state's climate that this gives visitors) claims that towns such as Swansea and Bicheno receive more hours of sunshine than other Australian coastal resorts. Hobart is Australia's second-driest capital after Adelaide.

Tasmania has four distinct seasons, although storms can bring wintry conditions at any time of year. In summer the days are generally warm rather than hot, while the nights are mild. This is the most pleasant time of year, and conditions often continue to improve right up until March, after which temperatures drop. The rest of autumn is generally characterised by cool, sunny days and occasional frosty nights.

Winter is wet, cold and stormy, particularly in the west. Overcast days are common in the east, despite its lower rainfall. Snow lies on the higher peaks but is usually not deep enough for skiing: the two ski resorts operate spasmodically.

Spring is windy. Storms still sweep the island in a winter pattern, but in between, the sun shines, and gradually warmth returns to the state. In some years, however, stormy spring weather continues well into summer.

## ECOLOGY & ENVIRONMENT

It is ironic that despite a long history of bad, and sometimes atrocious, environmental management, Tasmania is today famous for its pristine wilderness. Both the air and the water in certain parts of the state are claimed to be the purest on the planet, while its World Heritage Area, which covers approximately 20% of the island, is internationally renowned. Yet the preservation of much of what Tasmania has to be proud of in its environment has only been achieved by protracted campaigns in forests, on rivers, in the streets, in the media, in parliaments and in the courts. The fight to save Lake Pedder in the late 1960s and early 1970s was a watershed in the global history of the Green movement, while the Franklin River campaign of the early 1980s saw the conservation movement mature as a political force

and gain acceptance as a legitimate player in the policy-making process (see the History section earlier in this chapter). Recent changes to the number of state parliamentarians, however, resulted in three of the four sitting Green independents losing their seats in the 1998 election (see the Government & Politics section later in this chapter), and there are fears that the environment may suffer as a result.

## Conservation Groups

**Tasmanian Conservation Trust** The Tasmanian Conservation Trust (TCT, ☎ 6234 3552, 102 Bathurst St) is the state's peak nongovernment conservation organisation. In addition to managing its own campaigns, the TCT hosts the Tasmanian offices of two other Australian environmental organisations: the Threatened Species Network, which undertakes public education programs aimed at students, landholders and the wider community; and the Marine and Coastal Community Network, which has particular interests in the establishment of no-take marine reserves and the promotion of safe marine waste management practices.

**The Wilderness Society** The Wilderness Society in Tasmania (☎ 6234 9366, 130 Davey St) is presently attempting to ensure the preservation of three important areas: the Southern Forests, which are the tallest hardwood eucalypt forests on Earth, with specimens reaching in excess of 90m; the Tarkine Wilderness, which is 350,000 hectares of forest in the Arthur-Pieman region, including 80,000 hectares of cool-temperate rainforest (the largest single area of such forest in Australia), over 70% of which is unprotected and threatened by logging and mining; and the Great Western Tiers (also known by its Aboriginal name of Kooparoona Niara, meaning Mountain of Spirits), where long battles over the Mother Cummings Peak area have resulted, if not in the total protection of the area, then at least in the use of far more sensitive logging practices than might otherwise have been employed.

## Lake Johnston Nature Reserve

In 1987, an exceptional stand of Huon pines was discovered at Lake Johnston on Tasmania's west coast by Forestry Tasmania forester Mike Peterson. Unusually, the stand has been found to be exclusively male, which means that it must be reproducing itself vegetatively rather than sexually. Further tests have revealed very limited genetic diversity within the trees in the area, suggesting that the hundred or so existing specimens are all descended from remarkably few individuals. According to Parks and Wildlife Service (PWS) botanist Jayne Balmer (commenting on the work of former PWS botanist Alison Shapcott), all the trees in the main stand are likely to be clones of a single ancestor. This lack of diversity in the trees' DNA and the absence of females indicate that the stand is extremely old, possibly dating from the last deglaciation 10,000 years ago. As such, it is of enormous importance, both botanically and for the contribution it has made to a 5000-year record of climate change. For this reason, Lake Johnston Nature Reserve – a small area now managed by PWS – has been excised from the mining lease of which the stand was originally a part. Unfortunately, the area is so sensitive that access to it must be strictly controlled.

The Wilderness Society encourages travellers to help out in its campaigns or behind the counter in its Salamanca shop. In return, it says it will show interstate and overseas helpers some great bushwalks.

## Regional Forest Agreement

The Regional Forest Agreement (RFA), between the state and federal governments, was signed in November 1997. Essentially, it traded the complete or partial protection of forests with significant environmental and/or heritage values for guaranteed access to certain forests for commercial operators such as loggers and miners. As a result of the RFA, at the time of writing, the World Heritage Area and some national parks were being extended and two new national parks were being declared: Savage River and the Tasman.

## Marine Issues

**CCAMLR** The Hobart-based Commission for the Conservation of Antarctic Marine Living Resources (CCAMLR) meets in Hobart every spring and is responsible for managing the ecologically sustainable exploitation of the marine living resources of the Southern Ocean.

## Patagonian Toothfish & Albatrosses

One of the TCT's major concerns in recent times has been the illegal fishing of the Patagonian toothfish, a bottom-dwelling fish found around sub-Antarctic islands. The toothfish is caught on longlines that can cause the deaths of vast numbers of albatrosses, which take the baits intended for the fish and are hooked and drowned as a result. Licensed fishing boats must take measures to minimise these deaths, but pirate vessels have no interest in the fate of the albatrosses and are thought to be responsible for both the overfishing of the toothfish itself and the destruction of as many as 100,000 sea birds a year. In a remarkable display of cooperation, private fishing companies licensed to trawl for Patagonian toothfish, the Australian Antarctic Division and Environment Australia have joined forces to support the TCT in its efforts to collect and disseminate information on the illegal harvesting of the fish.

## Introduced Pests

Bass Strait is a significant obstacle to feral pests – so much so, in fact, that it was front-page news in 1998 when a single fox found its way to Tasmania aboard a container ship. Until then the state had prided itself on being entirely fox free – quite an achievement in a country where foxes pose a major threat to native fauna.

While feral dogs, goats and pigs can be found in Tasmania, they are not nearly so widespread here as on the mainland. Even rabbits, which are indeed a problem in rural areas, have had trouble penetrating the state's natural forests; this is just as well, because it appears scientists' latest weapon against the pest – calici virus – is not particularly effective in cool, wet areas.

By far the biggest threat to native wildlife in Tasmania is the cat, which has established itself throughout the state, including on the Overland Track and Macquarie Island. European carp, which are now flourishing in Lake Crescent, are a major headache for Inland Fisheries because of the impact they have on trout stocks and native fish. And the trout themselves, so prized by recreational fishers, pose a threat to such important species as Pedder galaxias (see Threatened Species in the 'Flora, Fauna, National Parks & Reserves' special section).

The European wasp is perhaps more of a nuisance than anything else, although it is a threat to native bees, which it will kill. It is disheartening to hear reports that it has been spotted even in such remote areas as the Franklin River.

The root rot *phytophthora* and weeds such as willow and gorse are the major introduced threats to Tasmanian flora: two new species of the former are thought to be responsible for the massive destruction of pencil pines near Pine Lake on the Central Plateau, which is now under quarantine.

### Energy
During the later years of 'hydro-industrialisation', energy production in Tasmania was controversial (see earlier in this section and in the History section of this chapter). Today, however, further dam building for electricity production no longer appears to be an option, and the government is looking to gas and wind generation for power.

## GOVERNMENT & POLITICS
Australia has a federal system of government with elements of both the US and Westminster systems. The federal government controls areas of national importance such as defence and foreign affairs. It collects income tax and shares a portion of this revenue with the states. The state government controls most internal affairs within the state. If there is a dispute between the two levels of government, then the high court studies the problem and the constitution and makes a ruling.

Tasmanian state elections are held every four years. The lower house is the House of Assembly, which has 25 members – five from each of the five electorates. The majority party in this house forms government, and its leader becomes premier. Members are elected by a system of proportional representation: candidates must achieve a quota of votes to gain a seat. In the past, this system resulted in smaller parties and independent candidates being well represented in parliament. However, at the 1998 election, the number of members in each electorate was reduced from seven to five; as a result, the number of votes required to meet a quota increased, and this has made it much harder for candidates who are not members of one of the two major parties to be elected. Only one of the four sitting Green Independents was re-elected in the 1998 election, which saw the government change from Liberal to Labor.

The upper house is the Legislative Council, members of which review government legislation.

## ECONOMY
Tasmania's economy is based primarily on mining and agriculture. There are only a couple of heavy industries, and they employ only a small proportion of the population. Tasmania has difficulty encouraging large industry, because the major markets are on the Australian mainland and Bass Strait is a real obstacle (and expense) to cross.

Mineral production has always been an important part of the economy, although the fortunes of particular mines have fluctuated alarmingly in recent times. The other main earner has been agricultural products and Tasmania's economy has always been affected by price trends on the competitive world market. In the 1960s Tasmania was the primary supplier of apples to Europe, but when prices plummeted the economy suffered. Farmers have learnt from experience and the state produces a diverse range of products – including cheese, pickled onions, fruit and lavender – many of which are of a very high quality.

Tasmania has some of the cleanest air and water in the world, and exports pollution-free, bottled rainwater. The clean ocean waters support a healthy fishing industry. A recently developed industry that has become a major export earner is fish farming. Atlantic Salmon from these farms is now sold around the world. Dairying is a major industry, with King Island cheese being world famous. Vegetables and potatoes are major crops in the north, with the produce being mainly sold to mainland Australia.

Tourism is another industry making a major contribution to the economy. Tasmania has come to realise it has in abundance what is now rare: huge, undeveloped areas that are wild and beautiful. The industry is dominated by many small family-style businesses that offer good value for money as well as friendly personal service.

One of the most notable Tasmanian success stories in recent years has been International Catamarans (Incat), the company that built the *Devil Cat*, which operates the car and passenger ferry service between George Town and Melbourne. However, the company has been so successful at selling its vessels lately that the Tasmania Government may have to look elsewhere for a catamaran in future. Today Incat sells its catamarans around the world. See the boxed text 'Little Devils & Great Big Cats' in the Hobart chapter.

## POPULATION & PEOPLE

Tasmania has a population of around 471,900 and was the only Australian state to record a population decrease in the 1997-98 financial year. The greater Hobart area has a population of around 200,000, while about 100,000 people live in greater Launceston.

There is some uncertainty about how many descendants of Tasmanian Aborigines are living in Tasmania: published estimates range from 6500 to 9000.

Most Tasmanians have a British background, and there are fewer non-British migrants here per head of population than in any other Australian state. Perhaps partly as a consequence, Tasmanians who live outside Hobart and Launceston can sometimes seem parochial to 'mainlanders' and other visitors. Technology and travel, however, are rapidly broadening the experiences and outlook of regional residents, while a concerted effort on the part of the government to encourage hospitality and service in the tourism industry is already having an impact, even in some of the remotest communities.

## EDUCATION

The University of Tasmania is particularly strong in the fields of geology and Antarctic science and policy; at Franklin, south of Hobart, the skills of wooden boatbuilding are taught at the highly regarded Shipwright's Point School of Wooden Boatbuilding; and at Beauty Point in the Tamar Valley near Launceston, the Australian Maritime College trains students in the techniques of fishing and navigation.

## SCIENCE

Hobart is a centre for the study of marine science, climate change, geology and Antarctic science in all its forms.

The Australian Antarctic Division has its headquarters in Kingston, just outside of Hobart; the Commonwealth Scientific and Industrial Research Organisation (CSIRO) Division of Marine Research has the office of its chief and one of its three marine laboratories in Castray Esplanade, next to Princes Wharf; and a national cooperative research centre, the Antarctic CRC, is located on the campus of the University of Tasmania. The Antarctic Division's research and resupply vessel the *Aurora Australis* and the CSIRO's research vessels the *Southern Surveyor* and the MV *Franklin* can often be seen docked at the wharfs, as can a number of international research vessels.

At the University of Tasmania is the Centre for Ore Deposit Research, a national research centre with close links to the School of Earth Sciences at the university.

# ARTS
## Aboriginal Arts & Crafts

Unfortunately, relatively little is known about the arts and culture of the Tasmanian Aborigines, which included rock engravings (petroglyphs), body decoration and possibly some bark painting. Some Aboriginal 'craft' traditions have survived and have been revitalised in recent years, notably basketry and shell necklace-making.

Tiagarra, the Tasmanian Aboriginal & Cultural Museum (☎ 6424 8250) in Devonport, was set up to preserve the art and culture of the Tasmanian Aborigines. It has artefact exhibits, a rare collection of more than 250 rock engravings, and sales of contemporary craftwork.

## Painting & Sculpture

Tasmania's art scene flourished from colonial times, particularly in the early 19th century under the governorship of Sir John Franklin and the patronage of his wife Lady Jane Franklin. One of the first artists to successfully capture the Australian landscape's distinctive forms and colours was John Glover, an English artist who migrated to Tasmania in 1830. The English sculptor Benjamin Law also arrived in Tasmania in the 1830s, and he sculpted busts of two of the last full-blood Tasmanian Aborigines, Truganini and Woureddy.

Benjamin Duterrau is best known for his somewhat coarse paintings of Tasmanian Aborigines, including *The Conciliation*, which commemorated the rounding up of the Aborigines by George Robinson. Successful convict artists included portraitists TG Wainewright (a convicted forger and reputed poisoner), Thomas Bock, and WB Gould, who executed charmingly naive still-lifes.

Hobart-born William Piguenit has been called 'the first Australian-born professional painter'. He painted romantic Tasmanian landscapes including Lake St Clair

and Lake Pedder in the 1870s, and his works were among the first exhibited by the Art Society of Tasmania, founded in 1884. Other early exhibitors were J Haughton Forrest, who painted 'chocolate-box' landscapes and maritime subjects, and Belgian-born modernist Lucien Dechaineux, who also founded the art department at Hobart Technical College.

Major mainland Australian artists who visited Tasmania for inspiration early this century included Tom Roberts, Arthur Streeton and Frederick McCubbin.

In 1938 the Tasmanian Group of Painters was founded to foster the work of local artists. Founding members included Joseph Connor, a Hobart-born landscape watercolourist who was one of the early Australian modernists. Other innovators of the time were the under-recognised women artists Edith Holmes and Dorothy Stoner.

Since the 1940s a strong landscape watercolour school has developed in Tasmania, with artists such as Max Angus and Patricia Giles among the best known.

Launceston-born artist and teacher Jack Carington Smith won Australia's coveted Archibald Prize for portraiture in 1963. Tasmanian sculptor Stephen Walker has produced many bronze works that adorn Hobart's public spaces. Renowned Australian landscape painter Lloyd Rees spent his final years living and working in Tasmania, where he was also involved in the conservation movement.

Notable contemporary artists include Bea Maddock, whose serialised images incorporate painting and photography, and Bob and Lorraine Jenyns, both sculptors and ceramicists. Since the early 1980s Tasmania's art culture has been revitalised, and the new wave includes printmaker Ray Arnold, painter David Keeling, photographer David Stephenson and video-maker Leigh Hobbs.

The Tasmanian Museum & Art Gallery (☎ 6235 0777) in Hobart has a good collection of Tasmanian colonial art, and exhibits relating to Tasmanian Aboriginal culture. Also worth visiting are the Queen

Victoria Museum & Art Gallery in Launceston and the Gallery & Arts Centre in Devonport.

## Crafts

A strong crafts movement has existed in Tasmania since the turn of the century. Studio potters Maude Poynter and Mylie Peppin were active in the 1940s, and furniture-making has been particularly important, with cedar pieces from colonial times highly prized today. Contemporary furniture designers such as Leslie Wright, John Smith, Gay Hawkes and Peter Costello are nationally recognised for their highly refined and often sculptural use of Tasmania's superb native timbers, such as Huon pine and sassafras.

The Design Centre of Tasmania (☎ 6331 5506) in Launceston displays and sells work by Tasmanian artists and craftspeople.

The galleries, shops and craft market at Salamanca Place show and sell crafts.

## Literature

Tasmania's unique culture and landscape and its tragic convict and Aboriginal history have inspired writers of both fiction and nonfiction.

Marcus Clarke, a prolific writer who was born in London but spent most of his life in Australia, visited Tasmania in the 1870s and wrote *For the Term of His Natural Life*, an epic novel about convict life.

Queensland-born poet Gwen Harwood lived in Tasmania from 1945 until her death in 1996, and much of her work, such as *The Lion's Bride* (1981) and *Bone Scan* (1988), explores the island's natural beauty and the tragic history of its Aboriginal population.

Robert Drewe's novel *The Savage Crows* (1976) also explores the oppression of Tasmanian Aborigines by the Europeans, while Hal Porter's *The Tilted Cross* (1961) is a novel set in old Hobart Town.

Christopher Koch is a Hobart-born author. His novels include *The Boys in the Island* (1958), an account of growing up in Tasmania, and *The Year of Living Dangerously* (1978), which was made into a film .

Carmel Bird, born in Launceston but now living in Melbourne, is known for the quirky black humour of her stories and novels, including *Cherry Ripe* (1985) and *The Bluebird Cafe* (1990), which is set in a fictional Tasmanian mining ghost town.

James McQueen's novels include *Hook's Mountain* (1982), which has as a subplot the struggle to save Tasmania's forests.

*Down Home: Revisiting Australia* (1988), by academic Peter Conrad, is an evocative recollection of the author's childhood in Tasmania. It describes the island's cultural isolation and the sense of displacement of its people.

Tasmanian Amanda Lohrey's novels include *Morality of Gentlemen* (1984), set against the backdrop of Tasmania's waterfront disputes, and *Camille's Bread* (1995).

Hobart author Richard Flanagan's award-winning novel *Death of a River Guide* (1995) weaves together Tasmanian history and myths in a story set on the Franklin River that makes an excellent introduction to Tasmanian history and life. More recently, his novel *The Sound of One Hand Clapping* (1997) has won a prestigious national literary award; the film of the same name has also been very well received (see the Films section of the Facts for the Visitor chapter).

In 1999 Tom Gilling released his first novel, *The Sooterkin*. The setting for the novel is Hobart Town in the early 1800s.

Tasmania has a thriving literary scene, with annual events such as the Salamanca Writers' Festival (Hobart, in August) and Tasmanian Poetry Festival (Launceston, in October) providing opportunities for discussion and readings. The Writers' Weekend is organised by the Tasmanian Writers' Centre and the University of Tasmania, in the Salamanca Arts Centre, on Salamanca Place, Hobart (☎ 6224 0029). Local writers' work is published in the literary magazine *Island*.

## Performing Arts

The Tasmanian Symphony Orchestra is highly regarded and tours nationally and internationally. It gives regular performances at Hobart's ABC Odeon and in Launceston's Princess Theatre. The Odeon is not a good venue, but a new concert hall is due to be constructed in Hobart in the near future.

Tasmania's professional contemporary dance company is Tasdance, which is based in Launceston and tours statewide and interstate. It performs dance and dance theatre, and often collaborates with artists in other fields. Another innovative company is IHOS Opera in Hobart, which is an experimental music and theatre troupe.

At the time of writing there was no professional state adult theatre company in Tasmania. The Terrapin Puppet Theatre, however, is a leading Australian contemporary performing arts company that has created puppetry productions for audiences of all ages. Its works combine a variety of theatrical styles, including object theatre, black theatre, shadow puppetry and mobile interactive performances. In recent years it has toured Hungary, Sri Lanka, Malaysia and South Korea.

# FLORA, FAUNA, NATIONAL PARKS & RESERVES

T asmania's diverse flora ranges from the dry forests of the east through the alpine moorlands of the centre, to the rainforests of the west. Many of the state's plants are unlike those found in the rest of Australia, and have ties with species that grew millions of years ago, when the southern continents were joined as Gondwanaland; similar plants are found in South America and as fossils in Antarctica.

Tasmania's fauna is not as varied as that of the rest of Australia, and it has relatively few large mammals. Its best known marsupial, the **Tasmanian tiger**, has been extinct since earlier this century, the last known specimen dying in Hobart zoo in 1936. It resembled a large dog or wolf and had dark stripes and a stiff tail. It is rumoured that tigers still exist, but despite many recent intense searches, there have been no official sightings.

**Title Page:** Wildflowers framing Cradle Mountain and Lake Dove in the Cradle Mountain-Lake St Clair National Park (photograph by SJ Cleland)

Tasmanian tiger

# FLORA

Many of Tasmania's trees are unique to the state, and its native pines are particularly distinctive. Perhaps the best known is the **Huon pine**, which can live for thousands of years (see Huon Pine later in this section), but there are other slow-growing Tasmanian pines, including **King Billy pines**, **pencil pines** and **celery-top pines**, all of which are commonly found in the higher regions and live for about 500 years.

The dominant tree of the wetter forests is **myrtle beech**, which is similar to the beeches of Europe.

One of Tasmania's many flowering trees is the **leatherwood**, which is really rather nondescript most of the year but can be positively eye-catching in season, when it is covered with a mass of white and pale pink flowers that are the source of a unique and fragrant honey highly prized by beekeepers.

While many of the eucalyptus trees in Tasmania also grow on the mainland, those in this state are often extremely tall. The **swamp gum** (*Eucalyptus regnans*, known as **mountain ash** on the mainland) grows to around 100m in height and is the

Tasmanian blue gum

Huon pine

tallest flowering plant in the world. It is readily seen in the forests of the south-east, where you will also find the state's floral emblem, the **Tasmanian blue gum**.

In autumn you might see the **deciduous beech**, the only truly deciduous native plant in Australia. It usually grows as a rather straggly bush with bright green leaves. In autumn, however, the leaves change colour, becoming golden and sometimes red, providing a bright splash of colour in the forest. The best places to look for examples of this plant are Cradle Mountain and Mt Field.

A notable component of the understorey in Tasmanian forests is the infamous **horizontal scrub** (see Horizontal Scrub later in this section), a plant that can make life hell for bushwalkers attempting to avoid established tracks. More familiar to bushwalkers, but also considerably more benign, is **buttongrass**. Growing in thick clumps up to 2m high, this unique Tasmanian grass prefers broad, swampy areas such as the many flat-bottomed valleys left by ice ages. Buttongrass plains are usually so muddy and unpleasant to walk over that in many places the Parks and Wildlife Service (PWS) has found it necessary to incorporate sections of elevated boardwalk into tracks that cross such areas, for both the comfort of the walker and the protection of the environment.

Another interesting specimen is the **cushion plant**, which is found in alpine areas and at first sight resembles a green rock. In fact, it is an extremely tough, short plant that grows into thick mats ideally suited to helping it cope with its severe living conditions.

## Huon Pine

This is perhaps the most famous of all Tasmania's native flora. The water repellent qualities of its oily yellow wood are responsible for its reputation as an exceptional boatbuilding timber, but it is also prized by furniture-makers and woodturners. Unfortunately it grows very slowly and so barely survived the massive logging that was undertaken in the early years of the colony, when its timber was at a premium for shipbuilding. Some trees remain, however, and one 2500-year-old specimen can be viewed during a cruise on the Gordon River. (See also the 'Lake Johnston Nature Reserve' boxed text.)

# King's Lomatia

This endemic Tasmanian plant, which is a member of the *Proteaceae* family and has flowers similar to those of the grevillea, only grows in the wild in one small area of the south-west World Heritage Area. Studies of the plant's chromosomes have revealed that it is incapable of reproducing sexually, which is why it must rely on sending up shoots to create new plants. Further research has shown that there is absolutely no genetic diversity within the population, which means that every King's lomatia in existence is a clone. The plant itself is now believed to be the oldest known clone in the world and is thought to have been around for at least 43,600 years.

# Horizontal Scrub

This slender plant is a feature of the undergrowth in many parts of Tasmania's south-west. It grows by sending up thin, vigorous stems whenever an opening appears in the forest canopy. The old branches soon become heavy and fall, after which they put up shoots of their own. This continual process of growth and collapse creates dense, tangled thickets that are a notorious obstacle to bushwalkers who venture off the beaten track.

There are some good examples of this plant on the nature walks in the south-west and in the Hartz Mountains. One adventurer to record his experience of horizontal scrub was Alex Sklenica, who walked from Lake Pedder to the Gordon River by way of the Olga River valley in 1959 and who described crawling on top of it like a monkey, bending tea trees down over it to cushion his hands and knees, and occasionally even slipping down into it a couple of feet under the weight of his pack.

# FAUNA

The distinctive mammals of mainland Australia, the marsupials and monotremes, are also found in Tasmania. **Marsupials** including wallabies and pademelons give birth to partially developed young that they then protect and suckle in a pouch. **Monotremes** – platypuses and echidnas – lay eggs but also suckle their young. Most are nocturnal and the best time to see them in the wild is around

Pandani plants

Tree ferns in the Donaldson Valley

dusk. The smaller mammals can be very difficult to find in the bush, but there are plenty of wildlife parks around the state where they can be seen.

# Kangaroos & Wallabies

The species found in Tasmania are related to those found on the mainland, but are usually smaller. The largest marsupial is the **Forester kangaroo**, which at one stage looked like becoming extinct because it favoured farmland for grazing. National parks at Asbestos Ranges and Mt William have been set aside to preserve this kangaroo.

In the colder regions, the **Bennett's wallaby** thrives and this is the animal you are most likely to see begging for food at the Cradle Mountain-Lake St Clair National Park. Do not give it bread, as this causes a terrible disease called 'lumpy jaw', which kills the animal. You can feed it healthier food, which is available at the kiosks in the park. It stands just over 1m in height and seems very friendly, but be careful, as these and other native animals are not tame, and can sometimes be aggressive.

If you spy any shorter, rounder wallabies hiding in the forest, then you will have seen either a **rufous wallaby** or a **pademelon**. These smaller species are shyer than their larger relatives.

Bennett's wallaby

# Tasmanian Devils

This marsupial is mainly a scavenger: its diet consists of carrion, insects and small birds and mammals, and it can often be seen at night feasting on roadkill – a habit that can lead to it becoming roadkill itself. Its bad temper and unpleasant odour are among some of its most distinctive features. It's about 75cm long, has a short, stocky body covered in black fur with a white stripe across its chest. You'll spot plenty in the wildlife parks around the state.

Tasmanian devil

# Possums

There are several varieties of possums in the state, one of which is the **sugar glider**, which has developed webs between its legs, enabling it to glide from tree to tree. The most common and boldest is the **brush-tail possum**. They live and sleep in the trees, but will come down to the ground in search of food. Possums show little fear of humans and, at times, steal food from tents and camping grounds.

# Wombats

These are very solid and powerfully built marsupials with broad heads and short stumpy legs. They live in underground burrows that they excavate. Most of the time they seem very slow moving animals, but then they do not have any natural predators to worry about.

Common wombat

# Platypuses & Echidnas

The platypus and the echidna are the only living representatives of the monotreme mammals. Monotremes are often regarded as living fossils, and although they display some intriguing features from their reptile ancestors, such as laying eggs, they are now recognised as a distinct mammalian lineage rather than a primitive stage in mammalian evolution. Although they lay eggs as reptiles and birds do, they suckle their young on milk secreted from mammary glands.

The **platypus** lives in water and has a duck-like bill, webbed feet and a beaver-like body. You are most likely to see one in a stream or lake, searching out food in the form of crustaceans, worms and tadpoles with its electrosensitive bill.

**Echidnas** are totally different and look similar to porcupines, being covered in sharp spikes. They primarily eat ants and have powerful claws for unearthing their food and digging into the dirt to protect themselves when threatened. They are common in Tasmania but if you approach one, all you are likely to see up close is a brown, spiky ball. However, if you keep quiet and don't move you might be lucky: they have poor eyesight and will sometimes walk right past your feet.

Platypus

# Southern Right Whales

These majestic creatures migrate annually from Antarctica to southern Australia to give birth to their calves in the shallow waters. So named because they were the 'right' whale to kill, they were hunted to the point of extinction. They are sometimes seen off the Tasmanian coast and occasionally beach themselves.

# Rare Birds

Some extremely rare birds are found in Tasmania: one of the best known is the **orange-bellied parrot**,

SJ CLELAND

ROB BLAKERS

**Top:** Banksia trees can be found throughout Tasmania.

**Bottom:** Cradle Mountain-Lake St Clair National Park

LINDSAY BROWN

ROB BLAKERS

RICHARD I'ANSON

**Top:** Snowgums in winter, Mt Field National Park

**Middle:** Autumn in Cradle Mountain-Lake St Clair National Park

**Bottom:** Pencil Pine Falls, Cradle Mountain-Lake St Clair National Park

CHRIS KLEP

SJ CLELAND

**Top:** Anniversary Bay, Rocky Cape National Park

**Middle:** Barn Bluff, Cradle Mountain-Lake St Clair National Park

**Bottom:** Tree ferns at Nelson Falls, Franklin-Gordon Wild Rivers National Park

RICHARD I'ANSON

CHRIS MELLOR

PAUL SINCLAIR

**Top:** Wineglass Bay and the surrounding forest, Freycinet National Park

**Bottom:** The view of Mt Oakleigh from Pelion Plains, Cradle Mountain-Lake St Clair National Park

Orange-bellied parrot

of which only a small number survive on the button-grass plains of the south-west. They winter on the mainland and must make the treacherous crossing of Bass Strait to reach their breeding grounds in south-west Tasmania. More common, but also threatened with extinction, is the **ground parrot**. To see this you will need to fly to Melaleuca in the south-west and wait in the specially constructed bird-hide.

On the eastern side of Tasmania many birdwatchers come to catch a glimpse of the very rare **forty-spotted pardalote**, which is mainly found on Bruny Island and in Mt William National Park. They prefer dry sclerophyll forest as their residence.

## Black Currawongs

The black currawong is only found in Tasmania. The currawong lives primarily on plant matter and insects, but will sometimes kill small mammals or infant birds. You will often see this large, black, fearless bird around picnic areas.

## Mutton Birds

An interesting bird is the mutton bird, which is more correctly called the short-tailed shearwater. This little bird lives in burrows in sand dunes and migrates annually to the northern hemisphere. They provide spectacular displays as they fly back to their burrows in their thousands at dusk. They are still hunted for food by Tasmanians, and you will occasionally see cooked mutton bird advertised for sale.

## Penguins

The little fairy penguin is the smallest penguin in the world and lives in burrows in the sand dunes. There are plenty of penguin rookeries around Tasmania where you can see them waddle from the ocean to their nests just after sunset. Bruny Island, Bicheno, Penguin and King Island all have rookeries you can visit to see these birds.

## Other Birds

There is a very wide variety of sea birds, parrots, cockatoos, honeyeaters and wrens. Birds of prey such as falcons and eagles are readily seen. There are many excellent publications available on Australian birds both in the form of field guides and large-format picture books.

## Snakes

There are only three types of snakes found in Tasmania and they are all poisonous. The most dangerous and largest is the **tiger snake**, which will sometimes attack, particularly in late summer. The other snakes are the **copperhead** and the smaller **white-lipped whipsnake**. Fortunately, bites are very rare, as most snakes are generally shy and try to avoid humans. If you do get bitten, do not try to catch the snake, as there is a common antivenene for all three; instead, get to hospital for treatment. See the section on Dangers & Annoyances in Facts for the Visitor.

## Threatened Species

Among Tasmania's threatened birds are the **forty-spotted pardalote**, the **orange-bellied parrot** and the **wedge-tailed eagle**. Tasmania is also home to the largest invertebrate in the world, the giant **freshwater crayfish**, whose numbers have been so depleted by recreational fishing and habitat destruction that it is now illegal to take any specimens from their natural habitat.

**Pedder galaxias** is a small, extremely rare fish discovered shortly before the inundation of Lake Pedder, which appears to have been its only natural habitat. It has since become virtually extinct in the enlarged lake and its feeder streams – Inland Fisheries has been unable to locate any specimens in these waters for a number of years – but attempts to establish a viable population in another lake in the south-west seem to have been successful.

# PARKS & RESERVES

About one quarter of the state falls inside reserves and parks. Because the largest parks are considered to be of international importance, the federal government provides financial assistance.

## National Parks

There are 18 national parks in the state and they are all worth visiting. The 13 parks outside the World Heritage Area of the south-west are all small and easily accessed by vehicle. Mt Field, South Bruny, Tasman, Maria Island, Freycinet and Rocky

CHRIS KLEP

Waldheim Chalet, Cradle Mountain

Cape are the most popular of the smaller parks. They all have interesting scenery and marked, maintained walking tracks of a few minutes to several hours in duration.

National parks are managed by the PWS (☎ 6233 6191) and fees apply to all of them, even when there is no ranger's office. A permit system has also been proposed for bushwalking tracks, but at the time of writing its introduction was expected to be some years off.

There are two types of fees: per vehicle and per person. For vehicles with up to eight people the charge for 24 hours is $9; a holiday pass that is valid for two months is $30 and an annual pass is $42. For individuals who arrive by bus, bicycle, motor bike or boat, entry fees are $3 for 24 hours, $12 for two months and $15 a year.

The fees are fairly high if you are only spending a day or two in the park, but if you're staying longer or visiting several parks, then the multiple-entry passes provide worthwhile savings. For most visitors the holiday pass is the best value. Passes are available at any park entrance, at many visitors' centres and at Service Tasmania (☎ 6233 3382, 134 Macquarie St, Hobart).

A huge amount of information on Tasmania's national parks is available on its Web site at www .parks.tas.gov.au.

## World Heritage Area

Covering 20% of the state, this is a huge and significant area. It contains the four largest national parks in the state – South West, Wild Rivers, Cradle Mountain-Lake St Clair and the Walls of Jerusalem national parks – plus the Hartz Mountains National Park and the Central Plateau Protected Area.

The region was first accepted for listing as a World Heritage Area in 1982. To be accepted, a nomination must satisfy at least one of the criteria for listing. The western Tasmania World Heritage Area was deemed to have outstanding natural and cultural values, and satisfied a record seven categories out of the 10 possible criteria. In 1989 the World Heritage Area was enlarged to 1.38 million hectares and renominated as the Tasmanian Wilderness World Heritage Area.

The area is managed by the same government agency that runs the national parks, the PWS. Most

The Hazards, Freycinet National Park

Russell Falls, Mt Field National Park

of the area is managed as a wilderness that the public are allowed to visit. However, being so large, most of it is accessible only to bushwalkers who can carry at least one week's food. One excellent and easy way to obtain a quick look over the area is to take a joy flight on a light aeroplane. Regular flights operate from Strahan and Hobart over the World Heritage Area.

## Other Protected Areas

The PWS also manages a set of conservation areas and state reserves around the state. These reserves usually have one feature that is to be protected – often wildlife – but allow activities such as mining, farming, forestry and tourism development. Many of these places are very small and include caves, waterfalls, historic sites and some coastal regions. Usually there are no entry fees to these areas, except those where the government has actively restored or developed the area.

## Forest Reserves

Forest reserves are usually small areas that have been given some protection inside larger regions of state forests. These forests are on crown land and their primary purpose is for timber production. Many of the waterfalls and picnic areas on the scenic forest drives are in this type of reserve. None of these reserves have real protection from future alterations. During weekdays some forestry roads are closed to private vehicles; if the roads are open, drive slowly and give way to logging trucks. There are no entry fees to the forests.

## Marine Reserves

Tasmania is becoming increasingly aware of the significance and vulnerability of its marine environment. Marine reserves aim to protect fragile ecosystems, and fishing or the collection of living or dead material within their boundaries is illegal. There are marine reserves at Tinderbox near Hobart, at Ninepin Point near Verona Sands south of Hobart, in the waters around the northern part of Maria Island, and around Grovernor Island off the coast at Bicheno.

Mt Amos, Freycinet National Park

# TASMANIA'S NATIONAL PARKS

Same Scale as Main Map

Cape Wickham

Yambacoona

Currie

Grassy

**King Island**

Stokes Point

To King Island (70km)

Furneaux Group

Cape Frankland

Flinders Island

Emita

Whitemark

Lady Barton

STRZELECKI NATIONAL PARK

Cape Barren Island

Cape Barren

Clarke Island

Cape Portland

Banks Strait

BASS STRAIT

Hunter Island

Three Hummock Island

Woolnorth Pt

Robbins Island

Stanley

The Nut

Marrawah

Smithton

ROCKY CAPE NATIONAL PARK

Arthur River

A2

SAVAGE RIVER NATIONAL PARK

ARTHUR PIEMAN PROTECTED AREA

C249

Pieman

Corinna

Pieman River

Rosebery

Queenstown

Strahan

Lake Burbury

Cape Sorell

Macquarie Harbour

Waratah

Savage River

Cradle Valley

CRADLE MOUNTAIN-LAKE ST CLAIR NATIONAL PARK

Lake St Clair

Franklin River

Derwent Bridge

Lake King William

FRANKLIN-GORDON WILD RIVERS NATIONAL PARK

Gordon River

Strathgordon

Lake Gordon

Lake Pedder

SOUTHERN

OCEAN

Burnie

Devonport

Ulverstone

ASBESTOS RANGE NATIONAL PARK

Port Sorell

George Town

Beaconsfield

Tamar River

MT WILLIAM NATIONAL PARK

Bridport

Gladstone

Derby

A3

St Helens

A3

Deloraine

C132

Mole Creek

Mersey River

MOLE CREEK KARST NATIONAL PARK

Longford

Launceston

South Esk River

BEN LOMOND NATIONAL PARK

St Marys

Fingal

Great Lake

WALLS OF JERUSALEM NATIONAL PARK

Arthurs Lake

Macquarie River

Campbell Town

A4

DOUGLAS APSLEY NATIONAL PARK

Bicheno

Lake Leake

Lake Sorell

Lake Echo

A5

Bothwell

River Derwent

A10

MT FIELD NATIONAL PARK

Hamilton

Westerway

B61

New Norfolk

HOBART

Sorell

A9

Lake Tiberias

Melton Mowbray

Triabunna

Swansea

Coles Bay

FREYCINET NATIONAL PARK

Great Oyster Bay

Schouten Island

MARIA ISLAND NATIONAL PARK

Bridgewater

Huonville

Huon River

Kettering

Geeveston

SOUTH-WEST NATIONAL PARK

Port Davey

Bathurst Harbour

South West Cape

HARTZ MOUNTAINS NATIONAL PARK

Southport

A6

Alonnah

Bruny Island

SOUTH BRUNY NATIONAL PARK

Tasman Head

Storm Bay

Tasman Peninsula

Port Arthur

TASMAN NATIONAL PARK

Cape Pillar

TASMAN SEA

South East Cape

D'Entrecasteaux Channel

To Macquarie Island (1500km)

0  25  50km

Spirit of Tasmania (Overnight trip to Melbourne; approx 14.5 hours or 429km)

# Facts for the Visitor

## HIGHLIGHTS

Tasmania's diversity and small size make it the perfect holiday destination. In the space of a week, you can walk to views of dazzling coastal scenery, pamper yourself in a high-class resort, eat your way through some of the best seafood in the country and still have time to visit Hobart's Salamanca Market and spend a day wine tasting in the Tamar Valley.

The rich legacy of Tasmania's convict era is evident throughout the state, but particularly in places such as Port Arthur and Richmond in the south and Ross in the Midlands. The 1830s warehouses of Hobart's waterfront are brimming with arts and crafts shops, cafés and restaurants, while many of the historic cottages in the fishing village of Stanley have been reborn as B&Bs, making it a charming place to stay overnight. Elsewhere, grand houses classified by the National Trust dot the countryside and are open for inspection.

The east of the state is justly popular for its beaches, but it's the more remote northeast that boasts some of the most stunning combinations of sweeping white sand and seas of aqua, deep blue and green.

The spectacular cliffs of the Tasman Peninsula attract ocean kayakers, abseilers and divers, while completing the famous Overland Track in Cradle Mountain-Lake St Clair National Park is the single objective of many visiting bushwalkers. The wild Franklin River in the west draws rafters from around the world, and the thriving tourist hub of Strahan attracts those who prefer the more sedate option of cruising the famous Gordon River.

If you're a foodie and have a yen for the great outdoors and a love of history, both architectural and social, you'll find no better holiday destination in Australia than its island state of Tasmania. There really is something for everyone.

## SUGGESTED ITINERARIES

In the following itineraries, the last destination listed for each day is the suggested place to stay overnight.

**Two days:**
    Day 1 – Arrive Launceston
    Day 2 – Tamar Valley (George Town); depart
            from Launceston
or
    Day 1 – Arrive Hobart
    Day 2 – Tasman Peninsula (Port Arthur); depart
            from Hobart

**One week:**
    Day 1 – Arrive Launceston
    Day 2 – Launceston, Mole Creek & Deloraine
    Day 3 – Longford, Evandale & Bicheno
    Day 4 – Freycinet Peninsula & East Coast
    Day 5 – Tasman Peninsula (Port Arthur) & Hobart
    Day 6 – Mt Field or Bruny Island & Hobart
    Day 7 – Hobart & Richmond; depart from Hobart

**Two weeks:**
    Day 1 – Arrive Launceston or Devonport
    Day 2 – Deloraine & Mole Creek
    Day 3 – Cradle Mountain
    Day 4 – Cradle Mountain
    Day 5 – Table Cape, Boat Harbour, Rocky
            Cape & Stanley
    Day 6 – Zeehan, Henty Dunes & Strahan
    Day 7 – Strahan
    Day 8 – Hobart
    Day 9 – Hobart or Bruny Island
    Day 10 – Hobart & Richmond
    Day 11 – Tasman Peninsula (Port Arthur)
    Day 12 – East Coast & Freycinet Peninsula
    Day 13 – Evandale & Launceston
    Day 14 – Depart from Launceston or Devonport

**One month:**
    Day 1 – Arrive Launceston or Devonport
    Day 2 – Launceston
    Day 3 – Tamar Valley (George Town)
    Day 4 – Pipers River wineries, Bridport &
            Scottsdale
    Day 5 – Derby, Mt William National Park, St
            Columba Falls, Pub in the Paddock
    Day 6 – Bay of Fires, St Helens, St Marys,
            Bicheno

Day 7 – Freycinet Peninsula, Swansea
Day 8 – Maria Island, Tasman Peninsula
Day 9 – Tasman Peninsula (Port Arthur)
Day 10 – Richmond & Hobart
Day 11 – Hobart
Day 12 – Bruny Island
Day 13 – Woodbridge, Cygnet, Hastings
Caves, Cockle Creek & Hobart
Day 14 – Midlands & Evandale
Day 15 – Longford, Great Lake, Bothwell &
Hamilton or Mt Field
Day 16 – Mt Field
Day 17 – Lake Pedder, Gordon Dam & Maydena
Day 18 – Lake St Clair & Derwent Bridge or
Bronte Park
Day 19 – Queenstown & Strahan
Day 20 – Strahan
Day 21 – Henty Dunes, Zeehan, Corinna (Pie
man River), Western Explorer &
Arthur River or Marrawah
Day 22 – Arthur River, Marrawah & Stanley
Day 23 – Rocky Cape, Boat Harbour, Table
Cape & Cradle Mountain
Day 24 – Cradle Mountain
Day 25 – Penguin, Gunns Plains & Ulverstone
Day 26 – Deloraine & Mole Creek
Day 27 – Launceston
Day 28 – King Island or Flinders Island
Day 29 – King Island or Flinders Island
Day 30 – Depart from King Island or Flinders
Island, or return to Launceston and
depart from Launceston or Devonport

# PLANNING
## When to Go

Tasmania is most popular during summer, because it's warm enough for swimming and it's great to be outdoors. Most days are fine in the major towns and cities. The exception is the south-west and west where only about half the days are fine; the other days are often rainy and cloudy.

December, January and February are therefore the busiest times for tourism. Accommodation is heavily booked (and often more expensive) and the popular venues and restaurants are more crowded, but as compensation you can expect to see an amazing variety of sporting events, including the finish of the Sydney to Hobart Yacht Race, and enjoy the festivities on the docks in Hobart.

The winter months are generally cold, wet and cloudy. Nevertheless, in some years, many winter days are clear, crisp and sunny – ideal for sightseeing and short bushwalks. The great advantage of visiting in winter is that tourist numbers and prices are low, and it seems as if you have the entire island to yourself. In addition, any peaks and ranges you pass in your travels are likely to be all the more attractive for being covered in snow (when they are not hidden by cloud).

Spring is the windiest time in Tasmania. Temperatures in early September are quite cold, the weather can be changeable and snowfalls are still common. Daffodils, tulips and lavender bloom in the north of the state, and the *Blooming Tasmania* brochure, available from Tasmanian Travel & Information Centres (TTICs), outlines all the floral festivals and horticultural events that take place at this time of the year.

Autumn is often pleasant, with mild temperatures, and is the season in which many festivals are held (see the Cultural Events section of this chapter for more information). From late April to early May, the deciduous beech changes from mid-green to glorious gold and red. It can be seen in Mt Field and Cradle Mountain-Lake St Clair national parks. Towards the end of autumn, the days (even sunny ones) are usually quite cold and windy.

The other major consideration when travelling is school holidays. Australian families take to the road (and air) en masse at these times; many places are booked out, prices rise and things generally get a bit crazy. Holidays vary somewhat from year to year, but the main holiday period is from mid-December to late January; the other two-week periods are roughly early to mid-April, late June to mid-July, and late September to early October. Tasmanians love to holiday in their own state, and camping in national parks is particularly popular at such times.

## Maps

The selection of maps available is wide, but many are of average quality. The best road map of the state, produced by the Royal

Automobile Club of Tasmania (RACT), is on sale in its offices around the island. (To the chagrin of some bushwalkers, its 1998-99 edition features on its cover a picture of Lake Oberon in the Western Arthurs – a destination that is an extremely tough full day's bushwalk from any roads.) TTICs stock a similar product published by the Department of Environment & Land Management (DELM). Both include maps of main city centres.

The *Tasmanian Towns Street Atlas* ($24.95), published by DELM and updated in 1998, contains excellent, clear maps of every town of significance and is better than most other commercially produced Tasmanian city street guides. It's available in selected newsagencies, bookshops and TTICs, at Service Tasmania (☎ 6233 3382, 134 Macquarie St, Hobart) and at the Tasmanian Map Centre (☎ 6231 9043, 96 Elizabeth St, Hobart).

TASMAP's topographic sheets are appropriate for bushwalking, ski-touring and other activities requiring large-scale maps. Many of the more popular sheets, including day walks and bushwalks in national parks, are available over the counter at shops specialising in bushwalking gear and outdoor equipment. Otherwise, purchase copies at TTICs, national park information centres, Service Tasmania or the Tasmanian Map Centre.

## What to Bring

Generally, Australians are casual dressers (shorts or jeans and T-shirts are very common) and neat, casual clothes will suffice in most hotels and restaurants. The casinos and more expensive restaurants will require long trousers, a neat shirt and shoes for men (ties and jackets are rarely needed).

You'll definitely need a warm jumper (pullover, sweater) or jacket, as well as something wind-proof and waterproof, no matter what time of the year you visit Tasmania. Often in autumn, spring and early summer you will be quite warm during those times in the day when the sun is shining and there is no wind, but the moment it becomes cloudy, the wind rises or you stand in the shade, you will need another layer of clothing; you may find yourself putting on and taking off your jumper or wind jacket all day long.

UV radiation in Tasmania is strong and dangerous, so a good sunscreen (15+) or zinc cream, a hat and sunglasses are essential.

If you are intending to bushwalk, you should bring a sturdy, comfortable pair of boots. The ubiquitous rubber sandals known as thongs (easily purchased here, and known as jandals or flipflops elsewhere) are suitable beach or casual wear, but aren't allowed in most pubs or restaurants and are not good for sightseeing or walking long distances.

## RESPONSIBLE TOURISM

Tasmania's 'disease-free' status is one of the things that makes its produce attractive to buyers, and the state government has stringent rules in place to ensure that the island maintains its advantage in this regard. To this end, plants, fruit and vegetables cannot be brought into the state without certification. Essentially, this means tourists must discard all such items prior to their arrival.

Live fish that can breed in Tasmanian waters cannot be brought into the state. (Carp infestation in Lake Crescent is thought to be a result of this regulation being flouted.) Anglers must not bring live bait into Tasmania, and in order to prevent the introduction of disease into native and recreational fisheries and aquaculture industries, they should also wash, disinfect and dry their gear before packing it for their trip.

*Phytophthora* is a root rot that is spread in soil and is devastating flora in some parts of the state. Always clean dirt off your shoes and equipment before and after you spend time in the bush. For more information about responsible bushwalking, see the Bushwalking section of the Activities chapter.

For details about responsible 4WD touring, read *Cruisin' Without Bruisin'*, a free brochure available at many tourist offices. Whether you are travelling in a 4WD on bush tracks or in a conventional vehicle on a highway, watch out for wildlife on the road and if possible avoid driving at dusk, when animals are likely to be active and difficult to see.

Be sure never to disturb or remove items from sites of significance to Aborigines.

## TOURIST OFFICES
### Local Tourist Offices
The TTICs are privately run, and the Hobart centre is on the corner of Davey and Elizabeth Sts (☎ 6230 8233). There are also centres in Launceston, Devonport and Burnie. As well as supplying brochures, price lists, maps and other information, they will often book transport, tours and accommodation for you. They are generally open from around 8.30 or 9 am to 5 or 5.30 pm weekdays and slightly shorter hours on the weekend.

In addition to the main centres mentioned above, there are visitors' centres in many smaller towns that are members of the Tasmanian Visitor Information Network. The standard of service they provide varies enormously from place to place. Centres such as those at Bicheno, Kettering and Geeveston are very efficient, while many others are staffed by volunteers, who can either be excellent sources of information or well intentioned but vague. Opening hours for the centres staffed by volunteers are often irregular.

The Department of Tourism publishes an invaluable bimonthly newspaper called *Tasmanian Travelways*, which is available at all information centres around the state. Along with interesting articles, it is packed with information, including comprehensive listings of accommodation, visitor activities, public transport, connecting transport facilities and vehicle hire, all with an indication of current costs throughout the state; best of all, it's free!

The travel centres also stock a host of free tourist literature, including the monthly magazine *This Week in Tasmania*. The annual *Tasmania Visitors Guide*, which has a good fold-out touring map of Tasmania, is particularly useful and is also free.

## Interstate Tourist Offices
On the mainland, there are branches of the government-run Tasmanian Travel Centre in:

Australian Capital Territory
 (☎ 02 6209 2133)
 165 City Walk, Canberra 2601
New South Wales
 (☎ 02 9202 2033)
 149 King St, Sydney 2000
Queensland
 (☎ 07 3405 4122)
 239 George St, Brisbane 4000
South Australia
 (☎ 08 8400 5533)
 1 King William St, Adelaide 5000
Victoria
 (☎ 03 9206 7922)
 259 Collins St, Melbourne 3000

These travel centres have information on just about everything you need to know about Tasmania and are also able to book accommodation, tours and even airline, boat and bus tickets.

## Tourist Offices Abroad
The Australian Tourist Commission (ATC) is the government body that informs potential visitors about the country. There's a very definite split between promotion outside Australia and inside it. The ATC is strictly an external operator; it does minimal promotion within the country and has little contact with visitors who are in Australia. Within the country, tourist promotion is handled by state or local tourist offices.

ATC offices overseas have a useful free booklet called *Australia Travellers Guide*, which details things of interest for backpackers around Australia.

The ATC publishes *Australia Unplugged*, which is a good introduction to Australia for young people, giving some information about the country in general and snapshots of the major cities.

The ATC also publishes a number of fact sheets on various topics, such as camping, fishing, skiing, disabled travel and national parks – and these can be a useful introduction to the subject. It also provides a handy map of the country for a small fee. This literature is intended for distribution overseas only; if you want copies, get them before you come to Australia. The ATC's Web site is www.australia.com.

## VISAS & DOCUMENTS

All visitors to Australia need a visa. Only New Zealand nationals are partially exempt, and even they receive a 'special category' visa on arrival.

Visa application forms are available from either Australian diplomatic missions overseas or travel agents, and you can apply by mail or in person. There are several different types of visa, depending on the reason for your visit.

## Visas

**Tourist Visas** Tourist visas are issued by Australian consular offices abroad; they are valid for a stay of either three or six months within a 12 month period, or occasionally for a full 12 months, and cost $50.

It may be possible to arrange a visa that allows you to enter the country a number of times within a 12 month period.

When you apply for a visa, you need to present your passport and a passport photo and sign an undertaking that you have an onward or return ticket and 'sufficient funds' to cover your stay – the latter is obviously open to interpretation.

You can also apply for a long-stay visa, which is a multiple-entry, four year visa that allows for stays of up to six months on each visit. These also cost $50.

### Electronic Travel Authority (ETA)

Visitors who require a tourist visa of three months or less can make the application through an IATA-registered travel agent, who can then make the application direct and issue the traveller with an ETA, which replaces the usual visa stamped in your passport. This system operates in about 30 countries – make inquiries with you local IATA-registered travel agent.

**Working Visas** Young, single visitors from the UK, Canada, Korea, Holland and Japan may be eligible for a 'working holiday' visa. 'Young' is fairly loosely interpreted as around 18 to 25, although exceptions are made and people up to 30, and young married couples without children, may be given a working holiday visa.

A working holiday visa allows for a visit of up to 12 months, but the emphasis is meant to be on casual employment rather than a full-time job, so you are only supposed to work for one employer for three months. This visa can only be applied for outside Australia (preferably but not necessarily in your country of citizenship), and you can't change from a visitor visa to a working holiday visa.

You can apply for a working holiday visa up to 12 months in advance, and it's a good idea to do it as early as possible because there is a limit on the number issued each year. Conditions attached to a working holiday visa include having sufficient funds for a ticket out, and taking out private medical insurance; a fee of $145 is charged when you apply for the visa.

See the section on Work later in this chapter for details of what sort of work is available and where.

**Visa Extensions** The maximum stay allowed to visitors in Australia is one year, including extensions.

Visa extensions are made through Department of Immigration & Multicultural Affairs offices in Australia and, as the process takes some time, it's best to apply about a month before your visa expires. There is an application fee of $145 – and even if they turn down your application they can still keep your money! To qualify for an extension you are required to show that you have sufficient funds to cover the period of the extension, and have a ticket out of the country. Some offices are more strict in enforcing these conditions than others.

If you want to remain in Australia in the long term, the books *Temporary to Permanent Resident in Australia* and *Practical*

*Guide to Obtaining Permanent Residence in Australia*, both published by Longman Cheshire, might be useful.

## Travel Insurance

A travel insurance policy to cover theft, loss and medical problems is a good idea. Some policies offer lower and higher medical-expense options; the higher ones are chiefly for countries such as the USA, which have extremely high medical costs. There is a wide variety of policies available, so check the small print.

Some policies specifically exclude 'dangerous activities', which can include scuba diving, motorcycling, even trekking. A locally acquired motorcycle licence is not valid under some policies.

You may prefer a policy that pays doctors or hospitals directly rather than your having to pay on the spot and claim later. If you have to claim later make sure you keep all documentation. Some policies ask you to call back (reverse charges) to a centre in your home country where an immediate assessment of you problem is made.

Check that the policy covers ambulances or an emergency flight home.

## Driving Licence

You can use your own foreign driving licence in Australia, as long as it is in English (if it's not, a translation must be carried). As an International Licence cannot be used alone and must be supported by your home licence, there seems little point in getting the international one.

## Medicare Card

Under reciprocal arrangements, residents of the UK, New Zealand, the Netherlands, Finland, Ireland, Sweden, Malta and Italy are entitled to free or subsidised medical treatment in Australia under Medicare, Australia's compulsory national health insurance scheme. To enrol in the system you need to show your passport and health care card or certificate from your own country, you are then entitled to receive a Medicare card.

Once you have a card you can get free necessary public hospital treatment and visits to a private doctor's practice. Claim methods vary between doctors and you may have to pay the bill first and then make a claim yourself from Medicare. You also need to find out how much the doctor's consultation fee is, as Medicare only covers you for a certain amount and you will need to pay the balance. Clinics that advertise 'bulk billing' are the easiest to use as they charge Medicare direct.

For more information phone Medicare (☎ 13 2011).

## Photocopies

All important documents (passport data page and visa page, credit cards, travel insurance policy, air/bus/train tickets, driving licences etc) should be photocopied before you leave home. Leave one copy with someone at home and keep another with you, separate from the originals.

## EMBASSIES & CONSULATES
### Australian Embassies and Consulates

Australian consular offices overseas include:

Canada
   (☎ 613 236 0841, fax 236 4376)
   Suite 710, 50 O'Connor St, Ottawa K1P 6L2, also in Toronto and Vancouver
China
   (☎ 10-6532 2331, fax 6532 4349)
   21 Dongzhimenwai Dajie, Sanlitun, Beijing 100600, also in Guangzhou and Shanghai
Denmark
   See Germany
France
   (☎ 01-4059 3300, fax 4059 3310)
   4 Rue Jean Rey, 75724 Paris Cedex 15 Paris
Germany
   (☎ 0228-81 030, fax 810 3130)
   Godesberger Allee 107, 53175 Bonn, also in Frankfurt and Berlin
Greece
   (☎ 01-644 7303, fax 646 6595)
   37 Dimitriou Soutsou, Ambelokipi, Athens 11521
Hong Kong
   (☎ 2827 8881, fax 2585 4459)
   Harbour Centre, 25 Harbour Rd, Wanchai, Hong Kong Island

India
  (☎ 11-688 8223, fax 688 7536)
  Australian Compound, No 1/50-G Shantipath,
  Chanakyapuri, New Delhi 110021, also in
  Mumbai (Bombay)
Indonesia
  (☎ 021-522 7111, fax 522 7101)
  Jalan H R Rasuna Said Kav C 15-16, Jakarta
  Selatan 12940
  (☎ 0361-23 5092, fax 23 1990)
  Jalan Prof Moh Yamin 51, Renon, Denpasar,
  Bali
Ireland
  (☎ 01-676 1517, fax 678 5185)
  Fitzwilton House, Wilton Terrace, Dublin 2
Italy
  (☎ 06-852 721, fax 8527 2300)
  Via Alessandria 215, Rome 00198,
  also in Milan
Japan
  (☎ 03-5232 4111, fax 5232 4178)
  2-1-14 Mita, Minato-ku, Tokyo 108
  (☎ 06-941 8601, fax 941 8602)
  Twin 21 MID Tower, 29th Floor, 2-1-61 Shi-
  romi, Chuo-ku, Osaka 540-6129
Malaysia
  (☎ 03-242 3122, fax 241 5773)
  6 Jalan Yap Kwan Seng, Kuala Lumpur 50450,
  also in Kuching and Penang
Netherlands
  See Germany
New Zealand
  (☎ 04-473 6411, fax 498 7118)
  72-78 Hobson St, Thorndon, Wellington
  (☎ 09-303 2429, fax 377 0798)
  Union House, 132-38 Quay St, Auckland 1
Papua New Guinea
  (☎ 325 9333, fax 325 3528)
  Godwit Rd, Waigani NCD, Port Moresby
Philippines
  (☎ 02-750 2840, fax 754 6269)
  Dona Salustiana Ty Tower, 104 Paseo de
  Roxas, Makati, Metro Manila
Singapore
  (☎ 737 9311, fax 737 5481)
  25 Napier Rd, Singapore 258507
South Africa
  (☎ 012-342 3740, fax 342 4222)
  292 Orient St, Arcadia, Pretoria 0083, also in
  Cape Town
Sweden
  See Germany
Switzerland
  See Germany
Thailand
  (☎ 02-287 2680, fax 287 2029)
  37 South Sathorn Rd, Bangkok 10120

UK
  (☎ 020-7379 4334, fax 465 8217)
  Australia House, The Strand, London WC2B
  4LA, also in Edinburgh and Manchester
USA
  (☎ 202-797 3000, fax 797 3168)
  1601 Massachusetts Ave NW, Washington DC
  20036, also in Los Angeles and New York
Vietnam
  (☎ 04-831 7755, fax 831 7712)
  66 Van Thuc Compound, Ba Dinh District,
  Hanoi, also in Ho Chi Minh City

## Foreign Embassies & Consulates in Australia

The principal diplomatic representations to Australia are in Canberra. There are also representatives in various other major Australian cities – particularly from countries like the USA, UK and New Zealand, which have strong links with Australia. Visa applications, however, are generally handled in Canberra.

In Hobart there are consulates for Belgium, the Czech Republic, Denmark, Finland, Germany, Greece, Italy, Japan, the Netherlands, the Philippines, Sweden, Switzerland and the UK. Their addresses and phone numbers can be found in the Hobart telephone directory.

## CUSTOMS

When entering Australia you can bring most articles in free of duty provided that Customs is satisfied they are for personal use and that you'll be taking them with you when you leave. There's also the usual duty free per person quota of one litre of alcohol, 250 cigarettes and dutiable goods up to the value of A\$400.

With regard to prohibited goods, there are two areas you need to pay particular attention to. Number one is, of course, dope – Australian Customs has a positive mania about the stuff and can be extremely efficient when it comes to finding it. Unless you want to make first-hand investigations of conditions in Australian jails, don't bring any with you. This particularly applies if you are arriving from South-East Asia or the Indian Subcontinent.

## Your Own Embassy

As a tourist, it's important to realise what your own embassy – the embassy of the country of which you are a citizen – can and can't do.

Generally speaking, it won't be much help in emergencies if the trouble you're in is remotely your own fault. Remember that you are bound by the laws of the country you are in. Your embassy will not be sympathetic if you end up in jail after committing a crime locally, even if such actions are legal in your own country.

In genuine emergencies you might get some assistance, but only if other channels have been exhausted. For example, if you need to get home urgently, a free ticket home is exceedingly unlikely – the embassy would expect you to have insurance. If you have all your money and documents stolen, it might assist with getting a new passport, but a loan for onward travel is out of the question.

Embassies used to keep letters for travellers or have a small reading room with ome newspapers, but these days the mail holding service has been stopped and even newspapers tend to be out of date.

Problem two is animal and plant quarantine. You will be asked to declare all goods of animal or vegetable origin – wooden spoons, straw hats, the lot – and show them to an official. The authorities are naturally keen to prevent weeds, pests or diseases getting into the country – Australia has so far managed to escape many of the agricultural pests and diseases prevalent in other parts of the world. Flowers are also unpopular, along with fresh food, particularly meat, sausages, fruit and vegetables. There are also restrictions on taking fruit and vegetables between states.

Weapons and firearms are either prohibited or require a permit and safety testing.

Other restricted goods include products (such as ivory) made from protected wildlife species, non-approved telecommunications devices and live animals.

## MONEY
### Currency
Australia's currency is the Australian dollar, which comprises 100 cents. There are coins for 5c, 10c, 20c, 50c, $1 and $2, and paper notes for $5, $10, $20, $50 and $100.

Although the smallest coin in circulation is 5c, prices are still marked in single cents, and then rounded to the nearest 5c when you come to pay.

There are no notable restrictions on importing or exporting travellers cheques, but cash amounts in excess of $5000 must be declared on arrival and departure.

### Exchange Rates
The Australian dollar fluctuates quite markedly against the US dollar, but seems to stay pretty much around the 60c to 80c mark – this is a disaster for Australians travelling overseas but a real bonus for inbound visitors.

| country | unit | dollar |
|---|---|---|
| Canada | C$1 | $1.05 |
| euro | €1 | $1.64 |
| France | 10FF | $2.63 |
| Germany | DM1 | $0.88 |
| Hong Kong | HK$10 | $2.02 |
| Japan | ¥100 | $1.28 |
| New Zealand | NZ$1 | $0.85 |
| United Kingdom | UK£I | $2.54 |
| United States | US$1 | $1.57 |

### Exchanging Money
Changing foreign currency or travellers cheques is no problem at almost any bank. It's done quickly and efficiently.

**Travellers Cheques** There are a variety of ways to carry your money around. If your stay is limited then travellers cheques are the most straightforward way, and they generally enjoy a better exchange rate than foreign cash in Australia.

American Express, Thomas Cook and other well-known international brands of travellers cheques are all widely used in Australia. A passport will usually be adequate for identification; it would be sensible to carry a driving licence, credit cards or some other form of identification in case of problems.

Fees for changing foreign currency travellers cheques seem to vary from bank to bank and year to year. Tasmania's Trust Bank does not charge a fee. Currently of the 'big four', ANZ charges $6.50, Westpac charges $7, the National charges $10 and the Commonwealth charges $5.

Buying Australian dollar travellers cheques is an option worth considering. These can be exchanged immediately at the bank without being converted from a foreign currency and incurring commissions, fees and exchange rate fluctuations.

**Banks, ATMs & EFTPOS** Banks exist in many towns in Tasmania, but in the smaller centres they are often only open one or two days a week. The most common bank is Tasmania's own Trust Bank. Post offices act as agents for the Commonwealth Bank, although like banks, post offices in many of the smaller towns are only open restricted hours on weekdays. Even ATMs are few and far between outside the largest of the state's centres. However, there's usually at least one general store, petrol station or newsagent in town that offers an Electronic Funds Transfer at Point of Sale (EFTPOS, see the following Local Bank Accounts section) service and will allow you to make small cash withdrawals with EFTPOS purchases (although you should not count on this on weekends, when cash supplies can run low).

**Credit Cards** Credit cards are widely accepted in Australia and provide an alternative to carrying large numbers of travellers cheques. Visa, MasterCard, Diners Club and American Express are all widely accepted.

Cash advances from credit cards are available over the counter and from many automatic teller machines (ATMs), depending on the card.

If you're planning to rent cars while travelling around Tasmania, a credit card makes life much simpler; they're looked upon with much greater favour by rent-a-car agencies than cash, and many agencies simply won't rent you a vehicle if you don't have a card.

**Local Bank Accounts** If you're planning to stay longer than a month, it's worth considering other ways of handling money that give you more flexibility and are more economical. This applies equally to Australians setting off to travel around the country.

Most travellers these days opt for an account that includes a cash card, which you can use to access your cash from ATMs. You put your card in the machine, key in your personal identification number (PIN), then complete the transaction from your account. Westpac, ANZ, National and Commonwealth banks have branches with ATMs in Hobart, Launceston and a few other centres around the state, and there are multibank ATMs at various locations in Hobart and Launceston.

ATM machines can be used day or night, and it is possible to use the machines of some other banks: Westpac ATMs accept Commonwealth Bank cards and vice versa; National Bank ATMs accept ANZ cards and vice versa. There is a limit on how much you can withdraw from your account. This varies from bank to bank but is usually $800 to $1000 per day.

Many businesses, such as service stations, supermarkets and convenience stores, are linked into the EFTPOS system and at places with this facility you can use your bank cash card to pay for services or purchases direct, and sometimes withdraw cash as well. Bank cash cards and credit cards can also be used to make local, STD and international phone calls in special public telephones.

Opening an account at an Australian bank is not all that easy, especially for overseas visitors. A points system operates and you need to score a minimum of 100 points before being given the privilege of letting the bank take your money. Passports, driving licences, birth certificates and other 'major' IDs earn you 40 points; minor ones such as credit cards get you 20 points. Just like a game show really!

If you don't have an Australian Tax File Number (see the section on Work later in this chapter), interest earned from your funds will be taxed at the rate of 47%.

## Costs

Compared with the USA, Canada and European countries, Australia is cheaper in some ways and more expensive in others. Manufactured goods tend to be more expensive: if they are imported they have all the additional costs of transport and duties, and if they're locally manufactured they suffer from the extra costs entailed in making things in comparatively small quantities. Thus you pay more for clothes, cars and other manufactured items. On the other hand, food is both high in quality and low in cost.

The biggest expense in any visit to Tasmania is the cost of actually getting over Bass Strait. You only have two choices: to fly or catch the ferry. Either way you'll be a couple of hundred dollars out of pocket before arriving.

On average you can expect to spend about $40 per day if you budget fiercely and *always* take the cheapest option; $70 gives you much greater flexibility. Obviously if you stay for longer periods in each place and can take advantage of discounts given on long-term accommodation, this helps to keep your costs to a minimum.

## Tipping

In Australia tipping isn't entrenched in the way it is in the USA or Europe. It's only customary to tip in more expensive restaurants and only then if you want to. If the service has been especially good and you decide to leave a tip, 10% of the bill is the usual amount. Taxi drivers don't expect tips (of course, they don't hurl it back at you if you decide to leave the change).

## POST & COMMUNICATIONS
### Postal Rates

Post offices are open from about 9 am to 5 pm Monday to Friday (slightly longer in Hobart and Launceston). In addition, the Launceston post office and the Sandy Bay post office in Hobart are open on Saturday mornings. There are also many post office agencies in general stores and newsagencies. In larger towns and cities, these are usually open from 9 am to 5 pm and on Saturday morning, but in the small towns they may only be open for a couple of hours a day, or in some cases just two days a week. You can often buy stamps from newsagencies and local shops.

In the major towns the post offices also have stamp vending machines. You must have the correct change.

### Sending Mail

Australia's postal services are relatively efficient but not too cheap. It costs 45c to send a standard letter or postcard within Australia.

Air-mail letters/postcards cost 75/70c to New Zealand, 85/80c to Singapore and Malaysia, 95/90c to Hong Kong and India, $1.05/95c to the USA and Canada, and $1.20/1 to Europe and the UK.

The rates for posting parcels abroad from Tasmania are not too exorbitant. To New Zealand by economy air/air it's $11/12 for 1kg, $21/23 for 2kg and $33/38 for 5kg. To the US by sea/economy air/air it's $13/15/20 for 1kg, $25/29/39 for 2kg and $43/53/78 for 5kg. To the UK and Europe it's $13/17/23 for 1kg, $25/33/45 for 2kg and $43/43/93 for 5kg.

### Receiving Mail

The poste restante service at the post office in Hobart is quite good. While it can be busy, particularly in the summer months, you usually do not have to wait too long. The post office will hold your mail for one month before returning it to the sender. Alternatively, you can pay a $5 monthly fee to have your mail forwarded to you within Australia (or by surface mail overseas). All post offices will hold mail for visitors, so it could be more convenient for you to have your mail sent to a suburban post office – just have it addressed care of that post office and include the postcode. If you own an American Express Card or buy Amex travellers cheques you can have mail sent to you care of American Express Travel (☎ 6234 3711, 74a Liverpool St, Hobart 7000).

## Telephone

The Australian telecommunications industry is deregulated and there are a number of providers offering various services. Private phones are serviced by the two main companies, Telstra and Optus, but in the mobile phone and payphone markets other companies such as Vodafone, One.Tel, Unidial, Global One and AAPT are operating, and it's where you'll find the most competition.

**Payphones & Phonecards** There are a number of different cards issued by the various telecommunications companies, and these can be used in any Telstra public phone that accepts cards, or from a private phone by dialling a toll-free access number. There's a wide range of local and international phonecards. Lonely Planet's eKno Communication Card (see the insert at the back of this book) is aimed specifically at travellers and provides cheap international calls, a range of messaging services and free email – for local calls, you're usually better off with a local card. To join eKno call ☎ 1800 674 100. To access the eKno service from Tasmania, dial ☎ 1800 114 478. For further information, visit the eKno Web site at www.ekno.lonelyplanet.com.

Long-distance calls made from pay phones are generally considerably more expensive than calls made from private phones. If you will be using payphones to make a large number of calls, it's wise to consider the various cards available from providers other than Telstra.

Some public phones are set up to only take bank cash cards or credit cards, and these too are convenient, although you need to keep an eye on how much the call is costing, as it can quickly mount up. The minimum charge for a call on one of these phones is $1.20.

**Local Calls** Local calls from public phones cost 40c for an unlimited amount of time. Local calls from private phones cost 25c. Calls to mobile phones are more expensive.

**Area Codes** All Tasmanian telephone numbers have eight digits, and the area code for Tasmania is 03, which is the same code as Victoria. When calling from one area of Tasmania to another, there is no need to dial 03 before the local number. Local numbers start with the following digits: 62 in Hobart and southern Tasmania, 63 in Launceston and the north-east, and 64 in the west and north-west.

There are three other Australian area codes: 02 covers New South Wales, 07 covers Queensland, and 08 covers South Australia, Western Australia and the Northern Territory.

**STD Calls** It's also possible to make long-distance (STD – Subscriber Trunk Dialling) calls from virtually any public phone. If you're not using a Telecom Phonecard, have plenty of coins handy and be prepared to feed them through at a fast rate. STD calls are cheaper in off-peak hours – see the front of a local telephone book for the different standard rates. With deregulation of the telephone system there is a price war on and even larger discounts are offered at times – watch the media advertising for such specials.

**International Calls** From most STD phones you can also make ISD (International Subscriber Dialling) calls. Dialling ISD you can get through to overseas numbers almost as quickly as you can to local numbers and, if your call is brief, it needn't cost very much.

All you do is dial 0011 for overseas, the country code, the city code and then the telephone number. And have a Phonecard, credit card or plenty of coins to hand.

International calls from Australia are among the cheapest you'll find anywhere.

Off-peak times, if available, vary depending on the destination – see the back of any White Pages telephone book, or call ☎ 0102 for more details. Sunday is often the cheapest day to ring.

Country Direct is a service that gives travellers in Australia direct access to operators in nearly 60 countries, to make collect or credit card calls. For a full list of the countries hooked into this system, check any local White Pages telephone book.

**Toll-Free Calls** Many businesses and some government departments operate a toll-free service, so no matter where you are ringing from around the country, it's a free call. These numbers have the prefix 1800. Many companies, such as the airlines, have six-digit numbers beginning with 13 or 1300, and these are charged at the rate of a local call.

**Mobile Phones** Phone numbers with the prefixes 014, 015, 016, 018, 019 or 041 are mobile or car phones. The three mobile operators are the government's Telstra, and the two private companies Optus and Vodaphone. Calls to mobile numbers are charged at special STD rates and can be expensive.

**Information Calls** Other odd numbers you may come across are numbers starting with 190. These numbers, usually recorded information services and the like, are provided by private companies, and your call is charged at anything from 35c to $5 or more a minute (more from mobile and payphones).

## Fax
All post offices (but few agencies) send faxes. If you send a fax to another fax machine it costs $4, which is also the rate for sending a fax to a postal address. For the latter, the fax is sent to the local post office and delivered in the normal mail service, usually the next day. You can send a same-day fax to some postal addresses if you deliver it by 1 pm ($12), and there's a two hour courier delivery service within metropolitan districts open until 4 pm ($20).

These rates apply to the first page of any fax. Subsequent pages cost $1 no matter which service you use.

## Email & Internet Access
Travelling with a portable computer is a great way to stay in touch with life back home, but unless you know what you're doing it's fraught with potential problems. If you plan to carry your notebook or palmtop computer with you, remember that the power supply voltage in the country you visit may vary from that at home, risking damage to your equipment. The best investment is a universal AC adaptor for your appliance, which will enable you to plug it in anywhere without frying the innards. You'll also need a plug adaptor – often it's easiest to buy these before you leave home.

Also, your PC-card modem may or may not work once you leave your home country – and you won't know for sure until you try. The safest option is to buy a reputable 'global' modem before you leave home, or buy a local PC-card modem if you're spending an extended time in any one country. Keep in mind that the telephone socket in each country you visit will probably be different from that at home, so ensure that you have at least a US RJ-11 telephone adaptor that works with your modem. You can almost always find an adaptor that will convert from RJ-11 to the local variety. For more information on travelling with a portable computer, see www.teleadapt.com or www.warrior.com.

Major Internet service providers such as AOL (www.aol.com), CompuServe (www.compuserve.com) and IBM Net (www.ibm.net) have dial-in nodes; it's best to download a list of the dial-in numbers before you leave home. If you access your Internet email account at home through a smaller ISP or your office or school network, your best option is either to open an account with a global ISP, like those mentioned above, or to rely on cybercafés and other public access points to collect your mail.

If you do intend to rely on cybercafés, you'll need to carry three pieces of information with you to enable you to access your Internet mail account: your incoming (POP or IMAP) mail server name, your account name and your password. Your ISP or network supervisor will be able to give you these. Armed with this information, you should be able to access your Internet mail account from any net-connected machine in the world, provided it runs some kind of email software (remember that Netscape and Internet Explorer both have mail modules). It pays to become familiar with the process for doing this before you leave home. A final option to collect mail through cybercafés is to open a free Web-based email account such as HotMail (www.hotmail.com) or Yahoo! Mail (mail.yahoo.com). You can then access your mail from anywhere in the world from any net-connected machine running a standard Web browser.

In Tasmania there is an Internet café ($2 for 10 minutes or $10 an hour) and an Internet access centre ($5 an hour) in Hobart (see the Hobart chapter for details). However, government lending libraries around the state now provide free Internet access. To use this service, you must first obtain a card, available at any library; bookings must then be made for periods of access during the normal opening hours of the library.

If you want to access your email or surf the Net, there are service providers in all Australia's capital cities, and in many regional areas too. Online costs vary, but a typical price structure is a $25 joining fee, then $10 per seven hours online, with no minimum charge. Major players that service Tasmania include:

Oz Email
 (☎ toll-free 1800 805 874, www.ozemail.com.au)
Pegasus Networks
 (☎ toll-free 1800 812 812, www.peg.apc.org)
CompuServe users who want to access the service locally should phone CompuServe (☎ 1300 307 072) to get the local log-in numbers.

## INTERNET RESOURCES
The World Wide Web is rapidly expanding to become one of the major sources of information on anything you care to name. Although things on the Net change rapidly, some sites that currently provide a range of information on Australia include:

Lonely Planet
 www.lonelyplanet.com.au
 (Our own site is not specific to Australia but is still definitely worth a look. Well, we would say that, wouldn't we?)
Guide to Australia
 www.csu.edu.au/education/australia.html
 (This site, maintained by the Charles Sturt University in NSW, is a mine of information, with links to Australian government departments, weather information, books, maps, etc.)
The Aussie Index
 www.aussie.com.au/aussie.htm
 (This site is a fairly comprehensive list of Australian companies, educational institutions and government departments which maintain Web sites.)
Australian Government
 www.fed.gov.au
 (The federal government has a Web site, which is predictably unexciting, but it is wide-ranging and a good source for things such as visa information.)
National Parks
 www.parks.tas.gov.au
 (Details all the parks and current regulations and is a mine of information if you intend to bushwalk.)

Other useful Web site addresses are listed under appropriate headings throughout the text.

## BOOKS
Most books are published in different editions by different publishers in different countries. As a result, a book might be a hardcover rarity in one country while it's readily available in paperback in another. Fortunately, bookshops and libraries search by title or author, so your local bookshop or library is best placed to advise you on the availability of the following recommendations.

### Lonely Planet
Lonely Planet publishes many books that you might like to refer to when planning your trip to Tasmania.

If you intend to spend any time in Sydney or Melbourne on your way, you will probably want to check out our *Australia, New South Wales* or *Victoria* guide or our *Sydney* or *Melbourne* city guide.

*Bushwalking in Australia* by John & Monica Chapman has a chapter on walks in Tasmania that will complement the briefer walk descriptions provided in this book (see Bushwalking in the following Activities chapter for more details), while the Pisces diving and snorkelling guide *Australia: Southeast Coast and Tasmania* is a must for those interested in taking advantage of the many diving opportunities the island has to offer. Finally, anyone intending to use Hobart as a departure point for a visit to Antarctica would be well advised to buy a copy of our fascinating and comprehensive *Antarctica* guide by Jeff Rubin.

## Guidebooks
In Hobart and Launceston bookshops and TTICs you'll find a host of general travel guides, many of which will give a brief overview of the state while focussing on a specific aspect of travel such as colonial accommodation, vineyards or guesthouses. For details about guides to particular activities (cycling, bushwalking etc), see the Activities chapter.

## Travel Accounts
The *Australian Geographic Book of Tasmania* by Lindsay Simpson (photographs by Bruce Miller) is the author's personal account of her travels around the state and features her partner's excellent photographs. It includes a useful lift-out map and some travel information.

*Down Home: Revisiting Tasmania*, by internationally recognised ex-Tasmanian academic, journalist and critic Peter Conrad, combines autobiography and history in a penetrating account of his return to the island after an absence of 20 years. This is a contemplative book that will appeal particularly to those with a love of language.

For something less weighty, you might consider *Travelling Tales* by journalist and former Tasmanian Charles Wooley, whose affection for his home state finds expression in chapters on such subjects as Lake Pedder and fly fishing on the Meander River.

*The Ribbon and the Ragged Square* by Linda Christmas is an intelligent, sober account of a nine month investigatory trip around Australia – including Tasmania – by a *Guardian* journalist.

## History
The most comprehensive and accessible history of Tasmania is the two volume work of that name by L Robson. Alternatively, try WA Townsley's *Tasmania: From Colony to Statehood*.

For a good introduction to Australian history generally, read Manning Clark's *A Short History of Australia* or Robert Hughes' bestselling account of the convict era, *The Fatal Shore*.

Geoffrey Blainey's book *The Peaks of Lyell*, described on its jacket as 'a landmark in Australian industrial history', gives a compelling account of the Mt Lyell Mining and Railway Company and a century of mining in western Tasmania. It's a great introduction to Queenstown for anyone with a particular interest in that intriguing community.

A number of books documenting Port Arthur's recent bloody history and the aftermath of the massacre are available, notably *Port Arthur: A Story of Strength and Courage* by Margaret Scott.

Books about Aboriginal and environmental history are listed under Aboriginal People and Environment respectively.

## Aboriginal People
There are many books on the history of Tasmania's Aborigines: *The Aboriginal Tasmanians* by Lyndall Ryan is one of the best, but you may also like to refer to *Blood on the Wattle* by Bruce Elder and any of Brian Plomley's works.

In *Fate of a Free People*, Henry Reynolds re-examines history from an Aboriginal perspective and puts a case for Tasmanian Aboriginal land rights, while Cassandra

Pybus' book *Community of Thieves* considers the fate of the Nuenone people of southeastern Tasmania from her perspective as a descendant of Richard Pybus, a European who took up a large land grant on Bruny Island, the traditional home of the Nuenone.

## Flora & Fauna

Among the many guides to Tasmania's fauna are *The Fauna of Tasmania: Birds* and *The Fauna of Tasmania: Mammals* by RH Green and *Tasmanian Mammals – A Field Guide* by Dave Watts.

If you are interested in the now extinct Tasmanian tiger, you might like to browse through *Thylacine: The Tragedy of the Tasmanian Tiger* by Eric Guiler, available in the Tasmaniana Library in the State Library in Hobart. The author draws together a diverse array of scientific knowledge and anecdotal evidence about the marsupial carnivore to argue that one of the greatest tragedies of its sorry history is that nobody bothered to study it thoroughly when they had the chance.

Among guides to Tasmania's flora are *Native Trees of Tasmania* by JB Kirkpatrick & Sue Backhouse, and a number of pocket-sized plant identi-kits by Phil Collier, including *Alpine Flowers of Tasmania, Orchids of Tasmania* and *Wildflowers of Mt Wellington*.

## Environment

For a summary of the legacy of early European exploration, read *Trampled Wilderness* by Ralph & Kathleen Gowlland.

The Australian Conservation Foundation's *The South West Book* provides a plethora of information about the southwest, from scientific debate to reproductions of newspaper articles and posters printed at times of conflict over the region's future. Published in 1978, the book is already something of an historical document itself and can be viewed in Hobart in the Tasmaniana Library in the State Library or in the library of the Tasmanian Environment Centre (102 Bathurst St).

*The Rest of the World is Watching*, edited by Richard Flanagan & Cassandra Pybus, covers the history to 1990 of the groundbreaking Tasmanian Green movement.

If you are at all interested in the original Lake Pedder, you must take the time to visit the State Library in Hobart and view the magnificent collection of photographs compiled by Bob Brown in the large-format publication entitled simply *Lake Pedder*. The accompanying article 'I saw my Temple Ransacked', written by Kevin Kiernan (and reprinted in an abridged form in *The Rest of the World is Watching*), is a first-hand account of the Pedder campaign including a brief but harrowing description of the drowning lake that will remain with you long after you have finished reading the book.

Among the photographers featured in *Lake Pedder* is Olegas Truchanas, an adventurer and conservationist whose exceptional images of Pedder were one of the conservationists' most powerful weapons in their fight to save the lake. If you like his work, you may also be interested in a more extensive collection of his wilderness photographs compiled by Max Angus in *The World of Olegas Truchanas*.

Truchanas died photographing the Gordon River in 1972, which was the year Lake Pedder was flooded, but his protégé, Peter Dombrovskis, continued in his footsteps, producing work of a similarly high standard now ubiquitous in Tasmania on postcards, greeting cards, posters and calendars. *Wild Rivers* by Bob Brown contains photographs of the Franklin taken by Dombrovskis during his three full-length trips down its course and is accompanied by the author's account of his own experiences on that river.

Like his mentor, Dombrovskis died in the pursuit of his art. *On the Mountain*, published after his death in the Western Arthurs in 1996, is a selection of images of Mt Wellington, which was his home for the greater part of 50 years. This book also contains a personal reflection on the mountain and its significance by Richard Flanagan and a natural history by academic Jamie Kirkpatrick.

## Fiction

Christopher Koch uses Tasmania as the setting for large sections of many of his novels, including *The Doubleman*, *Highways to a War* and *The Boys in the Island*. Richard Flanagan's novels *Death of a River Guide* and *The Sound of One Hand Clapping* and Amanda Lohrey's novel *Morality of Gentlemen* are also set in the state. For more information about these authors and their works, see the Arts section of the Facts about Tasmania chapter.

*The Potato Factory* by Bryce Courtenay (author of the blockbuster *The Power of One*) is a fictionalised account of the life of Tasmanian convict Ikey Solomon.

## Souvenir Books

Bruce Miller's photographs in Lindsay Simpson's *The Australian Geographic Book of Tasmania* (mentioned under Travel Accounts earlier in this section) make this glossy, soft-cover book an appealing keepsake. For pictures of the World Heritage Area, buy a coffee-table book like *South West Tasmania* by Richard Bennett or *The Mountains of Paradise* by Les Southwell. The Wilderness Shop always has a good range of the latest books about the Franklin River and Lake Pedder.

## FILMS

Richard Flanagan's film *The Sound of One Hand Clapping*, released in 1998, was shot in Tasmania and ran for extended periods in Australia's capital cities following its world premier at the Berlin Film Festival. A harrowing exploration of both the power and the limitations of love between parents and children, it traces the impact on successive generations of war, displacement and abandonment by recounting the story of a single family of European migrants from the time their grief finally becomes unendurable in a remote construction camp in the Tasmanian highlands.

Another Tasmanian film for which the highlands provide a grim setting is *The Tale of Ruby Rose*, the story of a woman brought up in harsh isolation coming to terms with marriage to a reclusive trapper.

Two excellent documentaries that consider Tasmanian Aboriginal history and experience are *The Last Tasmanian* (1978) and *Black Man's Houses* (1992). The former was widely acclaimed when it was first released, but the version of history it provides is now dated. The latter documents racial tensions on Flinders Island, where the graves of members of the Wybalenna Aboriginal settlement of the 1830s (see the History section of the Facts about Tasmania chapter) were desecrated shortly after they had been restored by the island's present-day Aboriginal community.

## NEWSPAPERS & MAGAZINES

In Hobart and the south, the main daily is the *Mercury*; in Launceston and the north-east, it's the *Examiner*; and in Burnie and the north-west, it's the *Advocate*. All are tabloids covering local, national and international news, with an emphasis on the local. Larger newsagents in Hobart and Launceston stock major mainland dailies.

*40° South* is a glossy quarterly magazine packed with articles about the state, many of which will be of interest to travellers. At $7.50, it's not cheap, but some cafés and takeaways keep copies for patrons to browse through.

If you are interested in the performing and visual arts or fine dining, look out for the free monthly magazine *Artswatch Tasmania*. It's available at arts venues and in some cafés throughout the state. You may also be able to pick up a copy in similar outlets in Sydney and Melbourne.

Good outdoor and adventure magazines that regularly include articles about Tasmania are *Wild*, *Rock* and *Outdoor Australia*.

About every two years the Hobart Walking Club publishes *Tasmanian Tramp*, a journal of various trips undertaken by club members containing valuable information on out-of-the-way walks and articles on conservation, history and humorous episodes. Back issues are held in the State Reference Library and as a collection are a fascinating record of how the experiences available to bushwalkers in the South-West have been altered by the construction of successive dams.

## RADIO & TV

The national advertising-free TV and radio network is the Australian Broadcasting Corporation (ABC).

### Radio

In major centres there are usually a number of stations, both AM and FM, featuring everything from rock to talkback to 'beautiful music'. Triple J is a government youth FM radio station broadcast nationally that plays excellent music (Australian and international) from outside the pop mainstream and plugs into Australia's youth culture. ABC Classic FM plays classical music, while Radio National is an Australia-wide service featuring current affairs and information. All three are commercial-free and can be received in most larger Tasmanian towns, though reception of Triple J and Classic FM may be poor in Queenstown and on parts of the east coast.

The FM Information Station, which runs individual services for Hobart, Launceston and Devonport, may be of interest to visitors. It provides useful basic information in a single tape replayed hourly.

### TV

The ABC (the main national public broadcaster), Southern Cross and Win Television (the state's two commercial stations), and SBS (a national government-sponsored multicultural service) are all available in Hobart and Launceston. Tasmania is very hilly, however, and elsewhere reception of the commercial stations and SBS can be poor: some remoter towns receive only the ABC.

### VIDEO SYSTEMS

Australia uses the PAL system, and so pre-recorded videos purchased in Australia may be incompatible with overseas systems. Check this before you buy.

## PHOTOGRAPHY & VIDEO

Australian film prices are not too far out of line with those of the rest of the western world. Including developing, 36-exposure Kodachrome 64 or Fujichrome 100 slide film costs around $25, but with a little shopping around you can find it for around $20 – even less if you buy it in quantity.

There are several camera shops in Hobart and Launceston and standards of camera service are good. Developing standards are also high, with many places offering one hour developing of print film and similar service for repeat prints. Photoforce (☎ 6234 6234, 178 Campbell St) is one of the higher-quality labs in Hobart and can have slide film developed the same day.

The best photographs are obtained early in the morning and late in the afternoon. As the sun gets higher, colours begin to appear washed out. You must also allow for the intensity of reflected light when taking shots at coastal locations. Especially in the summer, allow for temperature extremes and do your best to keep film as cool as possible, particularly after exposure.

As in any country, politeness goes a long way when taking photographs; ask before taking pictures of people. Note that many Aborigines do not like to have their photographs taken, even from a distance.

If you come from a country that uses a video system other than PAL, and you wish to buy a camera in Australia to record details of your holiday, you should shop for this in Melbourne or Sydney, as it is very difficult to find such items in Tasmanian retail outlets.

## TIME

Australia is divided into three time zones: Western Standard Time is plus eight hours from GMT/UTC (Western Australia), Central Standard Time is plus 9½ hours (Northern Territory, South Australia) and Eastern Standard Time is plus 10 (Tasmania, Victoria, NSW, Queensland). When it's noon in Western Australia it's 1.30 pm in the

Northern Territory and South Australia and 2 pm in the rest of the country.

During the summer things get slightly screwed up as daylight saving time (when clocks are put forward an hour) does not operate in Western Australia or Queensland, and in Tasmania it starts a month earlier and finishes up to a month later than in the other states. The main problem occurs with airline schedules and it pays to read your ticket carefully as the time shown will be correct but might be different from the published schedules in the crossover months.

## ELECTRICITY
Voltage is 220-240V and the plugs are three-pin, but not the same as British three-pin plugs. Users of electric shavers or hairdryers should note that, apart from in fancy hotels, it's difficult to find converters to take either US flat two-pin plugs or the European round two-pin plugs. Adaptors for British plugs can be found in good hardware shops, chemists and travel agents.

## WEIGHTS & MEASURES
Australia uses the metric system. Petrol and milk are sold by the litre, apples and potatoes by the kilogram, distance is measured by the metre or kilometre, and speed limits are in kilometres per hour (km/h).

If you need help with metric there's a conversion table at the back of this book.

## TOILETS
Tasmania has flushing toilets (either connected to sewers or septic tanks) just about everywhere except in national parks and reserves, where pit or composting toilets are often found. Composting toilets are set high off the ground and reached by a walkway or steps. After you use one of these, you should add a scoopful of wheat husks from the bag beside the toilet (if there is such a bag) and ensure that the lid is left down.

## HEALTH
Australia is a remarkably healthy country to travel in, considering that such a large portion of it lies in the tropics.

So long as you have not visited an infected country in the past 14 days (aircraft refuelling stops do not count) no vaccinations are required for entry.

Medical care in Australia is 1st class and only moderately expensive. A typical visit to the doctor costs around $35. If you have an immediate health problem, phone or visit the casualty section at the nearest public hospital. If you are bushwalking or rafting in remote areas in Tasmania, remember that help can be several days away, so be prepared to deal with your own medical emergencies.

Visitors from the UK, New Zealand, Malta, Italy, Sweden, Ireland, Finland and the Netherlands have reciprocal health rights in Australia and can register at any Medicare office. This entitles them to free medical treatment at public hospitals.

Ambulance services in Australia can be frightfully expensive, so you'd be wise to take out travel insurance for that reason alone. Make sure the policy specifically includes ambulance, helicopter rescue and a flight home for you and anyone you're travelling with, should your condition warrant it. See the Travel Insurance section the Visas & Documents section earlier in this chapter for more details.

### Medical Kit
While facilities in cities and towns are generally of a very high standard, doctors and hospitals are few and far between in the remote areas. If you're heading off the beaten track into the western half of the state, at least one person in your party should have a sound knowledge of first-aid treatment, and in any case you'll need a first-aid handbook and a basic medical kit. See the boxed text for items you should take.

### Health Precautions
The contraceptive pill is available on prescription only, so a visit to a doctor is necessary. Doctors are listed in the Yellow Pages section of the phone book or you can visit the outpatients section of a public hospital. Condoms are available from chemists, many convenience

## Medical Kit Check List

Following is a list of items you should consider including in your medical kit – consult your phamacist for brands available in your country.

- ☐ **Aspirin** or **paracetamol** (acetaminophen in the US) – for pain or fever.
- ☐ **Antihistamine** – for allergies, eg hay fever; to ease the itch from insect bites or stings; and to prevent motion sickness.
- ☐ **Antibiotics** – consider including these if you're travelling well off the beaten track; see your doctor, as they must be prescribed, and carry the prescription with you.
- ☐ **Loperamide** or **diphenoxylate** – 'blockers' for diarrhoea; **prochlorperazine** or **metaclopramide** for nausea and vomiting.
- ☐ **Rehydration mixture** – to prevent dehydration, eg due to severe diarrhoea; particularly important when travelling with children.
- ☐ **Insect repellent**, **sunscreen**, **lip balm** and **eye drops**.
- ☐ **Calamine lotion**, **sting relief spray** or **aloe vera** – to ease irritation from sunburn and insect bites or stings.
- ☐ **Antifungal cream** or **powder** – for fungal skin infections and thrush.
- ☐ **Antiseptic** (such as povidone-iodine) – for cuts and grazes.
- ☐ **Bandages**, **Band-Aids (plasters)** and other wound dressings.
- ☐ **Water purification tablets** or **iodine**.
- ☐ **Scissors**, **tweezers** and a **thermometer** (note that mercury thermometers are prohibited by airlines).
- ☐ **Cold** and **flu tablets**, **throat lozenges** and **nasal decongestant**.
- ☐ **Multivitamins** – consider for long trips, when dietary vitamin intake may be inadequate.

stores, and vending machines in the public toilets of many hotels and universities.

**Water** Tap water is safe to drink in towns and cities throughout the state. Always beware of water from rivers, creeks and lakes, as it may have been infected by stock or wildlife. If there's any doubt, the surest way to disinfect water is to thoroughly boil it for 10 minutes.

### Health Problems

**Hypothermia** Too much cold can be just as dangerous as too much heat. In Tasmania it can occur if you are caught in a blizzard while bushwalking.

Hypothermia occurs when the body loses heat faster than it can produce it and the core temperature of the body falls. It is surprisingly easy to progress from very cold to dangerously cold due to a combination of wind, wet clothing, fatigue and hunger, even if the air temperature is above freezing. It is best to dress in layers; silk, wool and some of the new artificial fibres are all good insulating materials. A hat is important, as a lot of heat is lost through the head. A strong, waterproof outer layer (and a 'space' blanket for emergencies) are essential. Carry basic supplies, including food containing simple sugars to generate heat quickly and fluid to drink.

Symptoms of hypothermia are exhaustion, numb skin (particularly toes and fingers), shivering, slurred speech, irrational or violent behaviour, lethargy, stumbling, dizzy spells, muscle cramps and violent bursts of energy. Irrationality may take the form of sufferers claiming they are warm and trying to take off their clothes.

To treat mild hypothermia, first get the person out of the wind, rain and/or water, remove their clothing if it's wet and replace it with dry, warm clothing. Give them hot liquids – not alcohol – and some high-kilojoule, easily digestible food. Do not rub victims; instead allow them to warm themselves slowly. This should be enough to treat the early stages of hypothermia. The early recognition and treatment of mild hypothermia is the only way to prevent severe hypothermia, which is a critical condition.

**Motion Sickness** Eating lightly before and during a trip will reduce the chances of motion sickness. If you are prone to motion sickness try to find a place that minimises movement – near the wing on aircraft, close to midships on boats, near the centre on buses. Fresh air usually helps; reading and cigarette smoke don't. Commercial motion-sickness preparations, which can cause drowsiness, have to be taken before the trip commences. Ginger (available in capsule form) and peppermint (including mint-flavoured sweets) are natural preventatives.

**Sunburn** You can get sunburnt surprisingly quickly in Tasmania, even through cloud. Use a sunscreen, hat, and barrier cream for your nose and lips. Calamine lotion or stingose are good for mild sunburn. Protect your eyes with good quality sunglasses, particularly if you will be near water, sand or snow.

**Sexually Transmitted Diseases** Gonorrhoea, herpes and syphilis are among these diseases; sores, blisters or rashes around the genitals, discharges or pain when urinating are common symptoms. In some STDs, such as wart virus or chlamydia, symptoms may be less marked or not observed at all, especially in women. Syphilis symptoms eventually disappear completely but the disease continues and can cause severe problems in later years. While abstinence from sexual contact is the only 100% effective prevention, using condoms is also effective. The treatment of gonorrhoea and syphilis is with antibiotics. The different sexually transmitted diseases each require specific antibiotics. There is no cure for herpes or AIDS.

## Cuts, Bites & Stings
**Insect Bites & Stings** Bee and wasp stings are usually painful rather than dangerous. However, in people who are allergic to them, severe breathing difficulties may occur and require urgent medical care. Calamine lotion or Stingose spray will give relief and ice packs will reduce the pain and swelling.

**Cuts & Scratches** Wash well and treat any cut with an antiseptic such as povidone-iodine. Where possible avoid bandages and Band-aids, which can keep wounds wet.

## Women's Health
**Gynaecological Problems** Sexually transmitted diseases are a major cause of vaginal problems. Symptoms include a smelly discharge, painful intercourse and sometimes a burning sensation when urinating. Male sexual partners must also be treated. Medical attention should be sought and remember in addition to these diseases HIV or hepatitis B may also be acquired during exposure. Besides abstinence, the best thing is to practise safe sex using condoms.

Antibiotic use, synthetic underwear, sweating and contraceptive pills can lead to vaginal fungal infections when travelling in hot climates. By maintaining good personal hygiene, wearing loose-fitting clothes and cotton underwear you can help to prevent these infections.

Fungal infections, characterised by a rash, itch and discharge, can be treated with a vinegar or lemon-juice douche, or with yoghurt. Nystatin, miconazole or clotrimazole pessaries or vaginal cream are the usual treatment.

**Pregnancy** It is not advisable to travel to some places while pregnant as some vaccinations normally used to prevent serious diseases are not advisable in pregnancy, eg yellow fever. In addition, some diseases are much more serious for the mother (and may increase the risk of a stillborn child) in pregnancy, eg malaria.

Most miscarriages occur during the first three months of pregnancy. Miscarriage is not uncommon, and can occasionally lead to severe bleeding. The last three months should also be spent within reasonable distance of good medical care. A baby born as early as 24 weeks stands a chance of survival, but only in a good modern hospital. Pregnant women should avoid all unnecessary medication, vaccinations and malarial prophylactics should still be taken where needed. Additional care should be taken to prevent illness and particular attention should be paid to diet and nutrition. Alcohol and nicotine, for example, should be avoided.

## EMERGENCY
In the case of a life-threatening situation dial ☎ 000. This call is free from any phone and the operator will connect you with either the police, ambulance or fire brigade. To dial any of these services direct, check the inside front cover of any local telephone book.

For other telephone crisis and personal counselling services (such as sexual assault, poisons information or alcohol and drug problems), check the Community pages of the local telephone book.

## WOMEN TRAVELLERS
Tasmania is generally a safe place for women travellers, although it's probably best to avoid walking alone late at night in any of the major towns. Sexual harassment is unfortunately still sometimes a problem. While the farther you get from 'civilisation' (ie Hobart and Launceston), the less enlightened your average Tassie male is likely to be about women's issues, things are slowly changing.

Female hitchhikers should exercise care at all times (see the section on hitching in the Getting Around chapter). In the event of misfortune, a useful contact is the Sexual Assault Support Service in Hobart (☎ 6231 1811).

## GAY & LESBIAN TRAVELLERS
On 1 May 1997 the Tasmanian parliament at last repealed Tasmania's anti-gay laws, thereby complying with the 1994 United Nations ruling on this issue and eliminating Australia's only remaining state law banning same sex relations. Tasmania is now considered by gay and lesbian-rights groups to have greater equality in the criminal law for homosexual and heterosexual people than most of the other Australian states.

You can pick up a free copy of the *Tasmanian Gay and Lesbian Business and Service Directory* at some cafés.

The Tasmanian Gay & Lesbian Rights Group (TGLRG) has a great Web site at www.tased.edu.au/tasonline/tasqueer. The site lists all the Tassie gay and lesbian organisations and groups and Tassie gay venues and events. For local information or assistance, you can call the Gay Information Line (☎ 6234 8179) or the Lesbian Line (☎ 6231 4228).

## SENIOR TRAVELLERS
The majority of attractions listed in this book have reduced rates for senior citizens, so make sure you ask whether a discount is available whenever you purchase a ticket. You will usually need to show some authoritative identification, such as a pensioner concession card, to qualify for the discount.

Discounts are also often available to senior travellers using public transport.

## TRAVEL WITH CHILDREN
If your children enjoy national parks and beaches, they will have a wonderful time in Tasmania. Otherwise, you will probably have to pay some money to keep them entertained. In Launceston there's the Penny Royal Gunpowder Mill and Cataract Gorge; in the Mole Creek area, there are caves and a wildlife park; at Paradise there's a deer farm; near Lake Barrington there's an extensive maze; just outside Devonport there's the Don Railway; and in Hobart there's the Cadbury chocolate factory and Antarctic Adventure. These are just a few of the many places of interest to children. More places are listed in the following chapters.

There are also a number of accommodation options around the state that would appeal to children because they have animals

## Disabled Travellers in Tasmania

Tasmania is a great tourist destination with an improving awareness of access issues. There are a number of agencies that provide information and/or assistance to disabled travellers.

### Transport

Transport options are limited so it is best to take your own vehicle on TT-Line's ferry *Spirit of Tasmania* (☎ toll-free 13 2010), which sails between Port Melbourne and Devonport. Four cabins are accessible with the 'flood step' removed, a wheel-in shower and grab-rails. TT-Line staff will drive your vehicle on and off the vessel for you. Qantas and Ansett service the airports at Hobart and Launceston but there are no air bridges so wheelchair passengers are boarded and disembarked using forklifts. The *Devil Cat* is accessible, quick (6hr trip) and operates from December to mid-April, but has not yet been commissioned for 1999/2000.

Three wheelchair accessible maxi-cabs (☎ 6234 3633) are available in Hobart but must be booked 24hrs in advance. AVIS (☎ toll-free 1800 22 5533) provides hand-controlled vehicles at Hobart and Launceston. Mobility Maps and Eating Out Guides are available from Launceston City Council Access and Advisory Committee (☎ 6323 3000) and City of Devonport Mersey Access Advisory Committee (☎ 6424 0511). *Easy Access Australia – A Travel Guide to Australia* has a chapter about Tasmania (write to PO Box 218, Kew Vic 3101, $24.85).

### Information

Tourism Tasmania (☎ toll-free 132 010), has *Tasmania – Tourist Information for People with Disabilities*, listing accommodation (rated by NICAN and RACT), attractions and available services.

The Royal Automobile Club Of Tasmania (RACT, ☎ 6232 6300) has some information for travellers with disabilities. The Paraplegic and Quadriplegic Association (☎ 6272 8816, fax 6272 8511) is a key information source with accommodation, accessible toilets, mobility maps and attractions, and can help with specific requests from travellers. You can also try the Australian Council for Rehabilitation of the Disabled (ACROD, ☎ 6223 6086) and The Aged & Disability Care Information Service (☎ 6234 7448, toll-free in Tasmania 1800 80 6656). Other organisations to contact are the Tasmanian Society for the Deaf (☎ 6249 5144/TTY 6249 1174) and the Royal Guide Dogs for the Blind Association (☎ 6232 1299).

### Attractions & Accommodation

The Tasmanian Parks and Wildlife Service (PWS, ☎ 6233 3275) publishes *Tasmania's National Parks, Forests, Walks and Waterways – A Visitors' Guide*, which indicates accessible facilities. Mt Field National Park (ranger ☎ 6288 1149), about 80km north-west of Hobart, has an accessible 500m-long bitumen track leading to spectacular Russell Falls. A Tall Tree walk takes visitors past some of the world's tallest flowering plants.

The Port Arthur Historical Site (☎ 6250 2363, toll-free 1800 65 9101) is the most significant attraction in Tasmania. Management are making the site accessible with dedicated parking spaces, accessible toilets, a wheelchair available to borrow and accessible entrances to many historic buildings. There is also access on the nightly Ghost Tour and on the Isle of the Dead tour.

Purpose built accommodation is available at **Helvetia Retreat** (☎ 6491 1806), in Sheffield, with two self-catering units. At Cradle Mountain-Lake St Clair National Park **Cradle Mountain Lodge** (☎ 6492 1303) has two accessible self-catering chalets. The visitors' centre and Rangers Station (☎ 6492 1110) has an accessible toilet and a ramp leads to the Rainforest Pencil Pines Walking Track, a 500m, accessible boardwalk through some spectacular rainforest.

**Bruce Cameron**

or other attractions on site, and these too are listed in the appropriate chapters.

## USEFUL ORGANISATIONS

There are many organisations in Tasmania that you may find useful during your visit. Most have their head office in Hobart. If you are looking for a particular group, check in the Yellow Pages telephone book under 'Organisations'. Most useful organisations noted in this book are listed under appropriate headings in relevant chapters.

### Royal Automobile Club of Tasmania

The RACT (☎ 6232 6300) is on the corner of Patrick and Murray Sts in Hobart. It provides an emergency breakdown service and has reciprocal arrangements with services in other Australian states and some from overseas. It also provides literature, excellent maps and detailed guides to accommodation and camping grounds.

### National Trust

The National Trust is dedicated to preserving historic buildings in all parts of Australia. The Trust actually owns a number of buildings throughout the country that are open to the public. Because of the large number of well-preserved buildings in Tasmania, the National Trust has many sites around the state.

The National Trust also produces some excellent literature, including a fine series of walking-tour guides. These guides are often available from local tourist offices or from National Trust offices and are usually free whether you're a member of the National Trust or not. Membership is well worth considering, however, because it entitles you to free entry to any National Trust property for your year of membership. If you're a dedicated visitor of old buildings this could soon pay for itself. There is a $30 joining fee, and annual membership costs $42 for individuals ($20 concession) and $60 for families and includes the monthly or quarterly magazine put out by the state organisation that

you join. The state head office is in Franklin House (☎ 6344 6233, 413 Hobart Rd, Launceston 7249).

## DANGERS & ANNOYANCES

### Snakes

The best known danger in the Australian bush, and the one that captures visitors' imagination, is snakes. Although all snakes in Tasmania are venomous, they are not aggressive and, unless you have the bad fortune to stand on one, it's unlikely that you'll be bitten. The tiger snake, however, will sometimes attack if alarmed.

To minimise your chances of being bitten always wear boots, socks and long trousers when walking through undergrowth where snakes may be present. Don't put your hands into holes and crevices, and be careful when collecting firewood or going to the toilet.

Snake bites do not cause instantaneous death and antivenenes are usually available. Keep the victim calm and still, place a pad on the bite site, wrap the bitten limb firmly (to compress the muscle tissues, but not constrict the blood flow), as you would for a sprained ankle, and then attach a splint to immobilise it – do not remove the splint or bandages once applied. Seek medical help. Do *not* try to catch the snake. Never wash, cut and suck the poison out or use tourniquets. These treatments are now comprehensively discredited.

### Flies

March flies are large and very persistent. They are prevalent in the summer months and are attracted to blue clothing, so you're better off wearing other colours. They can viciously attack the unsuspecting traveller and bite any uncovered area, leaving behind large, red lumps (similar to leech bites). Repellents such as Aerogard and Rid go some way to deterring these pests, but it's better to cover up. Calamine lotion can soothe the bites.

### Mosquitoes

Just when you think the flies have gone (around sunset) and it's safe to come out, the 'mossies' appear. Repellents usually keep them at bay.

## Leeches

These are very common in the damp rainforest and marsh areas around the state. Although they will suck your blood they are not dangerous and are easily removed by the application of salt or heat. Do not pull them off as the wound will continue to bleed for quite some time. A leech bite can be a very itchy, swollen lump, but will go down in a few days – apply calamine lotion or cream to soothe the itching and try not to scratch it! Insect repellent, such as Rid, seems to stop them from getting hold quickly and gives you a chance of removing them before they attach.

## Bushfires

Bushfires happen almost every year in Tasmania, even with the higher average rainfalls in this state. Don't be the mug who starts one. In hot, dry, windy weather, be extremely careful with any naked flame – no cigarette butts out of car windows, please. On a Total Fire Ban day (listen to the radio or watch the billboards on country roads), it is forbidden even to use a camping stove in the open. The locals will not be amused if they catch you breaking this particular law; they'll happily dob you in, and the penalties are severe.

If you're unfortunate enough to find yourself driving through a bushfire, stay inside your car and try to park off the road in an open space, away from trees, until the danger's past. Lie on the floor under the dashboard, covering yourself with a wool blanket if possible. The front of the fire should pass quickly, and you will be much safer than if you were out in the open. It is very important to cover up with a wool blanket or wear protective clothing, as it has been proven that heat radiation is the big killer in bushfire situations.

Bushwalkers should take local advice before setting out. On a day of Total Fire Ban, don't go – delay your trip until the weather has changed. Chances are that it will be so unpleasantly hot and windy, you'll be better off anyway in an air-conditioned pub sipping a cool beer.

If you're out in the bush and you see smoke, even at a great distance, take it seriously. Go to the nearest open space, downhill if possible. A forested ridge is the most dangerous place to be. Bushfires move very quickly and change direction with the wind.

## Blizzards

At the other end of the scale, blizzards can occur in Tasmania's mountain regions even in summer. A white Christmas is not unheard of in places like Cradle Mountain National Park. Some summer storms are severe enough to deposit snow on the Lyell and Murchison highways.

Bushwalkers in particular need to be prepared for Tasmania's infamous weather, particularly those venturing into the southwest. Take warm clothing such as thermals and wind jackets as well as wind and waterproof garments and be sure to eat, drink and rest regularly. High quality tents suitable for snow camping are advisable and the best preparation is to carry enough food for two extra days, allowing you to wait for better weather.

## BUSINESS HOURS

Most shops close at 5 or 6 pm on weekdays, and either noon or 5 pm on Saturday. In some places Sunday trading is starting to catch on, but it's currently limited to small shops and hardware stores. In the larger towns, many shops stay open until 9 pm on Friday. Many large supermarkets also stay open late on Thursday night.

Banks are open from 9.30 am to 4 pm Monday to Thursday, and until 5 pm on Friday, except in small towns where they may only open one or two days a week.

Of course there are some exceptions to the unremarkable opening hours and all sorts of places stay open late and all weekend – particularly milk bars, convenience stores, small supermarkets, delis and city bookshops.

## PUBLIC HOLIDAYS & SPECIAL EVENTS

The Christmas holiday season is part of the long summer school vacation and the time you are most likely to find accommodation booked out and long queues. There are three other shorter school holiday periods during the year but they vary by a week or two from year to year, falling from early to mid-April, late June to mid-July, and late September to early October.

Public holidays are as follows:

| | |
|---|---|
| New Year's Day | 1 January |
| Australia Day | 26 January |
| Regatta Day | second Tuesday in February (southern Tasmania) |
| Launceston Cup | last Wednesday in February (Launceston only) |
| Eight Hour Day | first Monday in March |
| King Island Show | first Tuesday in March (King Island only) |
| Easter | Good Friday, Easter Saturday, Sunday, Monday & Tuesday |
| Anzac Day | 25 April |
| Queen's Birthday | second Monday in June |
| Burnie Show | first Friday in October (Burnie only) |
| Launceston Show | second Thursday in October (Launceston only) |
| Flinders Island Show | third Friday in October (Flinders Island only) |
| Hobart Show | third Thursday in October (southern Tasmania) |
| Recreation Day | first Monday in November (northern Tasmania) |
| Christmas Day | 25 December |
| Boxing Day | 26 December |

Major annual festivals and events include the following:

### January

**Sydney to Hobart Yacht Race**
The arrival (29 December to 2 January) in Hobart of the yachts competing in this annual New Year race is celebrated with a mardi gras.

**Melbourne to Hobart Westcoaster Yacht Race**
The competitors arrive on the same days as those in the Sydney to Hobart.

**Hobart Summer Festival & Taste of Tasmania**
Starts around the time of the completion of the yacht races and lasts for 10 days at Hobart's waterfront.

**Australia Day**
This national holiday, commemorating the arrival of the First Fleet, in 1788, is observed on 26 January.

### February

**Royal Hobart Regatta**
This is the largest aquatic carnival in the southern hemisphere and is held over four days, with boat races and other activities.

**National Penny Farthing Championships**
Evandale holds the strangest of bicycle races when people on these tall bikes race around the town. There are plenty of spills and other entertainment.

**Cradle Mountain Overland Run**
A hardy band of people attempt to run the entire 80km of the Overland Track in one day. If you

## Wild Waters on the Windy Westcoaster

The Westcoaster yacht race, commencing in Melbourne, heads south across Bass Strait and down Tasmania's wild and windy west coast. The Southern Ocean kicks up some big swells straight from the depths of the Antarctic and the Roaring 40s really puts wind into the sails. With only a few harbours in which yachts can take shelter, it is indeed one of the toughest yachting races around.

The race concludes at the same time – New Year's Eve – as its more famous counterpart, the Sydney to Hobart. Constitution Dock comes alive as people gather to watch and cheer the yachts as they arrive. Some hardy spectators even come to the dock in the wee small hours to add to the atmosphere of the finish.

are walking it, don't get put off by the speeding runners – they don't get to enjoy the views.

## Food & Wine Fun Festa

Held at Devonport, many of the better restaurants on the northern coast participate in this popular event, which also has live music.

## March

### Fingal Valley Coal Shovelling Festival

The small town of Fingal hosts this unusual festival. See some unusual events like roof bolting, coal shovelling and double-handed sawing.

## April

### Anzac Day

This is a national public holiday, on 25 April, commemorating the landing of Anzac troops at Gallipoli in 1915. Memorial marches by the returned soldiers of both world wars and the veterans of Korea and Vietnam are held all over the country.

### Three Peaks Race

A combined event where the competitors have to sail their yachts and also run up three of Tasmania's higher mountains. Starts from Beauty Point north of Launceston.

### Targa Tasmania

A car rally for exotic cars that runs for one week around the whole state. It is popular and receives wide press coverage.

## June

### Bicheno Festival

Local festival.

### Suncoast Jazz Festival

The east coast has the mildest winter weather in the state and is further warmed by this popular three day jazz festival.

## September

### Blooming Tasmania

Lasting three months, this is more of a coordinated set of festivals and displays rather than a single event. A special brochure is produced every year detailing when each festival and garden is open to the public.

### Tasmanian Football League Grand Final

A visit to a grand final is an exciting and interesting way to see this fast-paced game. The final is held in North Hobart.

## October

### Royal Shows

The royal agricultural and horticultural shows of Hobart, Burnie, Flinders Island and Launceston are held during this month.

### Herald Sun Tour

A major two week professional bicycle race around Victoria and Tasmania. The local section is mainly through tough hilly sections on the northern coast.

### Melbourne to Stanley Yacht Race

Yachts dash across Bass Strait in early October.

### Wynyard Tulip Festival

At this time of the year, the tulips are in flower and you can also visit the tulip farm at nearby Table Cape as well.

### Derby River Derby

Around 5000 people cram into this old mining town to watch the assorted fleet raft down the river. There are no rules to the race and everybody usually gets wet but has a great time.

### Tasmanian Craft Fair

Held in Deloraine over four days in late October and/or early November, this is claimed to be Australia's largest working craft fair.

## November

### Melbourne Cup

On the first Tuesday in November, the whole country comes to a virtual standstill for the three minutes or so when Australia's premier horse race is run (in Melbourne). Even Tasmania stops while the Cup runs.

### Australian Wooden Boat Festival

Held in even-numbered years at the Hobart docks, it features vessels from around Australia and celebrates Tasmania's boat-building heritage.

## December

### Carols by Candlelight

Evening services are held in both Hobart and Launceston before Christmas.

### Latrobe Wheel & Latrobe Gift

Professional bicycle races held when most other towns are having Christmas meals.

## COURSES

The Shipwright's Point School of Wooden Boatbuilding offers a two year accredited Diploma in Wooden Boatbuilding (see the 'Wooden Boats' boxed text in the South-East Coast chapter). The school was established in 1992, and its students have produced boats such as a 30 foot carvel yacht, a 32 foot gaff cutter and many dinghies.

Tasmania also has particular strengths in Antarctic science and policy, which can be studied through the Institute of Antarctic and Southern Ocean Studies at the University of Tasmania.

## WORK

If you come to Australia on a 12 month 'working holiday' visa you can officially only work for three out of those 12 months. Working on a regular tourist visa is strictly forbidden, but many travellers on tourist visas do find casual work. It is very difficult to find a job in Tasmania as it has the highest unemployment level in the country at around 12%.

With the current boom in tourism, casual work is sometimes easy to find in the high season (summer) at the major tourist centres. Other good prospects for casual work include factories, bar work, waiting on tables or washing dishes, childcare, fruit-picking and collecting for charities.

If you are coming to Tasmania with the intention of working, make sure you have enough funds to cover your stay, or have a contingency plan if the work is not forthcoming. Jobs can be hard to find and there is a lot of competition from locals.

The Commonwealth government's employment service, Centrelink (☎ 13 2850), has offices in the larger towns and cities and staff usually have a good idea of what's available where. Try the classified section of the daily papers under situations vacant too.

The various backpackers' magazines, newspapers and hostels are good information sources – some local employers even advertise on their notice boards. As with all short jobs, be wary of those who are ripping off workers with low pay or attached conditions (such as stipulating you must stay at a particular place).

## Tax File Number
It's important to apply for a Tax File Number (TFN) if you plan to work (or open a bank account – see the Money section for details) in Australia, not because it's a condition of employment, but without it tax will be deducted from any wages you receive at the maximum rate, which is currently set at 47%! To get a TFN, contact the Tasmanian branch of the Australian Taxation Office (☎ 13 2861, 200 Collins St, Hobart) for a form. It's a straightforward procedure, and you will have to supply adequate identification,

such as a passport and driving licence. The issue of a TFN takes about four weeks.

## Paying Tax
Yes, it's one of the certainties in life! If you have supplied your employer with a TFN, tax will be deducted from your wages at the rate of 29% if your weekly income is below $397. As your income increases, so does the tax rate, with the maximum being 47% for weekly incomes over $961. For nonresident visitors, tax is payable from the first dollar you earn, unlike residents who have something like a $6000 tax-free threshold. For this reason, if you have had tax deducted at the correct rate as you earn, it is unlikely you'll be entitled to a tax refund when you leave.

If you have had tax deducted at 47% because you have not submitted a TFN, chances are you will be entitled to a partial refund if your income was less than $50,000. Once you lodge a tax return (which must include a copy of the group certificate all employers issue to salaried workers at the end of the financial year or within seven days of leaving a job), you will be refunded the extra tax you have paid. Before you can lodge a tax return, however, you must have a TFN.

## Fruit & Vegetable Picking Seasons
In Tasmania the main harvest times for the crops where casual employment is a possibility are: February to May in the Huon Valley and Tasman Peninsula (apples, pears), and December to January in the Huon Valley and Kingston (soft fruit). For more information, inquire at Centrelink.

## ACCOMMODATION
Tasmania is very well equipped with youth hostels, backpackers hostels and caravan parks with camping grounds. There are plenty of motels and hotels as well as comfortable B&Bs around the state.

Despite the variety of places to stay, Tasmania's major tourist centres are often fully booked in summer, so it's wise to make reservations. In other seasons it can be an advantage to play it by ear, as you can get large discounts, particularly on more expensive accommodation, if you make inquiries late in the day.

For more comprehensive accommodation listings, the RACT has a state-wide directory listing caravan parks, hotels, motels, holiday flats and a number of backpackers hostels in almost every town. It's updated every year so the prices are generally fairly current. It's available from the club for a nominal charge if you're a member (or a member of an affiliated club enjoying reciprocal rights). Alternatively, check the free bi-monthly guide for visitors called *Tasmanian Travelways*, which includes most accommodation places.

### Prices

Accommodation prices quoted throughout this edition are high season prices obtained at the time of writing. However, even these are somewhat unreliable, as on occasion different prices were obtained for the same accommodation in the same season in the space of a couple of days. Use our prices as a guide, and remember that stand-by rates and low season rates will usually be considerably lower than anything quoted in this book. (Tasmania's economy is in such bad shape at the moment that even standard prices will sometimes go down rather than up from one high season to the next.)

### Heating

If you are travelling around Tasmania in the cooler months, you may occasionally find your accommodation very cold when you arrive, particularly if you are staying in a cottage or self-contained unit heated by a wood heater. Always ask about heating when you make your booking, and if you know when you are likely to arrive, ask your hosts to light the fire in advance. Once these fires have been burning for an hour or so, they are usually very effective.

The heating in cheap hotel rooms, cabins and hostels can sometimes be just plain inadequate; if you have your own transport and intend to stay in such accommodation, consider packing a small heater of your own as a back-up.

The important thing to remember is that if you feel the cold, you should always ask how a room is heated before making a booking.

### Camping & Caravanning

Camping in Tasmania can be really good or very poor! There are a great number of caravan parks and you'll almost always find a camping space. It's also the cheapest form of accommodation, with nightly costs for two for unpowered sites being around $10 or $12.

Unlike other states (and probably due to its size), most cities in Tasmania have caravan and camping parks conveniently close to the city centre.

In general, Tasmanian caravan parks are well kept, conveniently located and excellent value. Most have on-site vans that you can rent for the night. On-site cabins are also widely available. These usually have one bedroom, or at least an area that can be screened off from the rest of the unit – just the thing if you have kids. The price difference is not always that great – say $35 for an on-site van, $55 for a cabin.

### YHA Hostels

YHA hostels are part of an international organisation, the International Youth Hostel Federation (IYHF, also known as HI, Hostelling International), so if you're already a member of the YHA in your own country, your membership entitles you to use the hostels in Australia. The annual *YHA Accommodation and Discounts Guide* booklet, which is available from any Australian YHA office and from some YHA offices overseas, lists all the YHA hostels with useful little maps showing how to find them. Tasmania's YHA office (☎ 6234 9617, 28 Criterion St, Hobart) provides brochures and information to travellers as well as an Australia-wide hostel-to-hostel booking service. If you wish to use the hostel at Coles Bay, you must book it here.

YHA hostels provide basic accommodation, usually in small dormitories or bunk rooms, although more and more of them are providing twin rooms for couples. The nightly charges are very reasonable – usually between \$12 and \$15 a night per person.

Most YHAs take non-YHA members for an additional nightly fee of \$3 per person. When staying at a hostel nonmembers receive an Aussie Starter Card, to be stamped each night by the YHA. Once the card has been stamped 12 times, you are given a year's free membership.

You can become a full YHA member for \$27 a year (there's also a \$17 joining fee, although if you're an overseas resident you can join without having to pay this). You can join at the main office in Hobart, or at any youth hostel.

YHA members are also entitled to a number of handy discounts around the country – on things such as car hire, activities, accommodation etc – and these are detailed in the *YHA Accommodation & Discounts Guide* mentioned earlier.

You must have a regulation sheet sleeping bag or bed linen – for hygiene reasons a regular sleeping bag will not do. If you haven't got sheets they can be rented at many hostels, but it is cheaper to have your own. YHA offices and some larger hostels sell the official YHA sheet bag.

All hostels have cooking facilities, 24 hour access and laundry facilities, and there's usually a communal area where you can sit and talk. Most have excellent noticeboards and lots of brochures available.

The hostels range from tiny places to big, rambling buildings, and most have a manager who checks you in when you arrive and keeps the peace.

Accommodation can usually be booked directly with the manager or through the YHA office in Hobart.

## Backpacker Hostels

Tasmania has plenty of backpacker hostels, and the standard of these varies enormously. Some are run-down, inner-city hotels where the owners have tried to fill empty rooms; others are former motels, so each unit, typically with four to six beds, will have a fridge, TV and bathroom; still others are very similar to YHA hostels.

Prices at backpacker hostels are generally in line with YHA hostels – typically \$12 to \$15 – although some have discount rates for staying several nights.

## Guesthouses & B&Bs

It has become almost impossible to keep track of the number of B&Bs in Tasmania.

New places are opening all the time, and the network of accommodation alternatives includes everything from restored convict-built cottages, renovated and rambling old guesthouses and upmarket country homes to a simple bedroom in a family home.

Only in the cheapest B&Bs are you likely to have to share bathrooms and toilets – *en suites* are now very much the norm in this market, though it pays to check. If your room doesn't have an *en suite*, it may still have its own private facilities across the hall.

Breakfast may be continental or cooked and is often supplied in the form of provisions that you must cook or serve yourself. Prices are between about \$60 and \$120 a double. However, there is a lack of B&B accommodation at the lower end of this price range, which is unfortunate, because cheaper B&Bs should be an excellent alternative to hotel accommodation, which is so often bland and impersonal.

## Hotels & Pubs

Not every pub has rooms to rent, although many still do. If you're staying in a hotel that is not a new upmarket place like the Hilton, its rooms will often be older in style and drab; occasionally, however, you will strike one with real character. It is also true that publicans in Tasmania are slowly seeing the advantages of making their accommodation more pleasing to the eye, so although you will usually have to share facilities, you may find that the paint, curtains and bed linen are new and there's a TV in the corner. If the hotel has nothing resembling a reception desk or counter, just ask at the bar.

Generally, older-style hotels will have rooms for around $30 to $60 a double. (The upmarket hotels, of course, frequently charge over $100 a double.) Often breakfast is included in the price of a cheap room, and this may be continental or cooked. If you are being offered a continental breakfast, it might be worth checking out the provisions while you are assessing the room: particularly in the winter months, hotel guests can be few and far between, and breakfast provisions that are stale or past their use-by date have occasionally been found in guests' kitchens.

## Motels, Holiday Units & Cottages

Motels are usually some distance from the centre of town. Prices vary, but you'll rarely find anything for less than about $50 a double. Most provide at least tea and coffee-making facilities and a small fridge and all have *en suites*.

Holiday units are usually self-contained, and many are rented on either a daily or a weekly basis. Paying for a week, even if you stay only for a few days, can sometimes still be cheaper than having those days at a higher daily rate. If there are more than just two of you, another advantage of holiday units is that they often have two or more bedrooms. A two bedroom holiday unit is typically priced at about 1½ times the cost of a comparable single bedroom unit. Prices given in this guide are for single night stays and are often in the range of about $60 to $80 a double. Historic cottages can be anything up to about $130 a double. Unlike prices for holiday units, prices for historic cottages usually include breakfast.

## Colleges

During the summer university vacations (from November to February) you can also stay at university colleges during uni vacations. These places can be relatively cheap and comfortable and provide an opportunity for you to meet people. Costs are typically from about $30 to $35 for B&B.

## Other Possibilities

There are lots of less conventional accommodation possibilities. For example, there are plenty of national parks where, providing you have a park pass, you can camp for free. Roadside rest areas provide emergency, short-term camping. If you want to spend longer in Tasmania, the first place to look for a shared flat or a room is in the classified advertising section of the daily newspaper. Wednesday and Saturday are the best days for these ads. Noticeboards in universities, hostels and cafés are good places to look for flats/houses to share or rooms to rent.

## FOOD

The culinary delights can be one of the real highlights of a visit to Tasmania. There are many fine restaurants offering a wide variety of fresh, local produce. On King Island, for example, are fine quality meat, cheese and cream, from which scrumptious meals are put together to tempt your taste buds. Tasmania is renowned for its superb range of seafood: fish like blue-eye (previously called trevalla) and striped trumpeter are delicious, as is the Tasmanian salmon. Rock lobster, crayfish and oysters are among the shellfish available.

Food is high in quality and relatively low in cost. A takeaway sandwich or pie and a drink will cost around $4. Main meals in local pubs will cost between $12 and $18 in the lounge, but there will often be cheaper meals and snacks available at the bar. Mid-range restaurants usually charge between $15 and $18 a main course, while upmarket restaurants charge $20 or more.

The cities have a selection of cafés and restaurants serving food that can be termed 'modern Australian'. These are dishes that borrow from a wide range of foreign cuisines but have a definite local flavour. At some places seemingly anything goes, so you might find Asian-inspired curry-type dishes sharing a menu with European or Mediterranean-inspired dishes. It all adds up to exciting dining.

Vegetarians are generally well catered for in most parts of the state. While there are few dedicated vegetarian restaurants, most modern cafés and restaurants have some vegetarian dishes on the menu.

## Takeaway Food

Around the state you'll find all the well-known international fast-food chains – McDonald's, KFC, Pizza Hut etc – all typically conspicuous.

On a more local level, you'll find a milk bar on (almost) every corner in the centre of towns, and most of them will sell pies, pasties, sandwiches and milkshakes. Then there are the speciality sandwich bars, delicatessens, bakeries and health-food shops, which are all worth seeking out if you want something a little more exotic than a pie.

Most shopping centres have a fish and chip shop and a pizza joint. If the food is cooked for you while you wait it's usually reasonably good. Absolute rock bottom is the kept-lukewarm-for-hours food found at roadside cafés and roadhouses. Give it a miss unless you have absolutely no choice, then ask for something that's not in the warmer trays so they cook a fresh batch.

## Restaurants & Cafés

The best Tasmanian eateries serve food as exciting and as innovative as anything you can find anywhere, and it doesn't need to cost a fortune. Best value are the modern and casual cafés, where for less than $20 you can get an excellent feed.

While eating out is a pleasure in the big cities, in many smaller country towns it can be something of an ordeal. The food will be predictable and unexciting, and is usually of the 'meat and three veg' variety. There are, of course, exceptions, with superb restaurants in many out-of-the-way tourist locations.

All over the state, you'll find restaurants advertising that they're BYO. The initials stand for 'Bring Your Own' and it means that you are permitted to bring your own alcohol with you. This is a real boon to wine-loving but budget-minded travellers because you can bring your own bottle of wine from the local bottle shop or from that winery you visited last week and not pay any mark-up,

although some restaurants make a small 'corkage' charge (typically $1 to $2 per person) if you bring your own.

## Pubs

Most pubs serve two types of meals: bistro meals, which are usually in the $12 to $18 range and are served in the dining room or lounge bar, where there's usually a self-serve salad bar; and bar (or counter) meals, which are filling, simple, no-frills meals eaten in the public bar, and which usually cost less than $10, sometimes as little as $4.

The quality of pub food varies enormously, and while it's usually fairly basic and unimaginative, it's generally pretty good value. The usual meal times are from noon to 2 pm and 6 to 8 pm.

## DRINKS

Alcohol drinkers should be aware that, in Australia, people who drive under the influence of alcohol and get caught lose their licences. The maximum permissible blood-alcohol concentration level for drivers is 0.05%.

## Beer

Australian beer will be fairly familiar to North Americans; it's similar to what's known as lager in the UK. It may taste like lemonade to the European real ale addict, but it packs quite a punch and is invariably chilled before drinking.

In Tasmania, there's Cascade in the south and Boags in the north, both having their fair share of loyal drinkers. The Cascade Brewery, near Hobart, produces Cascade Premium and Pale Ale. Visitors tend to ask for 'Cascade' expecting to get the one with the distinctive label bearing the Tasmanian tigers, but you are unlikely to get Premium unless you ask specifically for it. Cascade Brewery also conducts an informative tour. When you travel north, you cross an invisible line where all the hotels serve beer from Boags Brewery. They produce similar style beers such as Boags Export Lager and James Boags Premium.

Standard beer generally contains around 4.9% alcohol, although the trend in recent years has been towards low-alcohol beers, with an alcohol content of between 2% and 3.5%.

## Wine

If you don't fancy the beer, then try the wine. The wine industry was started by a few pioneers in the mid-1950s and is quickly gaining recognition for producing quality wines. Tasmanian wines are characterised by their full, fruity flavour, plus the high acidity expected of cool, temperate wine regions.

Grapes are grown all over the state, with the largest wine-growing region being at Pipers Brook in the north east, and the West Tamar region being the second largest. Notable vineyards, with cellar door tastings, include Pipers Brook, Rochecombe & Heemskirk and St Matthias. There are also wineries dotted down the east coast from Bicheno to Dunally, including the well-respected Freycinet, and farther south to the Huon Valley area where you'll find Hartzview Vineyard, among others. The Derwent River valley also has major wineries, including Meadowbank and Moorilla Estate. The Moorilla vineyard is the oldest in the southern part of the state, having been established in 1958.

Tasmania's wines are quite expensive, compared to similar mainland wines. You'll be set back more than $20 for an acceptable bottle of wine, but the best of them are superb.

The most enjoyable way to get to know Tasmanian wines is to get out to the wineries and sample the wine at the cellar door. Many wineries have tastings: you just zip straight in and say what you'd like to try. However, free wine tastings are no longer common and certainly do not mean open slather drinking. The glasses are generally thimble-sized and it's expected that you will buy something. Many wineries and tasting centres now charge a small 'tasting fee' of a couple of dollars, refundable if you buy any wine.

## ENTERTAINMENT
### Discos & Nightclubs

These are confined to the cities. Clubs range from the exclusive 'members only'

variety to barn-sized discos where anyone who wants to spend money is welcomed with open arms. Admission charges range from around $10 to $20.

Some places have certain dress standards, but it is generally left to the discretion of the people at the door – if they don't like the look of you, bad luck. The more 'upmarket' nightclubs attract an older, more sophisticated and affluent crowd, and generally have stricter dress codes, smarter décor – and, inevitably, higher prices. Many of these nightclubs double as winebars and cafés earlier in the evening.

## Casinos

In Hobart, the Wrest Point Casino is on the shores of Sandy Bay, and you can go in as long as you are dressed neatly. There are also live shows and discos. A similar standard of dress applies to the Country Club Casino at Launceston.

## Live Music

Many suburban pubs have live music, and these are often great places for catching live bands – either nationally well-known names or up-and-coming performers trying to make a name for themselves. Most of the famous bands in Australia have played the pub circuit.

The University of Tasmania Student Union building and the Derwent Entertainment Centre are the venues used by the more famous visiting artists.

The best way to find out about the local scene is to get to know some locals, or travellers who have spent some time in the place. Otherwise there are listings in local newspapers.

## Cinema

In Hobart, only one of the major commercial cinema chains operates. The Village Cinema Complex (181 Collins St) shows mainstream popular films. There is also a modern cinema complex in Launceston. Smaller towns usually have only one cinema, open intermittently. These theatres are often in grand old buildings. Seeing a new-release mainstream film costs around $10

($7.50 for children under 15) in Hobart, although often less in country areas and on certain nights.

Also in Hobart, you'll find art house and independent cinemas, and these places generally screen either films that aren't made for mass consumption or specialise purely in reruns of classic and cult movies. The State Cinema in Elizabeth St, North Hobart, is part of the art-house cinema scene.

## SPECTATOR SPORTS
If you're an armchair – or wooden bench – sports fan, Tasmania has much to offer. The football season runs from about March to September and when it ends, it's just about time for the cricket season to begin.

### Australian Rules
A very unique form of football is Australian Rules – only Gaelic football is anything like it. It's a team sport on an oval field with an oval ball that can be kicked, caught, hit with the hand or carried and bounced. You get six points for kicking a goal and one point for a 'behind' (kicking it through side posts). There are four quarters of 25 minutes each. Fast, tactical, skilful, rough and athletic, it can produce gripping finishes when even after 100 minutes of play the outcome hangs on the very last kick.

Tasmania has a northern and a southern league, and the two winning teams meet in the Tasmanian Football League Grand Final in late September at North Hobart Football Oval. Match details and tickets to games are available from the Tasmanian Football League (☎ 6234 9177). You'll only need to book for final games.

### Cricket
This is played during the other (non-football) half of the year. Tasmania held its first international test in Hobart in 1995, though one-day matches had been played at Bellerive Oval in the past. Tasmania takes part in the interstate Sheffield Shield competition and also has district cricket matches. Tasmania has never won the Sheffield Shield, but has pro-

duced two outstanding Australian Test side batsmen: David Boon and Ricky Ponting. Contact the Tasmanian Cricket Association (☎ 6244 7099) for tickets and match fixtures.

### Horse Racing
Major race meetings are the Hobart Cup at Elwick in January, the Launceston Cup in February and the Devonport Cup in January. Regular meetings are held about once every month at the Elwick racecourse in Hobart. You can't book tickets; just go along to the course. Most towns have a horse-racing track or a Totalisator Agency Board (TAB) betting office where you can bet on the races.

### Yachting
Hobart is the finishing line of the famous Sydney to Hobart yacht race and the lesser-known Westcoaster race at New Year. For the three weeks after New Year, regular, short races are held on the Derwent River and spectators can get reasonable views from the hills. In February the Royal Hobart Regatta is worth seeing.

The Three Peaks race in April combines sailing with marathon running.

### Tennis
The tennis courts at the Domain in Hobart are the venue for the state championships in March and for an international women's tournament in January, the latter being a warm-up tournament for the Australian Open. For bookings, contact the Domain Tennis Centre (☎ 6234 4805).

## SHOPPING
There are lots of things definitely *not* to buy, and a check of where it was actually manufactured should be made! Far too many of the supposedly authentic 'Australiana' items are actually made in Asia.

### Australiana
The term 'Australiana' is a euphemism for souvenirs. These are the things you buy as gifts for all the friends, aunts and uncles, nieces and nephews, and any other sundry bods back home. They are supposedly

representative of Australia and its culture, although many are extremely dubious. A typical example in Tassie is the stuffed toy Tasmanian devil.

## Huon Pine

Many woodworkers have taken to producing carvings and wood turnings from the local Huon pine. Some of the work is truly magnificent. Good examples, some of which are available for purchase, can be found at the Esperance Forest & Heritage Centre in Geeveston, the stores in Richmond or the craft shops at the Salamanca Market. Items from other uniquely Tasmanian timbers such as blackwood should also be considered. The timbers have rich colours and are all produced locally.

## Killecrankie 'Diamonds'

These 'diamonds' come from Flinders Island. They're beautiful stones, but not actually diamonds. They are really topaz – a semi-precious stone that comes in pale blue, pale pink and white varieties – and can be purchased on Flinders Island. The Gem Shop in Whitemark and Killiecrankie Enterprises (the general store in Killecrankie) can show you a selection of 'diamonds'. The Gem Shop also conducts fossicking tours where you get to look for your own. See the Flinders Island section of the Islands chapter for more details.

## Blundstones

These heavy-duty boots made in Tasmania wear well and are reasonably cheap. Intended for use on construction sites, they became something of a fashion item a few years ago and are still quite popular footwear. See the Shopping section of the Hobart chapter for details of retails outlets.

## Other Gifts

For those last-minute gifts, drop into a deli and buy some Tasmanian leatherwood honey (it is one of a number of powerful local varieties). The local cheeses are often magnificent, with King Island Brie being internationally famous. The cheeses produced at Pyengana and Lactos are also well worth finding in the delicatessens.

There are plenty of photographic calendars and coffee table books about Tasmania, many of them displaying the wilderness areas.

Antique stores exist all over the state and there is lots of old furniture to be found. This resulted from the large number of settlers who migrated here from Europe in the 19th century and brought their furniture with them. However, the fact that something is old does not mean it's good quality or worth a high price. Before buying antiques, you really need to know what is good value.

# Activities

However much you might enjoy wandering the streets of historic towns and lazing about in quaint cafés, you won't feel you've really experienced Tasmania until you've ventured into the mountains and onto the rivers, oceans and cliffs that are the greatest attractions of this beautiful island.

Bushwalks here are among the best (and at times the most treacherous) in the country: try tackling Federation Peak or the Western Arthurs if you really want to test your endurance. White-water rafting on the Franklin River has a deserved reputation for grandeur and excitement, while abseiling and rock climbing on the Tasman and Freycinet peninsulas is literally dazzling.

For those who want something less demanding, there's boating on the Arthur and Pieman rivers in the north-west, ocean kayaking on the waters around Port Arthur in the south-east, caving at Hastings in the south and diving with seals at George Town in the north.

If you have a yacht, or can afford to charter one, you'll be able to spend lazy days exploring the many bays and inlets of the D'Entrecasteaux Channel, while if you're a trout fisher with a desire for seclusion, you'll find plenty of remote lakes well stocked with fish.

## THE TASMANIAN TRAIL

The Tasmanian Trail is a 477km route from Devonport to Dover intended for walkers, cyclists and horse riders. Most of the trail is on forestry roads, fire trails or country roads. It passes towns, pastoral land and forests, and there are camping spots about every 32km. All the information you need to follow the trail is in the *Tasmanian Trail Guide Book*, available in visitors' centres throughout the state. See the Bushwalking, Cycling and Riding sections of this chapter for specific details on those activities.

## BUSHWALKING

Tasmania is a mecca for walkers from all over the world, and its most famous track is undoubtedly the superb Overland Track in Cradle Mountain-Lake St Clair National Park. Most of the best walks are in national parks, which you can read more about in the 'Flora, Fauna, National Parks & Reserves' special section earlier in this book.

### Bushwalking Gear

As bushwalking is so popular in Tasmania, there are many shops selling outdoor gear. Paddy Pallin (76 Elizabeth St, Hobart, and 110 George St, Launceston), Mountain Design (74 Elizabeth St, Hobart), Snowgum (104 Elizabeth St, Hobart), Allgoods (corner St John and York Sts, Launceston) and the Backpackers Barn (12 Edward St, Devonport) all have a very good range of bushwalking gear and plenty of invaluable advice. Snowgum, the Backpackers Barn and the Launceston City Youth Hostel (36 Thistle St, Launceston) hire bushwalking gear, while Goshawk Gear (55 Liverpool St, Hobart) sells mostly second-hand clothing and equipment and will buy it back for about half the price you paid if it's returned in a similar condition to that in which it was sold.

### Maps

The Department of Environment & Land Management produces and sells an excellent series of topographic maps available at visitors' centres, Service Tasmania (☎ 6233 3382, 134 Macquarie St, Hobart), the Tasmanian Map Centre (☎ 6231 9043, 96 Elizabeth St, Hobart) and some shops specialising in bushwalking gear and outdoor equipment.

### Books

Lonely Planet's guide *Bushwalking in Australia*, by John & Monica Chapman, describes nine walks of different lengths and difficulty in Tasmania. Among these are two-day strolls through Mt Field National Park or around the beaches of Freycinet Peninsula, as well as the Overland Track and more difficult walks such as the 11 to 14 day coastal trek along the South Coast and Port Davey tracks, and three to four-day walks to the summits of Frenchmans Cap and Mt Anne.

If you prefer shorter walks of one day or less, the books by Jan Hardy & Bert Elson are worth finding. Two of these cover the Hobart area, one covers Launceston and the north-east and a fourth covers the north-west. Some other writers also produce small books on specific areas, such as the Tasman Peninsula, and the mines of the west coast. One very popular book of shorter walks throughout the state is *A Visitor's Guide to Tasmania's National Parks* by Greg Buckman.

Another popular book describing walks throughout the state is *100 Walks in Tasmania*, by Tyrone Thomas. It covers a wide variety of short and multi-day walks, and Tyrone's descriptive passages are a joy to read.

There are also many detailed guides to specific walks or areas, including *South West Tasmania* by John Chapman and *Cradle Mountain – Lake St Clair & Walls of Jerusalem* by John Chapman & John Siseman.

## National Park Passes

Entry fees apply to all Tasmanian national parks. See the National Parks section of the 'Flora, Fauna, National Parks & Reserves' special section for details. At the time of writing walker permits were also being proposed, but it was not expected that they would be introduced for a number of years.

## Guided Walks

There are plenty of companies offering guided walks that range from one-day excursions to multi-day camping trips. Well established companies are Craclair Walking Holidays (☎ 6424 7833) and Tasmanian Expeditions (☎ 6334 3477), both of which offer trips along the Overland Track, to the Walls of Jerusalem and to some other popular destinations. Tasman Bush Tours (☎ 6423 4965) is a fairly new

company operating out of Tasman House Backpackers in Devonport.

If sleeping in a tent is not your style, Cradle Huts (☎ 6331 2006) can offer you a guided walk along the Overland Track staying in privately owned huts. See the Cradle Mountain-Lake St Clair section of the West chapter for details.

There are plenty of smaller companies, such as Taswalks (☎ 6363 6112), which provide more personal service for small bushwalking groups.

## Code of Ethics & Safety Precautions

The Tasmanian Parks and Wildlife Service (PWS) publishes a booklet called *Welcome to the Wilderness – Bushwalking Trip Planner for Tasmania's World Heritage Area*, which has sections on planning, minimal impact bushwalking and wilderness survival. Also included is a very useful equipment checklist that is essential reading for bushwalkers who are unfamiliar with Tasmania's notoriously changeable weather.

The PWS (☎ 6233 6191, GPO Box 44A, Hobart 7001) can send you this booklet and other leaflets, including the *Bushwalking Code*, free of charge. You can also pick up PWS literature at Service Tasmania (☎ 6233 3382, 134 Macquarie St, Hobart) or any national park visitors' centre or ranger station. Their useful Web site is at www.parks.tas.gov.au.

In 1997 the Tasmanian World Heritage Area and Freycinet National Park were declared 'fuel stove only' areas. A brochure outlining regulations relating to areas under this classification is available from the PWS.

In Tasmania (particularly in the west and south-west), a fine day can quickly become cold and stormy in any season, so it is essential that you carry warm clothing, waterproof gear and a compass year-round. In addition, you should never rely on finding a place in a hut; always carry a tent, particularly on popular walks such as the Overland Track.

On all extended walks, you must carry extra food in case you have to sit out a few days of especially bad weather. This is a very important point, because the PWS routinely hears of walkers running out of food in such instances and relying on the goodwill of better-prepared people they meet along the way to supplement their supplies. In the worst of circumstances, such lack of preparation and disregard for others puts lives at risk: if bad weather continues for long enough, everyone suffers, including those who have been kind enough to share their food.

Tasmanian walks are famous for their mud. Be prepared for this: waterproof your boots, wear gaiters and watch where you're putting your feet. Even on the Overland Track, long sections of which are covered by boardwalk, you can find yourself up to your hips in mud if you're not careful.

Following are some additional guidelines that you should adhere to whenever you walk in the Tasmanian bush.

- Bushwalkers should stay on established trails, avoid cutting corners and taking short cuts, and stay on hard ground where possible.
- Before tackling a long or remote walk, tell someone responsible about your plans and arrange to contact them when you return. Make sure you sign the PWS register at the start and finish of your walk.
- Keep bushwalking parties small.
- Where possible, visit popular areas at low-season times.
- When camping, always use designated camping grounds where provided. When bush camping, look for a natural clearing.
- When driving, stay on existing tracks or roads.
- Don't harm native birds or animals; these are protected by law.
- Don't feed native animals.
- Carry all your rubbish out with you – don't burn or bury it.
- Avoid polluting lakes and streams; don't wash yourself or your dishes in them, and keep soap and detergent at least 50m away.
- Use toilets provided; otherwise bury human waste at least 100m away from waterways.
- Boil all water for 10 minutes before drinking it, or use water purifying tablets.
- Don't take pets into national parks.
- Do not light fires in the World Heritage Area and Freycinet Peninsula National Park; use only fuel stoves for cooking. In other areas, don't light open fires unless absolutely necessary; if you do, keep the fires small, burn only dead fallen wood and use an existing fireplace. Make sure the fires are completely extinguished before moving on.
- On days of total fire ban, do not light any fire whatsoever, including a fuel stove.

## The Walks

**Mt Wellington (half a day)** Many walkers visiting Tasmania ignore Mt Wellington because of its proximity to Hobart. By doing so, they deprive themselves of some dramatic views. If scenery is your objective, take the level Organ Pipes Walk from the Chalet to its junction with the Zig Zag Track and follow that track to the summit. The Organ Pipes Walk takes you along the base of the cliffs, which from this vantage point are truly majestic. The views of the city and river spread out below are expansive from both sections of the walk, and on the upper reaches of the Zig Zag Track you really can hear the wind moan through the Organ Pipes like mournful music. (See the Mt Wellington section of the Hobart chapter for information about the mountain and a map of these tracks.)

**Hartz Peak (half a day)** This is a good day walk that you can drive to from Hobart. The views from the peak are panoramic, but because the mountain is so often in cloud, you should wait for a forecast of clear skies before setting off. (See the South-East Coast chapter for details of Hartz Mountains National Park.)

**Tarn Shelf (one day)** This is a wonderful walk at any time of year but particularly in fine weather when there are still patches of snow about the crags and tarns that adorn the shelf. You can drive to Mt Field National Park from Hobart, complete the walk and return to Hobart in one long day, but you might prefer to camp or stay in one of the huts in the park for a couple of nights so that you can really appreciate your time on the shelf. See the Mt Field National Park section of the South-West chapter for details of this and other walks in the area.

**Peninsula Walks** The **Freycinet Peninsula Circuit** (two days) takes walkers past the red granite peaks of the Hazards to some gorgeous white-sand beaches, including **Wineglass Bay**, which can be a stunning day walk in itself. Freycinet has some of the best weather in the state – another excellent reason for putting this walk at the top of your list. (See the East Coast chapter for information about Freycinet National Park.)

The **Tasman Peninsula Walk** (four days) from the Devils Kitchen to Waterfall Bay, Fortescue Bay, Cape Huay, Cape Pillar and back to Fortescue Rd is famous for its views of magnificent coastal cliffs and rock formations. (See the Tasman Peninsula section of the Around Hobart chapter for details of other, shorter walks in this area.)

Both these walks are reasonably easy and are in popular national parks well served by public transport.

**Walls of Jerusalem (one day or more)**
Many Tasmanian bushwalkers who value solitude regard the Walls of Jerusalem National Park as the most beautiful park in the state. The 'walls' surround a central basin entered through the pass known as Herods Gate. Inside, the various peaks that comprise the 'walls' tower above lakes, tarns and valleys, creating a scene of exquisite grandeur. Once you've reached the park itself, you can camp for any length of time and take day walks to features you wish to visit. See the Walls of Jerusalem National Park section of the North chapter for details of road access and public transport to the start of the two hour walk into the park. It is also possible to walk to the Walls from Cradle Mountain-Lake St Clair National Park. Unfortunately, this park is very exposed and so can be dangerous in extreme weather conditions.

**Frenchmans Cap (three to five days)**
Part of the reason this walk is so alluring is that Frenchmans Cap can be seen to great advantage from the Lyell Hwy between Hobart and Queenstown. However, steep climbing is required to reach the peak. (See the Franklin-Gordon Wild Rivers National Park section of the West chapter for details of bus services to the start of the walk.)

**Overland Track (five to six days)** This is the most popular long bushwalk in Tasmania, drawing between 6000 and 7000 walkers a year. It extends 80km from Cradle Mountain south to Lake St Clair and features craggy mountains, beautiful lakes and tarns, extensive forests and moorlands, and side walks to waterfalls, valleys and still more mountains, including Mt Ossa (1617m), the highest mountain in Tasmania. Because it is adequately served by public transport, well managed and signposted for its entire length, the Overland Track is suitable for those undertaking their first long-distance walk, provided they are reasonably fit and properly equipped. It was walked for this edition in December 1998, and track notes are provided in the Cradle Mountain-Lake St Clair section of the West chapter.

This is such a popular walk that gregarious trekkers are likely to have as much fun socialising in the huts at night as they have walking the track during the day.

**South Coast Track (10 days)** This is a relatively undemanding long track by Tasmanian standards but should still only be undertaken by walkers who have experience of hiking in dreadful weather. The track extends from Port Davey to Cockle Creek and is renowned for its remoteness and its views of magnificent beaches. Public transport is available to Cockle Creek from early November until early April (see the Lune River section of the South-East Coast chapter) but the only transport from Port Davey is light plane or boat.

**Difficult Walks** The **Western Arthurs Skyline Traverse, Frankland Traverse** and **Federation Peak** are difficult long walks in Tasmania's rugged and remote south-west that will take up to 12 days to complete and should only be attempted by extremely experienced walkers. Some writers claim that

## The Beginner's Guide to the Overland Track

The Overland Track is a great walk for first-time long-distance bushwalkers: Kathy Chisholm, who accompanied me when I walked the track in December 1998 to make track notes for this edition, is a fit mother of two in her early 30s who'd never done an overnight walk before, and she managed it in four days.

Kathy and I experienced perfect weather conditions. Lonely Planet author Graeme Cornwallis was not so lucky: he encountered drenching rain and, consequently, far more mud, both of which added to the length and difficulty of his walk.

The Overland Track is well graded by Tasmanian standards but many new walkers will find it challenging. Some sections, such as that near Narcissus Hut, are across boardwalk and are easy walking. However there are other sections, such as that around Pelion Hut, where conditions are difficult. Long sections of the track are muddy and wet, some sections are relatively steep, and in many places walkers must pick their way through tree roots. This can make it quite tiring for the inexperienced, especially if their packs are heavy (and remember: the smaller your party, the more each member will have to carry).

The huts always seem to be busy during the walking season. They are basic, but they're heated (either by coal or gas) and dry – very important if the weather is persistently wet. The beds are simply long wooden benches you must usually share with others; there are no mattresses. Huts also have tables and benchtops that are very useful when you are cooking.

**Hugh Sibly**

As a novice bushwalker and vocal critic of sleeping in tents, I was not an obvious choice for a walking partner. My ignorance worked in my favour, however, because the first time I put on my pack (or any pack) was in Waldheim car park. It was unbelievably heavy, and I couldn't imagine carrying it all the way to Lake St Clair. But it was too late to turn back.

The walk was satisfying without being gruelling. In fact, I found my mind more challenged than my body. Bad weather, snakes, leeches, mosquitoes – something to torment everyone.

At the Du Cane Hut we met two young men who were walking south to north, and so had already been where we were heading. They spoke with enthusiasm of waterfalls and mountains, but thing that most impressed them, though, was the toilet at Du Cane Hut. They *loved* the toilet at Du Cane Hut. In hindsight, they didn't describe it to us, but they left us in no doubt as to how much they admired it.

The prospect of discovering for myself the pleasures of this famous toilet seemed to lighten my pack. When we finally got to Du Cane Hut and found a spot to camp, I took my soggy toilet paper (I was the only person on the whole track who didn't have their toilet paper in a zip-lock bag) and followed the sign to the toilet up a little hill.

On top of the hill, overlooking the path into the Du Cane Hut site, was the toilet to which I'd been so looking forward. On a concrete slab was a huge chunk of wood crudely chiselled into what could have been the lid to a giant rectangular canister. It was fastened to the slab with two leather straps, hinge-like. Obviously, it covered a foul hole over which one was meant to squat.

It was only after squatting that I realised there was a small bush in front of this excuse for a toilet that obscured the user from view. Then I understood the primal pleasure of tending nature out in the open with only a small bush to acknowledge that we have been domesticated. At least, that's what I figure appealed to my young friends; I didn't particularly like it.

**Kathy Chisholm**

Federation Peak is the most difficult walk in Australia.

All three walks feature spectacular scenery, but the weather in this region is notoriously unpredictable and often appalling. Before Lake Pedder was inundated, it was possible to walk down to its famous beach from the Frankland Traverse. Today, however, the waters of the flooded lake are so extensive that there is no way to escape the track when the weather turns foul: all you can do is return to the beginning, continue to the end, or huddle up in your tent until conditions improve.

## CYCLING

Brake Out Cycling Tours (☎ 6239 1080) has a great Mt Wellington descent for $35, while Tasmanian Expeditions (☎ 6334 3477, toll-free 1800 030 230) has a variety of overnight and extended cycling tours available. It also offers cycling, canoeing, rafting and/or walking combination packages throughout the state.

Cycling around Tasmania can be a fantastic way to see the countryside up close and at your own pace.

If you intend to cycle between Hobart and Launceston via either coast, count on it taking around 10 to 14 days. For a full circuit of the island, allow 14 to 28 days. If you are planning a circuit, consider following the Giro Tasmania, which is detailed on the excellent 'giro' page of Bicycling Tasmania's Web site at www.netspace.net.au/~dmurphy/bt.htm.

Rent-a-Cycle at the Launceston City Youth Hostel (☎ 6344 9779, 36 Thistle St) has mountain bikes plus all the equipment you'll need for short or long trips. It charges $95 a week, including helmet and panniers. There's a reduced rate for each additional week, and a bond of $100 applies to all rentals. Lonely Planet has had some good reports about the service offered here.

In Hobart, Adelphi Court hostel (☎ 6228 4829) hires out bicycles for $20 a day, Derwent Bike Hire (☎ 0419 008357) charges $100 a week and Brake Out (☎ 6239 1080) charges $20 a day. Jim's Car Rentals also (☎ 6236 9779) hires out bicycles; its rate is $15 a day.

See the Bicycle section in the Getting Around chapter for more information.

## SKIING

There are two small ski resorts in Tasmania: Ben Lomond, which is 60km from Launceston; and Mt Mawson, in Mt Field National Park, 70km from Hobart. Both offer cheaper, although less-developed, ski facilities than the major resorts in Victoria and New South Wales (NSW); for example, rope tows are still used on some runs. Despite the state's southerly latitude, snowfalls tend to be fairly light and unreliable. For more information, see the Ben Lomond National Park section of the Launceston & Around chapter and the Mt Field National Park section of the South-West chapter.

## SWIMMING

The north and east coasts have plenty of sheltered, white-sand beaches that are excellent for swimming, although the water is rather cold. There are also some pleasant beaches near Hobart, such as Bellerive and Sandy Bay, but these tend to be polluted, so it's better to head towards Kingston, Blackmans Bay or Seven Mile Beach for safe swimming. On the west coast the surf can be ferocious and the beaches are unpatrolled.

## SURFING
Tasmania has plenty of good surf beaches. Close to Hobart, the best spots are Clifton Beach and the surf beach en route to South Arm. The southern beaches of Bruny Island – particularly at Cloudy Bay – can be good when a southerly swell is rolling. The east coast from Bicheno past St Helens has excellent beaches and fine surf. The greatest spot of all is Marrawah on the west coast, where the waves are often huge, as the ocean here is uninterrupted all the way to South America. The only problem is that it's a long way from anywhere else in the state, but that's part of its charm. See the Marrawah section of the North-West chapter for more information.

## SCUBA DIVING & SNORKELLING
On the east coast and around King and Flinders Islands there are some excellent scuba diving opportunities. In addition, underwater trails have been marked at Tinderbox near Hobart and on Maria Island.

Diving equipment can be rented to licensed divers in such places as Hobart, Launceston, Wynyard and on the east coast. If you want to learn to dive, go on a diving course; they are considerably cheaper here than on the mainland. In Hobart, courses are run by Southern Tasmanian Divers (☎ 6234 7243, 212 Elizabeth St). Other courses are run on the Tasman Peninsula and in Bicheno, St Helens and Wynyard; see the relevant chapters for details.

## SAILING
Since Tassie is surrounded by water, it's not surprising that sailing is so popular here. Fleets of white sails often dot the Derwent River in the sailing season and many Hobart residents own yachts and consider

Built from local Huon pine, the *Olive May* is Australia's oldest working vessel and is now used primarily for cruises.

Hobart's sailing opportunities among its greatest attractions. The D'Entrecasteaux Channel is wide and deep and exceptionally beautiful. Its waters are sheltered by Bruny Island, although conditions can be difficult south of Gordon.

There are many good anchorages in the Channel where you can spend a night or two, but it's best not to anchor overnight in the Derwent River between North Bruny and the Tasman Bridge except in Ralph's Bay; moor at one of the yacht clubs or the city docks instead. A berth at the Royal Hobart Yacht Club (☎ 6223 4599) is $15 a night, with the first night free. The Hobart Ports Corporation (☎ 6235 1000) charges by the week: for a 13m yacht it's $40, while for a 20m vessel it's $50. North of the bridge, you can anchor in Cornelian Bay or New Town Bay. At the pretty town of Kettering, in the Channel south of Hobart, there's a good marina, but it's usually crowded and it's not very easy to find a mooring there.

If you are planning a sailing trip to or around Tasmania, ring Paul Kerrison, the commodore of the Cruising Yacht Club of Tasmania (☎ 6273 4192) for advice. The club puts out detailed publications about sailing in various parts of the state that list, among other things, good anchorages.

If you are a capable sailor, you can hire a Beneteau Oceanis 320 or 350 from Yachting Holidays (☎ 6224 3195, 0417 550 879) in Hobart or Kettering from Friday evening to Sunday afternoon for $700 or $825 respectively. If you are not a sailor yourself, you can take a cruise on the *Prudence* (☎ 6223 4568), a Huon pine motor-sailer usually docked at Waterman's Dock in Hobart. Rates for Bruny Island cruises for a minimum of eight people start at $85 a person. Another option is the *Olive May*, a Huon pine boat operated by the South West Passage Cruising Company (☎ 6298 1062). It runs tours from Dover around the southern end of Bruny Island. (See the Dover section of the South-East Coast chapter for details.)

## CANOEING, KAYAKING & RAFTING

Tasmania is famous for its white-water rafting on the wild Franklin River in the west, but there are many other rivers that are popular for rafting and boating. The Arthur and Pieman rivers in the north-west and Ansons River in the north-east are great for a long, lazy paddle through picturesque scenery. For medium-paced rides on the Arthur, you can set off from Kanunnah Bridge or Tayatea Bridge for down-river trips of two or four days respectively. Rivers popular with rafters and kayakers, and closer to population centres, are the Picton, Huon, Weld, Leven, Mersey and North Esk, all of which are well served by rafting companies.

You can hire canoes at Arthur River (see the Arthur River section of the North-West chapter of this book). In Hobart you can hire kayaks of all descriptions from Snowgum (☎ 6234 7877, 104 Elizabeth St) for $10 an hour or $65 a day.

The most challenging river to raft is the Franklin. Most rafting trips are now run by commercial groups, as it takes a lot of effort to organise your own trip. See the Franklin-Gordon Wild Rivers National Park section of the West chapter for details of rafting companies: those that tackle the Franklin usually offer trips on other rivers as well.

Ocean Kayaking is popular in Hobart (Aardvark Adventures Tasmania, ☎ toll-free 018 127 714), at Kettering (Roaring 40°s Ocean Kayaking Company, ☎ toll-free 1800 653 712), on the Freycinet Peninsula (Coastal Kayaks, ☎ 6239 1080) and near Port Arthur on the Tasman Peninula (Baidarka Experience, ☎ 6250 2612). For more details, see the relevant chapters.

Hypothermia can be a serious risk if you end up in the water when it's particularly cold. Always be aware of rapidly rising river levels, particularly when rafting on the Franklin, as waters can reach flood height at any time of year. You should also be careful when water levels are very low, as logs, rocks and other entrapments can be major threats at such times. The information on rafting in the Franklin River section of the PWS Web site at www.parks.tas.gov.au is invaluable for anyone considering rafting anywhere in the state.

## FISHING

Brown trout were introduced into Tasmania's Plenty River in 1866 and into Lake Sorell between 1867 and 1870. Since then, innumerable lakes and rivers have been stocked, including many of the artificial lakes built by the Hydro Electric Commission (HEC) for hydroelectricity production. Needless to say, the fish have thrived, and today anglers travel from all over Australia to make the most of the state's abundant and often beautiful inland fisheries.

Tasmanian trout (brown and rainbow) can be difficult to catch, as they are fickle about what they will eat; the right lures are needed in the right season. If you find you just can't hook them yourself, there are experts who can take you around to some good fishing places and teach you the local tricks. Peter Hayes of Peter Hayes Guided Fishing (☎ 6259 8295) is at the Central Highlands Lodge near Great Lake. His rates start at $175 per day, which includes transport and all fishing gear but not accommodation. The Tasmanian Fly-Fishing School & Guiding Service (☎ 6362 3441) runs guided trips starting at $250 per person per day (this service was operating out of Deloraine at the time of writing, but the owner was planning to move to Brady's Lake near Bronte Lagoon in the near future). Alluring Trout Tours (☎ 6260 2431) operates out of Richmond and Hobart and offers day tours and multi-day tours from August to April starting at $340 per person. Among the many other operators around the state are Dragonfly Trout Adventures (☎ 6228 2264) and Red Tag Trout Tours (☎ 6229 5896).

A licence is required to fish in Tasmania's inland waters, and there are bag, season and size limits on most fish. Licences cost $45 for the full season, $35 for 14 days, $20 for three days and $12 for one day, and are available from sports stores, post offices, visitors' centres and some country shops and petrol stations.

In general, inland waters open for fishing on the Saturday closest to 1 August and close on the Sunday nearest 30 April. Different dates apply to some special places and these are all detailed in the *Fishing Code* brochure. The lakes in the centre of the state are some of the best-known spots for both brown and rainbow trout – Arthurs Lake, Great Lake, Little Pine Lagoon (fly fishing only), Western Lakes (including Lake St Clair), Lake Sorell and Lake Pedder. On some parts of the Great Lake you are only allowed to use artificial lures. You are also not allowed to fish in any of the streams flowing into that lake.

One of the best books available on the subject of trout fishing in Tasmania is *Tasmanian Trout Waters* by Greg French. In Hobart, a good place to stock up on lures and information is The Fishing Connection (☎ 6234 4880, 87-91 Harrington St).

London Lakes (☎ 6289 1159) at Bronte Park is an upmarket private trout fishing resort where you can stay and fish for $320 a day. Bronte Park Highland Village (☎ 6289 1126) is a popular and much cheaper accommodation-only option for fishers.

Rod fishing in salt waters is allowed all year without a permit but size restrictions and bag limits apply. Recreational sea fishing licences, available from post offices, Service Tasmania and the Marine Building on Franklin Wharf, are required if you are diving for abalone, rock lobsters or scallops or fishing with a net. There are now on-the-spot fines for breaches of the fishing regulations.

For more information on fishing in Tasmania, refer to the *Fishing Code* brochure you will be given when you buy your licence.

## HORSE RIDING

Horse riding is allowed in some of the national parks and all of the protected areas. There are several companies that will provide horse riding, ranging from hour-long trips to multi-day treks across the Central Plateau. Rates are around $25 per hour for short rides and $150 per person for overnight rides (including food) on guided treks. Horseback Wilderness Tours (☎ 0418 128 405), Central Highland Trail Rides (☎ 6369 5298), and Saddletramp Horseback Tours (☎ 6254 6196) all run short rides and overnight trips through different areas of the state.

## ROCK CLIMBING & ABSEILING

Dry weather is desirable for rock climbing, and Tasmania's weather is often wet. Nevertheless, rock climbing and abseiling seem to be the thing to do in Tassie at the moment.

Some excellent cliffs have been developed for rock climbing, particularly along the east coast where the weather is usually best. The Organ Pipes on Mt Wellington (above Hobart), the Hazards at Coles Bay and the cliffs on Mt Killiecrankie on Flinders Island provide excellent climbing on firm rock. Many visitors, having seen photos of the magnificent rock formations on the Tasman Peninsula, head straight for that region, but while the coastal cliffs there are indeed spectacular, it should be noted that it may be impossible to climb them at certain times if the swell is too big. At Adamsfield, on the road to Strathgordon, there are lots of bolted, steep, overhanging climbs on conglomerate rock and also opportunities for bouldering. The really keen climbers drag all their gear onto the huge cliffs of Frenchmans Cap on the western side of the state and wait for a break in the rain. The inexperienced, on the other hand, can hone their skills at places like Kingston and Blackmans Bay beaches close to Hobart, or even at the Climbing Edge indoor climbing venue (54 Bathurst St) in the city itself. Guide books exist to Frenchmans Cap, Coles Bay and Mt Killiecrankie.

If you want to climb or abseil with an experienced instructor, try Aardvark Adventures Tasmania (☎ 018 127 714), Freycinet Adventures (☎ 6257 0500), the Climbing Company (at the Climbing Edge, ☎ 6234 3575), or Summit Sports (☎ 0418 362 210). And if you're after something different, ask Phil at Aardvark Adventures about abseiling down the silos in Battery Point or the massive wall of the Gordon Dam in the south-west.

## CAVING
Tasmania's caves are regarded as being among the most impressive in Australia. The caves at Mole Creek, Gunns Plains and Hastings are open to the public daily, but gems such as the Kubla Khan and Croesus caves (near Mole Creek) and the extremely large Exit Cave are only accessible to experienced cavers. Permits are needed to enter these caves; they are not places for the inexperienced and most are locked. Apply through your speleological club or association in your own state or country for permits.

You can visit an underdeveloped (wild) cave with Huon Magical Mystery Tours (☎ 6298 3117, see the Hastings section of the South-East Coast chapter) or Wild Cave Tours (☎ 6367 8142, see the Mole Creek section of the North chapter). Expect to get wet and muddy, as these caves have no walkways or ladders and often have to be entered through streams.

## BIRDWATCHING
The eastern and south-eastern regions are the most popular birdwatching areas because the forest cover is thinner there and birds are easier to see. There are interesting birds throughout the state, though in the rainforest you can often hear them but rarely see them. Bruny Island Neck in the south and the Mt William National Park in the northeast are excellent places for finding the rare spotted pardalote and for general bird-watching. If you want to see the orange-bellied parrot, one of the world's rarest birds, fly to Melaleuca in the south-west, where you should be able to catch a glimpse of one from the special bird-hide near the airstrip.

Penguin viewing at dusk is also popular at many locations on Tasmania's north and east coasts, including Bruny Island Neck, Stanley and George Town (see the relevant chapters for details).

## SCENIC FLIGHTS
Scenic flights in four and six-seat planes are popular and range from one hour to half a day in length. In fine weather they are a great way to see the wilder regions of the state. See the Strahan section of the West chapter for details of flights above the Gordon River to the site of the Franklin Blockade.

From Hobart, Par-Avion (☎ toll-free 1800 646 411) operates from Cambridge airport (near Hobart airport) and runs scenic flights as well as some interesting trips into the South-West National Park. You can charter a flight for $190 an hour for up to three passengers. Alternatively, you can spend a day in the wilderness with a flight into the southwest and a cruise around Bathurst Harbour for $240 per person including lunch. The company also has a fully-catered camp beside Bathurst Harbour, where you can spend two days and one night for $485 or three days and three nights for $745. Tasair (☎ toll-free 1800 062 900) is another company operating out of Cambridge airport. It offers southwest, Freycinet and Tasman Peninsula flights.

There are other scenic flights available from most airports around the state. For example, from Wynyard or Cradle Mountain you can fly over the Cradle Mountain region (see those sections of the North-West and West chapters respectively).

## SEAL WATCHING

Seals congregate in 'haul-outs' (non-breeding sites) at various spots on Tasmania's north and east coasts. They can be observed, according to the PWS, by kayak, yacht or power boat, but it may be more sensible to take an organised tour. Sharks often swim with seals, so you should only dive in their presence in a shark-proof cage (see the George Town section of the North chapter for details). The PWS publishes a useful brochure about observing seals that is available at Service Tasmania and some visitors' centres.

# Getting There & Away

For most visitors, getting to Tasmania means flying first to mainland Australia.

## AIR (INTERNATIONAL)
### Airports
The main problem with getting to Australia is that it's a long way from anywhere. If you're coming from Asia, Europe or North America, you'll find lots of competing airlines and a wide variety of air fares – but there's no way you can avoid those great distances. Australia's current international popularity poses another problem – flights are often heavily booked. If you want to fly to Australia at a particularly popular time of year (the middle of summer, ie Christmas time, is notoriously difficult) or on a particularly popular route (like Hong Kong or Singapore to Sydney or Melbourne) then you need to plan well ahead.

Australia has a large number of international gateways. Sydney and Melbourne are the two busiest international airports. Perth also gets many flights from Asia and Europe and has direct flights to New Zealand and Africa. Other international airports are Adelaide, Port Hedland (Bali only), Darwin, Cairns and Brisbane. One place you can't arrive at directly from overseas is Canberra, the national capital.

Sydney is the busiest gateway and it makes a lot of sense to avoid arriving or departing there. Sydney's airport is stretched way beyond its capacity and flights are frequently delayed on arrival and departure. Unfortunately many flights to or from other cities (Melbourne in particular) still go via Sydney. If you're planning to explore Australia seriously, then starting at a quieter entry port like Cairns in far north Queensland or Darwin in the Northern Territory can make a lot of sense. If you're coming specifically to explore Tasmania, avoid the northern ports as it's expensive to get from them to Tasmania because of the distances involved. Instead fly into Melbourne, which is the closest major port.

## Buying Tickets
**Discount Tickets** Buying airline tickets these days is like shopping for a car, a stereo or a camera – five different travel agents will quote you five different prices. Rule number one if you're looking for a cheap ticket is to go to an agent, not directly to the airline. The airline can usually only quote you the absolutely by-the-rule-book regular fare. An agent, on the other hand, can offer all sorts of special deals, particularly on competitive routes.

Ideally an airline would like to fly all its flights with every seat in use and every passenger paying the highest fare possible. Fortunately, life usually isn't like that and airlines would rather have a half-price passenger than an empty seat. When faced with the problem of too many seats, they will either let agents sell them at cut prices, or occasionally make one-off special offers on particular routes – watch the travel ads in the press.

Of course what's available and what it costs depends on what time of year it is, what route you're flying and who you're flying with. If you're flying on a popular route (like from Hong Kong) or one where the choice of flights is very limited (like from South America or, to a lesser extent, from Africa) then the fare is likely to be higher or there may be nothing available but the official fare.

Similarly, the dirt cheap fares are likely to be less conveniently scheduled, will go via a less convenient route or be with a less popular airline. Flying London-Sydney, for example, is most convenient with airlines like Qantas, British Airways, Thai International or Singapore Airlines. They have flights every day, operate the same flight straight through to Australia and are good, reliable, comfortable, safe airlines. At the other extreme you could fly from London to an Eastern European or Middle Eastern city on one flight, switch to another flight from there to Asia, and change to another airline from there to Australia. It takes longer, there are delays and changes of aircraft along the way, the airlines may not be so good and furthermore the connection only works once a week, so you'll be leaving London at 1.30 am on Wednesday. The flip side is it's cheaper.

**Round-the-World Tickets** Round-the-World (RTW) tickets are very popular these days and many of these will take you through Australia. The airline RTW tickets are often real bargains and since Australia is pretty much on the other side of the world from Europe or North America it can work out no more expensive, or even cheaper, to keep going in the same direction right round the world rather than U-turn to return.

The official airline RTW tickets are usually put together by a combination of two airlines, and permit you to fly anywhere you want on their route systems so long as you do not backtrack. Other restrictions are that you (usually) must book the first sector in advance and cancellation penalties then apply. There may be restrictions on how many stops you are permitted and usually the tickets are valid from 90 days up to a year. A typical price for a South Pacific RTW ticket is around US$2010 to US$4400.

An alternative type of RTW ticket is one put together by a travel agent using a combination of discounted tickets from a number of airlines. A UK agent like Trailfinders can put together interesting London-to-London RTW combinations including Australia stopovers for between £799 and £1099.

## Departure Tax

There is a $27 departure tax when leaving Australia, but this is incorporated into the price of your air ticket and so is not paid as a separate tax.

## The UK

The cheapest tickets in London are from the numerous 'bucket shops' (discount ticket agencies) that advertise in magazines and papers like *Time Out, Southern Cross* and *TNT*. Pick up one or two of these publications and ring round a few bucket shops to find the best deal. The magazine *Business Traveller* also has a great deal of good advice on air fare bargains. Most bucket shops are trustworthy and reliable but the occasional sharp operator appears – *Time Out* and *Business Traveller* provide some useful advice on precautions to take.

Trailfinders (☎ 020-7938 3366, 46 Earls Court Rd, London W8) and STA Travel (☎ 020-7581 4132, 74 Old Brompton Rd, London SW7 and ☎ 020-7465 0484, 117 Euston Rd, London NW1) are good, reliable agents for cheap tickets.

The cheapest London to Sydney or Melbourne (not direct) bucket-shop tickets are about £339/550 one way/return. Cheap fares to Perth are around £309/549 one way/return. Such prices are usually only available if you leave London in the low season – March to June. In September and mid-December, fares go up by about 30%, while the rest of the year they're somewhere in between. Average direct high-season fares to Sydney and Melbourne are £554/700 one way/return, and from Perth £459/699.

Many cheap tickets allow stopovers on the way to or from Australia. Rules regarding how many stopovers you can take, how long you can stay away, how far in advance you have to decide your return date and so on, vary from time to time and ticket to ticket. Most return tickets allow you to stay away for any period between 14 days and one year, with stopovers permitted anywhere along your route. As usual with heavily discounted tickets, the less you pay the less you get.

From Australia you can expect to pay around A$895/1075 one way/return to London and other European capitals, with stops in Asia on the way. Again, all fares increase by up to 30% in the European summer and at Christmas.

## North America

There are a variety of connections across the Pacific from Los Angeles, San Francisco and Vancouver to Australia, including direct flights, flights via New Zealand, island-hopping routes and more circuitous Pacific-rim routes via Asia. Qantas, Air New Zealand and United all fly USA-Australia; Qantas, Air New Zealand and Canadian Airlines International fly Canada-Australia. An interesting option from North America's east coast is Northwest's flight via Japan.

On the US airlines, if your flight goes via Hawaii, the west coast to Hawaii sector is treated as a domestic flight. This means that you have to pay for drinks and headsets – goodies that are free on international sectors. An advantage of the Qantas and Air New Zealand flights via Hawaii is that they are international flights all the way through.

To find good fares to Australia, check the travel ads in the Sunday travel sections of papers like the *Los Angeles Times, San Francisco Chronicle-Examiner, New York Times* or *Toronto Globe & Mail*. You can typically get a one-way/return ticket from the west coast for US$998/1498, or US$1179/1378 from the east coast. At high seasons – particularly the Australian summer/Christmas time – seats will be harder to get and the price will probably be higher. In the USA good agents for discounted tickets are the two student travel operators, Council Travel and STA Travel, which have lots of offices around the country. Canadian west-coast fares out of Vancouver will be similar to those from the US west coast. From Toronto fares go from around C$1790/2200 one way/return.

If Pacific island-hopping is your aim, check out the airlines of Pacific Island nations, some of which have good deals on indirect routes. Qantas can give you Fiji or Tahiti along the way, while Air New Zealand can offer both these and the Cook Islands as well.

One-way/return fares that are available from Australia include: San Francisco A$1030/1830, New York A$1200/2080 and Vancouver A$1030/1830.

## New Zealand

Air New Zealand and Qantas operate a network of trans-Tasman flights linking Auckland, Wellington and Christchurch in New Zealand with most major Australian gateway cities. You can fly directly between a lot of places in New Zealand and a lot of places in Australia.

Fares vary depending on which cities you fly between and when you fly, but from New Zealand to Sydney you're looking at around NZ$345/459 one way/return, and to Melbourne NZ$495/730 one way/return. There is a lot of competition on this route – United, British Airways, Qantas and Air New Zealand all fly it, so there should be some good discounts.

Cheap fares to New Zealand from Europe will usually be for flights via the USA. A straightforward London-Auckland return bucket-shop ticket costs around £800. Coming via Australia you can continue right around on a RTW ticket, which will cost from around £895 for a ticket with a comprehensive choice of stopovers.

## Asia

Ticket discounting is widespread in Asia, particularly in Singapore, Hong Kong, Bangkok and Penang. There are a lot of fly-by-nights in the Asian ticketing scene so a little care is required. Also the Asian routes have been particularly caught up in the capacity shortages on flights to Australia. Flights between Hong Kong and Australia are notoriously heavily booked while flights to or from Bangkok and Singapore are often part of the longer Europe-Australia route so can be very full. Plan ahead. For much more information on South-East Asian travel and on to Australia see Lonely Planet's *South-East Asia on a shoestring*.

Typical one-way fares to Australia from Singapore are S$638 to Darwin or Perth, S$895 to Sydney or Melbourne.

From Australia return fares from the east coast to Singapore, Kuala Lumpur and Bangkok range from A$700 to A$1200, and to Hong Kong from A$1065.

## Africa

There are a number of direct flights each week between Africa and Australia, but only between Perth and Harare (Zimbabwe) or Johannesburg (South Africa). Qantas, South African Airways and Air Zimbabwe all fly these routes.

Some other airlines that connect southern Africa with Australia include Malaysia Airlines (via Kuala Lumpur), Singapore Airlines (via Singapore) and Air Mauritius (via Mauritius).

From East Africa, the options are to fly via Mauritius or Zimbabwe, or via the Indian subcontinent and on to South-East Asia, then connect from there to Australia.

## South America

Two routes operate between South America and Australia. The Chile connection involves Lan Chile's twice-weekly flight, from where you fly Qantas or another airline to Australia. Alternatively there is the route that skirts the Antarctic circle, flying from Buenos Aires to Auckland and Sydney, operated twice-weekly by Aerolineas Argentinas.

## AIR (DOMESTIC)

The airlines that fly to Tasmania are Ansett (☎ 13 1300), Qantas (☎ 13 1313), Kendell (☎ toll-free 1800 338 894), King Island Airlines (☎ 9580 3777), Aus-Air (☎ toll-free 1800 331 256), Island Airlines (☎ toll-free 1800 818 455) and Southern Australian Airlines (☎ 13 1313). Some of these are subsidiaries of the big two, Ansett and Qantas. At the time of writing, Ansett was planning to withdraw all its services to Tasmania, leaving the way free for its subsidiary, Kendell, to operate the vacated routes.

Ansett and Qantas fly to Tasmania from most Australian state capitals, while the other smaller airlines operate from various airports in Victoria. Flights are to Hobart, Launceston, Devonport, Burnie/Wynyard, Flinders Island or King Island.

Air fares to Tasmania are constantly changing, but because of the number of operators, prices are competitive and you can get some good deals – especially if you book well in advance or if you are planning a trip in the winter months. Discounts are

not uniform, with advertised 'rock bottom' fares ranging from 45% to 55% off, depending on the route, day of the week and time. When discount seats are unavailable, students under 26 years can get a 25% discount with the two main airlines.

## Hobart

The standard one-way economy fare with Ansett and Qantas from Melbourne is $260, although much cheaper fares are often available. From Sydney the standard fare is $376 and from Brisbane $504.

## Launceston

Ansett and Qantas fly from Melbourne for $225 one way, but it's around $260 return if you book well in advance. The smaller airlines flying out of Melbourne generally use one of the city's second-string airports such as Moorabbin and have lower base rates but offer fewer discounts. It's worth noting that Aus-Air runs flights between Traralgon in country Victoria and Launceston via Flinders Island which, at $254, is only a little more expensive than flying direct from Melbourne to Launceston with the major airlines. Although this is considerably more expensive than Aus-Air's full economy Traralgon to Launceston fare of $185, it gives you the option of a stopover on the island. Island Airlines has a similar arrangement.

## Burnie/Wynyard

There are flights from Melbourne to Devonport and Burnie/Wynyard by Kendell Airlines ($199 and $186), Southern Australian Airlines ($199 and $186) and Aus-Air ($166 and $155).

## The Islands

Kendell Airlines, Aus-Air and King Island Air fly to King Island from Melbourne, with full economy fares starting at around $110. Aus-Air and Island Airlines fly to Flinders Island from Melbourne, with fares starting at around $153. Aus-Air and Island Airlines also fly from Traralgon in country Victoria to Flinders Island, with fares starting at around $129. Some discounts are available, but as you'll need to book accommodation and hire a car, the best deal is to buy a fly, drive and accommodation package.

## SEA

Bass Strait is known as one of the roughest shipping channels in the world, so travellers prone to seasickness should beware.

### Ferry

The *Spirit of Tasmania*, which operates between Melbourne and Devonport, can accommodate 1300 passengers and over 600 vehicles. It has nine decks and, with its swimming pool, saunas, restaurants, gaming machines and bars, is more like a floating hotel than a ferry. The public areas of the ship have been designed to cater for wheelchair access, and four cabins have been specially designed for this purpose.

The ferry departs from the TT-Line terminal (☎ 13 2010, email reservations@tt-line.com.au) at Melbourne's Station Pier at 6 pm on Monday, Wednesday and Friday and from the terminal on the Esplanade in Devonport at 6 pm on Saturday, Tuesday and Thursday. The journey takes 14½ hours, arriving at 8.30 am.

The prices depend on whether you're buying a high, shoulder or low-season fare. The high season is from late December to late January, and Easter. One-way fares range from $106 ($136 in the high season) in hostel-style accommodation (20-bed cabins) to $232 ($317) in suites. Discounts apply for students travelling in cabins but not for those in hostel accommodation. All fares include an evening buffet dinner and a continental breakfast, or you can go to the formal restaurant and pay extra for your meal.

The cost for accompanied vehicles depends on the size of the vehicle. The standard size is 5m or less, for which the rate in 1999 was $30 ($40 in the high season). Motorcycles cost $25 ($30) and bicycles $20 ($25).

Over the 1997-98 and 1998-99 Christmas to Easter period, a vehicular catamaran, the *Devil Cat*, operated between George Town, on the Tamar River near the central north coast, and Melbourne. At the time of writing, there was some doubt as to whether this service would be available in 1999-2000: check with the TT-Line (☎ 13 2010). The catamaran that was used in 1998-99 carried 200 standard cars and 550 passengers, and the crossing took six hours. In the busiest period, between late December and late January and at Easter time, it left Melbourne at 7.30 am daily except Monday and George Town at 4 pm daily except Monday. The rest of the time it departed George Town at 1 pm on Wednesday and Friday and 4 pm on Saturday and Sunday; and Melbourne at 1 pm on Tuesday and Thursday and 7.30 am on Saturday and Sunday.

### Yacht

An interesting way to get to the state is by yacht. Every year hopeful adventurers head to Sydney to find a berth on a yacht in the Sydney to Hobart Yacht Race, but most have no hope as the yachts use their regular crews. You will have far more luck crewing a boat from Hobart back to its home port after the race has been completed, when many of the regular crew fly home. This is far more pleasant as the boats are cruising home, not racing.

## PACKAGE DEALS

Tourist agencies offer various package deals to Tasmania – transport there, accommodation and car hire – which are often considerably cheaper than purchasing each component separately. As you would expect, the biggest discounts apply in the quieter periods of autumn, winter and spring. In summer the package deals rise in price. Most package deals have conditions attached to them, of which the most common is twin share (two people). Sometimes an itinerary is fixed at booking.

### Air

Qantas and Kendell Airlines offer fly, drive and accommodation packages from Melbourne. A seven day package with Qantas is around $1100. These packages allow you to alter your itinerary and fly in and out of different airports; accommodation is with the larger motel chains. You should be able to get better deals from travel agents in your home town. For information on car and accommodation packages without air fares included, see the Getting Around chapter.

When visiting the two major islands in Bass Strait – King and Flinders Island – package deals should be seriously considered. This is because you have to fly there and you really need a car to get around. Booking these separately is considerably more expensive than a package deal; car hire on both islands is around $65 a day with no discounting.

High-season twin share packages from Melbourne to King Island with two nights accommodation and car hire start at around $400 a person and similar deals to Flinders Island are around $450.

Island Airlines (☎ toll-free 1800 818 826, for Flinders Island packages only) has air fare, accommodation and car hire high-season packages from Melbourne for $803 for five nights. Aus-Air has packages from Melbourne that include air fares, accommodation and car hire on Flinders and King islands and in Launceston, and other packages that visit both islands from Melbourne.

### Ferry & Catamaran
In 1998-99, TT-Line (☎ toll-free 1800 811 580, fax 1800 636 110, reservations@ tt-line.com.au) offered a Backpacker's Value Pack for $248. This was available to full-time students and members of YHA, VIP and Z Card, and covered return hostel accommodation on the *Spirit of Tasmania* or return travel on the *Devil Cat* and five days travel on scheduled services of Tasmanian Wilderness Travel.

There is also an infrequent ferry service between Bridport and Port Welshpool (see the Getting Around chapter for details).

### WARNING
The information in this chapter is particularly vulnerable to change – prices for travel are volatile, routes are introduced and cancelled, schedules change, rules are amended, special deals come and go. Airlines and governments seem to take a perverse pleasure in making price structures and regulations as complicated as possible and you should check directly with the airline or travel agent to make sure you understand how a fare (and the ticket you may buy) works. For non-refundable fares it's often wise to purchase insurance. Please note: since publication the airline industry is in a particular state of flux.

In addition, the travel industry is highly competitive and there are many lurks and perks. The upshot of this is that you should get quotes and advice from as many airlines and travel agents as possible before you part with your hard-earned cash. The details given in this chapter should only be regarded as pointers and cannot be any substitute for your own careful, up-to-date research.

# Getting Around

Tasmania is decentralised and its population very small. While public transport is adequate between most larger towns and popular tourist destinations, many people who wish to visit more remote and interesting sights find air and bus schedules frustrating. There are plenty of car rental companies that offer cheap rates for early-model vehicles, and you should seriously consider car hire as an option when planning your itinerary, particularly if your time is limited.

## AIR

Flights around the island are limited now that Airlines of Tasmania is no longer operating, and it is often a much better option to

travel by bus (except, of course to Flinders or King Island). There are now no scheduled flights to or from the west coast or Smithton.

Tasair Regional Airlines (☎ toll-free 1800 062 900) flies the following routes daily except Saturday: Hobart-Burnie/Wynyard ($99), Hobart-Devonport ($99), Hobart-King Island ($175), Burnie-King Island ($95) and Devonport-King Island ($95).

Aus-Air (☎ toll-free 1800 331 256) flies from Launceston to Burnie/Wynyard ($65), Flinders Island ($113) and King Island ($149), and between Burnie and King Island ($125).

Par Avion (☎ toll-free 1800 646 411) flies Hobart-Burnie/Wynyard ($119) daily except Saturday. Island Airlines (☎ toll-free

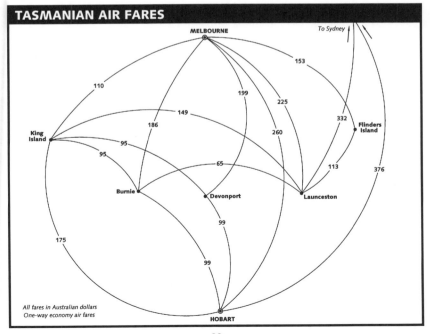

TASMANIAN AIR FARES

All fares in Australian dollars
One-way economy air fares

89

1800 818 455) flies Launceston-Flinders Island ($112) daily.

## BUS

Tasmania has good services to major centres, but weekend services to smaller towns may be infrequent or nonexistent. Getting to out-of-the-way places can sometimes be inconvenient and expensive; however, there are usually more services to such destinations in summer than in winter.

Two main bus companies cover most of the state: Tasmanian Redline Coaches (TRC, ☎ 1300 360 000) and TassieLink (☎ 1300 300 520). TassieLink offers a range of Explorer Passes ranging from 7 days to 21 days to be used within 10 to 30 days. Prices start at $150 for a 7 day pass. The pass is valid on all TassieLink services, and services operate regardless of minimum numbers. Explorer Pass holders are also en-

titled to substantial discounts off Tigerline sightseeing tours from Hobart and Launceston.

Explorer Passes can be bought in advance on the mainland from YHA and STA offices, Tasmanian visitors' centres and most travel agents. If you're intending to buy an Explorer Pass, ask for timetables in advance and plan your itinerary exhaustively before making your purchase. This is the only way to ensure that you will be able to get where you want to go within the life of the pass. The free newspaper *Tasmanian Travelways* (available at Tasmanian visitors' centres within and outside the state) has details of timetables and fares for major routes, but you'd be better off using one of the company's own printed timetables.

Buses run along most major highways all year. TassieLink services the Lyell Hwy from Hobart and Launceston to the west

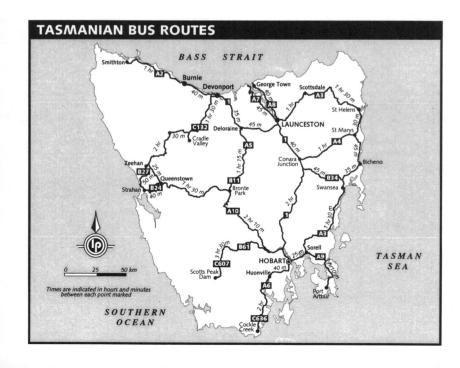

TASMANIAN BUS ROUTES

coast (Cradle Mountain, Strahan, Queenstown, Lake St Clair); and to the east coast (St Helens, Bicheno, Coles Bay etc); from Hobart to Port Arthur; and down the Huon Valley. TRC services the Midland Hwy from Hobart to Launceston ($19.50); the north coast from Launceston to Smithton ($29); and the east coast. Hobart Coaches (☎ 6234 4077) services the Tasman and Arthur Hwys from Hobart to Port Arthur ($11.50). See the Getting There & Around and Getting There & Away sections at the start of relevant chapters for details of these and other services.

Buses also run along a large number of minor roads to popular bushwalking destinations, and TassieLink offers special fares that will enable you to be dropped off at the start of a walk and picked up at the end. National Park passes can be purchased from TassieLink to cover the duration of the walk. These services are not as frequent as those that run between main towns and often only operate between December and April. Buses take the link road from Devonport past Cradle Mountain to the Lyell Hwy, and the direct route from Launceston past the Great Lake to Derwent Bridge and Cynthia Bay. Buses also run from Hobart past Maydena to Scotts Peak, and from Hobart past Dover to Cockle Creek in the south. See the sections on the relevant destinations later in this book for details of these services.

During winter there is a special TassieLink service to the ski fields (when there is snow!). Details of regional services are described in the relevant Getting There & Away and Getting Around sections of each chapter.

All bus fares quoted here should be treated as a guide only – prices change frequently.

## TRAIN

For economic reasons there are no longer any passenger rail services in Tasmania, which probably accounts for the number of model railways and train exhibitions in the state. Once a month there is a tourist train from Hobart to Parattah near Oatlands and back; see the Hobart chapter for details.

## TAXI

Taxis are available at all the major towns and can be a handy way of getting to places otherwise not easily reached. However, you should not seriously consider using a taxi to get around the state unless you have buckets of money.

## CAR
### Rental

Although you can bring cars from the mainland to Tasmania, it might be cheaper to rent one for your visit, particularly if your stay is a short one. Tasmania has a wide range of national and local car-rental agencies, and the rates (along with parking fines) are considerably lower here than they are on the mainland.

*Tasmanian Travelways* lists rental options, but before you decide on a company, don't forget to ask about any kilometre limitations and what the insurance covers – ensure that there are no hidden seasonal adjustments. It is, however, quite normal for smaller rental companies to ask for a bond of around $300. Also remember that the insurance offered by most companies does not cover accidents that occur on unsealed roads, which is a considerable disadvantage in a state where so many of the best destinations can only be visited by using such routes.

If possible, book in advance and ask first about rates for smaller cars. Outside the high holiday season, the large national firms like Budget and Hertz have rates starting at around $43 a day with a seven day minimum. In summer, rates are generally higher, being around $60 a day for multi-day hire but still considerably cheaper than the full advertised rates. Although these are more expensive than rates offered by many smaller companies, there's no bond and you get unlimited kilometres, comprehensive insurance and reliable cars. The larger companies also have offices at the main airports and near the ferry terminal in Devonport.

Tasmania has a number of companies renting older cars for around $20 or $30 a day depending on the length of time and season. In this bracket, Rent-a-Bug, with offices in Hobart (☎ 6231 0300), Launceston and Devonport, has a good reputation, but remember that old Volkswagon Beetles are rather noisy and can smell of petrol fumes when their heaters are turned on. Selective Car Rentals (☎ 6234 3311) is another firm that offers cheap older cars. Jim's Car Rentals (☎ 6236 9779) is also popular. To get the best deals, you need to book early. The smaller companies don't have desks at arrival points but can usually arrange for your car to be picked up at airports and terminals.

Another very popular option is to invest in an accommodation and rental car package. These can be arranged on the mainland or in Tasmania by travel agents or Tasmanian visitors' centres and often work out to be extremely economical. And for backpackers who don't want to walk too far, there's now the Tasmania Adventure Freedom Pass available from the YHA office in Hobart (☎ 6234 9617), which offers various combinations of YHA hostel accommodation and rental of a Nissan Pulsar or Toyota Camry including insurance (with a large excess) and unlimited kilometres: seven nights accommodation and seven days rental of a Nissan Pulsar, for example, is $280.

**Campervans** Campervans are a popular way to travel around the state. Check *Tasmanian Travelways* for details of campervan rental companies.

## Road Rules

Australia has country-wide road rules. Australians drive on the left-hand side of the road. There are a few local road rules to take special note of.

The main one is the 'give way to the right' rule. This means that if you're driving on a main road and somebody appears on a minor road on you right, you must give way to them unless they are facing a give-way or stop sign. When you are turning left, you have right of way over any vehicles that are turning right but you must still give way to vehicles on your right that are going straight

ahead. Another exception is at T-junctions where the through road has right of way over all traffic on the approaching road. Confused? Some local drivers still are and most major roads are now signposted to indicate the priority road.

In towns and cities, the general speed limit is 60km/h while on the open road the general limit is 100km/h, although on major highways such as the Midlands it's 110km/h. For provisional licence holders the speed limit is 80km/h. Speed cameras operate in Tasmania and are usually carefully hidden.

Australia was one of the first countries to make the wearing of seat belts compulsory. If you don't wear a seat belt then fines can be imposed by the police. The other main law applies to drinking and driving, where a strict limit of 0.05 for blood alcohol content applies. For exceeding the limit, heavy fines apply – your licence will be cancelled and jail sentences are imposed on offenders who are convicted several times. Random breath tests are conducted by police. The best policy is not to combine drinking and driving.

Overseas licences are acceptable in Australia for genuine overseas visitors. If you are staying for more than 12 months you will need to obtain a local licence; apply at any police station.

## On the Road

While you're driving around the state, watch out for the wildlife which, all too often, ends up flattened on the roadside. Many of the animals are nocturnal and often cross roads around dusk. Try to avoid driving in the country just after sunset; if you must drive then, slow down. Hitting a wombat not only kills the unfortunate animal, but also makes a mess of your car.

Many roads, including some highways, are fairly narrow with many sharp bends not signposted, and there are still some one-lane bridges that are not clearly signposted. Cycling is popular on some roads (particularly on the east coast), and when encountering bicycles you should wait until you can pass safely. It's wise to drive a little more slowly and allow more time to react to these hazards. Distances are short, so there is no need to speed.

Anyone considering travelling on 4WD tracks should read the free publication *Cruisin' Without Bruisin'*, available in the Parks and Wildlife Service (PWS) section of Service Tasmania (134 Macquarie St, Hobart) and at other visitors' centres around the state. It gives details of 23 tracks and also explains how to minimise your impact on the regions you drive through.

## Fuel Supplies

Petrol is available in most towns across the state every day of the week. In small towns there's often just a pump outside the general store, while the larger towns and cities have conventional service stations and garages. Most are open from 8 am to 6 pm on weekdays. Fewer are open on weekends, and fewer still are open late at night or 24 hours a day, something to keep in mind if you are travelling long distances at night.

LPG (gas) is available in some locations, and a list of these can be obtained from Boral Energy (☎ 6228 6255).

## BICYCLE

Tasmania's compact size makes it a tempting place to cycle around. It's a great way to get close to nature (not to mention, it has to be said, log trucks, rain and roadkill), and provided you are prepared for steep climbs and strong headwinds in certain sections, you should enjoy the experience immensely.

If you're planning an extended ride it's worth considering buying a bike and reselling it at the end. See the Cycling section of the Activities chapter for more information.

If you bring a bike over on the *Spirit of Tasmania* or the *Devil Cat* it will cost you $20 to $25 each way, depending on the season. By air, Ansett charges between $10 and $20 to carry a bicycle one way to Hobart or Launceston, while Qantas charges $10; however, you should be aware that your bicycle may be off-loaded at the last minute if there is too much other freight to be carried.

While the same road rules that apply to cars also apply to bicycles, riders should also follow another rule; if in doubt either give way or get out of the way. Even if you are in the right, you will almost certainly come off second best in any collision. When cycling on the narrow, winding roads, always keep your eyes and ears open for traffic. Also watch out for wooden bridges with gaps between the slats: these can trap bicycle wheels, causing accidents. Remember always to wear a helmet (it's compulsory) and try not to cycle at night. Full notes and lots of practical advice for cycling around the state can be found in *Bicycling Tasmania* by Ian Terry & Rob Beedham.

## FERRY

There is a regular car ferry from Kettering to Bruny Island. It operates several times each day and is free for passengers. However, you'll need a car or bicycle to explore this rather long island. See the Bruny Island section of the South-East Coast chapter for details.

Another useful ferry runs from the east coast near Triabunna to Maria Island. This also operates daily and will carry passengers and bicycles. This island is much smaller and is a national park. Vehicles are not allowed, so you can only explore it on foot or by bicycle. See the Maria Island section of the East Coast chapter for details.

Southern Shipping Company (☎ 6356 1753) operates a small ferry from Bridport in the north-east to Flinders Island and on to Port Welshpool in Victoria. Ring the company for details.

## HITCHING

Travel by thumb in Tassie is generally good, but you'll need to wrap up in winter and keep a raincoat handy. A good number of the state's roads are still unsurfaced and the traffic can be very light, so although these roads sometimes lead to interesting places, you normally have to give them a miss if you're hitching.

Hitching is never entirely safe in any country in the world, and we certainly don't recommend it. Travellers who decide to hitch should understand that they are taking a small but potentially serious risk. Women should be particularly careful. People who do choose to hitch will be safer if they travel in pairs and let someone know where they are planning to go.

## ORGANISED TOURS

There are many companies offering tours of Tasmania and you should check in *Tasmanian Travelways* if you have a good idea of the particular type of tour you'd like to join.

One company that provides transport and lunches, but not accommodation, is Under Down Under (☎ 6369 5555). It offers a five day state tour for $335, which departs from Devonport and Launceston on Thursday.

Tassie Experience & Eco Tours (☎ 6250 2766) has a seven day state tour that includes hostel accommodation and takes in many national parks for $660.

For more information on organised tours to King Island and Flinders Island, see the Islands chapter.

# Hobart

HOBART

- **pop 128,600**

Hobart is the second-oldest, second-driest, smallest and most southerly of Australia's capitals. Straddling the mouth of the Derwent River and backed by mountains offering excellent views over the city, Hobart has managed to combine the progress and benefits of a modern city with the rich heritage of its colonial past. The beautiful Georgian buildings, the busy harbour and the easy-going atmosphere all make Hobart one of the most enjoyable and engaging cities in the country.

## History

The first inhabitants of the city area were members of the Aboriginal Mouheneer tribe, who lived a semi-nomadic lifestyle. The first European colony in Tasmania was founded in 1803 at Risdon Cove, but a year later Lieutenant-Colonel David Collins, Governor of the new settlement in Van Diemen's Land, sailed down the Derwent River and decided that a cove about 10km below Risdon and on the opposite shore was a better place to settle. This, the site of Tasmania's future capital city, began as a village of tents and wattle-and-daub huts with a population of 262 Europeans.

Hobart Town, as it was known until 1881, was proclaimed a city in 1842. Very important to its development was the Derwent River estuary, one of the world's finest deep-water harbours, and many merchants made their fortunes from the whaling trade, shipbuilding and the export of products like corn and merino wool.

## Orientation

Hobart is sandwiched between the steep hills of Mt Wellington and the wide Derwent River. With a minimum of flat land, the city has spread along the shores of the Derwent River and is about 20km long but very narrow. Some development has spread into the hills and you will find many streets extremely steep.

## HIGHLIGHTS

- Eating in the restaurants and cafés on the waterfront
- Browsing through Salamanca Market
- Walking beneath the Organ Pipes on Mt Wellington
- Greeting the winners of the Sydney to Hobart Yacht Race
- Wandering the streets of historic Battery Point

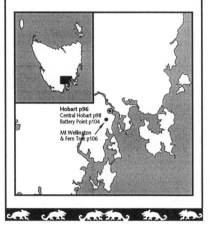

Hobart p96
Central Hobart p98
Battery Point p104

Mt Wellington
& Fern Tree p106

The city centre is fairly small, simply laid out and easy to find your way around. The streets in the city centre are arranged in a grid pattern around the Elizabeth St Mall. The Tasmanian Travel & Information Centre, Ansett Airlines, Qantas and the post office are all on Elizabeth St. Hobart has controlled the traffic in its narrow streets by making them one way: if you are driving, you should first study a map.

Salamanca Place, the famous row of Georgian warehouses, is along the waterfront, while just south of this is Battery

95

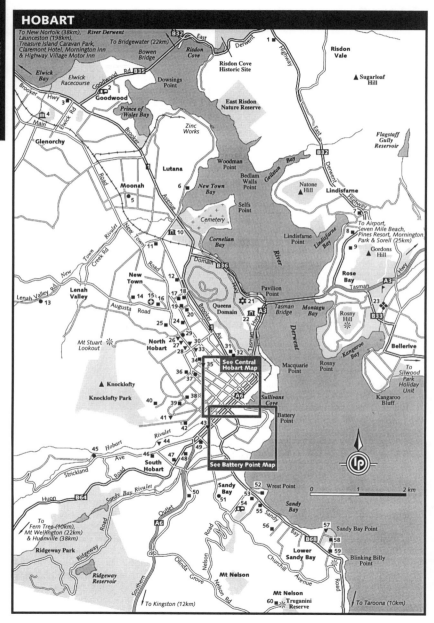

**HOBART**

To New Norfolk (38km),
Launceston (198km),
Treasure Island Caravan Park,
Claremont Hotel, Mornington Inn
& Highway Village Motor Inn

*River Derwent*

To Bridgewater (22km)

East

Derwent

1

Highway

**Risdon
Vale**

*Bowen
Bridge*

*Risdon
Cove*

▲ *Sugarloaf
Hill*

*Elwick
Bay*

*Elwick
Racecourse*

Goodwood Rd B35

*Dowsings
Point*

**Risdon Cove
Historic Site**

**Goodwood**

2

**East Risdon
Nature Reserve**

3

*Brooker*

Hwy

4

Main

*Prince of
Wales Bay*

*Flagstaff
Gully
Reservoir*

B32

**Glenorchy**

Elwick Rd

*Brooker*

Rd

*Zinc
Works*

*Woodman
Point*

*Gellston*

Bay

*Natone
Hill* ▲

**Lindisfarne**

**Lutana**

6

*New Town
Bay*

*Bedlam
Walls
Point*

To Airport,
Seven Mile Beach,
Pines Resort, Mornington
Park & Sorell (25km)

**Moonah**

5

New Town

Avenue

*Selfs
Point*

*Lindisfarne
Point*

*Lindisfarne
Bay*

8

9

*Gordons
Hill*

10

*Cemetery*

*Cornelian
Bay*

**Rose
Bay**

A3

Tasman

23

B33

**Lenah
Valley**

13

*Lenah Valley Rd*

New

Town

Creek Rd

Augusta

Road

11

Domain

B36

Derwent

River

**New
Town**

12

*Pavilion
Point*

*Montagu
Bay*

*Rosny
Hill*

**Bellerive**

To
Silwood
Park
Holiday
Unit

14 15 16

17 18

19

20

*Queens
Domain*

21

22

43

*Tasman
Bridge*

Hwy

*Kangaroo
Bay*

24

25

**North
Hobart**

26
27
29
28 30 33

31

32

35

*Macquarie
Point*

*Rosny
Point*

*Kangaroo
Bluff*

Mt Stuart
Lookout

34

**See Central
Hobart Map**

A6

36

37

▲ **Knocklofty**

**Knocklofty Park**

40

39 38

*Sullivans
Cove*

41

42

43

*Battery
Point*

Hobart

Rivulet

Ave

44

45

46

47
48

49

**See Battery Point Map**

**South
Hobart**

Strickland

Road

Huon

B64

*Sandy Bay Rivulet*

Outlet

50

**Sandy
Bay**

51

52 *Wrest Point*

53

54

55 Sandy

*Sandy
Bay*

To
Fern Tree (10km),
Mt Wellington (22km)
& Huonville (38km)

A6

56

57 *Sandy Bay Point*

B68

58

59

Bay

Road

**Ridgeway Park**

*Ridgeway
Reservoir*

Ridgeway

Road

Olinda

Grove

Nelson

Road

**Mt Nelson**

Southern

Nelson Rd

Churchill

**Lower
Sandy
Bay**

*Blinking Billy
Point*

0    1    2 km

**Mt Nelson**

60

*Truganini
Reserve*

To Kingston (12km)

Avenue

To Taroona (10km)

## HOBART

**PLACES TO STAY**
1  Bowen Park
2  Elwick Cabin & Caravan Park
3  Northside Holiday Villas
6  Marina Motel
7  Orana Accommodation
8  Lindisfarne Motor Inn
9  Roseneath Host Accommodation
11  Wendover
12  Hillpark House
14  Jutland House
16  Valley Lodge Motel
17  Adelphi Court
18  Hobart Tower Motel
19  Argyle Motor Lodge
20  Rydges Hobart
24  Domain View Apartments
25  Elms of Hobart
31  Wellington Lodge
32  Corinda Colonial Accommodation
34  Lodge On Elizabeth

36  Warwick Cottages
37  Waratah Hotel
38  Marquis of Hastings Hotel
39  Mayfair Hotel
40  Bay View Villas
42  Crows Nest B&B
46  Cascade Hotel
47  Islington Private Hotel
48  Jane Franklin Hall
49  Globe Hotel
50  Andersons
52  Wrest Point Hotel Casino
53  Amberley House
54  Sandy Bay Caravan Park
55  Sandy Bay Motor Inn
56  Mt Pleasant Mews
58  Antarctic Lodge
59  Beach House Hotel
60  Signalman's Cottage

**PLACES TO EAT**
26  Yabbies
27  Marti Zucco

28  Concetta's
30  Elizabeth St Restaurants
33  Republic Bar
35  Kaos Café
41  Round Asia
43  Flourishing Court
44  Le Provencal
57  Prosser's on the Beach

**OTHER**
4  Tasmania Transport Museum
5  Moonah Arts Centre
10  Runnymede
13  Lady Franklin Gallery
15  Calvary Hospital
21  Royal Botanical Gardens
22  Government House
23  Eastlands Shopping Centre
29  State Cinema
45  Cascade Brewery
51  University of Tasmania; Christ College

Point, Hobart's delightful, well-preserved early colonial district. If you follow the river around from Battery Point you'll come to Sandy Bay, the site of the yacht clubs, Hobart's university and the circular tower of Wrest Point Hotel Casino – one of Hobart's main landmarks.

The northern side of the city centre is bounded by the recreation area known locally as the Domain (short for the Queen's Domain), which includes the Royal Tasmanian Botanical Gardens and the Derwent River. From here the Tasman Bridge crosses the river to the eastern suburbs and the airport. North of the Domain the suburbs continue beside the Derwent River almost all the way to Bridgewater.

There are very few large industries and the ones that exist are well out of the main city area. Electrolytic Zinc , the Cadbury chocolate factory and paper mills at Boyer are beside the Derwent River but well upstream.

**Maps** The best maps of Hobart are the *Hobart Street Directory* and the Hobart maps in the *Tasmanian Towns Street Atlas*, both

of which are available at Service Tasmania (☎ 6233 3382, 134 Macquarie St, Hobart), the Tasmanian Map Centre (☎ 6231 9043, 96 Elizabeth St, Hobart), newsagencies and bookshops.

## Information
**Tourist Office** The Tasmanian Travel & Information Centre (TTIC, ☎ 6230 8233), on the corner of Davey and Elizabeth Sts, opens on weekdays from 8.30 am to 5.15 pm, and on weekends and public holidays from 9 am to 4 pm. You can also get tourist information from many accommodation and tourist establishments.

If you have an FM radio, you can pick up a tourist information broadcast on 88MHz within a 6km radius of the city centre.

**Useful Organisations** The Tasmanian YHA (☎ 6234 9617, 28 Criterion St) is open Monday to Friday from 10 am to 5 pm. For information about driving around the state, the Royal Auto Club of Tasmania (RACT, ☎ 6232 6300) is on the corner of Murray and Patrick St.

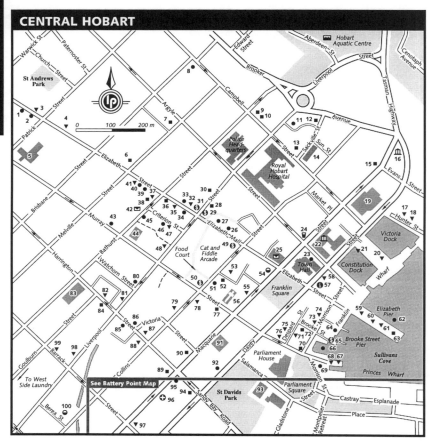

CENTRAL HOBART

**Money** Banks are open for business from 9.30 am to 4 pm Monday to Thursday and from 9.30 am to 5 pm Friday. Automatic Teller Machines (ATMs) can be used at any time and are available at the banks in the city centre and at some of the suburban branches. All the major banks have their offices near the mall on Elizabeth St. There are multibank ATMs next to the Cruise Company on Watermans Dock, and at the airport and at Antarctic Adventure in Salamanca.

**Post & Communications** The post office in the centre of the city, on the corner of Elizabeth and Macquarie Sts, is open weekdays from 8 am to 5.45 pm. The Sandy Bay post office, on King St opposite Purity supermarket, is open weekdays from 9 am to 5 pm and Saturday from 9.30 am to 1 pm; this is the only post office in Hobart open on Saturday. Hobart's STD area telephone code is the same as the rest of south-eastern Australia: ☎ 03. All numbers for the Hobart region begin with 62 and calls within the

## CENTRAL HOBART

**PLACES TO STAY**
6   Black Prince Hotel
7   Ocean Child Hotel
9   Royal Exchange Hotel
10  Hollydene House
12  Fountainside Motor Inn
13  Theatre Royal Hotel
15  Old Woolstore
19  Hotel Grand Chancellor
28  Alabama Hotel
30  Brunswick Hotel
36  Hobart Mid City Motor Inn;
    Stak a Jax
38  New Sydney Hotel
52  Central City Backpackers
63  Oakford on Elizabeth Pier
70  Customs House Hotel
72  Quest on Waterfront
77  Country Comfort Hadleys
    Hotel
83  Hobart Vista Hotel
84  Harrington Boutique
    Accommodation
89  Hobart Macquarie Motor Inn
90  Hotel Astor; Astor Grill
94  Welcome Stranger Hotel

**PLACES TO EAT**
3   Trattoria Casablanca
4   Rozzinis
17  Riviera Ristorante
18  Drunken Admiral
20  Mures Fish Centre
21  Floating Seafood Stalls
32  Banjos
35  Thai Hut
37  La Cuisine
41  Golden Bamboo
47  Cumquat
48  Kafe Kara

53  La Cuisine
55  Mersins
58  Palettes Studio Café
59  Fish Frenzy; Fusion
60  T-42°
61  A Splash of Paris
67  Waterline
68  Blue Skies; Sisco's
71  Areeba's
73  Brooke St Bar & Café
74  Rockerfeller's
75  Elbow Room
76  Roche's
78  Little Italy
79  Fortune Court
81  Vanny's
82  Tandoor Curry House
87  Café Toulouse
88  Little Bali; Little Salama
97  Bakers
98  Café Who
99  Zanskar's

**OTHER**
1   Mundy & Sons
2   Southern Tasmanian Divers
5   Royal Auto Club Tasmania
8   National Trust; Penitentiary
    Chapel & Criminal Courts
11  Hobart Coaches
14  Theatre Royal
16  Gasworks; Distillery &
    Museum
22  Tasmanian Museum & Art
    Gallery
23  Carnegie Building
24  Maloneys Hotel
25  Post Office
26  Ansett Airlines

27  Qantas Airlines
29  National Bank & ATM;
    Larder Café
31  Commonwealth Bank & ATM
33  Sport & Dive; Jolly Swagman;
    Seaworld
34  Paddy Pallin; Mountain
    Designs
39  Tasmanian Map Centre
40  Snowgum
42  Post Office
43  Rent-a-Bug
44  State Library
45  Environment Centre
46  Youth Hostel Association Office
49  ANZ Bank & ATM
50  Commonwealth Bank & ATM
51  Fullers Bookshop; Afterword
    Café
54  Metro Bus Terminus
56  St Davids Cathedral
57  Tasmanian Travel &
    Information Centre
62  *Lady Nelson*
64  Cruise Companies
65  Multi-Bank ATM
66  *Prudence; May Queen*
69  Harley Tours of Hobart
80  Odeon
85  Budget Rent-a-Car
86  The Fishing Connection
91  Service Tasmania
92  Royal Tennis Courts
93  Supreme Court
95  Chemists
96  St Helens Hospital
100 Transit Centre (Intercity
    Coaches); Transit Centre
    Backpackers

city are classed as local. Calls from Hobart to country regions are usually at STD rates, even when they begin with 62; rates are dependent on the distance involved. If you hear three pips at the start of a call, then STD rates are being charged and you should be ready to insert more coins if you are using a pay phone. Local calls from pay phones are 40c for unlimited time.

***Email & Internet Access*** There are several places in Hobart where you can access the Internet. You can log on at Drifters Internet Café (accessed either via The Galleria, 33 Salamanca Place, or Montpelier Retreat) for $2 per 10 minutes or $10 an hour. It's open from 7.30 am to 6 pm daily except Sunday, when it opens at 11 am. Internet access is also available at some hostels in Hobart and at Southern Internet Services ($5 an hour) in the Marine Board Building (ground floor, 1 Franklin Wharf). Free Internet access is available at the State Library (☎ 6233 7529 for bookings, 91 Murray St).

HOBART

**Bookshops** Fullers (☎ 6224 2488, 140 Collins St) has an extensive range of literature and travel guides, a café upstairs, and 'meet the author' afternoons every couple of Sundays. It's open from 9 am to 6 pm weekdays, 9 am to 5 pm Saturday and 10 am to 4 pm Sunday. The Hobart Book Shop (☎ 6234 9654, 22 Salamanca Square) and the Sandy Bay Newsagency & Bookshop (☎ 6223 6955, 197 Sandy Bay Rd) also have good literature, travel and Tasmania sections, and the latter is open long hours (from 7 am to 7 pm Monday to Saturday and from 9 am to 5.30 pm Sunday). Ellison Hawker (☎ 6234 2322, 90 Liverpool St), Angus & Robertson Bookworld (☎ 6234 4288, 96 Collins St) and Birchalls (☎ 6234 2122, 147 Bathurst St) are good general bookshops.

At the Wilderness Society Shop (☎ 6234 9370, The Galleria, 33 Salamanca Place) you'll find a range of environmental publications, wildlife posters, videos and calendars. At the other end of Salamanca Place, at No 77 (up a small arcade), is Deja Vu Books (☎ 6223 4766), an excellent secondhand bookshop. The Tasmanian Map Centre has a reasonable range of travel books.

**Library** The State Library of Tasmania (☎ 6233 7529, 91 Murray St) is open from 9.30 am to 6 pm Monday and Tuesday, from 9.30 am to 8 pm (lending library) or 9 pm (reference library) Wednesday to Friday and from 9 am to 12.30 pm Saturday.

**University** The University of Tasmania is on Churchill Ave, Sandy Bay. It has a theatre, gallery, bookshop, newsagency, Commonwealth Bank, multibank ATM, café and refectory and it is often the venue for visiting bands.

**Laundry** Westside Laundromat, on the corner of Goulburn & Molle Sts, is reasonably central and is open daily from 6.30 am to 9.30 pm. At the pleasant Machine Laundry Café on Salamanca Square you can have a coffee or a snack while you do your washing. The café is open from 8 am to 6 pm Monday to Thursday, from 8 am to 10 pm Friday and Saturday and from 9 am to 10 pm Sunday. The laundry opens half an hour before the café and the last wash is taken half an hour before the café shuts.

There are also laundrettes on Magnet Court in Sandy Bay, and in the Elizabeth St shopping centre in North Hobart.

**Medical Services** Hobart is not well served by after-hours doctors, but a service is provided by St John's Private Hospital (☎ 6223 7444, 30 Cascades Rd, South Hobart). There are a number of chemists near the corner of Harrington and Macquarie Sts that are open long hours (from 8 am to 10 pm at the latest).

**Emergency** On Argyle St, The Royal Hobart Hospital (☎ 6222 8308) has an emergency section, as does St Helen's Private Hospital (☎ 6221 6473, 186 Macquarie St) and Calvary Hospital (☎ 13 2205), which is on Honora Ave, Lenah Valley.

In the event of fire, or to contact the police or an ambulance in an emergency, dial ☎ 000.

## Walking Tours

There is a wealth of detailed historic walk literature available at the TTIC to will enable you to guide yourself around the docks and streets of the centre and Battery Point with ease. Among these are *A Sullivans Cove Walk*, *Hobart's Historic Places* and the *Historic Battery Point and Sullivan's Cove Trail of Discovery*. Of particular interest may be *In Her Stride*, which is a fascinating guide to a women's historic walk around the centre.

Two-hour guided walks, departing from the TTIC at 10 am daily from September to May, are $15 and can be conducted, by arrangement, in German, French, Italian, Dutch or Japanese. Another, and possibly more intimate, option is the $10 Footsteps Walking Tour of Battery Point (☎ 6224 0996), which takes 90 minutes and is available on demand; Elleanor is usually happy to conduct the walk for just one person if there are no other bookings.

The Hobart City Council runs $7 tours of the Hobart Rivulet at 4 pm on Thursday; bookings must be made at the council offices (☎ 6238 2711), on the corner of Davey and Elizabeth Sts. The rivulet runs under the central business district and the tour gives an insight into the historical development of the city from this very different perspective.

Yet another interesting option is the two hour Hobart Historic Pub Tour, which departs from the TTIC at 5 pm from Sunday to Thursday. It takes in Irish Murphy's, Knopwood's Retreat, the Customs House and the Brooke Street Bar and Café. The tour is $35 with four drinks along the way or $19 with one, and can be conducted in a foreign language by arrangement.

## Tasmanian Museum & Art Gallery

The excellent Tasmanian Museum & Art Gallery (☎ 6235 0777, 5 Argyle St – enter via Macquarie St) incorporates Hobart's oldest building, the Commissariat Store, built in 1808. The museum section features a Tasmanian Aboriginal display and artefacts from the state's colonial heritage, while the gallery has a good collection of Tasmanian colonial art. There are interesting displays of animals, including extinct and prehistoric ones, and a large mineral collection. The bookshop beside the entrance sells a wide range of books, many of which are not available elsewhere. The museum is free and opens daily from 10 am to 5 pm. Free guided tours are offered from Wednesday to Sunday at 2.30 pm.

## Other Museums

The **Allport Museum & Library of Fine Arts** (☎ 6233 7484, 91 Murray St) is based in the State Library. It has a collection of rare books on Australasia and the Pacific region, lots of antique furniture and a large collection of paintings. You can visit the museum on weekdays from 9.30 am to 5 pm; entry is free.

The **Van Diemen's Land Folk Museum** is the oldest folk museum in Australia. It's based in Narryna, a fine Georgian home (103 Hampden Rd, Battery Point). Dating from 1836, it stands in beautiful grounds and has a large and fascinating collection of relics from Tasmania's early pioneering days. It's open on weekdays except Monday from 10.30 am to 5 pm and at weekends from 2 to 5 pm; admission is $5 for adults, $2 for children or $10 for a family.

The **Maritime Museum of Tasmania** at Secheron House, on Secheron Rd, in Battery Point, was built in 1831 and is classified by the National Trust. It also contains an extensive collection of photos, paintings, models and relics depicting Tasmania's – and particularly Hobart's – colourful shipping history. Admission is $4 for adults (children free) and it's open daily from 10 am to 4.30 pm except Christmas Day and Good Friday. At the time of writing, the museum was intending to close down in the fourth quarter of 1999 and reopen in the Carnegie Building on lower Argyle St (near Constitution Dock) at about the end of 1999.

Close to Constitution Dock, the **Sullivans Cove Whisky Distillery & Museum** (2 Macquarie St) is open daily from 9 am to 7 pm, and self-guided tours with tastings are $5.

The **Tasmanian Transport Museum** on Anfield St, Glenorchy, is open on weekends from 1 to 4.30 pm. On the third Sunday of the month train rides are available, and on these days it's open from 11 am; admission is $2 for adults and $1 for children except on train ride days when it's $3 for adults and $1.50 for children. Take Metro bus No X1 from stop F on Elizabeth St: it's a short walk from Glenorchy bus station.

The **Lady Franklin Gallery**, on Lenah Valley Rd, was Australia's first museum and is open on weekends from 1 to 4.30 pm; entry is free. Take bus No 6, 7, 8, 9 or 10 to the Lenah Valley terminus from stop G on Elizabeth St. The **Moonah Arts Centre** (65 Hopkins St, Moonah) is open from 12.30 to 5 pm on weekdays; entry is free.

## Historic Buildings

One thing that makes Hobart so unusual among Australian cities is its abundance of old and remarkably well-preserved buildings. More than 90 buildings in Hobart are classified by the National Trust, and 60 of them, featuring some of Hobart's best Georgian architecture, are on Macquarie and Davey Sts. The National Trust's office (☎ 6223 5200) is on the corner of Brisbane and Campbell Sts, and it also has a shop in the Galleria on Salamanca Place.

An excellent booklet on both new and old buildings, *An Architectural Guide to the City of Hobart* (published by the Tasmanian Chapter of the Royal Australian Institute of Architects), is available from the National Trust shop for $3.20. The shop is open all day Monday to Friday and on Saturday morning.

Close to the city centre is **St Davids Park**, which has some lovely old trees, and some gravestones that date from the earliest days of the colony. On Murray St is **Parliament House**, which was originally used as a customs house (there is still a tunnel between Parliament House and the Customs House Hotel opposite, though the reason for the tunnel is unclear). Hobart's prestigious **Theatre Royal** (29 Campbell St) was built in 1837 and is the oldest theatre in Australia.

There's a **royal tennis court** on Davey St, one of only three in the southern hemisphere. Royal, or 'real', tennis is an ancient form of tennis played in a four-walled indoor court, and Hobart's court can be viewed as part of the Footsteps walking tour (see the Walking Tours section earlier in this chapter).

The historic **Penitentiary Chapel & Criminal Courts** (28 Campbell St) has daily tours run by the National Trust. The tour includes the buildings, cells, gallows and tunnels and runs between 10 am and 2 pm daily. It's $6 for adults – ring ☎ 6231 0911 for details. Ghost tours are also available for $10 but bookings are essential – ring ☎ 0417 361 392.

**Runnymede** (61 Bay Rd, New Town) is a gracious colonial residence dating from the early 1830s. It was built for Robert Pitcairn, who was the first lawyer to qualify in Tasmania, and named by a later owner, Captain

Charles Bayley, after his favourite ship. Now managed by the National Trust, it is open daily from 10 am to 4.30 pm; admission is $6 for adults, $4 for children and $12 for a family. It is closed during July and on major public holidays. To get there take bus No 15 or 20 from stop H in the Hobart bus station (Elizabeth St) and alight at the Old New Town station.

## Cascade Brewery

Australia's oldest brewery, on Cascade Rd close to the city centre, is still producing some of the finest beer in the country – although no doubt others would argue differently! Two-hour tours take place daily at 9.30 am and 1 pm, and bookings are essential (☎ 6224 1144); the tour costs $7.50 for adults and $1.50 for children. The tour requires climbing many stairs and flat shoes are recommended; thongs and open footwear are not suitable. The brewery is on the south-western edge of the city centre; take bus No 43, 44, 46 or 49 from Franklin Square and get off at bus stop 17.

## The Waterfront

Hobart's busy waterfront area, centring on **Franklin Wharf**, is close to the city centre and very interesting to walk around. At **Constitution Dock** there are several floating takeaway seafood stalls and it's a treat to sit in the sun munching fresh fish and chips while watching the activity in the harbour. At the finish of the annual Sydney to Hobart Yacht Race around New Year and during the Royal Hobart Regatta in February, Constitution Dock really comes alive. The docks also have some fine sit-down restaurants if you prefer something more formal.

Nearby **Hunter St** has a row of fine Georgian warehouses. They're similar to those on Salamanca Place, but haven't – yet – been developed as a tourist attraction. They are in a similar condition to that of the Salamanca Place buildings before they were restored.

The whole wharf area is actually reclaimed land. When Hobart was first settled, Davey St ran along the edge of the sea and

## Little Devils & Great Big Cats

In July 1998, fast ferry *Cat-Link V*, built by Tasmanian-based company International Catamarans (Incat), claimed the Hales Trophy for the fastest crossing of the Atlantic by a passenger ship. It was not the first time a vessel built by this company had won the trophy, and *Cat-Link*'s success came as no surprise to Hobart residents, for whom the spectacle of one of Incat's massive catamarans skimming along the Derwent at high speed during performance trials is a familiar sight.

Incat grew out of a company that made a name for itself providing a ferry service across the Derwent River in the two years following the 1975 collapse of the Tasman Bridge. When the bridge reopened, ferry operator Bob Clifford turned his attention from running ferries to designing them.

In 1983, the concept of the wave-piercing catamaran was developed, and a prototype of just 8.7m was built, tiny by comparison with the company's present day ferries, which can be 120m in length. The prototype was named *Little Devil*, and ever since, Incat's vessels have been regarded with an affection usually reserved for race horses – so much so, in fact, that the company actually talks of advances in technology as 'improving the breed'.

Incat has now built around 40% of the world's high-speed car ferries of more than 70m in length. It's Tasmania's largest private employer with 900 people employed directly and 300 as subcontractors and it's one of Tasmania's most successful enterprises.

Lyn McGaurr

Place were constructed. On Hunter St itself, there are markers indicating the position of the original causeway, built in 1820 to link Hunter Island with Sullivans Cove.

## Salamanca Place

The row of beautiful sandstone warehouses on the harbourfront at Salamanca Place is a prime example of Australian colonial architecture. Dating back to the whaling days of the 1830s, these warehouses were the centre of Hobart Town's trade and commerce. Only 25 years ago, many of these buildings were in a derelict state and under threat of demolition. Thankfully they were saved and today they have been tastefully developed to house galleries, restaurants, nightspots and shops selling everything from vegetables to antiques. Every Saturday morning a popular open-air **craft market** is held at Salamanca Place from 8.30 am to 3 pm in summer and to 2 pm in the other seasons. There are usually about 300 stalls in the market and the businesses in the warehouses are also open. Goods on sale range from the fresh vegetables grown by the Hmong community (a migrant group from Laos), to flowers, clothing and art works made by local artisans.

To reach Battery Point from Salamanca Place you can climb up the **Kelly Steps**, which are wedged between two of the warehouses about halfway along the main block of warehouses.

**Antarctic Adventure**, on Salamanca Square, is a combination of theme park and science centre. Inside, you can take a simulated blizzard ride downhill at 120km/h, experience temperatures of -5°C to -15°C and be blasted with snow in the cold room, and view Antarctica's night sky in the planetarium. It's expensive though, at $16 for adults, $8 for children and $40 for two adults and two children. It's open from 10 am to 5 pm daily.

Another venue for families is **Time Warp House**, also on Salamanca Square, which bills itself as 'Australia's first retro entertainment centre'. It's open from 10 am to 5 pm daily and is $8 for an adult and $4 for a child.

the Hunter St area was originally an island that was used to safely store food and other goods. Subsequent projects filled in the shallow waters and provided land upon which the warehouses of Hunter St and Salamanca

**HOBART**

## Battery Point

Behind Princes Wharf and Salamanca Place is the historic core of Hobart, the old port area known as Battery Point. Its name comes from the gun battery that stood on the promontory by the guardhouse. It was built in 1818, and is now the oldest building in the district. The guns were never used in battle and the only damage they did was to shatter the windows of nearby houses when fired during practice.

During colonial times, this area was a colourful maritime village, home to master mariners, shipwrights, sailors, fishers, coopers and merchants. The houses reflect their varying lifestyles, ranging from tiny one and two-room houses, such as those around Arthur Circus, to mansions. While most houses are still lived in by locals, a range of buildings are used for visitor accommodation, so you can stay here and experience the village atmosphere of this unique area. Battery Point's pubs, churches, conjoined houses and narrow winding streets have all been lovingly preserved and

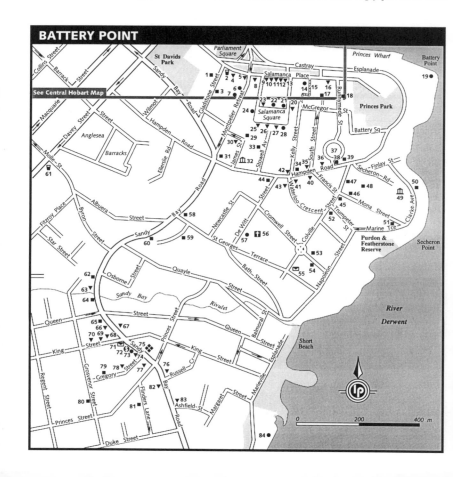

are a real delight to wander around, especially when you are able to get glimpses of the harbour between the buildings. There is so much to see here; don't miss out on **Arthur Circus** – a small circle of quaint little cottages built around a village green – or **St George's Anglican Church**.

**Anglesea Barracks** was built in Battery Point in 1811. Still used by the army, this is the oldest military establishment in Australia. There are no admission fees to the museum, which is usually open on Tuesdays from 9 am to 12.30 pm and, in summer, on Saturdays from 1.30 to 4.30 pm. There are guided tours of the restored buildings and grounds on Tuesday at 11 am. At other times you are free to wander around the buildings and look at the outside, but you cannot enter them as they are still in use.

The only way to see the place properly is to walk around, and the brochures listed in the earlier Walking Tours section of this chapter are well worth obtaining.

## Queen's Domain

When Hobart was originally settled, the high hill on the northern side of the city was reserved for the use of the governor. This stopped development of housing across the hill and today the area is known as the Queen's Domain and is reserved for public parkland.

This large park contains reserves and playing grounds for cricket and athletics as

---

## BATTERY POINT

**PLACES TO STAY**
1  Salamanca Mews Executive Suites
3  Salamanca Inn
17  Battery Point Guesthouse
18  Lenna of Hobart
29  Knopwood Apartment
31  Portsea Terrace
33  Hobart Town Guesthouse
34  Prince of Wales Hotel
38  The Grand Old Duke
39  Hampden Boutique Apartments
44  Barton Cottage
45  Colville Cottage
46  Ascot of Battery Point
47  Avon Court Holiday Apartments
48  Battery Point Holiday Flat
50  Jarem Waterfront B & B
51  Tantallon Lodge
52  Shipwright's Arms Hotel
53  Colonial Battery Point Manor
54  Cromwell Cottage
58  St Ives Motel
59  Crelin Lodge
60  Blue Hills
62  Woolmers Inn
64  Dr Syntax Hotel
65  Bay Arcade Holiday Units
79  Merre Be's
80  Grosvenor Court Holiday Apartments
81  Flinders Apartments

**PLACES TO EAT**
4  Zum Café
5  Retro Café
8  Knopwoods Retreat; Syrup; Round Midnight
9  Maldini
10  Parthenon
11  Salamanca Food Fair
12  Salamanca Café
13  Vietnamese Kitchen
16  Panache; Ball & Chain; Mikaku
20  Mr Woobys
23  All Bar One
25  Salamanca Bakehouse
26  Say Cheese
27  Toshi's Kitchen
30  Kelly's Restaurant
35  Da Angelo Ristorante
36  Tacos Mexican Restaurant
40  Dirty Dick's Steakhouse
41  Mozart on Hampden
42  Jackman & McRoss
43  Mummy's Coffee Shop
63  Dolphin In The Bay
66  Mykonos
67  La Bella Pizza; Caesar's Restaurant
68  The Fish Bar
69  Solo Pasta
70  Limelite Cafe; Poseidon's
74  Banjos
76  The French Lady
77  Nickelby's Wine Bar

78  Tasmanian Coffee Roasters
82  Garden of Earthly Delights
83  McDonald's

**OTHER**
2  Irish Murphy's
6  Wilderness Society
7  Drifters Internet Café
14  Salamanca Arts Centre: Long Gallery; Peacock Theatre; Foyer Espresso Bar
15  Kelly Steps
19  CSIRO Marine Laboratories
21  Time Warp House
22  Hobart Bookshop
24  Antarctic Adventure
28  Machine Laundry Café
32  Narryna & Museum
37  Arthur Circus
49  Maritime Museum
55  Battery Point Trading Post & Post Office
56  St Georges Anglican Church
57  St George's Park
61  Bridie O'Reilleys
71  Post Office
72  Commonwealth Bank & ATM
73  Sandy Bay Bookshop & Newsagency
75  Magnet Court Shopping Centre; Launderette; Golden Tulip Patisserie; Westpac Bank & ATM
84  Royal Yacht Club of Tasmania

well as wide areas of native grasslands. There are good views across the river and the city from many areas of the Domain; the best view is from the lookouts on top of the hill on the northern end of the park. If walking across the park, don't try to descend the northern end to New Town as deep road cuttings prevent pedestrian access. There are several pedestrian overpasses on the western side that provide good access to North Hobart.

On the eastern side, near the Tasman Bridge, are the **Royal Tasmanian Botanical Gardens**, which open at 8 am daily; admission is free. Established by the early governors, the gardens are a wonderful place to spend a few hours when you need a break from sightseeing. The massive brick walls were heated by wood fires to combat the effects of frost. Some of the newer features worth visiting are the Japanese Garden and the French Memorial Fountain.

Next door to the botanic gardens is **Government House**, which is the residence of the governor of the state. It is not open to the public and not visible from the road but you can get a good view of the turrets and towers on the building from high up on the hill of the Queen's Domain.

## Mt Wellington

Hobart is dominated by Mt Wellington (1270m), and there are many fine views and interesting walking tracks across it. You can walk from the city centre to the summit and back in a day, but this is really for fit, experienced walkers. The top is sometimes under cloud and in winter it often has a light cover of snow.

There is no year-round public transport to the top of the mountain. However, there are buses to Fern Tree, a small suburb of Hobart about halfway up the mountain. Metro bus Nos 48 and 49 leave from Franklin Square for Fern Tree. From there you can walk to the summit and back in about five to six hours via Fern Glade Track, Radfords Track then the Zig Zag Track. The Organ Pipes walk from the Chalet is an impressive flat walk below the Organ Pipes. Buy a copy of

the *Mt Wellington Walks* map for details of all tracks.

You can get to the top by joining a bus tour – see the Organised Tours section later in this chapter for details. Another enjoyable option is to get a taxi to the top – it costs around $23 for up to five people – and walk downhill back to the city. There are also buses to the top daily from December until mid-February for $6 each way from Franklin Square.

## Mt Nelson

If Mt Wellington is under cloud, the **Old Signal Station** on Mt Nelson, which is much lower, will still provide excellent views over the city. When Port Arthur was operating as a penal station, a series of semaphore stations using flags were positioned on all the high hills. These were used to transmit messages across the colony and Mt Nelson was the major link between Hobart and the rest of the colony.

Beside the signal station is a restaurant. The lookout can be accessed by a steep winding road from Sandy Bay, or via the

turn-off at the Southern Outlet on top of the hill. The outlet is the main road from Hobart to Kingston. From Franklin Square, Metro bus Nos 57 and 58 operate to the lookout.

## Alpenrail

This is one for the kids – a Swiss model village and railway at 82 Abbotsfield Rd, Claremont, open from 9.30 am to 4.30 pm daily. There are hands-on exhibits for the youngsters. Admission is $8.50 for an adult, $3 for a child (per person prices are reduced for larger groups). Take Metro bus No 42 from stop E on Elizabeth St.

## What's Free

Hobart is such a delight to discover on foot that just walking around the docks and Battery Point is probably the best free activity available. The Botanical Gardens and the museum are free, and there are also free guided tours of the museum (see that section earlier in this chapter). No park fees apply to Mt Wellington, which is a fantastic place to go for bushwalks, and swimming at Kingston Beach or Blackmans Bay is great if the weather is warm enough. Kids might enjoy watching the clockwork nursery rhyme characters that appear on the hour on the wall next to the clock in the Cat and Fiddle Arcade. Salamanca Market, held every Saturday morning on Salamanca Place, is free as long as you don't indulge yourself and actually buy something; there are usually buskers about to keep you entertained, and you can also browse in the nearby galleries and speciality shops, which are open at the same time.

## Sailing

The Derwent River and D'Entrecasteaux Channel are wonderful sailing waters; see the Sailing section of the Activities chapter for details.

## Cycling

There is a cycle route from central Hobart to the northern suburb of Glenorchy, part of which follows the banks of the Derwent River. Bikes can be hired at Derwent Bike Hire, at the Cenotaph in the Regatta Grounds, for $7 an hour, including helmet. It's open from 9 am on weekends from September to May. You can also take a $35 organised ride from the top of Mt Wellington with Brake Out Cycling Tours (☎ 6239 1090).

## Ocean Kayaking

Kayaking around the docks in Hobart, particularly at twilight, is gaining popularity. Two companies offering this activity are Aardvark Adventures Tasmania (☎ toll-free 018 127 714) and the Roaring 40°s Ocean Kayaking Company (☎ toll-free 1800 653 712).

## Train Rides

The Derwent Valley Railway Preservation Society (☎ 6234 6049) runs a passenger train to Parattah near Oatlands and return once a month for $25 an adult, $15 a child and $70 a family. A barbecue lunch is available at Parattah for a small additional cost.

## Organised Tours

**Cruises** Four cruise companies operate from the Brooke St Pier and Franklin Wharf and offer a variety of cruises in and around the harbour. One of the most popular cruises is the 4½ hour Cadbury's Cruise, run by the Cruise Company (☎ 6234 9294), which costs $33 for adults and $16 for children. The boat leaves at 10 am on weekdays and takes you on a slow return cruise to the Cadbury Schweppes factory in Claremont, where you can disembark and tour the premises.

Cruise timetables are unreliable. Some cruises have advertised running times but only operate if there are enough passengers; if you arrive to book just before it leaves, you may find the tour that day has already been cancelled. Harbour cruises are also available and vary in length from one to three hours.

The MV *Cartela* (☎ 6223 1914) runs morning cruises for $18, lunch cruises for $26, afternoon tea cruises for $12 and 2½ hour dinner cruises for $26. On Friday, it runs a counter-lunch cruise for a bargain $12.

**Cadbury Chocolate Factory Tour** You can go directly to the factory yourself and tour it without taking a cruise. Inspections are run on weekdays only at 9 am, 9.30 am, 10.30 am, 11.15 am and 1 pm. The factory is closed from the week before Christmas until late January. Admission is $10 for adults and $5 for children and tickets must be purchased at Cadbury's. Bookings are essential (☎ 6249 0333). You can get there by taking Metro bus No 37, 38 or 39 to Claremont from stop E at the Hobart bus station on Elizabeth St.

**Bus Tours** Day and half-day bus tours in and around Hobart are operated by Tasmanian Tours & Travel/Tigerline (☎ 6231 2200, 1300 653 633). Bus tours usually only run if there are bookings.

They offer half-day trips to Bonorong Wildlife Park and Richmond ($30), Bonorong ($45 with bush barbecue dinner), Richmond ($35 with afternoon tea), the City Sights and Mt Wellington ($25), Cadbury's ($25), the Channel ($35) and the Derwent Valley ($35).

Full-day tour destinations are Port Arthur ($45 or $55), the Huon Valley ($69) and Bruny Island ($95).

Another company offering coach tours of and from Hobart is Experience Tasmania (☎ 6234 3336), which has hotel courtesy pick-ups. It has half-day tours to Cadbury's; Mt Wellington (including Mt Wellington at sunrise); Mt Wellington and the Antarctic Adventure; Mt Wellington and Salamanca; Bonorong Wildlife Park and Richmond; and Mt Field National Park and the Bonorong Wildlife Park. Its full-day tours include those to Port Arthur; the Huon Valley; Cadbury's, Bonorong Wildlife Park and Richmond; and Mt Wellington and Richmond. It also offers twilight and evening tours of city sights, a coach tram tour and a combined coach tram tour and cruise.

**Motorcycle Tours** For something a bit different, you could try Harley Tours of Hobart (☎ 6224 1565) for a ride around Hobart in a Harley-Davidson sidecar. It operates from the waterfront and prices start at $15.

**Car Tours** If you're feeling particularly flush, you can take a day or half-day tour with the Tasmanian Limousine Service (☎ 6225 3131) for $40 an hour; it visits most of the places the bus tours go to. At the other extreme are the 1950s Holden Experience Tours (☎ 6247 9170). A two hour tour, tailored to suit your interests, is $30 an adult or $100 for four adults.

**Scenic Flights** Scenic flights are offered by Par Avion (☎ toll-free 1800 646 411) and Tasair (☎ toll-free 1800 062 900) from Cambridge airport, 15km from the city. See the Scenic Flights section of the Activities chapter for details.

## Special Events
From 29 December to 2 January, Hobart's waterfront area is alive with spectators and celebrating yachties at the finish of the annual New Year Sydney to Hobart Yacht Race and the Westcoaster Yacht Race. The festivities continue for 10 days with daily yacht races on the Derwent River and music and other events held around the waterfront.

The Royal Hobart Regatta, in early February, is a major four day aquatic carnival with boat races and other activities.

The biennial Australian Wooden Boat Festival is in November of even-numbered years at the docks. It features vessels from around Australia and celebrates Tasmania's vibrant boat-building heritage. There are displays, races, puppet shows and various other events with a nautical theme. See the 'Wooden Boats' boxed text in the South-East Coast chapter for details.

During January other sporting events such as the international Tasmanian Women's Open tennis tournament at the Domain, the Cadbury Marathon and sailing events for smaller boats are also held.

## Places to Stay – Budget
Hobart has a wide variety of accommodation catering for all tastes and price brackets.

The main areas for budget accommodation are the city centre and the older suburbs to the north and west. Middle and upper-end accommodation is spread all over town. The most popular suburb in which to stay is historic Battery Point, just south of the city and very close to the waterfront; almost all prices here are in the middle to upper range.

In the following listings, those places under the City subheading should be on the Central Hobart map, those under the Battery Point subheading should be on the Battery Point map, and most of those under the North, South, East and West subheadings should be on the Hobart map. The exceptions are a number of places in the vicinity of the Sandy Bay shopping centre, which are listed under the South subheading but are included on the Battery Point map.

**Camping & Cabins** All the camping grounds listed here except the Sandy Bay Caravan Park are out of walking distance of the centre.

**South** The handiest camping ground is the *Sandy Bay Caravan Park* (☎ *6225 1264, 1 Peel St, Sandy Bay)*, less than 3km from the city. It's popular because it's not only close to the city, but the casino at Wrest Point is just a short walk away. It charges $16 a double for a powered site, while on-site vans are $35 a double and cabins $55. To get there, take Metro bus No 54, 55 or 56 from Franklin Square or walk along Sandy Bay Rd for 40 minutes.

**North** The other parks are farther out of town and really only useful if you have your own wheels. The *Elwick Cabin & Caravan Park* (☎ *6272 7115, 19 Goodwood Rd, Elwick)* is 8km from the city and next to the road that leads across the Bowen Bridge. Powered sites are $15 a double, on-site vans $32 a double and cabins $58 a double.

Farther north, the *Treasure Island Caravan Park* (☎ *6249 2379)* is on a small peninsula at Berriedale, 14km north of the city. This is very close to the Moorilla Estate Winery and provides pleasant camping beside the Derwent River. Tent sites are $14, powered sites $16, on-site vans $34 and cabins $50 a double.

**East** If you prefer to stay on the eastern shore of the river then *Bowen Park* (☎ *6243 9879)* beside the East Derwent Hwy at Risdon has cabins for $55 a double. The other cabin park on the eastern shore is *Mornington Park* (☎ *6244 7070, 346 Cambridge Rd, Mornington)*. It's in the first suburb you come to when approaching the city from the airport. It's 5km from town and has cabins for $60 a double.

**Hostels** Hobart has a few good hostels right in the centre and a couple of hotels offering backpacker accommodation.

**City** The *Central City Backpackers* (☎ *6224 2404, 138 Collins St)* is a huge, rambling place in the middle of town that was previously called the Imperial Private Hotel and has excellent facilities and friendly staff. There are spacious communal areas, as well as a laundry and individual safe-deposit boxes. The cost is $14 or $16 for a dorm bed, $19 per person in a twin, and $30/38 for a single/double. There is a refundable key deposit of $5. Security is good here and it's clean and quiet, but there is no parking.

The *New Sydney Hotel* (☎ *6234 4516, 87 Bathurst St)* charges $14 a night for very basic bunks and facilities on the 1st floor of a hotel that's close to the shopping centre and outdoor equipment shops. It's rather cramped but is worth considering if you want to spend some time before bed in a popular, relaxed pub that has live music every night except Monday. The main dorm is right above the stage, but the performers are usually fairly laid back and are supposed to finish by midnight.

There is another hostel above the Transit Centre called *Transit Centre Backpackers* (☎ *6231 2400, 199 Collins St)*. It has beds for $13 per night and a very large communal area that lacks atmosphere but has good facilities. Security is provided by a digitally coded lock and reception is open until 10 pm

HOBART

(11 pm in summer). If your plane arrives late and it's clear you won't get into town on the shuttle bus before closing time, ring from the airport and make arrangements to be admitted after hours.

The cheapest backpackers in town is the *Ocean Child Hotel (☎ 6234 6730)*, on the corner of Argyle and Melville Sts, which has bunks for $12 a night.

**Battery Point** The *Hobart Town Guesthouse (☎ 6224 8331, 1 Stowell Ave)* has dorm beds for $15 a night with a continental breakfast included. It also has basic rooms with shared facilities for $25/40 with breakfast.

**North** The *Adelphi Court (☎ 6228 4829, 17 Stoke St, New Town)* is 2.5km from the city. It's an excellent hostel with good facilities and it charges $14 for a dorm bed, $38 a double for a twin room with shared facilities and $42/48 for *en suite* rooms. To get there, take Metro bus No 15 from stop H on Elizabeth St to stop 8. Any bus leaving stop E on Elizabeth St will take you to stop 13, which is close to Stoke St. Tasmanian Redline Coaches (TRC) also provides a drop-off and pick-up service on the airport bus.

**Colleges** During the longer school and university holidays periods you can stay in the hostels and halls of residence used by the students.

**City** The most convenient university hostel is *Hollydene House (☎ 6234 6434, 55 Campbell St)*, which offers B&B for around $25 plus $10 for each extra adult in a room, or a dormitory bed for $15.

**South** Next to the university on College Rd, Sandy Bay, *Christ College (☎ 6221 4567)* has single rooms with shared facilities for $32 each, which includes breakfast. *Jane Franklin Hall (☎ 6223 2000, 6 Elboden St, South Hobart)*, next to Davey St, charges $35/45 for B&B in rooms with shared facilities.

## Places to Stay – Mid-Range

**Hotels** Hobart has a large number of old hotels built from sandstone or brick and usually two to four storeys in height. Most were built last century and are close to the city centre. The cheaper ones generally offer single and double rooms with shared bathroom and vary in standard depending on how long ago the last major renovation was done. Often the hotel area downstairs is very classy while the rooms upstairs are fairly plain. The more expensive hotels have *en suite* rooms similar to motel rooms.

**City** The *Brunswick Hotel (☎ 6234 4981, 67 Liverpool St)* is pretty central and has average rooms costing $35/50 with a continental breakfast. Across the road, the *Alabama Hotel (☎ 6234 3737, 72 Liverpool St)* is a little more comfortable and charges $28/44. The *Hotel Astor (☎ 6234 6611, 157 Macquarie St)* is only two blocks from the mall; all rooms have shared toilets; singles/doubles with private shower are $60/65, while singles without private shower are $55. A continental breakfast is included in the price.

Nearby, the *Welcome Stranger Hotel (☎ 6223 6655)*, on the corner of Harrington and Davey Sts, has rooms for $49/59.

Over near the hospital the *Theatre Royal Hotel (☎ 6234 6925, 31 Campbell St)* has rooms for $35/45. One block away on the same street, the *Royal Exchange Hotel (☎ 6231 4444)*, on the corner of Campbell and Bathurst Sts, charges $49/59 for B&B in rooms with their own facilities.

The *Hobart Macquarie Motor Inn (☎ 6234 4422)*, on the corner of Macquarie and Harrington Sts, has rooms with *en suite* for $85/95. In a similar kind of multistorey building is the *Hobart Mid City Motor Inn (☎ 6234 6333)*, on the corner of Bathurst and Elizabeth Sts, which has rooms with *en suite* for $88/138.

Good value in the middle to upper range is *Country Comfort Hadleys Hotel (☎ 6223 4355, 34 Murray St)*. Rated as a four star hotel, the 140-year-old building has a lot more charm than many of the large new hotels. Single or double rooms with *en suite* are $105.

If you want to stay near the docks, the *Customs House Hotel* (☎ *6234 6645, 1 Murray St*) charges $50/65 with shared facilities and a continental breakfast, $70 a double with *en suite*.

**Battery Point** The *Shipwrights Arms Hotel* (☎ *6223 5551, 29 Trumpeter St, Battery Point*) is a popular local pub with rooms with shared facilities for $40/60. The *Prince of Wales Hotel* (☎ *6223 6355, Hampden Rd, Battery Point*) is 2km from town and provides basic accommodation with *en suites* for $60/70 including breakfast.

**North** Within walking distance but just out of town are several reasonable hotels. The *Waratah Hotel* (☎ *6234 3685, 272 Murray St*) has rooms with *en suite* for $52/65 with a cooked breakfast. If you prefer to be well out of the city you could try the *Claremont Hotel* (☎ *6249 1119, 1 Main Rd, Claremont*), which is 12km out and is close to the Cadbury chocolate factory; rooms with *en suite* are $20 per person with breakfast. Beside the Tasman Hwy on the eastern edge of the city, the *Mornington Inn* (☎ *6244 3855, 322 Cambridge Rd*) has rooms with *en suite* for $40/50.

**South** There are a couple of moderately priced hotels in Sandy Bay. The *Dr Syntax Hotel* (☎ *6223 6258, 139 Sandy Bay Rd*) is very close to Battery Point (see the Battery Point map). It has comfortable rooms with *en suite* for $43/59. The *Beach House Hotel* (☎ *6225 1161, 646 Sandy Bay Rd*) is 2km south of the casino and has good rooms with TV and continental breakfast for $48/58.

A bit classier is the *Cascade Hotel* (☎ *6223 6385, 22 Cascade Road, South Hobart*), where rooms with *en suite* are $58/68. It's 3km from town and easy to find, as Cascade Rd is the continuation of Macquarie St.

**West** Up on the hill, 1km west of the city, is the *Marquis of Hastings Hotel* (☎ *6234*

*3541*), on the corner of Brisbane and Hill Sts. Motel-style rooms with a view across the city are $60/70.

The *Globe Hotel* (☎ *6223 5800*) is a bit more basic; rooms with shared facilities are $23/33 with breakfast.

**Motels** There are plenty of motels in Hobart, but the majority are rather a long way out; you'll need your own transport to reach most of them. Some are attached to licensed hotels and often have their own restaurants.

**City** On the northern edge of the city centre is the *Fountainside Motor Inn* (☎ *6234 2911, 40 Brooker Ave*). It's at the large roundabout where the highways enter town. Rooms in the multistorey motel are $89/99.

**Battery Point** Two good, central motels on Sandy Bay Rd but within walking distance of the city and docks are *Blue Hills* (☎ *6223 1777, 96A Sandy Bay Rd*) and *St Ives Motel* (☎ *6224 1044, 86 Sandy Bay Rd*). Both are good options: singles/doubles in the former are $80/100, while in the latter they are $89 a double.

**North** As you would expect, the cheapest motels are all well out of town. Way north of the city, the *Highway Village Motor Inn* (☎ *6272 6721, 897 Brooker Hwy, Berriedale*) is in a pleasant spot beside the Derwent River and has budget rooms for only $48/58. Other rooms are up to $89/99.

The *Marina Motel* (☎ *6228 4748, 153 Risdon Rd, Lutana*) is 4km from town and is beside the Derwent River; rooms are $39/49. Just around the corner from the Adelphi Court YHA is the *Hobart Tower Motel* (☎ *6228 0166, 300 Park St, New Town*). This is in a good location beside the Brooker Hwy, about 2km from town; rooms are $58/68. Nearby, *Argyle Motor Lodge* (☎ *6234 2488*), is on the corner of Lewis and Argyle Sts, which has doubles ranging from $75.

**West** Closer to the city centre is the *Mayfair Motel* (☎ *6231 1188, 17 Cavell St, West*

*Hobart)*, which is on the hill and has rooms for $70/95.

**South** Near the casino is the pink, four storey *Sandy Bay Motor Inn (☎ 6225 2511, 429 Sandy Bay Rd)*. The rooms have good views of the casino and the Derwent River and are $80/90 with continental breakfast.

**East** On the eastern side of the Derwent River, the *Shoreline Motor Motel (☎ 6247 9504)*, on the corner of Rokeby Rd and Shoreline Drive, Howrah, is 7km from town. It's beside a major road junction, not beside the river as the name suggests; rooms are $55/65 with continental breakfast. The other motel on this side is *Lindisfarne Motor Inn (☎ 6243 8666, 101 East Derwent Hwy, Lindisfarne)*. It's beside the main highway 1km north of the Tasman Bridge and rooms are $65/75.

**Guesthouses & B&Bs** These are often housed in buildings of historical significance. The facilities vary widely but are often of a fairly high standard. Price is usually a good guide to quality, except around Battery Point where you must pay a little bit more to stay in this popular historic area. Most B&B places are fairly small with two to five rooms available for hire. Most guesthouse and B&B rooms now have *en suites* or private bathrooms nearby. Check-in times for guesthouses and B&Bs are often early afternoon, so remember to ask about this when you make your booking if you expect to be arriving in the morning.

**City** The inner city *Harrington Boutique Accommodation (☎ 6234 9240, 102 Harrington St)* has B&B for up to $115 a single or double.

**Battery Point** You can stay in some beautiful colonial guesthouses and cottages in Battery Point. While there is a wide selection from which to choose, there are no real bargains during the main tourist seasons. During winter discounts are sometimes available.

*Barton Cottage (☎ 6224 1606, 72 Hampden Rd)* is a two storey building that dates back to 1837 and is classified by the National Trust. There are six rooms and B&B accommodation costs $95/110. It also has a renovated self-contained coach house out the back; it sleeps four and is $135 a double.

A similar place worth considering is *Cromwell Cottage (☎ 6223 6734, 6 Cromwell St)*. This two storey townhouse dates from the late 1880s and is in a beautiful position overlooking the Derwent River. Rooms (some of which have views) are $85/110, which includes a cooked breakfast. One of the hosts speaks Japanese, French and German.

*Colville Cottage (☎ 6223 6968, 32 Mona St)*, which is very attractive and set in lovely gardens, has B&B for $95/115. Farther down the same street, *Tantallon Lodge (☎ 6224 1724, 8 Mona St)* is an imposing building with good views; rooms are $80/114.

**West** The *Crows Nest B&B (☎ 6234 9853, 2 Liverpool Crescent)* is within walking distance of the city in a quiet suburban street with good views over the casino and the river and has rooms with *en suite* for $55/75.

**North** Around the corner from the Adelphi Court hostel is *Hillpark House (☎ 6228 7094, 344 Park St, New Town)*. It has two double rooms with private bathrooms, which are $70/$90 with a cooked breakfast.

*Jutland House (☎ 6228 4970, 53 Montagu St, Lenah Valley)* is 4km from the city, off Augusta Rd. B&B here is $45/75. Close to the city in the small suburb of Glebe is *Wellington Lodge (☎ 6231 0614, 7 Scott St)*, only a 10 minute walk from town. It's in a nice location with good views across the city and is close to the nearby Queen's Domain parkland. Rates for B&B are $75/95.

**South** In Sandy Bay, up on the hill next to the Southern Outlet (the highway from Hobart to Kingston), is *Andersons (☎ 6223 6715, 5 Richardsons Ave)*. The one unit has views and a kitchenette, and the price with breakfast is $70/$75.

View of Hobart from Mt Wellington

Georgian warehouse on Hunter St, Hobart

Arthur's Circus at Battery Point, Hobart

Lively Salamanca Market

CHRIS KLEP

Salamanca Market

LINDSAY BROWN

Constitution Dock, Hobart

RICHARD I'ANSON

Beautiful sandstone warehouses make a great setting for the market.

An interesting option is the *Signalman's Cottage* (☎ *6223 1215, 685 Nelson Rd*) on the top of Mt Nelson. It's a self-contained, one bedroom unit and the cost is $60/70. The view over the city is excellent – especially in the evening – and the place is convenient if you have your own transport. Buses do operate to Mt Nelson; take No 57 or 58 from Franklin Square.

**East** Just across the Tasman Bridge, *Roseneath Host Accommodation* (☎ *6243 6530, 20 Kaoota Rd, Rose Bay*) has fine views across the river and is actually quite close to the city if you have your own vehicle. The rates for B&B are $75 a double for a room or $95 a double for a self-contained unit. In the same area is *Orana Accommodation* (☎ *6243 0404, 20 Lowelly Rd, Lindisfarne*). It's just off the East Derwent Hwy and this stately mansion has good value B&B starting at $65/110.

**Holiday Units** Hobart has a number of self-contained holiday flats with fully equipped kitchens. Prices vary, as does what's on offer. The cheaper units are normally flats in apartment blocks while the dearest are historic cottages.

**Battery Point** The biggest concentration of units can be found on the narrow streets of Battery Point. The *Knopwood Apartment* (☎ *6223 2290, 6 Knopwood St*) is a three bedroom upstairs flat overlooking beautiful Salamanca Place. Its view has been built out considerably in the past few years, but the garden is still lovely. It costs $70 a double and $20 for each extra person. Slightly dearer is *Crelin Lodge* (☎ *6223 1777, 1 Crelin St*), which is on a street that runs off St Georges Terrace. The lodge has units at $80 a double plus $10 for each extra adult. *Battery Point Holiday Flat* (☎ *6223 6592, 15 Secheron Rd*) is $90 for a single or a double.

Close to Hampden Rd is *Portsea Terrace* (☎ *6234 1616, 62 Montpelier Retreat*), which has nine apartments for $70/95. The price includes breakfast.

**North** The best bargains are well out of the city. *Northside Holiday Villas* (☎ *6272 4472, 9 McGough St, Glenorchy*) is 8km from Hobart. It's beside the Brooker Hwy and the units are $55/75. About 2km from town, *Domain View Apartments* (☎ *6234 1181, 352 Argyle St, North Hobart*) charges $60 a double.

**South** Sandy Bay is a convenient location; it is fairly close to town and has some good shops and units. *Grosvenor Court Holiday Apartments* (☎ *6223 3422, 42 Grosvenor St*) is just one block from the main shopping centre at Magnet Court on Sandy Bay Rd (see the Battery Point map). The apartments are $89/110. Just around the corner in a rather unattractive lane is *Flinders Apartments* (☎ *6234 6882, 4 Flinders Lane*), which has two plain units for $59 a single or double (see the Battery Point map).

In the middle of the Sandy Bay shopping centre is *Bay Arcade Holiday Units* (☎ *6223 2457, 163 Sandy Bay Rd, Sandy Bay*), which has self-contained units for $79 a double (see the Battery Point map).

In Lower Sandy Bay is *Antarctic Lodge* (☎ *6221 6222, 5 Beach Rd*), which is a good place for families because it's close to beaches and a popular playground. Two bedroom units are $85 a single or a double.

**West** About 8km from town the *Bay View Villas* (☎ *6234 7611, 34 Poets Rd, West Hobart*) has rooms for $99 a double with a garden view, $109 with a harbour view.

**East** On the eastern shore of the Derwent River, *Silwood Park Holiday Unit* (☎ *6244 4278, 7 Silwood Ave, Howrah*) is cheap at $49/54 and $62 a family. It can sleep five people and is close to the Howrah Beach.

## Places to Stay – Top End
Compared with other capital cities in Australia, the top end accommodation in Hobart is cheap and basically starts at around $120 a double. Prices are low enough even for the budget traveller to splash out on a luxury night. The four and five-star hotels

and luxury B&Bs are all fairly close to the city. Outside of the holiday seasons many of these places offer special deals, particularly for weekends. You'll find that either the rates are reduced or romantic dinners are included.

**Hotels** Hobart has several high-standard hotels close to the city's centre, the most well-known of which is the Wrest Point Hotel Casino.

*City* The *Hotel Grand Chancellor (☎ 6235 4535, 1 Davey St)* is an accommodation, bar and restaurant complex that dominates the city centre and has rooms priced from $220 a double. *Hobart Vista Hotel (☎ 6232 6225)*, on the corner of Bathurst and Harrington Sts, is another large hotel with suites from $128 a double.

*Battery Point* Just behind Salamanca Place, the *Salamanca Inn (☎ 6223 3300, 10 Gladstone St)* has rooms starting at $188 a double. About half of the 60 suites have kitchens. If none of these appeal, there's always the wonderful *Lenna of Hobart (☎ 6232 3900, 20 Runnymede St, Battery Point)*, which is an old mansion that is steeped in history and luxury and charges $140 for a double room.

*North* The *Rydges Hobart (☎ 6231 1588)* is on the corner of Argyle and Lewis Sts. It's in a restored building and offers antique furnished suites as well as modern hotel rooms and costs $135 a double with breakfast.

*South* The well-known *Wrest Point Hotel Casino (☎ 6225 0112, 410 Sandy Bay Rd)* is 5km south of the city centre. Rooms in the tower are $218 a double, while motel units are around $100 a double.

*West* If you would like something small and intimate then try the *Islington Private Hotel (☎ 6223 3900, 321 Davey St)*. The hotel has only eight suites and was constructed in 1845; the tariff is $75/150 and includes breakfast.

**Apartments** Quite a few inner city apartments have opened in Hobart over the past few years. The *Quest on Waterfront (☎ 6224 8630, 3 Brooke St)* is opposite the Brooke Street Bar & Café and has rooms for $135 a double. On the end of Elizabeth Pier itself, and consequently at the very heart of any dockside festivals that might be happening during your visit, is *Oakford on Elizabeth Pier*, with suites for $155 a double.

The *Old Woolstore (☎ 6235 5355, 1 Macquarie St)* has retained the façade of the original Sullivans Cove building but inside it's all brand new. Rooms are $130 a double, while one bedroom apartments are $155 a double.

**B&Bs** The very best restorations of Hobart's older mansions provide some fine accommodation. All these places are rated from four to five-star and provide very good quality accommodation.

*Battery Point* The *Colonial Battery Point Manor (☎ 6224 0888, 13 Cromwell St, Battery Point)*, built in 1834, has fine views to the south-east over the Derwent River; B&B is priced from $120/145; the *en suites* vary in size, so if this is a consideration, ask for a room with a large *en suite*. Just around the corner and almost as luxurious is *Ascot of Battery Point (☎ 6224 2434, 6 Colville St)*. The rate includes a cooked breakfast and is $100/140.

Very close to Salamanca Place is the *Battery Point Guesthouse (☎ 6224 2111, 7 McGregor St)*. Hidden down a side lane and with a rather startling view of the silos from its driveway, this was originally the coach house and stables for the nearby Lenna of Hobart. A cooked breakfast is included for $95/120 and families with young children are catered for.

If you prefer a new unit then try *Avon Court Holiday Apartments (☎ 6223 4837, 2 Colville St)*. Recently constructed from sandstone to blend in with the older buildings, the apartments include kitchens and are $118/125. The *Hampden Boutique Apartments (☎ 6224 2824, 27-29 Hampden*

*Rd)*, in the heart of Battery Point, has rooms with provisions for a continental breakfast for $110.

*Jarem Waterfront B&B (☎ 6223 8216, 8 Clarke Ave)* lives up to its name by being right on the edge of the water. It's modern and has lovely guest areas overlooking the river. Singles with private bathrooms are $95, while doubles with *en suite* are $120. The breakfast menu changes regularly.

**South** Close to the Sandy Bay shopping area is *Merre Bes (☎ 6224 2900, 24 Gregory St)*, which offers colonial accommodation in an 1880s house furnished with antiques (see the Battery Point map). It has B&B for $90/120. It has a dining room, but unfortunately the view is of a car park.

Near the casino is *Amberley House (☎ 6225 1005, 391 Sandy Bay Rd)*, which has rooms with *en suite* for $106/120. It's very attractive, but its location opposite a hotel on busy Sandy Bay Rd is a little at odds with the style of the property.

**North** An unusual area to stay in is Glebe, on the steep hill on the northern side of the city, where *Corinda Colonial Accommodation (☎ 6234 1590, 17 Glebe St, Glebe)* is conveniently located next to the Queen's Domain, and the botanical gardens and the city are both within walking distance. Apartments are $160 a double and a continental breakfast is provided.

Close to the city in North Hobart is the *Lodge on Elizabeth (☎ 6231 3830)*, on the corner of Elizabeth and Warwick Sts. It's an old mansion full of antiques. Large rooms with *en suite* are $115 a double. A bit farther up the road is *Elms of Hobart (☎ 6231 3277, 452 Elizabeth St)*, another old mansion, even more luxurious, and classified by the National Trust. The rate here with a cooked breakfast is $112/130.

If you want to stay in one of the oldest houses in Hobart then make your way to *Wendover (☎ 6278 2066, 10 Wendover Place, New Town)*; it's about 4km north of the city. The mansion is one of the original houses of the region, being built in

1815, and is much older and more beautiful than the nearby Runnymede. While New Town is not a fashionable suburb, the house is on a pleasant, leafy little street off a main road. The four spacious apartments contain kitchens and cost $140 a double with breakfast.

**Holiday Units & Cottages** There's a fairly small selection of holiday units and cottages in this price bracket.

**Battery Point** The most centrally located holiday units are the *Salamanca Mews Executive Suites (☎ 6227 9595, 5 Gladstone St, Battery Point)*, where an apartment costs $160 a double.

*The Grand Old Duke (☎ 6424 1606, 31 Hampden Rd)* is a self-contained historic apartment in the centre of Battery Point that charges $150 a single or double.

**South** If you would like a secluded, colonial cottage for two, then stay at *Mt Pleasant Mews (☎ 6225 1467, 32 Maning Ave, Sandy Bay)*. It's up on the hill about 1km south of the casino and is $156 a single/double. Closer to town is *Woolmers Inn (☎ 6223 7355, 123 Sandy Bay Rd)*, where the units are $120 a double (see the Battery Point map).

**West** Within walking distance of town is *Warwick Cottages (☎ 6254 1264, 119 Warwick St, West Hobart)*. The two units can each hold four guests and cost $145 a double with breakfast.

**East** The *Pines Resort (☎ 6248 6222)* at Seven Mile Beach is a good place to stay if you want to be out of the city. Complete with its own tavern, it's 18km from the centre but very close to the main airport and a good swimming beach; units are $120 a double.

## Places to Eat
**Takeaways & Light Meals** *Banjos (85 Elizabeth St)* is a central bakery open from 5 am to 7.30 pm weekdays and 4 am to 6.30 pm weekends. It has the usual bakery items,

sandwiches and light breakfasts, as well as a bottomless cup of coffee for $1.50. Across the road is *Stak a Jax*, which has a breakfast special of pancakes, eggs and maple syrup with coffee or tea for $5. It's open daily from 7 am until late, and pizzas are sold on the same premises.

Around the corner on Bathurst St is *La Cuisine*, which serves bakery items and light meals and is open for breakfast and lunch daily except Sunday. It also sells great sourdough bread. There is another La Cuisine in the Trafalgar Arcade on Collins St.

*Little Bali (41a Harrington St)* has excellent Indonesian takeaway, while right next door is *Little Salama*, which sells kebabs. Across the road and around the corner on Liverpool St is *Vanny's*, a Cambodian restaurant with a lunch takeaway special for $3.50. If pasta is more to your liking, then *Little Italy (152 Collins St)* is the place to go for cheap meals, though it's closed on weekends. On the opposite side of Collins street and back towards Harrington St is *Fortune Court*, which is a Chinese takeaway that avoids the use of MSG. It's open for lunch and dinner from Monday to Saturday.

In Murray St, opposite parliament house on the way down to the docks, is *Roche's* bakery and takeaway, which serves sandwiches, pies, pastries and light meals that you can eat inside or outside. It's open weekdays from 7.30 am to 3.30 pm.

In Battery Point is *Jackman & McRoss* (☎ *6223 3186, 57-59 Hampden Rd)*, a bakery café open weekdays from 7.30 am to 7 pm and on weekends to 5 pm. It has pies such as lamb shank and rosemary for $3.50 and gourmet sandwiches such as smoked beef and salad for $7.

There are a number of takeaways in the main section of Salamanca Place, most of which have outdoor tables. Among these is the *Vietnamese Kitchen*, which is a good place for cheap Asian food. Behind these buildings, on Salamanca Square, is *Toshi's Kitchen*, an excellent Japanese takeaway with sushi for $4 per two pieces. It's open for lunch and dinner daily except Sunday.

*Salamanca Bakehouse*, on the same square, is remarkable by Hobart standards for being open 24 hours a day. It sells the usual sandwiches, pies, pasties and pastries.

On the newly redeveloped Elizabeth Pier is *Fish Frenzy*, which serves cones of fresh seafood and chips that can be eaten inside or out. Across the bridge, on Constitution Dock, are a number of *floating takeaway seafood stalls*. Close by is Mures Fish Centre, where you can get excellent fresh fish and chips and other seafood at the bistro on the *Lower Deck*. The blue-eye is usually particularly good.

Other places that sell good fresh fish and chips are *Yabbies (410 Elizabeth St, North Hobart)* and *The Fish Bar (46-48 King St)*. For cheaper fish and chips and other kinds of takeaway in Sandy Bay, you could try *Mykonos (165 Sandy Bay Rd)*, which is open until the early hours of the morning, and the *Dolphin In The Bay (141 Sandy Bay Rd)*.

You can get takeaway pizzas at many places around town, including *Marti Zucco* and *Concettas*, both of which are on the Elizabeth St shopping centre in North Hobart, *Da Angelo Ristorante (47 Hampden Rd)* in Battery Point, *La Bella Pizza (172 Sandy Bay Rd)* and *Solo Pasta (50 King St)* in Sandy Bay. All have Italian restaurants on the premises, of which the best (though not the cheapest) is Da Angelo.

**Cafés & Café Wine Bars** The décor at *Kafe Kara (119 Liverpool St)* is surprisingly innovative for Hobart, and the food is excellent. It's licensed and is open from 8 am to 5 pm weekdays and from 9 am to 3 pm Saturday. Another gem, just around the corner, is *Cumquat (10 Criterion St)*, which has imaginative food and a pleasant atmosphere; it's open weekdays from 9 am until customers leave after dinner.

*Café Toulouse (79 Harrington St)* is central and has a wide selection of croissants and quiches. The *Larder Café* on the Elizabeth St Mall is also a possibility for lunch; it has small platters of Tasmanian produce for $9 and large ones for $16.

If you enjoy spending time browsing in good bookshops, you may like to stop for coffee and cake in the *Afterword Café (140 Collins St)* upstairs in Fullers Bookshop. It's open from 9 am to 5 pm Monday to Saturday and from 10 am to 4 pm Sunday.

A little north of the centre is *Kaos Café (273 Elizabeth St)*, a casual café that serves excellent light meals and is popular with all age groups. It has a generous turkey salad with bacon and Brie for $11.50 and is open weekdays from noon to midnight, Saturday from 10 am to midnight and Sunday from 10 am to 10 pm.

If you're after vegetarian food in abundance, head for *Zanskar's (39 Barrack St)*, a great place to relax over a slow meal or snack. It's open from 10 am to 9 pm daily; Sunday night is curry night, and a plate of mixed Indian curry with rice and salad is $10.50.

Also on the western edge of town is *Café Who*, a wine bar and café open for dinner from Tuesday to Saturday and for lunch from Wednesday to Friday.

In Battery Point you can eat or drink coffee until late at *Mummy's Coffee Shop (☎ 6224 0124, 38 Waterloo Crescent)*. This has been transformed recently and no longer has quite the charm (nor, it has to be said, any of the mustiness) of its previous incarnation. Today it is a thriving, modern, licensed café serving mains such as beer battered fish and chips for $11 and quiche and salad for $8.50. It's closed on Monday.

Also in Battery Point, and decidedly upmarket, is *Mozart on Hampden (☎ 6224 7124, 60 Hampden Rd)*, where you can eat high tea in the rose garden, or indulge in 'the maestro's breakfast', featuring champagne and caviar, for $25. It's open from 9 am to 11 pm Wednesday to Friday, from 8.30 am to 11 pm Saturday and from 8.30 am to 5 pm Sunday.

Possibly the most popular café in Hobart is the *Retro Café*, on the corner of Salamanca Place and Montpelier Retreat, which has something of the feel of the cafés on Brunswick St, Melbourne. It's often so crowded that you can't get a table, but locals who like its atmosphere and food are usually devoted enough to wait for one to become vacant. It's open daily from 8 am to 6 pm. Farther along Salamanca Place, in the direction of parliament house, *Zum Café* another very popular eatery with outdoor tables. It serves great pastries, salads, risotto, and eggplant stacks, and can be crowded for brunch on Saturday and Sunday.

Back towards the silos, there are a few more cafés with outdoor tables, and also an espresso bar called the *Foyer* inside the Salamanca Arts Centre.

Behind these buildings is Salamanca Square, where there are yet more cafés serving coffee, tea and light meals. Among them is *Say Cheese*, which sells Tasmanian wines and cheeses and is open for lunch from 11.30 am to 3 pm daily for mixed platters, salads etc. Opposite is *All Bar One*, a wine bar with a spacious café section. Call in here for wood-fired gourmet pizzas for $13 or platters of Tasmanian produce for $11. On Saturday and Sunday a cooked brunch is available. The kitchen is open until 11 pm from Monday to Thursday and midnight Friday and Saturday. The bar section is very popular with office workers.

In the new development on Elizabeth Pier is *Fusion*, open from 6.30 am to 1 am daily for breakfast, lunch, dinner, wine and coffee. Farther along the pier is *T-42°*, a wine bar and café open from 11.30 am until late. Both have outdoor tables, and the latter has the advantage of having views to both sides of the pier.

In the Sandy Bay shopping centre there are quite a few good cafés that attract a slightly older crowd, including *Lime Lite Café (54 King St)*, *Tasmanian Coffee Roasters (14 Gregory St)* and the *Golden Tulip Patisserie* on Magnet Court. On the edge of the shopping centre is the vegetarian *Garden of Earthly Delights (247 Sandy Bay Rd)*, which is below street level and gives the impression that it might be just the place to conduct an illicit romance. It's open for 'snacks, meals or just sweet indulgence', and boasts a garden eating area and, in winter, a log fire.

A popular wine bar right in the Sandy Bay shopping centre is *Nicklebys Wine Bar (217 Sandy Bay Rd)*, which has tables on its veranda and serves lunches and dinners daily.

**Pub Meals** Nearly all the hotels on the three Hobart maps serve counter meals, and many also have attractive restaurants or bistros. In the city, the *Brunswick Hotel (67 Liverpool St)* has meals from $4. The *New Sydney (87 Bathurst St)* is popular for cheap, filling counter meals. It serves lunches on weekdays and dinners daily. *Montgomery's (87 Macquarie St)* has bar meals for $9 or $10 and snacks such as rolls and focaccias for $4.50. Other good pubs in the city are the *Customs House (1 Murray St)*, which has a seafood restaurant with children's meals and also very cheap counter meals (around $6 for a main course); the lively *Brooke Street Bar & Café (19 Morrison St)*; *Irish Murphy's (21 Salamanca Places)*; the ever-popular old standard, *Knopwood's Retreat (39 Salamanca Place)*; *Bakers*, on the corner of Barrack and Macquarie Sts; and the stylish *Theatre Royal Hotel (31 Campbell St)*, right next door to the Theatre Royal, Australia's oldest functioning performing arts theatre.

The *Coupe de Ville Bar and Grill (145 Elizabeth St)*, in the Black Prince Hotel, is worth dropping into for a meal or a drink just so you can see the amazing décor (as the name suggests, it's nearly bursting with motoring memorabilia), but you'll have to be quick: it's due for redevelopment late in 1999.

The best medium-priced hotel meals in North Hobart can be had at the *Republic Bar (299 Elizabeth St)*, while in Battery Point the *Shipwright's Arms (29 Trumpeter St)* is a favourite with the locals for steak and seafood.

**Restaurants** Many new restaurants have opened in Hobart over the past few years, and the restaurant centre of the city is now very much concentrated on the waterfront streets and the docks and piers themselves. A number of upmarket restaurants have

recently introduced double sittings in the evenings, so check on this when you make your booking.

*Seafood* There is endless debate about which is the best seafood restaurant in Hobart, but *Prosser's on the Beach (☎ 6225 2276, Beach Rd, Lower Sandy Bay)* is always high on the list, despite being some distance from the city. Its excellent meals are served in attractive, unpretentious premises overlooking the water.

On the waterfront, the licensed *Drunken Admiral (☎ 6234 1903, 17 Hunter St)* is open every evening, while nearby in the Mures Fish Centre is the very popular *Upper Deck Restaurant (☎ 6231 2121, Victoria Dock)*, which has fine seafood and is justifiably famous.

*Kellys Restaurant (☎ 6224 7225)*, on the corner of James and Knopwood Sts in Battery Point, is in an 1849 sailmaker's cottage on the corner of back streets that run off Hampden Rd and Montpelier Retreat. It's open for dinner daily and for lunch on Friday.

*Italian* For reasonably cheap pasta and Italian dishes try *Casablanca (☎ 6234 9900, 213 Elizabeth St)*, open from 5.15 pm until late every evening. Nearby, another good Italian place is *Rozzini's (☎ 6234 1366, 201 Elizabeth St)*.

An exceptionally popular Italian restaurant in Battery Point is *Da Angelo (☎ 6223 7011, 47 Hampden Rd)*, which serves pasta for $8 to $12, small pizzas for $8.50 and large pizzas for $18. Come early or book, as it's often full.

Other good Italian restaurants include *Maldini (☎ 6223 4460, 47 Salamanca Place)*, which is open daily for lunch and dinner, and the laid-back *Riviera Ristorante (☎ 6234 3230, 15 Hunter St)*.

*Asian* Some of the best Indian curries in town are those available at the *Tandoor & Curry House (☎ 6234 6905, 101 Harrington St)*, where the banquets are $20 and $25 a person. Another good curry house is *Round Asia (☎ 6234 9385, 182 Goulburn*

*St)*, but make sure you let the chef know if you prefer your curries hot.

The ***Thai Hut*** *(☎ 6234 4914, 80 Elizabeth St)* is right in the middle of town and is reasonably cheap. It's open weekdays for lunch and dinner and Saturday for dinner only. Meat or vegetable mains are around $13, while seafood mains are priced from $14 to $18.

North Hobart has plenty of Asian restaurants. The Indonesian ***Rasa Asli*** *(☎ 6236 9833, 305 Elizabeth St)* has a Sunday special for $8.50 and takeaway from $5.50. Farther north is ***Vanidols*** *(☎ 6234 9307, 353 Elizabeth St)*, a comfortable BYO restaurant specialising in Thai, Indian and Indonesian cuisine and open Tuesday to Sunday. Farther along still is another BYO Asian restaurant, ***Dede*** *(☎ 6231 1068, 369 Elizabeth St)*, which has delicious sticky rice balls for $5 and mains for between $10 and $15.

A few Chinese restaurants you might like to try are ***Fortuna Restaurant*** *(275 Elizabeth St)*, the ***Golden Bamboo*** *(116 Elizabeth St)* and ***Flourishing Court*** *(252 Macquarie St)*. Flourishing Court cater well for children. The Chinese selection at the ***Asian Restaurant*** *(☎ 6225 0122, 410 Sandy Bay Rd)* at Wrest Point Casino is well regarded.

***The Sushi Bar*** *(☎ 6231 1790, Victoria Dock)* in the Mures Fish Centre and ***Mikaku*** *(☎ 6224 0882, 85-87 Salamanca Place)* serve reasonable Japanese meals.

**Mexican** The most central Mexican restaurant is ***Areeba's*** *(☎ 6224 4484, 7 Despard St)*, which is open from 5 pm until late from Tuesday to Saturday and specialises in seafood. Mains are around $16 or $18.

In North Hobart, you can get a good Mexican meal at ***Amigos*** *(☎ 6234 6115, 329 Elizabeth St)*, which is open daily for dinner and has burritos for $10.50 a half serve and $13.90 a full serve. Vegetarian enchiladas are $12.90.

***Tacos*** *(☎ 6223 5297, 41 Hampden Rd)*, in Battery Point, is open daily from 5.30 pm and also sells takeaway.

**Turkish** Turkish restaurants in Hobart are not cheap by Melbourne or Sydney standards. Two you may like to try are ***Mersins*** *(☎ 6223 2883, 121 Macquarie St)*, at the end of a short lane opposite Franklin Square, and ***Anatolia*** *(☎ 6231 1770, 321 Elizabeth St, North Hobart)*.

**French** The suburban ***Le Provencal*** *(☎ 6224 2526, 417 Macquarie St, South Hobart)* has wonderful, hearty fare with an emphasis on couscous ($17). Unfortunately the couscous is not available during December and January, when set menus predominate.

***A Splash of Paris*** *(☎ 6224 2200, Elizabeth Pier)* is the former Paris Restaurant minus the intimacy. The food is still excellent, however, and the views to either side of the pier delightful, particularly when the *Lady Nelson* sailing ship is docked just outside the window. It's open daily for lunch and dinner and mains are around $18.

The ***French Lady*** *(☎ 6224 1255)*, in Mayfair Arcade, Sandy Bay, would probably be a much more popular restaurant if it were in a more appealing location. Its advantage is the wide selection of traditional dishes you are able to choose from if you decide to have its $20 three course special.

**Other Restaurants** The ***Mit Zitrone*** *(☎ 6234 8113, 333 Elizabeth St, North Hobart)* is one of the most popular and trendy restaurants in town. Its menu is modern and innovative and its cakes are especially good. Highly recommended are the twice-cooked eggs ($8.50) as an entrée.

***Rockerfellers*** *(☎ 66234 3490, 11 Morrison St)* is a big, informal place down near the docks open for lunch and dinner daily. It has tapas for $4.50, fish and chips for $9.80 and venison and duck sausages for $9.80. It has jazz entertainment on Sunday and Monday from 6 pm. With food that is similar but cheaper and simpler is the nearby ***Syrup*** *(☎ 6224 8249, 39 Salamanca Place)*, above Knopwood's Retreat.

***Blue Skies*** *(☎ 6224 3747, Murray St Pier)*, right on the water, is another informal eatery. It serves coffee and snacks as well as lunches and dinners daily. Behind it, but still with excellent views, is the more formal *Waterline Restaurant*, which is part of the same establishment and serves seafood and steaks.

*Panache (☎ 6224 2929, 89 Salamanca Place)* is a bright, licensed café restaurant with an outdoor eating area by the adjoining rock walls. *Mr Wooby's (☎ 6234 3466, Wooby's Lane)*, tucked away in a side lane, is another pleasant, licensed Salamanca eatery.

*Sisco's (☎ 6223 2059, Murray St Pier)* upstairs on the docks, has an excellent reputation for its Mediterranean meals, and many of its tables overlook the water.

Down a stairway in a lane that runs off Murray St, opposite parliament house, is the intimate *Elbow Room (☎ 6224 4254, 9 Murray St)*, which has an emphasis on Tasmanian produce. Mains here are priced between $17.50 and $23.50.

There are a few steakhouses around town that pride themselves on grilling your meat to perfection, including the *Ball & Chain (☎ 6223 2655, 87 Salamanca Place)* and *Dirty Dicks (☎ 6224 9900)*, on the corner of Hampden Rd and Francis Sts.

The *Astor Grill (☎ 6234 3809, 157 Macquarie St)* features both steak and seafood. It serves lunch on weekdays and dinner daily and has a mixed seafood grill for $21.50 and venison fillets for $23. A set two course lunch is $19.50 and a three course dinner $27.50.

A little difficult to get to, but well worth the effort, is the historic *Mt Nelson Signal Station Licensed Restaurant (☎ 6223 3407, 700 Mt Nelson Rd)*, on the summit of Mt Nelson, which has spectacular panoramic views of Hobart and the surrounding area. Buses Nos 57 and 58 operate to the lookout.

Even farther from town but a real treat when there are leaves and grapes on the vines is *Moorilla Estate Vineyard (☎ 6249 2949, 655 Main Rd Berriedale)*, where you can sample the wonderful selection of Moorilla wines with your meal. Buses travelling on route X1 from stop F on Elizabeth St can take you there for lunch, which is served from Tuesday to Sunday.

Most of the expensive hotels have expensive restaurants, including Lenna's *Alexander's Restaurant (☎ 6232 3900, 20 Runnymede St, Battery Point)*, Wrest Point Casino's *The Point Revolving Restaurant (☎ 6225 0112, 410 Sandy Bay Rd)* and the Hotel Grand Chancellor's *Meehan's Restaurant (☎ 6235 4535, 1 Davey St)*. The $35 buffet dinner at *The Cove*, also at the Grand Chancellor, is literally a feast, and includes an array of fresh seafood.

## Entertainment

The *Mercury* newspaper, which is published daily, lists the details of most of Hobart's entertainment.

The *New Sydney Hotel (87 Bathurst St)* has low-key live music most nights. *Irish Murphy's* is a popular Salamanca Place pub with live bands from Wednesday to Sunday, while *Bridie O'Reilly's (124 Davey St)* has bands most nights.

*Round Midnight (39 Salamanca Place)*, above Knopwood's Retreat, is open until the early hours of the morning Tuesday to Saturday and is as popular for its live music as it is as a place to drink late into the evening on Friday nights. Around the corner on Salamanca Square is *All Bar One*, a bustling wine bar open until 11 pm or midnight every night.

There are 17 bars at the Wrest Point Hotel Casino, and some, like the *Birdcage*, need to be seen to be believed. The casino also has a disco every night except Monday and Tuesday, with a cover charge on Friday and Saturday only.

In North Hobart you'll find the *State Cinema (☎ 34 6318, 375 Elizabeth St)*, which screens art-house films, while in the city there's the large *Village* complex (☎ 34 7288, 181 Collins St), which shows the mainstream releases.

The acclaimed Tasmanian Symphony Orchestra presently performs at the inadequate *ABC Odeon (☎ 6235 3646, 167 Liverpool St)*, but at the time of writing a lavish new venue was due to be constructed in the near future in the car park of the Hotel Grand Chancellor.

Live theatre can be seen at a number of venues around town, including the *Theatre Royal* on Campbell St, the *Peacock Theatre* in the Salamanca Arts Centre and in the *Stanley Burbury Theatre* at the University of Tasmania.

## Shopping

Most of the speciality shops and services are in the city centre. The main shopping area extends west from the mall on Elizabeth St and shopping arcades are dotted through the blocks. There are also major shopping centres to the south at Sandy Bay, to the north at Glenorchy and on the eastern side of the river at Bellerive. There are many shops and galleries on Salamanca Place selling fine Tasmanian arts and crafts and souvenirs.

If you need bushwalking or outdoor equipment, see the Bushwalking section of the Activities chapter. Blundstone boots can be bought in the city from Country Comfort (104 Elizabeth St) and Tradewear (135 Elizabeth St).

For some ideas about what to buy in Tasmania, see Shopping in the Facts for the Visitor chapter.

## Getting There & Away

**Air** For information on international and domestic flights to and from Hobart see the Getting There & Away chapter. Ansett (☎ 13 1300) has an office on the Elizabeth St Mall, as does Qantas (☎ 13 1313).

**Bus** The main bus companies operating from Hobart are TRC (☎ 1300 360 000) and TWT (☎ 6334 4442), both operating out of the Transit Centre at 199 Collins St, and Hobart Coaches (☎ 6234 4077) at 4 Liverpool St. See the Getting Around chapter for general information about the services offered by these companies, then turn to the section in this book relating to the specific destination you wish to travel to for details of services from Hobart.

**Car** There are a large number of car rental firms in Hobart. Some of the cheaper ones

are Rent-a-Bug (☎ 6231 0300, 105 Murray St) and Selective Car Rentals (☎ 6234 3311, 132 Argyle St). See the Car section of the Getting Around chapter for more details.

**Hitching** To start hitching north, take a Bridgewater or Brighton bus from the Elizabeth St bus station. To hitch along the east coast, take a bus to Sorell first. With the regular and reasonably priced bus routes that visit many places, we do not recommend hitching. Lifts on some roads are few and far between and there is always the chance of a potentially dangerous situation.

## Getting Around

**To/From the Airport** The airport is in Hobart's eastern suburbs, 16km from the city centre. TRC runs a pick-up and drop-off shuttle service between the city centre (via Adelphi YHA and some other accommodation places on request) and the airport for $7. It also takes bicycles for $7. A taxi to or from the airport should cost around $23.

**Bus** The local bus service is run by Metro. The main office (☎ 13 2201) is at 9 Elizabeth St, inside the post office. Most buses leave from this area of Elizabeth St, known as the Metro City Bus Station, or from around the edges of the nearby Franklin Square.

If you're planning to bus around Hobart, it's worth buying Metro's user-friendly timetable, which only costs $1. For $3.10 ($9 for a family), you can get a Day Rover ticket that can be used all day on weekends and between 9 am and 4.30 pm and after 6 pm on weekdays. It cannot be used at peak hours so you do need to plan carefully. If you are staying in Hobart for a while you can get a Day Rover pass for $24, which is valid for any 10 days (not necessarily consecutive) and has the same restrictions on peak-hour travel. An alternative is to buy a book of 10 discounted tickets that can be used at any time of the day.

If you want to go to Mt Wellington without taking a tour, take bus No 48 from Franklin Square on Macquarie St; it will get you to Fern Tree halfway up the mountain,

HOBART

and from there it's still a 13km return walk to the top!

**Taxi** Taxi Combined Services can be reached on ☎ 13 2227. City Cabs' phone number is ☎ 13 1008, and Arrow Taxis' is ☎ 13 2211.

**Bicycle** The Adelphi Court hostel (☎ 6228 4829) hires bicycles for $20 per day, Derwent Bike Hire (☎ 0419 008357) charges $100 a week and Brake Out (☎ 6239 1080) charges $20 a day. Jim's Car Rentals (☎ 6236 9779) also hires bicycles; its rate is $15 a day. See the Activities and Getting Around chapters for more details.

**Boat** Catching a ferry can be a fun way to get around town. The *West Point Wanderer* (☎ 6223 1914) runs a ferry service that departs from the Brooke St Pier daily at 90 minute intervals from 10.30 am to 3 pm. It visits the Botanical Gardens ($2.50), Bellerive ($5), Wrest Point Casino ($7.50) and Battery Point ($9.50). The round trip is $12, and you can get on and off as many times as you desire. There are additional services on Saturdays to cater for people wishing to visit the Salamanca Market. The same boat also operates the Bellerive Ferry Service, which is run primarily in order to get residents to and from work.

# Around Hobart

One of Hobart's great advantages is its proximity to some of the best scenery and most popular sites in the state. Getting out of the city takes no time at all, and the lush countryside and water views between the capital and its satellite suburbs are attractions in themselves. The historic penal settlement of Port Arthur and the stunning cliffs of the Tasman Peninsula are an easy day trip away. But even if you only have a couple of hours to spare, you can immerse yourself in convict history by visiting the little town of Richmond, which has an excellent historic jail and is famous for its convict-built bridge.

## South of Hobart

The Channel Hwy is the continuation of Sandy Bay Rd and hugs the coastline as it heads south. The construction of the Southern Outlet from Hobart to Kingston and beyond has removed most of the traffic and today it's a pleasant tourist drive. The winding road is benched into the lower slopes of Mt Nelson, so drive slowly.

Six kilometres south of Hobart but still in Sandy Bay is **Tudor Court** (☎ 6225 1194). This model of a village in England was constructed by John Palotta, a polio victim with very limited mobility. It took about 12 years to build and has been on display for more than 30 years. It is still worth a look as it has much intricate detail including the building interiors. It's open every day from 9 am to 5.30 pm and entry is $4, children $2. To get there, take bus No 56 or 60 from Franklin Square and disembark at stop 30.

### TAROONA
Eleven kilometres from Hobart, on the Channel Hwy, is the satellite suburb of Taroona, which gained its name from an Aboriginal word meaning 'seashell'.

- Climbing the shot tower
- The beautiful riverside drive from Taroona to Tinderbox
- Learning to abseil in the blowhole at Blackmans Bay
- The ruins and ghost tours at Port Arthur
- Ocean kayaking on the Tasman Peninsula

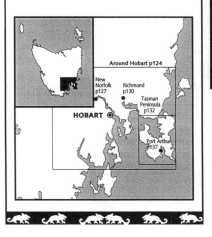

Around Hobart p124

New Norfolk p127    Richmond p130

Tasman Peninsula p132

**HOBART**

Port Arthur p137

### Shot Tower
Just past the town is one of the region's most famous landmarks, the Shot Tower (☎ 6227 8885). It's made from sandstone with every block curved and tapered. It was completed in 1870. From the top of the 48m-high tower, there are fine views over the Derwent River estuary. Lead shot for use in guns was once produced in high towers like this by dropping molten lead from the top which, on its way down, formed a perfect sphere.

Care should be taken if you are climbing the tower with small children, as the railing around the deep stairwell would not stop them falling if they strayed too close to the edge.

The tower, small museum, craft shop and beautiful grounds are open daily from 9 am to 5 pm and admission is $4 (children $2). There is also a tearoom that advertises 'convictshire' teas. Take bus No 60 from Franklin Square near Elizabeth St and get off at stop 45.

## Alum Cliffs

From the Taroona Beach, you can walk for approximately 5km around to the lovely Kingston Beach right along the **Alum Cliffs Track**. At some points the track runs right along the top of the cliffs, where you will be able to get good views of the Derwent River all the way across to Opossum Bay. Allow for around two to three hours each way.

## Places to Stay & Eat

One kilometre north of the Shot Tower is the **Taroona Hotel** (☎ *6227 8748*), which has basic rooms for $35/60 a single/double, which includes a continental breakfast. The bistro here serves counter lunch daily and offers dinner daily, except on Sunday. The hotel is right beside the highway and it's easy to find. Opposite the Shot Tower, you can rent the entire ground floor of the comfortable and self-contained **Hillgrove Colonial Accommodation** (☎ *6227 9043*) for $75/95, which includes provisions for a cooked breakfast.

## KINGSTON
- pop 12,900

The town of Kingston, 11km south of Hobart, has expanded rapidly in recent years because the Southern Outlet expressway has provided fast and easy access to the

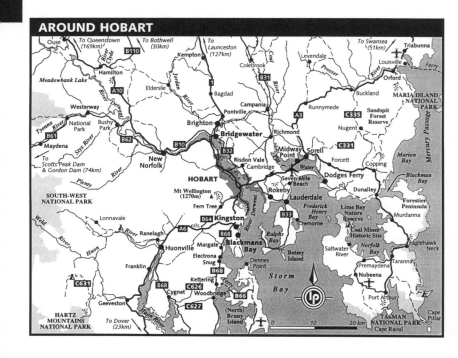

### AROUND HOBART

town. Today, it is a large, sprawling outer suburb of Hobart that is largely bypassed by the highways.

## Antarctic Division

In the town is the headquarters of the Australian Antarctic Division, which is beside the Channel Hwy, 2km south of the Southern Outlet (follow the sign on the Outlet towards Blackmans Bay instead of turning off to Kingston). This department administers Australia's 42% portion of Antarctica. Australia has had a long history of exploration and scientific study of the frozen continent and is one of the original 12 nations who set up the Antarctic Treaty in 1961. An excellent display (☎ 6232 3209), which features original equipment, is open for free inspection on weekdays from 9 am to 5 pm. The cafeteria at the centre is open to the public for a snack or a coffee from 8.30 am to 4.30 pm.

## Kingston Beach

As you branch off from the Southern Outlet and approach Kingston, continue straight ahead at the first set of lights instead of turning right onto the Channel Hwy: this road will take you all the way to **Kingston Beach**, at the finish of the Alum Cliffs Track from Taroona. This is a popular suburban swimming and sailing spot, with attractive wooded cliffs at each end of a long arc of white sand. Behind the clubhouse at the southern end is the start of a short, pretty walk to a much smaller and more secluded beach called **Boronia**, which has a deep rock pool. Farther south by road is **Blackmans Bay**, where there is another good beach and a blowhole. The water at these beaches is usually quite cold, and there is rarely any surf.

Many of the Hobart abseiling and rock climbing companies offer abseiling instruction on the cliffs and in the blowhole at Blackmans Bay – see the Activities chapter earlier in this book for more information.

## Tinderbox

If you have time, drive through Blackmans Bay to Tinderbox. The river views along the

way are gorgeous, particularly on sunny days, and at Tinderbox itself there's a small beach where you can snorkel along an underwater trail marked with submerged information plates. Bruny Island is just across the water from this beach, and locals often launch their outboard motor boats here to cross to Dennes Point.

From Tinderbox, you can continue around the peninsula to Howden and return to Kingston along the Channel Hwy.

## Places to Stay & Eat

The *Beachside Hotel* (☎ 6229 6185), on the corner of Beach Rd and Osborne Esplanade, has the advantage of being right opposite Kingston Beach. The plain motel-style rooms, which can sometimes be noisy, are $45/55. Just one block away along the beach is *Tranquilla Guesthouse* (☎ 6229 6282, 30 Osborne Esplanade), where room-only is $45/79. *On the Beach* (☎ 6229 3096, 38 Osborne Esplanade) is a self-contained unit with a large lounge room. It's in a pleasant weatherboard house right opposite the beach and is $80 a double.

Two kilometres west of Kingston, near the Southern Outlet as it heads towards Huonville, is the modern *Welcome Inn* (☎ 6229 4800) on Kingston View Drive. The complex has an à la carte restaurant, views across the river and sporting facilities next door, but is rather out-of-the-way. Motel rooms are $70 a double.

At last Kingston has a real café down by the beach! For years this has been the one thing lacking from the village section of this pretty suburb. So even though the *Echo Café* is on Beach Rd rather than opposite the water, it's the perfect place for a coffee or lunch between swims or walks along the esplanade. It's open from 10 am to 5.30 pm Wednesday to Friday and from 11 am to 5.30 pm on the weekend.

*Counter meals* are available in all the hotels and at the bar in the Welcome Inn. There are *Chinese restaurants* and other *takeaways* in Kingston's Channel Court and Blackmans Bay's little shopping centre. For surprisingly good curry, head for *Goa*

*Curry* on Beach Rd, just up from the Kingston Beach.

### Getting There & Away
Hobart Coaches (☎ 6234 4077) runs a regular bus service from Hobart to Kingston and Blackmans Bay at about one hour intervals on weekdays and less frequently on weekends. Buses leave Hobart from Murray St between Davey and Macquarie Sts.

### MARGATE
* pop 740

Eight kilometres south of Kingston on the Channel Hwy is the small town of Margate. Train buffs will be interested in taking a look at the last passenger train to be used in Tasmania. It now stands on a piece of railway track beside the highway on the northern side of town. It now houses bric-a-brac shops and a café.

On weekdays, Hobart Coaches runs several bus services from Hobart through Margate to Kettering. On Saturday there is a morning and evening service in both directions but only as far as Margate itself. There are no services on Sunday.

# Derwent Valley

### NEW NORFOLK
* pop 5800

Set in the lush, rolling countryside of the Derwent Valley, New Norfolk is an interesting historical town. It was first visited by Europeans in 1793 and was soon settled after Hobart was established. In 1808 an Irish convict became the first police constable and built the first house. By the 1860s the valley became an important hop-growing centre, which is why the area is dotted with old oast houses used for drying hops. Hops are very sensitive to winds, and trees were planted for wind protection. The most distinctive are the rows of tall poplars that today mark the boundaries of the former hop fields.

Originally called Elizabeth Town, New Norfolk was renamed after the abandoned Pacific Ocean colony on Norfolk Island. Over 500 people arrived from that colony in 1807 and 1808 to settle in the area. Today the town is a mixture of the old and the new and has some interesting sights that are unique to this area.

Visitors' information is available at the Council Chambers on Circle St.

### Visitors' Historical & Information Centre
This centre, next to the Council Chambers on Circle St, has an interesting photographic and memorabilia display. The key is held by the Council office.

### Oast House
The Oast House (☎ 6261 1030), just off the highway on the Hobart side of town, is devoted to the history of the hop industry. It also has a tearoom and a fine-arts gallery. The timber building dates back to the 1820s. In 1867, the first hop kiln was built and hops were dried here for 102 years, until 1969, when the kilns closed. You can go on a self-guided tour of the kilns and follow the story of how hops were processed. It's open Wednesday to Sunday from 9.30 am to 6 pm and admission is $3.50 for adults and $1.50 for children. The building itself has been classified by the National Trust and is worth seeing from the outside, even if you don't go in.

### Historic Buildings
**St Matthew's Church of England**, built in 1823, is Tasmania's oldest existing church. It's been extensively altered since its construction, and its best features today are its excellent stained glass windows.

The **Bush Inn**, on Montagu St, was built in 1815 and is claimed to be the oldest continuously licensed hotel in Australia. The **Old Colony Inn** (21 Montagu St) is a museum of colonial furnishings and artefacts. It also has a great dolls' house and a tearoom (see Places to Eat section). The inn is open from 9 am to 5 pm and admission is only $1 for adults, children get in for free. If you are approaching from Hobart and

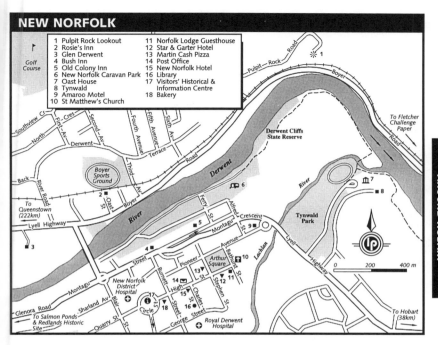

**NEW NORFOLK**

1 Pulpit Rock Lookout
2 Rosie's Inn
3 Glen Derwent
4 Bush Inn
5 Old Colony Inn
6 New Norfolk Caravan Park
7 Oast House
8 Tynwald
9 Amaroo Motel
10 St Matthew's Church
11 Norfolk Lodge Guesthouse
12 Star & Garter Hotel
13 Martin Cash Pizza
14 Post Office
15 New Norfolk Hotel
16 Library
17 Visitors' Historical & Information Centre
18 Bakery

**AROUND HOBART**

wish to park directly outside, you must make a tight U-turn at the top end of the road division on Montagu St.

### Paper Mill

The Fletcher Challenge Paper's Boyer Mill (☎ 6261 0433) is one of the area's major industries. Two-hour tours can be arranged Tuesday to Friday if you give at least 24 hours notice. It's located on the northern side of the river, 5km from town.

### Salmon Ponds

In 1864, the first rainbow and brown trout in the southern hemisphere were successfully bred in the Salmon Ponds (☎ 6261 1076) at Plenty, 9km west of New Norfolk. You can feed the fish in the six display ponds and visit the hatchery. There is also the museum to investigate. The ponds and museum are on Salmon Ponds Rd and are

open daily from 9 am to 5 pm, and admission is $5 for adults and $3 for children. You can also eat at the restaurant (see Places to Eat later).

### Lookout

You can get a fine view over New Norfolk by following the road along the northern side of the river eastwards for 1km, then up a steep side road to Pulpit Rock. This overlooks a sweeping bend of the Derwent River and is the spot from where most photos of the town are taken.

### Jet-Boat Rides

Devil Jet (☎ 6261 3460), behind the Bush Inn, runs 30-minute jet-boat rides 10km up-river and back at $44 for adults and $22 for children. They leave approximately every half-hour during summer; ring and book at other times of the year.

## Places to Stay – Budget

*New Norfolk Caravan Park (☎ 6261 1268)*, on the Esplanade, about 1km north of town, has tent sites for $8, powered sites for $12, on-site vans for $30 and cabins for $40 (all prices are for doubles). It's a great place if you want to fish in the river.

*Norfolk Lodge Guesthouse (☎ 6261 1877, 93 High St)* also provides accommodation. At the time of writing it was for sale.

The *Bush Inn (☎ 6261 2011, 49 Montagu St)* has plain rooms for $28/48 including a cooked breakfast, while the *Amaroo Motel (☎ 6261 2000)*, on the corner of Lyell Hwy and Pioneer Ave, has rooms for $48/58.

## Places to Stay – Mid-Range

The *Old Colony Inn (☎ 6261 2731, 21 Montagu St)* has just one double room called Honeymoon Cottage. It's $70 for B&B, or $100 for B&B plus a three course evening meal. The upper floor was added in 1835 and has great character with its small doors and low ceilings.

On the other side of the river to the main town, *Rosie's Inn (☎ 6261 1171, 5 Oast St)* has plenty of rooms for $80/90 with a cooked breakfast. Four kilometres north of town at Magra is *Denmark Hill (☎ 6261 3313)*, with B&B for $85 a double, with *en suite*.

## Places to Stay – Top End

Near the Oast House is *Tynwald (☎ 6261 2667)*. It's a three storey house dating back to the 1830s and oozing character. For many years it was the residence of the operators of the nearby Oast House and was altered in the 1890s, with wide verandas, lace work and bay windows. The rooms are well furnished, and it has a heated swimming pool and a tennis court. It costs $125 a double, which includes a cooked breakfast. For the same price you can stay in the nearby *Old Granary*, which was part of the original flour mills and is still part of Tynwald.

Beside the Lyell Hwy just west of the bridge over the Derwent River is the luxurious *Glen Derwent (☎ 6261 3244)*. Hidden behind a hawthorn hedge in extensive grounds, this mansion has a wide range of accommodation options starting at $124 a double for B&B.

Nine kilometres west of town, near the Salmon Ponds, is *Redlands Historic Site (☎ 6261 1122)*, a privately owned estate with buildings dating from 1823 and constructed of convict bricks. Here you can get B&B for $125 a double in self-contained historic units; the price includes provisions for a cooked breakfast. An attraction of the property is the large garden of mature trees and shrubs that children are encouraged to enjoy.

## Places to Eat

There's a *bakery* and a *coffee lounge* on High St, while *Martin Cash Pizza*, near the corner of Stephen and High Sts, serves Italian-style meals and takeaway.

The *Star & Garter* and *New Norfolk* hotels have counter meals some days, while at the *Bush Inn* you can eat good meals overlooking the water any lunch or dinner time except Sunday evening (Sunday dinners are only available during the months of daylight saving). There are tearooms where you can get snacks and lunches at the *Old Colony Inn* and the *Oast House*. The *Salmon Ponds* has a licensed restaurant where you can eat good food at reasonable prices between 9 am and 5 pm. (By doing this, you can watch the fish being fed by others without paying the entry fee yourself.)

*Tynwald* has a fine à la carte restaurant open every evening.

## Getting There & Away

Hobart Coaches is the main operator between Hobart and New Norfolk and on weekdays there are six buses in both directions. At weekends there's a morning and evening service on Saturday only. A one-way/return fare costs $4.30/6.90. In New Norfolk, the buses leave from Circle St. In Hobart they depart from the Hobart Coaches terminal at 4 Liverpool St.

## BUSHY PARK TO WESTERWAY

As you proceed farther west from New Norfolk towards Mt Field you leave the Derwent River and follow the narrow valley of

Derwent River Valley

Tasman's Arch

View from Remarkable Cave, near Port Arthur

Historic Richmond Bridge

Tessellated Pavement, Eaglehawk Neck on the Tasman Peninsula

RICHARD I'ANSON

RICHARD I'ANSON

CHRIS MELLOR

RICHARD I'ANSON

RICHARD I'ANSON

RICHARD I'ANSON

JOHN HAY

Droving sheep Tasmanian style

CHRIS MELLOR

Prison cells, Port Arthur

Church, Port Arthur

JON MURRAY

Grave of a free settler

RICHARD I'ANSON

View of the Port Arthur Historic Site

the Tyenna River. The three historic villages of Bushy Park, Glenora and Westerway are small, rural communities where you can see old barns, a water wheel and extensive hop fields. Many of the buildings are of shingles and still in use, allowing you to see how farms of the nineteenth century were built. Most features are right next to the road and are easily seen, but are on private property.

Hop growing has vanished from much of Tasmania but over recent years the company Bushy Park Estates has invested in a new kiln and adopted improved techniques to help it maintain viability. In late summer and autumn you can see the hops growing up the thin leader strings. Bushy Park and Glenora are so close that they are really one town.

A new industry to the area is wine making: **Meadowbank Vineyard** is open daily from 11 am to 5 pm. It's well off the main road, being 7km down a gravel road, but the drive is pleasant and the wine worth a taste.

*Hawthorn Lodge* (☎ 6286 1311) is on Salmon Ponds Rd in Bushy Park and provides comfortable B&B accommodation for $105 a double for a room with *en suite* and a cooked breakfast. It was the home of the pioneer hop grower Robert Shoobridge and was built in 1869; today the house is set in beautiful gardens off the road.

Westerway is a more substantial town with a general store and petrol station. You can also stay here at the *Haven Tea Garden* (☎ 6288 1120), where B&B is $35/50. For transport information, see Getting There & Away in the Mt Field National Park section of the South-West chapter.

# North of the Derwent

## PONTVILLE & BRIGHTON
* **pop 1125**

Twenty-five kilometres north of Hobart, on the Midland Hwy, is Brighton, and just north of it the historic town of Pontville. Both were once considered possible capitals of Van Diemen's Land and have some interesting buildings dating from the 1830s. Much of the freestone used in Tasmania's early buildings was supplied from quarries at Pontville, and the town boasts some sandstone buildings of its own.

Beside the river in Pontville, the *Barracks* (☎ 6268 1665) is an impressive Georgian sandstone building that originally housed soldiers. Today you can stay overnight in one of the three stone barracks for $90/100, which includes breakfast. The Pontville and Brighton area is still used by the military with some large bases nearby.

In Pontville, up on top of the hill, is **St Mark's Anglican Church**, where there is an excellent view of Mt Wellington. The church was built in 1841 and there are also other sandstone buildings in the area. North of the church on Rifle Range Rd is the *Sheiling* (☎ 6268 1951), a cute two storey house covered in ivy where B&B is $80 a double. This is one of the oldest houses in the state, being built in 1819.

Brighton is less interesting, composed mostly of recently built houses to serve the nearby military base. You can stay at the *Brighton Hotel Motel* (☎ 6268 1201) for $40/60, which includes breakfast. Nearby, 3km down side roads that are well signposted, you will find the **Bonorong Park Wildlife Centre** (☎ 6268 1184) on Briggs Rd. It is neatly laid out and caters particularly for children. Bonorong comes from an Aboriginal word meaning 'native companion' and you can feed the wombats, koalas and Tasmanian devils. It is open daily from 9 am to 5 pm; admission is $8, children $4. *The Bush Tucker Shed* restaurant is open from 10 am to 4 pm daily, and serves such treats as billy tea and damper. You can get to Bonorong by bus; from Hobart take any service to Glenorchy bus station, where you take bus No 125 or 126.

## RICHMOND
* **pop 750**

Richmond is just 24km from Hobart and, with more than 50 buildings dating from the 19th century, is Tasmania's premier historic

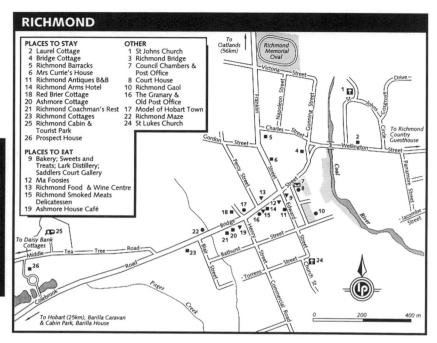

RICHMOND

**PLACES TO STAY**
2  Laurel Cottage
4  Bridge Cottage
5  Richmond Barracks
6  Mrs Currie's House
11  Richmond Antiques B&B
14  Richmond Arms Hotel
18  Red Brier Cottage
20  Ashmore Cottage
21  Richmond Coachman's Rest
23  Richmond Cottages
25  Richmond Cabin &
     Tourist Park
26  Prospect House

**PLACES TO EAT**
9  Bakery; Sweets and
    Treats; Lark Distillery;
    Saddlers Court Gallery
12  Ma Foosies
13  Richmond Food  & Wine Centre
15  Richmond Smoked Meats
     Delicatessen
19  Ashmore House Café

**OTHER**
1  St Johns Church
3  Richmond Bridge
7  Council Chambers &
    Post Office
8  Court House
10  Richmond Gaol
16  The Granary &
     Old Post Office
17  Model of Hobart Town
22  Richmond Maze
24  St Lukes Church

## Things to See & Do

The **Richmond Bridge** is the most famous construction in town and is still used for road traffic. You can freely walk around it and under it and there are good views on both sides. Built by convicts in 1823, it is the oldest road bridge in Australia. When it was first built it formed a vital link for the young colony and encouraged construction of the many buildings seen today.

The northern wing of **Richmond Gaol** was built in 1825, five years before the settlement at Port Arthur, and is the best preserved convict jail in Australia. It has not been modified and has original locks, cells and relics. Displays describe the old penal system, and the gaol is open daily from 9 am to 5 pm; admission is $4, children $1.50, or $9.50 for a family.

Other places of historical interest include **St John's Church** (1836), the oldest Catholic church in Australia; **St Luke's Church of England** (1834); the **courthouse** (1825); the **old post office** (1826); the **Bridge Inn** (1817); the **granary** (1829); and the **Richmond Arms Hotel** (1888).

town. Straddling the Coal River, on the old route between Hobart and Port Arthur, Richmond was once a strategic military post and convict station. The much photographed Richmond Bridge is the highlight of the town.

With the completion of the Sorell Causeway in 1872, traffic travelling to the Tasman Peninsula and the east coast bypassed Richmond. The town was not abandoned, as it was still the centre for a farming community, but it ceased to grow. For more than 100 years the town changed very little. It has since been discovered by tourists, but it remains a delightful spot to visit.

**AROUND HOBART**

**Richmond Historical Walks** (☎ 6248 5510, mobile 0419 312 041) departs from the council chambers in the centre of town at 11.30 am and 1 pm most days. The guided walk takes one hour and costs $4.

There's also a **model village** (designed from original plans) of Hobart Town as it was in the 1820s. It's worth a look, as the detail is excellent and you can see how much Hobart has changed in 170 years. The waterfront has seen the most dramatic changes with the reclamation of most of the shallow waters. It's open daily from 9 am to 5 pm and admission is $6 for adults and $3.50 for children. The **Richmond Maze**, on Bridge St, is fun but has wooden walls, not hedges; admission is $3.50 for adults and $2.50 for children, and it's open from 9.30 am to 5 pm. It also has a tearoom.

There are several arts and crafts places around the town selling paintings, carved timber bowls and trinkets, leather goods, books and furniture. Prices are not particularly cheap but then many items are of good quality and locally made. Saddlers Court Gallery on Bridge St has some exquisite items for sale. It is open from 9.30 am to 5.30 pm in summer and from 10 am to 5 pm in winter.

The **Lark Distillery** is a working distillery that is open from 10 am to 5 pm daily. It produces malt whisky, as well as liqueurs distilled from native ingredients such as the pepperberry.

## Places to Stay – Budget
*Richmond Cabin & Tourist Park* (☎ 6260 2192), on Middle Tea Tree Rd opposite Prospect House, has tent sites for $14, powered sites for $16, on-site vans for $38, standard cabins for $40 and self-contained cabins for $62 a double.

Back at Cambridge, about 12km south of Richmond, is the *Barilla Caravan and Cabin Park* (☎ 6248 5453). It's beside the road to Richmond and close to the noisy airport road, but the grounds are enhanced by trees and bird calls. Tent sites are $12, on-site vans $30, cabins without *en suite* $40 and cabins with *en suite* $50 a double.

## Places to Stay – Mid-Range
The cheapest B&B is *Richmond Country Guesthouse* (☎ 6260 4238), on an attractive rural property on the gravel surfaced Prossers Rd, 4km north of town. You'll feel like part of the family here, in a room with its own bathroom across the hall. Rooms are $45/70 with a continental breakfast.

Motel-style units behind the *Richmond Arms Hotel* (☎ 6260 2109, 42 Bridge St) are $85 a double.

There are a couple of other places in town in this price range but they are not particularly impressive. *Richmond Antiques B&B* (☎ 6260 2601, 25 Edward St) has rooms above the shop in a residential-style brick house for $75 a double, while *Richmond Coachman's Rest* (☎ 6260 2729) is a dated unit behind 30 Bridge St for $60 a double.

## Places to Stay – Top End
In the upper price group, the best known is *Prospect House* (☎ 6260 2207), which is a two storey Georgian country mansion with rooms around an appealing courtyard. It's just outside Richmond, on the Hobart road, and charges $122/144. The house also has a well-known restaurant with à la carte menu for lunch and dinner every day except lunchtime Tuesday. There is also a self-contained three bedroom cottage for $140 a double.

In the centre of town you can stay in some of the historic cottages: *Richmond Cottages* (☎ 6260 2561, 12 Bridge St) is $115 a double, *Laurel Cottage* (☎ 6260 2397) is $110 a double, while *Bridge Cottage* (☎ 6260 2247, 47 Bridge St) and *Ashmore Cottage* (☎ 6260 2247, 32 Bridge St) are $130 a double. Of the modern cottages, *Red Brier Cottage* (☎ 6260 2349, 15 Bridge St) is one of the most pleasant: it's spacious and attractive and costs $116 a double. Prices for all the above cottages include breakfast.

*Mrs Currie's House* (☎ 6260 2766, 4 Franklin St) is a beautiful, central historic B&B with rooms with private bathroom as an *en suite* for $96/116.

**AROUND HOBART**

*Richmond Barracks* (☎ *6260 2453, 16 Franklin St*), built in 1830, has B&B in rooms with *en suite* for $95 a double. If you don't mind being a little distance from town, you might like *Daisy Bank Cottages* (☎ *6260 2390*), where there are two very attractive units in a converted sandstone barn for $110 or $130 a double.

North of the caravan park in Cambridge and at the end of a side road signposted off the road to Richmond is *Barilla House* (☎ *6248 5654*), on Denholms Rd. It overlooks the wide estuary of Pitt Water, and has B&B rooms with *en suite* in a modern home for $86/96.

### Places to Eat

In Richmond you can get something to eat and drink at the *Richmond Food and Wine Centre* on Bridge St. This new building is set back from the street and is a good place for breakfast and lunch. It specialises in Tasmanian produce and wines, and is open from 8 am to 5 pm daily except Friday and Saturday, when it's also open for dinner.

There are several tearooms with light meals; try *Ma Foosies* or the *Ashmore House Café* on the main street. The town also has a *bakery* hidden behind the saddlery building. If you have a sweet tooth then the old-fashioned lolly shop called *Sweets and Treats* on Bridge St will be tempting. If the lollies don't appeal then try the wide variety of ice cream.

The *Richmond Arms Hotel* provides lunches and dinners every day in its pleasant dining room, with mains at around $15.

### Getting There & Away

If you have your own transport, you will find that Richmond is an easy day trip from Hobart. If not, you can take a bus tour from Hobart with Tasmanian Tours & Travel/Tigerline (☎ 6231 2200, 1300 653 633). Hobart Coaches runs three regular buses a day to and from Richmond on weekdays only. There is also a Metro service from the Elizabeth St bus station Monday to Saturday from late December to mid-February that is $6 each way.

# Tasman Peninsula

The Arthur Hwy runs 100km from Hobart through Sorell to the Tasman Peninsula, the most popular tourist region in the state. Port Arthur, the infamous 'escape proof prison' of the mid-19th century, draws 200,000 visitors a year. Yet the region is also famous for its 300m-high cliffs, which are the tallest in Australia and which, together with its delightful beaches and beautiful bays, make this a fantastic place for bushwalking, diving, ocean kayaking and rock climbing.

Much of the best bushwalking on the Tasman Peninsula is through areas that are now national park, and of couse the usual national park entry fees apply (see the National Parks section of the 'Flora, Fauna, National Parks & Reserves' special section for prices).

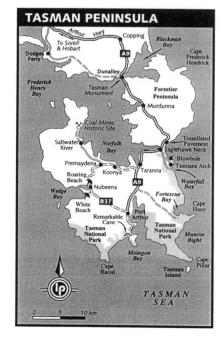

**TASMAN PENINSULA**

## Information

The main information centre for the region is the Eaglehawk Neck visitors' information centre (☎ 6250 3722, 443 Pirates Bay Drive) at the Officers Mess restaurant and store. Information is also available at Know-How Travel (☎ 6265 3370, 23 Gordon St) in Sorell and at the Copping Colonial and Convict Exhibition.

**Triple Pass** You can save around 10% on the cost of passes to the Historic Site, the Bush Mill and the Tasmanian Devil Park and Wildlife Rescue Centre by purchasing a Triple Pass at any of those sites. The price is $31.95 for adults, $15.75 for children and $82.50 for families.

## Getting There & Away

Hobart Coaches has a weekday service that departs Hobart at 4.15 pm and Port Arthur at 6.40 pm and stops at all the main towns on the Tasman Peninsula.

Another way that you can visit the area is to join a coach tour run by Tasmanian Tours & Travel/Tigerline (☎ 6231 2200, 1300 653 633).

## SORELL

* pop 3200

This is one of the oldest towns in Tasmania but little of interest remains. It has good facilities, including banks and supermarkets. Visitors' information is available at Know-How Travel (☎ 6265 3370, 23 Gordon St).

## Things to See

A few 19th century buildings near the centre of town have survived and are worth a look. Behind the high school is **Scots Uniting Church**, built in 1841. Also near the school are the **Barracks** and the **Blue Bell Inn** (circa 1829). In the main street is **St George's Anglican Church** and next door is an interesting graveyard with many headstones of early settlers.

## Places to Stay & Eat

The *Blue Bell Inn* (☎ 6265 2804, 26 Somerville St) is a two storey sandstone building offering B&B with *en suite* and a cooked breakfast for $85 a double. It also provides à la carte dining for both guests and visitors.

*Flimby Host Home* (☎ 6265 1632), on Rosendale Rd, is 3km from town in rural countryside. It caters for families or groups of up to five people and B&B is $75 a double.

For most visitors, Sorell is a stopping place for stocking up on food and this is reflected in a very wide range of reasonable takeaways along the main street.

## Getting There & Away

There are plenty of buses passing through this town. Hobart Coaches' Hobart to Port Arthur service passes through here, as does Tasmanian Redline Coaches' (TRC, ☎ 1300 360 000) Hobart to Dunalley service.

## COPPING

This tiny village has only one feature for visitors: the **Copping Colonial and Convict Collection** (☎ 6253 5373). Stop here to get into the convict mood or pick up some visitor information. Admission for adults is $5, while those under 18 accompanied by an adult are admitted free.

## DUNALLEY

The timbered Forestier Peninsula is connected to Tasmania by an isthmus known as Dunalley. A canal complete with an opening bridge cuts across the isthmus, providing a short cut for small boats.

## Places to Stay

It's all B&B around this isthmus. On the highway about 3km from town on the Hobart side of Dunalley, *Potters Croft* (☎ 6253 5469) is beside the water and has a self-contained cottage for up to five guests for $95 a double, plus $20 for each extra adult. Above a gallery on the site there are also *en suite* rooms with lovely water views for the same price.

If you are travelling from Hobart and you continue straight through Dunalley onto the gravel Fulham Rd instead of turning right to cross the bridge, you will come to **Fulham Shearers Quarters** (☎ *6253 5247*), which is a five bedroom cottage on a working sheep and cattle farm about 3km from the town. B&B here is $80 a double plus $20 for each extra person.

### Getting There & Away

TRC has services to Dunalley every day except Sunday and public holidays. Hobart Coaches stops in Dunalley on the way to Port Arthur on weekdays.

## EAGLEHAWK NECK

Another isthmus, this connects the Tasman Peninsula to the Forestier Peninsula. In the days of convict occupation, the 100m-wide neck had a row of fierce dogs chained across it to prevent escape. Some dog platforms were also placed in narrow Eaglehawk Bay to the west to prevent convicts from wading around the barrier. Rumours were circulated that the waters were shark-infested (it's not true) to discourage swimming. Despite the precautions, a few convicts did escape.

### Information

Information is available at the visitors' information centre (☎ 6250 3722, 443 Pirates Bay Rd), which is in the Officers Mess restaurant, takeaway and store, which is clearly visible on the north-eastern side of the isthmus.

### Things to See

As you approach from the north, turn off east onto Pirates Bay Drive to the **lookout**. From here you get a wonderful view of Pirates Bay and the rugged coastline beyond.

The only remaining structure here from the convict days is the **Officer's Quarters**, a building dating from 1832 that is the oldest wooden military building in Australia. It's diagonally opposite the Officers Mess car park.

At the northern end of Pirates Bay, below the hotel, is the **Tessellated Pavement** – a rocky terrace that has eroded to look like tiled paving. At low tide it is worth walking farther along the foreshore to **Clydes Island**,

from where there are fine views of the coastline; you can see as far south as Cape Huay.

Follow the side roads to **The Blowhole** and **Tasmans Arch** for some famous close-up views of the spectacular coastal cliffs. Take great care around The Blowhole, as several people have died here; at the other features keep behind the fences, as the cliff edges are rather crumbly.

On the road to the Blowhole is a sign marking the turn-off to the 4km gravel road to **Waterfall Bay**, one of the best of the more easily accessible views in this area (see the following Bushwalking section).

### Bushwalking

**Waterfall Bluff** From the car park at Waterfall Bay, take the 1½ hour return walk to Waterfall Bluff. While much of the walk is through a forest of tall, slender trees that obscure the view somewhat, the track stays close to the bay, and there are plenty of places to stop and view the magnificent scenery from the clifftops, which are unfenced except at the car park. Make sure you continue to the bluff itself before returning to the part of the walk that takes you down past the falls, as the views from here are breathtaking.

**Tasman Trail** Waterfall Bay is also the start of the Tasman Trail, which climbs over Tatnells Hill then follows the coast to Fortescue Bay. This is a full day's walk, with some camp sites along the way. If you need to return to your car, walk only as far as Tatnells Hill, where you can enjoy a wonderful view all the way from Eaglehawk Neck to the stunning rock formations of Cape Huay (7km, one day return). Track notes to this walk and many others in this area are available in *Tasman Tracks* by Shirley and Peter Storey.

### Diving

The erosion processes that have formed the impressive cliff faces have also created some amazing caves and canyons, which are mainly underwater. The best way to see these is to go diving with Eaglehawk Dive

Centre (☎ 6250 3566), on the scenic Pirates Bay Drive, north of the neck. Regular dive sites include caves, kelp forests, a sea lion colony and shipwrecks. A full day's dive of two dives with all equipment is $127. Diving tickets are required for diving in Australia and full instruction is provided: a basic course is $375 for either two weekends or five days, and the fee covers the hire of all gear but not passport-sized photos or a medical. A one day Discover Scuba Diving course for people without a certificate is $130.

## Places to Stay

While there is not a lot of accommodation around the Neck, what is there is varied enough to suit most people's needs. Its advantages are that it's far more scenic than Port Arthur, that it's not crowded, and that it is very close to all major features.

The *Eaglehawk Neck Backpackers* (☎ 6250 3248), on Old Jetty Rd, is located on the northern side of the isthmus, down the side road to the west. It's a small and friendly hostel charging $12 a night, and a good base from which to explore the Eaglehawk Neck area. The managers hire out bicycles, which are ideal for visiting the remoter parts of the peninsula. There is also a small camping ground on the site.

For great views, the *Lufra Holiday Hotel* (☎ 6250 3262), perched above the Tessellated Pavement, is hard to beat. It's $80 a double for *en suite* rooms with a continental breakfast. The bistro here serves lunch and dinner seven days a week.

Farther along this road towards the lookout is the turn-off to *Wunnamurra Waterfront* (☎ 6250 3145) and *Osprey Lodge Beachfront B&B* (☎ 6250 3629). Both are situated in attractive private gardens and overlook the bay. B&B in rooms with *en suite* is $80 to $94 a double at Wunnamurra and $90 to $110 a double at Osprey Lodge.

The *Pirates Bay Motel* (☎ 6250 3272) on Blowhole Rd provides rooms for $55/70 or family rooms for four for $100. For an entire house, *The Neck Beach House* (☎ 6250 3541) near the hotel is $100 a night for up to four people and $10 a night for a fifth person.

## Places to Eat

The *Officers Mess* provides takeaway and meals in a large café, while the *Pirates Bay Motel* has tearooms and a licensed restaurant open daily for lunch and dinner. The licensed *Eaglehawk Café* is in an attractive building overlooking Norfolk Bay and serves breakfast, lunch and dinner daily.

## Getting There & Away

See the Port Arthur Getting There & Away section for details, as most bus services to Port Arthur stop at Eaglehawk Neck.

## TARANNA

Taranna is a tiny village spread along the shores of Norfolk Bay and its name comes from an Aboriginal word meaning 'hunting ground'. Ten kilometres north of Port Arthur, this is an historically important village, as it was the terminus for a convict-powered tramway that ran from Long Bay, near Port Arthur, to this village. It was Australia's first railway and was powered by convicts: they pushed the carriages uphill, then jumped on for the ride down. The line ended at a jetty and the remainder of the route to Hobart was then by sea. In those days Taranna was called 'Old Norfolk'.

**Dart Island** was used as a semaphore station to relay messages from Port Arthur to Hobart. Today the waters near the island are used for oyster farming.

The major attraction of the village is the **Tasmanian Devil Park and Wildlife Rescue Centre** (☎ 6250 3230). This is not a zoo, but a refuge for injured and orphaned animals and is linked to the World Wide Fund for Nature. The major feature for most visitors is the feeding of the Tasmanian devils at 10 and 11 am. Other features are a video about the Tasmanian tiger, an arboretum of endemic Tasmanian plants, a kiosk and barbecue facilities. The park is open every day, entry is $11 for adults, $5.50 for children and $29.50 for families. The associated World Tiger Snake Centre is a biomedical research centre that has approximately 100 snakes in winter and 1000 in summer.

## Places to Stay & Eat

*Taranna Escapes Bar & Café* has backpacker accommodation with basic shared facilities for $25 per two people, but you'd probably prefer to stay at one of the hostels, which are more appealing and better situated. Counter lunches and dinners are served daily.

On the highway on the way into town from Eaglehawk Neck is *Taranna Mason's Cottages B&B* (☎ 6250 3323), which has modern self-contained brick units built close together for $65 a double.

*Teraki Cottages* (☎ 6250 3436) are a couple of small, well-presented one-bedroom self-contained cabins with tiny *en suites* for $60 a double, including ingredients for a cooked breakfast. They have the advantage of being a little off the highway, at its junction with the road to Nubeena.

*Norfolk Bay Convict Station* (☎ 6250 3487) provides B&B in an historic building for $100 a double, which includes a cooked breakfast.

## FORTESCUE BAY

Hidden 12km down a gravel road is one of the gems of the peninsula, with a sweeping sandy beach backed by thick forests. Apart from swimming and lazing on the beach, the main activity here is walking. Excellent tracks lead to some of the best coastal scenery in the state. The cliffs are taller and more impressive than those around Eaglehawk Neck. For those with their own boats, this is an excellent base for fishing, since it has a boat ramp and calm waters.

The sheltered bay was one of the semaphore station sites used during the convict period to relay messages to Eaglehawk Neck. Early this century a timber mill was in operation and the boilers and jetty ruins are still visible near Mill Creek. Timber tramways were used to collect the timber and some of their remains are still visible today. The mill closed in 1952. A fish factory was also in operation in the 1940s in Canoe Bay. Fortescue Bay is part of the Tasman National Park, and the usual park entry fees apply.

## Bushwalking

Several walking tracks start from the bay. The best walk is to **Cape Huay** and takes four hours return. A well-used track leads out to the sensational sea stacks, the **Candlestick** and **The Needle**. To see rainforest, follow the same track towards Cape Huay and then the side track to Mt Fortescue, which takes six to seven hours return. To the north a good track follows the shores of the bay to Canoe Bay (two hours return) and Bivouac Bay (four hours return). The tracks extend all the way to **Cape Pillar**, where the sea cliffs are 300m high. This requires at least two days to visit. For track notes see Lonely Planet's *Bushwalking in Australia* by John & Monica Chapman.

## Places to Stay

At Fortescue Bay there is a camping ground at *Mill Creek* (☎ 6250 2433). There's no power, but cold showers and firewood are available. The charge is $10 per site, in addition to national park entry fees. Bookings are advised at major holiday periods. There are no stores or kiosks so bring all your food with you. There is no public transport to the bay; it is a 12km walk to the highway, from where buses run to Port Arthur.

## PORT ARTHUR

Port Arthur is the name of the entire small settlement in which the Port Arthur Historic Site is situated.

In 1830, Governor Arthur chose the Tasman Peninsula as the place to confine prisoners who had committed further crimes in the colony. He called the peninsula a 'natural penitentiary' because it was connected to the mainland only by a strip of land less than 100m wide: Eaglehawk Neck.

Between 1830 and 1877 about 12,500 convicts served sentences at Port Arthur, and for some of them it was a living hell. In reality, convicts who behaved well lived in better conditions than those that had come from Britain and Ireland. The soldiers who guarded them lived in similar conditions, and they too were often imprisoned for what would be regarded today as minor offences.

The penal establishment of Port Arthur became the centre of a network of penal stations on the peninsula, but was much more than just a prison town. It had fine buildings and thriving industries, including timber milling, shipbuilding, coal mining, brick and nail production and shoemaking.

A semaphore telegraph system allowed instant communication between Port Arthur, the penal out-stations and Hobart. Convict farms provided fresh vegetables, a boys' prison was built at Point Puer to reform and educate juvenile convicts, and a church, one of the most readily recognised tourist sights in Australia, was erected.

Port Arthur was again the scene of tragedy in April 1996, when a lone gunman opened fire on visitors and staff at the historic site, killing 35 people, either there or close by, and injuring several others. The gunman was finally captured after he had burned down a local guesthouse; he is now in prison.

## Historic Site

Today, the well-presented and informative historic site at Port Arthur is Tasmania's premier tourist attraction.

**Information** The site is open daily from 8.30 am to dusk. You can drive to the car park behind the visitors' centre, eat in the café/restaurant and visit the gift shop without paying an admission charge. From there, you can pay and go through a turnstile to enter the site and its extensive Interpretation Centre.

**Prices** For a fee of $16 ($8 for children or $38 for a family) you can visit all the restored buildings including the Asylum (now the Museum) and the Separate Prison. The ticket is valid for the day of purchase and the following day, and entitles you to free admission to the Museum, a guided tour of the settlement and a 20 minute harbour cruise. Tickets can be converted to annual passes at the visitors' centre for an extra $5. If you arrive late in the day, you should be offered a half-price Twilight Ticket, which will only be valid on the day of purchase. There is also a Triple Pass available (see the

**AROUND HOBART**

**PORT ARTHUR**

To Sorell & Hobart
Garden Point Road
Stewarts Bay State Reserve
Stewarts Beach Road
Stewarts Beach
Garden Point
Stewarts Bay
North Street
Fryingpan Point
To Nubeena
Sports Ground
Nubeena Road
Port Arthur Historic Site
Scorpion Rock
Tramway Street
Cove Road
Champ St
Stewarts Bay
Walking Track
To Isle of The Dead
Mason Cove
Commandants Point
Safety Cove Road
Bond St
Creek
Radcliffe
To Palmers Lookout
Lookout Rd
To Andertons Accomodation & Remarkable Cave
Carnarvon Bay

0   250   500 m

| **PORT ARTHUR** |
|---|
| 1  Fox & Hounds |
| 2  Bush Mill |
| 3  Port Arthur Caravan & Cabin Park |
| 4  Public Toilets; Launching Point for Ocean Kayaks |
| 5  Port Arthur Holiday World |
| 6  Post Office |
| 7  Port Arthur YHA Hostel |
| 8  Ruined Church |
| 9  Visitor Centre; Kiosk |
| 10  Ruins of Broad Arrow Cafe |
| 11  Port Arthur Villas |
| 12  Port Arthur Motor Inn |
| 13  Separate Prison |
| 14  Museum |
| 15  Penitentiary |
| 16  Commandants Cottage |

Tasman Peninsula Information section earlier in this chapter).

**Penal Settlement** Take the free historic tour, or refer to the brochure *Port Arthur Historic Site 1830: The Australian Convict Experience* for a detailed account of the site and its buildings. Briefly, the **Museum**, which contains many displays and a coffee shop open from 10 am to 4 pm, was originally the Asylum, housing patients from throughout the colony; the **Separate Prison** was built as a place of punishment for difficult prisoners, following a decision to discipline by isolation rather than by flogging; the **Church** was built in 1836 but was gutted by fire in 1884; while the **Penitentiary**, converted from a granary in 1857, was gutted by fire in 1897-98.

**Broad Arrow Café** The Broad Arrow Café – the scene of many of the 1996 shootings – was gutted following the massacre. Today, just the shell of the café remains, alarmingly in keeping with the other damaged buildings on the site. Yet in many ways it is even more grim, if only because the tragedy it commemorates happened so recently in the town's history.

**Organised Tours** The informative and worthwhile 40-minute free tours of the historic site leave hourly from the visitors' centre (☎ 6250 2539) between 9.30 am and 3.30 pm daily.

Ghostly apparitions, poltergeists and unexplained happenings have been recorded at Port Arthur since the 1870s, and nightly lantern-lit Ghost Tours (☎ toll-free 1800 659 101) of the buildings and ruins are fun, but also pretty spooky. Ninety-minute tours leave on most days from the visitors' centre at dusk and are well worth the $12 for adults, $4 for children and $20 for a family.

In all but the winter months you can take a $7 Isle of the Dead Landing Cruise to the island that was once the settlement's cemetery. In addition, there is a seaplane pontoon in the harbour: inquire about scenic flights at the visitors' centre.

**Bush Mill**
The Bush Mill (☎ 6250 2221), north of the historic site, has a steam train providing a 4km ride through the bush. The site has recreated much of the pioneer heritage with a sawmill, blacksmith and bush doctor exhibits illustrating what life was like in the Australian bush around 1890. The site is open every day with trains leaving at 10.15 and 11.15 am and 2.30 pm. Entry is $14 for adults, $6 for children and $32 for a family, including train rides.

**Ocean Kayaking**
Baidarka Experience (☎ 6250 2612, fax 6250 2030), which has been recommended by Lonely Planet travellers, offers well-equipped kayak tours of the Port Arthur coast tailored to suit experienced paddlers or novices. It's an interesting way to view the historic site, not to mention the spectacular cliffs of the region. Kayaks are launched at Stewarts Bay, 2km north of the historic site, and trips cost $45 for two hours and $90 for half a day.

**Places to Stay**
The *Port Arthur YHA Hostel (☎ 6250 2311)* is very well positioned on the edge of the historic site and charges $13 a night. To get there, continue half a kilometre past the Port Arthur turn-off then turn left onto Remarkable Cave Rd at the sign for the hostel and the Port Arthur Motor Inn. You can buy your historic-site entry ticket at the hostel. The hostel often offers package deals such as two nights accommodation, bus to and from Hobart and Port Arthur entry fee, all for $54.

The *Port Arthur Caravan and Cabin Park (☎ 6250 2340)* is 2km north of Port Arthur in lovely bushland above quiet Stewarts Bay beach. It's one of the most pleasant and well-kept caravan parks in Tasmania. It has a cooking shelter, laundry and games area. The bunkhouse has full cooking facilities, and costs $13 for adults and $8 for children. Tent sites are $12, powered sites $14 and cabins $70 a double. From the park you can follow a walking track south for 40 minutes to Port Arthur.

The most conveniently located motel is the ***Port Arthur Motor Inn*** (*☎ 6250 2101, toll-free 1800 030 747*), on Remarkable Cave Rd, which overlooks the historic site and has rooms starting at $110 a double. In the same area, but without the views of the ruins, is ***Port Arthur Villas*** (*☎ 6250 2239, 52 Remarkable Cave Rd*). Its self-contained units sleep four to six people for $95 a double.

***Andertons Accommodation*** (*☎ 6250 2378, 20 Remarkable Cave Rd*), which has been recommended by Lonely Planet travellers, is some distance from the historic site but is right on Carnarvon Bay, not far from a beach. B&B in a large bedroom with *en suite* and lounge room is $70 a double with a cooked breakfast, while a self-contained two bedroom holiday unit on an adjoining block is $60 a double.

Self-contained log cabins are the main feature of ***Port Arthur Holiday World*** (*☎ 6250 2262*). It is tucked into a quiet area away from the crowds and above the swimming beach of Stewarts Bay. The 18 units cost $95 a double, plus $15 for each extra person.

Near the Bush Mill is the mock-Tudor ***Fox & Hounds*** (*☎ 6250 2217*), which has motel rooms for $80/90 and two-bedroom self-contained units for $110 a double.

### Places to Eat
At the historic site, there's a large *café/restaurant* in the visitors' centre and a *café* in the Museum. Takeaway is available at the *General Store*, snacks and country-style meals at the *Bush Mill*.

For more formal dining, try the ***Port Arthur Motor Inn***, next to the youth hostel, which often has specials on the menu. ***The Fox and Hounds*** serves counter lunches and à la carte dinners daily.

### Getting There & Away
Tasmanian Tours and Travel/Tigerline runs tours to Port Arthur.

Hobart Coaches has a service from Monday to Friday that travels via most towns on the Tasman Peninsula.

## REMARKABLE CAVE
South of Port Arthur at the end of Remarkable Cave Rd is Remarkable Cave, a series of arches that the sea has eroded. A boardwalk provides access to a metal viewing platform. From the car park you can follow the coast east to Maingon Blowhole (two hours return) or farther on to Mt Brown (five hours return), where there are excellent views.

On the return it is worth deviating to **Palmers Lookout**, which provides good views of the entire Port Arthur and Safety Cove area.

## NUBEENA
* **pop 230**
This is the largest town on the peninsula yet it is a much quieter place than Port Arthur. It's really just a holiday destination for locals. The name Nubeena is the Aboriginal word for 'crayfish'. The town itself is spread along the seashore.

The main activities are swimming and relaxing on **White Beach**. Fishing from the jetty or the foreshore is another popular pastime. To the south, down a side road, is some fine walking to **Tunnel Bay** (five hours return), **Raoul Bay Lookout** (two hours return) and **Cape Raoul** (five hours return). *Tasman Tracks* by Shirley & Peter Storey contains detailed notes.

### Places to Stay
South of the town, ***White Beach Caravan Park*** (*☎ 6250 2142*) has tent sites for $11 a double, powered sites for $12 a double, on-site vans for $30 a double and cabins for $50 a double. At the other end of the beach ***White Beach Holiday Village*** (*☎ 6250 2152*) has self-contained villas in a quiet, secluded setting. Units cost $68 a double.

***Parson's Bay Country Accommodation*** (*☎ 6250 2261*) has B&B for $75 a double. ***Fairway Lodge Country Club*** (*☎ 6250 2171*), a low-key resort on the edge of town, has motel rooms for $89 and self-contained units for $99 a double.

For takeaway and snacks you could try ***Gorman's Bakehouse*** near the B&B. The

*Nubeena Tavern* near the Country Club has counter meals.

## Getting There & Away

The Hobart Coaches service described in the earlier Port Arthur section travels through Nubeena.

## SALTWATER RIVER

The ruins of the dreaded **coal mines** are the most powerful and dominant reminders of the past in this section of the peninsula. Started in 1833, the mines were used to punish the worst of the convicts, who worked in terrible conditions in a poorly managed mining operation. The mining operation was not economic: in 1848 it was sold to private enterprise and within 10 years it was abandoned. Some buildings were demolished, while fire and weather took a toll on the rest.

## Things to See & Do

The old mines are interesting to wander around and provide a dramatic contrast to the developments at Port Arthur. Be sure not to enter any of the mine shafts because they have not been stabilised and could be potentially dangerous. You can, however, enter some very well-preserved cells, which are small, dark and often described as being underground, although in fact they are at basement level.

Apart from the mines, the main attractions of the area are **rare birds** and **butterflies**, and easy **walks** across gentle coastal country. From Lime Bay the two to three hour return walk to Lagoon Beach is the most popular walk.

## Organised Tours

Nearby, the Seaview Lodge (☎/fax 6250 2766) offers daily $20 lantern-lit night tours of the coal mines and basement cells, which include spotlighting of fauna and some role-play. Written translations of the commentary are available in Chinese, Japanese and Vietnamese on request. Bookings are essential.

## Places to Stay

Bush *camping* is allowed near the mine site at Plunkett Point and farther north along a sandy track at Lime Bay. Camping is very basic, with pit toilets and fireplaces. Water must be taken in, as there is no permanent fresh water. Fees apply.

## KOONYA

There is little for visitors at this tiny settlement apart from the interesting accommodation. The budget *Seaview Lodge Host Farm* (☎ 6250 2766), signposted off the main road, has fantastic views: bunks are $15 each, double rooms $35. School groups often stay here in the low season.

## Sculpture by the Sea

Windgrove, at Roaring Beach near Nubeena on the Tasman Peninsula, is a peaceful coastal property owned by Peter Adams, a creator of beautiful wooden benches that sell for upwards of $10,000. Peter attempts to produce works that express a link between art, ecology and theology and in November and May each year displays them in 100 acres of revegetated coastal heath as part of the Australian Open Garden Scheme. During a 1998 national program entitled Sculpture by the Sea, not only Peter's benches, but innovative pieces by many local artists were placed along a path overlooking the ocean and the property opened to the public for nine days of viewing, music and lantern parades. In time, Peter hopes to develop Windgrove as an artists' retreat. Meanwhile, if you are in the area when his property is open, you should take the time to follow the signs from the main road to this garden gallery: there is no better artists' space in the state.

*Cascades* (☎ *6250 3121)* was originally an out-station of Port Arthur, with around 400 convicts working there at one time. The historic buildings are all on private property and some of the quarters have been restored in period style and are used for accommodation. B&B is $95 a double. There is also a private museum that you can visit.

Nearby, you can get good self-contained accommodation at the two bedroom *Boronia Cottage* for $50 a double.

### Getting There & Away

The Hobart Coaches service described in the earlier Port Arthur section travels through Premaydena and Koonya from Monday to Friday.

AROUND HOBART

# South-East Coast

This region of the state is often neglected, but it has much to offer, particularly if you have your own transport and enjoy driving through idyllic countryside, chatting in village tearooms and browsing through roadside produce stores. Spectacular rainbows in the Huon Valley, water views from the mountain passes of the peninsula and all the attractions of Bruny Island make the region the perfect destination for such laid-back visitors. However, the more energetic will not be disappointed either: Hartz Peak, the caves at Hastings, and the South Coast Track from magnificent Recherche Bay, are just a few of the major attractions an easy day trip south of Hobart.

The wide Huon River dominates the region, carving the hills into deep valleys and wide waterways. Synonymous with this river is the famous Huon pine, a unique tree that can exceed 2000 years in age. Sadly, those trees were logged out many years ago and only a few young specimens remain. The area is also known for its spectacular rainbows, which are probably due to a combination of southern latitude and abundant waterways.

In the 1960s, it was apple growing in the Huon Valley that put Tasmania on the international export map. At one stage there were over 2000 orchards exporting eight million boxes of apples, mainly to the United Kingdom. When demand from Europe declined, so did the orchards.

In recent years, farmers have diversified into other fruit crops, along with Atlantic salmon, wine and tourism. Tasmania's reputation for clean air and low pollution has led to these new products finding markets in Asia. The abundance of high-quality local produce is a bonus for the region's restaurateurs, many of whom make a feature of it in their menus.

From around the end of December to April or May fruit-picking work is available here, but competition for jobs is stiff. Grape-

## HIGHLIGHTS

- Lazy drives beside the D'Entrecasteaux Channel
- Camping at Cockle Creek or Recherche Bay
- Bushwalking on Bruny Island and in the Hartz Mountains
- Exploring the caves at Hastings
- Jams, berries, apples and wholefood at stalls and cafés

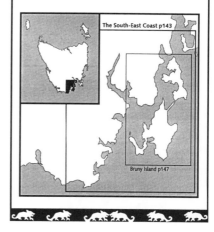

The South-East Coast p143

Bruny Island p147

picking jobs are sometimes available in late autumn and early winter, as most wineries are still hand-picking their crops. Hostels are good sources of information on how to find such jobs. Be warned though: fruit-picking is a tough way to earn a few dollars and pay is proportional to the quantity and quality picked. Many pickers struggle to earn enough to pay for their accommodation.

## Getting There & Around
**Bus** The region south of Hobart has two distinct areas: the peninsula, which includes

Kettering and Cygnet, and the coastal strip followed by the Huon Hwy from Huonville to Cockle Creek.

Hobart Coaches (☎ 6234 4077) runs several buses on weekdays from Hobart south through Margate, Snug and Kettering to Woodbridge. There are no weekend services. One bus each weekday runs from Hobart to Snug and inland across to Cygnet.

A different set of buses is run by Hobart Coaches from Hobart through Huonville and Franklin to Geeveston. There are five

services each weekday as far as Geeveston and one bus continues on to Dover. On school days extra services run between Dover and Hobart. There is also a service to Geeveston on most Sundays.

Tasmanian Wilderness Transport (TWT, ☎ 6334 4442) also runs buses along the Huon Hwy from Hobart through Huonville, Geeveston and Dover all the way to the end of the road at Cockle Creek. This is a Wilderness service, which means that it will only run if there are four full-fare-paying

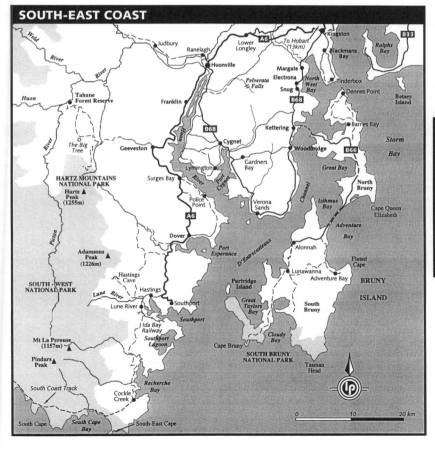

passengers on board. It operates on Monday, Wednesday and Friday from early November to early April.

There is no regular public transport from Geeveston to the Hartz Mountains.

**Car** The views from the highway between Hobart and Woodbridge are lovely, particularly on sunny days during seasons of adequate rainfall. At such times, the contrast between the lush green of the pastures and the deep blue of the channel waters is dazzling. If you then take the road from Woodbridge to Gardeners Bay on the way to Cygnet, you will be rewarded with stunning water views on both sides of the ridge. Another road across the peninsula to Cygnet leaves the highway just before Kettering, but it's less scenic. You can also follow the coast around from Woodbridge through Verona Sands to Cygnet on a road that passes very close to the channel at some points; if the water is choppy, this can be an impressive detour.

Farther south, some sections of the side route from Surges Bay through Police Point and on to Dover are gravel, but this should not deter you, as the road is in good condition and the views are great. The 19km road from Lune River to Cockle Creek has been surfaced with very coarse gravel, which can put pressure on older vehicles. Check your tyres before you start out, and make sure your spare is in good condition.

**Organised Tour** The Bottom Bits Bus company (☎ toll-free 1800 777 103) offers a three day tour of this entire area for $175. This covers one night's camping, one night's accommodation at the Lune River YHA, meals, park entry fees and transport.

## SNUG
• **pop 767**
Early European explorers found that this area provided a safe, sheltered anchorage for their ships, hence the name Snug. The town became famous in the 1967 bushfires when 80 houses (most of the town) were burnt to the ground. A temporary village was

established in caravans beside the oval and this led to the creation of the caravan park.

Since then the town has been rebuilt and is a popular holiday place, with sheltered waters and good boating facilities.

The nearby **Oyster Cove** has little for visitors but is historically important as it was the home of the last of Tasmania's full-blood Aborigines (see the History section of the Facts about Tasmania chapter). Prior to European settlement, the quiet cove had been a favoured site of the Aborigines because it was rich in shellfish.

### Things to See & Do
The nearby **Snug Falls** are worth a visit and are located 3.5km off the highway on a minor side road. An easy 1km walk each way, complete with seats and picnic shelters, leads to the foot of the falls.

One kilometre south of the town, beside the highway, the **Channel Historical and Folk Museum** (☎ 6267 9169) illustrates the history of the timber, ship building and fishing industries as well as recording the huge 1967 fires. It's open daily except Wednesday in summer; entry is $3 for adults and 50c for children.

Just south of Snug, there is a good swimming beach at **Conningham**.

### Places to Stay & Eat
The **Snug Beach Caravan Park** (☎ 6267 9138) has shady, grassed sites beside the beach. Tent sites are $12 a double ($15 with power) and on-site vans are $45 a double plus $7 for each extra person. Self-contained cabins are $65 a double.

Takeaway and sit-down meals are available from **Mothers Favourites**, where curried, fresh scallop pie is the speciality ($2.95). This shop has, on occasion, been declared independent of Tasmania by its owner – have a chat if you stop here and find out what its current status is.

The **Snug Tavern** has counter meals available for reasonable prices: a three course special is $11.50. Lunch is available from Wednesday to Sunday, dinner from Thursday to Saturday.

## KETTERING
- **pop 295**

The small port of Kettering lies at the head of the scenic Little Oyster Cove. This sheltered bay contains a marina for fishing boats and yachts as well as the terminal for the Bruny Island car ferry. It's a reasonable place to base yourself for exploring the region.

### Information
The excellent Bruny D'Entrecasteaux visitors' centre (☎ 6267 4494) at the ferry terminal sells books, park passes, Tasmanian wines and crafts.

### Ocean Kayaking
The Roaring 40°s Ocean Kayaking Company (☎ toll-free 1800 653 712) has an office in the same building as the visitors' centre. It offers an interesting range of kayaking options, including evening and weekend packages. On one such organised paddle, you can explore the channel and eat lunch on Bruny Island for $80 (YHA discounts apply). Children can be included on some of the shorter trips.

If you'd prefer to plot your own course, you can hire a kayak for $10 an hour.

### Places to Stay & Eat
The *café* (☎ 6267 4494) at the Bruny D'Entrecasteaux visitors' centre at the ferry terminal is surprisingly pleasant. Don't be put off by the bland exterior – inside the décor is attractive, and you can sit at tables overlooking the marina. Light lunches, snacks and Tasmanian wines are available from 9 am to 5 pm daily. (In winter it may be closed on Monday and Tuesday – ring and check.)

The *Oyster Cove Inn* has beautiful views and reasonable restaurant meals for $15 to $17 a main course; cheaper meals are available at the bar. The inn was once the residence of a wealthy grazier and dominates the end of the bay. The B&B accommodation upstairs has great views over the marina but seems little more than a sideline. It's $30 a head.

*The Old Kettering Inn* (☎ 6267 4426), on the road to the ferry terminal, is a guest-house in which only one bedroom (with *en suite*) is rented out. It's in a fantastic position, and the large guests' lounge room overlooks the marina: accommodation and a cooked breakfast is $89 a double.

*Heron Rise Vineyard* (☎ 6267 4339) offers luxury B&B accommodation in two self-contained units for $125 a double. The vineyard was established in 1984, and wine tastings as well as dinner can be provided to guests upon request: a three course meal is $25 a person. The vineyard is 1km north of the town on Saddle Rd.

### Getting There & Away
On weekdays, Hobart Coaches runs four buses daily from Hobart to Kettering, continuing farther south to Woodbridge. They arrive at and depart from the Kettering General Store on the main road and the fare is $5.40. Two services in each direction meet the ferry.

## BRUNY ISLAND
- **pop 520**

Bruny Island is almost two islands, joined by a sandy isthmus less than 100m wide. Locals refer to the two sections as North Bruny and South Bruny, as they are also different in character. North Bruny consists of rolling hills that are extensively farmed, while South Bruny is more scenic, with higher, steeper hills that are forested.

In between is the narrow isthmus, which is over 5km in length and is the home of mutton birds and other waterfowl. It is a peaceful and beautiful retreat. South Bruny National Park is renowned for its varied wildlife, including fairy penguins and many species of reptile. It has great natural appeal and is well worth visiting.

The island's coastal scenery is superb and there are plenty of fine swimming and surf beaches, as well as good sea and freshwater fishing. There are also a number of signposted walking tracks within the national park and reserves, especially the southern Labillardiere Peninsula and at Fluted Cape.

The island was sighted by Abel Tasman in 1642 and later visited by Furneaux,

Cook, Bligh and Cox between 1770 and 1790, but was named after Rear-Admiral Bruni D'Entrecasteaux, who explored and surveyed the area in 1792. Confusion existed about the spelling, and in 1918, it was changed from Bruni to Bruny.

The Aborigines called the island Lunawanna-Alonnah and this name has been retained in the form of the names of two settlements. However, the Aborigines were hopelessly outnumbered and had no defence against diseases introduced by the settlers. By the 1840s they had been forced off the island and transported to Flinders Island. The many landmarks named after them are the only reminder of their tragic clashes with European culture.

The island has seen several commercial ventures come and go during its history. Sandstone was mined from one of the rocky points and used in prominent buildings such as the post office and the Houses of Parliament in Melbourne. Coal was also mined, but these industries declined as transportation costs were high. Only the farming and forestry operations proved viable over the long term.

Proper roads were not constructed on the island until the car ferry started running in 1954. Today there are over 200km of roads to explore.

Tourism has now become an important part of the island's economy but it is still fairly low key. There are no massive resorts; instead, there are interesting cottages and houses, most of which are self-contained. Unless you're staying at Adventure Bay you should bring food with you. Also, it is wise to book accommodation in advance, as managers often don't live next door.

This island is not an overdeveloped tourist destination; instead it is a peaceful place with an interesting past and many unpopulated and unpolluted beaches. Major activities for visitors include walking in the national park and reserves and along beaches, looking for rare birds and just enjoying the relaxed lifestyle. Even so, you really need more than one night on the island to appreciate it.

## Information

The visitors' centre for the island is actually the Bruny D'Entrecasteaux visitors' centre (☎ 6267 4494) at the ferry terminal in Kettering. Here you can pick up handouts about the wildlife and walks on the island and a useful one page description of a self-drive tour.

The island's police station (☎ 6293 1142) is in Alonnah, as is the health centre, which is open from 8.30 am to 4.30 pm daily and should be contacted if an ambulance is needed.

The general stores in Alonnah and Adventure Bay, South Bruny, are Australia Post and Commonwealth Bank agencies. They also have EFTPOS and sell petrol.

National park passes should be available from the above stores, though it's probably safer to purchase them at the visitors' centre in Kettering.

Petrol, EFTPOS (no cash withdrawals) and limited fishing supplies are available at Kelly's Village Store, at Dennes Point, North Bruny.

## Museums

The island was one of the first places that European explorers visited and its history is recorded in the **Bligh Museum of Pacific Exploration** (☎ 6293 1117) at Adventure Bay, South Bruny (past the general store and across the bridge). Constructed of bricks made by convicts, it has a display on European exploration in the South Pacific. The collection includes maps, charts and globes and information on the early Antarctic explorations. Many of the books and manuscripts are originals or first editions and well worth seeing. It's open daily from 10 am to 4 pm except for Thursday and public holidays; entry fee is $4 for adults, $2 for children and $10 for a family.

At the council offices in Alonnah there is a small **history room** open daily from 10 am to 4 pm.

## Lighthouse

Also of historical interest is South Bruny's lighthouse, which was built in 1836 and is

# BRUNY ISLAND

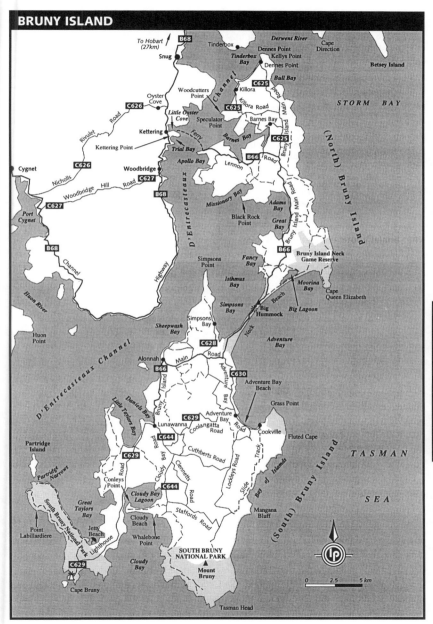

the second oldest in Australia. Built from local stone, it's located on the stormy southern end of the island. It's worth a visit just to see the rugged coastline. The lighthouse reserve is open to the public.

## National Park & Reserve
The **Neck Beach Game Reserve** is the home of mutton birds and fairy penguins that nest in the sand dunes. The best time and place to see these birds is at dusk in the warmer months at Highest Hummock Lookout (park at the Bruny Island Neck Game Reserve sign). Climb the 273 timber steps to the lookout and **Truganini Memorial**, where there are sweeping views of both parts of the island. A timber walkway also crosses the Neck to the other beach. You should keep to the boardwalks in this area, as the mutton birds dig deep holes into the sand. The holes can be very hard to see and stepping into them can result in a broken ankle.

The popular **Fluted Cape**, part of South Bruny National Park, is at the east of the small township of Adventure Bay. Here you can walk along the shore to **Penguin Island**, which is accessible at low tides or complete a more difficult circuit and climb the cape for more extensive views.

The south-western portion of the park is the large Labillardiere Peninsula, which features rugged coastal scenery and a lighthouse. Walks range from leisurely beach explorations to a seven-hour circuit of the entire peninsula.

Other attractions include a waterfall behind Adventure Bay and habitat of the rare forty-spotted pardalote. Many birdwatchers come here to catch a glimpse of this endangered species.

## Camel Rides
For something different, camel rides are available at Camel Tracks (☎ 6260 6335), which is north of the isthmus, beside the main road linking North Bruny to South Bruny. Open all year and operating on demand, short rides start at $5/4 for adults/children, one hour is $25/20, and a 2½ hour trek to the beach is $45/35. Day rides and overnight rides are also available.

## Organised Tour
If you have limited time and no transport, then an organised day tour around the island with Bruny Island Ventures (☎ 6267 1999 or 015 872 870) might appeal. With a maximum group size of seven, this tour visits all major features. The cost from Hobart is $95 each for the day with discounts available to YHA members.

## Places to Stay
This is a popular holiday destination for some Tasmanian families, as shown by the large number of self-contained cottages for hire that offer economical rates for one week rentals. Many of these are suitable for medium-size groups. Rentals for shorter periods are available for most places but prebooking is essential. Look in the *Saturday Mercury* newspaper's classified ads section for details.

Adventure Bay on the southern part of the island is the main accommodation area, but there are also individual places dotted around the island. Alonnah is the other main settlement on South Bruny, while Dennes Point is the main area on North Bruny.

## Places to Stay – Budget
**National Park & Reserve** If you have a vehicle and a tent, the cheapest place to stay is at any of the free *camping grounds*. To prevent the island's foreshores being damaged by indiscriminate tent sites, camping is restricted to specified locations that have pit toilets, some water and fireplaces (bring your own firewood). They are: **Neck Beach**, which is at the southern end of the sandy isthmus (signposted to the left as you head towards Alonnah); **Jetty Beach**, which is 3km north of the lighthouse at Cape Bruny and a safe swimming beach for children; and **Cloudy Bay** at the southern end of South Bruny. These are all signposted. The last two are in the national park, where park passes are required. There are no camping grounds on North Bruny.

**Adventure Bay** The appealing *Adventure Bay Holiday Village* (☎ *6293 1270*) is beside the beach at the end of the road at Adventure Bay. It has tent sites for $10, powered sites for $13, backpacker cabins for $45, on-site vans for $50 and self-contained cabins for $90. All these prices are for two people.

The *Captain James Cook Memorial Caravan Park* (☎ *6293 1128*) is closer to town and less interesting, being mostly just a large, flat, grassed area. Tent sites are $7, powered sites are $10 and on-site vans are $32 a double (linen and pillows required).

The YHA hostel on the island is the *Lumeah Hostel* (☎ *6293 1265*) in Adventure Bay, which is a 115-year-old sawmiller's cottage right opposite the water. The host, Simon, is making an effort to offer a complete Bruny Island service. Ocean kayaks can be hired for $10 an hour or $50 a day, mountain bikes for $15 a day and fishing rods for $5 a day. Three-hour nightly penguin tours are available from November to February for $15; island tours can also be arranged. Simon should also be able to provide transport from here to any of the main walking tracks, though minimum numbers apply. The hostel itself has recently been renovated, and dormitory beds are $14, while the family room is $40 double. Simon will pick you up from Hobart ($25 return) or Kettering ($10 return) on Monday, Wednesday or Friday afternoon (minimum numbers apply) provided you book. Alternatively, you can ring the hostel, book a room and ask Simon to book you a $5 place on the mail bus (he will give you details about how to connect with the mail bus using a Hobart Coaches service from Hobart).

## Places to Stay – Mid-Range

**Adventure Bay** There are plenty of self-contained cottages or houses around Adventure Bay. It is best to book ahead, as managers and keys are not always easily located. Cottages include *Rosebud Cottage* (☎ *6293 1325*) at $70 a double and *Mavista Cottage* (☎ *6293 1347*) at $90 a double.

Some cottages require a minimum stay of two nights; these include *Adventure Bay Holiday Home* (☎ *6243 6169*) at $60 a double and $10 for each extra person, and *Bruny Island Quiet Corner Units* (☎ *6264 2011*), which cost $70 a double.

**Lunawanna & Alonnah** The two main settlements on the eastern side of South Bruny are very small villages that are not as attractive for visitors as the Adventure Bay area. The best value accommodation in the area is *Coolangatta Cottage* (☎ *6293 1164*), which is in an uninspiring location in the middle of nowhere beside the Cloudy Bay Road and costs only $60 a night for up to five people. On the same road is *Mill Cottage* (☎ *6293 1156*) for $70/80 a single/double plus $10 each extra person, and *Inala – Bruny Island* (☎ *6293 1217*) for $80/90 plus $10 each extra person.

In Alonnah the *Hotel Bruny* (☎ *6293 1148*) charges $40/60 for basic motel rooms in an unattractive position.

**North Bruny** Barnes Bay was once the ferry terminal but is now a peaceful location, and *Barnes Bay Villas* (☎ *6260 6287*) has one well equipped but uninspiring unit for five adults available for $70 a double plus $10 for each extra person.

If you want a bit of privacy, rent the large *Christopher Lumsden Cottage* (☎ *6239 6547*), which is beside the main road north of the isthmus. The charge of $70 a double plus $10 for each extra adult is very reasonable for this interesting two storey house. A minimum stay of two nights applies from November to April.

## Places to Stay – Top End

**South Bruny** At Lunawanna, *Belmont* is a high quality cottage for $80/100. Also at Lunawanna is *St Clairs* (☎ *6293 1300*), a luxurious cottage for $125 a double.

*Morella Island Retreats* (☎ *6293 1131*), beside the entrance road to Adventure Bay, has two beautiful units for couples for $170 and $195 a double with breakfast. It also has upmarket accommodation suitable for families for $110 a double plus $10 for each extra person (breakfast $10 a person). The historic gardens here are open to the public from 10 am to 4 pm daily, and admission is $3.

**North Bruny** On the eastern road to Dennes Point is *Kellys Lookout (☎ 6267 4494)*. It's a modern house with magnificent views over Bull Bay that you can rent for $100 a double.

### Places To Eat
Most visitors bring their own provisions, as the range of food available on the island is very limited. Standard takeaways are available at the *Lunawanna General Store*, *Alonnah General Store*, *Adventure Bay General Store*, *The Dozing Dog Caravan* (which is beside the road leading to the ferry terminal) and *Kelly's Village Store* at Dennes Point.

For excellent lunches and afternoon teas including Devonshire teas and continental cakes, the *Penguin Tearoom and Craft Shop* in Adventure Bay next to the general store is well worth visiting. It's closed from June to August but opens daily the rest of the year from 10 am to 5 pm. A two course Sunday roast is $14.50, soup with herb scones $4.50 and smoked salmon, Brie and salad $11.

The *Hotel Bruny*, at Alonnah, South Bruny, serves counter dinners daily in the high season and Thursday to Saturday the rest of the year. Lunches are available daily year-round. Mains are quite cheap: steaks are $9 to $14, roasts $9 and scallops $14. Takeaway is also available.

### Getting There & Away
Access to the island is by a modern car ferry (☎ 6273 6725) from Kettering to Roberts Point on North Bruny and takes only 15 minutes. There are 10 services a day from Monday to Saturday, except Friday, when there are 11. On Sunday there are eight services. The first ferry to Bruny departs Kettering at 6.50 am (8 am on Sunday), while the last ferry to Kettering departs Roberts

Point at 7 pm (7.50 pm on Friday, 6.50 pm on Sunday). The timetable may vary at any time, however, so it's best to check on the day. An extra service is run on Friday nights. The ferry can carry 75 cars and has an interesting propulsion system using the unusual 'Voith Schneider' propellers. These look like vertical paddle wheels and provide excellent manoeuvrability.

All fares are for return trips and a car costs $18 except on public holidays and public holiday weekends, when the fare is $23. Bicycles are taken across for $3 and this can be a very good way to see the island. The charge for motorcycles is $11 ($14 during public holidays). There is no charge for passengers.

At least two buses a day from Hobart to Kettering will stop at the ferry terminal on request, but the Roberts Point terminal on Bruny is a long way from anywhere. You'll need a vehicle to get around the island, as there are no buses. There is little traffic, except around the time of ferry arrivals and departure, when there is a flurry of such magnitude that you may hardly notice it. Most roads are gravel and in good condition. Drive carefully and if possible, schedule at least a few days for a full exploration of the island.

### WOODBRIDGE
Over the past decade or so, it is the *Woodbridge Hotel (☎ 6267 4604)* that has put this little village on the map. Its tranquil setting beside the water has made it a popular lunch spot for tourists and Hobart residents alike. The dining room overlooks the channel, and prices for mains are a reasonable $10 to $15. Lunches are available daily, dinners from Thursday to Saturday. The dining room is closed on public holidays. The proprietors also own a small vineyard, and you can taste their wines here.

For more wine tasting, try the **Hartzview Vineyard & Wine Centre** (☎ 6295 1623), in the hills behind the town off the road to Gardners Bay. It features fruit ports and liqueurs under the Pig & Whistle label as well as wines from the smaller nearby vineyards. It's open every day from October to February from 9 am to 5 pm; in other months it's open only at weekends.

## Places to Stay

The *Woodbridge Hotel* has standard hotel rooms with shared facilities for \$27.50/50 without breakfast. Just around the corner, on the road to Gardners Bay, is *The Old Woodbridge Rectory*, which offers B&B in rooms with *en suite* (one with wheelchair access) for \$108 a double.

If you are after something really special then stay at the *Hartzview Vineyard Homestead* (☎ 6295 1623) near the wine centre. Complete with antiques, a log fire, complimentary wines and views over Gardners Bay, the price for B&B in this self-contained cottage is \$140 a double plus \$30 for each extra adult. There are also some pleasant bushwalks on the property.

## Getting There & Away

See Getting There & Away in the Kettering section of this chapter. Buses arrive at and depart from the general store and the fare from Hobart is \$5.50.

## CYGNET
* pop 924

This small township was originally named 'Port de Cygne Noir' (Port of the Black Swan) by the Frenchman Rear-Admiral D'Entrecasteaux because of the many swans seen on the bay. Now known as Cygnet, the town and surrounding area have many apple and other fruit orchards and offer excellent fishing, plenty of easy bushwalks, flat-water canoeing and some fine beaches, particularly farther south at Randalls Bay and Verona Sands.

The town is the largest on this peninsula and provides a good range of services. Travellers who are interested in antiques will enjoy browsing in the stores around the town selling old furniture. Another attraction is the Cygnet Folk Festival, held in January each year. You can check out the program by calling ☎ 6295 0280 or see the Web site on www.cygnetfolkfest.southcom.com.au.

## Things to See & Do

The **Talune Wildlife Park & Koala Garden** is in the hills 6km south-east of the town on the road to Woodbridge. Animals on display include Tasmanian devils, wallabies, koalas and wombats. It's open every day except Christmas Day from 9.30 am to 5 pm; entry is \$7 for adults, \$2.50 for children and \$16.50 for families.

Woodturning and handmade dolls are a speciality produced at **The Deepings**. It's open every day except Sunday morning and entry is free. It's on the Nichols Rivulet Rd, which is the first road between Cygnet and the eastern side of the peninsula you come to when heading out of town towards Deep Bay and Verona Sands.

After heavy rain the nearby **Pelverata Falls** are well worth visiting. Located 12km north of the town, a 4km walk leads to the base of the 81m-high waterfall. Allow three to four hours for the return walk.

## Places to Stay

*Huon Valley (Balfes Hill) YHA & Backpackers* (☎ 6295 1551) is on the Channel Hwy, about 5km north of the town. The backpacker accommodation here is now separate from the fruit-pickers' accommodation, and boasts a spacious new communal area with lovely views. Bunks here are \$15 a night, and rooms and facilities have wheelchair access. There are also new rooms with *en suite* for \$18 a person. Meals are available at the hostel if required. Bunks in the fruit-pickers' quarters are \$12 a night, and the host is willing to help you find work and provide transport to farms. The hosts here also organise day trips to the Hartz Mountains, Hastings Caves and the Snowy Range.

The *Cygnet Hotel* (☎ 6295 1267) has basic rooms for \$25/50 with a cooked breakfast. Opposite is the very basic *Cygnet Holiday Park* (☎ 6295 1869), with tent sites for \$7 and powered sites for \$10. Also at the northern end of the main street is *Howard's Cygnet Central Hotel* (☎ 6295 1244). Here modern motel units will cost you \$50 a double.

*Cygnet Guesthouse* (☎ 6295 0080, 89 Mary St), on the main street, has attractive rooms with private facilities across a hall for $70/79 with a cooked breakfast.

The *Talune Wildlife Park* (☎ 6295 1775) has three self-contained prefabricated cabins in a grassy paddock near the entrance for $55 a double plus $5 for each extra person.

*Leumeah Lodge* (☎ 6295 0980) has modern accommodation in a peaceful setting by the water at Crooked Tree Point just south of town. B&B is $85/95. Farther south, on the road from Gardners Bay to Woodbridge and just past the turn-off to Talune Wildlife Park, is the turn-off to *Lower Bagot Farm* (☎ 6295 1615), a commercial flower farm. Here you can get B&B in a tiny cabin with *en suite* for $50 a double.

You can also stay out of town at *The Deepings* (☎ 6295 1398), on Nichols Rivulet Rd in the hills east of town; B&B in self-contained units is $98/106.

### Places to Eat

The *Old School House Coffee Shop* in the centre of town makes good light lunches and bakehouse produce. It is all made on the premises.

*The Red Velvet Lounge*, on the main street, is a wonderful wholefood café in an old weatherboard place set well back from the road. It's open weekdays from 9 am to 6 pm and weekends from 10 am to 6 pm. Next door is the *Old Bank Teashop*, where you can get lasagne and salad for $5 and Devonshire tea for the same price. It's open from 10 am to 5 pm daily in the high season and from Wednesday to Sunday during the rest of the year except August, when it's closed.

The modern *Howard's Cygnet Central Hotel*, at the northern end of the main street, has cheap counter meals daily in its spacious bistro.

### Getting There & Away

Hobart Coaches (☎ 6234 4077) has one weekday-only service between Hobart and Cygnet via Snug.

## CYGNET COAST RD

To take the scenic route to Cradoc (on the way to Huonville) past Petchys Bay and Glaziers Bay, follow the sign on the main street pointing south to Lymington. Between January and March, you may be able to pick your own fruit at one of the **blueberry farms** along the way, but these farms are also worth seeing in autumn, when the bushes turn a spectacular shade of red. Farther around the coast is the beautiful *Scented Rose B&B*, where one room is available for $140 a double. Its impressive **rose garden** featuring David Austin roses is open to the public from 10 am to 5 pm on weekdays from November to March. Admission is $2.50. Also on this road (just 1km from Cradoc junction) is **Panorama Vineyard** (☎ 6266 3409), which has tastings between 10 am and 5 pm from Wednesday to Monday.

## HUONVILLE
* pop 1524

Straddling both banks of the Huon River, the major reason for this town's existence is that it is situated beside the first rapid on the river and was an important crossing point. Today a modern bridge crosses the Huon River enabling access to the south. The valuable softwood, Huon pine, was first discovered here.

The Huon and Kermandie rivers were named after Huon D'Kermandec, the second in command to the explorer D'Entrecasteaux. Prior to that the Aboriginal people called the area Tahune-Linah. As the region was originally covered in tall forests, timber milling was the first major industry to develop. At first the Huon pine was wasted, but once its properties were understood it became the major forestry product. Being very slow-growing, with a typical tree being over 800 years old, it didn't take long for Huon pine to be virtually wiped out, and today only immature trees can be found along the river. Once the forest was cleared, apple trees were planted and this began the orcharding industry, which is still the primary agricultural product of the region.

## Information

The visitors' centre for the town is Huon River Jet Boats (☎ 6264 1838), which is down on the Esplanade.

## Things to See & Do

For the visitor, one of the main attractions of Huonville is a jet-boat ride through the rapids on the river. For $38 for adults and $28 for children you get a thrilling 40 minute ride. Other options are 15-minute rides for $7 and 30-minute rides for $12. In theory they are available daily from 9 am to 5 pm, but you should book, as often they only run on demand. You can also hire pedal boats and aqua bikes from the same office (☎ 6264 1838) on the Esplanade.

If you like old cars, then visit the **Tasman Antique Motor Museum** (☎ 6264 1346) at Ranelagh, 2km north-west of Huonville; entry is $5, children $2. There are over 40 cars, mostly American and dating back to 1923. If you find it difficult to catch fish then you should visit the **Snowy Range Trout Fishery** (☎ 6266 0243) where your catch is guaranteed! It's in the hills 15km west of Huonville, signposted off the road to Judbury, and is open from 9 am until dark Wednesday to Sunday and public holidays, except in January, when it's open daily, and July, when it's closed. You pay a small admission fee and then pay by weight for the fish you catch. There is also a one day package for $25 per car, which includes admission, two rods for half a day, bait and up to 1kg of fish.

In the nearby hills (turn left at the roundabout if heading south) are Horseback Wilderness Tours (☎ 0418 128 405), on Sale St, which follow quiet trails near the Huon River on tours of from one hour to six days. Rates are $25 an hour, $60 for half a day (including lunch) and $90 for a full day (including lunch).

**Grove**, a small settlement 6km to the north, has become the tourist capital of the apple industry. Beside the highway, the **Huon Valley Apple & Heritage Museum** is crammed with displays about apples and also depicts life in the 1800s; entry is $3, $1.50 for children. It's open daily, from 9 am to 5 pm from September to May and from 10 am to 4 pm from June to August. It's closed in July.

Also at Grove is Australia's oldest jam company, **Doran's** (☎ 6266 4377), on Pages Rd, open from 10 am to 4 pm daily. Its strawberry conserve is out of this world, while the spiced apple butter is a real taste sensation. There's an observation platform where you can watch the jam being made.

## Places to Stay & Eat

The town itself is the commercial centre of the region but is not a major overnight stop for visitors. The ***Grand Hotel*** *(☎ 6264 1004)*, near the river, is an old brick pub with plenty of basic rooms for $25/35. B&B at ***Constables*** *(☎ 6264 1691, 12 Crofton Court)*, the old police residence, is $60/90, while ***Crabtree House***, a circa-1870 farmhouse 7km north of Huonville, is $95 a double.

There are the usual takeaways and roadhouses. Pizza and pasta are available at ***Tower Pizza*** *(☎ 6264 1949)*, on the main street, from 5 pm till late. For a more substantial meal, ***Huon Manor*** *(☎ 6264 1311)*, opposite the hotel near the river, provides à la carte lunch and dinner daily except Wednesday and Sunday evenings in winter. A light lunch of home-made pie of the day with salad and French fries is $8.50, grilled blue-eye is $16.50, and a 'Tasmanian Experience' is $36.50 for two. Local wine is sold by the glass.

The ***Apple Valley Teahouse*** at the Huon Apple near Grove is worth a stop for its excellent egg & bacon pies and cakes. Another pleasant café is ***JJ Café*** at Doran's jam factory, where you can get muffins with jam for $2.50, and curry puffs with Mediterranean antipasto-style salad, and plum, port and chilli dipping sauce for $7.50.

## Getting There & Away

See the Getting There & Around section at the start of this chapter for details. Buses arrive at and depart from the Huonville

Newsagency on the main road and the fare from Hobart is $6.30.

## FRANKLIN
• pop 462

The highway follows the Huon River south for a long way passing through the tiny settlements of Franklin, Castle Forbes Bay and Port Huon. These were once important shipping ports for exporting apples. Today the wharves and packing sheds are rarely used.

Franklin is the oldest town in the Huon area and the peaceful, wide river provides the venue for one of Australia's best rowing courses. The town itself is fairly large for its small population and there has been little change to the buildings in the last 100 years. The main street with its Federation architecture is worth stopping to view.

The Shipwright's Point **School of Wooden Boatbuilding** (☎ 6266 3586) runs two-year courses in traditional boatbuilding using some of Tasmania's excellent boatbuilding timbers, including Huon pine and King Billy pine (see Courses in the Facts for the Visitor chapter). Depending on what stage the course is at, you may be able to see a boat under construction – ring for details.

There's also a toymaker in town; his shop, **Terrys Crafted Wooden Toys**, is open daily from 10 am to 6 pm and sells wooden trucks, dolls' house furniture and rocking horses. Other local crafts can also be seen daily at the **Huon Showcase**, which is on the highway as you travel south.

### Places to Stay & Eat

The *Franklin Lodge* (☎ 6266 3506) is a lovely building that started in the 1850s and was extended around 1900 into the grand Federation building seen today. Bed and continental breakfast is provided here for $75/134 a double plus $41 for each extra person. The nearby inviting *Franklin Grill* (☎ 6266 3645) is open for dinner from Wednesday to Sunday.

The *Franklin Tea Gardens* are a favourite stop for Hobart residents spending the day down south. It's inside a nursery,

## Wooden Boats

Tasmania has a fine tradition of wooden boatbuilding, the result of the availability on the island of many exceptional boatbuilding timbers. Foremost among these is Huon pine, one of the most durable boatbuilding timbers in the world, famous for its resistance to borers and rot. There are many Huon pine craft in existence that are more than 100 years old and still in excellent condition.

Other Tasmanian timbers prized for boatbuilding are celery top and King Billy pines, though the latter, like Huon pine, is extremely slow growing and now difficult to come by (due to excessive logging). Blue gum, stringy bark and swamp gum are also employed by local craftspeople.

In November every two years, the state celebrates its boatbuilding heritage with the Australian Wooden Boat Festival at the docks in Hobart. Equipment is displayed, techniques of boatbuilding are demonstrated and antiques and artefacts are exhibited. And the tradition itself is kept alive at the Shipwright's Point School of Wooden Boatbuilding south of Hobart in Franklin, where already more than 360 students have helped produce dinghies and sailing vessels using skills perfected over generations.

and serves wholesome meals such as a huge plate of interesting salads and cold meat, with damper on the side, for $6.50. Fruit smoothies ($3) are also a speciality.

Farther south, at Castle Forbes Bay, is *Castle Forbes Bay House* (☎ 6297 1995), which provides B&B for a reasonable $50/70. This is a former schoolhouse and is off the highway and surrounded by an apple orchard. A little more upmarket is *Camellia Cottage* (☎ 6297 1528, 119 Crowthers Rd), in lovely rural countryside, where B&B is $75 a single or double.

## Getting There & Away
See the Getting There & Around section at the start of this chapter for information. You can flag buses down from the main street, and the fare is $7.50.

## PORT HUON
In the heyday of the apple industry this small village was famous as being its biggest export port. The wharf and cool stores remain as a legacy of those busy times and today are a rarely-used facility. For visitors the **Shipwright Reserve** picnic ground beside the river is a good place to stop and enjoy the view.

Huon River Cruises operates from the **Kermandie Lodge** (☎ *6297 1110*). A one hour river cruise runs at 11 am and 2 pm daily. It visits the Atlantic salmon farms, and costs $18 for adults and $9 for children. The lodge itself has a swimming pool, golf course and tennis courts; hotel rooms cost $45/75 and villas are $60/95. Lunches and dinners are available daily.

## GEEVESTON
- **pop 826**

Located 31km south of Huonville, this is the administrative centre for Australia's most southerly municipality and the gateway to the Hartz Mountains National Park. While most towns have declined as apple sales dropped, this town has reversed the trend and grown. It has always been an important base for the timber industry and today its economy is based on forestry industries and the tourists who come to see both the forests and nearby wilderness.

This town was founded in the mid-19th century by the Geeves family; their descendants are still prominent in local affairs. In the 1980s the town was the centre of an intense conservation battle over the forests of Farmhouse Creek. At the height of the controversy some conservationists spent weeks living in the tops of the 80m-tall eucalypts to prevent them from being cut down. In the end the conservation movement won, Farmhouse Creek is now protected from logging and peace has returned to this busy little town.

On the main street there is a post office that is a Commonwealth Bank agency and a library with public Internet access.

## Things to See
The town's main attraction is the **Forest & Heritage Centre** on the main street. It has comprehensive displays on all aspects of forestry such as logging practices and land management. There is also a wood-turning workshop where you can watch the experts or try it yourself. In the foyer there are often exhibitions of crafts. The centre is also the visitors' centre for the region (☎ 6297 1836) and is open daily from 9.30 am to 5 pm (10 am to 4.30 pm in the low season); admission is $4, children $2.50. It's interesting and well worth the visit. Here you can pick up park passes, maps and descriptions of walks in the Hartz Mountains. You can also purchase an interesting tape that will guide you along the Arve Rd and its walks; it's $8, and there is a $2 refund if you return it to the centre.

The grandiose gateway to the town, with its swamp gum logs, also has an adjacent reserve where a short walking track highlights the range of forest plants. There are also picnic tables and barbecues.

## Places to Stay
*Forest House* offers backpacker accommodation for $12 a night. It's close to town, on the road to the Hartz Mountains.

## Getting There & Away
See the Getting There & Around section at the start of this chapter for details. Buses arrive at and depart from Geeveston Electrical and the fare is $9.40.

## ARVE RD
From Geeveston this gravel road heads westward through rugged, timbered country to Hartz Mountains and the Huon River. The road was constructed for extracting timber from the extensive forests and although it's a dead-end road, it's an interesting drive. Logging trucks also use the road; drive slowly.

Follow the road to the **Arve River Picnic Area**, which has picnic tables and a short forest walk. Just past here you can turn left for the climb to Hartz Mountains. If you stay on the Arve Rd, it will take you over the next ridge to the Tahune Forest Reserve on the banks of the Huon River, which you can visit without a park pass.

Along the road to Tahune there are several short tracks (about 10 minutes each) worth walking. **Keogh's Creek Walk** is a short circuit with an all-weather covered bridge for viewing the forest. The **Big Tree Walk** leads to a timber platform beside a giant 87m-high swamp gum. The **West Creek Lookout** provides different views, with a bridge extending out onto the top of an old tree stump. At the end of the road is Tahune Forest Reserve; cross the bridge to do an easy 20 minute circuit walk to view ancient Huon pines.

## TAHUNE FOREST RESERVE

The name of this reserve is derived from Tahune-Linah, which was the Aboriginal name for the Huon River. The picnic ground has tables, toilets and a shelter (it often rains here). There are two signposted walks, one of 20 minutes, the other of one hour. The longer tracks can be muddy. On the first walk, you can view Huon pines, which grow beside the river. There are plenty of younger trees, recognisable by their feathery foliage and weeping branches.

## HARTZ MOUNTAINS NATIONAL PARK

This national park, classified as part of the World Heritage Area, is very popular with weekend walkers and day-trippers as it's only 84km from Hobart. The park is renowned for its rugged mountains, glacial lakes, gorges, alpine moorlands and dense rainforest. Being on the edge of the South-West National Park, it is subject to sudden changes in weather, so even on a day walk take waterproof gear and warm clothing. The normal national park entry fees apply.

**Waratah Lookout** is only 24km from Geeveston and is an easy five minute walk

from the road – look for the jagged peaks of the Snowy Range and the Devils Backbone. Other good walks on well-surfaced tracks are **Arve Falls**, 20 minutes return and **Lake Osborne**, 40 minutes return. For the more adventurous, a rougher track leads to **Hartz Peak**, three hours return.

## POLICE POINT

The main road from Geeveston to Dover heads inland at Surges Bay and is an uninteresting but quick route to Dover. The more scenic alternative is to leave the highway at Surges Bay and follow the Esperance Coast Rd through Police Point and Surveyors Bay. Some of this road is unsealed but has a firm, gravel surface. The road provides many fine views over the very wide Huon River and passes many scenic places like **Desolation Bay** and **Roaring Bay**. Along the way you will obtain very close views of the pens of the commercial salmon farms.

### Places to Stay & Eat

The rustic *Huon Charm Waterfront Cottage* (☎ 6297 6314) is much more aptly named than its location, Desolation Bay, which is actually a delightful, secluded little bay. Suitable for four, this self-contained cottage is $80 a double plus $20 for each extra person. Just around the next point is the more modern brick unit of *Huon Delight Holiday Cottage* (☎ 6297 6336), which has fine views over the river and is also $80 a double.

Farther down the road, the friendly people at *Emma's Choice* (☎ 6297 6309) will let you watch the jam-making process, using local fruit. They also provide excellent Devonshire teas in *Emma's Tearoom* beside the house. Seven varieties of jam are produced here. It's open daily from 9 am to 5 pm.

## DOVER
- **pop 570**

This picturesque fishing port, 21km south of Geeveston on the Huon Hwy, has some fine beaches and makes an excellent base to explore the area. Originally it was called

Port Esperance after one of the ships in Admiral D'Entrecasteaux's fleet, but that name is now only used for the bay. The three small islands in the bay are known as Faith, Hope and Charity.

Last century, the processing and exporting of timber was Dover's major industry. Timber was milled and shipped from here and also in the nearby towns of Strathblane and Raminea. While much of it was Huon pine, hardwoods were also harvested and sent to countries like China, India and Germany and used as railway sleepers. If you have your own car and are heading farther south, it's a good idea to buy petrol and food supplies here.

Today the major industries are fruit growing, fishing and the Atlantic salmon fish farms. The fish factories near the town support 2000 workers and produce Atlantic salmon, which is exported to many Asian countries. The town centre has reasonable services available with supermarkets and some bank agents.

## Yacht Cruises
From September to May, the South West Passage Cruising Company (☎ 6298 1062) runs a two hour cruise twice daily to inspect the salmon farms in the bay. This is a rare chance to see how salmon farms are managed; it costs $35 for adults and $17 for children. The yacht, the *Olive May* is a 42ft Huon pine vessel that cruises under sail or motor. Twilight and Bruny Island cruises are also available.

## Places to Stay
This is the major base for the region and has a wide range of accommodation to suit all tastes and budgets. The attractive *Dover Beachside Caravan Park* (☎ 6298 1301), on Kent Beach Rd, is on flat ground opposite the beach and has tent sites for $10, powered sites for $12, on-site vans for $30, and self-contained cabins for $55 a double. It also has a backpacker section, with bunks for $12.50.

Nearby, *Dover Bayside Lodge* (☎ 6298 1788) is in a building right opposite the water that used to provide dormitory accommodation. It now offers B&B in plain room with *en suite* for $75 a double with water views, $60 a double without. One room has wheelchair access.

The *Dover Hotel* (☎ 6298 1210), on the Huon Hwy just south of the town, has several levels of accommodation. B&B in hotel rooms with shared facilities is $35 a person with a cooked breakfast, $30 with continental. One of its $75 double rooms has good views of the water, as does the large unit it calls the 'housefront', which is $95 a double.

*Annes Old Rectory* (☎ 6298 1222) is homely accommodation where you share the house with the owners. It's beside the road as you approach the town from the north, and charges $60 a double for rooms with shared facilities. Dinner is available upon request for guests.

If you prefer a flat, *3 Island Holiday Apartments* (☎ 6298 1396), near the foreshore, has three units with reasonable facilities for $65 a double. The much more modern *Driftwood Cottages* (☎ 6298 1441), opposite the water on Bay View Rd, has four studio apartments with all facilities for $120. *Beach House* and *Cove House* are self-contained units owned by the same people; they cost $160 a double.

For somewhere special, try *Riseley Cottage* (☎ 6298 1630, 170 Narrows Rd, Strathblane), signposted off the highway south of Dover. It's on a hill overlooking the water in a bush setting and provides rooms with *en suite* and a cooked breakfast for $65/85 a night, which is great value for this standard of accommodation.

## Places to Eat
The *Dover Hotel* has a fairly good blackboard menu featuring local produce such as oysters and Atlantic salmon, as well as Tasmanian wines. Breakfast and lunch is available daily, while dinner is available daily except Sunday.

*The Gingerbread House*, on the main bend as you come into town, is a pleasant bakery and café open daily except Monday from 8.30 am to 5 pm. It has burgers for $7.50 and fruit salad for $4.50.

Light lunches and Devonshire teas are also available in the plain little tearoom adjacent to *Anne's Old Rectory*. It's open daily except Thursday in the high season but only intermittently in the low season.

### Getting There & Away
See the Getting There & Around section at the start of this chapter for details. Buses arrive at and depart from the Dover Store on the main street and the fair is $12.50.

## SOUTHPORT
Originally, Southport was called 'Baie des Moules' (Bay of Mussels) and has been known by several names during its history. Its current name is fairly descriptive as it's located at the southern end of the sealed highway. In fact, most visitors don't even pass through the town as there is a major road junction 2km to the north. It has limited appeal and exists primarily to serve the sparsely populated local area.

The bluff south of the town has a memorial to an early shipwreck in which 35 people perished. The aptly named **Burying Ground Point** on Lady Bay Rd is a convict burial ground.

The *Southport Tavern* is the hotel, general store and caravan park. The hotel is open every day providing both lunch and dinner; at the bar, meals are $11 to $13, while in the restaurant there is a better range of similar food for $12 to $16. The general store is open daily from 8 am to 6 pm and also sells petrol. Behind the hotel, the caravan park is in a rather ordinary grassed paddock; tent sites are $5, powered sites $10.

## HASTINGS
Today, it's the spectacular **Hastings Cave & Thermal Pool** that attracts visitors to the once-thriving logging and wharf town of Hastings, 21km south of Dover. The cave is found among the lush vegetation of the **Hastings Caves State Reserve** (☎ 6298 3209), 10km inland from Hastings and well signposted from the Huon Hwy. Daily tours

of the cave (adult $10, children $5, or family $25 – prices include admission to thermal pool) leave at 11 am and 1, 2 and 3 pm, with up to four extra tours daily from December to April. From the thermal pool allow 10 minutes drive, then five minutes walk through rainforest to the cave entrance. For the more energetic a short track continues past the cave to a viewpoint overlooking the forest. Don't forget to pick up your tickets from the kiosk near the entrance to the pool.

The thermal pool ($2.50, children $1.50, or family $6), about 5km before the cave, is filled daily with warm water from a thermal spring. Near the pool are a kiosk and restaurant. The 10 minute sensory walk near the pool is well worth doing. This is a feel-and-smell walk, which can also be completed by visually impaired people.

### Organised Tours
The hostel at Lune River runs Huon Magical Mystery Tours (☎ 6298 3117) to Mystery Creek Cave, where you can see plenty of glow worms. This is a wild cave tour, and all gear is supplied. The tours take three to four hours and will depart up to twice daily on demand.

## LUNE RIVER
A few kilometres south-west of Hastings is Lune River, a haven for gem collectors and the site of Australia's most southerly post office and youth hostel. From here you can take a 6km ride on the **Ida Bay Railway** (☎ 6298 3110) through scrub and light bush to the beach at Deep Hole Bay. The train runs every Sunday at noon and 2 and 4 pm. The 1½ hour ride (time includes break at the beach) is $12 for adults, $6 for children and $30 for a family.

The most southerly drive you can make in Australia is along the secondary gravel road from Lune River to **Cockle Creek** and beautiful **Recherche Bay**. This is an area of spectacular mountain peaks and endless beaches – ideal for camping and bushwalking. This is also the start (or end) of the challenging **South Coast Track**, which, with the right preparation and a week or so to spare, will take you all the way to Port Davey and beyond in the south-west. See Lonely Planet's *Bushwalking in Australia* by John & Monica Chapman for more information, including track notes.

Cockle Creek provides a good base for several day walks. You can follow the shoreline north-east to the lighthouse at **Fishers Point**, which is three hours return. The South Coast Track can also be followed to **South Cape Bay** and takes five hours return.

### Places to Stay & Eat

The *Lune River Youth Hostel* (☎ 6298 3163) charges $12 a night. It's a cosy place, and there's certainly plenty to keep you occupied here – ask the managers about hiring mountain bikes or kayaks, or about bushwalking, fishing or caving. The hostel is known for its full moon feasts: the managers have built a large beehive-shaped mud-brick pizza oven out the back, and on any full moon night you should be able to get a meal of oysters, mussels, abalone, salmon, pizza, salads and crumble for $12. At any other time, however, you should bring your own food, as there's little available in the area. The hostel runs a shuttle bus connecting with the Hobart Coaches' Dover service; bookings are essential. B&B is available in *Lune River Cottage* (☎ 6298 3107), at the post office, for $60 a double.

### Getting There & Away

See the Getting There & Around section at the start of this chapter for details of the TWT service to Cockle Creek. For $5 the managers of the hostel will provide transport to or from Dover to meet the daily Hobart Coaches bus. They will also drop off or pick up from Cockle Creek for a flat rate of $25 for any number of passengers; if you want to be picked up on completion of the South Coast Track, ring from Cockle Creek when you arrive there.

# Midlands & Lake Country

The inland region of Tasmania has a definite English atmosphere, due to the diligent efforts of early settlers who planted English trees and hedgerows. The agricultural potential of the area contributed to Tasmania's rapid settlement, and coach stations, garrison towns, stone villages and pastoral properties soon sprang up.

This mainly agricultural region extends from the Midlands Hwy in the east to the Derwent River in the south-west and north to the edges of Launceston. At the centre of this triangle is an elevated, sparsely populated region known as the Lake Country. Three major highways traverse the region: the Lyell Hwy to Queenstown, the Lake Hwy, which climbs onto the high Central Plateau and the Midlands Hwy, which connects Hobart to Launceston.

## Midlands Hwy (Heritage Hwy)

Hobart was founded in 1804, Launceston in 1805. By 1807 the need for a land link between the two resulted in surveyor Charles Grimes mapping out a route. The road was constructed by convict gangs and by 1821 was suitable for horses and carriages. Two years later a mail cart operated between the two towns, and this became the first coach service, as it sometimes carried passengers. The main towns along this road were all established in the 1820s as garrisons for prisoners and guards. The Midlands is a fairly dry area and produces fine wool, beef cattle and timber. These products put the Midlands on the map, and along with the modern industry – tourism – are still the main sources of income.

If you are interested in antiques and old wares, you will find plenty of opportunities along the way to stop and browse. There are antiques shops in most of the towns mentioned in this section, and also in **Kempton**,

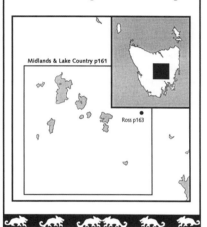

Midlands & Lake Country p161

Ross p163

### HIGHLIGHTS

- Fishing on the Central Plateau
- Browsing in antique shops
- The hydroelectricity power scheme display at Waddamana
- Detailed carvings on the Ross Bridge

signposted off the highway between Hobart and the Oatlands turn-off.

The course of the Midlands Hwy has changed slightly from its original route and many of the historic towns are now bypassed; actually this is a welcome change as you can now safely cross the streets without having to dodge the highway traffic. It's definitely worth making a few detours to see these quiet historic towns. The route is now marketed as the Heritage Hwy, and you can pick up a free tourist map of the region at most information centres around the state.

### Getting There & Away

Tasmanian Redline Coaches (TRC, ☎ 1300 360 000) runs up and down the Midlands

160

## MIDLANDS & LAKE COUNTRY

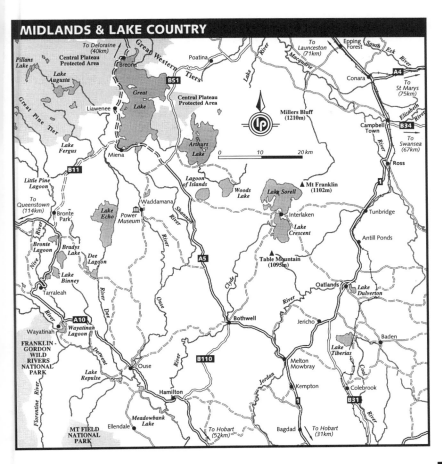

Hwy, and you can be dropped off at any of the main towns provided you are not travelling on an express service. The fare from Hobart to Launceston is $19.50.

## OATLANDS

- pop 545

With the largest collection of Georgian architecture in Australia, and the highest number of buildings dating from before 1837, the town of Oatlands is an interesting place for a brief visit. On the main street

alone, there are 87 historic buildings and the oldest is the 1829 convict-built **courthouse**, the oldest Supreme Court courthouse in Australia. Much of the sandstone for these early buildings came from the shores of **Lake Dulverton**, a wildlife sanctuary, which is beside the town. Unfortunately, the lake is now virtually dry. This may be a result of low rainfall over many years, but some people believe that blasting for the highway diversion cracked its base, allowing its waters to seep away.

The town site was chosen in 1821 as one of four military posts on the road from Hobart to George Town, but was very slow to develop. In 1832 a proper survey of the town was made and surveyor Sharland marked out 50 miles of streets, imagining it would become the capital of the Midlands. Many residents moved in the 1830s and, with the help of the former convicts and soldiers who were skilled carpenters and stonemasons, a large number of solid buildings were erected. The town did not grow into the planned capital, and today is a charming, small town. Some of its historic properties are occupied by residents.

## Information
The visitors' centre in Oatlands is the Central Tasmanian Tourism Centre (☎ 6254 1212, 77 High St), and you can pick up a detailed brochure about the town that includes directions for a self-guided historic tour. The post office, ANZ Bank and Trust Bank are on the main street, but the banks have restricted opening hours.

## Things to See & Do
**Callington Mill**, the restoration of which was to be Tasmania's main bicentennial project, still isn't open to the public. The mill was built in 1837 and was used until 1891. After a century of neglect, its restoration was begun by the Parks and Wildlife Service (PWS), but the project seems to move in fits and starts, according to what funding is available. It is hoped that when restoration is complete, the mill will feature a cap with a fantail attachment that will automatically turn its sails into the wind.

An unusual way of seeing Oatlands' sights is to go on one of Peter Fielding's daily historical Ghost Tours, which visit the gaol, courthouse and other convict sites (☎ 6254 1135). It starts at 8 pm in winter and 9 pm in summer, and costs $8 for adults and $4 for children. Candles are used for lighting on the tour.

At the time of writing, there were also plans to start up wildlife tours from Oat-

lands to Lake Crescent and Lake Sorell. Check at the visitors' centre for details.

## Places to Stay – Budget
The *Oatlands Youth Hostel (☎ 6254 1320, 9 Wellington St)* is a couple of hundred metres off the main street and charges $12 a night. The *Midlands Hotel (☎ 6254 1103, 91 High St)* is close to Callington Mill and charges $35/45 for singles/doubles with continental breakfast.

## Places to Stay – Mid-Range
*Oatlands Lodge (☎ 6254 1444, 92 High St)* has four classy rooms with private bath for $85 a double including breakfast.

*Woodbine House (☎ 6254 1534)* is signposted off the main road towards the northern end of town. It's a small but attractive sandstone building set in paddocks. B&B is $75 a double. All rooms come with private facilities.

As you approach Oatlands from Hobart you pass the Jericho turn-off, where there is also a signpost to *Ellesmere (☎ 6254 4140)*, a timber cottage on a sheep farm 2km along a gravel road; accommodation is $80 a double.

## Places to Stay – Top End
*Waverly Cottages (☎ 6254 1264)* has a number of cottages for $125 a double, including *Amelia Cottage (104 High St)*, opposite the hotel, and *Forget-Me-Not Cottage (17 Dulverton St)*, which is behind Amelia. The same people have accommodation 6km west of town.

Between Jericho and Oatlands, its name spelt out on the ground beside the highway in huge letters formed with white stones, is the 1842 *Commandant's Cottage (☎ 6254 4115)*. B&B is $90 a double and $25 for each extra person for the whole house, which can sleep 12.

## Places to Eat
The cramped little *Midlands Hotel* has counter lunches and dinners daily.

*Blossom's Cottage Restaurant (☎ 6254 1516)*, at the northern end of the main street, is an attractive place for lunch and morning and afternoon tea. À la carte evening meals can be arranged on any night if you book ahead. It's open from 10 am to 4.30 pm daily except Monday in summer. For the rest of the year it's open from 10 am to 3 pm Tuesday, Friday, Saturday and Sunday .

Opposite is the *White Horse Inn*, which has tearooms and a gallery open daily from 10 am to 5 pm.

### Getting There & Away

Catch one of TRC's Midlands Hwy services between Hobart and Launceston. Make sure you ask if you can be dropped off when making your booking, as some services are express. Buses arrive at and depart from the takeaway opposite the hotel. The fare to Launceston is $14.10, to Hobart $10.90.

## ROSS
* **pop 282**

This ex-garrison town, 120km from Hobart, is steeped in colonial history. The realignment of the Midlands Hwy to bypass the town has added to the peaceful charm of this little settlement. The town has strict rules on development and does not have a commercial feel to it at all.

It was established in 1812 to protect travellers on the main north-south road and was strategically important, being the crossing point for the Macquarie River. Originally the crossing was a ford, then in 1821 a low-level bridge was made with logs laid on stone buttresses. In 1836 this rough structure was replaced with the current stone bridge.

In the days of horse and carriage, Ross was also important as a staging post and most of the buildings are from the 1820 to

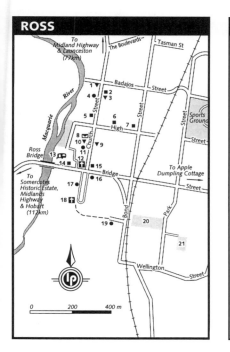

**ROSS**

**PLACES TO STAY**
2   Ross Bakery Inn
5   Captain Samuel's Cottage
6   Hudson Cottage
7   Church Mouse Cottage
13  Ross Caravan Park
14  Ross Barracks Cottage
15  Man-o'-Ross Hotel

**PLACES TO EAT**
1   Village Fine Arts Tearoom Gallery
3   Ross Village Bakery & Tearooms
9   Old Ross General Store
    Bakery Tearooms
10  Oppys Café

**OTHER**
4   Reception for Colonial Cottages
    of Ross
8   Post Office
11  Scotch Thistle Inn
12  Catholic Church
16  Town Hall
17  Tasmanian Wool Centre
    Visitor's Centre
18  St Johns Church of England
19  Ross Female Factory Site
20  Cemetery
21  Original Burial Ground

**MIDLANDS & LAKE COUNTRY**

1870 era and are of sandstone construction. The town then remained a local centre for the wool industry, but ceased to grow in size, remaining a village. In recent years, Ross has realised the historic value of its buildings and has refused development along the main street, therefore keeping its village feel.

## Information
The visitors' centre is the Tasmanian Wool Centre (☎ 6381 5466). It's open from 9 am to 5.30 pm daily in the high season and 4 pm the rest of the year. The centre has a free brochure that includes details of the historical buildings in the town.

## Ross Bridge
The best way to see this town is to walk around it; it's small and cars seem out of place. The town is famous for the convict-built Ross Bridge, the third-oldest bridge in Australia and one of the most beautiful, with its unique, decorative carvings. The graceful proportions of the bridge were designed by John Archer and it was built by two convict stonemasons, Colbeck and Herbert, who were granted their freedom for the work. Herbert has also been credited with the intricate detailed work on the 186 panels that decorate the arches. Each panel is different: Celtic symbols, animals and faces of notable people are carved into the sandstone. At night the bridge is floodlit and worth visiting as the carvings really stand out.

## Historic Buildings
In the heart of town is a crossroads that can lead you in one of four directions – 'temptation' (represented by the Man-o'-Ross Hotel), 'salvation' (the Catholic church), 'recreation' (the town hall) and 'damnation' (the old gaol).

Other interesting historic buildings include the **Scotch Thistle Inn**; the **old barracks (Ross Barracks Cottage)**, restored by the National Trust; the **Uniting Church** (1885); **St John's Church of England** (1868); and the **post office** (1896), which is

still in use. The three churches are all worth a visit and are floodlit at night.

## Tasmanian Wool Centre
The Tasmanian Wool Centre (☎ 6381 5466) on Church St is both a museum and craft shop. It contains displays of the convict era, including mouldings of some of the carvings from the Ross Bridge, and also of the wool industry in Australia. There are bales of wool you can touch, and an audiovisual display about wool. The Wool Centre also runs guided tours around the town. Admission and a guided tour of the museum (or just admission, if you haven't booked a tour) is $4; the town tour is $3; a combined town and museum tour is $6.

## Ross Female Factory Site
This is one place many visitors miss. It was the site of one of only two female prisons in the convict period, and one building still stands. It's open daily and free. Although there is little to see inside, a few simple descriptive signs and a model of the prison give you sufficient idea of what it was like.

To walk to the site, follow the sign at the top of Church St, just near St John's Church. Up the hill on the other side of the site is the original **burial ground**, where you can see more stone carvings on the headstones; these were done by the same stonemasons who worked on the bridge.

## Places to Stay – Budget
Adjacent to the Ross Bridge is the *Ross Caravan Park* (☎ 6381 5462), which has tent sites for $10, powered sites for $14 and units without *en suites* for $25 a double ($15 for students or backpackers).

## Places to Stay – Mid-Range
The *Man-o'-Ross Hotel* (☎ 6381 5240), on the corner of Church and Bridge Sts, has rooms with shared facilities for $40/60.

The only true B&B in town is the *Ross Bakery Inn* (☎ 63 81 5246) on Church St, originally a coaching inn built in 1832. Rooms with *en suite* are $55/89, which includes a bakery breakfast.

## Places to Stay – Top End

There are quite a few old cottages around town that are available for hire and provide continental breakfast. The following are run by *Colonial Cottages of Ross* (☎ *6381 5354, 12 Church St)*: *Apple Dumpling Cottage* on Bridge St ($110 a double); *Captain Samuel's Cottage* on Church St ($140 a double); *Hudson Cottage* on High St ($120 a double); and *Church Mouse Cottage* on the corner of High and Bond Sts ($115 a double).

*Ross Barracks Cottage* (☎ *6381 5420)* is near the bridge and is $130 a double, including a continental breakfast. At the time of writing it was for sale.

*Somercotes Historic Estate* (☎ *6381 5231)*, just off the highway 5km south of Ross, has B&B in 1820s cottages on an attractive property for $110/120. A free cultural and garden tour is included.

## Places to Eat

The *Man-o'-Ross Hotel* has a variety of meal options available every day: its bar meals are of the cheap fish and chips variety, its light lunches are between $5.50 and $10, while its lunch and evening à la carte main meals are around $15. One attraction of its light lunches is that they can be eaten in the pleasant beer garden at the back of the hotel.

*Oppys* is a fairly plain café and takeaway serving burgers etc until 9 pm daily. The *Old Ross General Store Bakery Tearooms* is a bit more interesting, with the usual bakery items and pies such as scallop and venison. A little farther down the main street is *Ross Village Bakery & Tearooms*, which boasts a wood fired oven, a courtyard eating area and good coffee. Diagonally opposite is the *Village Fine Arts Tearoom Gallery*, which is a more formal café open from 10 am to 4 pm Thursday to Saturday.

## Getting There & Away

TRC runs several buses every day between Hobart and Launceston along the Midlands Hwy, arriving at and departing from the Ross newsagency. The fare to Hobart is $14.60, to Launceston $9.80.

## CAMPBELL TOWN

* pop 879

Twelve kilometres north of Ross is Campbell Town, another former garrison settlement on the Midlands Hwy. Today it is the commercial centre of a cattle and sheep farming area and has reasonable services with two hotels, a supermarket and general stores.

## Information

The Heritage Highway Museum & Visitor Information Centre (☎ 6381 1353) on High St (the highway) is open from 10 am to 3 pm from Monday to Friday (and Saturday in the high season).

## Things to See & Do

The town has many buildings over 100 years old, but they are scattered and display a variety of architectural styles. Most buildings can be seen by travelling along High St and returning along Bridge St. They include the **Grange** (1847), **St Luke's Church of England** (1835), the **Campbell Town Inn** (1840), the building known as the **Fox Hunters Return** (1829), and the **old school** (1878). The main bridge across the Elizabeth River is almost as old as the bridge at Ross, being completed in 1838. While not as beautiful, the 'Red Bridge', as it's known, was constructed by convicts from bricks made on site.

You can visit one of the oldest farms in the area, **Winton** (☎ 6381 1221), which was founded in 1835 as a merino sheep stud and still operates today. Tours of the original buildings and gardens cost $6 for adults and $2 for children and must be booked in advance.

The showgrounds (behind the high school) stage the annual Campbell Town Show in early June. This has been held every year since 1839 and is the oldest continuous show in Australia. The town also runs a country music festival in November.

## Places to Stay & Eat

There are not many accommodation options to choose from in town. *Powells Hotel* (☎ *6381 1161)*, on the main street, has

MIDLANDS & LAKE COUNTRY

basic, old-fashioned motel rooms for $30/40, and counter meals for lunch and dinner every day except Sunday evening.

The historic *Grange* (☎ 6381 1686), in the middle of town but a little off the main street, has B&B in attractive rooms with *en suite* for $99 a double. It's open intermittently for tea, coffee and light meals – if the huge 'Open' sign's out (you can see it from the main road), drop in – you might be lucky.

The *Fox Hunters Return* (☎ 6381 1602), on the left as you enter town from Hobart, was built with convict labour between 1834 and 1840. It has rooms in the main house for $95/125 with breakfast. One twin has an *en suite*, while the other twin and the double share a rather luxurious bathroom down the hall. There are also larger rooms with *en suite* in newer wings of the building for the same price. The formal restaurant has mains for up to $19 and is open daily for dinner.

Beside the highway on the northern side of town is *The Gables* (☎ 6381 1347), which provides B&B for $80/85. It also hires out cottages for $95 a single or double with breakfast provisions supplied.

Thirteen kilometres north-west of town, on the farm of Winton mentioned earlier in this section, you can rent *Elizas Cottage* (☎ 6381 1221) for $110 a double, with breakfast provisions included.

*St Andrews Inn* (☎ 6391 5525) is 10km north, at Cleveland, which is just past Conara Junction, on the highway as you head towards Launceston. Built in 1845, this old coaching inn is classified by the National Trust and is a good place for Devonshire tea, lunch or dinner from Wednesday to Sunday. It also has B&B for $95 a double in rooms with *en suite*.

### Getting There & Away

TRC's Midlands Hwy services arrive at and depart from the BP service station on the main street. The fare to Hobart is $16.50, to Launceston $8.50.

There's a secondary road from Campbell Town, through the excellent fishing and bushwalking area around **Lake Leake** (32km), to Swansea (67km) on the east coast. Some TRC buses travel this route and can drop you at the Lake Leake turn-off, 4km from the lake. Another highway, the A4, runs from Conara Junction, 11km north of Campbell Town, east to St Marys. Buses running from Launceston to Bicheno follow the A4, as well as buses from Hobart and Launceston to St Helens.

# Lake Country

The sparsely populated lake country of Tasmania's Central Plateau is a region of breathtaking scenery, comprising steep mountains, hundreds of glacial lakes, crystal-clear streams, waterfalls and a good variety of wildlife. It's also known for its fine trout fishing, and for its ambitious hydroelectricity schemes, which have seen the damming of rivers, the creation of artificial lakes, the building of power stations, both above and below ground, as well as the construction of massive pipelines over rough terrain.

Tasmania has the largest hydroelectricity power system in Australia. The first dam was constructed on Great Lake in 1911. Subsequently, the Derwent, Mersey, South Esk, Forth, Gordon, King, Anthony and Pieman rivers were also dammed. If you want to inspect the developments, go along to the Tungatinah, Tarraleah and Liapootah power stations on the extensive Derwent scheme between Queenstown and Hobart.

On the western edge of the Central Plateau is the **Walls of Jerusalem National Park**, which is a focal point for mountaineers, bushwalkers and cross-country skiers. There's excellent fishing all over the Central Plateau. Most of the larger lakes have good access and the Great Lake, Lake Sorell, Lake Crescent, Arthurs Lake and Little Pine Lagoon are popular spots. The plateau itself actually contains thousands of lakes; many are tiny, but most contain trout. To get to many of the smaller lakes you must walk in. You'll need to be well equipped with lightweight camping gear, as the region is prone to regular snowfalls.

At Waddamana, on the road that loops off the Lake Hwy between Bothwell and Great Lake, there's the Hydro Electric Commission's (HEC) **Waddamana Power Museum** (☎ 6259 6175). It's a former hydroelectricity power station that was constructed from 1910 to 1916. Originally it was a private venture but financial difficulties resulted in the government taking over and creating the Hydro-Electric Department, which today is the HEC. The power station has operational turbines and an interesting display of the state's early hydroelectricity history; it's open weekdays from 10 am to 4 pm, Sundays and public holidays to noon.

## BOTHWELL
• pop 396

Bothwell, in the beautiful Clyde River valley, is a charming and historic town, with 53 buildings recognised or classified by the National Trust. Places of particular interest include the beautifully restored **slate cottage** of 1835; a **bootmaker's shop**, fitted out as it would have been in the 1890s; the delightful **St Luke's Church** (1821); and the **Castle Hotel**, first licensed in 1821.

The visitors' information centre (☎ 6259 4033) is in the Australian Golf Museum on Little Alexander St. You can pick up a map marking all the buildings of interest, many of which have descriptive plaques outside.

Although Bothwell is probably best known for its great trout fishing, it also has Australia's oldest golf course. This was built by the Scottish settlers who established the town in the 1820s. The course is still in use today and is open to members of any golf club. The associated **Australian Golf Museum** on Little Alexander St is open daily except Saturday from 10 am to 4 pm.

### Places to Stay

The *Bothwell Caravan Park* (☎ 6259 5503) is behind the Golf Museum. It's small and ugly but very cheap: tent sites are $3 a double, powered sites $6 a double. Check in at the council chambers between 8 am and 5.20 pm. After-hours you will have to track down the caretaker, who lives on Queen St,

across the park (there are no street numbers in Bothwell, so look for the house with the trucks parked out the front).

In town, *Bothwell Grange* (☎ 6259 5556), on Alexander St, provides B&B at $100 a double. It was built in 1836 as a hotel and today provides comfortable accommodation and à la carte meals.

*Mrs Gatenby's Repose* (☎ 6259 5624), on Arthur Crescent, is a cottage that sleeps five and is available for $98 a double.

A great option out of town is *'Nant' Highland House* (☎ 6259 5506), which is an attractively furnished five bedroom cottage well away from the main house on a working sheep station. The whole cottage is just $80 a double with breakfast.

Farther out of town is *Mrs Wood's Farmhouse* (☎ 6259 5612), in Dennistoun, which is 8km from Bothwell. Accommodation in a basic cabin set in paddocks is $25 a person.

### Getting There & Away

Hobart's Metro (☎ 6233 4232) has a weekday bus service (No 640) to Bothwell, but it would only be useful if you were planning to stay in Bothwell overnight. It departs stop F in Hobart at 4 pm and arrives in Bothwell at 5.30 pm; the return service departs Bothwell at 7 am. The fare is $9.20.

## LAKES
### Great Lake

Located 1050m above sea level on the Central Plateau this is the largest natural, freshwater lake in Australia. The first European to visit the lake was John Beaumont in 1817; he sent a servant to walk around the lake and this took three days. In 1870, brown trout were released into the lake and it soon became famous as a great trout fishing area. In 1910, rainbow trout were added to the waters and they thrived. Attempts were also made to introduce salmon but these failed as the fish did not multiply. The trout have now penetrated most of the streams across the plateau and some of the best fishing is in the smaller streams and lakes west of the Great Lake.

A small dam was constructed on the Great Lake to raise the lake level near Miena for the early power schemes. The lake is linked to the nearby Arthurs Lake by canals and a pumping station, and supplies water to the Poatina Power Station on the north-eastern side of the lake.

While the plateau has interesting plants and excellent fishing, there are no rugged mountains around its shores Nevertheless, many people consider it very beautiful. Well-equipped bushwalkers can walk across the plateau to the Walls of Jerusalem National Park and also into the Cradle Mountain-Lake St Clair National Park. The PWS visitors' centre at Liawenee, on the western side of the Great Lake, is worth visiting. There are no PWS camping areas on Great Lake, and no general store.

## Other Lakes

**Lake Crescent**, **Lake Sorell** and **Arthurs Lake** are other popular fishing spots. Unfortunately, Lake Crescent has been closed indefinitely as a result of carp infestation. There is a lakeside *camping ground* at Dago Point that has toilets and, during the fishing season, hot showers; unpowered sites for tents or caravans are $3. There is another camp with similar facilities and the same prices at Pumphouse Bay on Arthurs Lake. At Jonah Bay, also on Arthurs Lake, there is a more basic camping ground with toilets only, where sites are $2. Book at the Liawenee visitors' centre (☎ 6259 8148).

## Fishing

A wide variety of regulations apply to fishing in this area. They are aimed at ensuring there is plenty of fishing for all, and to allow fish to breed future generations. On some parts of Great Lake you are only allowed to use artificial lures and you are not allowed to fish in any of the streams flowing into the lake. The lake is closed to fishing in June and July each year. On the Central Plateau some waters are reserved for fly-fishing only and bag and size limits apply for all waters. Details of all regulations are provided when you purchase your fishing licence (see the Activities chapter for details), which you will see advertised

## Tackle the Trout

It should be easy to catch a trout as most of Tasmania's rivers and lakes have been stocked with brown and rainbow trout. However, you need to organise your fishing gear, and be in the right place at the right time. There are restrictions on the types of tackle that can be used in various areas, at different times of the year.

Fishing using live bait is probably the oldest form of fishing. It requires a grasshopper, grub or worm to be attached to the hook. However, this form of fishing is banned in most inland waters.

Artificial lures come in many different shapes, sizes, weights and colours. This is probably the easiest way to fish. You cast the lure from a river bank or boat and reel them in. Depending on the season, you might find that a 'Cobra' wobbler or Devon-type 'spinner' works well in the lakes, whilst in the streams, the 'Celta'-type lures are often effective.

One of the most challenging forms of fishing is fly fishing. Keen anglers make their own artificial flies, but you can purchase a large variety. There are many areas in Tasmania specifically reserved for this form of fishing, which most often involves wading the shallow rivers and lake shores in the early morning and stalking the wary fish.

Remember to always be prepared for Tasmania's notorious changes of weather, especially in the Lake Country. Take warm and waterproof clothing, even in the middle of summer.

for sale at petrol stations and stores in the wider area.

The fish can be very difficult to catch, and local knowledge of lures and locations is a considerable advantage. Peter Hayes Guided Fishing (☎ 6259 8295) is at the Central Highlands Lodge. Rates start from $175 per day, which includes transport and all fishing gear but not accommodation. Extended trips into remote areas requiring camping are also available. Another operator is Gary Castles (☎ 6259 8245), who works out of the Great Lake Hotel.

### Places to Stay
At Swan Bay, near Miena, is the *Great Lake Hotel (☎ 6259 8163)*, which has a range of accommodation: powered sites are $7.50, fishermen's cabins are $20 per adult, motel rooms are $65 a double with continental breakfast, and self-contained units are $95 a double. Also close to Miena is the *Central Highlands Lodge (☎ 6259 8197)*, which operates from October to April. It has packages that include accommodation and all meals for $175 a double. Room-only is $125 a double.

### Getting There & Away
Tasmanian Wilderness Travel's (TWT, ☎ 6334 4442) Wilderness service between Lake St Clair and Launceston goes via Bronte Park, Miena, Great Lake and Deloraine. This service runs on Monday, Tuesday, Thursday and Saturday in summer only (early December to early April) and only operates if there are four full-fare-paying passengers on board. Therefore bookings are essential.

# Derwent Valley Hwy

This highway follows the rich farmlands and valley of the Derwent River from New Norfolk to the southern edge of the Central Plateau. From there it continues past Derwent Bridge to Queenstown.

## HAMILTON
This is another National Trust classified historic town that was originally laid out on a grand scale to be a major centre, yet never became more than a small, sleepy village. Today the few buildings that exist are mostly old, well spread out and closely surrounded by farms, with excellent views of the mountain ranges and peaks farther west. There are some good historic buildings from the 1830s and 1840s to visit. It's not somewhere you would spend a lot of time exploring, but it makes an interesting overnight stop.

The area was settled in 1807 when New Norfolk was established, and by 1835 had a population of nearly 800, with 11 hotels and two breweries. Many streets were surveyed, but the rich, yet dry, soils near the town defeated many farmers and the town did not grow as expected. As roads and transport improved, the town declined further and many historic buildings were removed. The ones that remain today are a reminder of what was a boom town during the 1830s and 1840s. The major buildings are floodlit at night and well worth venturing out to see.

The **Hamilton Heritage Centre** is open from 1.30 pm to 3.30 pm on Sunday during the high season. Admission is $2 for adults and $1 for children.

### Places to Stay & Eat
The historic *Hamilton Inn (☎ 6286 3204)*, off the highway on Tarleton St, still operates as a hotel and provides B&B for $45 with shared facilities or $65 a double with *en suite*. All the floors slope and the walls lean a little, but then, that's the character of the place. It's also the only place in town that serves dinner, with counter lunches daily except Monday and dinners daily except Sunday. The inn has a series of underground cellars that can sometimes be inspected by guests, and they also bottle and export mineral water from an underground spring beneath the hotel.

There are plenty of sandstone cottages for hire. *Emma's*, *George's*, *Victoria's* and

*Edward's* are beside the highway and are run by the same people *(☎ 6286 3270)*; they cost $90 a double plus $25 for each extra adult. On the other side of the highway is the larger *McCauley's Cottage (☎ 6286 3258)*, which charges $140 a double. One block south, along the main highway, is the *Old School House (☎ 6286 3292)*, which was built in 1856 and served as the school until 1935. It was condemned in 1972, but was saved by being sold and restored and now operates as an unusual B&B for $110 a double. If you prefer to stay on a farm, 4km west of the town is *Over the Back Holiday Cottage (☎ 6286 3230)*. It's on the Hamilton Sheep Farm overlooking Lake Meadowbank and at popular periods, like holidays and weekends, must be booked for at least two nights. Rates are $105 a double plus $20 for each extra adult.

During the day, light meals are available from *Glen Clyde House* at the sharp bend at the northern end of town. This former hotel now houses tearooms providing home-cooked food and a well-stocked craft gallery.

## Getting There & Away

TWT's Tuesday, Thursday, Saturday and Sunday Hobart to Queenstown and Queenstown to Hobart services pass through Hamilton and Ouse. From Queenstown, you can catch connections to Strahan and (except on Sunday) to Cradle Mountain Lodge, Devonport and Launceston. The fare from Hobart is $7.90.

## ELLENDALE

This tiny village is on a quiet link road that joins the Lyell Hwy to Westerway. The signposted Ellendale Rd leaves the Lyell Hwy about midway between Hamilton and Ouse and is a convenient short cut to Mt Field, and the town is a good place to stay if you are planning a day trip to that national park. The road is narrow, but sealed, for its entire length. Shortly after leaving the Lyell Hwy you cross Lake Meadowbank, which is part of the Derwent River hydroelectricity power scheme. It's quite

pretty on a calm day and you can see the piers of the original Dunrobin Bridge next to the current bridge crossing. The original bridge was built in 1850 and marked the start of Dawsons Rd, which led to Gordon Bend in the south-west. It was intended to continue to Port Davey but was abandoned after settlers decided that the south-west was too rugged to farm.

Ellendale was once a hop-growing area and just north of the town is a huge abandoned hop kiln; next door is a pretty sandstone church and graveyard. There is little in town apart from a picnic shelter beside the creek, a general store and *Hopfield Cottages (☎ 6288 1223)*, which provides good rooms for $100 a double. Just out of town, 3km along a side road, is Old Macdonald's Farm (☎ 6288 1199), which is open weekdays. Admission is $3 for adults and children. The farm also has accommodation: its *Hillcrest Holiday Cabins* are $50 a double plus $10 per extra person.

*Hamlet Downs (☎ 6288 1212)* at Fentonbury, 6km south of Ellendale, has B&B for $75 to $100 a double in a farmhouse where you can go bushwalking or try your hand at fishing in the dam. The hosts grow their own organic herbs and vegetables and enjoy using these in dishes they cook for guests by prior arrangement.

## Getting There & Away

In summer, TWT runs daily Wilderness services in both directions between Hobart, Mt Field and Lake St Clair, and these pass through Ellendale. Bookings are essential, and services only operate when there are four full-fare-paying passengers on board.

## OUSE

While this area was also settled early, for a long time there was no town and Ouse (pronounced 'ooze') was little more than a river crossing. Most buildings were erected in the last 100 years and are weatherboard, so this town does not have any historic charm. The Ouse River was originally called the Big River and the area was home to a tribe of Aborigines who were known by the same name. They were forced into other areas following the arrival of European settlers.

The town is a popular stop for food along the highway and has several takeaway shops and cafés. The picnic ground beside the river is the best place to eat or rest. The *Lachlan Hotel* (☎ *6287 1215)* has B&B for \$25/50, and counter meals Wednesday to Saturday. The only other places to stay are cottages: *Rosecot* (☎ *6287 1222)*, opposite the hotel, is \$92 a double for B&B; *Sasso-del-Gallo* (☎ *6287 1263)* is \$70 a double but less attractive, being beside the garage. The only alternative is the *Cawood Farm Cottage* (☎ *6287 1499)*, 3km from town, which is \$100 a double.

### Getting There & Away
See the Hamilton Getting There & Away section earlier in this chapter for details. The fare from Hobart is \$9.60.

### WAYATINAH
This is the permanent village from which the HEC runs the power stations of the Lower Derwent Power Scheme. It is lkm off the Lyell Hwy on a side road; the buses along the highway do not deviate into this town. There is a shop open weekdays and a tavern open daily except Monday. The only place to stay is the *Wayatinah Camping Ground* (☎ *6289 3317)*. With water frontage onto the Wayatinah Lagoon, this is a very pleasant place to camp and for your camping fee you are allowed to use all the town's facilities such as the tennis courts and heated swimming pool. Tent sites are \$7, powered sites \$10 a double.

### TARRALEAH
Tarraleah was constructed as a residential village for HEC staff at the nearby power stations and dams. In 1998 much of the town was sold off and today it is little more than a scruffy collection of prefabricated houses.

The main features of interest are the **power stations** of Tarraleah and Tungatinah in the bottom of the deep gorge north of the town. These are next to each other yet receive water from different catchments. The Tarraleah power station is the oldest.

The huge pipelines feeding the power stations are also major features and the one that runs past the town has two tall surge tanks that dominate the town. The only place to stay here is the *Tarraleah Chalet* (☎ *6289 3128)*, which has rooms for \$30/55. Counter meals are available at the tavern in the chalet.

### Getting There & Away
See the Hamilton Getting There & Away section earlier in this chapter. The fare from Hobart is \$19.

# East Coast

Tasmania's scenic east coast, with its long, sandy beaches, fine fishing and exceptional peacefulness, is known as the 'sun coast' because of its mild climate. The area boasts more than 2250 hours of sunshine a year – an average of six hours every day. The red granite peaks and glorious bays of the Freycinet Peninsula are among the state's most attractive features, but even from the highway the water views are often magnificent. And if you have a yen for seaside towns, this is the place to indulge it.

Settlement of the region, which was suitable for grazing, proceeded rapidly after the establishment of Hobart in 1803. Offshore fishing and whaling became important, as did tin mining and timber cutting. Many convicts who served out their terms in the area stayed to help other settlers establish the fishing, wool, beef and grain industries that are still significant today.

The major towns along the coast are Orford, Triabunna, Swansea and Bicheno. There are also three national parks: Maria Island National Park has been reserved as much for its interesting history as its natural beauty; the large, dramatic peninsula of Freycinet National Park is an excellent place for walking; and Douglas Apsley National Park farther north has waterfalls and remnant rainforest, and also features examples of the dry eucalypt forests that once covered the east coast region.

There is plenty of accommodation here. Expect to pay up to 50% more during the high season around December and January. As this coast is a holiday destination for many Tasmanians, it is best avoided at Easter, and during the last week of December and most of January, when it is crowded. If you must come then, book well ahead.

Banking facilities on the east coast are limited and in some towns the banks are only open one or two days a week. There are agencies for the Commonwealth Bank at all post offices, though most have restricted

## HIGHLIGHTS

- The white-sand beaches at Scamander
- Exploring red granite Hazards at Freycinet Peninsula
- Convict ruins on Maria Island
- Eating pancakes high above the coast in the Mt Elephant Pancake Barn

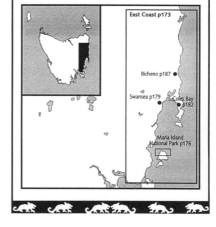

opening hours. EFTPOS is available at many places frequented by tourists.

## Getting There & Around

**Bus** Tasmanian Redline Coaches (TRC, ☎ 1300 360 000) and Tasmanian Wilderness Travel (TWT, ☎ 6334 4442) are the main bus companies operating on the east coast. TRC runs at least one service each weekday (and Sunday from January to Easter Sunday) from Hobart to Swansea and Bicheno and return via the Midland Hwy and inland linking roads. There are similar runs from the same towns to Launceston and return. You must change buses in Campbell Town, where you will have to wait anything from a couple of

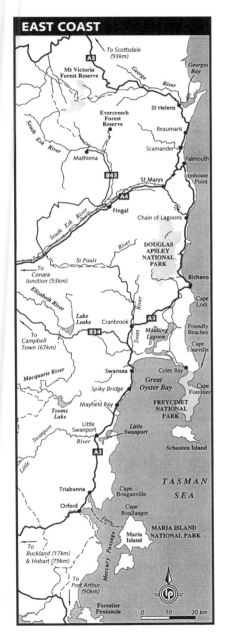

EAST COAST

minutes to 1½ hours depending on the service. TRC also runs services every day except Saturday from Hobart and Launceston to St Helens and return via St Marys.

TWT has a service to Swansea via Richmond, Orford and Triabunna on weekdays except public holidays. It has an additional service to all these towns (except Richmond) and on to Bicheno and St Helens on Wednesday, Friday and Sunday all year and Monday from 1 December to early April.

TWT also has a service between Bicheno and Launceston via Avoca, Fingal and St Marys. This runs on Wednesday, Friday and Sunday, and there is also a Monday service from Launceston to Bicheno in summer.

Neither major bus company services the Freycinet Peninsula. For this route, you must rely on Bicheno Coach Service (☎ 6257 0293), which runs from Bicheno to Coles Bay. This service connects with all TRC services. It will also meet TWT services, provided you book. The TRC fare from Hobart to the Coles Bay turn-off is $30.20.

Because services are limited at weekends, it might take a little longer to travel between towns than you anticipate. Also, some services do not connect, making overnight stops necessary. In some cases the same buses are used by school children, so most buses run in the early morning or late afternoon. During school terms some extra buses operate.

**Bicycle** Cycling along the east coast is one of the most enjoyable ways of seeing this part of Tasmania. Traffic is usually light and the hills are not too steep, particularly if you follow the coastal highway from Chain of Lagoons to Falmouth.

If you are planning to cycle between Swansea and Coles Bay, there's an informal boat service for cyclists and hikers (☎ 6257 0239) from Dolphin Sands across the Swan River to Swanwick, 6km north of Coles Bay, which will save you 65km. The approximate cycling time from Swansea to Dolphin Sands is one hour. The service operates from October to late April, weather permitting. Ring first.

## BUCKLAND

This tiny township, 63km from Hobart, was once a staging post for coaches on the way to the east coast. **Ye Olde Buckland Inn**, at 5 Kent St, welcomed coach drivers and travellers a century ago and today offers a good counter lunch every day, and dinner on Friday and Saturday nights. On Sunday, a $10 three course lunch is served between noon and 1.30 pm. Light meals are also available in the roadhouse beside the highway.

The large east-facing window behind the altar of the 1846 sandstone church of **St John the Baptist** has a fascinating history. How it came to be here is a mystery. It is originally believed to have been installed in Battle Abbey on the site of the Battle of Hastings in England. Some of the windows from that abbey were rescued just before Cromwell destroyed the building. What is certain is that it was made in the 14th century and was undoubtedly hidden for a long time before appearing in this church in around 1850. The church is usually open. Entry is free, but donations are welcome.

## ORFORD
* **pop 500**

The highway approaches this low-key resort by following the Prosser River through the impressive rock-lined **Paradise Gorge**. In the gorge, close to the town on the northern side of the river, are the remains of an incomplete **convict-built road** that is now a pleasant riverside walk.

The town was once an important sea port, serving the whalers and the local garrison on Maria Island. The **Prosser River** was named after an escaped prisoner who was caught on its banks. The area has good fishing, swimming and diving. Pretty **Spring Beach**, 4km south of the town, is a good surfing location with great views of Maria Island. The water is cold and wetsuits should be used for water sports.

The beaches close to town are sheltered and ideal for swimming or walking. A 2km walking track has been constructed from Shelley Beach around the cliffs of Luther Point to Spring Beach. This passes the site of an old quarry, which was the primary source of sandstone for many of the older buildings in Melbourne and Hobart.

### Places to Stay – Budget

There's plenty of accommodation in Orford in the form of flats, cabins and motels. The caravan park is north of the town, beside the beach and has fine views of Maria Island. **Raspins Beach Camping Park** (*☎ 6257 1771*) has sandy tent sites for $9 a double or powered sites for $11 a double.

On the Tasman Hwy, the **Blue Waters Motor Hotel** (*☎ 6257 1102*) has singles/doubles at $35/50. Almost next door, the fancier looking **Island View Motel** (*☎ 6257 1114*) has similar standard rooms for $52/64.

### Places to Stay – Mid-Range

Right on the highway, diagonally opposite the river, is **Prosser Holiday Units** (*☎ 6257 1427*). Self-contained units are $76 for four people ($300 a week). On the opposite side of the river, in bush at the start of the convict road, is **Riverside Villas** (*☎ 6257 1655, toll-free 1800 817 533*), which charges only $90 a double for self-contained units of a very high standard. Hire of a motorised dinghy is included.

More private is **Holkham House** (*☎ 6225 1248*), in farmland on the edge of town. It's $85 a double plus $25 for extra adults and $12 for each child. The nearby **Miranda Cottage** is run by the same people and charges the same rates.

### Places to Stay – Top End

**Spring Beach Holiday Villas** (*☎/fax 6257 1440*), on Rheban Rd, about 4km south of town, has modern, self-contained units for $100. Each unit has fine views of Spring Beach and Maria Island, and its tranquillity, play areas and resident wildlife make it especially appealing for children. To get here on the way from Hobart, turn right instead of crossing the bridge.

The **Eastcoaster Resort** (*☎ 6257 1172*), on Louisville Point Rd, 6km north of the post office, was once a kelp-harvesting factory and now has the usual resort facilities, including swimming pools. Hotel rooms are $75/90 a single/double, while self-contained villas range from $100 to $140 a double. The main interest here for most visitors is the *Eastcoaster Express* (☎ 6257 1589), the ferry to Maria Island (see the later Maria Island section).

## Places to Eat

*East Coast Seafoods*, beside the highway, offers both takeaway and eat-in seafood meals. Diagonally opposite, counter meals are available seven days a week at the *Blue Waters Motor Hotel*. The *Eastcoaster Resort* serves counter meals and also has a fully licensed seafood restaurant.

## Getting There & Away

See the introductory Getting There & Around section at the start of this chapter. TWT coaches arrive at and depart from the Orford Roadhouse and the fare from Hobart is $11.

## WIELANGTA FOREST

There is a direct link from the Tasman Peninsula area to Orford. It leaves the Tasman Hwy at Copping and follows quiet gravel roads north through the Wielangta Forest, which is managed for timber harvesting. Significant portions of the forest have been kept in reserves for recreation use and some walking tracks have been marked.

About halfway from Copping to Orford, the **Sandspit River Reserve** has a picnic shelter, a 20 minute rainforest walk that begins at an impressive bridge constructed of massive logs and passes rock formations once used as shelters by Aborigines. There is also a longer walk along the river valley. The other main site of interest, **Thumbs Lookout**, is only 6km from Orford. A rough side road leads to a picnic ground and lookout from which there are good views of Maria Island. A two hour return walk to the open, rocky summit of the highest 'thumb' will reward you with even better panoramic views of the coast.

There are no bus services along this road. It is a pleasant route that is highly recommended for cyclists as there is little traffic.

## MARIA ISLAND NATIONAL PARK

This peaceful island was declared a national park in 1972. It features some magnificent scenery: fossil-studded sandstone and limestone cliffs, beautiful white, sandy beaches, forests and fern gullies. There are some lovely walks on the island, including the fairly rugged Bishop & Clerk Mountain Walk and the historical Fossil Cliffs Nature Walk; brochures are available for both. A visit to the Painted Cliffs is also a must. The marine life around most of the island is diverse and plentiful, and is now protected in a marine reserve.

On a day trip to Maria Island, you can see many of its restored buildings and a variety of wildlife. But if you have time, it's well worth staying here for a few nights. There are no shops on the island.

## History

At various times, Maria Island has been a penal settlement, the location of factories and a farming district.

The island was originally occupied by Aborigines, who called it Toarra Marra Monah. They were members of the Oyster Bay Tribe, and lived primarily on shellfish. They crossed to the mainland in canoes and rested on the tiny Lachlan Island.

In 1642 Abel Tasman discovered the island for Europeans and named it after Anthony Van Diemen's wife. The Aborigines then remained undisturbed until the early 19th century. In 1821 the island was selected as Tasmania's second penal settlement and four years later the first convicts arrived and founded Darlington.

Over the next seven years many major buildings including the Commissariat Store (1825) and the Penitentiary (1830) were constructed from locally made bricks. A water race, mill pond and jetty were also built. In 1832 it was decided that the costs involved in running three penal settlements outside Hobart were too great and the convicts were moved. For the next 10 years, whalers, farmers and smugglers used the island.

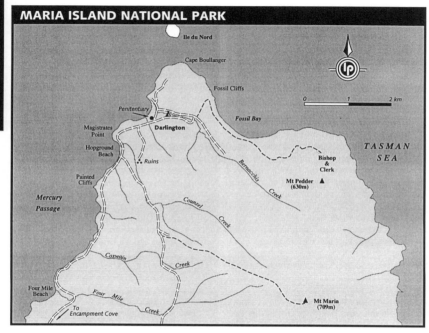

## MARIA ISLAND NATIONAL PARK

Reopened in 1842, Darlington was once again used by the penal system, this time as a probation station. The existing buildings underwent renovation while new structures were established. During this time, agriculture was the main industry. In 1845 a second settlement was established at **Long Point** and by 1850 a road connecting the two sites had been created. The road gave more ready access to the island and extra land was cleared to allow sheep to graze. At one stage there were more than 600 convicts at Darlington. However, in 1850 the flow of convicts to Tasmania reduced and Darlington was closed in that year, with Long Point closing the following year. The island was then leased for grazing.

In 1884 an enterprising businessman, Signor Bernacchi, leased the island to set up a silk and wine-making industry. The Darlington buildings were renovated and the town of 260 was renamed San Diego. Over the next 40 years there were various industries here, the most notable being a cement plant, established in 1922. By 1930 the Great Depression had begun: the cement plant closed down and the island reverted to being a farming district.

In the 1960s the government gradually bought the properties on the island. Since European occupation none of the larger animals or birds had existed on the island, so in the late 1960s, Forester kangaroos, Bennett's wallabies, Cape Barren geese and emus were introduced. These have since thrived and are often seen by visitors. In 1971 the island was declared a wildlife sanctuary. It's popular with birdwatchers, being the only national park in Tasmania where you can see 11 of the state's native bird species, including the endangered forty-spotted pardalote.

## Things to See

The only way to get around is by walking. The old township of **Darlington** is well worth wandering around for a couple of hours. The best short walk of 1½ hours return is to the **Painted Cliffs** at the southern end of Hopground Beach. The sandstone has been stained with iron oxide, forming intricate colourful patterns. This walk is a must.

There's a good circuit walk of 1½ hours to **Cape Boullanger**, the **Fossil Cliffs** and return via the old brickworks. If the peaks are clear, you'll be rewarded with great views by climbing **Bishop & Clerk**. A good track leads to the summit and takes about four hours return from Darlington. A walk of six hours return takes you to **Mt Maria**, the highest point on the island.

The coastline from Return Point to Bishop & Clerk is a marine reserve, which means no fishing is allowed, including in the Darlington area. The reserve, together with the giant kelp forests and caves around **Fossil Bay**, has created an excellent area for scuba diving and snorkelling. The water is cold and wetsuits are essential.

## Places to Stay

The rooms in the Penitentiary at Darlington and some of the other buildings have been converted into bunkhouses. These are called the *Parks, Wildlife & Heritage Penitentiary Units* (☎ 6257 1420) and cost $8 a night, children $4. The cells have mattresses only; bedding is not supplied and there are no cooking facilities or electricity. You must bring your own stove to cook on. The units are very popular and it's essential to book ahead.

There is also a basic *camping ground* at Darlington with fees of $4 per adult or $10 per family. Fires are only allowed in designated fireplaces and during summer these are often banned. A portable stove is therefore recommended. For those who are prepared to walk, there are other camping areas three to four hours away. French's Farm and Encampment Cove have only small water supplies and are all fire-free areas where only portable stoves are allowed for cooking. There are no camping fees at these grounds.

You'll need to take all your refreshments with you as there are no shops on the island. There is a public telephone close to the centre of Darlington. You'll also need clothing suitable for cool, wet weather, but remember the hat and sunscreen too!

A current national park pass is also required here.

## Getting There & Away

The *Eastcoaster Express* ferry (☎ 6257 1589) is operated by the Eastcoaster Resort from Louisville Point, 6km north of Orford. It departs daily from Louisville Point at 10.30 am, 1 pm and 3.30 pm and returns from Darlington 30 minutes later.

In summer (December to April) an extra service departs daily at 9 am. There is no service on Christmas Day. The 10km crossing takes about 20 minutes each way. Fares for day trips are $17 per adult and $10 for children. If staying on the island and returning on a different day, fares are $20 for adults and $13 for children. Bicycles and kayaks are taken over for $3 each.

TWT east coast coach services will stop at the Eastcoaster Resort provided you book in advance (see the Getting There & Around section at the start of this chapter for details of the services).

It is also possible to land on the airstrip near Darlington by light plane. These can be chartered from Triabunna or farther away at Hobart or Launceston.

## TRIABUNNA
* pop 830

Just 8km north of Orford is Triabunna, a larger town but not as attractive to visitors. It's at the head of the very sheltered inlet of Spring Bay, and as such is a useful port. Originally a whaling station, it served as a military base in the penal era. Today it is the commercial centre of the region, with woodchip processing and scallop and cray fishing being the major industries.

The town's name comes from an Aboriginal word meaning native hen. It once boasted the largest apple orchard in the southern hemisphere.

## Information
The attractive and well stocked visitors' centre (☎ 6257 4090) is on the corner of the Esplanade and Charles St, right on the water.

## Boat Charter
You can charter boats such as the *Crescent* (☎ 6257 1137) for $500 a day for bottom fishing or cruising and $750 for tuna fishing.

## Places to Stay & Eat
The *Triabunna Caravan Park* (☎ 6257 3575), on the corner of Vicary and Melbourne Sts, is a bargain with tent sites for $10, powered sites for $11 and on-site vans for $25 a double. The *Triabunna YHA Hostel* (☎ 6257 3439, 12 Spencer St) is an old house in farmland, across the bridge and a 10 minute walk from the main part of town. It's comfortable and quiet, if a bit rundown, and charges $12 a night.

Down by the waterfront near the jetty, the *Spring Bay Hotel* (☎ 6257 3115, 1 Charles St) has rooms with shared facilities for $30/45 with a continental breakfast. It also has counter dinners daily except Sunday.

Beside the highway, *Tandara Motor Inn* (☎ 6257 3333) has rooms for $50/60 and counter meals on Friday and Saturday nights and Sunday lunchtime.

In Henry St, near the council offices, is *Girraween Gardens & Tearooms*, a relaxing place for light meals. *Sufi's*, on the corner of Charles and Vicary Sts, has snacks and Devonshire teas and is open daily from 10 am to 5 pm.

## Getting There & Away
See the introductory Getting There & Around section at the start of this chapter. TWT buses arrive at and depart from the Shell Service Station and the fare from Hobart is $11.70.

## LITTLE SWANPORT
The tiny hamlet of Little Swanport is set around the Little Swanport River, which flows into a large lagoon. Its attractions are its great natural beauty and the fact that although it's undeveloped, it has easy access to the coastline. There are some fine uninhabited beaches in the area, particularly at Mayfield Bay, Kelvedon Beach, Raspins and Cressy beaches. All these beaches can be accessed by side roads.

The only place to stay is the *Gum Leaves* (☎ 6244 8147 or 6244 4167), a resort set in bushland south of Little Swanport. It has an adventure playground, deer park, horse museum and its own lake. The log-cabin hostel costs $20; self-contained cabins are $98 a double.

## SWANSEA
* pop 420

On the shores of Great Oyster Bay, with superb views across to the Freycinet Peninsula, Swansea is a popular place for camping, boating, fishing and surfing. European settlers came here in the 1820s and the town became the administrative centre for Glamorgan. It is Australia's oldest rural municipality. In 1993 it merged with Spring Bay and the administration moved to Triabunna.

Swansea, originally known as Great Swanport, has a number of interesting historic buildings including the original council chambers and the lovely three storey, red-brick Morris's General Store, which was built in 1838.

Because it's a popular holiday destination, prices for accommodation and food are generally higher in Swansea than in other towns along the coast. Several dominating accommodation blocks have been built near the waterfront and the town has lost some of its historic character. However, it's still one of the nicest towns on the coast. People come from around the state to eat at Shouten House, and the B&Bs here are great.

## Information
The Swansea Wine & Wool Centre (☎ 6257 8677, 96 Tasman Hwy) is the local visitors' information centre.

## Historic Buildings

The best way to see the town is to walk along Franklin and Noyes Sts, passing many of the older buildings in the town, including **Morris's General Store** and the **council chambers**. Most of Swansea's historic buildings are privately owned but the **Glamorgan Community Centre and War Memorial Museum**, dating back to 1860, houses the Museum of Local History and is worth a visit. The major feature here is the only oversized billiard table in Australia.

When it was being made, the builders did not want to trim the four pieces of slate and instead made the table larger. You can play a game on the table after 5 pm for $2 if you book. The museum also contains Aboriginal artefacts and possessions belonging to early settlers. There is also a war memorial room and an interesting display of old photographs of Swansea. The museum is open from Monday to Saturday and admission is $3 for adults and 50c for children; ring the bell for entry.

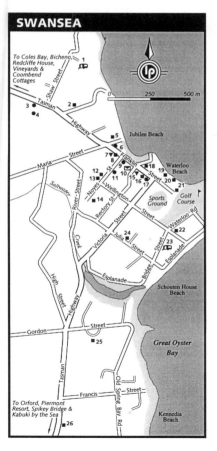

SWANSEA

## Swansea Bark Mill & East Coat Museum

In the front section of the Swansea Bark Mill & East Coast Museum (☎ 6257 8382, 96 Tasman Hwy) the processing of black-wattle bark is demonstrated on restored original machinery. This bark produces tannic acid, a basic ingredient used in the tanning of heavy leathers. The mill was made from scavenged materials and what you see today is how it actually operated. During the Great Depression the bark mill was one of the few industries in the area to continue operation, and it kept the town of Swansea alive. Behind the bark mill is a museum featuring displays of Swansea's early history, including some superb old photographs. It's open daily from 9 am to 5 pm and admission is $5 for adults, $2.75 for children and $12 for a family.

## Other Attractions

**Duncombes Lookout**, 3km south of town, provides panoramic views of Oyster Bay and Freycinet Peninsula. On the highway 7km from town is **Spiky Bridge**, built by convicts in 1843 using thousands of local fieldstones but no mortar. The nearby beach and headland is popular for picnics and rock fishing.

## Wine Tasting

The **Swansea Wine & Wool Centre** at the Bark Mill site sells sheepskin and woollen products. It also sells local wines, and wine tastings are available at $2. It's open daily except Christmas Day; entry is free.

There are also several wineries on the Tasman Hwy to the north. Best known is **Freycinet Vineyard** (☎ 6257 8574) 28km away, which has cellar door sales on most days and tea, coffee and pâtés in spring, summer and autumn. From August to May it's open weekdays from 9 am to 5 pm and weekends from 10 am to 4.30 pm. In June and July it's open from 9 am to 4.30 pm weekdays. Next door is **Coombend Estate** (☎ 6257 8256), which is open by appointment. Closer to town is **Spring Vale Vineyard** (☎ 6257 8208), 15km north of Swansea on the Tasman Hwy. It has cellar

door sales on weekends and public and school holidays, or by appointment.

## Places to Stay

There is a large amount of accommodation around the town. Because it's a popular holiday resort, bookings are essential at Easter and Christmas.

## Places to Stay – Budget

**Camping** The *Swansea Cabin & Tourist Park* (☎ 6257 8177), on Shaw St, on the northern edge of town, is by the beach and has a lovely outlook. Tent sites are $12, powered sites $16, cabins $55 and self-contained units $70 a double. In town, *Swansea-Kenmore Caravan Park* (☎ 6257 8148) isn't so well positioned but has good facilities. Tent sites are $13, powered sites $16, on-site vans $35 and cabins $61 a double. Both have playgrounds and barbecue areas.

**Hostels** The *Swansea Youth Hostel* (☎ 6257 8367, 5 Franklin St) is in the centre of town right by the sea and charges $13 a night.

## Places to Stay – Mid-Range

**Hotels & Motels** Right on the beach is *The Swan Inn* (☎ 6257 8899, 1 Franklin St), with budget motel rooms for $50 a double.

Next door, the two storey *Swansea Motor Inn* (☎ 6257 8102) has dated rooms with water views from $60 a single and double. *Amos House & Swansea Ocean Villas* (☎ 6257 8656, 3 Maria St) has small but pleasant motel rooms above a restaurant close to the beach for $89 a double.

**B&Bs** Swansea is a great place for high-standard B&Bs. For a little seaside sophistication in the centre of town, try *Freycinet Waters Beachside Cottage* (☎ 6257 8080, 16 Franklin St), across the road from the beach. Once the post office and post master's residence, it has a nautical colour scheme and a simplicity of décor that is a pleasant change from the frills and flowers favoured by so many B&Bs. Rooms have water views and *en suites*, and are $65/80 with a cooked breakfast.

The large 1836 *Oyster Bay Guesthouse* (☎ 6257 8110), almost opposite the youth hostel on Franklin St, is a friendly, colonial-style place with rooms with *en suite* for $55/95 with a cooked breakfast.

*Braeside* (☎ 6257 8008, 21 Julia St), south of the centre, has two lovely rooms with *en suite* and a cooked breakfast for $75/95. Retired hosts Ronnie and Hetty (from 'somewhere near Glasgow') have a dry sense of humour. When they learnt the price of the dry-stone wall they'd had constructed around the guests' swimming pool, the structure immediately became known as Ronnie's Indiscretion. (Ronnie is equally proud of another aptly named garden feature, but you'll have to ask Hetty for details of that one.)

## Places to Stay – Top End

**B&Bs** The *Meredith House* (☎ 6257 8119, 15 Noyes St), which is classified by the National Trust, is a charming guesthouse offering B&B for $90/130. It's a short walk uphill from the main street. A home-cooked evening meal featuring local food and wine is available by arrangement.

*Schouten House* (☎ 6257 8564, 1 Waterloo Rd), in the southern part of town, is first and foremost a fine restaurant, but it also has excellent rooms with *en suite* for $96/126 with provisions for a continental breakfast. There are also a couple of great B&Bs outside town. *Redcliffe House* (☎ 6257 8557), 1km north of town beside the Meredith River, has large rooms with *en suite*, private gardens and a hearty breakfast for $112 a double. *Kabuki by the Sea* (☎ 6257 8588), in a fantastic location above some of the best coastline along the Tasman Hwy, is 12km south of Swansea. It has self-contained cabins with continental breakfast for $85/120. A package including dinner at the Japanese restaurant is $100/175.

**Holiday Units & Cottages** Near the water, Amos House and Swansea Ocean Villas (☎ 6257 8328, 43 Franklin St) has attractive self-contained villas for $125 a double.

Next door to Meredith House is *Meredith Mews* (☎ 6257 8119, 15 Noyes St), which

has apartments that are slightly larger than the rooms in the guesthouse for $130 a double with breakfast. They have spas, kitchenettes and small back verandas overlooking gardens.

Nearby, in a quiet lane, is the inviting *Scarecrow Cottage* (☎ 6257 8473, 22 Noyes St), which is available for $125 a double with breakfast provisions supplied. Both Meredith Mews and Scarecrow Cottage are only a short walk uphill from the main street.

Three kilometres south of town, on the Tasman Hwy but in attractive gardens, are a number of cottages, two of which were constructed in the 1860s. For details ring *Wagners Cottage* (☎ 6257 8494). They start at $120 a double with provisions for a cooked breakfast. Nearby is the *Lester Cottages Complex* (☎ 6257 8105, 42 Gordon St), with B&B in cottages or units starting at $100 a double.

*Coombend Cottages* (☎ 6257 8256) is near Freycinet Vineyard, on the Tasman Hwy 28km north of Swansea. It has two self-contained cottages set in rolling farmland close to Great Oyster Bay. The weatherboard George's Cottage is the most appealing of the two. Both are $116 a double with provisions for a cooked breakfast.

The upmarket resort here is *Piermont Resort* (☎ 6257 8131), on the Tasman Hwy. It's 3km south of town and has self-contained stone villas in lovely grounds overlooking the water. Prices start at $160 a double with breakfast provisions.

**Hotels** The *Swansea Waterloo Inn Hotel* (☎ 6257 8577) has motel rooms from $99 to $150 a double.

## Places to Eat

There are several good places in and around the town for afternoon tea and light meals. On Franklin St, *Just Maggies* has coffee, cakes and light lunches in a clean, modern shop. There's a *takeaway* just down the road.

At the Swansea Bark Mill, *Millers' Pantry* serves light lunch, snacks and Devonshire tea in the old Swansea Roller Flour Mill.

The **Swan Inn** has an à la carte restaurant with seafood mains for between $13.50 and $16.50. This and the pleasant **Viewpoint Restaurant**, at Amos House and Swansea Ocean Villas, both have water views and are relaxed enough for children.

The licensed **Shy Albatross Restaurant** (☎ 6257 8110), in the Oyster Bay Guesthouse, has an Italian and seafood menu and an extensive selection of fine Tasmanian wines in a casual and relaxed atmosphere. You can also get breakfast here from 8 to 10 am.

Schouten House has a highly regarded licensed restaurant named **Fidler's** (☎ 6257 8564) that specialises in seafood and game. It's open for dinner daily (book by 6 pm) and for lunch by appointment. It has an inviting cocktail bar and an excellent wine list.

**Kabuki by the Sea** (☎ 6257 8588), 12km south of Swansea, has a unique Japanese-style, fully licensed restaurant open daily for lunch and morning and afternoon tea. From December to April it's open for dinner from Tuesday to Saturday, and for the rest of the year Friday and Saturday only. Local wine is available by the glass.

**Kate's Berry Farm**, 3km south of Swansea, is open daily from 9 am to 6 pm for tastings and sales of its berries, jams, sauces, ice cream and wine.

### Getting There & Away
**Bus** See the introductory Getting There & Around section at the start of this chapter. All coaches arrive at and depart from the Swansea Corner Store. The TWT fare to/from Hobart is $16.50. The TRC fare to Hobart is $26.40.

**Bicycle** See the Bicycle section of Getting There & Around at the start of this chapter.

### COLES BAY & FREYCINET NATIONAL PARK
The township of Coles Bay is both dominated and sheltered by the spectacular 300m-high red granite mountains known as The Hazards. These mark the start of the beautiful Freycinet National Park, noted for its magnificent scenery, fine weather, coastal heaths, orchids and other wildflowers. The local fauna includes black cockatoos, yellow wattlebirds, yellow-throated honeyeaters and Bennett's wallabies, which will steal the food right out of your hands if you're not careful.

### History
The Oyster Bay tribe of Aborigines lived here as hunters and gatherers. The Freycinet area was important to them, because in winter they could live off the abundant shellfish. The large shell middens along Richardsons Beach are one of the few visible signs of Aboriginal occupation.

The first European to visit this area was Abel Tasman in 1642; he named Schouten Island, but also mistook Freycinet for an island. Later, in 1802, a French expedition

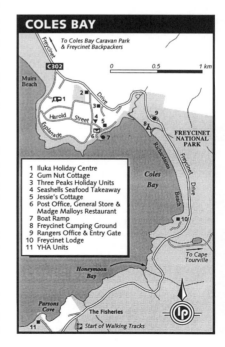

**COLES BAY**

To Coles Bay Caravan Park & Freycinet Backpackers

0    0.5    1 km

Muirs Beach

Harold Street

Esplanade

FREYCINET NATIONAL PARK

Coles Bay

Richardsons Beach

Freycinet Drive

1 Iluka Holiday Centre
2 Gum Nut Cottage
3 Three Peaks Holiday Units
4 Seashells Seafood Takeaway
5 Jessie's Cottage
6 Post Office, General Store & Madge Malloys Restaurant
7 Boat Ramp
8 Freycinet Camping Ground
9 Rangers Office & Entry Gate
10 Freycinet Lodge
11 YHA Units

To Cape Tourville

Honeymoon Bay

Parsons Cove

The Fisheries

Start of Walking Tracks

discovered that Freycinet was a peninsula and named it and many other features. When other expeditions noted the number of seals in the vicinity, sealers arrived from Sydney and quickly wiped out most of them. Some of these sealers stole Aboriginal women from their communities, and by the time European settlers arrived, the Aboriginal population had already decreased severely.

In 1824 a whaling station was established at Parsons Cove. By the 1840s the whales had been wiped out and the station had closed. The town of Coles Bay was named after Silas Cole, who came here in the 1830s and burnt some of the midden shells to produce lime. Mortar made from this lime was used in the construction of many of Swansea's older buildings.

Schouten Island was mined for coal from 1840 to 1880 and for tin in the 1870s. Both Freycinet and Schouten Island were also used for farming. In 1906 both areas were declared game reserves to stop the over-hunting of animals. In 1916 Freycinet shared honours with Mt Field to become Tasmania's first national park; Schouten Island was added much later, in 1977. To complete protection of the coastal regions, the Friendly Beaches were added to the national park in 1992.

### Information
The township of Coles Bay is 31km off the Tasman Hwy on a sealed side road and has reasonable amenities for visitors. It is the gateway to the many white-sand beaches, secluded coves, rocky cliffs and excellent bushwalks on the Freycinet Peninsula.

At the time of writing it was intended that a visitors' information and interpretation centre would be constructed near the ranger station in the national park by 2000. Until the centre opens, visitors' information will be available at the post office and at the supermarket at Iluka.

The town has a post office and general store open daily. It sells groceries and other basic supplies. The Iluka Holiday Centre has its own mini-supermarket with takeaway food and it also sells petrol.

### Friendly Beaches
The signposted turn-off to the Friendly Beaches is 22km north of Coles Bay. From the car park at Isaacs Point, a five minute walk leads to a vantage point from which there are uninterrupted views of the expanse of white sand and blue water. If you are here in autumn and have plenty of money, you might consider spending four days at Freycinet Experience's *Friendly Beaches Lodge* (☎ toll-free 1800 506 003). Accommodation, food, wine, boat trips and transport from Hobart are provided for around $1000 a person.

### Cape Tourville Lighthouse
The best short drive is to follow the 6km road out to Cape Tourville Lighthouse. The road enters the park (and national park fees apply) and is in reasonable condition, but care must be taken in places. The extensive views along the coastline make the trip worthwhile.

### Fishing
The shores of Great Oyster Bay offer excellent fishing: charter a boat or hire a dinghy and go out to catch your meal yourself.

From March to May, Coles Bay is a great base for big game fishing, especially when the giant bluefin tuna run, and Freycinet Sea Charters (☎ 6257 0355) can take you to some of the best spots. The bay is also famous for crayfish, but unless you go diving you will find it easier simply to buy one from the local boats.

### Water Sports & Cruises
Coles Bay is at the head of a large, sheltered bay where you can swim, windsurf and water-ski in safe ocean waters. This is a great place to learn these activities.

Freycinet Sea Charters (☎ 6257 0355) offers half-day/full day scenic and marine wildlife cruises for $60/100 a person. In addition to viewing the wonderful scenery, you may see dolphins, seals, sea eagles, albatrosses, penguins (in flat conditions) and/or whales (in winter).

Kayaking is superb in this area. Coastal Kayaks (☎ 6239 1080) has half-day/full-day tours for $60/105 that leave from Coles Bay and a limited number of three-day packages that leave from Hobart for $540.

## Rock Climbing & Abseiling

The Freycinet Peninsula is regarded as one of the best rock climbing and abseiling spots in Australia. The tempting granite peaks of **The Hazards**, as well as other cliffs in the area, attract both experienced climbers and novices. Rafting Tasmania/ Coastal Kayaks (☎ 6239 1080) caters for both, offering $70 half-day expeditions, with all equipment and transport from Coles Bay provided.

## Bushwalking

Roads only penetrate a small way into the park and the only way to visit the many features is to walk. Well-used tracks lead to the best features.

One of the most beautiful walks in the entire state is to **Wineglass Bay**, which takes from 2½ to three hours return. If that's too far, you can walk along the same track only as far as the **Wineglass Bay Lookout**, which has wonderful views and is only one hour return. Another superb walk, if you're fit, is to the summit of **Mt Amos**, from which the views are spectacular. It takes about three hours return along a marked track. Instead of driving, you can follow the shore from Coles Bay to Honeymoon Bay to the main walking tracks; this takes about 1½ hours each way.

There are also plenty of shorter walks. **Sleepy Bay**, just off the Cape Tourville Road, is well worth a visit. The lookout on top of the hill in Coles Bay is also good.

For any walk in the national park, remember to sign in (and out) at the registration booth at the car park. A current Tasmanian National Parks permit is also required. For more information contact the ranger's office (☎ 6257 0107).

The Freycinet Peninsula also has some excellent overnight walking. Bush camping is allowed south of The Hazards. The scenery at the free camp sites of Wineglass Bay (one to 1½ hours), Hazards Beach (two

to three hours) and Cooks Beach (about 4½ hours) is well worth the walk.

If you are here in summer and would prefer a guided luxury walk, you could try Freycinet Experience's Walk Freycinet, a four day walk along the peninsula including a boat trip to Shouten Island, accommodation in standing tents, meals and wine for around $1000 from Hobart.

Alternatively, guide yourself around the peninsula by following the 27km circuit described in Lonely Planet's *Bushwalking in Australia* by John & Monica Chapman.

At the time of writing, a toilet block was being constructed at the walking track's car park.

**Warning** There's no permanent drinking water at any of the free camp sites. There is a water tank at Cooks Beach, but this can run dry. As a result, you should be prepared to carry your own water, and you should also remember that occasionally in late summer you might not be able to get supplies from anywhere on the peninsula.

## Other Activities

If you wish to go cycling, you can hire a bike at the post office for $10/$15 for a half-day/full day. Freycinet Four Wheelers (☎ 6257 0111) gives one/two hour four-wheel motorbike guided tours (driving licence essential) for $30/50. And scenic flights over the area are available from $49 from Belarine Aviation (☎ 6375 1694).

## Places to Stay – Budget

Inside the national park is *Freycinet Camping Ground (☎ 6257 0107)*, a series of tent sites in the dunes behind Richardsons Beach. Bookings can be made at the ranger's office. Tent sites are $10 for two ($12.50 a family) and powered sites $12 ($15 a family). Amenities are very basic – pit toilets and cold water (no showers) – but at the time of writing, the camping ground was under review: it is possible that by the time you read this it will have been shifted or upgraded. A national park permit is required if you wish to camp here. Children will love the often overly friendly native animals; you will need to lock all food away, as the possums will break into tents and packs to get a feed. If you want to feed the animals, don't give them bread, as this brings on a disease called 'lumpy jaw'. Ask the ranger what food is suitable.

Farther north, at the Friendly Beaches, are two extremely basic camping areas. These have pit toilets and no fresh water. This camping site was also under review at the time of writing, and it was hoped that the toilets would be improved. Bring your own water if you're staying here. While there are no camping fees, national park entry fees apply.

In town the only place to put up your tent is *Iluka Holiday Centre (☎ 6257 0115)*, above the eastern end of Muir's Beach. Tent sites are $12 a double, powered sites $14 a double. It also has a new YHA hostel, with beds for $13.

*Coles Bay Caravan Park (☎ 6257 0100)* is 3km out of town, at the western end of Muir's Beach. A tent site costs $11 a double and on-site vans are $30. A free bus ticket to the walking tracks is provided. On the same site is *Freycinet Backpackers*, with bunks for $14 for the first night and $10 a night thereafter.

In addition to the hostel at Iluka, there are two very basic *YHA units* at Parsons Cove. They're in a wonderful spot, overlooking a beach, but have no running hot water and only pit toilets. Bookings are essential and must be made in advance at the YHA state office in Hobart (☎ 6234 9617).

## Places to Stay – Mid-Range
Iluka Holiday Centre (☎ 6257 0115) has both some cheap older accommodation that's a bit rough around the edges and some newer, more attractive options. Its wide variety of on-site vans, cabins and units are priced from $35 to $85 a double. Linen is $5 extra.

*Three Peaks Holiday Units (☎ 6257 0333)* charges $90 a double, while *Gum Nut Cottage (☎ 6257 0109)* is $80 a double. On the Esplanade, *Jessie's Cottage (☎ 6257 0143)* is $100 a double for a one bedroom unit, $120 for a two bedroom unit.

On the road into Coles Bay, and 10 minutes drive from the town, is *Churinga Holiday Cottages (☎ 6257 0190)*, where you can stay in spacious self-contained cabins in an open, bushy setting for $80 a double.

## Places to Stay – Top End
*Freycinet Lodge (☎ 6257 0101)* is at the southern end of Richardsons Beach and has magnificent views over the bay and The Hazards. There is a variety of cabins, some suitable for wheelchairs, some with spas and others with kitchens. Rates range from $155 to $200 a double per night if you stay two nights or more. The price is rather high for the standard of accommodation offered, but you are paying for the location. Meals are available.

*Cottages by the Sea (☎ 6257 0102)* is a resort just north of Coles Bay on good swimming beaches and with views of The Hazards. It has bicycles, tennis courts and a children's playground; doubles are $160.

## Places to Eat
*Madge Malloy's (☎ 6257 0399, 3 Garnet Ave)* licensed restaurant/café, open from 6 pm Tuesday to Saturday, specialises in freshly caught seafood. It's next door to the general store, which does takeaway. *Seashells Seafood Takeaway* across the road has fish and chips, oysters, crayfish rolls etc.

More expensive is the *Freycinet Licensed Restaurant* at Freycinet Lodge. The views from the restaurant and the à la carte seafood and steak make it an ideal place to eat if you want to splash out. For a cheaper option, try the bistro here, which shares the great views.

Back in Coles Bay, the *Iluka Tavern* has counter lunches and dinners daily and gives YHA members a 10% discount.

## Getting There & Away
**Bus** See the introductory Getting There & Around section at the start of this chapter. Bicheno Coach Services runs the school bus

service from Coles Bay to Bicheno and this has evolved into a handy bus service. From June to October there are up to three services on weekdays, up to two on Saturday and one on Sunday. From November to May extra services are scheduled but only run if needed.

Some services only run if bookings exist and it is wise to book ahead at least the night before. The fare each way is $5 ($6 to the walking track's car park). Pick-ups can be made from accommodation if requested. In Bicheno, buses depart from the Bicheno Take-Away and Caravan Park on Burgess St; in Coles Bay they leave from the general store.

It's more than 5km from the town to the national park walking track's car park, and Bicheno Coach Services has a weekday shuttle bus running two or three times daily from Monday to Saturday if required. Bookings are advised and the cost is $2 one way, $3 return. Park entry fees apply.

**Bicycle** See Bicycle in the introductory Getting There & Around section at the start of this chapter.

## BICHENO
• pop 750

This town has everything a holiday resort needs: the scenery is picturesque, the climate mild and the sunshine abundant. Fishing is one of the mainstays of the community, and the fleet shelters in a tiny, picturesque harbour called The Gulch. With reasonable prices for food and accommodation, it's a great place to stay for a few days.

### History

The town began as a sealers' port and was called Waubs Bay Harbour after an Aboriginal woman, Waubedebar, who was enslaved by sealers as a wife and servant in the early 19th century. A strong swimmer, she later became famous for rescuing two sealers when their boat was wrecked 1km offshore. Years after her death, the town honoured her by constructing a grave, which you can still visit.

In 1854 the town became a coal mining port but in 1855 most of the miners left and joined the gold rush in Victoria. The town shrank and almost vanished, which is why so few historic buildings remain. Around the 1940s, the town's fortune changed as it began to develop into the holiday destination it is today.

### Information

Staff at the Visitors' Information Centre (VIC, ☎ 6375 1333), on the Tasman Hwy, are enthusiastic and knowledgeable and can book most organised activities. The centre is open from 9.30 am to 5.30 pm daily except in June and July, when it's only open from 1 pm. Internet access is available at the library.

### Wildlife Centres

The small **Sea Life Centre**, on the Tasman Hwy and Waubs Bay, is open daily from 9 am to 5 pm and features Tasmanian marine life swimming behind glass windows. There's also a restored trading ketch. Admission is $4.50. Seven kilometres north of town is the 32 hectare **East Coast Birdlife & Animal Park**, which is open daily from 9 am to 5 pm; admission is $7.50 for adults and $4 for children.

### Walks

The best walk follows the **Foreshore Footway**, constructed as part of the Bicentennial celebrations of 1988. It's 3km long and goes from one end of town to the other. The most interesting section extends from the Sea Life Centre east to **Peggys Point**. This takes you through The Gulch and along to the **Blowhole**, where there's a large granite boulder that is rocked by the sea. You return along footpaths with panoramic views over the town. In whaling days, passing whales were spotted from **Whalers Hill**, which can still be climbed today.

### Fishing

**The Gulch** is an interesting place. Although it's simply a channel behind a low rocky island, it provides a sheltered anchorage for the fishing fleet. When the boats return they will often sell fresh crayfish, abalone, oysters etc directly to the public. Alternatively, you can do the fishing yourself: three hours on a sharkcat costs $75 – book at the VIC.

## Water Sports

Bicheno is great for all sorts of water sports. Waubs Beach and Rice Beach are fairly safe ocean beaches for swimming. For warmer water, the sheltered and shallow Denison River beside the highway 8km north of town is popular. When the surf's up, Redbill Point has good surfing breaks. Body boards can be hired at the VIC for $12 a day. Water-skiing is also popular.

The **Bicheno Dive Centre** (☎ 6375 1138, 2 Scuba Court), up a lane opposite the Sea Life Centre, runs courses more reasonably priced than those in warmer waters on the mainland, and you can also hire or buy diving equipment from its shop. Scuba tank fills are $6 per tank and diving charges are $24 per boat dive. Diving trips leave twice daily during summer.

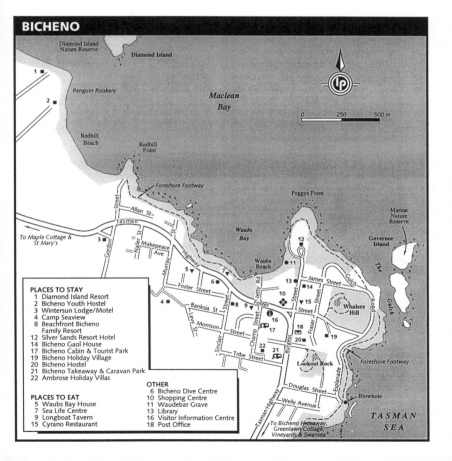

**BICHENO**

PLACES TO STAY
1 Diamond Island Resort
2 Bicheno Youth Hostel
3 Wintersun Lodge/Motel
4 Camp Seaview
8 Beachfront Bicheno Family Resort
12 Silver Sands Resort Hotel
14 Bicheno Gaol House
17 Bicheno Cabin & Tourist Park
19 Bicheno Holiday Village
20 Bicheno Hostel
21 Bicheno Takeaway & Caravan Park
22 Ambrose Holiday Villas

PLACES TO EAT
5 Waubs Bay House
7 Sea Life Centre
9 Longboat Tavern
15 Cyrano Restaurant

OTHER
6 Bicheno Dive Centre
10 Shopping Centre
11 Waudebar Grave
13 Library
16 Visitor Information Centre
18 Post Office

## Cycling

You can hire a mountain bike for $15/20 half-day/full day – inquire at the VIC.

## Wine Tasting

See the earlier Swansea section of this chapter for details of vineyards south of Bicheno.

## Organised Tours

Guided tours of the nearby **Oyster Farm** (☎ 6257 0140) are run on demand around 4 pm daily. Tours include a barge trip to the cages and oyster tastings. Book with Bicheno Coach Services or at the VIC.

Guided penguin tours to local rookeries depart from the VIC every evening and cost $12 a person. The centre also arranges one-hour glass bottom boat tours of Bicheno's marine park and The Gulch for $12 a person.

Historic coach tours of the town depart daily and cost $25 a person. Once again, inquire at the VIC.

## Places to Stay – Budget

**Caravan Parks & Hostels** The *Bicheno Takeaway & Caravan Park* (☎ 6375 1280), on the corner of Tasman Hwy and Tribe St, has tent sites for $8, powered sites for $10 and on-site vans for $28 a double. More central and attractive is the *Bicheno Cabin & Tourist Park* (☎ 6375 1117), on Champ St. Tent sites are $12, powered sites $14, on-site vans $40 and cabins $60 a double. This is also the *Waubs Harbour Backpackers*, where beds in a small, new hostel with limited communal space are $14 ($10 key deposit).

The most popular hostel seems to be *Bicheno Hostel* (☎ 6375 1651), on Morrison St, in a short but steep street close to town. It's clean, cosy and has some lock-up storage space. Rates are $13 per person.

Three kilometres north of town, beside the beach opposite Diamond Island, is the YHA *Bicheno Youth Hostel* (☎ 6375 1293). It's a pretty spot but the hostel itself is looking its age and provides only basic accommodation. It charges $11 and is often booked out in summer. In a bushland setting on the edge of town, *Camp Seaview*

(☎ 6375 1247), on Banksia St, has hostel accommodation for $12 per person. With bunks for 80 people, a bed is often available here when the smaller hostels are filled. However, it is popular with schools, so if you are booking in advance, ask whether there will be any large groups visiting during the time you are planning to stay.

**Hotels** The *Silver Sands Resort Hotel* (☎ 6375 1266), on Burgess St, will sometimes provide budget accommodation if you ask for it specifically.

## Places to Stay – Mid-Range

**Holiday Units & Cottages** The *Ambrose Holiday Villas* (☎ 6375 1288), on the corner of Tribe and Champ Sts, which is tucked in behind the caravan parks, has doubles for $80. More secluded and tranquil is *Bicheno Hideaway* (☎ 6375 1312), 3km south of town and down a side road. It has three arc-shaped holiday units with great ocean views. The hosts speak six European languages and rates are $80 a double.

**Hotels & Motels** Silver Sands Resort Hotel (☎ 6375 1266), on Burgess St, has the best position, right beside the water. Rooms are reasonable and range from $70 to $95. *Beachfront Bicheno Family Resort* (☎ 6375 1111), beside the highway in town, is poorly named. It's a motel, not really a resort, and it's not right on the beachfront. Prices range from $85 to $95 a double, and some rooms have good views of the ocean.

## Places to Stay – Top End

**Holiday Units & Cottages** The *Bicheno Gaol House* (☎ 6375 1430), on Burgess St, is the town's oldest building (1845) and offers colonial accommodation for $115 a double with provisions for a cooked breakfast. In town and set in bushland between the two lookout hills is *Bicheno Holiday Village* (☎ 6375 1171), which is surprisingly hidden for such a large development. The A-frame holiday units are about the same standard as most other places in town but the green, leafy grounds set them apart. Doubles are $128.

*Maple Cottage* (☎/fax 6375 1172, 160 Tasman Hwy) is west of the centre in lovely suburban gardens opposite the water. The cottage, which is separate from the main house, is $105 a double with provisions for a cooked breakfast.

*Greenlawn Cottage*, 7km south of Bicheno, is signposted off the highway. This attractive cottage is separate from the main house and set amid trees and gardens on a working farm. B&B is $116 a double.

**Resorts** Out near the Youth Hostel, *Diamond Island Resort* (☎ 6375 1161, toll-free 1800 030 299) is a series of two-storey, self-contained, Tudor-style units priced from $80 to $140 a double.

### Places to Eat

There are *coffee shops* and *takeaways* in the main shopping centre.

For lunch or dinner you can try the *Sea Life Centre* on the foreshore in town. Nearby *Waubs Bay House* has fresh seafood meals. It has a bargain speciality on Wednesday nights of a two/three course roast dinner for $10/12.

The *Longboat Tavern*, beside the highway in the centre of town, has very good, reasonably priced counter meals. The *Silver Sands Resort Hotel* at the northern end of Burgess St also has counter meals. For a char grill visit the *Bicheno Holiday Village*. For à la carte, try *Cyrano Restaurant* or the *Diamond Island Resort*.

### Getting There & Away

See the introductory Getting There & Around section at the start of this chapter. TWT coaches arrive at and depart from the Bicheno Four Square Store on Burgess St and the fare is $20.30 to Hobart and $19 to Launceston. TRC coaches arrive at and depart from the Bicheno General Store on Forster St. The TRC fare to Launceston is $21.60, while to Hobart it's $31.50. Bicheno Coach Service buses to Coles Bay arrive at and depart from the Bicheno General Store; see Getting There

& Away in the earlier Coles Bay & Freycinet Peninsula section for details.

## DOUGLAS APSLEY NATIONAL PARK

This is a large area of undisturbed dry forest typical of much of the original land cover of the east coast. It was declared a national park in 1989 after much public concern over wood chipping and the large-scale clearing of the remaining original forests. The southern end was donated by Arthur Jones. In addition to the forests, major features include rocky peaks, river gorges and beautiful waterfalls. As it has only been a park for a short while, there has been little development and this is one of its appealing features.

Access to the park is by quiet gravel roads. To reach the southern end, the **Apsley Waterhole**, turn left off the highway 5km north of Bicheno and follow the signposted road for 7km to the car park. A basic camping ground with a pit toilet is provided. The nearby waterhole provides excellent swimming. To access the northern end, at **Thompsons Marches**, turn left off the highway 24km north of Bicheno onto E Rd. This is a private road, so obey any signs as you follow it to the car park and boom gate beside the park border. There are no suitable places to camp near the car park. As with all other parks, entry fees apply. Open fires are not permitted in this park from October to April, when cooking is only allowed on fuel stoves.

### Bushwalking

As with most national parks the only way to see anything is to walk. At **Apsley Waterhole** a wheelchair-standard track of five minutes leads to the lookout, which has a great view over the river. A walk of two to three hours return leads to **Apsley Gorge**.

At the northern end, the best walk is to **Heritage Falls**, which takes four to six hours return. There is a good bush camping ground near the falls.

The major walk in the park is the **Leeaberra Track**, which takes three days; you are requested to walk from north to south to prevent further spreading of a plant disease. Full track notes are available in the third edition of Lonely Planet's *Bushwalking in Australia* by John & Monica Chapman.

## ST MARYS
• **pop 630**

St Marys is a charming little town 10km inland from the coast, near the Mt Nicholas range. There's not much to do there except enjoy the peacefulness of the countryside, visit a number of waterfalls, and take walks in the state forest.

There are some rocky hills surrounding the town that provide fine views and are well worth climbing. The **South Sister** towers over the road leading to Seaview Farm. It's only a 10 minute walk from the car park to the top. East of the town, **St Patricks Head** is a longer climb of three hours return. Cables and a ladder add some excitement to the climb.

### Places to Stay & Eat

The superbly positioned *Seaview Farm* (☎ *6372 2341*), on a working cattle farm surrounded by state forest, is 8km from St Marys on Germantown Rd, and commands magnificent views of the coast, ocean and mountains. It costs $13.50 a night for a bunk in the cottage, $35 a double for a room with *en suite*.

Accommodation is also available in the *St Marys Hotel* (☎ *6372 2181*), where rooms are $25/40 for B&B. The pub also has counter dinners on Friday, Saturday and Sunday. There's a *takeaway* on the main street, and also a *bakery/coffee shop* open daily, except in the low season, when it's closed on Saturday.

To the south, beside the highway to Bicheno in Elephant Pass, is the famous *Mt Elephant Pancake Barn* with splendid views and delicious pancakes of all varieties. The sign out the front of the shop says it all: 'Good food – fresh coffee. Relax. No Arts, No Crafts, No Souvenirs.' The barn is open every day from 8 am to 6 pm. See the boxed text in this section for more information.

## Mt Elephant Pancake Barn

There's something of the British Raj about the Mt Elephant Pancake Barn: set high up Elephant Pass, amid lush forest and overlooking Tasmania's gorgeous east coast, it needs only sweltering heat and drenching humidity to complete the illusion. Or perhaps there is no illusion but merely a hint of the exotic, suggested by an abundance of timber, an evocative name and a couple of amazing chairs with massive carved elephants' heads protruding from their backs. They're not toys, but they'll fascinate kids who are prepared to look and not touch. Whatever its mystique, the barn is the perfect place to pull over for a snack between St Marys and Bicheno. It seems to be in the middle of nowhere, yet it has good coffee, pancakes of every description and sweeping views. And the best part is, it's open long hours every day.

### Getting There & Away

See the introductory Getting There & Around section at the start of this chapter for details of these services from Hobart and Launceston that run via St Marys. The TRC fare from Launceston to St Marys is $15.50, from Hobart $29.40. Broadby's (☎ 6376 3488) runs a service from St Helens to St Marys return on weekdays. Buses depart from the BP service station in St Helens at around 7.45 am and return from the post office in St Marys at 9 am; the fare is $3 each way.

**Warning** Cyclists travelling on Elephant Pass should take extreme care. The road is steep, narrow and winding, and it's difficult for vehicles – particularly trucks – to negotiate their way around bicycles.

## FINGAL
• **pop 430**

This inland town 21km west of St Marys is near the site of the state's first worthwhile gold strike in 1852. It has seen boom and bust times and today is a peaceful settlement serving the local community. For visitors its main attraction is the annual Coal Shovelling Championships held in early March. This one day event attracts many spectators.

The surrounding valley contains several abandoned towns from the mining era. Mangana, Rossarden and Storys Creek display piles of tailings, mine machinery and tiny cottages that are rarely used. If these sights are too depressing then visit the **Evercreech Forest Reserve** to the north near Mathinna. A 20 minute circuit walk takes you to the White Knights, the highest white gums in the world, which reach 89m. Evercreech Falls are also worth walking to, taking about one hour return.

The *Fingal Hotel* (☎ *6374 2121)* has rooms for $30/40 and also serves counter meals. Unfortunately, the once impressive collection of Scotch whisky bottles has been sold.

### Getting There & Away

See the introductory Getting There & Around section at the start of this chapter for details. The fare from Launceston is $13.20, from Hobart $26.40.

# The North-East

It is remarkable that the north-east receives so little attention from visitors: it is conveniently and seductively close to the wines and restaurants of the Pipers Brook and Pipers River vineyards, yet it boasts some of the most secluded and magnificent white-sand beaches in the state. Encompassing the pretty seaside town of St Helens, Mt William National Park and Eddystone Point, the historic mining town of Derby, the truly grand St Columba Falls, and a couple of hostels on working farms with views that will take your breath away, the appeal of north-eastern Tasmania may well endure beyond that of many of the more popular tourist destinations you visit in your journey around the state.

The area is often overlooked because it is bypassed by the usual route from Launceston to the east coast, which takes you along the A4 as far as the tiny town of St Marys, before heading south-east to Chain of Lagoons and Bicheno. Instead, take the Tasman Hwy (A3) to Scottsdale and branch out from there: north to the holiday town of Bridport, from which you can head west to the vineyards (see the Tamar Valley section of the North chapter) or east to the coastal Waterhouse Protected Area and Tomahawk; east to Derby then north and north-east to the national park, Ansons Bay and the Bay of Fires; or east and south-east to the waterfalls around Ringarooma and Pyengana, then on to St Helens. If you have your own transport, you will have no trouble devising loops to take in all these attractions in comfortable day trips from most accommodation centres in the region.

## Getting There & Around

**Bus** Tasmanian Redline Coaches (TRC, ☎ 1300 360 000) runs buses from Launceston to Conara Junction, then through Fingal ($13.20) and St Marys ($15.50) to St Helens ($19.20). It also runs a bus to Scottsdale ($9.30), Derby ($13) and Winnaleah, where

## HIGHLIGHTS

- Snorkelling in the Bay of Fires
- Sweeping arcs of white sand and aqua water
- St Columba Falls and the Pub in the Paddock
- Trying to sink rival rafts in the Derby River Derby
- Blue Lake and Cube Rock

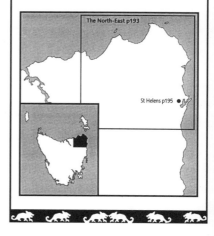

The North-East p193

St Helens p195

you can catch the Suncoast bus to St Helens (see later in this section).

TRC fares from Hobart are: Fingal ($26.40), St Marys ($29.40) and St Helens ($31.70).

Broadby's (☎ 6376 3488) runs a service from St Helens to St Marys and back from Monday to Friday. It departs from the BP service station in St Helens at 7.45 am and leaves the post office in St Marys at 9 am; the fare is $3 each way. The same company also runs a bus from St Helens through Derby and Winnaleah and back to St Helens. This service connects with TRC's

The Hazards and wild flowers, Swanick

RICHARD I'ANSON

Devils in love

JON MURRAY

Old Mill, Campbell Town

GLENN BEANLAND

Spikey Bridge was built by convicts in 1843

CHRIS MELLOR

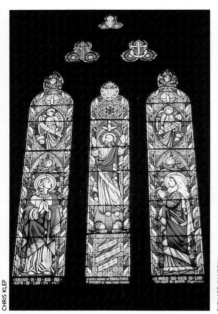

CHRIS KLEP

Stained glass at Ross Uniting Church

RICHARD l'ANSON

Sleepy Bay near Coles Bay

CHRIS KLEP

Darlington, Maria Island National Park

north-east service at Winnaleah. It departs from the post office in St Helens from Monday to Friday at 10.45 am, leaves Derby at 12.45 pm and leaves Winnaleah at 1 pm. The fare is $5 one way to/from either Derby or Winnaleah.

Tasmanian Wilderness Travel (TWT, ☎ 6334 4442) has a service from Hobart to St Helens via the east coast on Wednesday, Friday and Sunday, and also on Monday from early December to early April. The fare is $29.40.

**Bicycle** The Tasman Hwy is a winding narrow road that crosses two major passes as it heads west through Weldborough and Scottsdale. Cyclists need to be vigilant on this road because it can be dangerous. One alternative is to follow the rough unsealed roads around the coast. There is little traffic and you have fewer hills to climb. However, you'll need to carry a tent because there is no accommodation around the coast between St Helens and Bridport; camping areas exist at both ends of Mt

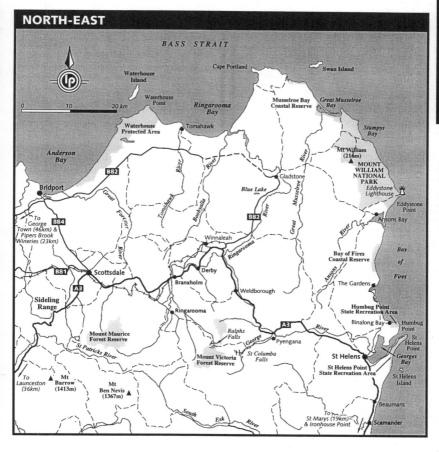

William National Park and at Tomahawk on the route from St Helens to Bridport.

**Organised Tours** North-East Adventure Tours (☎ 6353 2340) has day and half-day 4WD tours of many of the region's sights and will pick up within a 50km radius of Ringarooma (near Scottsdale).

## IRONHOUSE POINT

The road following the coast from Chain of Lagoons (north of Bicheno) to Falmouth then Scamander passes through some excellent coastal scenery. It also avoids the slow climb over the two passes to St Marys. Much of the coastline is rocky and the best place to stop along it is at Ironhouse Point and **Four Mile Creek**, where the beaches begin. Ironhouse Point is named after the first house in the region to have an iron roof.

The *Cray Drop-In Village* (☎ 6372 2228) is near the Point and has holiday units for $50 to $65 a double. There are 27 units in all so it caters for large groups. There is a licensed restaurant and bar in the village.

## SCAMANDER & BEAUMARIS

• **pop 407**

Scamander and Beaumaris townships are stretched along some lovely white-sand beaches in a coastal reserve. No more than a collection of buildings that almost merge, these holiday towns lack even a fishing port, but you can take long walks along the beach, take a $12 one to two hour scenic cruise with Scamander River Cruises (☎ 6372 5297), fish for bream from the old bridge over the Scamander River or try your luck at catching trout farther upstream. The wide ocean beach in front of both towns is excellent for swimming, while water-skiing is good on the lagoons north of Beaumaris.

For a fine view of the St Helens area and the coast around Scamander, a 5km drive from Beaumaris along gravel Forestry roads takes you to a fairly steep five minute walk to the **Skyline Tier Scenic Lookout**. The drive is attractive on a sunny day, and the view from the lookout is great.

## Places to Stay & Eat

The *Kookaburra Caravan and Camping Ground* (☎ 6372 5121), 1.5km north of the river, has camp sites for $5 a person and on-site vans for $28. It's only a short walk to the beach.

About 500m from the ocean, on Pringle St, are the neat but dated *Carramar Holiday Units* (☎ 6372 5160), which are $65 a double. Up on the hill on the northern side of the river, *Blue Seas* (☎ 6372 5211) has fine views and offers self-contained units for $75 a double. *Pelican Sands* (☎ 6372 5231, toll-free 1800 816 561), on the other side of the highway and beside the river, charges $55/75 a single/double. The units are very plain but have the advantage of being right on the beach. It also has fishing rods for hire.

Dominating the river foreshore is the *Scamander Beach Resort Hotel* (☎ 6372 5255). This three storey building is a bit of an eyesore, but has marvellous views. Rooms are $50 to $75 a double, depending on which floor they are on, and bar meals are available.

For something more upmarket try *Bensons* (☎ 6372 5587) in Beaumaris. This modern two storey house has sweeping views and elegant décor. B&B is $120 to $140 a double.

The *Surfside Motor Inn* (☎ 6372 5177), on the outskirts of Beaumaris on the way to St Helens, charges $50/60. It also has a family restaurant that serves lunch and dinner.

## ST HELENS

• **pop 1145**

St Helens, on Georges Bay, was settled in 1830 by sealers and whalers. By the 1850s, farmers had arrived to create a permanent settlement. In 1874 it was discovered that the inland hills were rich in tin and many arrived to try their luck at mining. St Helens, with its sheltered bay, was the port used for shipping tin. When the mines stopped operating, St Helens continued to grow while the mining towns died. Today it is the largest town in the area and Tasmania's largest fishing port, with a big fleet based in the bay.

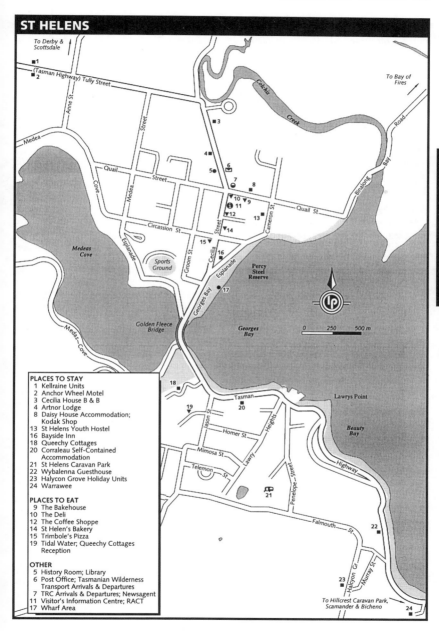

ST HELENS

To Derby &
Scottsdale
(Tasman Highway) Tully Street
To Bay of
Fires
Anne St
Medea
Quail
Street
Cove
Medea
Street
Circassion St
Colchis Creek
Binalong Bay Road
Quail St
Cameron St
Cecilia
Groom St.
Circassion St
Medeas
Cove
Esplanade
Sports
Ground
15
16
Esplanade
Percy
Steel
Reserve
Georges Bay
17
Golden Fleece
Bridge
Medeas Cove
Georges
Bay
0    250    500 m

Lawrys Point

Tasman
Heights
Homer St
Mimosa St.
Jason St
Telemon St.
Lawry
Beauty
Bay
Highway
Penelope Street
Falmouth St
18
19
20
21
22
23
24
Halcyon Gr.
Muray St.
To Hillcrest Caravan Park,
Scamander & Bicheno

PLACES TO STAY
1  Kellraine Units
2  Anchor Wheel Motel
3  Cecilia House B & B
4  Artnor Lodge
8  Daisy House Accommodation;
   Kodak Shop
13 St Helens Youth Hostel
16 Bayside Inn
18 Queechy Cottages
20 Corralleau Self-Contained
   Accommodation
21 St Helens Caravan Park
22 Wybalenna Guesthouse
23 Halcyon Grove Holiday Units
24 Warrawee

PLACES TO EAT
9  The Bakehouse
10 The Deli
12 The Coffee Shoppe
14 St Helen's Bakery
15 Trimbole's Pizza
19 Tidal Water; Queechy Cottages
   Reception

OTHER
5  History Room; Library
6  Post Office; Tasmanian Wilderness
   Transport Arrivals & Departures
7  TRC Arrivals & Departures; Newsagent
11 Visitor's Information Centre; RACT
17 Wharf Area

## Information

The visitors' information centre (☎ 6376 1329) in the Royal Automobile Club of Tasmania (RACT) office on Cecilia St is open from 9 am to 5 pm Monday to Friday, from 10 am to 2 pm Saturday and from noon to 4 pm Sunday in the high season but closed from noon on Saturday and all day Sunday in the low season.

The post office and banks are also on Cecilia St. The Trust and Westpac banks have branches with ATMs, but ANZ only has a branch. EFTPOS facilities are available at petrol stations and supermarkets.

## Things to See & Do

St Helens' interesting and varied history is recorded in the **History Room** (☎ 6376 1744, 59 Cecilia St), adjacent to the town library. It's open weekdays from 9 am to 4 pm and admission is $4 (children $2). It offers tours of Blue Tier that include walks through temperate rainforest and grasslands and take in remnants of tin mining in the region.

Both sides of the wide entrance to Georges Bay have been designated state recreation areas and provide some easy walking. A good track circles around St Helens Point, and takes about one hour return. On the north side, **Skeleton Bay** and **Dora Point** are good places from which to explore the coastline.

While the beaches in town are not particularly good for swimming, there are excellent scenic beaches at **Binalong Bay** (10km north of St Helens) and **Cosy Corner** (12km north of St Helens) and at **Stieglitz** (7km east of St Helens), as well as at St Helens and Humbug points.

Georges Bay, with its flat waters, is excellent for canoeing and windsurfing. Its clear waters are also good for diving. Colin Lester, at Eastlines (☎ 6376 1720), runs diving courses.

Boats can be chartered from Professional Charters (☎ 6376 3083), which provides all gear for reef, game, deep sea and bay fishing. Prices vary considerably according to group numbers and the type of fishing undertaken.

Tuna fishing, for example, is $190 a person per day for a minimum of four people.

For overnight fishing, hire the *Norseman III* (☎ 6424 6900), which is a 53-foot cruiser. It can take a maximum of 6 passengers (12 for day trips) and costs $1200 per day. You need to take your own food.

Among the best attractions of St Helens, however, are the day trips and half-day trips you can take from here: see the Pyengana, Mt William National Park, Bay of Fires and St Marys sections of this chapter.

## Places to Stay – Budget

**Camping & Hostels** The *St Helens Caravan Park* (☎ 6376 1290) is on Penelope St, south of the bridge. It offers no views but is well laid out. Camp sites are $12 a double, on-site vans $20/30 a single/double and cabins $50 to $60 a double. The other caravan park, *Hillcrest Caravan Park* (☎ 6376 3298), has tent sites for $11 and holiday cabins for $50 to $55. It's 7km out of town at Stieglitz on the side road to St Helens Point.

The *St Helens Youth Hostel* (☎ 6376 1661, 5 Cameron St) is in a quiet spot by the water and is close to town. The cost is $13 a night and $15 for nonmembers.

**Motels** The best deal for motel units is *Anchor Wheel Motel* (☎ 6376 1358), which is beside the highway on the western side of town. Here rooms are $40/45.

The St Helens Hotel/Motel on the main street was closed at the time of writing and up for auction.

**Holiday Units** For budget-priced, self-contained units with a kitchen, try the fairly new *Kellraine Units* (☎ 6376 1169) beside the highway on the western side of town. At $35 a double they are a real bargain despite being away from the town and the water.

Behind the Kodak shop on the main street there are also a number of modest-looking, self-contained cottages called *Daisy House Accommodation* (☎ 6376 1371, 0417 392387).

## Places to Stay – Mid-Range

**Motels** The *Bayside Inn* (☎ 6376 1466, 2 Cecilia St) is conveniently located opposite the wharf and charges a reasonable $48/58 for rooms overlooking the water. (It also has more expensive rooms.)

**Holiday Units** On the highway between Jason St and Lawry Heights is *Corraleau Self-Contained Accommodation* (☎ 6376 1363), which has older-style conjoined units with wood heaters for $55 a double.

Good self-contained units with views can be found at *Halcyon Grove Holiday Units* (☎ 6376 1424, 16 Halcyon Grove) and cost $55 a double. Back towards town, *Queechy Cottages* (☎ 6376 1321) has higher standard self-contained units with fine views of Georges Bay, tennis courts and a playground for children for $70/75.

**Guesthouses & B&Bs** The *Artnor Lodge* (☎ 6376 1234) is a guesthouse on the main street charging $35/45 for rooms with shared facilities that are accessed along a covered veranda and $50/65 for rooms with *en suite* (cooked breakfast included). Diagonally opposite is *Cecilia House B&B* (☎ 6376 1723), which provides comfortable rooms with *en suite* and a cooked breakfast for $60/80.

## Places to Stay – Top End

Just south of the bridge and off the highway is the Edwardian *Wybalenna Guesthouse* (☎ 6376 1611). Set in peaceful gardens among tall trees alive with birds, it has water views from the dining room and the veranda and also from the best of the bedrooms. All rooms have *en suites*, and a cooked breakfast is included in the price; singles range from $85 to $110, while doubles range from $95 to $130. Wybalenna does not cater for children under 14.

A bit farther down the highway is *Warrawee* (☎ 6376 1987), a colonial house set in spacious grounds, which has doubles with *en suites* for $95 to $150, including a cooked breakfast. (It also has a self-contained cottage for $75 a double.)

## Places To Eat

**Town** On Quail St, *The Bakehouse* is open seven days a week and sells pastries, bread, cakes and flat white or black coffee. *St Helens Bakery*, on the main street, is also open seven days a week and has pies and cakes you can eat on the premises or takeaway and a cooked breakfast that is a real bargain at $6.

Also on the main street, *The Coffee Shoppe* is an attractive café serving meals, while nearby is *The Deli*, where you can eat in or takeaway from 7.30 am to 7 pm weekdays and from 8 am to 4 pm weekends.

*Trimbole's Pizza*, near the corner of Cecilia and Circassion Sts, has pizza and pasta, and you can get fish and chips in the other takeaways around town.

*The Bayside Inn* serves counter meals seven days a week in a pleasant restaurant overlooking the water. The *Anchor Wheel Motel* has a restaurant that boasts two menus: go there if you want a reasonably cheap night and choose a main course from its $8 family menu. For something special, try *Tidal Water*, the seafood restaurant at Queechy.

**Out of Town** At the time of writing the *St Columba Falls Hotel*, better known as the Pub in the Paddock, was changing hands but was still serving great counter meals, with eight types/styles of vegetable and massive steaks grilled to order. If you are staying in St Helens for a couple of days, consider driving to this hotel for a meal. See the Pyengana section in this chapter for information.

Similarly, even if you won't be driving through St Marys and down Elephant Pass for any other reason, you should do it just so you can enjoy a light lunch at the wonderful *Mt Elephant Pancake Barn*. See the St Marys section in the East Coast chapter for more details.

## Getting There & Away

See the Getting There & Around section at the start of this chapter for details. TWT buses arrive at and depart from Roberts Real Estate, next to the post office on Cecilia St, while TRC buses arrive at and depart from the newsagency on Cecilia St.

Broadby's (☎ 6376 3488) runs a Monday to Friday service from St Helens down to St Marys, back to St Helens then across to Derby and back again. This is a very handy service if you want to travel across the hilly but interesting Tasman Hwy towards Launceston. Broadby's buses depart from the BP service station on Cecilia St. See the Getting There & Around section at the start of this chapter for more details.

## BAY OF FIRES

From St Helens a minor road heads north-east to meet the coast at the start of the Bay of Fires and continues up as far as The Gardens. The northern end of the bay can be reached on the C843, the road to the settlement of Ansons Bay and Mt William National Park. The bay was named by early explorers to describe the number of Aboriginal fires they had seen along the shore. It is a series of sweeping beaches, rocky headlands, heathlands and lagoons. As well as being popular with today's tourists it was also popular with the Aborigines, who left behind high piles of shells (middens). The foreshore, lagoons and heathlands are all part of a coastal reserve. If you are after something very cheap, as well as extremely scenic, then this is a great place to camp for a few days.

The ocean beaches provide some good surfing. The lagoons provide safe swimming; it is not advisable to swim in the ocean, due to the many rips along the beaches.

There are many places along the bay where free *camping* is allowed, although it's pretty basic, with no toilets or fresh water. Just before Ansons Bay is the turn-off to **Policemans Point**, a camping spot in a beautiful location, close to gorgeous beaches. This and Deep Creek (see the Mt William National Park section of this chapter) are among the most attractive free-range camping spots on the north-east coast.

A little farther on, the road crosses the **Ansons River Reserve**. Just before the floodway, on the left as you drive towards Ansons Bay, is a tiny picnic area with a lovely outlook upriver. Ansons River is a charming,

gentle river to paddle along – you can launch your boat at the picnic area.

## PYENGANA & ST COLUMBA FALLS

This small settlement lies in an isolated valley in the hills. It's worth a detour to see the cheese factory, an interesting hotel and one of the state's best waterfalls. The name Pyengana derives from an Aboriginal word that describes the meeting of two rivers in the valley.

Over a hundred years ago, the pioneers of the region recognised that this beautiful green valley was ideal dairy country. However, transporting milk from the isolated valley was impractical. When converted into cheese and butter, the produce survived the slow journey to the markets. Today, Cheddar cheese is still produced using the old methods at **Healey's Pyengana Cheese Factory**. It's open daily for tastings and sales.

Farther down the road is the *St Columba Falls Hotel (☎ 6373 6121)*, which is more generally known as the Pub in the Paddock, an apt description. Originally a house, it has been a hotel for well over a century and has good hotel rooms with new, clean shared facilities for $20/30. At the time of writing, the hotel was changing hands, but the counter lunches and dinners, available daily, were still exceptionally generous: nothing fancy, but plenty of it, and steaks that came the way you asked for them.

The best known feature of the valley is St Columba Falls, 6km past the hotel. At around 90m high, they are believed to be the state's second highest falls. Although you can see them from the road, you get an entirely different and more impressive view from the platform at their base, an easy 10 minute walk from the car park. These falls are as good as, if not better than, Russell Falls in Mt Field National Park and not to be missed. The rivers in the valley provide good trout fishing.

Following the completion of a small section of road through the Mt Victoria Forest Reserve, it is now possible to drive from St Columba Falls to Ralph's Falls. See the

'Ringarooma Community Spirit' boxed text for details.

## WELDBOROUGH

The road approaching the **Weldborough Pass** on the Tasman Hwy follows a high ridge with wonderful views of the surrounding mountains. As you descend to the south, you can stop at the **Weldborough Pass Rainforest Walk**, a 10 minute circuit marked with interpretive signs describing the myrtle rainforest through the eyes of 'Grandma Myrtle'.

Last century, the town boomed when tin was discovered nearby, but today it is virtually deserted. At one stage there were 800 Chinese here, many of whom were miners; they brought with them many examples of their own culture, including an ornate joss house, now on display in Launceston's Queen Victoria Museum & Art Gallery. There were also other mining towns in the area: the cemetery at **Moorina** to the north has an interesting Chinese section.

The *Weldborough Hotel* (☎ 6354 2223), the town's only pub, calls itself the 'Worst Little Pub in Tassie'. It serves lunch and dinner – and don't be put off by the Irish menu, which advertises delicacies like 'blow fly sponge', 'gum leaf soup' and 'maggot-mornay'. The hotel also provides accommodation for $20/35 with shared facilities. The *Weldborough Camping Ground* is operated by the pub and has tent sites for $5 and powered sites are $8, which is cheap, but then there's not much there.

## GLADSTONE

About 25km to the north, off the Tasman Hwy between St Helens and Scottsdale, is the tiny town of Gladstone. It was one of the last tin-mining centres in north-eastern Tasmania, until the mine closed in 1982. The surrounding area also had a number of mining communities and a large Chinese population. Today, many old mining settlements are just ghost towns, and Gladstone shows signs of heading in the same direction. If you decide to spend the night here then the *Gladstone Hotel* (☎ 6357 2143) provides accommodation for $30/45 with shared facilities; the price includes a cooked breakfast.

On the road between the Tasman Hwy and Gladstone, you can spend a minute or two viewing Blue Lake, which is an astonishing shade of blue. While you're there, look for Cube Rock, perched incongruously on the ridge of South Mt Cameron, which you can also observe close up by taking the two hour return walk to the mountain's summit.

THE NORTH-EAST

### Ringarooma Community Spirit

The main reason to visit the tiny town of Ringarooma, signposted off the highway east of Scottsdale, is to drop into the White House and get local historian Norm Brown to tell you the inspiring story of his community's long and ultimately successful struggle to complete a road through Mt Victoria Reserve, creating a scenic loop linking Ralphs Falls and St Columba Falls. The road was begun during the Depression, and sections finished at that time feature extensive hand-built dry-stone walls. In the 1990s, the people of the area made a tremendous personal effort to ensure the success of the project by clearing vegetation with their own machinery and helping with the actual construction. The completed road was opened in 1998, and the community's contribution is acknowledged in a plaque at the Falls car park. The unsealed road is indeed very scenic, but it's also rough in parts and subject to thick fog.

Norm believes that Ralphs Falls are the highest single-drop falls in the state, and possibly Australia. They splash down the cliff face in a narrow jet that can be seen to great effect from a viewing platform an easy 10 minute walk from the car park.

## MT WILLIAM NATIONAL PARK

This little-known park in Tasmania's north-eastern corner consists of sweeping sandy beaches, low ridges and coastal heathlands. The highest point, Mt William, is only 216m high, yet there are some breathtaking views from it. The area was declared a national park in 1973 for the prime purpose of protecting the endangered Forester kangaroo. This animal prefers open, grassy areas, the very lands preferred by farmers, and there are now only a few places where it is found. Thankfully the kangaroos have flourished here and can now be seen throughout the park.

The best seasons here are spring and early summer when the wildflowers in the heathlands are at their peak. Mt William provides good views of the Furneaux Group of islands, including Flinders Island. When sea levels were lower, these formed part of a land bridge to mainland Australia, which the Aborigines used to migrate to Tasmania. **Musselroe Point** has a very large midden, which illustrates how long Aboriginal people occupied the region.

The main activities include birdwatching, animal watching, surf and boat fishing, swimming, surfing at Picnic Rocks and diving around Stumpys Bay and Cape Naturaliste. Horse riding is only allowed under permit, so contact the ranger first (☎ 6357 2108). Spotlighting (strictly in order to observe the animals at night, of course) is also permitted, but again, the ranger (who can supply lights) must be advised in advance.

On the road between the northern and southern ends of the park is **Tarrabah Park**, where you can see orphaned wildlife by appointment (☎/fax 6357 2131).

The easy climb to the rocky summit of **Mt William** takes one hour return. The view extends from St Marys in the south to Flinders Island in the north. Farther south is the impressive **Eddystone lighthouse**, built of granite blocks in the 1890s; if you follow the fence line at the car park down to the beach, you will find the quarry from which the granite was cut, and huge stone remnants

of the quarrying process. There is a small picnic spot here overlooking a beach of red granite outcrops, while a short drive away is the idyllic free camping ground of Deep Creek, beside a lovely tannin-stained creek and yet another magnificent arc of white sand and aqua water.

*Camping* in the park is very basic, with only pit toilets, bore water for washing and fireplaces provided. There is no power and no fresh water except at Deep Creek. Camping is allowed at four areas in Stumpys Bay, and also at Musselroe Top Camp and in the south at Deep Creek. Fires are only allowed in fireplaces and it is advisable to bring in your own wood or, preferably, a portable stove. On days of total fire ban only gas cookers are permitted.

### Getting There & Around

You can enter the park, which is well off the main roads, from the north or the south. The northern end is 12km from Gladstone, the southern end is 50km from St Helens. From Bridport, take the road towards Tomahawk and continue on to Gladstone. Try to avoid driving here at night, as that's the time the animals are most active. National park entry fees apply; on the access road there is a ranger station where you can obtain a park pass.

### DERBY

In 1874 tin was discovered in Derby (pronounced 'derby' rather than 'darby') and this little township flourished throughout the late 19th century. Several mines operated around the town and, like many other mining regions, these eventually amalgamated into one large mining company supporting a town of 3000 people. Operations continued smoothly until 1929, when the local dam burst, flooding the town and drowning many residents. The mine closed for five years, reopened, then closed again in 1940. Since then, most of the population has moved away. Instead of becoming a ghost town, Derby put the remnants of its past on display and ensured the town's future as a tourist destination.

## Information

Vegetarians and animal libbers beware!: the Derby information officer is the butcher. Drop into his shop any time from Monday to Friday and he'll give you all the hints you need, while continuing to wield his blade over the rack of ribs on the chopping block in the middle of the room.

## Things to See & Do

Derby is a classified historic town and some of the old mine buildings now form part of the excellent **Derby Tin Mine Centre** (☎ 6354 2262), which is a museum and shanty town. The museum is in the old school and displays old photographs and mining implements. The re-created shanty town is very interesting with shops, a mine office, cottages and a gaol. The centre is open daily from 9 am to 5 pm and is worth seeing. Admission is $4 (children $1.50, family $10). In winter, opening times are shortened to 10 am to 4 pm. The nearby mural beside the road is worth a look.

The region is famous for minerals and gemstones. Sapphire Safaris (☎ 6354 6238) runs gem-fossicking excursions on weekends and public holidays from nearby Branxholm. Tours are $45 including lunch.

Derby comes alive in late October when between 5000 and 10,000 people arrive for the annual **Derby River Derby**. Around 500 people compete in the derby in rafts of every description on an 8km course. It's like a battle with no rules and the art is simply to stay afloat; it's all immense fun with the main aim being to sink everyone else rather than to win.

At the nearby town of **Branxholm**, the Imperial Hotel has an impressive façade worth looking at and it's also a good place for a drink. The hop fields behind the hotel can be visited from mid-March to mid-April by prior arrangement (☎ 6354 6127).

## Places to Stay

Derby is also just 10km from a great farm hostel, *Merlinkei Home Hostel (☎ 6354*

THE NORTH-EAST

DOT BESWICK

**The annual Derby River Derby is a huge drawcard for the town. People flock to the town to see the race, which appears to be more about trying to sink the enemy than getting to the finishing line.**

*2152)*. It's about 6km from Winnaleah (take the road towards Banca and follow the signs), but the manager will pick you up from either Derby or Winnaleah. And it's worth the detour (provided you can appreciate the sound and smell of dairy cattle at close proximity), because the views from the hostel across the rural valley to the Blue Tiers are wonderful. Rates are $12 a night for YHA members.

The **Dorset Hotel** (☎ *6354 2360)* has rooms for $35/55 including breakfast.

Back on the highway, just west of Branxholm, is a sign advertising **Buttercup Farm Cottage** (☎ *6353 2263)*, which provides B&B in a self-contained cottage on a working dairy farm for $90 a double.

### Places to Eat
Perhaps one of the other activities that should be listed as a Derby attraction is eating, because the **Crib Shed Tearooms** (part of the mine centre) has an array of freshly baked cakes and scones that smell like heaven, while **Derby Sweet Thoughts** has old-fashioned lollies, hand-made chocolates, sweet and savoury pancakes, good coffee, pasta, pizza and ice cream desserts. The tearooms are open the same times as the mine centre, while the sweet shop is open from 11 am to 10 pm Wednesday to Friday, from 2 to 10 pm Saturday and from 11 am to 9 pm Sunday (although pizzas are only available from 5 pm).

The **Dorset Hotel** serves counter lunches and dinners.

### Getting There & Away
See the Getting There & Around section at the start of this chapter.

### SCOTTSDALE
- **pop 2020**

Scottsdale, the largest town in the northeast, was named after surveyor Scott, who opened the area for European settlement. The rich, fertile valleys supported farming and Scottsdale grew into the business centre of the region. Farming still has a very important role in the town.

In January and February, poppies provide a blaze of colour and there are extensive hop fields that are used to produce beer. In the town, the frozen vegetable factory produces mountains of frozen peas and French-fried potatoes. The Department of Defence also keeps its food laboratories here; they produce food for the armed services.

Recently a major industry has developed, with huge pine plantations supplying future timber needs. These look like a sea of uniform dark green trees and should be thought of as tree farms as that's really what they are. Just outside town, two large sawmills process this timber and some of the remaining hardwoods.

Westpac, ANZ, the Trust Bank and the Commonwealth Bank all have branches in Scottsdale, and Westpac and the Commonwealth have ATMs.

### Things to See
At Nabowla, 21km west of Scottsdale, is the **Bridestowe Lavender Farm** (☎ 6352 8182), the biggest oil-producing lavender farm in the southern hemisphere and the only source of perfumed lavender outside Europe. It's open from 9 am to 5 pm daily from November to April and from 10 am to 4 pm Monday to Friday in May, September and October (closed June, July and August). During the spectacular flowering season from mid-December to late January admission is $3, which covers a guided tour. At other times admission is free. The farm has a kiosk and toilets, and visitors can use the barbecues in the grassed picnic area.

The road from Scottsdale to Launceston crosses a pass called **The Sideling**. It's a good place to stop for a rest from the winding road. There are toilets, a shelter and good views. For even better views, take the road on the other side of the pass to **Mt Barrow**. A walk of about one hour return provides panoramic views over a third of Tasmania.

### Places to Stay
A camp site at the **North-East Park Camping Ground** costs $7.50, or $10 with power. Located beside the river on the road to

Derby and St Helens, the camping ground is pretty but has only very basic facilities. At least it's only a short walk to the hotels.

***Bellow's Backpacker & Budget Accommodation (☎ 6352 2263)*** is a spick and span hostel on King St opposite Anabel's. It charges $15 for a dorm bed and $35 for single or double rooms with good shared facilities. Linen is $5 extra. The communal kitchen is excellent.

***Lords Hotel (☎ 6352 2319)***, on the main highway junction in town, has basic rooms for $20/30 with shared facilities. Continental breakfast provisions are available for an extra $5 in the upstairs dining room, which has expansive rural views. Nearby, the ***Scottsdale Hotel/Motel (☎ 6352 2510)***, better known as Kendall's, has basic motel rooms for $39/51, continental breakfasts for $8 and cooked breakfasts for $12. Its large log fires are quite an attraction on cold nights, and David Kendall is a jovial host and a great source of information on the area.

If you don't mind staying out of town, you might like ***Kames Cottage (☎ 6352 2760)***, set in a beautiful garden on a small acreage 2.5km from Scottsdale on the road to Bridport. It charges $70/85, which includes provisions for a cooked breakfast.

***Anabel's of Scottsdale (☎ 6352 3277, 46 King St)*** has accommodation in attractive, modern rooms in a beautiful garden for $70/80 with en suite and $90 a double with en suite and kitchen. The price includes provisions for a continental breakfast. There is a good restaurant in the National Trust-classified main building.

***Beulah's B&B (☎/fax 6352 3723, 9 King St)*** is a lovely cottage run by friendly hosts who charge $95 a single or double for rooms with en suite and a cooked breakfast. Guests are invited to make use of the house's sauna and spa, and three-course evening meals are also available. The hosts are hoping to be able to offer tours of the Pipers Brook vineyards in the near future.

### Places to Eat
Both *hotels* serve lunch and dinner every day, while *Anabel's of Scottsdale (☎ 6352 3277)*,

mentioned in the earlier Places to Stay section, is an upmarket restaurant in a National Trust-classified building on King St that is open for dinner from Tuesday to Saturday.

### Getting There & Away
See the Getting There & Around section at the start of this chapter.

## TOMAHAWK
This low-key beach resort on the Tomahawk River is hidden halfway along the north-east coast, 40km from Bridport along straight, sealed roads. For most of the year its beaches are deserted, so it's a great place to get away from people, though possibly not worth the detour simply for a day trip. It provides some excellent fishing for keen anglers. The only place to stay is the ***Wanyeke Caravan Park (☎ 6355 2268)***, which has camp sites for $10, powered sites for $12, on-site vans for $35 and cabins for $40. Petrol is available and there is also a kiosk, but bring your own groceries and linen.

## BRIDPORT
• pop 1160
This well-developed holiday resort lies on the shore of Anderson Bay on the northern coast. Just 85km from Launceston, it's popular with Tasmanians, and there are many holiday houses in town.

Bridport has safe **swimming beaches**, and the sheltered waters are ideal for waterskiing. Sea, lake and river fishing are also popular here. The area is renowned for its native orchids, which flower from September to December.

### Places to Stay & Eat
The leafy ***Bridport Caravan Park (☎ 6356 1227)*** is right beside the beach and has camp sites for $9.50 and powered sites for $12.50, but can be crowded in summer. The hostel is the ***Bridport Seaside Lodge (☎ 6356 1585)*** on Main St. It is close to the town centre and has bunks for $13 each. It's $30 to $35 for double rooms without linen or $40 to $42 with linen. Basic rooms are available at the ***Bridport Hotel (☎ 6356 1114)*** with B&B for $25/35.

THE NORTH-EAST

For a higher standard B&B try ***Bridairre Modern B&B Accommodation*** (☎ *6356 1438*) on the hill on Frances St. It's rather suburban but has views of the bay; doubles (most with *en suite*) are $60 to $80 with a continental breakfast. Rooms with *en suite* at the ***Bridport Motor Inn*** (☎ *6356 1238*) cost $59/69, while self-contained units $80 a double.

***Indra*** (☎ *6356 1196, 53 Westwood St*) has self-contained units for $70 a double or single. The units are quite large, but not right in the centre.

For something different, try the ***Platypus Park Farm Chalets*** (☎ *6331 5650 or 6356 1873*) just out of town beside the Brid River. Set among the trees, these conjoined units start at $70 a double. Provisions for a cooked breakfast are $15 a person extra.

You can't miss the oceans of green gravel at the new ***Bridport Resort***, which has doubles in spacious self-contained units for $115. The resort also has a heated indoor pool, a games room, tennis courts etc.

The motor inn has a ***bistro*** that serves breakfast, lunch and dinner seven days a week, the ***hotels*** serve counter meals, and ***The Seaside Takeaway*** has fish and chips. ***Joseph's*** at the Bridport Resort is à la carte and fully licensed.

## Getting There & Away

From Monday to Friday, Stan's Coach Service (☎ 6356 1662 after 6.30 pm) runs from Scottsdale to Bridport. It connects with the TRC bus service from Launceston. See the Scottsdale Getting There & Around section at the start of this chapter for further details.

The Southern Shipping Company (☎ 6356 1753) runs a small passenger ferry from Bridport to Flinders Island and on to Port Welshpool in Victoria. Ring the company for details.

# Launceston & Around

## Launceston

- **pop 67,800**

Officially founded in 1805, Launceston is Australia's third-oldest city and Tasmania's second-oldest city. It is the commercial centre of northern Tasmania and is today a charming blend of the old and new.

The region was originally occupied by Tasmanian Aborigines, who arrived about 40,000 years ago. They lived primarily by hunting animals on the open plains of the regions. The first Europeans to visit the Tamar River were Bass and Flinders in 1798, who were attempting to circumnavigate Van Diemen's Land to show that it was not joined to the rest of Australia. A large swell south of Point Hicks in Victoria had long encouraged the belief that Tasmania was an island. Demonstrating that this was true meant that thereafter the passage from Europe to Sydney, which previously had rounded the coast of southern Tasmania, was shorter and less hazardous.

Around the same time the French were also exploring the coast. Out of fear that they would establish a colony, Colonel William Paterson set up a camp near the mouth of the Tamar River in 1804. Unfortunately, a poor site was chosen.

Launceston was the third attempt at a permanent settlement on the Tamar River and was originally called Patersonia, after its founder. In 1907, the city was renamed in honour of Governor King, who was born in Launceston, England, a town settled 1000 years before on the Tamar River in the county of Cornwall. The Aborigines' name for the area was Ponrabbel, and the fertile plains that the Europeans had occupied were also important Aboriginal hunting grounds. For several years there were skirmishes between the settlers and the Aborigines, and many Aboriginal women and children were kidnapped by sealers and whalers, with devastating results on their communtiy.

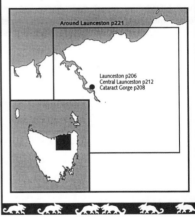

Around Launceston p221

Launceston p206
Central Launceston p212
Cataract Gorge p208

A notable event in Launceston's history occurred in 1835 when John Batman sailed from Launceston to Victoria and founded the town of Melbourne.

Launceston is situated at the end of the deep water channel of the Tamar River where the South Esk and North Esk Rivers join. It is a sheltered city, located among steep hills 64km inland from Bass Strait.

### Orientation

The city centre is arranged in a grid pattern centred around the Brisbane St Mall, between Charles and St John Sts. The main shopping centre is based around the mall and the nearby Quadrant Mall, which is a

**LAUNCESTON & AROUND**

semi-circular side street. Two blocks north, on Cameron St, there's another pedestrian mall in the centre of a block called the Civic Square, around which many of the public buildings such as the library, town hall and police station are to be found. Two blocks to the east of Civic Square is Yorktown Square, a charming and lively area of restored buildings that have been turned into shops and restaurants. The open space is not square and is fairly small but there are some good places in which to eat.

Parks and gardens are important to the city and close to the centre are formal gardens at City Park, the wide sweeping lawns of Royal Park and the smaller open spaces of Princes Square and Brickfields Reserve. To the west of the city is Cataract Gorge, a rugged natural river gorge, which is the best known of the city's features.

Although Launceston suffers from a lack of street signs, it's not difficult to find your way around and the city's main attractions are all within walking distance of the centre.

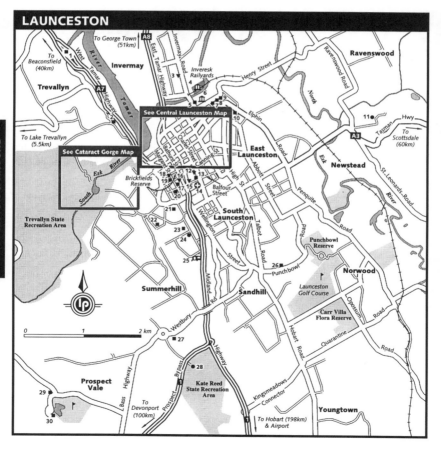

## Information

The Tasmanian Travel & Information Centre (TTIC, Gateway, Tasmania, ☎ 6336 3122), on the corner of St John and Paterson Sts, is open from 9 am to 5 pm weekdays, to 3 pm on Saturday, and to noon on Sunday and public holidays. Information can also be obtained by listening to radio station 99.3 FM.

The post office is at 107 Brisbane St, near the Quadrant, and is open from 9 am to 5.30 pm on weekdays and Saturday morning from 9.30 am to 1 pm.

Banks are open for business from 9.30 am to 4 pm Monday to Thursday and to 5 pm on Friday. Automatic Teller Machines (ATMs) can be used at any time and are available at most banks in the city area. Most banks have branches on St John St or Brisbane St near the mall.

The Royal Automobile Club of Tasmania (RACT, ☎ 6335 5633, 13 1111 for roadside help), on the corner of George and York Sts, provides services for members of automobile clubs from other states of Australia as well. It is also the place to go for road maps.

For bushwalking maps and camping gear, Paddy Pallin (☎ 6331 4240, 110 George St) and Allgoods (☎ 6331 3644), on the corner

of York and St John Sts, are both excellent. If you're in town at the weekend, there's a craft market on Yorktown Square every Sunday from 9 am to 2 pm.

The Wilderness Society Shop, which sells clothing, books, videos, cards and souvenirs with 'green' credentials, is at 174 Charles St.

## Cataract Gorge

At the entrance to the magnificent Cataract Gorge, only a 10 minute walk from the city centre, almost vertical cliffs line the banks of the South Esk River as it enters the Tamar. The area around Cataract Gorge has been made a reserve for native wildlife and is justly one of Launceston's most popular tourist attractions.

Starting at Kings Bridge, two walking tracks, one on either side of the gorge, lead up to **First Basin**, which is filled with water from the South Esk River. The walk takes about 30 minutes. The northern trail is easier and it took eight years for local residents to construct the track through the cliffs. The southern trail is known as the Zig Zag Track and has some steep climbs as it passes along the top of the cliffs. The waters of First Basin are very cold and deep, so you may feel safer swimming in

**LAUNCESTON & AROUND**

## LAUNCESTON

**PLACES TO STAY**
1  Tamar River Villa
2  Turret House
5  Andy's Backpackers; Mallee Grill
7  Cottage on the Park
8  Cottage on Cimitiere
9  Thyme Cottage
10 Kilmarnock House
13 Sportsman's Hall Hotel
17 The Mews Motel
19 Brickfields Terrace
20 Alice's Cottages & Hideaway Reception
21 Edenholme Grange
22 Clarke Holiday House
23 Launceston City Youth Hostel
25 Treasure Island Caravan Park
26 Aberdeen Court
27 Olde Tudor Motor Inn

29 Bass Villas
30 Launceston Country Club Casino

**PLACES TO EAT**
3  Me Wah Restaurant
12 Elaia Café
15 Quigley's
16 Golden Sea Dragon
18 Cucina Simpatica

**OTHER**
4  Inveresk Railyard; New Museum Site
6  National Automobile Museum of Australia
11 Waverley Woolen Mills
14 Launceston General Hospital
24 Old Coats Patons Building; Tamar Knitting
28 Silverdome

the nearby concrete pool. The landscaped area around the basin features picnic spots, the Gorge Restaurant (see Places to Eat), a café, rhododendrons and lots of peacocks. At night the gorge is lit up and is well worth a visit.

You don't have to walk to the First Basin – there is car parking at the entrance. From the city follow York St, Hillside Crescent, Brougham St then Basin Rd. Parking fees apply so buy a ticket at the machine.

Upstream of the First Basin, the **Alexandra Suspension Bridge** crosses the river and provides a fine view of another section of the gorge. Downstream of the basin there is a concrete causeway that crosses the river. When the river is in flood the causeway is closed.

There's also a **chair lift**, which crosses the basin to the reserve on the other side; the six minute ride costs $5 one way or return,

children $3. Good walking tracks lead farther up the gorge to the **Second Basin** and Duck Reach; these take 45 minutes each way. Duck Reach is the site of the first municipal hydroelectricity power station in Australia, which provided power from 1895 until 1955.

Tracks also lead from the northern side of the First Basin to several lookouts including Cataract and Eagle Eyrie from where there are fine views.

## Penny Royal World

The Penny Royal entertainment complex, which claims to take you back to a 'world of yesteryear', has exhibits including working 19th century water mills and windmills, gunpowder mills and model boats. You can take part in mock battles firing cannons on the man-o'-war sloop on the lake in the complex. You can also take a ride on a

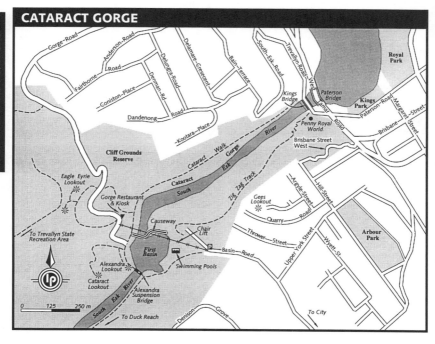

barge or on the restored city tram that provides transport between the different features. There is also a 45 minute cruise part-way up the gorge on the *Lady Stelfox* paddle steamer. The main complex is set into an old quarry beside the entrance to Cataract Gorge and is an imaginative use of the area.

Although some parts of the Penny Royal complex are interesting, overall it's not worth the $19.50 ($9.50 for children) admission, unless you plan to spend all day here. You can, however, just pay for one of the attractions; the gunpowder mill, for example, is $10 for adults and $6 for children, while the Mole Hill Fantasy is $4 for adults and $2 for children. The short tram ride is free.

### Ritchies Mill Art Centre
Near Penny Royal, beside the entrance to Cataract Gorge, is this 1834 flour mill and miller's cottage. It was originally powered by water that was delivered by a pipeline from Cataract Gorge. Inside is Gallery Two, a contemporary art and craft gallery open from 11 am to 5 pm Tuesday to Sunday except in winter, when it closes at 4 pm. Beside the mill is a huge 41m-tall blue gum; it's 160 years old and dominates the area. With the pleasant leafy grounds and a good restaurant and the art gallery in the mill, it's a nice place to spend an hour or two.

### Trevallyn Recreation Reserve
Farther upstream from Duck Reach is the Trevallyn Dam, which holds back the waters of Lake Trevallyn. Here, you can view a 90m-long elver ladder, constructed to help young eels negotiate the dam wall in their annual 3500km migration.

A reserve of 450 hectares beside the lake provides some natural forest and bushlands for recreational use. There are picnic grounds and a motorcycle track, and archery, horse riding and bushwalking are the main activities catered for. Water-skiing is allowed on the lake as well as general boating, windsurfing and canoeing.

At the Trevallyn Dam quarry in the reserve you can do simulated hang-gliding

(☎ 018 132 788) for $10. From December to April you can glide every day from 10 am to 5 pm, in other months it's open on weekends and public and Tasmanian school holidays from 10 am to 4 pm. The hang-glider is suspended on a 200m-long cable and is much safer than the real thing.

To get to the reserve follow the West Tamar Hwy past the entrance to Cataract Gorge, turn left onto Gorge Rd, then follow Bald Hill Rd, Veulalee Ave and then Reatta Rd to the reserve. The reserve is open daily from 8 am until dusk, except when the river is in flood, when access is restricted. Camping is not allowed within the reserve.

### Queen Victoria Museum & Art Gallery
The Queen Victoria Museum & Art Gallery (☎ 6331 6777) on Wellington St was built in the late 19th century and displays the splendour of the period both inside and out. It has a unique collection of Tasmanian fauna, Aboriginal artefacts and colonial paintings. A major attraction is the splendid joss house, donated by the descendants of Chinese settlers. At the time of writing, facilities were being developed for the display of galaxiids – tiny freshwater fish, many of which (such as the notable *Pedder galaxias*) are endemic to Tasmania.

The centre is open Monday to Saturday from 10 am to 5 pm, and from 2 to 5 pm on Sunday. The gallery and museum are free, and there are free guided tours of the Colonial Gallery at 2.30 pm most Saturdays and Sundays (ring first). The Queen Vic Café is inside the museum (see Places to Eat).

The museum has a planetarium, which is one of only five in Australia. It costs $3 for adults, $2 for children, or $7 for a family, and is open for showings at 3 pm Tuesday to Fri, 2 and 3 pm Saturday, and 3 pm Monday during school holidays.

At the time of writing, the Inveresk Railyards just across Victoria Bridge, to the right of Invermay Rd, were being extensively redeveloped to house much of the museum's

LAUNCESTON & AROUND

collection. The new premises, due to open in 2001, would triple the museum's exhibition space and would house its arts and crafts, and community history and technology collections. The fine art collection was to be moved to the Stone building (Stone being the name of the architect), also at the railyards. The natural history collection was to remain in the Wellington St building.

## Historic Buildings

There is less of an architectural heritage left in Launceston than in Hobart and other towns in Tasmania. The older buildings that still exist, however, are more varied than those seen elsewhere because they are from several architectural periods. In response to the local availability of materials, less sandstone has been used than elsewhere in Tasmania, and there has been a greater use of bricks.

In the Civic Square is **Macquarie House**, built in 1830 as a warehouse but later used as a military barracks and office building. At the time of writing, it was housing the Tasmanian Wood Design Collection. The historic **Johnstone & Wilmot warehouse**, on the corner of Cimitiere and St John Sts, dates from 1842.

The **Town Hall**, also on Civic Square, is an imposing building from 1864 in a Victorian Italianate style. Directly opposite the Town Hall on Cameron St, the **old post office** is an interesting building with its unique round clock tower.

One block away, at 35 Cameron St, is the 1848 **Batman Fawkner Inn**. Originally a hotel, it was built to commemorate the site of the historic meeting to plan the founding of Melbourne, and there are many mementos of that meeting on display. It is still used as a hotel today.

One corner of City Park contains **Albert Hall**, which was erected in 1891 for a trade fair. The hall has been in constant use as a public venue ever since and features an unusual water organ.

The **Old Umbrella Shop**, at 60 George St, was built in the 1860s and still houses a selection of umbrellas. Classified by the Na-

tional Trust, it is the last genuine period shop in the state. The interior is lined with Tasmanian blackwood timber, and the shop sells a good range of National Trust items. It's open from 9 am to 5 pm on weekdays and to noon on Saturday.

Many of Launceston's churches were constructed between 1830 and 1860. The wide range of religions and denominations represented reflect the influence of the 1837 Church Act which, in addition to acknowledging the existence of all religions, exempted places of worship from many taxes. By 1860 there were 12 churches. On the Civic Square block are the Pilgrim Uniting and St Andrews churches, and on St John St opposite Princes Square is St Johns Church.

The **Community History Branch** (☎ 6323 3727), on the corner of Cimitiere and St John Sts, is a branch of the Museum that has a foyer gallery and community access to business and personal papers, photos and maps. It's open from 10 am to 4 pm Monday to Friday.

On the Midland Hwy 6km south-west of the city is **Franklin House** (☎ 6344 6233), one of Launceston's most attractive two-storey Georgian homes. It was built in 1838 and has been beautifully restored and furnished by the National Trust. An outstanding feature of its interior is the woodwork, which has been carved from New South Wales (NSW) red cedar. The house is open daily from 9 am to 5 pm (4 pm in June, July and August) and admission is $6, children $4 or $12 for a family. To get there by bus, take Metro bus Nos 20, 22 or 25 from St John St near the mall.

## Parks & Gardens

Launceston is sometimes referred to as 'the garden city', and with so many beautiful public squares, parks and reserves, it's easy to understand why.

The six hectare **City Park** is a pleasant example of a Victorian garden and features an elegant fountain, a bandstand, a monkey enclosure, a wallaby enclosure and a conservatory. **Princes Square**, between Charles and St John Sts, features a bronze fountain bought at the 1855 Paris Exhibition.

Other public parks and gardens not mentioned earlier in this section include **Royal Park**, near the junction of the North Esk and Tamar rivers; the **Punchbowl Reserve**, with its magnificent rhododendron garden; and the **Windmill Hill Reserve**.

## Other Attractions

The **Design Centre of Tasmania**, on the corner of Brisbane and Tamar Sts, is a retail outlet displaying work by Tasmania's top artists and craftspeople.

The **National Automobile Museum** (☎ 6334 8888) is a little out of the centre, on the corner of Cimitiere and Willis Sts. It's open from 9 am to 5 pm daily from September to May and from 10 am to 4 pm daily the rest of the year; admission is $7.50 for adults and $4 for children.

The **Waverley Woollen Mills** (☎ 6339 1106) are on Waverley Rd, 5km to the east of the city centre. The mills were established in 1874 and are the oldest operating woollen mills in Australia. In 1889 the mill installed a hydroelectricity generating station, which is believed to be the first hydro plant in the southern hemisphere. Both places are open daily from 9 am to 5 pm; admission is free, as are tours, which run on the hour from 9 am.

The **Tamar Knitting Mills** (☎ 6344 8255), founded in 1926, are now located in the old Coats Patons building, on the corner of Glen Dhu and Thistle Sts, and are open to the public. The building also houses a number of other business, which together, take fine Tasmanian wool from its raw stage to the finished garment at a single location.

## Walking Tours

You can pick up a copy of the *Historic Walks* brochure from the visitors' centre and view the city's architectural heritage at your own pace or join a tour. Launceston Historic Walks (☎ 6331 3679) departs daily at the TTIC at 9.45 am. The tour finishes at 11 am and costs $10.

## Organised Tours

The Coach Tram Tour Company (☎ 6336 3122) has three tours leaving from the office of the TTIC. Its City and Suburbs Historical Tour is a three hour trip around the sights of Launceston. It costs $23 and leaves at 10 am daily all year, and also at 2 pm daily from 1 November to 30 April. The Historic Countryside Evening Tour leaves at 6 pm Tuesday, Thursday and Saturday and includes dinner for $45 (minimum of four), while the West Tamar Valley Day Tour departs at 10.30 am Tuesday, Thursday, Saturday and includes lunch for $49 (minimum of four).

Tasmanian Redline Coaches (TRC, ☎ 1300 360 000), on George St, has half and full-day Explorer Tours (minimum of four) of the Tamar Valley ($34), the north-west coast ($38), the north-east ($42), Cradle Mountain ($45), and the lavender farm at Brindelstowe ($25, late December and January).

Tasmanian Wilderness Travel (TWT, ☎ 6334 4442) has tours of the Tamar Valley ($39), the Tamar Valley vineyards ($39), Cradle Mountain ($45 and $55), the Mole Creek caves and animal park ($45), Stanley ($49), Longford ($39) and the Freycinet Peninsula ($45). It also runs two-day trips to Strahan and the Gordon River ($395 twin share) and two-day trips to Cradle Mountain ($230).

## Special Events

Cataract Gorge forms the backdrop for many of Launceston's events. In February there is the Basin Concert, a rock concert held at the First Basin. In March the same place is used for a more cultural concert called A Night in the Gorge with the Tasmanian Symphony Orchestra. Both of these events are popular with the local residents.

In February, race horses compete for the Launceston Cup and during Easter the trotting track comes alive for the Easter Cup Pacing Championship. Once winter is over there is a whole series of small festivals and art shows. The Launceston Spring Festival in September and the Royal Launceston Show in October are the major events.

LAUNCESTON & AROUND

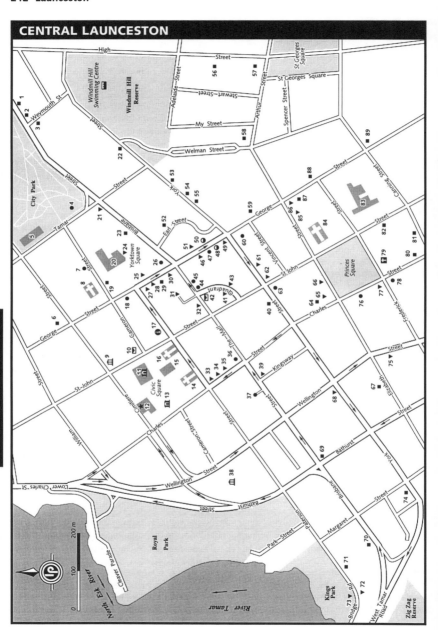

# CENTRAL LAUNCESTON

## CENTRAL LAUNCESTON

### PLACES TO STAY
| | |
|---|---|
| 1 | Sandors On The Park |
| 2 | North Lodge Motel |
| 3 | Parklane Motel |
| 6 | Lloyds Hotel |
| 19 | Batman Fawkner Inn |
| 20 | Novotel Launceston |
| 22 | Adina Place |
| 23 | The Maldon |
| 29 | Royal Hotel |
| 40 | St James Hotel |
| 52 | Great Northern Hotel |
| 53 | York Mansions |
| 54 | Alice's & Ivy Cottages |
| 55 | Balmoral Motor Inn |
| 56 | Windmill Hill Tourist Lodge |
| 57 | Ashton Gate Guesthouse |
| 58 | Highfield House |
| 59 | Fiona's B&B |
| 64 | Hotel Tasmania |
| 67 | YHA Summer Hostel |
| 69 | Irish Murphy's |
| 70 | Rose Lodge |
| 71 | Penny Royal Village |
| 74 | Old Bakery Inn |
| 80 | The Edwardian |
| 81 | Canning Cottage |
| 82 | Airlee Dorset Terrace |
| 87 | Colonial Motor Inn |
| 88 | Launceston City Backpackers |
| 89 | Hillview House |

### PLACES TO EAT
| | |
|---|---|
| 21 | Royal Oak Hotel |
| 24 | Tairyo Japanese Restaurant & Sushi Bar |
| 25 | La Cantina |
| 27 | Shrimps |
| 28 | Pierre's |
| 30 | Leo's Asian Food House |
| 31 | Croplines Coffee Roasters |
| 32 | Banjo's |
| 33 | Arpar's Thai Restaurant |
| 34 | Star Bar |
| 35 | Happy Pumpkin |
| 39 | Jilly's Pancake & Ice Cream Parlour |
| 41 | That Dear Little Coffee Shop |
| 43 | Pasta Resistance Too |
| 46 | Konditorei Café Manfred |
| 49 | O'Keefes Hotel |
| 51 | Pepperberry Café/Restaurant |
| 61 | Fu Wah |
| 62 | The Metz |
| 65 | Canton |
| 66 | The Happy Chef |
| 68 | Ball & Chain |
| 72 | Owl's Nest |
| 73 | Ripples Restaurant; Ritchies Mill Art Centre |
| 75 | Calabrisella |
| 77 | Fee & Me |
| 85 | Quill & Cane |
| 86 | Three Steps on George |

### OTHER
| | |
|---|---|
| 4 | Design Centre of Tasmania |
| 5 | Albert Hall |
| 7 | Advance Car Rentals |
| 8 | Holy Trinity Church |
| 9 | Community History Branch |
| 10 | Old Post Office |
| 11 | Town Hall |
| 12 | Police Station |
| 13 | Macquarie House |
| 14 | Pilgrim Uniting Church |
| 15 | Library |
| 16 | St Andrew's Church |
| 17 | Travel & Information Centre |
| 18 | Old Umbrella Shop |
| 26 | Traveland (Ansett Agent) |
| 36 | Qantas Airlines |
| 37 | Tamar Valley Coaches |
| 38 | Queen Victoria Museum & Art Gallery |
| 42 | Post Office; Commonwealth Bank |
| 44 | Kodak Shop; Petrarch's Bookshop |
| 45 | All Booked Up Bookshop |
| 47 | Paddy Pallin |
| 48 | Tasmanian Redline Coaches |
| 50 | Tasmanian Wilderness Travel; Skybus |
| 60 | Royal Automobile Club of Tasmania |
| 63 | Allgoods |
| 76 | Wilderness Society Shop |
| 78 | Coles Supermarket |
| 79 | Christ Church |
| 83 | St Vincent's Hospital |
| 84 | St John's Church |

LAUNCESTON & AROUND

## Places to Stay – Budget

**Camping & Cabins** The only caravan park in the city is the ***Treasure Island Caravan Park*** (☎ *6344 2600, 94 Glen Dhu St*), 2km south of the city beside the Midland Hwy. It has single/double tent sites for $9/14, powered sites for $13/16, standard cabins for $54 a single or double and deluxe cabins for $60 a single or double. As this is the only caravan park in Launceston, it can get crowded at times and, being right next to the highway, it is quite noisy.

**Backpacker Accommodation** Conveniently located on the edge of the city centre is the smoke-free ***Launceston City Backpackers*** (☎ *6334 2327, 173 George St*). It's an old house that has been thoughtfully renovated, and the cost is $14 per person in four-bed rooms or $30 a double for a separate room.

***Andy's Backpackers*** (☎ *6334 9289*), on the corner of Boland and Tamar Sts, above the Mallee Grill, has dorm beds for $14 a night, and rooms with shared facilities for $40 a double. There is a laundry and a kitchen. ***Irish Murphys*** (☎ *6331 4440, 211 Brisbane St*) has dorm beds for $14. ***Lloyds Hotel*** (☎ *6331 4966, 23 George St*) has backpacker beds for $12.

The rambling ***Launceston City Youth Hostel*** (☎ *6344 9779, 36 Thistle St*), which is not a YHA hostel, is 2km from the centre of town. It's just off Glen Dhu St and close to the caravan park. Dormitory beds and family rooms are $12 per adult and $5 for children. The building dates from the 1940s and used to be the canteen for the Coats Patons Woollen Mill. The hostel has mountain and touring bikes for hire as well as a comprehensive selection of bushwalking gear, including boots.

The *YHA summer hostel (☎ 6334 4505, 132 Elizabeth St)* only runs from 1 December to 29 January. It has 'apartments' consisting of two two-bed rooms, a kitchen and a bathroom. It charges from $14 a night, and advance bookings can be made through the Hobart YHA office (☎ 6234 9617).

**Hotels** One of the cheapest hotels in town is Irish Murphys (☎ 6331 4440, 211 Brisbane St), which has rooms with shared facilities for $30 a double. There is entertainment here five nights a week, so it can be noisy at times.

The *Sportsman's Hall Hotel (☎ 6331 3968, 252 Charles St)* is in a quiet part of town and it's an easy walk from the centre. It has rooms for $35/50, including a cooked breakfast. Bands sometimes play here on Friday and Saturday nights, but it claims to have good soundproofing. More central is the *Hotel Tasmania (☎ 6331 7355, 191 Charles St)*, which is better known as the Saloon. Rooms with *en suite* are $45/58, including breakfast.

There are several older centrally located hotels, all of which include breakfast in their tariff: the *Royal Hotel (☎ 6331 2526, 90 George St)* is $28/55 a single/double, Lloyds Hotel (☎ 6331 4966, 23 George St) is $30/54 with *en suite*, and *St James Hotel (☎ 6331 6122, 122 York St)* is $45/60 with *en suite*.

The historic *Batman Fawkner Inn (☎ 6331 7222, 35 Cameron St)*, right next door to Yorktown Square, has rooms for $42/65; or there are budget singles for $25 and standard singles for $35. The cheaper singles can be noisy on Friday and Saturday nights.

**Flats** The *Clarke Holiday House (☎ 6334 2237, 19 Neika Ave)*, about 1km out of town, is great value. The downstairs flat is spacious and comfortable, if a little dark, while the bigger house upstairs can sleep six. The flat is $30/35, while the house is $45 a double. To find it, follow the main road of Hillside Crescent then Brougham St towards the First Basin at Cataract Gorge. Neika Ave runs left off Brougham St just past where Basin Rd starts.

## Places to Stay – Mid-Range

**Guesthouses & B&Bs** Right in town is *Fiona's B&B (☎ 6334 5965, 141 George St)*, which has single/double rooms with *en suite* for $60/80 with a cooked breakfast. The *Rose Lodge (☎ 6334 0120, 270 Brisbane St)* has small but comfortable rooms with *en suite* and a cooked breakfast for $55/68. Around the corner, heading south down Margaret St, the *Mews Motel (☎ 6331 2861, 89 Margaret St)* is closer to a guesthouse than a motel. It has very clean, comfortable rooms and friendly hosts, and is $55/68, including a continental breakfast.

A 10 minute walk south of the city centre, in a set of terrace houses near Princes Square, is *Airlee Dorset Terrace (☎ 6334 2162, 138 St John St)*, where rooms with *en suite* and continental breakfast are $65/85. One block away is *Hillview House (☎ 6331 7388, 193 George St)*, where B&B is $55/85 in rooms with *en suite*. Even closer to town is *The Maldon (☎ 6331 3211, 32 Brisbane St)*, which provides good rooms with *en suite* in a grand Victorian building for $70 a single and $80 to $90 a double. *The Edwardian (☎ 6334 7771, 227 Charles St)* has rooms with *en suite* and continental breakfast for $70/85.

The eastern side of the city is bounded by a steep hill on which some of the earlier mansions were constructed. Today some of these provide good B&B accommodation. While you can walk into town, the hill is very steep. The *Windmill Hill Tourist Lodge (☎ 6331 9337, 22 High St)* charges $60/70 for rooms with *en suite*. The lodge also has self-contained holiday flats at $75 a double.

**Motels** There are a large number of motels, most of a similar standard. Those around the city centre are either refurbished old hotels or multistorey motels, while the motels in the suburbs are the more familiar two storey modern style.

Most motels are east of the city centre on either York or Brisbane St and are about 1km from town. *North Lodge Motel* (☎ *6331 9966, 7 Brisbane St)* has rooms for $75 a double. Next door is *Parklane Motel* (☎ *6331 4233, 9 Brisbane St)* where rooms are $85 a double and self-contained units are $95.

*Sandors On The Park* (☎ *6331 2055, 3 Brisbane St)* provides good standard rooms for $70/80. *Balmoral Motor Inn* (☎ *6331 8000, 19 York St)* is a multistorey motel with rooms for $71/75.

If you prefer to be south of the city then try the *Olde Tudor Motor Inn* (☎ *6344 5044, Westbury Rd)*, beside the old highway to Devonport. It's 4km from town and rooms are $75/88.

**Self-Contained Units** There are plenty of self-contained units of various sizes and styles at *Adina Place* (☎ *6331 6866, 50 York St)*. The rooms on the upper floors have excellent views across the city and start from $55/65.

Most other mid-range units are well away from the city centre. *Aberdeen Court* (☎ *6344 5811, toll-free 1800 006 042, 35 Punchbowl Rd)* in the suburb of Sandhill has units that are really motel rooms with kitchens. They are listed at $82/92, but even in the high season you should be able to negotiate a cheaper price.

To stay near the casino at a reasonable price you should consider the two units available at *Bass Villas* (☎ *6344 7259, 1 Casino Rise)*, where the rate is $85 a double. Each unit can sleep up to eight people. Approximately 5km north-east of the city is the *Tamar River Villa* (☎ *6327 1022, 23 Elouera St)*, which is beside the

West Tamar Hwy and has self-contained rooms for $79 a double.

**Cottages** At *Canning Cottage* (☎ *6331 4876, 26-28 Canning St)* there are two separate two-storey cottages, both of which are very cosy. These are original cottages, so there are lots of steep steps and narrow doorways. The cost is a very reasonable $85 a double including continental breakfast.

## Places to Stay – Top End
**Guesthouses & B&Bs** If you can afford the extra cost, there are some great guesthouses offering rather luxurious colonial accommodation, such as the cosy *Ashton Gate Guesthouse* (☎ *6331 6180)*, on the corner of High and Arthur Sts. With a cooked breakfast, singles/doubles cost $75/95 and $130 for the best rooms.

*Edenholme Grange* (☎ *6334 6666, 14 St Andrews St)*, which is classified by the National Trust, is on a side street off Hillside Crescent (the road to First Basin) and charges $100 for singles and $130 to $160 for doubles, with a five course cooked Tasmanian breakfast. Its theme rooms are so lavishly decorated that you may believe you've found your way into your very own bodice-ripper. The glassed-in *en suite* in the Captain's Room will delight some, but may not appeal to more modest guests. For the not so adventurous, they do have rooms with conventional *en suites*.

*Highfield House* (☎ *6334 3485)*, on the corner of Welman and Arthur Sts, has rooms with *en suite* for $100/120, which includes a cooked breakfast.

If you prefer to be out of town, then head for *Turret House* (☎ *6334 7033, 41 West Tamar Rd)*, 1.5km from the centre, on the western side of the Tamar River. Cataract Gorge is reasonably close and there are excellent views across the river. Rooms with *en suite* are $65/95 with a cooked breakfast.

*Kilmarnock House* (☎ *6334 1514, 66 Elphin Rd)* is 1.5km east of the city and charges $80/100 for lovely rooms with *en suite* and a continental breakfast.

**Hotels** The *Great Northern Hotel* (☎ *toll-free 1800 030 567, 3 Earl St)*, close to Yorktown Square, has rooms starting at $94 a double. At the *Novotel Launceston* (☎ *6334 3434, 29 Cameron St)*, rooms start at $145 a double, including a buffet breakfast.

If you really want to be pampered, then try the *Country Club Casino* (☎ *6344 8855)* at Prospect Vale, 5km south of the city. At $245 a double, you will need some extra cash for those gaming tables!

**Motels** At *Penny Royal Village* (☎ *6331 6699, 145 Paterson St)*, one-bedroom apartments are $95 a double, while motel rooms and two-bedroom apartments are $120 a double.

On the western side of the city is the *Old Bakery Inn* (☎ *6331 7900)*, on the corner of York and Margaret Sts, which was established as a bakery in 1870 and retains many historic architectural features. Motel-style rooms are $100 a single or double.

The *Colonial Motor Inn* (☎ *6331 6588)*, on the corner of George and Elizabeth Sts, has an attractive reception area and restaurant, but the rooms themselves are nothing out of the ordinary given their price of $120 a double.

Five kilometres north-east of the city is the *Riverside Motel* (☎ *6327 2522, 407 West Tamar Rd)*, which charges $90 a single or double with a continental breakfast.

**Self-Contained Units** The Edwardian (☎ 6334 7771, 227 Charles St) is close to town and has self-contained suites for $70/100 with continental breakfast. *York Mansions* (☎ *6334 2933, 9 York St)* has five apartments in an 1840 National Trust-classified building. The luxury and opulence is reflected in the $155 a double rate, which includes the provisions for a full cooked breakfast.

**Cottages** At *Alice's Cottages & Hideaways* (☎ *6334 2231, 129 Balfour St)* there are a number of places to choose from starting at $140 a double; its Ivy Cottage and Alice's Cottage on York St are close to the centre.

North-east of the city centre, near City Park, *Cottage on the Park* (☎ *6334 2238, 29 Lawrence St)* and *Cottage on Cimitiere* (☎ *6334 2238, 33 Cimitiere St)*, are both two-bedroom cottages that sleep up to five people. With breakfast provided the rates are $145 a double. For both cottages inquire at 27 Lawrence St. Nearby is *Thyme Cottage* (☎ *018 135 481, 31 Cimitiere St)*, which is $110 a double with provisions for a cooked breakfast.

On the opposite side of town is *Brickfields Terrace* (☎ *6331 0963, 64 & 68 Margaret St)*, two separate townhouses overlooking the Brickfields Reserve, where bricks were made last century. They are $140 a double with provisions for a cooked breakfast.

## Places to Eat
**Cafés & Takeaways** For good coffee, *Croplines Coffee Roasters* (76 Brisbane Court) has been recommended by travellers as the place to go. *Banjo's* bakery and café (Yorktown Square and 98 Brisbane St) is open daily from 6 am to 6 pm. At Yorktown Square, *Molly York's Coffee Shoppe* is another possibility for breakfast or lunch.

There are some excellent lunch spots around the city's Quadrant. *Pasta Resistance Too*, a tiny place that is always crowded, has serves for around $5 or $6. In fact, limited space must be a hearty recommendation in the Quadrant, because just opposite is *That Dear Little Coffee Shop*, a matchbox-sized café with a great reputation for its home-made cakes and soups.

The *Happy Pumpkin*, on Charles St near the Star Bar, is a chicken and vegetarian coffee house and takeaway, and here you can get breakfast from 9 am to 11 am for $6.50, or pick up a vegie pie or pastie for lunch. It also has a Mexican section.

*Leo's Asian Food House*, which opens out onto George St (opposite Traveland), has lunch-time takeaway priced from $3.50 to $6.50.

One of our favourite cafés is *Elaia Café* (238-240 Charles St), which is a little south of the centre, near the Sportsman's Hall

Hotel. It's colourful, open and sunny, and serves good coffee, lunches and dinners. Soup is $6.50, while restaurant-style mains are around $14. It's open from Monday to Thursday from 9 am to 6 pm, Friday and Saturday it's open till 9 pm and Sunday it's open from 10 am to 4 pm.

The *Queen Vic Café* in the museum has a pleasant outlook and seats on a balcony. Curries and gourmet pizzas are $9, pastas $7.50 and soup with olive bread $5.

*Ripples Restaurant*, in the Ritchies Mill Art Centre, opposite Penny Royal, specialises in light meals such as crêpes and pancakes, and there's a lovely view of the boats on the Tamar River from the outdoor tables.

If you have kids with you, try *Jilly's Pancake & Ice Cream Parlour (147 Brisbane St)*, just down the road from the cinema complex. It has savoury and sweet pancakes, burgers, nachos etc and is open daily (late on Friday and Saturday nights).

**Hotels** Most of Launceston's many hotels have filling, reasonably priced counter meals and most are open daily. The *South Charles Café* at the Sportsman's Hall Hotel serves à la carte lunches and dinners daily, or you can get a counter meal in the bar. Other pub options are *O'Keefes Hotel (124 George St)*, the *Hotel Tasmania (the Saloon, 191 Charles St)*, the *Royal Oak Hotel (14 Brisbane St)*, which specialises in seafood, and *Irish Murphys (211 Brisbane St)*.

Central and extremely popular is the *Star Bar (113 Charles St)*, which is spacious, appealing, and has a wood-fired pizza oven. It's open from 11 am to 11 pm Monday to Wednesday, to midnight Thursday to Saturday, and noon to 10 pm Sunday. In a similar vein is *The Metz*, on the corner of York and St John Sts, which is a bar, café and restaurant in what used to be the St George Hotel. It's open from 8 am to 3 am daily in the tourist season and from 10 am to 3 am the rest of the year. Its 'On York's Meateaters Platter' is $9 for one or $14 for two and features ostrich, quail and wallaby.

At the Great Northern Hotel, *Oscars Bistro (3 Earl St)* serves family fare daily in the $9 to $15 price range. At the back of the Batman Fawkner Inn is *Pascoes (35 Cameron St)*, which has grills and seafood.

**Restaurants** There are also some good restaurants in Launceston. One of the most popular for simple Italian food is *Calabrisella (☎ 6331 1958, 56 Wellington St)*. It opens at 5 pm every day except Tuesday and usually closes at midnight. It's a good place to go if you have children with you. You can also get takeaway pizza here.

The *Ball & Chain* charcoal grill *(☎ 6331 0303)*, on the corner of Wellington and York Sts, and the *Mallee Grill (☎ 6334 9288)*, on the corner of Tamar and Boland Sts, pride themselves on their steaks. (The Mallee Grill is below Andy's Backpackers.)

The *Konditorei Café Manfred (☎ 6334 2490, 106 George St)*, well-known for its delicious, inexpensive home-made German rolls and pastries, now has a licensed restaurant upstairs offering Mediterranean and traditional French fare. Mains are $13 to $20, and there is an outdoor dining area. Across the road is the *Pepperberry Café/Restaurant (☎ 6334 4589, 91 George St)*, which has an emphasis on Tasmanian produce and uses pepperberries hand-picked by the owner-chef in dishes featuring game such as wallaby. Wallaby pies are a speciality, and everything is cooked on the premises.

On the other side of town, just out of the centre, is *Cucina Simpatica (☎ 6334 3177)*, on the corner of Frederick and Margaret Sts. It's rather trendy but has a bright, relaxed atmosphere and great food. It's popular for lunch but is also open for dinner.

*Pierre's (☎ 6331 6835, 88 George St)* is a café, bar and restaurant open from 10 am Monday to Saturday. It closes at 7 pm Monday to Wednesday, at 9 pm Thursday and 10 pm Friday and Saturday (also closed from 2 to 6 pm Saturday). Mains are priced from $7.50 to $18.50.

The *La Cantina (☎ 6331 7835, 63 George St)*, beside Yorktown Square, is a popular licensed restaurant with pasta and other Italian dishes. *The Happy Chef (☎ 6331 9107, 68*

*Elizabeth St)* is open for lunch from Tuesday to Friday and for dinner Tuesday to Saturday, and has pastas for $7 to $10.50 and other mains for $13.50 to $17.50.

*Arpar's Thai Restaurant (☎ 6331 2786)*, on the corner of Charles and Paterson Sts, is well worth a visit. If you prefer Chinese, try the *Fu Wah (☎ 6331 6368, 63 York St)*. Other options for Chinese food are the up-market *Canton (☎ 6331 9448, 201 Charles St)*, which has a separate Chinese menu for those who prefer authentic dishes; the *Golden Sea Dragon (☎ 6331 7728, 97 Canning St)*, on the edge of town; and the *Me Wah Restaurant (☎ 6331 1308, 39 Invermay Rd)*, 2km out of town just north of Cataract Gorge. A great Japanese restaurant and sushi bar is the *Tairyo (☎ 6334 2620)*, at Yorktown Square, which is open every evening.

For Tasmanian wines and good food, try the *Owl's Nest (☎ 6331 6699, 147 Paterson St)*, next to the Penny Royal complex. The *Gorge Restaurant (☎ 6331 3330)*, at Cataract Gorge, has the best setting in all of Launceston with main courses starting at $17.50. It's open for lunch and dinner from Tuesday to Saturday and for lunch only on Sunday.

In the Colonial Motor Inn Reception building on Elizabeth St is the *Quill & Cane (☎ 6334 2084)*, which has a wide range of à la carte dishes. Next door is *Three Steps on George*, on the corner of George and Elizabeth Sts, which is another café, bar and restaurant.

For upmarket eating try *Shrimps (☎ 6334 0584, 72 George St)*, which has an intimate atmosphere, or *Fee & Me (☎ 6331 3195)*, on the corner of Charles and Frederick Sts, which is in a charming old building and is considered one of Launceston's best restaurants. *Quigley's (☎ 6331 6971, 96 Balfour St)*, in an 1860s terrace, specialises in game and is another restaurant with a fine reputation.

As you would expect, the Country Club Casino has several places to eat, including the *Terrace Restaurant (☎ 6335 5777)*, open Tuesday to Saturday.

## Entertainment

There's quite a good choice of evening entertainment in Launceston, most of which is advertised in the daily newspaper *The Examiner* and some are also announced in the free *Launceston Week* newspaper or in the free *This Week in Tasmania*.

The *Pavilion Tavern (Yorktown Square)* has bands and a cabaret-style nightclub on Friday and Saturday nights. Despite its trendy western setting, the *Hotel Tasmania (the Saloon, 191 Charles St)* isn't a country and western venue, but it does have standard pub bands on Wednesday, Friday and Saturday nights.

Places like the *Star Bar (113 Charles St)* and *The Metz (corner York and St John Sts)* are popular wine bars (see Places to Eat earlier in this chapter for opening hours).

Major events are held in the *Silverdome* at Prospect, south of the junction of the Bass Hwy to Devonport and the Midland Hwy to Hobart.

If you want to risk a few dollars, or just observe how the rich play, check out the *Launceston Federal Country Club Casino* at Prospect, 10km from the city centre. Most big-name bands touring from the mainland perform here. You don't have to pay to get in and dress standards have been relaxed. As long as you are tidy, clean and wearing appropriate footwear (no runners or thongs), you should be let in.

## Getting There & Away

**Air**  Daily flights operate from Launceston to Melbourne and connect to the other capital cities of Australia. For information on domestic flights to and from Launceston, see the Getting There & Away chapter at the beginning of this book. The agent for Ansett Airlines is Traveland (☎ 6331 9777) on the corner of Brisbane and George Sts, while Qantas (☎ 6332 9911, 140a Brisbane St Mall) is on the corner of Brisbane and Charles Sts.

Regular flights also operate from Launceston to Flinders Island (see The Islands chapter for details) as well as to the other major towns in Tasmania. Charter flights with the small airlines can also be arranged.

**Bus** The main bus companies operating out of Launceston are TRC (112 George St), TWT (101 George St) and Tamar Valley Coaches (☎ 6334 0828, 4 Cuisine Lane).

TRC runs several buses every day from Hobart to Launceston ($19.50), then it goes along the north coast to Devonport ($13.70) and Burnie ($18.30), from where you can catch a TRC service farther along the north coast to Wynyard ($20.90), Stanley ($29) and Smithton ($29). It also services Deloraine ($6.80).

TRC also runs buses from Launceston to Conara Junction, then through St Marys ($15.50) to St Helens ($19.20) on the east coast. It also runs a bus into the north-east to Scottsdale ($9) and Derby ($13), and Broadby's (☎ 6376 3488) runs a connecting service from there to St Helens (see the Getting There & Around section at the start of the North-East chapter).

On weekdays, Tamar Valley Coaches has at least one bus a day running up and down the West Tamar Valley, but there are no weekend services. The fare from Launceston to Beaconsfield is $5.70.

TRC runs three buses every weekday and one bus on Sunday along the eastern side of the Tamar River from Launceston to Dilston, Hillwood and George Town. There are no services on Saturday. On some services the bus will continue on to Low Head, but only if a booking has been made. The fare from Launceston to George Town is $7.20.

When the catamaran is running, a coach to or from Launceston meets the ferry each time it arrives or departs.

A small operator runs the service from Launceston to Longford but you should be able to get information from Tamar Valley Coaches. There are three services a day, and the fare is $3.30.

TWT runs a scheduled service from Launceston to Sheffield ($15.80), Gowrie Park ($18.60), Cradle Mountain ($36.50, plus $7 to Dove Lake), Tullah ($31.60), Rosebery ($33), Zeehan ($38.50) and Queenstown ($43.10) all year on Tuesday, Thursday and Saturday, and from Queenstown to Strahan on those days and also on Sunday ($5.60, or

$48.70 from Launceston). For details of other TWT services from Launceston, see the relevant sections of this book.

**Car** There are plenty of car-rental firms in Launceston. Prices range from $30 to over $100 for a single day, depending on the time of year and model. Most firms give discounts for multi-day hire except for the really cheap prices where a surcharge is applied for single-day hire. Ask before hiring if insurance is included in the rates because insurance is compulsory and can double the cheaper rental prices. Also ask about whether the insurance covers travel on gravel roads. (It's almost impossible to see the best of Tasmania without travelling on such surfaces.) Advance Car Rentals (☎ 6391 8000, 32 Cameron St and Airport) is one of the cheaper ones.

## Getting Around
**To/From the Airport** The airport is 16km south of the city. TWT and TRC operate $7 shuttle services that meet flights that land close to schedule. You can board the bus at either terminal or arrange to be collected from any of the major hotels in the city. The taxi fare to/from the city is around $20.

**Bus** The local bus service is run by Metro (☎ 6336 5888), and the main departure points are the two blocks on St John St, between Paterson and York Sts. For $3.10 you can buy a Day Rover ticket, which can be used for unlimited travel all day at weekends and between 9 am and 4.30 pm and after 6 pm on weekdays. Most routes, however, do not operate in the evenings, and Sunday services are limited. If you are staying in Launceston for some time, you can buy books of 10 tickets for about a 25% discount; these tickets do not have to be used consecutively and have no expiry date.

**Bicycle** Rent-a-Cycle, at the Launceston City Youth Hostel (☎ 6344 9779), has a good range of mountain bikes for $95 a week, including helmet and panniers. There's a reducing rate for each additional week, and a bond of $100 applies. Lonely Planet has had good reports about the service offered by Rent-a-Cycle.

# Around Launceston

## HADSPEN
• pop 1334

Fifteen kilometres south-west of Launceston is the popular residential area of Hadspen. Some attractive Georgian buildings from the 19th century survive, and the **Red Feather Inn**, **Hadspen Gaol** and the **Church of the Good Shepherd** are definitely worth looking at.

Two kilometres past Hadspen on the western side of the South Esk River is **Entally House**, one of Tasmania's best known historic homes. It was built in 1819 by Thomas Haydock Reibey but is now owned by the National Trust. Located in beautiful grounds, it creates a vivid picture of what life must have been like for the well-to-do on an early farming property. The home, its stables, church, coach house and grounds are open daily from 10 am to 12.30 pm and 1 pm to 5 pm. Admission is $6, children $4 or a family $12. The Reibeys have quite an interesting family history; for example, Thomas Haydock Reibey's mother was a convict.

### Places to Stay & Eat
In Hadspen, on the corner of the Bass Hwy and Main Rd, is the *Launceston Cabin & Tourist Park (☎ 6393 6391)*. The park has good facilities and charges $10 for a tent site, $12 for a powered site and $55 a double for a self-contained cabin.

On the other side of the South Esk River near Entally House is the resort complex of *Rutherglen Holiday Village (☎ 6393 6307)*. Motel rooms are $59/65. This is a fully self-contained resort, complete with a bar and bistro.

For international à la carte meals try upstairs in the *Red Feather Inn (☎ 6393 6331, 42 Main St)*. It was built in 1844 and is open every night from 6.30 pm to 8.30 pm. Downstairs, you can get counter meals.

## CARRICK
• pop 325

The area around this village, 19km southwest of Launceston on the old highway to Deloraine, was a major grain-growing area in the 19th century. Today it is home to several artists, and its most prominent feature is the large four storey mill beside the old Bass Hwy. Behind the mill, on Bishopsbourne Rd, is the grand and dramatic ruin known as **Archers Folly**. It's been burnt down twice but the owners still dream of restoring it; in the meantime they run the **Copper Art Gallery** (☎ 6393 6440), next door to the ruin. It's open daily and well worth a visit as the art is innovative and unusual, there are no entry fees and all works are for sale.

### Places to Stay & Eat
The *Carrick Inn* beside the highway has counter meals. Thirteen kilometres away, at Whitemore and well signposted off the main roads, is *Gossips Restaurant (☎ 6397 3148)*, which is highly regarded, especially for its hare. It has two-course set menus for $28 and three-course set menus for $35. It's open for dinner from Tuesday to Saturday and for lunch by arrangement.

Just off Bishopsbourne Rd is *Hawthorn Villa (☎ 6393 6150)* where B&B is available at $50/85 for singles/doubles, or you can hire a cottage for the same price.

## LIFFEY VALLEY
The Liffey Valley is a small farming community at the foot of the Great Western Tiers and is well known to most Tasmanians. What has made the valley famous is that it is the holiday home of Dr Bob Brown, the conservationist who turned to politics. It is no coincidence that the Western Tasmania World Heritage Area starts at the back fence of Dr Brown's property.

Of major interest to most visitors is the **Liffey Forest Reserve**, which features the impressive Liffey Valley Falls. There are two approaches to the falls, which are actually three separate waterfalls. From the upstream car park it's a one hour return walk on marked tracks. You can also follow the river upstream through forest; allow two to three hours return.

The valley is also a popular destination for fishing, and day-trippers are also attracted by an amazing fernery. The *Liffey Valley Fernery, Tearooms and Gallery* (☎ 6397 3213) were built from pine, tea tree and melaleuca timbers. You can sit in the tearooms, enjoy freshly made scones and take in the view of Drys Bluff, which, at 1297m, is the highest peak in the Great Western Tiers. The fernery and tearooms are open from 11 am to 4 pm most Saturdays, every Sunday and most public holidays but are closed from the June long weekend until the end of October. Liffey is 34km south of Carrick, via Bracknell, and is a good day trip from Launceston.

If you'd like to stay in the area, you can get B&B in a modern farmhouse at *Liffey Falls* (☎ 6369 5356) for $80/85. Guests can also get a two course dinner with wine here for $20 a person.

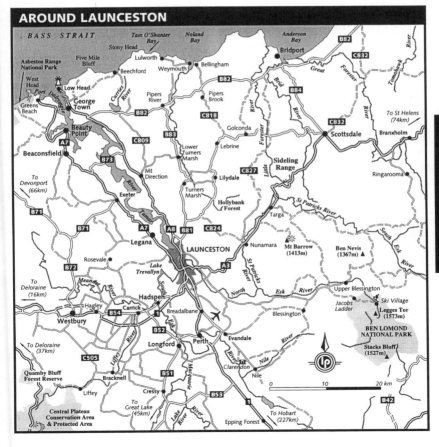

AROUND LAUNCESTON

LAUNCESTON & AROUND

## LONGFORD

* pop 2601

Longford is 27km south of Launceston and is classified as an historic town. The surrounding region is a rich pastoral area watered by the South Esk and Macquarie rivers, and it also has many historic farm houses and grand estates. The original inhabitants of the area were the Tasmanian Aborigines, and the plains provided good hunting grounds for them. Under their chief, Eumarrah, they actively resisted the Europeans until the 1830s, when the remaining tribal members were moved to Flinders Island.

The Europeans initially called the area Norfolk Plains because of land grants given in 1812 to settlers from the abandoned colony on Norfolk Island. Originally the town was called Latour and the road from Launceston to the town was built in 1813. With a reliable transportation route to Launceston, the site quickly grew into a town, and by 1823 over 500 people lived here. At that time, it was one of the few towns in the state established by free settlers rather than convicts.

### Information

One of the best ways to explore this historic town is to follow the National Trust's *The Path of History* brochure, which will take you past many colonial buildings. Along with other information, it is available from the visitors' centre at Heritage Corner (☎ 6391 1181, 1 Marlborough St) in the centre of town.

There is a post office and a Trust Bank in the town.

### Things to See & Do

Based around **Memorial Park**, the town is best known for its Georgian architecture. Buildings worth seeing are the **Baptist Church**, **Christ Church**, a large **warehouse** on Union St, the **town hall**, **library** and the **Queens Arms Hotel**.

In the early 1960s Longford's streets were used for motor car races and several Grand Prix races were held here. While there are no longer any races, the Country Club Hotel on Wellington St has a large collection of photos and relics of that period. Today the town is much quieter: the Longford Garden Festival in November is the highlight of the year.

The rich farming lands near the town supported many estates and two of the earliest are **Woolmers** (☎ 6391 2230) and **Brickendon** (☎ 6391 1251), both of which were established by William Thomas Archer. Tours of Woolmers operate daily at 11 am and 12.30, 2 and 3.30 pm and cost $10 for adults and $2.50 for children (self-guided inside, guided outside). If you intend to visit Brickendon also, pick up a voucher here that will give you a discount on admission to that estate (without the discount it is $7.50 for adults and $3.50 for children). Brickendon is only open from Wednesday to Sunday. The properties are south of Longford and are found by following Wellington St into the countryside. Both can be visited on day tours from Launceston or Hobart with TWT.

On Pateena Rd north-west of town is **Bowthorpe** (☎ 6391 1253), a country farm and gardens started in 1825. You can walk through the extensive gardens and lanes of the farm and have afternoon tea in one of the cottages. It's open every day from 10 am to 4 pm and entry is $5 each or $12 for a family.

### Places to Stay & Eat

The *Riverside Caravan Park* (☎ 6391 1470), on the banks of the Macquarie River, has quiet shady camping and is very close to the centre of town. Tent sites are $10, powered sites $15, on-site vans $30, cabins without *en suite* $35 and self-contained cabins $45 a double.

The *Country Club Hotel* has recently renovated rooms with shared facilities, a continental breakfast and a pleasant communal area for $20/40.

The remainder of the accommodation is of colonial style. *Kingsley House* (☎ 6391 2318, Wellington St), on the northern side of town beside the railway line, is well priced and appealing, and has some larger than average rooms and suites, some of which are ideal for people travelling with small children. All accommodation is in the main house, and one option includes two large rooms, a kitchen, a bathroom and a small fenced yard, all for the standard B&B price of $80 a double plus $30 for each extra adult.

In Marlborough St, on the southern side of town, is the private hotel *Racecourse Inn* (☎ 6391 2352), where B&B is $95/140.

Other places are out of town. West of town, on the other side of Back Creek, is the *Old Rosary* (☎ 6391 1662) at Longford Hall. It's found by following Malcombe St to where a private road leads to the hall, which was at one time a school and a monastery and is currently a residence. There is one lovely cottage for hire at $130 a double with provisions for a cooked breakfast. The cottage and residence are hidden among magnificent gardens that are part of the Australian Open Garden Scheme.

South of town on Wellington St are the *Brickendon Historic Cottages* (☎ 6391 1251), where B&B in a self-contained cottage is $130 a double. Farther out, at *Woolmers* (☎ 6391 2230), self-contained historic cottages are $125 a double with a continental breakfast or $130 with a cooked breakfast provided.

For light meals, *JJ's Bakery* on Wellington St has won several state awards for its bread and pies. The nearby Memorial Park is a good place to eat takeaway. For hotel meals the *Country Club Hotel* on Wellington St has a bistro with meals available every day.

### Getting There & Away

Ring TRC for details of the private service that runs from Launceston to Longford three times daily for $3.30.

## EVANDALE
• pop 850

Evandale, 22km south of Launceston in the South Esk Valley, is near Launceston's airport and is another town classified by the National Trust. Many of its 19th century buildings are in excellent condition and its narrow streets give it the atmosphere of an English country village.

### Information

The visitors' centre in Evandale is the Tourism and History Centre (☎ 6391 8128, 14 High St), which is open daily from 10 am to 3 pm and provides some excellent information. While you are there, pick up the $2 brochure *Evandale Heritage Walk*, which will guide you around the town's main features.

There is a post office and petrol station on the main street.

### Historic Buildings

Places worth seeing around the town are the brick **water tower**, the two **churches**, and historic houses such as **Solomon House**, **Ingleside** and **Fallgrove**.

The **Clarendon Arms Hotel** has been licensed since 1847 and has some interesting murals in the hall depicting the area's history. The locals may encourage you to see if you can spot the well-concealed rabbit in the stagecoach mural; have a go – it really is there!

Eight kilometres south of Evandale, on Nile Rd, is the National Trust property of **Clarendon** (☎ 6398 6220), which was completed in 1838 and is one of the grandest Georgian mansions in Australia. The house and its formal gardens are open daily from 10 am to 5 pm (closing an hour earlier in winter) and admission is $6, children $4 or $12 for a family.

### Market

A popular market is held every Sunday morning on Logan Rd, where children can get train rides between 9 am and 1 pm.

### Special Events

In keeping with its olde-worlde feel, Evandale hosts the Evandale Village Fair and the National Penny-farthing Championships in February each year, which attract national and international competitors. In March is another special event – the Evandale Picnic Races, featuring local horses.

LAUNCESTON & AROUND

## Places to Stay

Most places to stay are on Russell St. The *Clarendon Arms Hotel (☎ 6391 8181, 11 Russell St)* has basic rooms for $25/35.

*Bees Nees Cottage (☎ 6391 8088, 28 Russell St)* is an 1840s cottage close to the centre of town for $78/100 with breakfast. Two doors away is *Arendon Cottage (☎ 6391 8806, 30 Russell St)*, another attractive option for $80/100 with breakfast. *The Stables (☎ 6391 8048, 5 Russell St)* provides accommodation in modern self-contained units for $110 a double, including breakfast.

*Greg and Gill's Place (☎ 6391 8248, 35 Collins St)* is the antithesis of a resort and a good place to stay if you have children of around primary school age. The accommodation itself is hidden from the road by lovely gardens, and among the many unusual attractions of this unpretentious property are collections of cameras, vintage cars, model planes and toys. Host Greg Waddle also has his studio gallery here, where he works and gives classes. Next door, but essentially part of the same grounds, are the premises of the Evandale Light Rail and Steam Society, where the trains that operate at the Sunday market are garaged; Greg can easily be persuaded to bring them out for your children to see. B&B is $50/75.

*Solomon Cottage (☎ 6391 8331)*, opposite the corner of High and Russell Sts, used to be a bakery. It has since been elegantly renovated, and the area that was once the oven is now the perfect alcove for a queen-size bed. B&B in this large, comfortable unit that can sleep four is $70/95 and $25 for each extra person.

Three kilometres north-east of town is *Harland Rise (☎ 6391 8283)*, an impressive 1858 farmhouse in beautiful grounds on a working farm. The upstairs room is lovely and has an *en suite*. The room downstairs is small and its only window is a glass door opening onto the breakfast room. The private bathroom for the downstairs room is upstairs, but it's rather luxurious and includes a bathtub. B&B in either room is $50/80.

## Places to Eat

*Solomon House Tearooms*, opposite the corner of High and Russell Sts, and the *Colonial Bakery Tearoom*, on Russel St, are attractive, spacious cafés in historic buildings that serve light meals, tea, coffee and cakes. The former is open daily in the high season from noon to 5 pm (Sunday only in the low season), while the latter is open daily from 9 am to 5 pm.

Light meals are also available at the *Dalmeny Café & Gallery (14 Russell St)*, which has focaccias for $6 and mains for around $15. The only true restaurant in town is *Russells Restaurant (☎ 6391 8622, 3 Russell St)*, where main meals are around $16 to $20. It's open from Wednesday to Sunday for lunch and Wednesday to Saturday for dinner.

The *Clarendon Arms Hotel (☎ 6391 8181, 11 Russell St)* has counter lunches and dinners priced from $10 to $16 available daily except Sunday evening. Counter meals are also available at the *Prince of Wales Hotel* on the corner of High and Collins Sts.

## Getting There & Away

TRC operates buses on weekdays only between the town and Launceston. The bus takes only 15 minutes to travel between the two towns and runs from Monday to Friday, departing Launceston at 5.40 pm and Evandale at 7.55 am and 6 pm. Some extra services run on Monday, Thursday and Friday. Buses travel via Barclay, Macquarie and Russell Sts in Evandale and the fare is $2.40.

## BEN LOMOND NATIONAL PARK

This 165 sq km park, 50km south-east of Launceston, includes the entire Ben Lomond Range and is best known for its skiing. The range does not have any dramatic peaks; instead it is an elevated plateau about 14km long by 6km wide. The plateau is around 1300m high, with the gentle hills on the plateau being 1500m in height. The highest point is Legges Tor (1573m), which is the second highest peak in Tasmania and

Georges Bay, St Helens

GLENN BEANLAND

Rafting on the South Esk River

CHRIS KLEP

Pencil pines on the Central Plateau in winter

ROB BLAKERS

Fishing boats in Waub's Bay, Bicheno

CHRIS KLEP

Brisbane St, Launceston

Wood carving at Grindelwald, Launceston

Boats on the Tamar River, Launceston

Cataract Gorge, Launceston

well worth climbing in good weather for its panoramic views.

The scenery at Ben Lomond is magnificent all year-round. The park is particularly noted for its alpine wildflowers, which run riot in spring and summer.

Ben Lomond was named after its Scottish namesake by the founder of Launceston, Colonel Patterson, in 1804. From 1805 to 1806, Colonel Legge explored the plateau and named most of the major features after explorers of the Nile River in Africa and members of the fledgling Van Diemen's Land colony.

From Launceston, a good road leads to the foothills of the park where the road changes to gravel. This rough road is easily followed to **Carr Villa**, from where a walking track leads to the plateau above. You can also drive to the top via the unsealed and treacherous Jacobs Ladder. This is a set of six sharp hairpin bends; once above the ladder it's an easy drive to the ski village. In winter, chains are essential for the final climb.

## Things to See & Do
In summer, the plateau provides some easy walking. The most popular place to visit is the highest point, **Legges Tor**. It can be reached via a good walking track from Carr Villa, about halfway up the mountain, and takes about two hours each way. You can also climb to the top from the ski village on the plateau, which takes about 30 minutes each way on marked tracks.

You can easily walk across the plateau in almost any direction but there are no marked tracks and navigation is difficult in mist. Unless you are well equipped, walking south of the ski village is not advised.

During the ski season (early July to late September), a kiosk, tavern and restaurant are open in the alpine village at *Creek Inn* (☎ *6372 2444*). Bistro meals are available every day for both lunch and dinner. Rooms with continental breakfast are $180 for up to four people, while backpacker accommodation is $30 a person.

There are eight tows for skiers and a day-visitors' shelter with heating is provided. To check conditions for downhill or cross-country skiing, phone ☎ 190 229 0530. Lift tickets and ski equipment hire cost about half what they do on the mainland. There are three T-bars and five Poma lifts.

## Getting There & Away
In the past, TWT has run buses to Ben Lomond during the ski season for $29 return in a single day or $40 return with an overnight stay. At the time of writing, it was uncertain whether TWT would be continuing this service – ring for details. Bookings are essential, as this is a Wilderness Service, and so only operates if there are four full-fare-paying passengers on board. The service is cancelled when there is no snow on the mountain.

TWT also runs a shuttle service from the bottom of Jacobs Ladder to the alpine village and back. This is advertised as running on demand, but people have been known to wait two hours at the top for a bus to arrive take them down again.

# The North

The northern plains are actually rolling farmlands and hill country, which extend from the Tamar River valley north of Launceston west to the Great Western Tiers. There are some interesting towns and scenic spots, and the best way to explore this area is to leave the highways and follow the quiet minor roads through the small towns.

The Tamar River separates the east and west Tamar districts and links Launceston with its ocean port of Bell Bay. Crossing the river near Deviot is Batman Bridge, the only bridge on the lower reaches of the Tamar. The river is tidal for all of the 64km to Launceston and winds its way through some lovely orchards, pastures, forests and vineyards, as well as providing a habitat for black swans.

The Tamar Valley and nearby Pipers River are among Tasmania's main wine-producing areas, and the dry premium wines produced here have achieved national recognition.

Heading west from Launceston, the main highway skirts the foot of the Great Western Tiers then heads north to Devonport, the state's third-largest city. The terminal for the car ferry from Melbourne is here, and the town is the gateway to the well-known Cradle Mountain-Lake St Clair National Park. Between Devonport and that park are a series of small towns hidden in the hills, some of which are well worth passing through.

For thousands of years the Tasmanian Aborigines lived in this area and there are many middens of shells and rock carvings around Devonport.

European history in the region dates from 1798, when Bass and Flinders discovered the Tamar estuary. Settlement commenced in 1804. Slowly the valley developed, first as a port of call for sailors and sealers from the Bass Strait islands and then as a sanctuary for some of the desperate characters who took to the bush during the convict days. By the mid-19th century the Abori-

## HIGHLIGHTS

- Wine tasting and lunching in Pipers Brook and Tamar Valley vineyards
- The dramatic views of the Great Western Tiers
- Hop fields and lush countryside of Gunns Plains
- Seal viewing from George Town
- The wild caves of Mole Creek Karst National Park

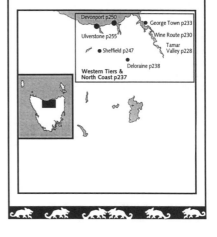

gines had been forced from their former hunting grounds by the Europeans, who slowly spread across the plains turning the forested land into farming country.

In the late 1870s, gold was discovered by William and John Dally at Cabbage Tree Hill, just west of present-day Beaconsfield, and the fortunes of the north took a new turn. The region boomed and for a time this was the third-largest town in Tasmania, before the mines closed in 1914. Further gold deposits have recently been discovered in the Beaconsfield area.

## Getting There & Around
**Bus** On weekdays, Tamar Valley Coaches (☎ 6334 0828) has at least one bus a day running up and down the West Tamar Valley, but there are no weekend services. The fare from Launceston to Beaconsfield is $5.70.

Tasmanian Redline Coaches (TRC, ☎ 1300 360 000) runs three buses every weekday and one bus on Sunday along the eastern side of the Tamar River from Launceston to Dilston, Hillwood and George Town. There are no services on Saturday. On some services the bus will continue on to Low Head, but only if a booking has been made. The fare from Launceston to George Town is $7.20.

When the catamaran is running, a coach to or from Launceston meets the ferry in Devonport each time it arrives or departs.

TRC has several services daily from Launceston to Devonport ($13.70), Ulverstone ($15.80) and Penguin ($16.20), some of which call at the ferry terminal in Devonport. It also runs weekday services from Launceston to Deloraine ($6.80).

Buses also run from both Launceston and Devonport to Cradle Mountain-Lake St Clair National Park. See the Getting There & Around section at the start of the West chapter and the Cradle Mountain-Lake St Clair Getting There & Away section of the same chapter for details.

**Bicycle** The ride north along the Tamar River is a gem. On the west bank, it is possible to avoid most of the highway and follow quiet roads with very few hills through the small settlements. On the eastern shore, follow the minor roads inland to Lilydale. There are plenty of hills but the different landscapes more than compensate for the hard work!

From Launceston to Deloraine, the construction of the new highway is a real plus for riders: most vehicles follow the new road, and riders can now enjoy the old highway. It's slower and climbs more hills, but it's far more interesting, passing through all the small towns. From Deloraine, the rebuilt highway that heads directly to Devonport is best avoided by travelling through the quieter towns of Sheffield or Railton.

# Tamar Valley

Running north from Launceston the Tamar Valley is off the normal tourist circuit and has some interesting sights. Tourism is just starting here but so far is very minor and you usually get good service and value in the region. You can drive up either side of the river and cross over on the unusual single-tower Batman Bridge.

## LEGANA
* **pop 1398**
Just 12km north of Launceston, this is fast becoming a satellite suburb of the nearby city. It originally consisted of orchards, but these days new houses are growing faster than anything else. There are some vineyards here, but the wineries are not open to the public.

The main tourist feature in the area is **Grindelwald**, a reproduction Swiss village sitting in a shallow valley on top of the nearby hills. It started as a residential village but has evolved into a convention and conference centre. It's really a bit out of place and not that special.

More interesting is a visit to **Notley Fern Gorge**. This is hidden in the hills 14km west of Legana and while only small it is the last remnant of the original forest that once covered the region. The big hollow tree in the park is reputed to have been the hiding place of Matthew Brady, a famous bushranger from the 19th century; who knows if it's true but it makes a good story. It's a nice cool place on a warm day and the marked circuit walk takes about 45 minutes.

## Places to Stay & Eat
The *Launceston Holiday Park* (☎ 6330 1714) is beside the highway. Tent sites are $10, powered sites $12, on-site vans are $35 and cabins are $35. In Legana, well off the highway overlooking the river, is *Freshwater Point* (☎ 6330 2200). It's an original homestead with sweeping views and is

impressive, but then so is the price: B&B is $120 a double.

***Grindelwald Holiday Village*** (*☎ 6330 1799, toll-free 1800 817 595*) has rooms for $115 and units at $135 a double with breakfast. At least you can eat at ***Alpenrose Restaurant***, where main meals cost from $15 to $18.

## ROSEVEARS

On the west side of the Tamar, it's worth leaving the highway and following the narrow sealed road that winds along the river banks, passing through the tiny town of Rosevears. This was the place where the *Rebecca*, John Batman's ship, was constructed; he sailed across Bass Strait in it to settle Melbourne.

The ***Rosevears Tavern*** was opened in 1831 and you can still get a beer and counter meal there seven days a week.

Within walking distance of the hotel, the **Waterbird Haven Trust** (*☎ 6394 4087*) is a sanctuary for marine birds. Entry is $4

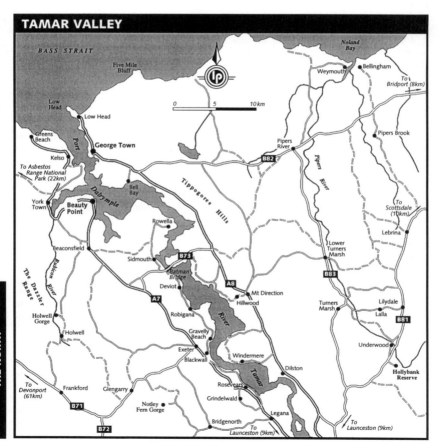

TAMAR VALLEY

(children $1). *B&B* is available beside the haven at $30/50 for a single/double, which includes entry to the haven.

Local wines can be tasted at the **Strathlynn Wine Centre** (☎ 6330 2388), which is open daily except Christmas Day. This is an outlet for Pipers Brook and Ninth Island. Excellent meals featuring Tasmanian produce are served in the *restaurant* overlooking the river. The nearby **St Matthias Vineyard** (☎ 6330 1700) is also open daily for tastings.

Next door to the vineyards is *Conmel Cottage (☎ 6330 1466)*, which can be rented for $95 a double, including breakfast. A little farther north, *Tamar House (☎ 6330 1744)* offers similar B&B for $100 a double.

When you again meet the highway, it is worth following the signs to the nearby **Bradys Lookout State Reserve**. Brady was a well-known bushranger who used this rocky outcrop to spy on travellers on the road below. You can do the same today and also enjoy the fine views over the Tamar River.

## EXETER
* **pop 400**

The Tamar visitors' centre (☎ 6394 4454), on the main street, is well stocked with information on the region.

If you're hungry visit the *Exeter Bakery*, which is open daily and bakes its own creations in a wood-fired oven – real country cooking. You can also eat at the *Exeter Country Kitchen*, on the main road. The *Tamar Court Restaurant*, on the highway, serves lunches from Wednesday to Sunday and dinners from Wednesday to Saturday.

On the second Sunday of every month a **market** is held in the show hall from 11 am till 3 pm.

There is nowhere to stay in town.

## ROBIGANA & DEVIOT

Instead of following the main highway from Exeter to Beaconsfield it's far more scenic to follow the minor roads beside the Tamar River. Turn off just south of Exeter and pass through Gravelly Beach, Robigana and Deviot.

Robigana – named after an Aboriginal word for 'swans' – is the spot where the road crosses the Supply River. From here there is a marked walking track beside the Tamar River to **Paper Beach**, which takes one hour return. If you prefer a shorter walk it's only 400m along the Supply River to the ruins of a **flour mill**. This was the site of the first water-driven flour mill in Australia. It's a pleasant walk under the trees, although there is not a lot to see at the ruins.

Farther upstream on the Supply River is *Norfolk Reach (☎ 6394 7681)*, which provides B&B for $80 a double. This is well hidden in quiet bushland and is a great place for birdwatching. Access is via Motor Rd.

At Deviot, **Marions Vineyard** (☎ 6394 7434) is open daily with a $2 fee for wine tastings. The fee is refunded if you make a purchase from its range of six or seven wines. The vineyard provides good free facilities, with a sheltered barbecue area, timber tables and sink.

## BATMAN BRIDGE

This is an important link between the two sides of the Tamar River. Its eye-catching design resulted from foundation problems. The east bank has poor foundations for a large bridge so it just supports a minor part of the span. Most of the bridge is supported by the 100m-tall west tower that leans out over the river. Opened in 1968, it was one the world's first cable-stayed truss bridges. There are good views and toilets on the eastern bank of the river.

Passing underneath the bridge on the western bank, a gravel road leads to **Sidmouth**. About all there is to see here is the Auld Kirk and graveyard and the nearby views of the Batman Bridge.

## BEACONSFIELD
* **pop 1358**

The once-thriving gold-mining town of Beaconsfield is still dominated by the ruins of its three original mine buildings. Two of these house the **Grubb Shaft Gold Museum** complex, which is open daily from 10 am to 4 pm; entry is $4, $3 for students and 50c

THE NORTH

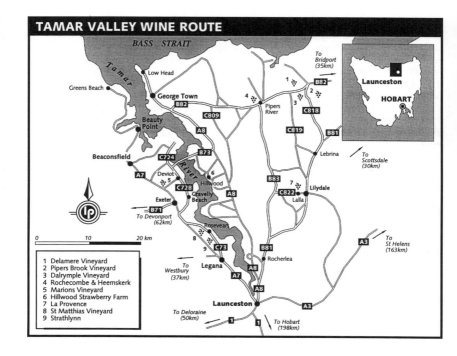

TAMAR VALLEY WINE ROUTE

1 Delamere Vineyard
2 Pipers Brook Vineyard
3 Dalrymple Vineyard
4 Rochecombe & Heemskerk
5 Marions Vineyard
6 Hillwood Strawberry Farm
7 La Provence
8 St Matthias Vineyard
9 Strathlynn

for children. This was Tasmania's largest gold mine, as seen in the size of the equipment and depth of the mine. The museum is staffed by volunteers and has some working machinery demonstrating how the mine operated. It's worth a visit. Opposite the mine buildings, a miner's cottage and old school are on display. The old Hart Shaft next to the museum has been opened up and, using today's technology, mining for gold is again under way. There is a viewing platform overlooking this shaft in the museum.

There is nowhere to stay overnight in town. The *Club Hotel* (☎ *6383 1191*), north of the gold mine on Weld St, serves counter meals daily. *Garwoods Bakery* produces some tasty breads. The supermarket sells takeaway meals, and there is a Chinese restaurant called *Red Ruby Chinese* (☎ *6383 4153*).

## HOLWELL GORGE
In the hills, 9km south of Beaconsfield, the small reserve of Holwell Gorge contains sections of original forest. There are some giant trees reaching 60m, many ferns and three waterfalls. A reasonable one-way track runs through the gorge and it takes about two hours return.

## BEAUTY POINT
• pop 1137
Initially the port for the nearby Beaconsfield gold mines, this town still has a wharf and ship-loading facilities. The name did not originate from the landscape; rather it was named after a bullock called Beauty. In spite of that, the name is definitely appropriate!

Beauty Point is home to the **Australian Maritime College**, which conducts training in fisheries, navigation and other maritime skills. With its many live-in students and three training vessels, the college is a significant supporter of the town's economy, as is shipping.

Just west of the town, *Redbill Point Van Park* (☎ 6383 4536) provides tent sites for $11 and on-site vans for $35. A room for two at the *Beauty Point Motor Hotel* (☎ 6383 4363), near the college, is $65, and *Riviera Hotel* (☎ 6383 4153), on the northern side of the town, charges $55 a double with breakfast. Both hotels have counter meals daily.

If you prefer somewhere more peaceful, the nearby holiday settlements of Kelso and Greens Beach might appeal. *Kelso Sands Caravan Park* (☎ 6383 9130) has tent sites for $12, powered sites for $15, on-site vans for $35 and cabins for $50 (all double rates). The more basic *Greens Beach Caravan Park* (☎ 6383 9222) has tent sites for $7. The *Holiday Lodge Hotel* (☎ 6383 4188), just south of Kelso, has B&B in rooms with *en suite* for $60 a double. It serves counter meals daily.

If you are cycling and wish to avoid using Batman Bridge, you can cross to George Town with Tamar Boat Hire (☎ 6383 4744), on Beauty Point Marina, for $10 to $12.

## ASBESTOS RANGE NATIONAL PARK

This little known park is located roughly midway between the Tamar River and Devonport. The scenery is not as sensational or rugged as in many other parks; instead it's a gentle landscape. Part of the park was once farmland, and the cleared land provides grasslands. The prime purpose of the park is to provide some habitat for Tasmania's larger animals, particularly the Forester kangaroo. Around dusk you will also see wombats, wallabies and pademelons grazing.

Park entry fees apply and permits are available from the ranger (☎ 6428 6277). The rangers provide guided walks, talks and activities during the summer months. Horse riding is allowed and corrals and a 26km

trail are also provided. Permits are needed for horse riding and bookings should be made with the ranger as facilities are limited. **Bakers Beach** provides the safest swimming area, and water-skiing is allowed there in summer.

There are some interesting walking trails in the park. **Badger Head** provides a four hour circuit walk. **Archers Knob** has good views of Bakers Beach and takes four hours return. The **Springlawn Nature Trail** is short and has an interesting boardwalk across a swamp. The **beach** from Griffiths Point to Bakers Point is good for beachcombing and is also a great place to watch the sun set.

Bush *camping* is allowed at three places in the western half of the park for $4 a person; pit toilets and bore water are supplied. The park can be reached from the Beaconsfield area or from Port Sorell near Devonport.

## LOW HEAD
• **pop 454**

Located on the eastern side of the Tamar River where it enters Bass Strait, this scattered settlement contains the historic **Pilot Station**. The station was established in 1805 and the current buildings were convict-built in 1835. Today the building contains the interesting **Pilot Station Maritime Museum**. With 10 rooms of displays it is good value; entry is $3 for adults and $2 for children, and it's open daily from 8 am until late.

At Low Head itself, the **lighthouse**, built in 1888, is worth a visit. It provides great views over the river mouth and surrounding area. There is good surf at **East Beach** on Bass Strait and safe swimming in calm water at **Lagoon Bay** on the river.

The town itself does not have a centre, but there are shops at George Town, which is only 5km away. Around the town are navigation lights, which look like mini-lighthouses and are very striking with their painted red stripes. You can watch the fairy penguins return to their nests near the lighthouse, or join the guided penguin tours (☎ 0418 361 860) one hour before sunset from July to April at a cost of $6 for adults and $3 for children. The departure point is

THE NORTH

signposted on the main road soon after you enter the town.

## Places to Stay & Eat

The **Golden Beach Pines Holiday Village** (☎ 6382 2602) is right by the sea at East Beach, facing Bass Strait. It has a kiosk and a family restaurant that is open daily. Tent sites are $6, sites with power $15 and cabins are $55/60. Less attractive is **Low Head Caravan Park** (☎ 6382 1573), which is about midway between George Town and Low Head. Tent sites are $10, powered sites $13, on-site vans $25 and self-contained cabins $50 a double.

The **Pilot Station** (☎ 0417 503 292) now offers self-contained accommodation in the Pilot's House. The house itself is rather plain, but it's large enough to sleep eight, has a water frontage and is right in the station grounds. It's $60/70 plus $20 for each extra adult, with provisions for a continental breakfast. There are plans to open a number of the other cottages here, including one with facilities for the disabled.

**Belfont Cottages** (☎ 6382 1841) provides B&B for $110 a double. If you phone in advance, a courtesy car from George Town can be provided. The décor here is very attractive, but the position is less appealing than that of the Pilot Station.

## GEORGE TOWN

- pop 5025

George Town, on the eastern shore of the Tamar River, close to the heads, is best known as the site where Colonel Paterson landed in 1804 to settle northern Tasmania. In 1811 the town was named after King George. It might have become the northern capital but for its lack of fresh water, which prompted Paterson to move south in 1825 and establish Launceston. Some of the older buildings in town date from the 1830s and 1840s, when it prospered as the port linking Tasmania with Victoria.

The opening of the aluminium smelter at nearby Bell Bay in 1949 revived the town, and today Bell Bay's industries continue to provide employment. In addition, for as long as the catamaran service to Melbourne continues, Gorge Town will be a bustling summer gateway to the state.

## Information

The visitors' information centre (☎ 6382 1700) is on Low Head Main Rd as you enter the town from the south. The post office, which is an agency for the Commonwealth Bank, is on Macquarie St, as is the Trust Bank.

## Things to See

**The Grove** on Cimitiere St is a lovely Georgian stone residence dating from the 1830s, which has been classified by the National Trust. It's open daily from 9.30 am to 5.30 pm in summer and from 10 am to 5 pm during the rest of the year; admission is $4 for adults, $1.50 for children and $10 for a family. Refreshments are available and lunch is served by staff in period costume. You can also stay here (see Places to Stay in this section).

The **old watch house** on Macquarie St dates from 1843 and has been turned into a community arts centre; it's open weekdays from 11 am to 3 pm and Saturday morning, and it costs nothing to look around. Also of interest is the **St Mary Magdalene Anglican Church** on Anne St. On the northern edge of town you will find a distinctive **water tower**. The mural is an innovative way of disguising what might otherwise be a dominant eyesore. For panoramic views visit **Mt George**, which has a restored semaphore mast on it.

## Organised Tours

**Bell Bay** The nearby industrial area of Bell Bay has Tasmania's only thermal power station, along with several other unattractive heavy industries; it can be clearly seen from the highway. In recent years these factories have been reducing their output of pollutants and improving their image. Temco (☎ 6382 0200) has a tour of its furnaces on the first Wednesday of every month at 11 am, and Comalco (☎ 6382 5111) has site tours of the aluminium smelter on the first Friday of each month – ring for details.

Make sure you wear enclosed shoes, long sleeves and pants for protection.

**Seal Spotting** Seal & Sea Adventure Tours (☎ 0419 357028) offers tours in which you can actually enter the water in a wetsuit and a perspex shark cage and view seals close up for $95 an adult (minimum of three). If you don't want to enter the water, you can still watch the wildlife through the glass bottom of the boat. Fishing and diving trips can also be arranged.

## Places to Stay & Eat

The hotels and motels in George Town are often booked by people working short term at Bell Bay, so don't take it for granted that you will find it easy to get accommodation, even midweek in the low season. And of course, when the catamaran is running all types of accommodation are likely to be in demand.

For caravan parks, see the previous section on Low Head, which is only 5km north.

The YHA hostel in town is the *Travellers Hostel* (☎ 6382 3261, 4 Elizabeth St). It's

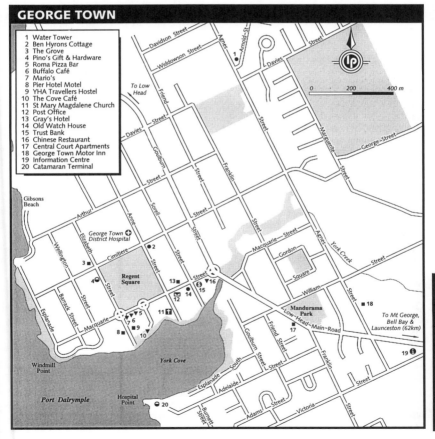

**GEORGE TOWN**

1 Water Tower
2 Ben Hyrons Cottage
3 The Grove
4 Pino's Gift & Hardware
5 Roma Pizza Bar
6 Buffalo Café
7 Mario's
8 Pier Hotel Motel
9 YHA Travellers Hostel
10 The Cove Café
11 St Mary Magdalene Church
12 Post Office
13 Gray's Hotel
14 Old Watch House
15 Trust Bank
16 Chinese Restaurant
17 Central Court Apartments
18 George Town Motor Inn
19 Information Centre
20 Catamaran Terminal

0    200    400 m

To Low Head

Gibsons Beach

George Town District Hospital

Regent Square

Gibsons Beach

Windmill Point

Port Dalrymple

Hospital Point

York Cove

Mandurama Park

To Mt George, Bell Bay & Launceston (62km)

**THE NORTH**

in an attractive restored house with pleasant gardens close to the waterfront and has tent sites for $10, beds for $14 and double and twin rooms for $40. The *George Town Motor Inn* (☎ *6382 1057*) has basic units on the edge of town for $45/55 and also has a family bistro. A little closer to the town centre, signposted off Main Rd, are more motel units at *Central Court Apartments* (☎ *6382 2155*).

If you prefer a hotel room, try *Gray's Hotel* (☎ *6382 2655, 75 Macquarie St*), which has rooms with *en suites* for $70. The family bistro serves lunches and dinners daily. The classiest hotel in town is the *Pier Hotel Motel* (☎ *6382 1300, 3 Elizabeth St*). The comfortable hotel rooms with shared facilities are in the old building and cost $40/50; the motel rooms, which are new and face the water, are $99 a single or double; and new self-contained villa units are $119 a single or double. The pub is open for breakfast and its bistro serves meals daily.

*The Grove* (☎ *6382 1336, Cimitiere St*) has accommodation for $60/75 with breakfast provisions. The licensed restaurant serves morning and afternoon teas and light lunches, with mains priced up to $11.

Apart from the hotels, there are *takeaways* and *Italian* and *Chinese restaurants* on Macquarie St, as well as the licensed *Buffalo Café*, which is open Thursday to Sunday from 10 am for coffee, lunch or dinner and has something of the atmosphere of a city wine bar. The *Cove Café* is a reasonable café along a short path down by the water.

## Getting There & Away

TRC runs three buses every weekday along the eastern side of the Tamar River from George Town through Hillwood and Dilston to Launceston. There are no services on Saturday. On Sunday evening one bus leaves Launceston at 5.15 pm for George Town then returns immediately to Launceston at 6.15 pm. On some services the bus will continue to Low Head for pick-ups, but only if it's prebooked.

When the catamaran is running, a coach to or from Launceston meets the ferry each time it arrives or departs.

The George Town agent for TRC is Pino's Gift & Hardware at 21 Elizabeth St. The fare to Launceston is $7.20.

## PIPERS RIVER REGION

This rural region is central to the Tasmanian wine industry. It started in 1974 with Pipers Brook and today the area produces about half of the state's wines. There are nine vineyards and seven have wine tastings. The countryside through which you drive to visit the vineyards is uninteresting, but some of the vineyards are particularly attractive, and the restaurant at **Rochecombe & Heemskerk Wines** is a beautiful place to stop for a meal. It has an outdoor vine-covered eating area and a playground for children. Wine tastings are available from 10 am to 5 pm daily. The *restaurant* is open daily from November to April and from Thursday to Monday during the rest of the year.

The most famous vineyard is **Pipers Brook**, which was started in the wake of an academic exercise by Dr Andrew Pirie comparing the famous wine regions of France with Australian regions. The architecturally arresting and innovative winery is open daily from 10 am to 5 pm and light lunches are available. Other vineyards worth visiting include **Delamere** and **Dalrymple**.

The Pipers River region is between the north and the north-east of the state. If you are travelling between these two regions, make sure you drop into a vineyard on the way. Alternatively, if you are spending time only in Bridport or George Town, visit the area as a day trip (what better way to spend a rainy day?).

## HILLWOOD

South of George Town, beside the Tamar River, is the attractive, rural area of Hillwood, where you can pick strawberries, raspberries and apples and sample Tasmanian fruit wines and cheese at the **Hillwood Strawberry Farm** (☎ *6394 8180*). It's open all year, but of course you can only pick fruit in season, which is mainly from December to March. The fruit wine is unusual and a real novelty – try it!

Next door to the farm is the Tasmanian Gourmet Cheese factory, which is not open to the public. The nearby airstrip provides ultralight aeroplane flights over the hills with Ultralight Aviation (☎ 018 120 199), but you should book a couple of days in advance. The village is also noted for its fishing and lovely river views.

## LILYDALE & LALLA

The tiny towns of Lilydale and Lalla, 25km north of Launceston, form the centre of an interesting region that is popular with visitors. There is something here for everybody, ranging from wine to flowers, and from easy strolls to strenuous walks.

At Lalla, the **WAG Walker Rhododendron Reserve** has superb floral displays from September to December. In other months it is less colourful but still worth a visit. Exotic and rare trees are a feature of

the reserve. Entry costs $2 a vehicle and it's open daily for much of the year, except in summer when it's only open on weekends.

Opposite the rhododendron reserve is **La Provence** (☎ 6395 1290), which was first planted in 1956, making it Tasmania's oldest vineyard. It is open for cellar-door sales daily.

Three kilometres from Lilydale is the **Lilydale Falls Reserve**, which has camping facilities and an easy 20 minute walk to two waterfalls. To the south of Lilydale is **Hollybank Forest**, which has fine picnic areas, numerous short tracks and an information centre. In its short history the reserve has been a sawmill, an ash forest producing wood for tennis racquets and cricket bats, and today it showcases the way forests are managed. While the displays are interesting, in our experience real forests are not as neatly managed as the reserve!

For a more energetic walk, climb **Mt Arthur**, which towers above Lilydale. A five to seven hour return walk leads to the

## How Do You Like Your Grapes?

Squeezed please! It doesn't really matter what colour they are so long as they have been lovingly processed and matured.

The Tasmanian wine industry is relatively young, with commercial crops first planted in the mid-1970s. Rapid expansion in the 1980s saw many new vineyards being developed and this has continued through the 1990s. There are now more than 100 grape growers in the state producing some 3000 tonnes of grapes.

Most of the vineyards in the state are tiny, but there are also a few very large ones, such as Pipers Brook, that produce wine under a number of labels. The vast majority of grapes come from the Tamar Valley and Pipers Brook regions.

While Tasmania's wine production is not yet on a grand scale, it has great potential owing to its cool-climate location. Tasmania's vineyards are at latitudes which, in the northern hemisphere, correspond to the French wine regions of Bordeaux and Burgundy. However, just as these cool climates offer potential, so too do they bring their share of difficulties as grape growers combat severe frost and high winds.

For the visitor, there is a good selection of wine tasting and cellar-door sale venues all around the state, and some of the larger companies have cool, green vineyard restaurants where their own wines complement wonderful fresh Tasmanian produce.

THE NORTH

summit from where there are lovely views if you ignore the towers on top.

## Places to Stay & Eat

For something different, stay near Lilydale at *Plovers Ridge Host Farm* (☎ *6395 1102).* With B&B, the self-contained units are $85/110. Vegetarian meals are available for guests. *Falls Farm* (☎ *6395 1598)* north-west of the town has B&B for $60/90. The landmark of the town is *Bardenhagen's General Store*, which is one of the few stores of its type still operating in Australia. It sells products from *Lilydale Bakery*, which is famous for its old-fashioned breads.

# Western Tiers & the North Coast

Between the northern coastal strip and the Great Western Tiers (which rise up to Tasmania's central plateau), there are some interesting towns and scenic places. Through the centre of this region, the Bass Hwy runs from Launceston to Deloraine then to Devonport. The best way to see the region is to leave the recently built highways from Launceston to Deloraine and follow the older roads through the small towns. Once you reach Deloraine, the most interesting route is through the hill country to the west of the Bass Hwy, through Sheffield.

## WESTBURY

- pop 1292

The historic town of Westbury, 32km west of Launceston, is best known for its **White House**, a property built in 1841 as a general store. It is now managed by the National Trust and features several collections, such as period furniture and old vehicles, including an 1888 penny-farthing. The house is open from 10 am to 4 pm daily except Monday; admission is $6 for adults, $4 for children and $12 for a family. An **historic walk** (☎ 6393 1053) departs from the White House corner; the $13 charge includes Devonshire tea and a tour of the White House.

In front of the White House is the **village green**, a long, narrow, grassy park that includes a maypole and war memorial.

The **Westbury Gemstone, Mineral & Mural Display**, on the Bass Hwy, has a huge collection, but it was for sale at the time of writing. However, if it's closed, at least you can walk down the side of the shed for a free look at the mural. Next door is **Pearn's Steam World**, which is open from 9 am to 4 pm daily. It costs $3 to inspect a wide range of working steam engines; you might even get to ride on one.

On the other side of the old highway is the **Westbury Maze**. This hedge maze is open daily from October to June; admission is $3.50 for adults, $2.50 for children and $14 for a family.

## Places to Stay

The *Westbury Hotel* (☎ *6393 1151, 107 Bass Hwy)* provides basic rooms for $25/45. For B&B, *Fitzpatricks Inn* (☎ *6393 1153),* an old building beside the highway at No 56, is good value at $40/70. It's not nearly as grand as it looks from the outside, but it has clean, comfortable *en suite* rooms sharing a veranda overlooking a lovely garden.

Slightly farther out of town is the Westbury Inn, but at the time of writing, it was not offering accommodation.

*The Olde Coaching Inn* (☎ *6393 2100, 54 William St)* has B&B for $79 a double. The first room, which has an *en suite,* has more of a period feel about it, as well as access to a lovely private courtyard. The other room has a nicer bathroom, but it's on the other side of the breakfast area.

The host of *Gingerbread Cottage* (☎ *6393 1140, 52 William St)* insists that this quirky little house is just like grandma's, and she's right! Out the back is a dense cottage garden and lots of potted plants that attract plenty of birds. Inside are kitchen appliances and ornaments that seem to have come straight from Clarke's Antiques next door, a separate business run by the same people. The old elegant fashioned toilet seat is an attraction in itself. Bed and provisions for a cooked breakfast are $114 a double.

THE NORTH

## Places to Eat

The *White House Bakery* is open from 9 am to 4.30 pm Wednesday to Sunday and sells pies, biscuits and bread.

The *Bass Bakery* on the main road is open 24 hours a day and serves pizza from 5 to 11 pm from Thursday to Sunday. Next door is *Hobnobs Coffee Shop & Licensed Restaurant*.

The *Westbury Hotel* serves counter lunches and dinners daily. On Thursday night it is possible to buy a Chinese meal

from a takeaway van outside and eat it in the hotel.

## Getting There & Away

See the Deloraine Getting There & Away section for information on bus services to the town.

## DELORAINE

* pop 2098

With its lovely riverside picnic area, superb setting at the foot of the Great Western

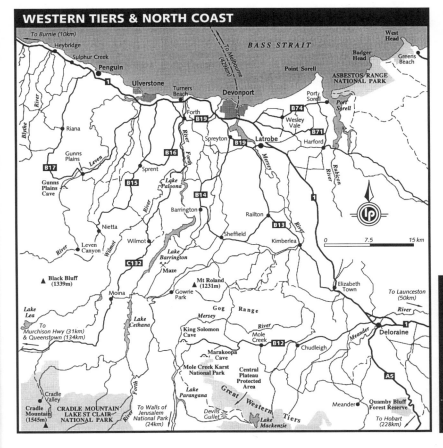

THE NORTH

Tiers and good amenities, Deloraine is a great alternative to nearby Launceston or Devonport, both of which could conceivably be enjoyed in a series of day trips from this beguiling smaller town. It is close to Cradle Mountain and even closer to a number of impressive waterfalls, caves and shorter walks, and although it may not always be the most convenient stopover for interstate or international travellers heading for the Overland Track, it has much to offer bushwalkers as a base for exploring the whole of the central north. (Unfortunately, the local lads can be rather noisy on Friday and Saturday nights, and at the time of writing the goods train passing through the town late in the evening was blowing its whistle at the level crossing loudly enough to wake all but the heaviest sleepers staying in accommodation in the centre of town.)

Deloraine owes a good deal of its charm to its Georgian and Victorian buildings, many of which have been faithfully restored. It was first settled by Europeans in the 1820s, and the older buildings date mainly from the 1830s and 1840s. Initially cattle grazing and wheat growing were the mainstays of the region but competition and disease closed the wheat mills. The farms have since diversified and now cultivate a wide variety of crops as well as raising livestock.

The main reason people come to Deloraine is to bushwalk and explore the nearby caves of the Mole Creek Karst National Park (see the following Mole Creek section for caving information).

If you are travelling in this area in spring, it's worth being aware that Deloraine's annual craft fair draws tens of thousands of visitors in late October and/or early November,

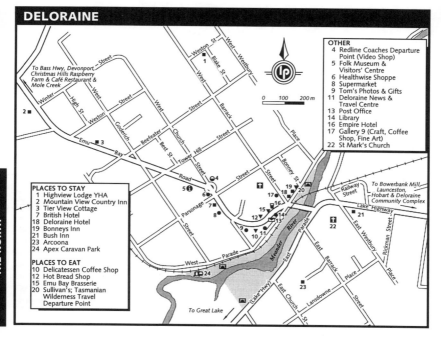

## DELORAINE

**OTHER**
4  Redline Coaches Departure Point (Video Shop)
5  Folk Museum & Visitors' Centre
6  Healthwise Shoppe
8  Supermarket
9  Tom's Photos & Gifts
11  Deloraine News & Travel Centre
13  Post Office
14  Library
16  Empire Hotel
17  Gallery 9 (Craft, Coffee Shop, Fine Art)
22  St Mark's Church

**PLACES TO STAY**
1  Highview Lodge YHA
2  Mountain View Country Inn
3  Tier View Cottage
7  British Hotel
18  Deloraine Hotel
19  Bonneys Inn
21  Bush Inn
23  Arcoona
24  Apex Caravan Park

**PLACES TO EAT**
10  Delicatessen Coffee Shop
12  Hot Bread Shop
15  Emu Bay Brasserie
20  Sullivan's; Tasmanian Wilderness Travel Departure Point

To Bass Hwy, Devonport, Christmas Hills Raspberry Farm & Café Restaurant & Mole Creek

To Bowerbank Mill, Launceston, Hobart & Deloraine Community Complex

To Great Lake

when accommodation can be booked out from Launceston to Devonport.

## Information

The Deloraine visitors' centre (☎ 6362 3471) is in the Folk Museum, by the roundabout on Emu Bay Rd. It's staffed by volunteers and is open Monday to Friday from 9.30 am to 4 pm, Saturday from 1 to 3.30 pm and Sunday from 2 to 4 pm.

Internet access is available at the library on Church St.

There are branches of the Trust and ANZ banks in town, and the post office is an agent for the Commonwealth Bank. EFTPOS withdrawals can be made at the Deloraine News & Travel Centre for a transaction fee of $1; this is also a travel agent and is open from 6 am to 6 pm Monday to Saturday and from 7 am to 1 pm on Sunday.

Bushwalkers can pick up food and gas supplies in Deloraine, but for specialised gear you will have to travel to Devonport or Launceston.

## Museum & Galleries

The small **Folk Museum** is on Emu Bay Rd, near the roundabout (see the previous Information entry for opening hours). Also in town is **Gallery 9**, featuring jewellery, art, theatre and occasional musical recitals. It is usually open from 10.30 am to 5 pm daily, though hours may be reduced in winter.

Two kilometres to the east of Deloraine, on the road to Launceston, is **Bowerbank Mill**. The corn mill was built in 1853 and is classified by the National Trust; these days it houses an art gallery, which is open from 10 am to 5.30 pm daily, and also provides accommodation (see Places to Stay in this section).

At the uninspiring Deloraine Community Complex on Alverston Drive you can see some impressive panels (3.5m by 4m) described as **Artwork in Silk**, in which embroidery, weaving, patchwork and a number of other techniques have been used to depict aspects of local history and the surrounding environment. The exhibition is open from 10 am to 4 pm Monday to Wednesday (and

from 1 to 5 pm Sunday from December to April), and admission is $3.

## St Mark's Church

This church, which is floodlit at night, is situated on high ground on the eastern side of the river and can be seen from most parts of the town. It is open to the public daily except school holidays, though you may have to find someone to let you in. The main part of the church was built in 1859, while the chancel and sanctuary were added in 1878. A detailed printed guide is available inside. Visitors are asked not to enter the sanctuary.

## Farms & Gardens

About 8km north of Deloraine, on the road to Devonport and just before Elizabeth Town, is the **Christmas Hills Raspberry Farm**, where you can pick your own fruit in December and January (see also Places to Eat in this section). A bit farther on is **Ashgrove Farm** (☎ 6368 1137), where you can see award-winning cheeses being processed. It is open daily from 9 am to 5.30 pm.

The beautiful gardens at **Villarett**, along a side road that departs the highway a farther 8km past Elizabeth Town, are well worth a visit even if you are not intending to eat or sleep there.

## Bushwalking

Dominating the southern skyline are the Great Western Tiers, which provide some excellent walking. Their Aboriginal name is Kooparoona Niara, meaning Mountain of the Spirits, and they feature many waterfalls, exceptional forest and some long climbs. The **Meander Forest Reserve** is the most popular starting point. From here Split Rock Falls can be visited in two to three hours, or you can walk farther to Meander Falls, which are four to five hours return. Overnight camping is allowed in the area.

Other good walks on the Great Western Tiers are to **Projection Bluff** (two hours), **Quamby Bluff** (five hours) and **Mother Cummings Peak** (three hours). There are many other walks described in various walking guides (see Bushwalking in the Activities chapter).

## Special Events
The impressive Tasmanian Craft Fair, held in Deloraine over four days in late October and/or early November, is claimed to be Australia's largest working craft fair. There are 200 stalls at 10 venues around town, the main venue being the Community Complex on Alveston Drive.

## Organised Tours
Bonneys Farm (☎ 6362 2122) runs half-day ($20) and day tours ($40 to $45) to many of the attractions listed in the Western Tiers & North Coast section of this chapter. Clients not staying at the farm itself (see Places to Stay – Mid-Range in this section) can be collected from accommodation in town.

## Places to Stay – Budget
**Camping** A basic tent site at the *Apex Caravan Park* (☎ 6362 2345) costs $7/9, while powered sites are $10/12; there are no on-site vans. This park's lovely position on the banks of the river means it is subject to flooding, but we're told the caretaker is expert at moving vans out in a hurry.

**Hostels** The YHA hostel is the *Highview Lodge Youth Hostel* (☎ 6362 2996, 8 Blake St). It's a steep walk from town, but the compensation is magnificent views of the Great Western Tiers. It charges $12, and its office hours are from 8 to 10 am and 5 to 10 pm. Since it changed managers a couple of years ago, it has been less involved in arranging tours, but mountain and touring bikes are still available for hire.

**Hotels** East of the bridge is the *Bush Inn* (☎ 6362 2365, 7 Bass Hwy), with good hotel accommodation for just $15 a head (a continental breakfast is $5 extra). Although a little farther from town, it is probably a quieter pub to stay in than the Deloraine Hotel, and its shared facilities look a bit better.

All the rooms in the circa 1848 *Deloraine Hotel* (☎ 6362 2022) are $25 a head

with continental breakfast, so try for one of the three pleasant rooms with *en suite*, as the others are smaller and the shared facilities pretty spartan. The *British Hotel* also has accommodation.

## Places to Stay – Mid-Range
**Rural Accommodation** If you want to stay out of town, try *Bonneys Farm* (☎ 6362 2122), 4km away. It has three units and a guesthouse for $40/60, plus $12 for each extra person. It also runs tours (see the earlier Organised Tours entry for details). To get there on the way in from Devonport, just follow the signs; on the way out of Deloraine on the road to Devonport, take the turn-off to Weetah.

At *Villarett*, along a side road that departs the highway 8km past Elizabeth Town, you can stay in a spacious, private, fairly modern unit overlooking lush, undulating countryside for $65/85, which includes a cooked breakfast.

**B&Bs** Right in the town centre is the circa 1830 *Bonneys Inn* (☎ 6362 2974), which was the first brick building in Deloraine. It charges $60/75 for recently upgraded colonial-style accommodation. The price includes a cooked breakfast in winter and a continental breakfast in summer. Some rooms have *en suites*, and it is very comfortable for the price.

A little out of the centre of town is *Tier View Cottage* (☎ 6362 2377, 125 Emu Bay Rd), which is a pleasant place to stay, despite being opposite a service station. It charges $70 a single or double for the whole cottage, with ingredients for a continental breakfast provided.

**Motels** The *Mountain View Country Inn* (☎ 6362 2633) charges $70/75 for older rooms with shower only and $80/85 for rooms with queen-size bed, shower and bath. Breakfast is extra, and there's a licensed restaurant (closed Sunday). The older rooms have views of the Tiers, which in our opinion makes them preferable to the more expensive rooms.

## Places to Stay – Top End

**B&Bs** The luxuriously appointed *Arcoona* (☎ 6362 3443, 018 463 347) is on a hill on the eastern side of the river (access from East Barrack St). This historic building was originally the town doctor's residence and then became the district hospital. An impressive feature is the billiard room, with its original table. B&B is $95/130 ($150 a double with spa).

Two kilometres out of town on the road to Launceston is the historic and wonderfully atmospheric *Bowerbank Mill* (☎ 6362 2628), built in 1853 as a flour mill. Here, B&B is $105/130, and three-course evening meals with coffee are available for $32.

## Places to Eat

The place visitors head for these days is the *Christmas Hills Raspberry Farm*. It's well signposted about 8km from town on the road to Devonport, and is open daily from 9 am to 5 pm (6 pm in summer). Desserts here are understandably heavy on the raspberries – raspberry sorbet, raspberry pavlova, raspberry crepes, raspberry waffles – but it's a relaxed little restaurant on a genuine farm and so far not at all gimmicky. A popular and filling winter choice is the $9.50 special of a hearty soup and damper followed by dessert.

Back in town there are plenty of takeaways on the main street. *Sullivan's* café is open daily from 9 am to 7.30 pm and serves everything from fish and chips to eye fillet. Counter meals are available at the three hotels in town, as well as at the *Elizabeth Town Hotel*, 10km north of town on the road to Devonport.

Self-caterers should be pleased with the variety of health food, organic vegetables, breads and dairy products available at *Healthwise Shoppe*, open Tuesday to Friday from 9 am to 5 pm and Saturday until noon.

One of the nicest places for a late breakfast, a light lunch or a snack is the *Delicatessen Coffee Shop*. Its menu features savoury pastries and Tasmanian produce, and it's open Monday to Friday from 9 am to 5 pm and Saturday from 9.30 am to 1.30 pm.

Also very popular and reasonably priced is the *Emu Bay Brasserie* (☎ 6362 2067), which is open for dinner. It has pastas for $8.50 and side salads for $3.50, as well as more expensive items such as salmon tails for $15. Its jovial hosts make everyone feel welcome, and there's a log fire in winter. It's open Monday to Saturday from 9 am (10 am in winter) to 2.30 pm for breakfast or lunch and from 6 pm for dinner.

For an earlier breakfast or a cheap Sunday lunch, try the *Hot Bread Shop*. It serves pies, pasties, rolls and pastries, and at the time we visited had cappuccino for $1. It's open from 8 am to 5 pm Monday to Friday and until 3 pm on Sunday (closed Saturday).

Back out of town, along a side road that departs the highway 8km past Elizabeth Town on the way to Devonport, is *Villarett*, which has a teahouse open daily except Friday for light meals from 10 am to 4, 5 or 6 pm, depending on the time of year.

## Getting There & Away

From Monday to Friday TRC runs up to five buses a day from Launceston through Westbury to Deloraine and return. The one-way fare is $6.80. Ask TRC about a shuttle service to Mole Creek.

From early December to early April Tasmanian Wilderness Travel (TWT, ☎ 6334 4442) runs buses through Deloraine on its Wilderness service between Launceston and Hobart via Great Lake, Lake St Clair and Mt Field on Monday, Tuesday, Thursday and Saturday. You can also get to Deloraine on TWT's Walls of Jerusalem service, which operates on Tuesday, Thursday and Saturday in summer and Monday and Friday the rest of the year. Both these services are Wilderness services, which means they only operate when there are four full-fare-paying passengers on board. TWT arrives at and departs from Sullivan's Restaurant.

## MOLE CREEK

* pop 249

About 25km west of Deloraine is Mole Creek, in the vicinity of which you'll find spectacular limestone caves, leatherwood honey and one of Tasmania's best wildlife parks. The town is tiny, with very few services, but it has excellent views of the Great Western Tiers and is a handy access point for caving and bushwalking.

## Mole Creek Karst National Park

The word 'karst' refers to the scenery characteristic of a limestone region, including caves and underground streams. Of the 300 caves in the Mole Creek area, about 50 have been included in the Mole Creek Karst National Park, declared in 1996. The park itself is in a number of small segments, and entry fees are incorporated into the prices of admission to public caves and fees for wild cave tours.

**Public Caves** There are two public caves: **Marakoopa** (from the Aboriginal word meaning 'handsome'), a wet cave 15km from Mole Creek featuring two underground streams and an incredible glowworm display; and **King Solomon**, a dry cave with amazing light-reflecting calcite crystals (and very few steps, making it the better cave for the less energetic). In the high season there are at least five tours daily of each cave, except on Christmas Day, when both are closed. The caves remain open in winter, but tour times may vary. Current tour times are prominently displayed on access roads: the earliest tour of Marakoopa is usually at 10 am, while the first tour of King Solomon usually departs at 10.30 am. The last tour for the day at both caves is usually at 4 pm. A tour of one cave costs $8 (children $4), or you can visit both for $12 (children $6). Family prices are $20 for one cave and $30 for two. For more details, ring the ranger on ☎ 6363 5182.

**Wild Caves** These are caves without steps or ladders, and among the better known in the Mole Creek area are Cyclops, Wet, Honeycomb and the magnificent Baldocks. The only way you can view such caves is with a caving club or as a member of a guided tour. Wild Cave Tours (☎ 6367 8142) provides caving gear and guides for

$65 a half-day or $130 a full day per person. Take spare clothing and a towel, as you will get wet. The tours, which must be booked, depart from outside Sam's Supermarket on the main street of Mole Creek at 9.30 am. Guide Deb Hunter does her utmost to cater for the interests of her clients, varying the number and type of caves visited to suit their requirements. It is, however, impossible for her to accommodate experienced cavers who wish to do vertical rope work; these people will have to make their own arrangements with cave clubs (see Caving in the Activities chapter). Deb does not collect clients from Launceston or Devonport.

## Stephens Leatherwood Honey Factory

The leatherwood tree only grows in the damp western part of Tasmania, so honey made by bees visiting its flower is unique to this state. From January to April, when the honey is being extracted, you can visit the factory (☎ 6363 1170) in Mole Creek and learn all about this fascinating industry. It's open on weekdays and admission is free.

## Trowunna Wildlife Park

Two kilometres from Chudleigh, east of Mole Creek on the way in from Deloraine, is the Trowunna Wildlife Park (☎ 6363 6162), which is worth a visit. It specialises in Tasmanian devils, wombats and koalas, the last of which are not native to the state and are only found here in captivity. The park also features many birds, including white goshawks and the wedge-tailed eagles. It's open daily, except Christmas day, from 9 am to 5 pm (8 pm in summer) and admission is $8.50 (children $4.50). Prebooked nocturnal tours (most of the animals are active at night) take place from January to April and also cost $8.50.

## Devils Gullet

In fine weather, those with transport should head for the Western Tiers. The only road that actually reaches the top of the plateau is the one to Lake McKenzie. Follow this road to Devils Gullet. The 30 minute return walk leads to a platform bolted to the top of a dramatic gorge: looking over the edge is not for the faint-hearted.

## Bushwalking

Popular short walks in the area are **Alum Cliffs Gorge** (one hour return) and **Westmoreland Falls** (two hours return). For information about the Walls of Jerusalem National Park, see the following section.

## Places to Stay & Eat

Three kilometres west of town beside Sassafras Creek, at the signpost to Paradise and Sheffield where the main road veers off to the caves and Cradle Mountain, is the *Mole Creek Caravan Park (☎ 6363 1150)*. It has basic facilities with coin-operated showers and charges $8 a family for tent sites and $10 for powered sites.

Rooms at the *Mole Creek Hotel (☎ 6363 1102)* have been nicely painted, and this, together with new linen, curtains and colour TVs, has made them a more comfortable but also more expensive option than they used to be. B&B is $30/55 with shared facilities and $60 a double with *en suite*. Downstairs in the lounge bar, counter meals are avail-

able daily, or you can sit down to standard roadside café fare just along the street at the *Mole Creek Tearooms & Takeaway*, which is open long hours seven days a week.

Nearby, the small *Mole Creek Guesthouse (☎ 6363 1399)* charges $70 a double for rooms with private bathroom across the hall and $92 a double for rooms with *en suite*. The price includes a cooked breakfast served in the restaurant. The tearoom and restaurant downstairs provide meals and snacks.

Back towards Deloraine, *Mole Creek Holiday Village (☎ 6363 6124)* has attractive timber units with mountain views for $68 a double; there is also a restaurant and tearooms on the premises.

Closer to Mole Creek is the turn-off to *Blackwood Park (☎ 6363 1208)*, where you can rent a single brick three bedroom cottage situated in lush farmland in sight of the main house but far enough away to feel private. It has beautifully crafted furniture, a stone floor with under-floor heating and excellent facilities. At just $96 a double for B&B, it's a real find.

Farther along the road is *Alum Cliffs Homestead (☎ 6363 6149)*, which offers B&B in a self-contained unit for $65.

## Leatherwood Honey

Under the canopy of the tall, rainforest trees in the wet, western half of Tasmania, grow the endemic leatherwood trees (*Eucryphia lucida*). The trees grow to a height of about 20m. From December to March the tree is covered in small, white, waxy flowers that have very pale pink stamens. The name 'Leatherwood' comes from the leathery nature of the tree's timber.

Leatherwood honey was first produced commercially in the early 1920s, but it was not until after the war that Tasmanian beekeepers commenced taking large numbers of hives into the leatherwood areas. Today, many thousands of hives are transported by truck or even semi-trailer annually.

Apiarists visit their sites several times during the flowering season to remove full boxes, known as 'supers', and replace them with empty ones for the bees to work on. At the end of the flowering period, all the hives are brought back to their home sites and the honey is extracted from the full supers.

Honey is extracted from the 'combs' inside the supers by spinning and is then packaged for sale and export. The resulting product is a distinctive, aromatic honey that will certainly tempt your taste buds!

THE NORTH

From the same turn-off on the main road, you can reach *Rosewick Cottage (☎ 6363 1354)*, which has B&B for $60 a double in a three bedroom cottage.

## Getting There & Away
See Getting There & Away in the earlier Deloraine section for details.

## WALLS OF JERUSALEM NATIONAL PARK
The most popular full day walk is to the Walls of Jerusalem National Park. This park comprises a series of glacial valleys and lakes on top of the plateau. If you have the time and equipment, it's worth camping in the park. This is a very delicate area, and a water catchment, so if you camp within the 'walls', you should remove all your waste when you leave. The park is also exposed, so you must be prepared for strong winds and snowfalls even in summer. Walks across the park are described in *Cradle Mountain Lake St Clair and Walls of Jerusalem National Parks* by John Chapman and John Siseman.

If you prefer a guided walk, Taswalks (☎ 6363 6112) at Chudleigh will help you to explore the bush. Rather than running set tours, the company varies the places it visits, so you are able to see the real bush.

## Getting There & Away
**Bus** See Getting There & Away in the earlier Deloraine section for details of the TWT service to the start of the track. Fares are $45/80 one way/return from Launceston and $40/75 from Deloraine.

**Car** The best access to the Walls is from Sheffield or Mole Creek. From Mole Creek take the B12, then the C138 and finally the C171 (Mersey Forest Rd) to Lake Rowallan; remain on this road, following the 'C171' and/or 'Walls of Jerusalem' signs to the start of the track, from where it's a two hour walk to Herod's Gate.

## MOLE CREEK TO SHEFFIELD
From Mole Creek you will pass through Paradise before arriving at a major T-intersection at which you must turn right to Sheffield or left to Gowrie Park and Cradle Mountain. If you have the time, and are not intending to travel this way to Cradle Mountain on some other occasion, you might like to make a loop through Gowrie Park and back past Lake Barrington to Sheffield instead of taking the more direct route indicated by the road sign. The views of Mt Roland alone will make it a worthwhile detour, but there are also a number of attractions along the way that may be of interest to children.

## Paradise
The first part of the trip from Mole Creek takes you through the pretty little settlement of Paradise, dominated, like much of the area, by the dramatic 1233m Mt Roland (see the following Gowrie Park entry). Here you'll find the **Paradise Park Deer Farm** (☎ 6491 1628), which has 500 deer, barbecues, a coffee shop, a play area complete with tame deer and a *camping area*. Admission is $5 (children free), camping costs $8, and it's open from September to May.

*Paradise Cottage (☎ 6491 1613 or 6491 1626, Jeffries Rd)* has two units at $45 to $60 a double.

## Gowrie Park
Gowrie Park, 14km south-west of Sheffield, is a good place to stay if you intend to climb Mt Roland. It's also the site of a huge 94m-long mural on the Hydro Electric Commission (HEC) maintenance shed. There are walks to the summits of Mt Roland and Mt Vandyke and to Minnow Falls, as well as shorter walks in the cool, shady forests of the lower slopes.

**Mt Roland** This mountain looks like it would be extremely difficult to climb but is, in fact, graded as medium, though it should not be climbed in winter. There are two access points. The first is at a place called Claude Rd, a short distance towards Gowrie Park from the T-junction at Paradise. To use this access, turn off at Kings Rd and head south for about 1.5km to the start of the Mt

Roland Track, which is 6.4km and takes 3½ hours. The other access point is Gowrie Park itself, where you turn off the main road just near the sports ground and travel 2km to a gate, which is the start of a 10km track that takes four hours.

**Places to Stay & Eat** The *Weindorfers Restaurant* (☎ 6491 1385) is behind the *Mt Roland Budget Backpackers* (same telephone number), and well signposted off the main road. This is a rustic restaurant run by cheerful hosts that serves hearty meals at reasonable prices.

The basic but cheap backpacker accommodation, run by the same people, is $10 a night. Neither the hostel itself, nor the views from its windows, are attractive, but it is a good base for anyone wishing to climb Mt Roland, and the owners claim that improvements are being made.

Three kilometres north of Gowrie Park is *Silver Ridge Retreat* (☎ 6491 1727, fax 6491 1925), which has wonderful views of the mountain, a licensed restaurant and a heated indoor pool. Its two-bedroom chalets, which are attractive and comfortable but not luxurious, are $140 to $160 a single or double, and bushwalking, horse riding and birdwatching can be arranged.

### Getting There & Away
TWT's west coast service runs through Gowrie Park. See the Getting There & Around section at the start of the West chapter for details.

### C140 & LAKE BARRINGTON
Approximately 10km down the road from Gowrie Park to Cradle Mountain, turn off onto the C140, which will take you back towards Sheffield. From the southern end of this road, there are great views of Mt Roland, and along the way you pass a **weaving studio**, Highland Trails Horse riding (☎ 6491 1533) and **Sheffield Stained Glass** workshop and showroom, the last of which is open from 9 am to 5 pm Monday to Friday and until noon Saturday all year except winter. At the same location is *The Gra-*

*nary*, with self-contained timber cottages for $92 a double. All feature stained-glass windows, but the older No 1 is set apart from the others and has more charm. Outside is a magnificent gum in which a huge tree-house has been constructed for the use of any children staying on the property.

Farther along the road, at Promised Land, is the turn-off to the lake and, right next to the turn-off, **Tazmazia**, which the owners claim is the largest maze complex in the world. This really is a place to take the kids. The mazes, which vary in complexity, are entertaining, while the miniature village on the site is extensive and detailed. There are also fields of lavender and a large pancake parlour. Admission is $7 for adults, $4 for children and $20 for a family, and it's open daily except Christmas Day and August.

On either side of **Lake Barrington** are steep, thickly forested slopes, which make this an attractive recreation area. The approach road from the turn-off near the maze leads to the section of the lake that has been marked out for international, national and state rowing championships. Other access roads lead to picnic areas and boat ramps.

Farther along the road is *Carinya Farm Accommodation* (☎ 6491 1593), where you can get B&B (cooked breakfast provisions) in one of two conjoined units for $92 a double. The views of Mt Roland from here are lovely.

### WILMOT
Wilmot, on the western side of Lake Barrington, is worth staying in if you're visiting Cradle Mountain and don't mind a long drive. *Antill Apartments* (☎ 6492 1473) offers an apartment the size of a house with large rooms and a view of the garden for $88 a double with breakfast.

*Jaquies* (☎ 6492 1117) has rooms with *en suite* for $75 a double. It also has a restaurant open daily for dinner.

### SHEFFIELD
* pop 992

For a town that really has little going for it in the way of unusual or significant natural features, Sheffield manages to attract a good number of tourists. For most of its history this town was a quiet farming backwater that struggled to exist. In the 1980s the shopkeepers decided to take positive steps and copied the idea of painting **murals** from the Canadian town Chemainus. The first mural was completed in 1986; it was a success with tourists and a craze started. There are now 20 murals around the town with a further 10 in the surrounding district. There are so many paintings that it's reaching the stage where new sites are becoming hard to find. Today the town is often referred to as 'the town of murals' or 'the outdoor art gallery'.

A few years ago the old public toilet block was demolished, and this resulted in the loss of four popular murals: Tasmanian Tigers and Devils, Kentish Nocturnal, Kentish Birds and Kentish Aquatic.

## Information

The Sheffield visitors' information centre (☎ 6491 1036) is on Pioneer St, in the same building as the Bluegum Gallery, and here you can get information on the whole region. It's open daily from 10 am to 4 pm.

There are branches of the Trust and Westpac banks in town but no ATMs. The post office is an agency for the Commonwealth Bank.

## Diversity Murals Theatrette

In this theatrette at the western end of the main street, you can see an interesting 18 minute documentary about the paintings. The theatrette is open all day from Monday to Saturday, and on Sunday afternoon; admission is free but donations are invited. A map with a brief description of the murals and how to find them is available from the theatrette.

## Magical Murals

Once upon a time, in a small, sleepy town called Sheffield in north-western Tasmania, the townsfolk called a special meeting to try to find some magical way to awaken the town and stop it slipping into eternal economic slumber. The Kentish Association for Tourism Inc (KAT) was formed at the meeting and named after the municipality. One member had heard of a Canadian town being transformed by a magical mural momentum and thought that the same might work for Sheffield.

In December 1986 the first mural was unveiled to the public. This was the start of a continuing commitment by KAT to retell the history of the town through these colourful murals. Some murals, such as 'The Smithy at Work' and 'Early Trading' depict the early settlers. Others, such as 'Cradle Mountain Beauty' and 'The Forth Falls' highlight the beauty that surrounds the town. Murals also depict events, such as the 'Cradle Mountain Rescue', which shows the rugged, snow covered scenery, and bushwalkers – as well as Snr Constable Harry Clark who was in charge of this first helicopter rescue in the park.

In the beginning, there was no shortage of stories to tell nor walls to paint. Today, however, while there are still many tales to tell, there are so many marvellous murals that it's getting harder to find space for more. Some artists have even ventured farther into the Kentish countryside: to Railton, Gowrie Park, Roland and Moina, to use sides of shops and sheds to present their work.

Hopefully for Sheffield, they will live happily ever after, thanks to the mural magic that has created substantial growth for the town. A look at this outdoor art gallery is a must for every visitor.

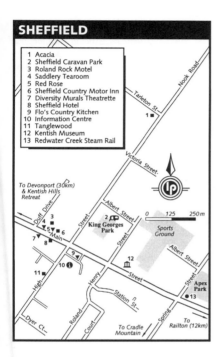

**SHEFFIELD**

1 Acacia
2 Sheffield Caravan Park
3 Roland Rock Motel
4 Saddlery Tearoom
5 Red Rose
6 Sheffield Country Motor Inn
7 Diversity Murals Theatrette
8 Sheffield Hotel
9 Flo's Country Kitchen
10 Information Centre
11 Tanglewood
12 Kentish Museum
13 Redwater Creek Steam Rail

## Kentish Museum

The museum (☎ 6491 1180), next to the high school on Main St, has a display on the Mersey-Forth hydroelectricity scheme. There is also a display about Gustav Weindorfer, the founder of Waldheim near Cradle Mountain, plus artefacts from the area. It is open daily except Saturday; admission is $2 for adults and 50c for children.

## Steam Train

At the eastern end of town is **Redwater Creek Steam Rail** (☎ 6491 1613), which has locomotives running on a narrow track. It's open from 11 am to 4 pm on the first weekend of each month and daily for the first two weeks in January.

## Special Events

On the Tasmanian Labor Day weekend (end February) each year Sheffield hosts a Steamfest, which includes displays of steam equipment, heritage games for children, stalls etc and coincides with the Gowrie Park Rodeo.

## Places to Stay

In town, the **Sheffield Caravan Park** (☎ 6491 1366) is tucked in behind the town hall. It's very basic and costs $8 to pitch your tent.

The **Roland Rock Motel** (☎ 6491 1821, 47 Main St), hidden behind the Sheffield Milk Bar & Tearoom, has hostel bunks for $15 and motel rooms for $45 a double. More hostel accommodation is available in Gowrie Park (see the Gowrie Park section earlier in this chapter).

The **Sheffield Hotel** (☎ 6491 1130), near the Diversity Murals Theatrette, has very basic rooms with shared facilities for $30/45 including a light breakfast. The **Sheffield Country Motor Inn** (☎ 6491 1800, 51 Main St) has standard motel rooms for $65 and units for $75 a double. A little out of the town centre, the new **Kentish Hills Retreat** (☎ 6491 2484, 2 West Nook Rd) has attractive modern motel units for $75 to $90 a single and $80 to $120 a double, with a continental breakfast.

**Tanglewood** (☎ 6491 1854, 25 High St) provides some luxury in an old timber home for $72/100, with a continental breakfast provided. Farther away from the town centre, **Acacia** (☎ 6491 2482, 113 High St) charges $40/70 with a cooked breakfast, and has wheelchair access.

There are many enticing rural accommodation options in the area around Sheffield – you can ask for details at the visitors' information centre.

## Places to Eat

Afternoon teas are available at the **Diversity Murals Theatrette**, where you can get a hot drink and a biscuit for $1, and the service is very friendly.

**Flo's Country Kitchen** on Main St is worth a visit for more than just its curiosity value: it's spacious and inviting, and the pumpkin scones are really great. It was established by former Queensland senator Flo Bjelke-Petersen, whose husband, Sir Joh, was for many years a controversial Queensland premier. It's open daily from 9 am to 4 pm, and is inexpensive. When we visited, there was an overabundance of Joh memorabilia on the walls, and two huge pumpkins on the floor in the middle of the room. According to the sign, the vegetables were Atlantic giants, and the largest weighed 81.6kg.

The Sheffield Hotel has counter lunches and dinners daily. The Irish-style *Red Rose* licensed café restaurant is open for lunch and dinner.

### Getting There & Away
TWT's west coast services run through Sheffield. See the Getting There & Around section at the start of the West chapter for more information.

### LATROBE
- **pop 2551**

Just 10km from Devonport, this historic town is, often overlooked in favour of its larger neighbour, yet is far more interesting. Founded in the 1830s, it was originally the region's port, with ships sailing up the Mersey River to its docks. It was also the location of the first ford across the river, and the discovery of coal nearby assured its development. It was named after Charles La Trobe, the first Lt Governor of the state of Victoria. By 1889 a railway line was established and the first hospital was opened. At this stage Latrobe was one of the state's largest towns.

The extension of the railway line and construction of a deep-water port at the river mouth at Devonport moved shipping business away from Latrobe. The town remained the business centre for the farming community. Today it's becoming an outer suburb of Devonport.

### Information
The Latrobe visitors' information centre (☎ 6426 2693), in the Barclays Building on Gilbert St, is open for varying periods on most days.

### Things to See
The town's history is depicted through the 600 prints on display in the **Court House Museum** next to the post office in the centre of town. It's open on Friday and Sunday from 2 to 5 pm; admission is $1, children 50c.

### Special Events
On Boxing Day, the town stages an annual bicycle race, the Latrobe Wheel Race, which attracts professional riders from all over Australia. Latrobe also hosts the Henley-on-the-Mersey carnival, which is held on Australia Day at Bells Parade, the site of the town's former docks.

### Places to Stay & Eat
Out of town, opposite the hospital, the *Old Latrobe Motel* (☎ 6426 2030) has rooms for $49/59. In town the *Lucas Hotel* (☎ 6426 1101), at the western end of Gilbert St, provides B&B in rooms with *en suite* for $75 a double. The restored hotel also has a moderately priced grill that is open daily for lunch and dinner.

On the edge of town, *Erica Cottage* (☎ 6426 2717 or 0418 133 895, 35 Gilbert St) can be rented for $115 a double. It's a quaint little self-contained cottage with a pretty garden. Alternatively, stay at *Lucinda* (☎ 6426 2285, 17 Forth St) where B&B is $95 a double.

There are quite a few restaurants and cafés in Latrobe. Among the best for à la carte is *Glo Glos* (☎ 6426 2120, 78 Gilbert St), which is open from Tuesday to Saturday for dinner and serves seafood, game and meat. *Kosmos* (☎ 6426 1236, 145 Gilbert St) is a café restaurant open for dinner from Tuesday to Saturday.

### PORT SORELL
- **pop 1494**

Just east of Devonport is Port Sorell and Hawley Beach, both of which are well-established holiday retreats and retirement villages on the shallow estuary of the Rubicon River. Named the First Western River in 1805, this was the first area to be settled by Europeans on the north-west coast. In

1822 it was renamed Port Sorell after the Governor of the day. In the 1840s, it was the largest town on the coast and home to the region's police headquarters. With the development of Latrobe, then later Devonport, this port declined and bush grew over much of the town. Modern transport has helped it gain favour as a holiday resort and as a place to retire.

The town is split into two sections by the flats of Poyston Creek. At Port Sorell there are several islands in the estuary that can be reached at low tide. The flats are rather muddy so you must return before the tide rises. An alternative walk is to follow the track along the shoreline north to Point Sorell, which takes three hours return. **Hawley Beach** has sandy and sheltered swimming beaches and coves.

## Places to Stay

The *Moomba Holiday Park* (☎ 6428 6140), on the corner of Kermode and Meredith Sts, has tent sites for $9 and holiday cabins for $48 a double. Closer to the foreshore, *Port Sorell Lions Caravan Park* (☎ 6428 6261) charges $9 for a tent site and $19 for a powered camp site.

Most other accommodation is west of town, in the hills. *Tudor Cabins* (☎ 6428 6390, 102 Appleby's Rd) has good value cabins for $43 a double. Nearby *Appleby Creek Lodge* (☎ 6428 7222) provides high-standard B&B for $80 a double. *Newcroft* (☎ 6428 6835, 39 Sunhaven Drive) has water views and B&B for $40/60.

## DEVONPORT

• **pop 25,400**

Devonport is Tasmania's third-largest city. Originally there were two separate towns on either side of the Mersey River; Formby was on the western side and Torquay was on the eastern side. In 1890 they merged to become Devonport, although the old town of Torquay is still referred to by locals as East Devonport.

Following the name change and the extension of the railway to the town, Devonport took over from Latrobe as port for the region. It is flat land, a rarity in Tasmania, aided the town's growth. The most dominant feature of the town is the lighthouse-topped Mersey Bluff, from where there are fine views of the coastline. The lighthouse was built in 1889 to aid navigation for the expanding port. Today, the port still remains important, handling much of the produce from the agricultural areas of northern Tasmania.

For many visitors the city is the site of the terminal for the *Spirit of Tasmania*, the vehicular ferry between Victoria and Tasmania. Devonport tries hard to attract tourists but its visitors are usually arriving or departing rather than actually staying.

## Information

For any information about Devonport and Tasmania in general, head for the Backpackers Barn (☎ 6424 3628, 10-12 Edward St). The Barn is open daily from 9 am to 6 pm Monday to Friday and Saturday till noon. The friendly staff can arrange transport and car rental, help organise itineraries or look after your backpack. It has a café, an excellent shop with all sorts of bushwalking gear, a great selection of books on Tasmania and a rest room with showers, which travellers can use for a small fee. If you would like to go bushwalking but didn't bring all your gear, you can hire major items like sleeping bags, backpacks, stoves and tents here. You can check out its Web site at www.tasweb.com.au/backpack/index.htm.

The Devonport Showcase (☎ 6424 8176, 5 Best St) also has a complete range of tourist information with displays and workshop demonstrations of arts and crafts. The centre incorporates the official Tasmanian Travel & Information Centre (TTIC, ☎ 6424 4466) and is open daily from 9 am to 5 pm. You can also tune in to the tourist radio station on 99.3 FM, which runs 24 hours a day and repeats a one hour tape about the city.

The post office is one block away from the mall, on the corner of Stewart St and Formby Rd.

# DEVONPORT

**PLACES TO STAY**
2 Mersey Bluff Caravan Park
4 Sunrise Motor Inn
5 Barclay Lodge
6 River View Lodge
7 Elimatta Motor Inn
8 Abel Tasman Caravan Park
9 Devonport's Vacation Village
10 Birchmore
13 Molly Molones; Inner City Backpackers
17 Edgewater Hotel & Motor Inn
21 Gateway Motor Inn
25 Alexander Hotel; Formby Hotels
29 Mac Fie Manor
30 Turton Cottage
34 Tasman House Backpackers
35 Rosalie Cottage
36 Rannoch House
37 Argosy Motor Inn
39 MacWright House (YHA)

**PLACES TO EAT**
11 Mallee Grill
12 Klaas's Bakehouse
14 Rialto Gallery Restaurant; Renusha's Indian Restaurant
26 China Garden
28 Golden Panda
31 Dangerous Liaisons
32 Chinese Chef
33 KFC

**OTHER**
1 Tiagarra
3 Maritime & Folk Museum
15 Devonport Bookshop
16 Tasmanian Travel & Information Centre; Devonport Showcase; Tasmanian Wilderness Travel
18 Spirit of Tasmania Ferry Terminal
19 Post Office
20 Backpackers Barn; Billabong Café
22 Tasmanian Redline Coaches Depot
23 Devonport Gallery & Art Centre
24 Warehouse & Spurs Saloon Nightclub
27 Taswegia
38 Home Hill

THE NORTH

## Tiagarra

The Tasmanian Aboriginal Culture & Art Centre is at Mersey Bluff, on the road to the lighthouse. It's known as Tiagarra, which is the Tasmanian Aboriginal word for 'keep', and was set up to preserve the art and culture of the Tasmanian Aborigines. The centre has a rare collection of more than 250 rock engravings, and is open daily from 9 am to 5 pm; it's well worth the $3 admission fee (children $2). From the centre a walking track leads to Aboriginal rock carvings on Mersey Bluff.

## Tasmanian Maritime & Folk Museum

Halfway between Mersey Bluff and the town centre, this excellent museum has models of sailing ships, both old and new, which have visited Tasmania. The Bass Strait ferries are a major feature and there are lots of marine items. It has recently been expanded, and is open Tuesday to Sunday from 1 to 4 pm April to September and to 4.30 pm the rest of the year. Admission is $3 for adults and $1 for children.

## Don River Railway & Museum

The Don River Railway (☎ 6424 6335), 4km out of town on the Bass Hwy towards Ulverstone, has lots of brightly coloured engines and carriages for kids to climb on and a workshop for them to view. Steam trains run on Sunday, public holidays and from Boxing Day to the end of January, while diesels run on the other days. Trains leave on the hour for 30-minute journeys along the Don River from 10 am to 4 pm inclusive. Rides are $7 for adults and $4 for children, or you can visit the site without taking a ride for $4. Occasionally there are special mainline tours to various destinations throughout the state.

## Devonport Gallery & Art Centre

The gallery, at 45-47 Stewart St, is open Monday to Saturday from 10 am to 5 pm and on Sunday afternoons from 2 to 5 pm; there is no entry fee. As well as its own permanent collection there are regular special exhibitions.

## Home Hill

At 77 Middle Rd, not far from the youth hostel, is Home Hill, which used to be the residence of Joseph and Dame Enid Lyons and is now administered by the National Trust. Joseph Lyons is the only Australian to have been both a state premier and the prime minister of Australia, and Dame Enid Lyons was the first woman to become a member of the House of Representatives and a cabinet minister. Home Hill is open from Tuesday to Thursday from 2 to 4 pm and at weekends from 2 to 4 pm; admission is $5.50 for adults, $3 for children and $10 for families.

## Taswegia

In a lovely old building at 55-57 Formby Rd is a commercial printing house with a gift shop. It's open daily from 9 am to 5 pm, and well-known resident illustrator David Hopkins is usually pleased to chat about his art or the convict or mining history of the state. There are still a couple of old printing machines on site, but the bulk of the collection is now at the Victoria Museum in Launceston.

## Arboretum

South of the city, beside the Don River at Eugenana (10km from Devonport), is the Tasmanian Arboretum, containing native and exotic trees; entry is free.

## Forest Glen Tea Gardens & Bird Sanctuary

This pretty sanctuary is 9km from Devonport on the road to Sheffield. Here, among three hectares of tall trees and gardens landscaped to be in harmony with nature, the endangered green swift parrot can be viewed feeding at trays provided by the owner, Bev Sharman. In 1991 Bev won a Greening Australia Award for her efforts to ensure the survival of the bird by organising the planting of 52,100 native trees between Wynyard and Sheffield. Today, her own little sanctuary rings with the sound of bird calls and is a great place to enjoy a Devonshire tea.

THE NORTH

## Walks

Most of the shoreline around the city is lined with parks and reserves that provide good walking. You can walk from the city centre along the Mersey River shore to Mersey Bluff. Walking tracks continue to Coles Beach then upstream along the Don River to the Don River Railway.

## Organised Tours

Many of the full-day tours from Devonport are to Tasmania's wilderness areas. Tarkine Tours (☎ 6423 4690, 0418 143057) goes to places like Cradle Mountain ($55), Pieman River ($70), Gordon River ($85), Arthur River ($65) and Leven Canyon ($50). From December to early February tours run daily, and in other months they're on Saturday and Sunday.

Tasman Bush Tours, operating out of Tasman House Backpackers, offers guided walks along the Overland Track (see the Cradle Mountain-Lake St Clair section of the West chapter for details). For more information about what's on offer, try the Backpackers Barn.

A great way to see most of the wilderness areas is by light plane. Bass Flight Services (☎ 6427 9777) flies from Devonport over Cradle Mountain and the surrounding areas. An hour's flight costs $100 per person for a minimum of two people and flights run on demand.

## Places to Stay – Budget

**Camping** On the western side of the river is the *Mersey Bluff Caravan Park* (☎ 6424 8655), in our view the most attractive of Devonport's camping spots. It's near Tiagarra and the lighthouse, 2.5km north of town and right next to some good beaches. It has powered camp sites for $15, vans for $40 and cabins for $50.

East Devonport has a number of caravan parks close to the beach. The most pleasant is the *Abel Tasman Caravan Park* (☎ 6427 8794, 6 Wright St). It has camp sites for $10 a double, on-site vans for $35 a double (without linen) and cabins for $56 a double.

**Hostels** The backpacker accommodation closest to the city centre is *Inner City Backpackers*, above Molly Malones Irish Pub. Here, a bunk in two or four-bed rooms with shared facilities is $13.

*MacWright House* (☎ 6424 5696, 155 Middle Rd), 400m past Home Hill, is Devonport's YHA hostel; it charges $10 a night for members. It's 3km from the city centre – about a 40 minute walk.

The other hostel accommodation option is *Tasman House Backpackers* (☎ 6423 2335 or 018 139 207, 169 Steele St through to 114 Tasman St)*, in the converted nurses' quarters of what was previously the regional hospital. Prices are $10 for a bunk in a dorm, $12 in a twin room and $28 for a room with an *en suite*. It's a 15 minute walk from town and transport can be arranged when booking.

**Hotels** Two good hotels close to the city centre are the *Alexander Hotel* (☎ 6424 2252, 78 Formby St)*, where a room with shared facilities is $30/40 with a continental breakfast (a cooked breakfast is $7.50); and the *Formby Hotel* (☎ 6424 1601, 82 Formby Rd)*, where singles with shared facilities are $35/45 with TV and cooked breakfast, and singles/doubles with new *en suites* are $50/65 with TV and cooked breakfast.

## Places to Stay – Mid-Range

**B&Bs** The friendly *River View Lodge* (☎ 6424 7357, 18 Victoria Parade)*, on the foreshore, charges $45/55 with shared facilities, and $55/70 with *en suite*, both include an excellent cooked breakfast. It's deservedly popular with travellers. If you like brewed coffee, mention this to the hosts and they will make some fresh for breakfast.

**Motels** There are quite a number of motels in the city centre and East Devonport. An easy walk from the city centre is the *Elimatta Motor Inn* (☎ 6424 6555, 15 Victoria Parade)*, which charges $55/60. There are many other motels nearby, in the area around Mersey Bluff, including the *Sunrise Motor Inn* (☎ 6424 8411, 140 North Fenton

*St)* and **Barclay Lodge** *(☎ 6424 4722, 112 North Fenton St).*

In East Devonport, the **Edgewater Hotel & Motor Inn** *(☎ 6427 8441, 2 Thomas St)* is not very attractive from the outside but is close to the ferry terminal and charges $45/50. The **Argosy Motor Inn** *(☎ 6427 8872),* on Tarleton St, charges $78 a double.

## Places to Stay – Top End

**Motels** Right in the city centre, **The Gateway Motor Inn** *(☎ 6424 4922, 16 Fenton St)* has deluxe rooms for $100/113 and standard rooms for $89/98.

**B&Bs** Very close to the city centre is the circa 1899 **Mac Fie Manor** *(☎ 6424 1719, 44 Macfie St).* A completely renovated, two storey Federation brick building with views, it charges $65/85 for lovely rooms with *en suite* and cooked breakfast. Even closer to town is **Birchmore** *(☎ 6423 1336, 10 Oldaker St),* which caters particularly for business people. Rates for doubles are $88 to $98. Singles start at $72. Prices are for *en suite* rooms and cooked breakfast.

In East Devonport, **Rannoch House** *(☎ 6427 9818, 5 Cedar Court)* is a bit out of town but has orchards and a large garden. Rates are $74/92 with an *en suite* and a cooked breakfast. Another great option is **Ochill Manor** *(☎ 6428 2660),* which about 10km west of town (see the following Forth section).

**Cottages** Both **Rosalie Cottage** *(☎ 6424 1560, 66 Wenvoe St)* and **Turton Cottage** *(☎ 6424 1560, 28 Turton St)* are managed by the same people, and can be rented for $130 a double, with a cheese platter and provisions for breakfast or a cooked breakfast supplied. Both cottages can sleep four and it's free for children under 12. Rosalie Cottage is on a more pleasant St but is a little farther from town. Both are furnished in period style and have attractive gardens.

## Places to Eat

**Cafés & Takeaways** There are plenty of coffee lounges and takeaways in the mall,

but for a good atmosphere try **Billabong Café** *(12 Edward St),* the café at the front of the Backpackers Barn. It's menu is mainly vegetarian and the meals are between $4 and about $7. The **Old Devonport Town Coffee Shop** in the Devonport Showcase is also open daily and is good for a drink or a snack. **Klaas's Bakehouse** *(11 Oldaker St)* is only open on weekdays, but has excellent cakes and pastries.

**McDonald's** *(1 Best St)* is beside the TTIC, while **KFC** is on the corner of William and Steele Sts. The Rialto's takeaway **Pizzaria** is just up from the restaurant itself, on Rooke St.

**Hotels** Most hotels have good counter meals for around $8 to $15; try **Molly Malones** *(34 Best St),* the **Alexander** *(78 Formby Rd),* or the **Formby** *(82 Formby Rd),* which has a family bistro. In East Devonport, the **Edgewater Hotel** *(2 Thomas St)* has cheap counter meals.

**Restaurants** Devonport has a good selection of moderately priced restaurants. If pasta's your choice, try the **Rialto Gallery Restaurant** *(159 Rooke St).* The service is so prompt that if you want to take your time over your meal, you should probably mention this to the staff. It's open from Monday to Friday for lunch and every evening for dinner until late, with main courses for $11.

For Chinese food, try the **China Garden** on King St, the **Chinese Chef** *(132 William St)* or the **Golden Panda** on Formby Rd. **Renusha's** is an Indian restaurant next door to the Rialto on Rooke St. It's BYO, and you can eat in or take away.

The **Mallee Grill** at the roundabout on the corner of Oldaker and Rooke Sts serves grilled steaks, gourmet sausages, kebabs and chicken. The $17 mixed grill is very generous, but if you like steak, order the cheaper single item and make the most of it.

In the more upmarket range is **Dangerous Liaisons** *(28 Forbes St),* which is open Tuesday to Saturday for lunch and dinner. It's a short distance from the city centre, but is very popular.

## Entertainment

Check the *Advocate* newspaper for Devonport's entertainment listings. The *Warehouse Nightclub* and *Spurs Saloon* are on King St. The *Elimatta Motor Inn (15 Victoria Parade)* occasionally has bands on weekends, and Irish bands often play at *Molly Malones*.

## Getting There & Away

**Air** For information on domestic flights to/from Devonport, see the Getting There & Away chapter earlier in this book. There are several daily flights to Melbourne with Qantas and Ansett, plus regular flights with smaller airlines to major regional towns around Victoria.

**Bus** TRC buses depart from and arrive at 9 Edward St, across the road from the Backpackers Barn. All buses also stop at the ferry terminal when the ferry is in town. It runs at least three services daily from Hobart to Launceston, on to Devonport and Burnie, and return. On weekdays most services continue to Smithton. At weekends, only one Saturday service operates to Smithton and there are no services on Sunday. The fare from Launceston to Devonport is $13.70.

TWT runs services to Sheffield, Gowrie Park, Cradle Mountain and the west coast. See the Getting There & Around and Cradle Mountain-Lake St Clair sections of the West chapter for details.

Similar services are also provided by Maxwells (☎ 6492 1431), which runs buses on demand to Cradle Mountain, Lake St Clair, Walls of Jerusalem, Frenchmans Cap and other walking destinations. See the West chapter for details.

Outside the summer period, or if none of the scheduled wilderness services suit your particular needs, you can charter a minibus from Maxwells or the Backpackers Barn. For example, if you hire a Maxwells bus from Devonport to Cradle Mountain, it will cost $120 for one to four people and $35 for each extra person.

**Car** There are plenty of cheap car-rental firms such as Range/Rent-a-Bug (☎ 6427

9034, 5 Murray St, East Devonport) where high-season rates for a VW Beetle start at $40 a day including insurance. Major companies like Avis, Thrifty and Budget deliver to the ferry terminal and hire out everything from new cars to old petrol guzzlers.

**Boat** See the Getting There & Away chapter at the beginning of this book for details on the *Spirit of Tasmania* ferry service between Melbourne and Devonport. It operates three times every week each way across Bass Strait. The TT-Line terminal (☎ toll-free 1800 030 344) is on the Esplanade, East Devonport. You can't miss seeing the ferry as it dominates the town when it's in port.

## Getting Around

An airport bus meets every flight. A shuttle bus runs between accommodation options and the ferry, but we've been told that people arriving on the *Spirit* often miss it because it doesn't wait long for passengers. Local buses, operated by Mersey Coaches, run from Monday to Friday – pick up a timetable at the Devonport Showcase.

**Ferry** There's a bridge across the Mersey River 2km south of town and it's a long walk from Devonport to the ferry terminal at East Devonport. It's much quicker to use the small ferry, the MV *Torquay*, which departs opposite the post office. On the eastern side it docks next to the *Spirit of Tasmania*. It runs on demand from 7.45 am to 6 pm weekdays and until 5 pm on Saturday. There are no Sunday services. One-way fares are $1.50 for adults, 70c for children and 50c for bicycles. The ferry also offers scenic trips in summer on Sunday only (subject to tides).

## FORTH

This tiny town off the highway 10km west of Devonport is worth driving through just because it's so pretty. But it also has a fine upmarket B&B called *Ochill Manor* (☎ 6428 2660). The property is on a hill and has extensive gardens and good views. À la carte meals are available. Rates are $85/120 with *en suite* and cooked breakfast.

## ULVERSTONE
• **pop 9923**

Ulverstone, at the mouth of the River Leven, is a great base from which to explore the surrounding area. The town's main features are its war memorials and spacious parklands. The visitors' information centre (☎ 6425 2839), on Car Park Lane, can be reached via an arcade from Reibey St. It's staffed by volunteers and its opening hours vary, so ring first if you are pressed for time. Inside are some clean public toilets,

and there are public telephones nearby. Public Internet access is available at the library, which is open from 9.30 am to 6 pm Monday to Wednesday and to 9 pm Thursday and Friday.

The **local history museum**, at 50 Main St, is open from 1.30 to 4.30 pm Wednesday to Sunday and 9.30 am to noon Tuesday. The display focuses on the lives of the Europeans who cleared the forests and created farms in the area; admission is $3 for adults and $1 for children.

**ULVERSTONE**

BASS STRAIT

PLACES TO STAY
1 Apex Caravan Park
2 Ocean View Guesthouse
3 Ulverstone Caravan Park
4 Beachway Motel
5 Willaway Apartments
8 Lighthouse Hotel
16 Furners Hotel
18 Winterbrook B&B

PLACES TO EAT
9 Domino's Pizza; TRC Terminal
13 Chinese Restaurant
14 Mrs Simpson's
15 Pedro The Fisherman;
   Pedro's the Restaurant
17 Chinese Restaurant

OTHER
6 Shrine of Remembrance
7 Local History Museum
10 Library
11 Visitors' Information Centre
12 Post Office

THE NORTH

## Places to Stay – Budget

**Camping** There are plenty of camping grounds in Ulverstone, including the *Apex Caravan Park (☎ 6425 2935)* on Queen St, West Ulverstone, where camp sites with or without power are $12 a double. The *Ulverstone Caravan Park (☎ 6425 2624)* on Water St is somewhat closer to town and has tent sites for $12, powered sites for $13, on-site vans for $35, cabins for $45 without linen and $52 with linen, and units for $57. (All these prices are for doubles.)

## Places to Stay – Mid-Range

**Hotels & Motels** The *Furners Hotel (☎ 6425 1488, 42 Reibey St)* has fairly simple rooms with *en suite* from $40/60, which includes a cooked breakfast.

If you prefer a motel, the *Bass & Flinders Motor Inn (☎ 6425 301, 49-51 Eastland Drive)* has rooms for $65 a double. Closer to the beach is *Beachway Motel (☎ 6425 2342, Heathcote St)*. Both are away from the town centre, but the latter is close to the beach.

**Holiday Units** Holiday units can be rented at *Willaway Apartments (☎ 6425 2018, 2 Tucker St)*. It's very close to the beach; it's $65 a double plus $5 for each extra adult and has a very pleasant atmosphere.

## Places to Stay – Top End

**Hotels** The *Lighthouse Hotel (☎ 6425 1197)*, on the corner of Victoria and Reibey Sts, has good rooms with *en suite* for $85/95 with a continental breakfast.

**B&Bs** For a great location try the *Ocean View Guesthouse (☎ 6425 5401, 1 Victoria St)*, 100m from the beach and an easy walk from the town centre. It's a lovely old house where rooms with *en suite* are $65/85 with a cooked breakfast. One of the rooms has facilities for disabled guests.

Not quite so close to the town centre but in an impressive circa 1800 house set in a large suburban garden and classified by the National Trust is *Winterbrook B&B (☎ 6425 6324, 28 Eastland Drive)*, which

has rooms with *en suite* and cooked breakfast for $75/90.

*Westella House (☎ 6425 6222, Westella Drive)* is close to the highway, but despite this, is not noisy. Set well back from the road, it's spacious, warm and inviting, and charges $110 to $128 a double for a room with *en suite* and a cooked breakfast. The hostess is a china painter, and you can sometimes chat with her as she works in the evenings.

## Places to Eat

*Pedro the Fisherman*, down by the wharf, has good takeaway fish and chips. And now there is *Pedro's the Restaurant* just next door, which has a great outlook over the water and is open for lunch and dinner.

There are *Chinese restaurants* on Reibey and King Edward Sts open daily. *Aromas* bakery and café on Reibey St is open daily from 6 am to 6 pm and is a good place for cheap light meals, including breakfast. And there's a *Domino's Pizza* on Victoria St (this is also the TRC terminal).

*Furners Hotel* on Reibey St has a family bistro with the usual steaks and seafood dishes. Similar fare is available at the *Lighthouse Hotel* on the corner of Reibey and Victoria Sts. This has a special menu for children and a good indoor play area.

Also on Reibey St is a combined deli, café and restaurant called *Mrs Simpson's*, with an interesting menu and lots of homemade goodies.

## Getting There & Away

See the Getting There & Around section at the start of this chapter. TRC buses arrive at and depart from Domino's Pizza at 33 Victoria St.

During the week, Metro Burnie (☎ 6431 3822) has regular local buses that go to Ulverstone for $2.80. You can hail a bus on the main street.

## AROUND ULVERSTONE
## Gunns Plains Scenic Circuit (B17)

If you are staying in Ulverstone for a couple of days and have your own transport, consider spending one day doing this circuit, particularly if you have children with you. Or better still, stay overnight at one of the many accommodation options along the way.

Begin by driving to Penguin along the **Old Bass Hwy**, a narrow, winding road that follows the coast and offers attractive views of the shores around Penguin Point. The three small islands known as the **Three Sisters** are particularly scenic, and there are some pretty roadside gardens as you enter the town. For details on Penguin itself, see the following section.

**Penguin to Gunns Plains** From Penguin, follow the signs to Riana and the Pindari Deer Farm. In the **Dial Range**, behind the town, there are some good walking tracks. If you want to hire a cottage on a farm, *Watercress Cottage* (☎ 6437 1145), on Browns Lane on the way to Riana, should suit. It's 3km inland from the coast, hidden at the end of a steep road, and charges $60/70, including breakfast. It is only large enough for two people.

Near Riana, you'll see the turn-off to *Pindari Deer Farm* (☎ 6437 6171, Wyllies Rd), 17km from Penguin. The kids should love this place, which has many birds and animals for them to interact with and plenty of space for them to stretch their legs. It's on a hilltop with panoramic views that take in Mt Roland in one direction and Table Cape in another. It has a café that is open from 10 am to 5 pm daily (except Monday and Tuesday in winter), a restaurant that is open the same days for dinner (but you must book) and B&B in attractively situated units for $110 to $135 a double. The farm is free to all resident guests, while admission is $7.50 for nonresidents ($5 for children and $18 for a family).

Back in Riana is the very pleasant little *Pioneer Park Camping Ground* (☎ 6437 6137 or 6437 6129), where tent sites are $3/5 and powered sites are $5.50/7.

**Gunns Plains** The drive down to the plains itself is picturesque, with views over the lush valley and some extensive hop fields.

In the valley is a captivating little camping ground called *Wings Farm Park* (☎ 6429 1335), where tent sites are $7 a double and powered sites are $9.50 a double. Cabins without *en suite* are $50 for up to five people, while with *en suite* they're $60 for up to five people; both have kitchens. Bunkhouse accommodation in small caravans is $10/15. There are plenty of farm animals wandering around the property, as well as deer, emu, ostriches and rabbits; there are trout and platypuses in the nearby Leven River.

On the road to the farm is a signpost marking the start of the **Penguin Cradle Trail**, a 20km walking track to Penguin via the Dial Range.

**Gunns Plains Caves** (☎ 6439 1388), 32km from Penguin and 25km from Ulverstone, are limestone caves. They are open daily from 10 am to 4 pm; admission is $8 for adults and $4 for children.

From the caves, return to the turn-off on the main road. From here continue the circuit back to Ulverstone, or cut across to the C125, which will take you to the road to Nietta and Leven Canyon.

## Leven Canyon

On the southern side of Gunns Plains, the River Leven emerges from a deep gorge. To view the gorge, follow roads through Nietta to the **Leven Canyon Lookout**, 41km from Ulverstone. The car park is a good picnic site and a well-graded track leads, after a 10 minute walk, to the sensational lookout on top of the gorge. You can walk through the gorge, but this takes at least 10 hours and is not recommended. Better nearby day walks lead to Winterbrook Falls (four hours return) or to Black Bluff (six hours return).

There are several other smaller waterfalls around Castra and Nietta, and Cradle Mountain is only a short drive away. Be warned that the road linking Upper Castra to Wilmot crosses a deep river gorge and is very steep; don't use it in very wet weather or with low-powered vehicles.

Accommodation nearby can be found at *Kaydale Lodge* (☎ 6429 1293) in Nietta,

THE NORTH

which has B&B for $100 a double with *en suite*, and *Mountain Valley Log Cabins* (☎ *6429 1394*) in Loongana, where cabins are $110 to $125 a double.

## Penguin
This is a pretty little coastal town with a concrete penguin on the foreshore on the main street that might interest the very young. Real penguins still appear around dusk each day during the warmer months of the year at **Penguin Point** (entry is $5 for adults and $2 for children). **Hiscutt Park**, beside Penguin Creek, has good playground equipment, plus a working windmill. In September, the tulip display around the windmill adds a touch of brightness. Near the *Penguin Caravan Park* (☎ *6432 2785*), which is below the highway and perched on a small cliff beside the ocean, is a miniature railway that operates on the second and fourth Sunday of the month, when there is also a popular market.

A good place to stay in town is the pretty *Beachfront Lodge* (☎ *6437 2672, 64 Main St*), which is opposite the beach and has

Aptly named, Penguin is a great place to view the little fellers.

B&B for $45/60 with shared facilities and $55/70 with *en suite*.

**Getting There & Away** See the Getting There & Around section at the start of this chapter.

During the week, Metro Burnie (☎ 6431 3822) has regular local buses to Penguin for $2.10. You can hail a bus on the main street.

# The North-West

Tasmania's magnificent north-west coast is a land as rich in history as it is diverse in scenery. Its story goes back 40,000 years to a time when giant kangaroos and giant wombats roamed the area, and Aboriginal tribes took shelter in the caves along the coast. Little remains of their long occupation – there are a series of rock engravings, and middens containing the leftovers of meals.

Europeans too realised the potential of the region, building towns along the coast and inland on the many rivers. The genocide of the Aboriginal people was quick, the last group was captured near the Arthur River in 1842. Originally heavily forested, the area was cleared and soon transformed into a vital part of the young colony's developing economy. Today it's a major producer of frozen vegetables and potatoes for Australia.

Along the coast itself, there are some impressive headlands providing spectacular views. From the north across to the Queenstown region the scenery is great but there are few towns. The wild area between the Arthur and Pieman rivers is known as the Tarkine Wilderness, and it was here that conservationists fought a protracted battle some years ago to prevent the upgrading of a road they called 'the road to nowhere', between Corinna and Balfour, within or close to the eastern border of that part of the Tarkine called the Arthur Pieman Protected Area. Their battle was ultimately unsuccessful, and the completed C249 now forms part of what has since been christened the Western Explorer (see the Western Explorer & Arthur Pieman Protected Area section later in this chapter), a route from the west coast to Smithton. However, although it can be negotiated by vehicles without 4WD and is promoted as a tourist road, the C249 is remote, mostly unsealed and can become potholed between maintenance, and so should probably not be attempted in bad weather or at night. If you are using this road to get to the west coast, see the

## HIGHLIGHTS

- Cruising on the wide, forested Arthur and Pieman rivers
- Savouring the quiet charm of Stanley
- Surfing at Marrawah
- Swimming at Boat Harbour
- Enjoying drives through patchwork farming landscape

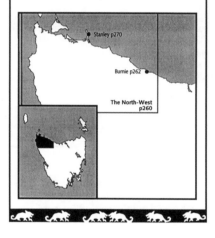

Stanley p270

Burnie p262

The North-West p260

Corinna section later in this chapter for information about the vehicular ferry across the Pieman River.

The other important road in the area is the CI32 from the Murchison Hwy (A10) through to Cradle Mountain Lodge. This is a link road that enables cars and buses to travel directly from Devonport to Queenstown, thereby avoiding the north-west coast altogether. However, if you have time it is far better to follow the older, slower roads that pass through this interesting region.

If you intend to spend a few nights on the northern north-west coast, you will probably prefer to stay in or around Stanley or

THE NORTH-WEST

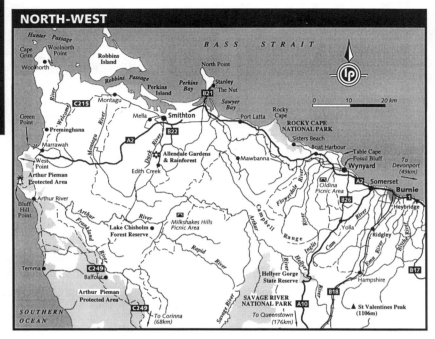

## NORTH-WEST

Boat Harbour. Both of these places may be booked out in the high season, however, in which case the little town of Wynyard, close to Table Cape, is a good alternative.

On the western north-west coast, the area from Marrawah to Arthur River is extremely scenic, and both of these towns have accommodation.

### Getting There & Around

**Air** The airport for the region is in Wynyard, and is known as both Wynyard and Burnie airport. See the Wynyard Getting There & Away section for details of the numerous airlines that have services to the north-west.

**Bus** Tasmanian Redline Coaches (TRC, ☎ 1300 360 000) runs several buses daily from Hobart to Launceston ($19.50), then along the north coast to Devonport ($13.70) and Burnie ($18.30), from where you can

catch another TRC service on weekdays and Saturday to Wynyard ($20.90), Stanley ($29) and Smithton ($29).

## BURNIE
- **pop 21,300**

Burnie, Tasmania's fourth-largest city, sits on the shores of Emu Bay but is not an attractive city, despite its backdrop of rich farming land. One of its main assets is its deep-water port, which makes cargo shipping an important industry. Until recently another major employer was 'the Pulp', the Australian Paper pulp mill that processed woodchips supplied by North Forest Products. The closure of the pulping operation in October 1998 cost 220 jobs and was a devastating blow to this small, economically vulnerable community.

The town (named after William Burnie, who was a director of the Van Diemen's

Land Company) started life quietly as a potato-growing centre. Forty years later, tin was discovered at Mt Bischoff in Waratah. In 1878 the Van Diemen's Land Company opened a wooden tramway between the mine at Waratah and the port of Burnie – the humble beginning of the important Emu Bay Railway that linked the port to the rich silver fields of Zeehan and Rosebery in the 1900s. Today, the Emu Bay Railway still transports ore from the west coast, travelling through some wild and impressive country on the way. Unfortunately, it does not carry passengers.

## Information

The Tasmanian Travel and Information Centre (TTIC, ☎ 6434 6111, fax 6431 6123), in the Pioneer Village Museum on Little Alexander St, has lots of information on Tasmania's north-west and Burnie itself, including a number of brochures outlining self-guided walking tours of the town. It is open from 9 am to 5 pm Monday to Friday, from 10 am to 1 pm and 1.30 to 4.30 pm Saturday and from 1.30 to 4.30 pm Sunday.

Internet access is available at the Burnie Library (☎ 6434 6412, 30 Alexander St); bookings are required.

## Pioneer Village Museum

This museum (☎ 6430 5746), on Little Alexander St near High St, has re-created an original village dated around 1900. It includes an authentic blacksmith's shop, printer, wash house, stage coach depot and boot shop, and should be of interest to children. This impressive museum with over 30,000 items on display is open from 9 am to 5 pm Monday to Friday, and from 1.30 to 4.30 pm at weekends. Admission is $4.50 for adults, $1.50 for children and $3.50 for pensioners.

## Art Gallery

The Burnie Regional Art Gallery, Wilmot St, is open daily the same hours as the Pioneer Village Museum and is also worth a look; admission is free.

## Parks & Gardens

**Burnie Park** features an animal sanctuary and the oldest building in town, the Burnie Inn. The inn was built in 1847 and moved from its original site to the park in 1973. It's classified by the National Trust and is open from 10.30 am to 4.30 pm daily except winter. Lunches and afternoon teas are available at the inn when it is open. The oval on the northern side of the park is the site of the annual Burnie Athletics Carnival, which has been held on New Year's Day for more than 100 years.

The lovely **Emu Valley Rhododendron Gardens**, 8km south of Burnie (on Breffny Rd, Romaine, via Mount Rd and Cascade Rd), are open daily between September and February from 10 am to 5 pm (admission is $3). They are managed by a branch of the Australian Rhododendron Society. Nearby are the **Annsleigh Gardens & Tearooms**, which are open daily from 9 am to 5 pm from September to May; admission is $4 (children free).

In the Burnie area, there are a number of waterfalls and viewpoints, including **Roundhill Lookout** and **Fern Glade**, just 3km from the town centre, and the impressive **Guide Falls** at Ridgley, 16km away.

## Lactos Cheese Factory

On weekdays between 9 am and 5 pm or at weekends between 10 am and 4 pm you can visit the Lactos cheese factory, on Old Surrey Rd, where you can taste and purchase the products (the tastings finish at 4.30 pm on weekdays).

## Places to Stay

For such a large town, the centre is small and restricted by the location of the highway, which means that many places to stay are quite a distance away.

## Places to Stay – Budget

**Camping & Hostels** To find the camping grounds and hostel, head west out of town to Cooee and Somerset. The *Treasure Island Caravan Park* (☎ 6431 1925) on the Bass Hwy at Cooee, 4km from town, has

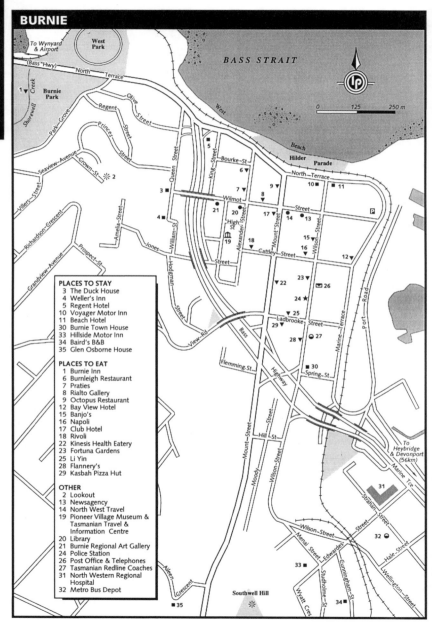

# BURNIE

BASS STRAIT

**PLACES TO STAY**
3 The Duck House
4 Weller's Inn
5 Regent Hotel
10 Voyager Motor Inn
11 Beach Hotel
30 Burnie Town House
33 Hillside Motor Inn
34 Baird's B&B
35 Glen Osborne House

**PLACES TO EAT**
1 Burnie Inn
6 Burnleigh Restaurant
7 Praties
8 Rialto Gallery
9 Octopus Restaurant
12 Bay View Hotel
15 Banjo's
16 Napoli
17 Club Hotel
18 Rivoli
22 Kinesis Health Eatery
23 Fortuna Gardens
25 Li Yin
28 Flannery's
29 Kasbah Pizza Hut

**OTHER**
2 Lookout
13 Newsagency
14 North West Travel
19 Pioneer Village Museum &
   Tasmanian Travel &
   Information Centre
20 Library
21 Burnie Regional Art Gallery
24 Police Station
26 Post Office & Telephones
27 Tasmanian Redline Coaches
31 North Western Regional
   Hospital
32 Metro Bus Depot

powered camp sites for $14 a double, on-site vans for $30/36 a single/double and cabins for $45/55. There is also hostel accommodation available for $12 a night.

A little farther out is *Somerset Gardens Caravan Park* (☎ *6435 2322*), 6km from Burnie, which has powered camp sites for $12 a double and timber cabins for $46 a double for the first night and $40 for each subsequent night. It's part of a nursery that also has a café and art gallery.

**Hotels** In town most cheap accommodation is in hotels. The *Regent Hotel* (☎ *6431 1933, 26 North Terrace*), overlooking West Beach, has rooms without *en suite* for $30/40 and with *en suite* for $35/45; a continental breakfast is $5 extra. Also overlooking West Beach is the *Beach Hotel* (☎ *6431 2333, 1 Wilson St*), which has rooms for $45/60.

West of town on the Bass Hwy at Somerset are the *Somerset Hotel* (☎ *6435 2346*), with self-contained rooms for $35/45, and the *Seabrook Hotel Motel* (☎ *6435 1209*), with self-contained rooms for $40/50.

**Motels** The *Hillside Motor Inn* (☎ *6431 3222*), on the corner of Edwards and Menai Sts, has basic rooms for a bargain $35/50 but is quite a walk from the town centre. A continental breakfast is $5 a person extra.

At Cooee, 4km from town on the same site as the Treasure Island Caravan Park, is the *Ocean View Motel* (☎ *6431 1925*), which has neat rooms for $55/65.

## Places to Stay – Mid-Range
**Motels** A bit of a walk uphill from town is *Weller's Inn* (☎ *6431 1088, 36 Queen St*), a large motel complex with rooms at $75/85 and units for $100 a double (all negotiable).

West of town, in a peaceful spot beside the Cam River, is the *Murchison Lodge Motor Inn* (☎ *6435 11069, 9 Murchison Hwy*), which has good rooms for $85/90.

**B&Bs** Within easy walking distance of the town centre, *The Duck House* (☎ *6431 1712, 26 Queen St*) provides B&B accommodation for up to four guests at $75/95.

## Places to Stay – Top End
**Motels** Overlooking West Beach, opposite the Beach Hotel, is the *Voyager Motor Inn* (☎ *6431 4866*), which has rooms for $100 a single or double. At the southern end of the town centre, near the highway, is the *Burnie Town House* (☎ *6431 4455, 139 Wilson St*), which has recently refurbished singles and doubles for $95.

**B&Bs** In the suburban hills south of the town centre, *Glen Osborne House* (☎ *6431 9866, 9 Aileen Crescent*) provides high standard B&B with *en suite* rooms and a cooked breakfast for $80/100 ($120 a double with spa). This large National Trust registered house in established gardens feels so secluded that you will forget you are in Burnie.

*Baird's B&B* (☎ *6431 9212, 22 Cunningham St*) is another B&B in suburban Burnie charging $80/100.

## Places to Eat
**Cafés & Takeaways** If you are staying in Burnie or just looking for somewhere to pick up a meal on your way farther west, drop into the wonderful *Kinesis Health Eatery* (☎ *6431 5963, 53 Mount St*). Its old club lounge chairs and country kitchen atmosphere are a welcome change from the more spartan décor of most of the town's cafés and takeaways. It has gourmet salad for $6 a bowl, focaccias for $5.50 to $7 and soup with toast for $4.80. Most of the menu items are available as takeaways – ring ahead and staff will have your order waiting. It opens at 8.30 am from Tuesday to Saturday and closes at 6 pm Tuesday to Thursday, late on Friday and at around 4 pm on Saturday.

There are plenty of other cafés in the town centre. The *Pioneer Museum Coffee Shop* has soups for $3, focaccias with salad for $4, sandwiches and espresso coffee. Other options include the *Napoli* in the Harris Scarfe department store and the *Rivoli* (*54 Cattley St*). *Praties* (*18 Alexander St*) specialises in baked jacket potatoes and is open every day. For fish and chips, head to *Octopus* near the corner of Mount St and North Terrace; it's open from 9 am to 7 or 7.30 pm every day except Sunday.

There are plenty of Chinese restaurants in town offering cheap lunch takeaway, including *Fortuna Gardens (66 Wilson St)*, the *Mandarin Palace (63 Wilson St)* and *Li Yin (28 Ladbrooke St)*.

The *Kasbah Pizza Hut (25 Ladbrooke St)* is open from 5 pm until late every day except Monday.

If you have transport you might like to try lunch at the *Grove Country Kitchen*, at the West Park Nursery, on Park Grove just past the Burnie Park.

**Hotels** West of town on the Bass Hwy at Somerset, the *Seabrook Hotel Motel* advertises $5 counter meals for lunch on Wednesday and Thursday and dinner on Friday. At other times expect to pay around $10.

In town, most hotels have reasonably priced counter meals from Monday to Saturday – try the *Bay View Hotel*, on the corner of Cattley St and Marine Terrace, or the *Beach Hotel (1 Wilson St)*. (The Club Hotel was under renovation when we visited.) The *Mallee Grill (26 North Terrace)* is in the Regent Hotel and serves grilled steaks, gourmet sausages, kebabs and chicken. The $17 mixed grill is very generous, but if you like steak, order the cheaper single item and make the most of it.

**Restaurants** *Flannery's (☎ 6431 9393, 104 Wilson St)* is an à la carte restaurant that caters for vegetarians. Gourmet pies and tarts start at around $7.50, steaks are $16 to $20 and seafood dishes are around $20.

At the other end of the town, the *Burnleigh Restaurant (☎ 6431 3947, 8 Alexander St)* also provides fine à la carte meals. It's easily missed, being a pink house set back from the street, and it's open for lunch from Tuesday to Friday and dinner Tuesday to Saturday.

*Moods* at the Burnie Town House has a four course carvery on Friday and Saturday nights for $18, while the *Rialto Gallery Restaurant (☎ 64317718, 46 Wilmot St)* has good pasta dishes for around $10.

## Getting There & Away

**Air** The nearest airport – known as either Burnie or Wynyard airport – is at Wynyard, 20km from Burnie. See the Wynyard Getting There & Away section later for details of services.

**Bus** See the Getting There & Around section at the start of this chapter for details of TRC services to/from Burnie.

During the week, Metro Burnie (☎ 6431 3822, 30 Strahan St) has regular local buses to Penguin ($2.10), Ulverstone ($2.80) and Wynyard ($2.80), which depart from outside Harris Scarfe department store on Cattley St. However, there are no weekend services.

## WYNYARD
- pop 4679

Sheltered by the impressive Table Cape and surrounded by beautiful patchwork farmland, Wynyard sits both on the seafront and on the banks of the Inglis River.

The area was first settled by Europeans in 1841, and for most of the 19th century, Wynyard was the principal port on this section of coast. While Burnie eventually took over the shipping trade, Wynyard remained the centre of a rich agricultural region. Butter, cheese, milk, vegetables and speciality crops such as tulips support the town's economy. There is a Tulip Festival in October each year that the locals would dearly love to see become more popular.

Wynyard is also the location of the airport that serves the north-west, known as either Wynyard or Burnie airport.

## Information

A good source of tourist information is the visitors' information centre (☎ 6442 4143) on Goldie St. It's run by volunteers and is open from 10 am to 4 pm from April to September and 9 am to 4 pm the rest of the year. Pick up the brochure *Scenic Walks of Wynyard and Surrounding Districts*, which explains how to get to Fossil Bluff and also details walks in the Oldina Forest Reserve, to Detention Falls and in Hellyer Gorge.

## Activities
You can hire scuba gear from the Scuba Centre (☎ 6443 3347, 62 Old Bass Hwy) and dive in Wynyard Bay, Boat Harbour or at Sisters Beach. The centre also runs occasional charters to Bicheno and Eaglehawk Neck.

Greg-Lea Park Trail Riding (☎ 6442 3085), on Calder Rd, runs hour-long or overnight rides through the surrounding area for an hourly rate of $15 a person.

## Organised Tours
Holiday Coast Tours (☎ 6442 2891) runs day and half-day tours to Circular Head and Stanley for $30, Marakoopa Caves for $30 and places south of Devonport like Cradle Mountain for $30. Bookings are necessary and a minimum of four people are required before a tour will run. Scenic flights over Cradle Mountain and the south-west can be arranged with Tasmanian Scenic Flights (Western Aviation, ☎ 6442 1111) next to the airport.

## Places to Stay
Close to town, on the Esplanade right beside the beach, is the *Wynyard Caravan Park* (☎ 6442 1998), which has camp sites for $10, on-site vans for $34 a double and cabins for $54 a double. It also has hostel beds for $14 each or $24 a double. The beds themselves are in comfortable individual prefabricated rooms, but you must go outside to reach all facilities.

*Leisure Ville* (☎ 6442 2291, 145 Old Bass Hwy) is some distance from town and is a modern, spick-and-span family resort with a children's playground, tennis courts etc. It has powered camp sites for $14 a double, camp sites with their own bathroom for $18 a double, on-site vans, cabins and villa units.

The *Wynyard Youth Hostel* (☎ 6442 2013, 36 Dodgin St), one block south of the main street, has rooms for $13. Its main advantage is that it is only a five minute walk from the airport and so is a good spot to spend your first night if you are flying into Wynyard.

The *Federal Hotel* (☎ 6442 2056, 82 Goldie St), in the middle of town, has rooms with shared facilities and cooked breakfast for $35/55. The *Inglis River Hotel Motel* (☎ 6442 2344, 4 Goldie St) has motel rooms for $30/45.

On the other side of Goldie St beside the river and adjacent to the wharf is the *Waterfront Wynyard Motor Inn* (☎ 6442 2351, fax 6442 3749), which has motel rooms for $55/65. The new proprietors, Gael and Debbie, are young and enthusiastic and have started to improve the look of the place since taking over.

The best quality B&B in Wynyard is *Alexandria* (☎ 6442 4411), which is on the northern side of town at the start of the road to Table Cape. Attractive rooms with *en suite* in a two bedroom bungalow behind the main house are $65/85.

## Places to Eat
On the way into town along the scenic route from Burnie, drop into the *Seaward Inn* (59-61 Old Bass Hwy) for Devonshire tea or a meal in a pleasant cottage atmosphere. Among the lunch dishes available are fettuccine with chicken and cashews for $7.50, while the dinner menu features Caesar salad for $7, vegetarian filo purses for $12 and marinated scotch fillet for $16. There's an open fire in winter, and the brave claim on the menu that this inn makes the best cappuccino in the whole of Tasmania somehow just adds to its charm.

Fish and chips is the speciality at *YT's Fish Place*, which is at the wharf, between the visitors' information centre and the Waterfront Wynyard, and is open daily. In the main shopping centre on Goldie St are several *coffee shops* and a *hot bread shop*. Pizzas are available at *Leisureville*, which is some distance from town, while other takeaway can be purchased at the *Wynyard Caravan Park shop*.

Good value counter meals for around $10 are available every day at the three hotels in town. In fact, the dining room at the *Federal Hotel* is open from 7 am until 8 pm every day except Sunday, when it shuts at 2 pm. It provides breakfast, lunch, dinner and snacks from a board, but will also try to cater for special requests.

*Toysun Chinese Restaurant* (☎ 6442 1101, 25 Goldie St) has takeaway as well as table service.

*Gumnut Gallery Restaurant* (☎ 6442 1177, 43 Jackson St) serves lunch (sandwiches, soups, nachos etc) from 10.30 am Monday to Friday and dinner from 6 pm Friday and Saturday. The evening menu features baked eggplant filled with semolina couscous and vegetables for $12.50 and emu fillet for $17.

The licensed restaurant at the *Waterfront Wynyard Motor Inn* is also à la carte: mains are $14 to $18 and old-fashioned desserts are $6.

### Getting There & Away

**Air** The airport is just one block from Wynyard's main street; about a five minute walk away. This is also the airport for Burnie (which is 20km away) and it is listed on many of the schedules as Burnie, not Wynyard, airport. Aus-Air (☎ toll-free 1800 331 256) runs regular flights between Wynyard and Moorabbin in Victoria, King Island and Launceston.

Southern Australian Airline (book with Qantas ☎ 131313) runs daily services between Wynyard and Melbourne, and Kendell Airlines (☎ toll-free 1800 338 894) also has flights between the two. Par Avion (☎ toll-free 1800 646 411) has flights between Wynyard and Hobart daily except Saturday, as does Tasair (☎ toll-free 1800 062 900). Tasair also has flights between Wynyard and King Island.

Badge's Skybus (☎ 041 950 1115) services all major airlines and most minor ones, transporting passengers between Wynyard and Burnie for $7. If you are in Burnie, ring and make a booking – you can arrange to be picked up from most accommodation options.

**Bus** See the Getting There & Around section at the start of this chapter for details.

During the week, Metro Burnie (☎ 6431 3822) runs regular local buses from Burnie to Wynyard for $2.80. You can hail a bus from the main street.

## AROUND WYNYARD
### Fossil Bluff

Three kilometres from the town centre is Fossil Bluff, where the oldest marsupial fossil found in Australia was unearthed. Some of the fossils that have been collected here are on display in the Tasmanian Museum & Art Gallery in Hobart. The soft sandstone also features numerous shell fossils deposited when the level of Bass Strait was much higher. At low tide you can walk along the foot of the bluff, observe the different layers in the rocks, and find fossils. It's also worth walking east along the rocks to the mouth of the Inglis River where there is a seagull rookery. If the tide is high, it is still worth climbing to the top of the bluff for the good views.

The Bluff is quite close to the town on the northern side of the river, and a pleasant two hour return walk to it is outlined in a brochure available from the visitors' information centre. It's a shame that a new housing development now extends all the way to the base of the bluff.

### Table Cape

If you have transport, ignore the highway and follow the minor roads towards Table Cape, which is 4km north of Wynyard. The narrow, sealed roads lead to the car park and lookout on top of the cape, 177m above the ocean. It's often windy here and the view over Wynyard and the coast is excellent. You can also visit the nearby lighthouse, which was built in 1885, although the views here are less impressive.

In September and October the **Table Cape Tulip Farm** (☎ 6442 2012) is in full flower and is worth visiting. It's beside the road to the lighthouse, and its fields are stripes of bright colours that contrast with the rich red soils of the cape. Do not enter the paddocks, as the farm is on private land. From late September to mid-October, the farm is open to the public from 10 am to 4 pm daily. Admission is $4 per adult or $10 per car and entitles you to wander around the paddocks and also view the large display of tulips in the greenhouses.

The best route from the cape to Boat Harbour is to follow Tollymore Rd north-west. There are some great views of the cliffs and rocky coast along this road.

**Places to Stay** Some of the best views on the cape are those you will have if you can afford to stay at *Skyescape (☎ 6442 1876, fax 6442 4118, 282 Tollymore Rd)*. This stylish, modern home with panoramic windows offers tranquillity, magnificent scenery and access to private beaches. Only one party of guests (of up to four adults) is accepted at a time and gourmet dinners are provided on request. Rates are $130 or $180 a double, depending on your choice of suite, and both options include a delicious breakfast, use of a separate living/dining room and either an *en suite* or a separate bathroom with spa.

## Flowerdale

Located inland from Table Cape near the Bass Hwy, there is little to see here except the **Flowerdale Valley Emu Farm** (☎ 6442 3911), where you can feed the birds and go on a guided tour of the farm. It's open Tuesday to Saturday from 9.30 am to 5 pm. The half-hour tour is $4 for adults, $2.50 for children, $3 for pensioners or $15 for a family; you can visit the shop free of charge without participating in the tour.

## Oldina State Forest

Most of the hills south of Wynyard are used for timber production and form part of the Oldina State Forest. Pines were first planted here in 1920 and willows, Douglas firs and poplars, as well as native trees, are a feature of the forest.

Some sections have been reserved for recreation, with separate zones for walking, horse riding and trail-bike riding. Each forest zone has its own parking and picnic site. The walking reserve features the **Noel Jago Walk**, which is a short nature walk beside Blackfish Creek. Passing under manferns and eucalyptus trees, it takes 30 to 45 minutes to complete. There are reputed to be platypuses in the creek.

## Lapoinya Rhodo Garden

Located in the hills 20km west of Wynyard, this 8½ hectare garden is well worth seeking out. Stocked with a wide variety of rhododendrons, azaleas and begonias, there is something in flower every month of the year. It is open every day except major holidays; entry is $2 for adults and 50c for children.

## BOAT HARBOUR BEACH

Just 14km from Wynyard, this holiday resort has a beautiful bay with white sand and crystal-blue water, and is a lovely spot for exploring rock pools and snorkelling. It was originally used in the 19th century as a port, but because the harbour is not sheltered from easterly winds it very quickly lost favour for this purpose. In the 1920s holiday-makers discovered the firm white sand and clear waters. Most buildings in the small village are holiday shacks.

Three kilometres off the Bass Hwy, the town consists of a single street, The Esplanade, which is the continuation of the steep access road. As you descend towards the town, a short path on the left leads to a timber platform and panoramic view over **Boat Harbour**.

## Places to Stay

The *Boat Harbour Beach Caravan Park (☎ 6445 1253)* is on an open, sunny site in view of the water and opposite a short walkway to the beach. Tent sites are $10, while on-site vans are $32. There is also a neat, new prefabricated cabin for $65 a double, but at the time we visited it was only fitted with a rather smelly chemical toilet. Also at the time we visited, the owners were building a campers' kitchen and games room and had plans to add a number of timber cabins. The existing laundrette is open to the public.

On the hill above the town is the *Backpackers Hostel (☎ 6445 1273)* on Strawberry Lane. From here there is a rough track down to the beach. Bunks are $14 per person and some double rooms are available for $38. The floor is concrete and there is limited wood heating, so it is likely to be fairly cold in winter. Pick-up from the highway is available.

On the same property as the hostel is *Cape View B&B* (☎ *6445 1273)*, which has a rather suburban feeling inside, despite its lovely rural setting. B&B is $95 a double in a modern upstairs room with attractive views. The somewhat less appealing downstairs room is $75 a double.

Back at the beach, the *Seaside Garden Motel* (☎ *6445 1111)* has small but cute holiday units in a large garden for $80 to $90 a double. There is also a larger self-contained cottage. The proprietors are extremely welcoming.

Next door, *Boat Harbour Beach Resort* (☎ *6445 1107)* has motel rooms for $79/99. It also has an indoor heated swimming pool, sauna and spa.

Behind the caravan park (and under the same management) is the large, comfortable *White Sands Cottage* holiday house (☎ *6445 1253)*, which can sleep six. From Christmas until the end of January, it's $100 a night; at any other time, the price is negotiable.

If you can't find a bed near the beach, try *Country Garden Cottages* (☎ *6445 1233)* back near the highway, where rooms are priced from $65/75.

Farther back towards Wynyard are *Killynaught Cottages* (☎ *6445 1041, fax 6445 1556)*. They are on the Bass Hwy and from the road look rather stark. From inside, however, the views to the rear are attractive and give the impression of rural seclusion. The cottages are all fully self-contained and have been lavishly decorated in federation style. There are open fireplaces in the lounge rooms, spas in the *en suites* and ingredients for a cooked breakfast in the kitchens. B&B is $124 a double.

## Places to Eat

If you continue along the road to Sisters Beach past the turn-off to Boat Harbour you'll come to the *Mallavale Farm Crafts Tearoom*, at the Strawberry Lane turn-off to the Backpackers Hostel. It has wholesome, cheap snacks and lovely views of Table Cape. The atmosphere is decidedly that of a country women's association craft stall, but that's half the fun. Tea is $1.30, coffee

$1.60, sandwiches $2 to $2.50 and chicken fillet and salad $6.50. It's open Monday to Saturday from 9.30 am to 4 pm and Sunday from 11 am to 4.30 pm.

The *Boat Harbour Store* at the caravan park sells takeaway and petrol, and has a new paved outdoor area where you can order from a café-style menu. *The Harbour Shop* on the beach serves takeaway and has a couple of tables. Outside is a fenced children's play area. It is closed in winter.

The *Avalon Restaurant* (☎ *6445 1111)* at the Seaside Garden Motel is open Tuesday to Saturday in the high season and intermittently the rest of the year (ring first). Its home-cooked main meals are around $12 and are served in a pleasant country-style dinning room.

*Jacobs Restaurant* (☎ *6445 1107)* at the Boat Harbour Beach Resort is à la carte; its main meals are between $13.50 and $24.

## Getting There & Away

See the Getting There & Around section at the start of this chapter for details. Unless you have your own transport, you will have to hitch to get to most of these places. The TRC service to Smithton will drop you at the turn-off to Boat Harbour (3km) and Sisters Beach (8km). Boat Harbour Beach Backpackers Hostel picks up from the highway.

## ROCKY CAPE NATIONAL PARK

This small area was declared a national park in 1967. Its major features are the rocky headlands, heath-covered hills, and caves that were once occupied by Aborigines. Excavations have shown the caves were first used 8000 years ago and were still used up until European occupation in the 19th century. The coast here is mostly rugged quartzite, and the park is believed to contain the only stands of *Banksia serrata* in the state.

There are a couple of beaches within the park, the best known of which is **Sisters Beach**, which is a beautiful, sweeping 8km expanse of white sand. The Sisters Beach village, which is reached by following the side road from the Bass Hwy that passes the turn-off to nearby Boat Harbour, is a popular resort surrounded by the national park.

In 1998 an intense fire, started by picnickers, swept through most of the park, and it is estimated that it will take 10 years for the vegetation to regenerate fully. Until the bush re-establishes itself, you will probably prefer to walk in the unburnt section east of Sisters Beach township. Usually, however, the western end is the most attractive, as it has a more rugged coastline; and even in the aftermath of fire, wildflowers and orchids bloom throughout the park in spring and summer.

On Rocky Cape, there is a lighthouse with road access. Overnight camping is not allowed, and as with all national parks, entry fees apply.

Sisters Beach is a good place for swimming and fishing. On the eastern side of the creek there are picnic tables and a shelter; a foot bridge crosses the creek, providing access to the beach.

In Sisters Beach village is the 10 hectare **Birdland Native Gardens** (☎ 6445 1270), which contains aviaries and also attracts native birds from the national park. It's open daily; admission is $2.50 for adults and 50c for children.

## Bushwalking

From Sisters Beach, the walk to **Wet Cave** and **Banksia Grove** takes 45 minutes. (To reach the start of these walks, follow the signs to the boat ramp.) You can continue farther along the coast to Anniversary Point, which is three hours return. It's also possible to follow the coast to Rocky Point and return along the Inland Track (eight hours return).

From the western end of the park at Rocky Cape Rd (accessed from a separate entrance off the Bass Hwy west of the turnoff to Sisters Beach) you can visit the two large Aboriginal caves; both are a 20 minute return walk away. There is also a good circuit of the cape itself; allow 2½ hours.

## Places to Stay & Eat

**Sisters Beach** The *Birdland Holiday Cottages* (☎ 6445 1471) are not in the Birdland Gardens themselves but in bush a short distance away. They have something of the atmosphere of a religious retreat, and are $50 a double. *Tasman Buray Holiday Units* (☎ 6445 1147) are less secluded but have more-attractive timber cottages costing $65 a double plus $10 each for extra adults. There are also *holiday shacks*, which can sometimes be rented short term; inquire at the *general store*, which sells takeaway and park passes.

**Western End** The *Rocky Cape Tavern & Caravan Park* (☎ 6443 4110), on the highway near the entrance to the western end of the national park, has tent sites for $8 a double, powered sites for $13 a double, onsite vans for $30 a double and motel units for $49 a double. The tavern serves counter lunches and dinners daily, with mains for between $7 and $14.

Two kilometres from the park and 27km from Stanley is *Araluen Holiday Camp* (☎ 6443 4197), which has self-contained family units for $20 per person or $40 a family. Full laundry facilities are provided free of charge.

*Tanfield Gardens* (☎ 64434319, 153 Montumana Rd) is signposted off the highway near the park entrance. It looks a little rough from the driveway, but the room is spacious and nicely decorated and has large windows overlooking broad gardens. It's $65/85 with a cooked breakfast.

## AROUND ROCKY CAPE

In the hills south of the national park, you can visit a number of waterfalls, including **Detention Falls**, 3km south of Myalla, and **Dip Falls**, near Mawbanna. The area also contains some giant eucalypts.

## PORT LATTA

This part of the coastline is a series of pretty little beaches and rocky coves marred by the ugly smoke and pollution from the industrial complex at Port Latta. This is the terminus for the 85km iron ore pipeline from Savage River. Fortunately, there is only one factory here, and away from the smokestack the coast is pleasant.

## Places to Stay

Just past Port Latta are two free camp sites: *Peggs Beach Coastal Reserve*, which has toilets, tables, fireplaces and water; and *Peggs Creek*, which has only pit toilets.

At Crayfish Creek, 2km east of Port Latta, *Caradale Caravan Park (☎ 6443 4228)* has on-site vans for $25/30, timber cabins for $45 to $90 and a small kiosk.

## STANLEY

- pop 600

Nestled at the foot of the extraordinary Circular Head (better known as The Nut), Stanley is a very appealing historic village that has changed very little since its early days. In 1826 it became the headquarters of the London-based Van Diemen's Land Company, which was granted a charter to settle and cultivate Circular Head and the north-western tip of Tasmania. The company built

its headquarters at Highfield, to the north of Stanley, and the town started at the same time, serving as the port.

For 30 years the company struggled with its vast land-holding and by 1858 had sold most of it. The area prospered when it began shipping large quantities of mutton, beef and potatoes to Victoria's goldfields in the 1850s and 1860s, and continued to prosper when settlers discovered rich dairying land behind Sisters Hills and tin reserves at Mt Bischoff.

Today Stanley is a charming fishing village with many historic buildings and great seascapes. The Circular Head Arts Festival is held here every March and this has become one of the major events in the state, featuring arts and crafts and live entertainment.

## Information

Fishing tackle, fishing licences and film are available from de Jonge's Country Store,

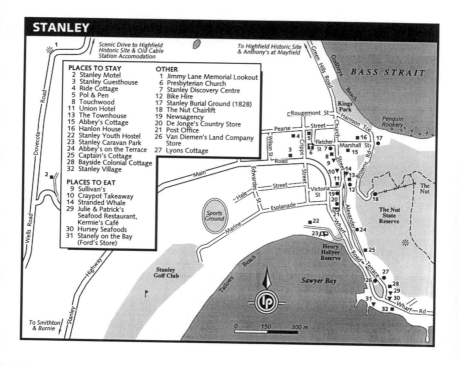

### STANLEY

PLACES TO STAY
2 Stanley Motel
3 Stanley Guesthouse
4 Ride Cottage
5 Pol & Pen
8 Touchwood
11 Union Hotel
13 The Townhouse
15 Abbey's Cottage
16 Hanlon House
22 Stanley Youth Hostel
23 Stanley Caravan Park
24 Abbey's on the Terrace
25 Captain's Cottage
28 Bayside Colonial Cottage
32 Stanley Village

PLACES TO EAT
9 Sullivan's
10 Craypot Takeaway
14 Stranded Whale
29 Julie & Patrick's Seafood Restaurant, Kermie's Café
30 Hursey Seafoods
31 Stanely on the Bay (Ford's Store)

OTHER
1 Jimmy Lane Memorial Lookout
6 Presbyterian Church
7 Stanley Discovery Centre
12 Bike Hire
17 Stanley Burial Ground (1828)
18 The Nut Chairlift
19 Newsagency
20 De Jonge's Country Store
21 Post Office
26 Van Diemen's Land Company Store
27 Lyons Cottage

open Monday to Friday from 9 am to 5.30 pm and Saturday until 5 pm.

There are no ATMs in town but EFTPOS withdrawals can be made at the newsagency, which is open Monday to Thursday from 7.30 am to 8 pm, Friday from 7.30 am to 9 pm, Saturday from 8 am to 8.30 pm and Sunday from 8 am to 8 pm. Beware, however: some B&Bs only accept cash, and the newsagency has been known to run dry as early as Saturday afternoon.

## The Nut
This striking 152m-high volcanic rock formation, thought to be 12.5 million years old, can be seen for many kilometres around Stanley. It's a steep 15 minute climb to the top, but the view is definitely worth it. For the less energetic, a chairlift (☎ 6458 1286) operates daily from 9 am to 5.30 pm in the high season and 10 am to 4 pm in winter; rides are $6 an adult, $2 a child and $15 a family. The best lookout is a five minute walk to the south of the chairlift. You can follow a path around the top, which is a 40 minute walk.

From September to June, Nut Buggy Tours (☎ 6458 1312) does a 2km circuit of the top for $5 a person.

## Stanley Discovery Centre
To learn more about the town, visit this folk museum on Church St. For most of the year, it is open daily from 10 am to 4.30 pm, but during June and July it's closed. Admission is $3.

## Scenic Drive
Follow Dovecote Rd past the Stanley Motel to the **Jimmy Lane Memorial Lookout**. This is a timber platform providing a reasonable view over the cape area. The road then passes Highfield, before winding back down to Stanley past some attractive scenery.

## Penguin Viewing
Penguins can be viewed at either end of Godfreys Beach from late September until February. Nut Buggy Tours (☎ 6458 1312) runs penguin tours during this time for $10 a

head. Phone bookings are necessary, but you will be collected from your accommodation.

## Highfield
The Van Diemen's Land Company headquarters were located on the high land north of Stanley. The company was formed in 1824 to establish a wool-growing venture and was granted 100,000 hectares of unexplored territory. In 1835 Highfield was built, but the company had great difficulty developing its land and in 1856 Highfield was leased, then eventually sold some years later.

In 1982 the state government purchased Highfield, undertook extensive restorations and made it into an historic site. The site is open daily, and for $2 you can see the stables, grain stores, workers' cottages and the chapel. For $5 an adult, or $12 a family (which includes the site fee), you can also wander through the historic house, from 9 am to 3 pm Tuesday, Wednesday and Thursday, and from noon to 4 pm on weekends.

## Historic Buildings
The old bluestone building on the seafront is the **Van Diemen's Land Company Store**, designed by John Lee Archer, Tasmania's famous colonial architect, and dating from 1844. Today it houses the Stanley Artworks Studio Gallery (☎ 6458 2000), where you can watch the resident artists at work (a watercolourist, a furniture-maker and a wood-turner) and view exhibitions of an even wider variety of arts and crafts.

Also near the wharf is the particularly fine old bluestone **Ford's Store**, which used to be a grain store. It is believed to have been built in 1859, although the plaque near its door dates it from 1835. Now the restaurant Stanley on the Bay, it was constructed from stones brought to Stanley as ship's ballast.

On Church St, next door to the Discovery Centre, is the restored **Plough Inn** (1840), which is now the Stanley Craft Centre.

Other buildings of historical interest are **Lyons Cottage**, on Church St, which was the birthplace of former Prime Minister Joseph Lyons and is open from 10 am to 4 pm

(11 am to 3 pm in winter, admission by donation); the **Union Hotel**, also on Church St, which dates from 1849; and the **Presbyterian Church**, which was probably Australia's first prefabricated building, bought in England and transported to Stanley in 1885.

The **Wiltshire Junction Railway Station** was saved from demolition by being transported to Stanley, where it is now part of the Stanley Village accommodation complex.

## Places to Stay

**Town Centre** Unless otherwise stated, the following establishments are within easy walking distance of the town centre.

On a great site right on Sawyer Bay overlooking the wharf is *Stanley Caravan Park* (☎ *6458 1266)*, where powered sites are $13, on-site vans $30 and cabins $40. Next door, the small *Stanley Youth Hostel* (☎ *6458 1266)* is part of the caravan park and charges $12 a night.

The *Union Hotel* (☎ *6458 1161)*, on the corner of Church and Victoria Sts, has basic hotel rooms for $25/40.

With views of north, *Pol & Pen* (☎ *6458 1186, AH 6458 1430, fax 6458 1286, 8 Pearse St)* has contemporary cottages for $55 to $65 a double without breakfast.

Close by, the whole of *Ride Cottage* (☎ *6458 1348, 12 Pearse St)* is available for $90 a double without breakfast. In the same area of town, *Hanlon House* (☎ *6458 1149, 6 Marshall St)* has a number of rooms for $75/100, including cooked breakfast, in an attractive home with welcoming hosts. Across the road, *Abbey's Cottage* (☎ *6458 1186, AH 6458 1430, fax 6458 1286)* has been tastefully decorated in period style and is quite lovely inside, despite its rather plain exterior. It sleeps up to six people and costs $114 a double (plus $25 for each extra person) with continental breakfast.

*Stanley Guesthouse* (☎ *6458 1488, 27 Main Rd)* is another B&B offering a number of rooms in the hosts' own home. It is a bit farther away from the town centre and charges $75/95 with a cooked breakfast.

*Abbey's on the Terrace* (☎ *6458 1186, AH 6458 1430, fax 6458 1286, 34 Alexander Terrace)* looks rustic from the outside but is modern inside. It has great views of the bay and is closer to town than its counterpart on Marshall St, but charges the same rates.

*Captain's Cottage* (☎ *6458 3230, fax 6458 3237, mobile 0419 871 581, 30 Alexander Terrace)* was built in 1838 and also has good views to the south. In 1998 it was bought by the people who own Gateforth (see later in this section), and guests staying at Captain's are welcome to visit the working farm on which its sister accommodation is situated. The cottage has recently been upgraded and is now $120 a double with continental breakfast, plus $30 for each extra adult.

Down the end of the street, next door to Julie & Patrick's Restaurant, *Bayside Colonial Cottage* (☎/fax *6458 1209, 44 Alexander Terrace)* is furnished in period style and charges $120 a double for the whole cottage, with ingredients for a cooked breakfast provided (no children).

Right in the middle of town is *The Townhouse* (☎/fax *6458 1455, 4 Church St)*, a cottage charging $125 a double, with ingredients for a cooked breakfast provided. Across the road, *Touchwood* is run by the same people as Ride Cottage. It was built around 1842 and smells a bit musty in parts. It is let in two sections, the Cottage and the Dairy, both of which cost $110 a double with continental breakfast. Alternatively, you can rent the modern *Pines* cottage out the back for the same price.

Finally, right on the water at the wharf itself, the modern *Stanley Village* has motel rooms with spa upstairs for $95/110 and without spa downstairs for $85/100.

**Out of Town** Not far from the town on the scenic Dovecote Rd, *Stanley Motel* (☎ *6458 1300)* has great views of the town and the Nut. Motel rooms are $80/90, while two-bedroom holiday cottages are $90 to $104 a double.

Near the lookout on Dovecote Rd is the turn-off to the *Old Cable Station Homestead* (☎ *6458 1312)*, where B&B in modern accommodation in rural surroundings is

$80/90 (no children). Farther along the road (though closer to town if you approach it from the other direction), *Anthonys at Highfield* (☎ 6458 12450) was built for the Van Diemen's Land Company in 1828. It's not luxurious but is pleasantly situated. B&B is $40/80.

Back towards the highway, on The Neck, *Beachside Retreat West Inlet* (☎ 6458 1350, mobile 019 407 094) should appeal to naturalists, being home to the rare striped marsh frog and many resident and migratory birds. The property operates commercially as a cattle stud and affords access to a large private beach for fishing, swimming and walking. Rates are $80 to $100 a single or $120 to $130 a double, for accommodation in modern self-catering units.

If you return to the Bass Hwy and head east to Black River, you will come to the turn-off to *Gateforth* (☎ 6458 3230, mobile 0419 871 581, fax 6458 3237), a working farm overlooking Stanley. Its two attractive cottages, which have lovely rural views, cottage gardens and a considerable degree of privacy despite their close proximity to one another, are $120 a double ($135 with spa). There is also an older-style house available. Farm tours are offered.

## Places to Eat
*Hursey Seafoods (2 Alexander Terrace)* sells takeaway and live seafood, and although viewing the wonderful variety of deep-sea fish, crayfish, crabs, eels and abalone on display in its tanks might be fascinating, eating the little guys is what it's all about.

Next door is *Kermie's Café*, where you can sit down to enjoy meals similar to those served in the takeaway. Upstairs is *Julie & Patrick's Seafood Restaurant*, where the best of the fish and crayfish are served in the evenings. All three businesses are run by the same people, and the café and seafood shop usually close at 6 pm, which is when the restaurant opens.

Counter meals are available every day at the *Union Hotel* on the corner of Church and Victoria Sts. Across the road is a pleasant little café called the *Stranded Whale*,

which is open daily and serves inexpensive light meals and snacks.

The *Dovecote Restaurant* at the Stanley Motel on Dovecote Rd has standard fare, while *Stanley on the Bay*, in Ford's Store down on the wharf, is more upmarket (closed mid-July to mid-August).

Right in town, *Sullivan's (25 Church St)* is open daily from 11 am to 9.30 or 10 pm, and serves light lunches, teas and dinner. For lunch, you can choose from a variety of dishes ranging from standard sandwiches for $2.50 to crayfish sandwiches for $9.90. All the restaurants in Stanley take advantage of the town's excellent fresh seafood and other local produce.

## Getting There & Around
**Bus** See the Getting There & Around section at the start of this chapter for details.

**Bicycle** Stanley is the perfect size for cycling around. Bergin's Bike Hire on Church St is open daily from 9 am to 5 pm. It charges $2.50 per half-hour, and mountain and beach bikes are available.

## SMITHTON
* pop 3495

Twenty-two kilometres from Stanley, Smithton serves one of Tasmania's largest forestry areas and is also the administrative centre for Circular Head.

Smithton is on Duck River, named after the wild ducks that frequent the estuary. The town started to develop in the 1850s after the Van Diemen's Land Company sold off most of its holdings. At first, clearing of the giant forests was the primary activity, but once this had been achieved the land was used for potato farming. Little happened until the 1890s, when the first sawmill opened; soon afterwards dairy farming began, and the Duck River Butter Factory came into production. In the 1940s vegetable dehydration and fish processing added to the town's economy.

You will find Commonwealth and Westpac banks on Emmett St, both of which have ATMs.

## Woolnorth

On the north-western tip of Tasmania, near Cape Grim, Woolnorth is a 220 sq km cattle and sheep property that is the only remaining holding of the Van Diemen's Land Company. This is the only surviving Royal Charter Company in the world, and today is a diversified business with sheep, cattle, crops and tree plantations. The 80-bail rotary dairy milks 1800 cows a day. Tours of the property can be booked by calling ☎ 6452 1493. Day tours, costing $90 a head and leaving from the Bridge Hotel in Smithton at 9.30 am and returning between 3.30 and 4.30 pm, include lunch and snacks and also visit Cape Grim and Woolnorth Point. Other tour options may sometimes be available.

## Montagu

The road heading north-west towards Woolnorth passes through farmlands, with views over the narrow waterways that separate Perkins and Robbins Islands. The only place of interest is **Montagu Blueberries** (☎ 6456 6187), where you can pick fruit from New Year to mid-February.

## Lacrum

A rich dairy (☎ 6452 2322) just 6km west of Smithton, this farm and factory produces cheese. During milking season, it's open daily from 3 to 5 pm, when you can see the turnstile dairy in operation, taste the cheese and enjoy afternoon tea. Entry is $7.50 for adults, $5 for children and $15 a family. It's usually open from November to the end of May.

## Allendale Gardens

South of Smithton on the road to Edith Creek, these gardens (☎ 6456 4216) are a good place to walk around and relax. The two hectare property includes impressive botanical gardens, a rainforest walk, a wildflower section and a café serving Devonshire teas. The centre is open from 10 am to 6 pm daily from October to April, and admission is $6.50 for adults and $3 for children.

## Milkshakes Hills Forest Reserve

Temperate rainforest and buttongrass moorland can be found at this reserve, 45km south of Smithton. There are several very short walking tracks around the picnic grounds and a longer track of one hour return to the top of Milkshakes Hills.

## Lake Chisholm

Even farther south of Smithton is this tranquil lake, which is actually a limestone sinkhole. It's located in beautiful rainforest and is a 15 minute walk from the car park. The gravel roads leading to the lake may be closed after heavy rain.

## Places to Stay & Eat

There are a few places to stay in town, but there's no budget accommodation. Close to town on the other side of Duck River, **Bridge Hotel** (☎ 6452 1389) has rooms with shared facilities for $25/40 and motel units for $50/60. Bistro meals are available every evening.

Two kilometres south of town on Scotchtown Rd, **Tall Timbers Hotel/Motel** (☎ 6452 2755) is more like a resort than a motel. The extravagant use of timber in the main building is rather impressive. Rooms are $60/70, and there is a family bistro. Live bands or a disco provide entertainment on Friday nights.

**Christie's Corner** (☎ 6452 3132, 46 Goldie St) is an attractive B&B on the main road into town. Rooms with a cooked breakfast are $60/80. The gardens are lovely, and the comfortable dining room is open to the public for meals and snacks from 10 am to 5 pm Monday to Friday and until 4 pm Sunday. There is another B&B at Sedgy Creek, 6km east of town, where **Rosebank Cottage** (☎ 6452 2660) has two cottages for $116 to $128 a double.

For light meals there are several coffee shops to choose from: you could try **Birda's Coffee Lounge** (5 Smith St) or **Gloryannas** (54a Emmett St). **Jade Dragon Chinese** (16 Smith St) is open for dinner every evening, and for lunch from Tuesday to Saturday.

## Getting There & Away

See the Getting There & Around section at the start of this chapter for details.

## MARRAWAH

Now this really is an undiscovered gem. Marrawah is where the wild Southern Ocean occasionally throws up the remains of ships wrecked on the dangerous and rugged west coast. Its nearby beaches and rocky outcrops can be hauntingly beautiful, particularly at dusk, and the seas are often huge. It was at the relatively small beach of Green Point that 35 sperm whales stranded themselves and died in February 1998, and it is at this same beach that the West Coast Classic, a notable round of the state's surfing championships, is held each year.

There is no regular public transport to Marrawah – a fact one can't help thinking is probably a blessing as well as a curse.

### Aboriginal Sites

The Marrawah area has seen minimal disturbance from European development. As a result, many signs of Aboriginal inhabitation remain, and particular areas have been proclaimed reserves to protect the relics, including rock carvings, middens and hut depressions. The main Aboriginal sites are at **Preminghana** (formerly known as Mt Cameron West), **West Point** and **Sundown Point**.

Preminghana has been returned to the Aborigines. If you wish to view the area, you can try driving down to the access point and asking the caretaker for permission for pedestrian access.

### Surfing

One of Marrawah's major attractions is its enormous surf: the West Coast Classic, a round of the state's surfing championships, is decided here, as is a round of the state's windsurfing championships. Green Point, 2km from the centre, has a break that works in southerly conditions, and there's also good surfing farther along the road at Nettley Bay. South of Marrawah, there's good surfing in an easterly at West Point, and

great reef surfing in similar conditions at Bluff Hill Point, which is said to be famous for its world-class waves. The West Point surf beach is reached by taking the left-hand branches of the road from the turn-off on the C214, while the Bluff Hill Point surf beach is to the right of the lighthouse at the end of another side road farther south.

### Bushwalking

There's a beach walk from Bluff Hill Point to West Point that takes four hours one way and a coastal walk from Bluff Hill Point to the mouth of the Arthur River that takes two hours one way. There is also a good walk of three or so hours return north along the beach from Green Point to Preminghana. These are beautiful areas well worth visiting even if you don't intend to do one of the walks.

### Fishing

The whole region is good for fishing. In winter you can catch Australian salmon at Nettley Bay or off the rocks at West Point, while in summer you can catch black-backed salmon here and at the mouth of the Arthur River. Estuary perch can be caught in the Arthur River.

### Organised Tours

Some of the roads past this town are rough vehicle tracks requiring a 4WD. Based at Marrawah, Blue Wren 4WD Tours (☎ 6457 1307) runs daily tours to the mining town of Balfour and along deserted beaches that are only accessible to 4WDs. Group size is limited to a maximum of five. The tour can be started from Smithton or Stanley if required. Rates are $50 for a half-day and $85 for a full-day tour. This is a good way to see the west coast.

### Places to Stay & Eat

The township of Marrawah consists of the *Marrawah Tavern* (☎ 6457 1102), which serves counter meals but doesn't offer accommodation, and a *general store* (☎ 6457 1122), which is an agent for Australia Post and the Commonwealth bank, and sells supplies and petrol. If you are planning to take the Western Explorer (see the Western Explorer & Arthur Pieman Protected Area section later in this chapter), fill up here, as there are no other petrol outlets for 184km. At the time of writing, the general store was doing up a bus for backpacker accommodation that would cost around $10 a person. It was also proposing to add a café and public toilet to its premises.

There is a basic *camping ground* behind the beach at Green Point, 2km from Marrawah, where there are toilets, water and an outdoor cold shower.

Just down the C214 towards Arthur River is *Glendonald Cottage (☎ 6457 1191)*, a comfortable house in pleasant rural surroundings where you can stay for $70 a double. If it's cold, ask the proprietors (Margo and Joe), who live nearby, to have the wood fire blazing before you arrive. The house has plenty of reading material on Aboriginal history and the ecology of the area, and Joe appears to have an intimate knowledge of both.

Back towards Smithton, near the Redpa Store on the Bass Hwy, *Rest-a-While (☎ 6457 1272)* has a cottage available for $70 a double.

## ARTHUR RIVER

The sleepy town of Arthur River, 14km south of Marrawah, is mainly a collection of holiday houses for people who come here to fish. It has acquired a few more accommodation options since the previous edition of this book was written, but there is still no regular public transport service from Smithton. There is, however, a Parks and Wildlife Service (PWS) ranger station on the northern side of the river, where you are able to get permits for off-road vehicles and camping.

**Gardiner Point**, signposted off the main road on the southern side of the bridge, has been christened 'The Edge of the World' by locals because the sea here stretches uninterrupted all the way to Argentina. There is a plaque at the point, and a great view of some rocky coastline.

### Arthur River Cruises

Arthur River Cruises (☎ 6457 1158) offers a scenic day cruise departing at 10 am and returning at 3 pm (see 'The Other West Coast Cruises' boxed text). The cruise is available most days as long as a minimum of eight people have booked. The cost is $40 a person. Arthur River cruises has been operating since 1985. Its boat, the MV *George Robinson*, is spacious and has plenty of character, and the barbecue lunch (included in the price) amid the trees at Turks Landing is a big drawcard.

There is now an alternative cruise available, offered by West Coast Scenic River Cruises (☎ 6457 1288). The attractive new MV *Reflections* travels farther upriver than its competitor but does not stop at Turks Landing. It departs at 10.15 am and costs $35 per person, which includes a barbecue lunch in the garden back at the kiosk.

### Canoeing

You can explore the river on your own with Arthur River Canoe & Boat Hire (☎ 6457 1312). It hires boats for $15 per hour or $100 per day, and canoes from $6, $8 or $10 per hour (depending on the craft) and $30, $40 or $50 per day. You can also be transported upriver for a 40km down-river paddle, which takes two or three days. If necessary, you can be picked up from Smithton or Stanley; bookings are essential for this service.

### Places to Stay & Eat

The town has a *kiosk* and a *camping ground* with basic facilities.

*Arthur River Holiday Units (☎ 6457 1288)*, at the kiosk, has self-contained units for $60/70 a double; breakfast provisions are an extra $5 a person.

*Ocean View Holiday Cottage (☎ 6452 1278 or 6457 1100, Lot 80 Gardiner St)* is a pleasant three bedroom house with a covered barbecue area. It's $85 as double and $15 for each extra person.

Back up the street is *Sunset Holiday Villas (☎ 6457 1197, Lot 23 Gardiner St)*, where you can get B&B in new self-contained units for $80 a double ($70 without breakfast).

## WESTERN EXPLORER & ARTHUR PIEMAN PROTECTED AREA

The Western Explorer is the name of the road linking Smithton and the Pieman River. Because there is a barge to carry cars across the Pieman at the tiny settlement of Corinna, it is possible to use this route to the west coast as an alternative to the Murchison Hwy. However, the road is an attraction in its own right, running through or close to the eastern boundary of the Arthur Pieman Protected Area.

The condition of the C249 – the 53km section from the C214 to Corinna that was upgraded from a 4WD track in 1995 – varies from season to season and month to month. Try asking the barge operator at Corinna or a PWS ranger at Arthur River for an up-to-date assessment. Its narrowness, sharp bends and steep ascents and descents justify its 50km/hour speed limit, and having to pass more than a few approaching vehicles would slow your progress considerably. Potholes can also be a hazard.

The other big hazard is the bleak, rugged terrain you pass at its southern end: in places it is so seductive that, despite the challenging nature of the drive, you just can't help snatching the occasional glance. The northern end, however, is far less scenic, and therefore not such a hazard.

Make sure you remember to fill your car's fuel tank at Zeehan in the south or at Marrawah in the north, because no petrol is available between these points. For more information about the barge across the Pieman see the Corinna section later in this chapter.

The attractions of the Arthur Pieman Protected Area include magnificent ocean beaches, waterfalls on the Nelson Bay River, Rebecca Lagoon, Temma Harbour, the old mining town of Balfour, the Pieman River and the Norfolk Ranges.

## CORINNA & PIEMAN RIVER CRUISE

Now that there is a small vehicular ferry across the Pieman River, the tiny idyllically situated settlement of Corinna seems as much part of the west coast as of the north-west, being only a 45 minute drive from Zeehan. The main reason to visit Corinna today is to take the Pieman River Cruise (☎ 6446 1170), a laid back alternative to the Gordon River cruises out of Strahan. Costing $30, the tour on the MV *Arcadia II* departs daily at 10.30 am and returns at 2.30 pm. It is definitely best to book 24 hours in advance; during summer it can be booked out and in winter it only runs if there are bookings. (See 'The Other West Coast Cruises' boxed text in this chapter for more information.)

### Places to Stay & Eat

The only accommodation in Corinna other than unpowered *camp sites* ($3 a person) is at the *Pieman Retreat Cabins* (☎ 6446 1170), although at the time of writing we were told that there were plans to build a lodge. Each of the existing cabins is self-contained and can sleep up to six people. They can smell quite musty at times but otherwise are adequate, although they only have electricity at night (their fridges and stoves run on gas). They cost $60 a double and $10 for each extra person, and there is an additional charge for linen. Basic supplies can be bought from the kiosk, but the only meals available are picnic lunches.

### Getting There & Away

There is no regular public transport to Corinna. It is approximately a 45 minute drive from Zeehan and a 1½ hour drive from Strahan in the south and a three to four hour drive from Smithton in the north. See the previous Western Explorer & Arthur Pieman Protected Area section in this chapter for more details.

The Pieman River Fatman is the small vehicular ferry across the Pieman River. If you are travelling through Corinna from the north-west, be sure to arrive here before it ties up for the night. Its operating hours are from 9 am to 7 pm from October to March and until 5 pm during the rest of the year. The charge for a standard car is $10 each

THE NORTH-WEST

## The Other West Coast Cruises

Strahan and the famous Gordon River cruises are a goldmine for tourist operators, but some visitors find them a bit too glitzy for their taste. So, if you're after a rather more rustic experience, consider taking either the Arthur River Cruise from Arthur River township on the north-west coast or the Pieman River Cruise from Corinna, near Zeehan.

For this edition, I took both cruises, just to get an idea of what they had to offer: both departure points are a long drive from anywhere, and if you're going to make the effort to get to either, you will want to know what to expect.

The Arthur River Cruise was the more comfortable, professional and interesting of the two, but the river itself was less impressive than the Pieman. A feast of a barbecue was provided at Turk's Landing on the Arthur, and mountainous surf at Pieman Heads pounded a beach littered with massive logs. The forest along the Pieman was more impressive than that along the Arthur, and the Pieman passed through a magnificent gorge on its way to the heads. The guided forest walk at Turk's Landing on the Arthur, however, was informative and entertaining, and birdlife seemed to be more abundant on the Arthur, where there were sea eagles and azure kingfishers, among other species.

On the Pieman River Cruise, the commentary was delivered with such a dead-pan voice and over such bad sound equipment that you could have been excused for failing to notice that it was actually rather quirky; the fascinating history of the Huon pine *Arcadia II* was not quite enough to make up for its mustiness and bad design; and the soggy cup of tea and dry biscuit that was meant to pass for a snack would have been better left back at Corinna.

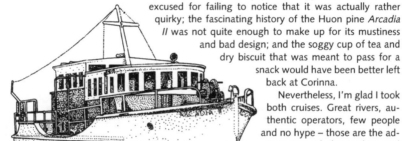

Nevertheless, I'm glad I took both cruises. Great rivers, authentic operators, few people and no hype – those are the advantages of the Arthur and Pieman river cruises, and the reason to drive all that way to take them.

**Lyn McGaurr**

way, although this amount will also cover the return crossing if you are visiting Corinna specifically to take the cruise.

## HELLYER GORGE

Seven kilometres west of Burnie is the small town of Somerset, at the junction of the Murchison and Bass Hwys. Hellyer Gorge is about 40km south of Somerset on the banks of the Hellyer River. The

Murchison Hwy winds its way through the impressive gorge. At the picnic area by the river, there are two pleasant very short walks that provide a welcome break if driving. The River Walk takes only 10 minutes and the Old Myrtle Forest Walk is 15 minutes return.

From Burnie to the Waratah area there is an alternative road that is faster but less scenic. It passes through Ridgley and

Hampshire on road B18 and avoids the winding road through the Hellyer Gorge. This has diverted traffic away from the peaceful reserves in the gorge.

About 40km south of Hellyer Gorge is the CI32 turn-off to Cradle Mountain. This is a major highway that was constructed in the 1980s providing a link from the west coast to the northern end of Cradle Mountain national park.

## WARATAH & SAVAGE RIVER

The Mt Bischoff mine, near Waratah, once the world's richest tin mine, opened in 1888 and was very profitable until 1929, when it was leased. The mine continued to be worked in a minor way until 1947. From a population of 4000 in the 1890s, Waratah almost vanished when the tin ran out.

The nearby development of the low grade iron ore at Savage River in 1968 revived the town and kept it alive. The extracted ore is pumped as a slurry along an 85km pipeline to Port Latta on the north coast. Savage River Mines is now owned by Australian Bulk Minerals.

In 1983 a rich lead-zinc-silver-copper ore-body was found near the junction of the Murchison Hwy and the link road to Cradle Mountain, and by 1989 the Aberfoyle Hellyer Mine (now owned by Western Metals, ☎ 6439 2222) had started operating. Today it employs 160 staff.

Waratah is built on both sides of a narrow lake. The townspeople have tried to attract tourists with a **museum** that contains relics of the boom days. It's open daily: collect the key at the council office on weekdays. Next door to the museum is the **Philosopher Smith's Hut**, a reconstruction of the way prospectors lived. There are some sign-posted walking tracks around town including one to the Power House, which is two hours return.

At the time of writing, an area around Savage River was soon to be declared a national park.

### Places to Stay & Eat

***Waratah Camping Ground*** (☎ 6439 1231) consists of tent sites behind the council offices and on the lawns beside Lake Waratah, and a gravelled area behind the council offices where you can park a caravan. Tent sites are $5, or $8 with the use of the amenities, and powered sites are $8. Keys to the amenities block are available at the council offices, or after hours at the Bischoff Hotel.

The ***Bischoff Hotel*** (☎ 6439 1188) on Main St is the main building remaining from the mining days. It serves daily counter lunches and dinners, and has hotel rooms with shared facilities for $25/40. It's $3 to $5 for a continental breakfast and $10 for a cooked breakfast.

# The West

Nature at its most awe-inspiring is the attraction of Tasmania's rugged and magnificent west. Formidable mountains, buttongrass plains, ancient rivers, tranquil lakes, dense rainforests and a treacherous coast are all features of this compelling and beautiful region, some of which is now World Heritage Area.

Centuries before the arrival of Europeans, this part of Tasmania was home to many of the state's Aborigines and some archaeological evidence is more than 20,000 years old. They lived through the last ice age in the caves along the Franklin River and undoubtedly lived elsewhere inland. In more recent times, they lived primarily along the coast.

When Europeans began to enter the region the Aborigines were killed and driven from their homes by force. Today there is little physical evidence of their existence, apart from the remains of their cooking fires and middens.

Prior to 1932, when the Lyell Hwy from Hobart to Queenstown was built, the only way into the west coast was by sea, through the dangerously narrow Hells Gates into Macquarie Harbour to Strahan. Despite such inaccessibility, early European settlement brought explorers, convicts, soldiers, loggers, prospectors, railway gangs and fishers to the region. The 20th century has brought outdoor adventurers, naturalists and environmental crusaders.

It was over the wild rivers, beautiful lakes and lonely valleys of Tasmania's south-west that battles between environmentalists and government raged. In the 1980s, the proposed damming of the Franklin and Lower Gordon rivers caused the greatest and longest environmental debate in Australia's history (for more information see the boxed text in the South-West chapter). Subsequently the area has seen ecotourism thrive in the harbourside town of Strahan. More recently, a guarantee of funding for the recon-

## HIGHLIGHTS

- The stunning walks and scenery along the Lyell Hwy as it passes through the Franklin-Gordon Wild Rivers National Park
- Walking the Overland Track during the day and socialising in the cabins at night
- Rolling down the giant Henty Dunes
- The fascinating mining history of Queenstown and Zeehan
- Cruises and seaplane flights from Strahan

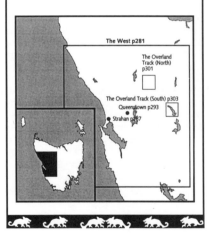

struction as a tourist venture of the historic Abt Railway between Queenstown and Strahan has inspired a little confidence among west coast residents, whose traditional faith in mining as a source of employment has been sorely tested in recent times.

## Getting There & Around

Tasmanian Wilderness Travel (TWT, ☎ 6334 4442) runs one bus a day on Tuesday, Thursday, Saturday and Sunday from Hobart to Bronte Junction ($20.60), Lake St Clair ($28.70), Derwent Bridge ($24.70), Queenstown ($36.20) and Strahan ($41.80). Buses run on the same days from Strahan to Queenstown ($5.60; Strahan to Launceston $48.70) and on to Hobart. Buses run on Tuesday, Thursday and Saturday from Queenstown to Zeehan ($5.60), Rosebery ($11), Tullah ($12.40), Cradle Mountain Lodge ($17.60), Gowrie Park ($24.70), Sheffield ($27.50), Devonport ($30.10) and Launceston ($43.10); there are return services on the same days.

For information about alternative services for those walking the Overland Track, see the Cradle Mountain-Lake St Clair section of this chapter.

## TULLAH

Originally, this old mining town was very isolated: for much of its history the only access was on foot or, later, by train. The town was first established in 1892 when a

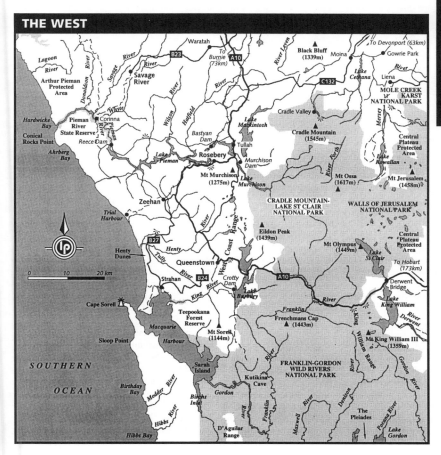

THE WEST

lead-zinc-copper-silver ore body was discovered on Mt Farrell; mining continued until the early 1970s.

In 1962 the construction of the Murchison Hwy from Burnie to Queenstown linked Tullah to the rest of Tasmania. When the mine closed, the town probably would have collapsed if it had not received a reprieve by being chosen as the accommodation site for the workers for several hydroelectricity schemes. In the 1970s and early 1980s there were 2000 construction workers residing here.

With the completion of the dams and power stations, the workers vanished and the town emptied. Many of the buildings were also removed and the streets were deserted. The remaining residents are now trying to survive on tourism, with the biggest drawcard being the large trout caught in the lakes around the town.

The name Tullah comes from an Aboriginal word meaning 'meeting of two rivers': today the rivers in question have been flooded to form Lake Rosebery (reportedly soon to be renamed Lake Tullah, as Tullah, not Rosebery, is the town on its shores), part of a large hydroelectricity scheme. The town offers great views of Mt Murchison and the surrounding ranges.

## Radford Woodcrafts

At this little gallery and workshop (☎ 6473 4344) opposite the pub, you can watch the woodturner at work and purchase souvenirs daily from 9 am to 5 pm.

## Scenic Drives

There are several scenic drives passing the major dams and lakes built for hydroelectricity generation. Three kilometres north of town you can follow a road for 55km west to the **Reece Dam**. The road crosses the dam wall and continues a farther 29km to Zeehan.

The other main scenic road starts 5km south of town and heads over the flanks of Mt Murchison towards Queenstown. Known as the Anthony Rd, it provides some extremely scenic views as it crosses the

West Coast Range. From town, minor roads also lead to the Murchison dam.

## Wee Georgie Wood

From 1908 until the 1960s, Tullah's only transport link with the rest of the world was a train line. Eventually, of course, a road was built and train services ceased, but in 1977 the residents decided to restore Wee Georgie Wood, one of the engines that had operated on the train line. From August to April, the train runs on about two or three days every month (it's always a Saturday or Sunday). Ring ☎ 6473 1229 after 6 pm for details. The 20-minute rides are available between noon and 4 pm, and fares are $2 for adults, $1 for children and $5 for a family.

## Horse Riding

One way to see the region around the town is to go horse riding with Tullah Horse Back Tours (☎ 6473 4289). Rides are $20 for the first hour and $15 for each extra hour. Bookings should be made at least 24 hours in advance.

## Places to Stay & Eat

The rather sad little Tullah Village on Farrell St houses the *Village Café*, which is an agency for Australia Post and the Commonwealth Bank, and where breakfast, other light meals and takeaway are available every day. In the same complex, *Tullah Village Bed & Breakfast* (☎ 6473 4377, AH 6473 4136) can sleep up to four people in one very large room with *en suite* for $20/35 a single/double.

Farther down Farrell St, the *Tullah Lakeside Chalet* (☎ 6473 4121, fax 6473 4130) overlooks the lake. The huge open fire in the lounge bar makes this a great place to relax and enjoy anything from a beer to a Devonshire tea, whether or not you are staying overnight. The rooms themselves, however, are the quarters used by Hydro Electric Commission (HEC) construction workers in the 1970s, and although they have *en suites*, and the more expensive ones have been extended slightly to give them better views of the water, they are not plush. Prices range from $90 a single or double for a lakeside room to $30 a single or twin for a traveller's room. The chalet specialises in functions, bus tours and special events, so if you prefer to avoid groups, you might like to ask if anything of this kind is planned before making your booking. The restaurant is open every day: a cooked breakfast is $11.50, a continental breakfast $6.50.

Around the corner on Meredith St, *Tullah Lakeside Cottage* (☎ 6473 4165) can be rented for $55 a double plus $15 for extra adults and can accommodate up to four.

Back on the highway, the tired-looking *Tullah Hotel* has counter meals on Tuesday, Thursday and Saturday from 6 to 6.30 pm only. On the opposite side of the highway and just north of the pub, *Wombat Lodge* (☎ 6473 4252) is an attractive two storey cottage, suitable for a couple only; it costs $60. Next door is the *Bush Nook Tearoom*, which is open from 10 am to 4 pm daily.

## Getting There & Away
See the Getting There & Around section at the start of this chapter. Buses arrive at and depart from the BP service station.

## ROSEBERY
• **pop 1637**
Gold was discovered in Rosebery in 1891. Further prospecting revealed rich sulphide deposits and the first mines opened in 1896. Mining started at the same time on Mt Read to the south. By 1899 the Emu Bay Railway from Burnie had reached the town and the lead-silver-copper-gold ore was shipped to Zeehan for smelting. However, when the Zeehan lead smelters closed in 1913, operations also closed in Rosebery, as did the nearby Hercules Mine on Mt Read.

In 1920 the Electrolytic Zinc Company bought both mines. It took many years for a mill to be designed and constructed, but in 1936 production resumed at both mines. An aerial ropeway from Mt Read transported the ore from the Hercules Mine to Rosebery. In 1986 the Hercules Mine was closed

and the aerial ropeway collapsed; it can still be seen from the highway.

Today the mine at Rosebery continues to employ around 300 people, and supports the town's economy.

## Information
The post office, open from 9 am to 5 pm Monday to Friday, is an agent for the Commonwealth Bank. There is a Trust Bank behind the post office, and an ANZ ATM inside the newsagency, which is open from 6 am to 6 pm Monday to Friday, until 1 pm Saturday and from 7 am to 1 pm Sunday.

## Things to See
Behind the Plandome Hotel, the high school has some interesting remnants from the old mines along its front fence, including a water wheel and railway carriage for steep inclines. The school also contains a mining museum displaying artefacts and old photos; entry is free – ask at the school office.

The picnic area on the southern side of town is the start of a walk down the Stitt River. This short walk leads to Park Rd and the **Stitt Falls** just beyond, which are good after recent rainfall. Otherwise there is not much else to see in and around the town.

Sealed roads lead to Williamsford, 8km south of Rosebery. This is the site of an abandoned mining town and also the start of an excellent walk to the impressively high but not voluminous **Montezuma Falls**. These are over 100m high and among the highest falls in the state. The excellent and easy return walk along an abandoned railway line takes about three hours return. You can explore the adit at the end of the walk if you bring a torch (flashlight).

If you prefer a guided walk to Montezuma Falls, Hays Bus Service (☎ 6473 1247) runs trips to the falls for $40 each, which includes lunch and takes 3½ hours. Hays Bus Service also runs tours of the **Pasminco Zinc Mine** at 9.30 am, 12.30 and 3.30 pm daily. The mine is an underground operation, but the two hour tour remains on the surface, visiting the above-ground operations. The tour costs $8 for adults, $5 for children and $24 for families. The Hays also have a boat and can take you trout fishing on any of the lakes that are part of the hydroelectricity schemes.

## Places to Stay & Eat
*Rosebery Caravan Park and Mountain Holiday Cabins (☎ 6473 1366)* on Park Rd has views of the mountains (and the mine, which is very close by). It has tent sites for $8, on-site vans for $28 and cabins for $45.

Right in the centre of town beside the highway, the *Plandome Hotel (☎ 6473 1351)* has reasonable rooms for $25/38. It serves daily counter meals too. The nearby *Rosebery Hotel* also provides daily counter meals.

*Miss Murchison (☎ 6473 1366)* is a cottage near the caravan park for which you will pay $60 a double plus $12 for each extra adult; it has six beds.

Nancy's Guesthouse, opposite the school, only provides accommodation for miners.

On Karlson St, *Miners Cottage (☎ 6473 1796)* charges $80 a double plus $25 for each extra adult; the price includes provisions for a continental or cooked breakfast. There is also a flat with single beds for $45 a person.

There are a number of *snack bars* etc on the main street, which provide a variety of snacks and takeaways.

## Getting There & Away
See the Getting There & Around section at the start of this chapter. Buses arrive at and depart from Mackrell's store (24 Agnes St).

## ZEEHAN
* pop 1132

In 1882 rich deposits of silver and lead were discovered around what today is Zeehan. By 1900 the town had a population of around 8000 (a third of Hobart's population) and was known as 'Silver City'. In its heyday, it had 26 hotels and its Gaiety Theatre seated 1000 people.

In 1908 the major mines started closing, the last large one ceasing operation in 1960. However, with the reopening and expansion of the Renison Tin Mine at Renison Bell 17km towards Rosebery later that decade, Zeehan experienced a revival, becoming the housing base for Renison Ltd.

## Orientation & Information
Zeehan is a very small town, but it's worth noting that the historic part of Main St is at the opposite end of the road from where you enter it on your way in from Queenstown or Strahan. The town is the administrative centre for the region run by the West Coast Council, and has branches of the ANZ and Trust banks and a library with public Internet access.

Now that there is a road right up to the Pieman River 48km away, and a barge to carry cars across the water to Corinna, Zeehan is a convenient place to spend the night if you are planning to take a cruise or go boating on that beautiful watercourse (see the Corinna section of the North-West chapter) or continue along the Western Explorer to the north-eastern corner of the state.

## West Coast Pioneers' Memorial Museum
The excellent West Coast Pioneers' Memorial Museum (☎ 6471 6225) is in the 1894 School of Mines building on Main St, and is open daily from 8.30 am to 5 pm. Admission is $5 for adults and $3 for children; donations are also welcome, and all proceeds go towards the restoration of the Grand Hotel and Gaiety Theatre (see the following entry). The museum features an interesting mineral collection and an exhibit of steam locomotives and carriages used on the early west-coast railways. Downstairs are displays of fauna and Aboriginal artefacts, while upstairs there are photographs of mining towns and the people who lived in them.

## Historic Buildings
The **Grand Hotel** and **Gaiety Theatre** are a single building known as the Gaiety Grand, a short distance up Main St from the museum.

The Gaiety was one of the biggest and most modern theatres in the world when it opened in February 1899, and what a bonus it must have been for the miners to be able to move between the pub and the theatre through connecting doors. In his book *The Peaks of Lyell*, historian Geoffrey Blainey notes that to mark the Gaiety's opening, a Melbourne troupe of 60 was brought to the town, where it played to a house of 1000 every night for a week, pulling audiences from as far afield as Queenstown, then a six hour journey away.

Today the building, which has been subjected to some appalling renovations over the years, is slowly being restored using funds from the museum and whatever government grants can be secured. The restorer, Pat Geraghty, is devoted to his task and happy to give tours of the premises whenever he is on site. In time, the West Coast Heritage Authority also hopes to restore the town's other historic buildings, including the **post office** (still in use), the **old bank** and **St Luke's Church**.

## Historic Walk

An excellent way to see more is to complete a circuit walk around town. Starting from the museum, follow Main St west, turn left towards the golf course and walk through **Spray Tunnel**, a former railway tunnel. Turn left again to follow the Comstock track (an old tramway) south to **Florence Dam**. Follow the right track at the fork, winding around Keel Ridge, then descend to the southern end of Main St. It takes two to three hours to walk and passes a lot of old mine sites.

More detailed notes to this walk and others around the mining sites of the west coast are available in *Historic Mines of Western Tasmania* by Duncan How, available at the museum for $8.95. Alternatively, take the drive suggested by the Museum (all the way or as far as Spray Tunnel from where you can continue on foot).

## Other Attractions

There are plenty of old mining relics farther out of town. Four kilometres to the south you will find some **old smelters** beside the highway. A cairn and display board details

their history. For panoramic views you can walk to the top of **Mt Zeehan**. The track starts near the smelters and follows a vehicle then walking track; it is three hours return.

At Renison Bell, 17km east of Zeehan, there is a signposted **Battery Mill Walk** starting 300m west of the mine entrance. This visits the old mill site where rock from the mine was crushed. A locomotive, railway sidings and old workings are described with the aid of photographic plaques beside the track. Allow about 45 minutes return for a visit.

North-west of Zeehan, a quiet sealed road leads to the **Reece Dam** on the Pieman River, part of the Pieman Hydro Electric Scheme. This road gives access to some rarely visited places like **Granville Harbour**, which is down a side road, and Corinna, the departure point for the Pieman River Cruise (see the Corinna section of the North-West chapter). Granville Harbour is a small coastal holiday place where you can camp. The road to Reece Dam also provides a view of **Heemskirk Falls**; a one hour return walk leads to the base of the falls.

For fishing enthusiasts, Granville Harbour is a good place for crayfish and Lake Pieman behind the Reece Dam has some fine trout. A gravel road heads west to **Trial Harbour**, the original port for Zeehan, where there are also some good fishing spots. This is a beautiful place to camp, with rocky outcrops to the right and a sandy beach past a couple more outcrops to the left.

From Zeehan, you can take Henty Rd (B27) to **Henty Dunes** (see the following Strahan section for more details).

**Warning** If walking off marked tracks in the bush close to Zeehan, beware of abandoned mine shafts hidden by vegetation.

## Places to Stay & Eat

At the *Treasure Island West Coast Caravan Park* (☎ 6471 6633), on Hurst St on the northern edge of town, there are camp sites for $8/14, powered sites for $12/16, on-site vans for $35 a double and cabins for $60.

*Hotel Cecil* (☎ 6471 6221) on Main St has rooms for $40/60 with shared facilities,

THE WEST

one double with *en suite* (also $60), and self-contained Miners Cottages for $80 a double. A continental breakfast is $7 a person, and counter meals are available daily.

The *Heemskirk Motor Hotel* (☎ 6471 6107), on Main St at the western entrance to town, has motel rooms from $73/79 and also offers bistro meals. The brick units at the *Zeehan Motor Inn & Lodge* (☎ 6471 6107) are motel units that cost $60 a double. Hostel beds in a nearby building on the same site are $14 each.

For a light meal go to the *Museum Coffee Lounge*, which is open every day and serves coffee and takeaway food. At the time of research, a new café, *The Coffee Stop*, was about to open. It is planning to operate from 9 am to 5 pm Tuesday to Sunday, and offer home-made cakes, pastries and sandwiches.

## Getting There & Away
See the Getting There & Around section at the start of this chapter. Buses arrive at and depart from Marina's Coffee Shop, on the main street near the ANZ bank.

## STRAHAN
• pop 597

Strahan is 40km from Queenstown, on Macquarie Harbour. Aborigines lived in this area for more than 40,000 years, surviving an ice age in the caves along the Franklin River. Yet, in less than 40 years of European settlement, the genocide of the Aborigines had devastated their community.

Macquarie Harbour was discovered by sailors searching for the source of the Huon pine that frequently washed up on southern beaches. In those days, the area was totally inaccessible by land, while its treacherous coast made it very difficult to reach by sea. In 1821 these dubious assets prompted the establishment of a penal settlement on Sarah Island, in the middle of the harbour, to isolate the worst of the colony's convicts and use their muscle to harvest the huge stands of Huon pine. The convicts worked upriver 12 hours a day, often in leg irons, felling the pines and rafting them back to

the island's saw-pits, where they were used to build ships and furniture.

Sarah Island, which featured in Marcus Clarke's novel about the convict experience, *For the Term of His Natural Life*, was one of Australia's most notorious penal settlements. The most dreaded punishment meted out there was confinement on tiny Grummet Island, little more than a windswept rock. In 1834, after the establishment of the 'escape-proof' penal settlement at Port Arthur, Sarah Island was abandoned.

Strahan prospered during the west-coast mining boom late last century, when ore was transported to its port along the Abt Railway from Queenstown. However, following the closure of many mines, the opening of the Emu Bay Railway from Zeehan to Burnie, and the construction of the Lyell Hwy between Hobart and Queenstown, the town became nothing more than a sleepy village.

Then, much to its own surprise, it shot to fame in the 1980s as the centre for the Franklin River Blockade. At that stage, the HEC had already constructed a large dam on the Gordon River and flooded Lake Pedder, and was about to construct a series of dams on the Franklin and lower Gordon rivers. Protesters set off from Strahan in rubber boats and canoes to physically prevent work from proceeding. In the summer of 1982-3, 1400 people were arrested in a widely publicised dispute. The conservationists eventually won and the Franklin River still flows free. (For more information see the boxed text in the South-West chapter.)

The town has since taken advantage of its nearby wilderness by offering a variety of tours on the Gordon River and developing its gorgeous harbourside main street into what is now called Strahan Village. Not surprisingly, Strahan today is reputed to be the second most popular tourist destination in the state after Port Arthur. As a result, it is expensive by west coast standards and has lost much of the charm it acquired during its transition from backwater to tourist hub. On the other hand, if you like a bit of luxury, you may find the polish of the new Strahan the perfect foil for the harsh landscape and uncompromising authenticity of the surrounding mining towns.

At the time of writing, the *Mercury* (the main daily paper for the Hobart area) was reporting that the success of existing ventures and the promise of funding for the reconstruction of the Abt Railway (see the boxed text) was encouraging still further development in Strahan: the Marine Board was planning to improve the wharf, jetty and harbour works, horseback tours through the Teep-

ookana Forest were being considered, and investors were talking of developing Risby Cove by building a marina and galleries and renting out ocean kayaks and canoes.

## Information
The architecturally unusual and innovative Strahan visitors' centre (☎ 6471 7488) on the waterfront is almost a tourist attraction in its own right. It was substantially renovated in 1998, when the gardens were rejuvenated or replanted, activities introduced

THE WEST

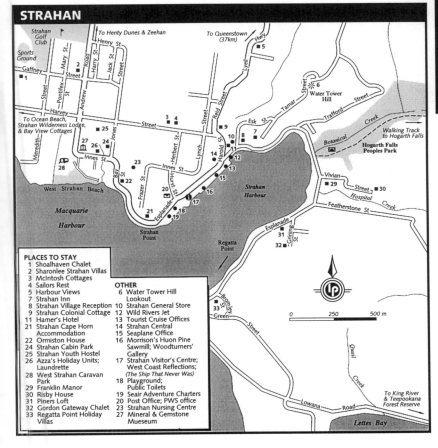

**STRAHAN**

To Henty Dunes & Zeehan
To Queenstown (37km)
Strahan Golf Club
Sports Ground
Gaffney St
Henry St
Harry St
Jack St
Mary St
Pontifex St
Andrew
Road
Harvey St
To Ocean Beach, Strahan Wilderness Lodge, & Bay View Cottages
Meredith
Jones Street
Innes St
Herbert St
Bay St
Frazer St
Esplanade
West Strahan Beach
Macquarie Harbour
Strahan Point
Regatta Point
Reid Street
Lyell Hwy
Esk St
Harold St
Lynch St
Tamar Street
Trafford St
Water Tower Hill
Creek
Walking Track to Hogarth Falls
Botanical
Hogarth Falls Peoples Park
Vivian
Street
Hospital
Featherstone St
Creek
Strahan Harbour
Esplanade
Grining St
Bromley St
Green St
Lowana
Road
Quail Creek
Lettes Bay
To King River & Teepookana Forest Reserve
0   250   500 m

**PLACES TO STAY**
1 Shoalhaven Chalet
2 Sharonlee Strahan Villas
3 McIntosh Cottages
4 Sailors Rest
5 Harbour Views
7 Strahan Inn
8 Strahan Village Reception
9 Strahan Colonial Cottage
11 Hamer's Hotel
21 Strahan Cape Horn Accommodation
22 Ormiston House
24 Strahan Cabin Park
25 Strahan Youth Hostel
26 Azza's Holiday Units; Laundrette
28 West Strahan Caravan Park
29 Franklin Manor
30 Risby House
31 Piners Loft
32 Gordon Gateway Chalet
33 Regatta Point Holiday Villas

**OTHER**
6 Water Tower Hill Lookout
10 Strahan General Store
12 Wild Rivers Jet
13 Tourist Cruise Offices
14 Strahan Central
15 Seaplane Office
16 Morrison's Huon Pine Sawmill; Woodturners' Gallery
17 Strahan Visitor's Centre; West Coast Reflections; *(The Ship That Never Was)*
18 Playground; Public Toilets
19 Seair Adventure Charters
20 Post Office; PWS office
23 Strahan Nursing Centre
27 Mineral & Gemstone Mueseum

for children, and the amphitheatre outside remodelled to make it an all-weather venue. The centre is open daily from 10 am to 6 pm (8 pm in summer). Its very friendly staff can help you find accommodation or issue you with a national park pass. See the Things to See and Entertainment entries in this section for more information on what the centre has to offer.

There is an office of the Parks and Wildlife Service (PWS, ☎ 6471 7122) in the old Customs House building close to the town centre. This building also houses the post office, which is also a Commonwealth Bank agency. The Strahan Wharf Centre and Strahan Village have EFTPOS facilities, as does the newsagency, which is an agency for ANZ and gives preference to ANZ clients when cash supplies are low.

## Things to See

**West Coast Reflections** is the museum section of the Strahan visitors' centre and presents all aspects of the history of the south-west, including the Franklin Blockade, in a way that really captures the imagination. You can gain some impression of the display by looking through the glass wall on the harbour side. It is open the same hours as the visitors' centre, and admission is $4.50 for adults or $9 a family (children free). Tickets remain valid for 24 hours allowing several visits.

Probably the finest old building on the west coast is Strahan's imposing **Customs House**, which now houses the post office. Near the Strahan Wharf Centre, **Morrisons Huon Pine Sawmill** (☎ 6471 7235) has a **woodturner's gallery** (☎ 6471 7244) and sales centre. You can also view the sawmill in operation.

The lookout over the town is **Water Tower Hill**, accessed by following Esk St beside the Strahan Village Reception Centre. It's less than 1km from the village and you can walk or drive to it.

**Hogarth Falls** is a pleasant 40 minute return walk through the rainforest beside Botanical Creek. The track starts at Peoples Park on the Esplanade, 700m east of Hamers Hotel.

The **Cape Sorell Lighthouse**, at the southern head of the harbour, is the third largest in Tasmania. A return walk of two to three hours along a vehicle track from the jetty at Macquarie Heads leads to the lighthouse. You will need a boat to cross the heads unless you can find a friendly fisher to take you over.

Opposite the caravan park, the **Mineral & Gemstone Museum** charges $2 admission. Next to the caravan park is **West Strahan Beach**, which has a gently shelving sandy bottom that provides safe swimming.

Six kilometres from town is the impressive 33km **Ocean Beach**, where the sunsets have to be seen to be believed. The beach is one continuous stretch of sand from Trial Harbour in the north to Macquarie Heads in the south. Due to rips and undertows, swimming at Ocean Beach is not recommended. The dunes behind the beach contain the nesting burrows of mutton birds. From mid-September, the mutton birds return from their 15,000km winter migration and – for the entire summer until April – provide an evening spectacle as they return to their nests at dusk.

Fourteen kilometres along the road from Strahan to Zeehan are the **Henty Dunes**, vast white sand dunes on Ocean Beach, many of which are more than 30m high. They are a soothing contrast to the harshness of so much of the scenery on Tasmania's west coast, and any children in your company will be wild with excitement at the prospect of rolling or running down their steep slopes. Unfortunately, off-road vehicles are permitted, but for this edition we visited mid-week in early and late September (the latter occasion a warm, sunny day) and both times were the only people on the entire expanse of sand. From the picnic area, you can take a 1½ hour return walk along a track through the dunes and out to Ocean Beach; remember to carry drinking water.

The **Teepookana Forest** surrounds the **King River** to the west of Strahan, and the narrow gravel road to this reserve begins at a turn-off a short distance past Regatta Point. The King River is a graphic example

Stanley stands at the foot of The Nut

Colonial Buildings, Stanley

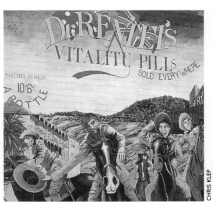

One of the many murals at Sheffield

Sunset at Wynyard, North-West Tasmania

The Pier Hotel, George Town

The Rocky Cape National park

Wild flowers in the North-West of Tasmania

View of Bass Strait from The Nut, Stanley

of that other famous west coast feature, environmental degradation: along each of its banks is a band of sludge in which nothing grows, the result of pollution from mining operations in Queenstown. Yet incongruous as it sounds, the forest and the river are still beautiful. In fact, when reconstruction of the scenic Abt Railway has been completed, an extensive section of the line will follow the King River and, in anticipation, state and federal governments and the mining company are redoubling their efforts to cleanse the river of its acid mine drainage.

## Organised Tours & Cruises

**River Cruises** A traditional way of experiencing the beauty of the Gordon River is on one of the cruises operating out of Strahan, and there is something available every day except Christmas day. All cruises that stop at Sarah Island include an informative guided tour.

Gordon River Cruises (☎ 6471 7187) operates three large launches, the *James Kelly II*, the MV *Gordon Explorer* and *Wilderness Seeker*. During winter only one or two boats run according to demand, with all three boats running in summer. There are half-day trips from 9 am to 2 pm (from 1 to 21 January, 2 to 7 pm) for $45 ($25 for children) including morning or afternoon tea; or full-day trips from 1 October to 31 May from 9 am to 3.30 pm for $61 ($30 for children) including a smorgasbord lunch. The booking office on the wharf has a display of some of the photographs from the Zeehan Museum, which is worth viewing if you're not going to Zeehan.

All trips run up the Gordon River as far as Heritage Landing, where a short walk takes you past a 2000-year-old Huon pine tree. They also visit Sarah Island where some walking tracks, complete with interpretive signs, pass among the ruins of the former penal settlement.

World Heritage Cruises (☎ 6471 7174) is a family business with a long association with the harbour; the first trip the family ran across Macquarie Harbour for tourists was in 1896. They operate the MV *Heritage*

*Wanderer II*, a new boat built to minimise the wake and the effect of this on the shore. They charge $36 ($16 for children) for a trip from 9 am to 3.30 pm. Lunch isn't included in the price, though you can bring your own or eat at the licensed dining area on board for $8 a person ($3 for children). This cruise also visits Heritage Landing and Sarah Island, and operates daily except during August and Christmas day.

A unique way to see the Gordon River is to sail along it with West Coast Yacht Charters (☎ 6471 7422). For $320 each (children $160) you will be taken on a two day and two night sail across Macquarie Harbour and up the river. If this is too much, there is also a 2½ hour crayfish dinner cruise around Macquarie Harbour for $50 each (children $30). Three-hour fishing trips are also available from 9 am to noon for $40 each (children $20). The yacht is generally available for hire from October through March and can also provide B&B while moored at the wharf (see Places to Stay in this section).

**Seaplane Tours** A highly recommended way to see the river and surrounding World Heritage Area is on a seaplane tour with Wilderness Air (☎ 6471 7280). The planes take off from Strahan's wharf every 1½ hours from 9 am onwards and fly up the river to Sir John Falls, where they land so that you can take a walk in the rainforest before flying back via Sarah Island, Cape Sorell, Hells Gates and Ocean Beach. The 80 minute flight is well worth the $105. Demand for flights is heavy, so it's good to book if possible. The office is diagonally opposite the hotel, just past the Gordon River Cruise Office. The flight path varies according to weather and the time of day. The seaplanes land much farther up the Gordon River than where the launches turn around. There are also some shorter and longer flights around Strahan and over the World Heritage Area.

**Jet-Boat Rides** With an office on the wharf, Wild Rivers Jet (☎ 6471 7174) operates 50-minute jet-boat rides up the King

River for $39, children $25 or $112 for a family of five. The boats can take a maximum of five passengers at a time and run from 9 am to 5 pm daily.

**4WD Wilderness Trips** South West Adventure Tours (☎ 6471 7612, AH 6471 7462) also runs 4WD tours to Henty Dunes for $40, to see the sunsets on Ocean Beach ($35), to Teepookana Forest Reserve on the King River ($40) and three-hour fishing tours on Macquarie Harbour for $65 to $95. Bookings can be made at Strahan Central.

**Helicopter & Light Plane Scenic Flights** Seair Adventure Charters (☎ 6471 7718 Strahan, ☎ 6442 1220 Wynyard) offers light-plane flights over Queenstown, Lake Burbury, Frenchmans Cap, Cradle Mountain, the Franklin and Gordon rivers, and Macquarie Harbour. These depart from Strahan Aerodrome. There are also helicopter flights departing from the landing pad opposite the post office in Strahan itself. These take in the Teepookana Forest and some of the gorges once negotiated by the Abt Railway from Queenstown (now being restored), and feature a 15 minute break in the flight to view Huon pines. The Strahan office is opposite the post office and is open daily from about 8.30 am to 5 pm, except in bad weather.

**Bus Tours** TWT offers various tours of Strahan's attractions for $29.

## Places to Stay

Although Strahan has a wide range of accommodation and plenty of it, it's extremely popular in summer and during school and public holidays, so always book ahead at such times.

Much of the accommodation in the central part of town is part of Strahan Village (☎ 6471 7191, fax 6471 7389) and can be booked through its new reservation office on the corner of the Esplanade and Esk St. Still more of the town's accommodation, including the hostel, is handled by Strahan Central (☎ 6471 7612), on the corner of the Es-

planade and Harold St. If you arrive late in the afternoon without a booking, call into these offices for a quick assessment of what's still on offer. By taking your chances with this stand-by option in the low season (don't risk it in summer), you should be able to secure a substantial discount on any available beds; accommodation near or in view of the water is expensive in Strahan, yet much of the rest of the town is rather drab, so such a strategy is worth considering.

You can also arrange accommodation through the Strahan visitors' centre.

## Places to Stay – Budget
**Camping** The unattractive *West Strahan Caravan Park* (☎ 6471 7239) charges $10 a double for tent sites and $12 a double for powered sites (there's also a $5 refundable deposit on the key to the shower block). The *camping ground*, 15km away at Macquarie Heads, has only very basic facilities.

**Hostels** The *Strahan Youth Hostel* (☎ 6471 7612) on Harvey St charges $13 a night for YHA members. It's about a 10 minute walk from the town centre and is set in reasonably attractive grounds but doesn't have a view of the water. It also has twin rooms for $36 and some tiny A-frame cabins for $42 a double.

## Places to Stay – Mid-Range
**B&Bs** Right in town, moored at the wharf, is a yacht managed by *West Coast Yacht Charters* (☎ 6471 7422) where you can get B&B for $30 a person ($10 for children). Because the yacht is used for charters, it has a 9 pm check in and 8 am check out.

Three kilometres from town, on Ocean Beach Rd, the historic *Strahan Wilderness Lodge* (☎ 6471 7142) has doubles with a continental breakfast for $40/50. The same people also run the *Bay View Cottages*, where B&B costs $60/70. Unless you have your own transport, staying here can be a bit inconvenient. Both are set in areas of low coastal vegetation.

Not as far out, but still inconvenient without transport, *Shoalhaven Chalet* (☎ 6471

7400) has B&B for $70 a double. *Harbour Views* (☎ 6471 7143), on the corner of Charles St and the Lyell Hwy, provides B&B for $70 a double with *en suite* only, or $80 a double in a self-contained unit.

**Hotels** The *Hamers Hotel* (☎ 6471 7191, fax 6471 7389), managed by Strahan Village, is opposite the wharf right in the middle of town and has comfortable, basic rooms with shared facilities for $48/65, including a continental breakfast.

**Holiday Units** Accommodation at *Azza's Holiday Units* (☎ 6471 7253, 7 Innes St), near the caravan park, is $60 a double. Around the corner, *Strahan Cabin Park* (☎ 6471 7442, 10 Jones St) offers portable cabins for $73 a double.

*Strahan Cape Horn Accommodation* (☎ 6471 7169) is perched above Strahan Point at the end of Frazer St and overlooks the harbour. It has one plain but comfortable brick unit for $50/70. It's just a short walk through bush to town.

*Sailors Rest* (☎ 6471 7237) on Harvey St is only a five minute walk from town. While the units appear ordinary from the outside, they are large (they sleep eight) and have good amenities, and cost $80 a double plus $20 for each extra person.

## Places to Stay – Top End
**B&Bs** A five minute walk from Hamers Hotel is *McIntosh Cottages* (☎ 6471 7358), an old house divided into two self-contained units, each costing $135 a double with provisions for a cooked breakfast. On Reid St (up the hill past Strahan Central), the very comfortable *Strahan Colonial Cottages* (☎ 6471 7612) range from $150 to $180 a double with breakfast provisions provided.

For a memorable stay, try the historic *Franklin Manor* (☎ 6471 7311, fax 6471 7267), on the Esplanade around the bay, 1km from the town centre. Rooms with *en suite* are $110 to $208 a double with a cooked breakfast. Nearby, the modern, two storey, celery-top pine *Piners Loft* (☎ 6471

7390) offers views of the harbour. The whole place is yours for $160 a double plus $35 for extra adults and $22 for children (sleeps six). Provisions for a continental breakfast are supplied. *Risby House* (☎ 6471 7340) is in the same part of town but up the hill. It offers B&B in your own house (sleeps seven) for $120 a double.

On the other side of town, the wonderful 1899 *Ormiston House* offers luxurious B&B for $180 to $210 a double (no children under 12 permitted), with a continental breakfast.

**Motels** Strahan Village now manages the *Strahan Inn* (☎ 6471 7191, fax 6471 7389), the motel at the end of Jolly St on the hill above its reservation office. Many of these rooms have magnificent views of the harbour. Prices are $85 to $95 a double. There are also units available at the *Strahan Village* reservation office itself.

Upstairs at *Strahan Central* (☎ 6471 7612) are a number of attractive split level suites for $120 to $130 a double; a continental breakfast is $10 extra per person.

**Holiday Units** On the corner of Andrew Rd and Gaffney St, *Sharonlee Strahan Villas* (☎ 6471 7224) has units for $105 a double plus $25 for each extra adult.

On the other side of the harbour, *Regatta Point Holiday Villas* (☎ 6471 7103) is located next to some old wharves, 2km from the town by road. It has units with good views for $120 a double plus $20 for extra adults.

In a much nicer spot closer to town but still on the way to Regatta Point, *Gordon Gateway Chalet* (☎ 6471 7165) has modern, attractive units with beautiful views across the harbour to the village for $110 a double plus $30 for extra adults. The larger chalets, which have similar views, are $150 a double plus $35 for extra adults.

*Strahan Village* (☎ 6471 7191, fax 6471 7389) has a large selection of self-contained units and cottages built close to the waterfront, many in period style, for $99 to $155 a double.

## Places to Eat

The *Strahan Bakery* in the hotel complex is open from 7.30 am to 8 pm. It has salad rolls and cakes, and from 5.30 pm doubles as a pizza and pasta shop.

*Hamers Hotel* on the Esplanade serves counter meals and is open daily for breakfast from 7.30 am, for lunch from noon to 2.30 pm and for dinner from 5.30 to 8.30 pm. Mains are priced from $10 to $18. The hotel's location in the heart of the village makes it a great place to relax over a meal or a drink, but the service is not always up to standard.

The *Regatta Point Tavern*, 2km around the bay on the Esplanade, serves plain counter meals daily, with mains around $14 (when we ate here the steak was great). It has an outdoor playground for children and a children's menu.

*Strahan Central* has a pleasant café serving coffee, cakes and interesting meals, such as Cajun dirty rice with pappadams for $6.50. The *Gordon River Cruises* café across the road from Hamers Hotel is open from 8 am to 6 pm. Until 10 am it serves a breakfast special of scrambled egg and bacon on toast and tea or coffee for $5.95. In summer it stays open until 9 or 10 pm and serves evening meals.

Overlooking the harbour, the *Macquarie Restaurant* (☎ 6471 7160) in the Strahan Inn has an à la carte menu. Both *Franklin Manor* (☎ 6471 7311) and *Ormiston House* (☎ 6471 7077) have excellent à la carte restaurants. Three courses at Franklin Manor cost $39. It's best to book at either. Ormiston House also serves morning and afternoon teas.

## Entertainment

The Strahan visitors' centre puts on daily performances of the play *The Ship That Never Was* at 5.30 pm (also 8.30 pm in summer). This is the story of some convicts who escaped from Sarah Island by building their own ship. The play is performed in the amphitheatre outside the centre and is intended to be fun for all ages. Tickets can be booked at the centre and cost $10 for adults and $5 for children.

## Getting There & Away

**Bus** See the Getting There & Around section at the start of this chapter. Buses arrive at and depart from the visitors' centre.

The YHA office (☎ 6234 9617, 28 Criterion St, Hobart) sometimes has two-day transport and accommodation deals from Hobart on offer.

**Hitching** If you are hitching, it can be a long wait between vehicles on both the Lyell and Murchison highways, and in winter it gets bloody cold; the bus services are an attractive alternative.

## QUEENSTOWN
* pop 3368

The final, winding descent into Queenstown from the Lyell Hwy is a memorable experience. With deep, eroded gullies and naked, multicoloured hills, there's no escaping the fact that this is a mining town, and that the destruction of the surrounding area is a direct result of this industry.

The discovery of alluvial gold in the Queen River valley in 1881 first brought prospectors to the area. Two years later, mining began on the rich Mt Lyell deposits, and for nearly a decade miners extracted a few ounces of gold a day from the Iron Blow and ignored the mountain's rich copper reserves. In 1891 the Mt Lyell Mining Company began to concentrate on copper but had trouble raising financial backing. A lucky discovery of a rich vein of silver rescued the company and in 1895 the first of the Mt Lyell smelters began operating. Copper had became the most profitable mineral on the west coast.

The initial township was at Penghana around the smelters, but a bushfire in 1886 wiped out the shanty town and the residents moved to the newly planned town on the Queen River, which became known as Queenstown.

In 1896 the company built a railway between Queenstown and Teepookana on the King River to transport copper to the coast. (The line was later extended to Strahan; see the 'Abt Railway' boxed text in this chapter.)

At the turn of the century, Queenstown had a population of over 5000 and was the third-largest town in Tasmania. It had 14 hotels, 28 mining companies working the Mt Lyell deposits, and 11 furnaces involved in the smelting process. The Mt Lyell Mining and Railway Company eventually acquired most of the mines or leases.

By the 1920s, after only 20 years of mining, the rainforested hills around Queenstown had been stripped bare: three million tonnes of timber had been felled to feed the

furnaces. Uncontrolled pollution from the copper smelters was killing any vegetation that hadn't already been cut down, and bushfires raged through the hills every summer, fuelled by the sulphur-impregnated soils and dead stumps, until there was no regrowth left at all. The rains then washed away the exposed topsoil until only bare rocky hills remained.

In 1969 the smelters closed, and for a long time there was no change to the barren hills around the town. In recent years,

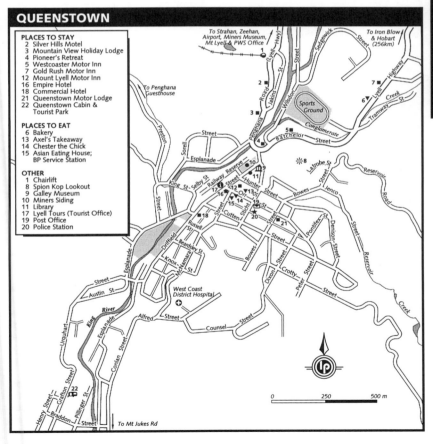

## QUEENSTOWN

PLACES TO STAY
2 Silver Hills Motel
3 Mountain View Holiday Lodge
4 Pioneer's Retreat
5 Westcoaster Motor Inn
7 Gold Rush Motor Inn
12 Mount Lyell Motor Inn
16 Empire Hotel
18 Commercial Hotel
21 Queenstown Motor Lodge
22 Queenstown Cabin & Tourist Park

PLACES TO EAT
6 Bakery
13 Axel's Takeaway
14 Chester the Chick
15 Asian Eating House; BP Service Station

OTHER
1 Chairlift
8 Spion Kop Lookout
9 Galley Museum
10 Miners Siding
11 Library
17 Lyell Tours (Tourist Office)
19 Post Office
20 Police Station

however, a bit of scrub and a few small trees have succeeded in recolonising the slopes. Already the landscape is less stark than it was just a decade ago.

The Mt Lyell mine closed in late 1994 and for some months the town's future looked bleak. In 1995 Copper Mines of Tasmania took over the lease and opened the mines again. It was good news for the community but by no means an assurance of prosperity. At the time of writing, copper prices were so low that they were hardly covering the cost of production and the mine had just been sold once again.

Today, Queenstown is making every effort to promote itself as a tourist destination, following news in 1998 that federal funding would be provided for the reconstruction of the historic Abt Railway to Strahan.

## Orientation

Orr St, which meets Driffield St opposite Lyell Tours, is the heart of the town; most shops, hotels and businesses are either on this street or very close by.

## Information

**Tourist Office** Lyell Tours on Driffield St (☎ 6471 2388) is the local visitors' centre and is open daily from 8.30 am. You can also get visitors' information at the Galley Museum (☎ 6471 1758) on the corner of Sticht and Driffield Sts.

**Money** The Trust Bank is on Orr St, while the post office is an agency for the Commonwealth Bank. Many businesses have EFTPOS available.

**Parks & Wildlife Service** The PWS ranger station and information centre (☎ 6471 2511) is on Penghana Rd, next door to the Mt Lyell Museum at the mine entrance. It's open from 8.30 am to 5 pm Monday to Friday. However, there is a ranger on duty at most other times, and a phone number to reach them after hours is posted on the door. At this office, you can find out about nearby walking tracks and buy passes to na-

McCall Rd, a controversial 4WD track from the southern end of Lake Burbury to the Franklin River, you should ring the office to arrange a ranger to issue you with a permit and a key to the gate, both of which are free.

**Climate** It rains a *lot* in Queenstown. Bring wet-weather gear and warm clothing no matter when you visit. In summer you should also be prepared for the occasional spell of sunshine and high temperatures.

## Galley Museum

This museum, which started life as the Imperial Hotel and was the first brick hotel in Queenstown, has a quaint jumble of photographs, mining equipment, household goods and clothing from Queenstown's past. Particularly impressive are the 800 or more B&W photographs collected by local identity Eric Thomas and displayed on the walls of seven rooms. Most date from before 1940 and have wonderfully idiosyncratic captions written by Mr Thomas. From October to May, the museum is open from 10 am to 6 pm Monday to Friday, and from 1 to 6 pm on Saturday. During the rest of the year, it's open from 10 am to 4.30 pm Monday to Friday, and from 1 to 4.30 pm on Saturday. Admission is $3 for adults, $2 for children aged 10 to 12 and free for children under 10.

## Miner's Siding

Opposite the museum, the Miner's Siding is a public park that features a restored Abt steam locomotive as well as various rock, bronze and Huon pine sculptures. This was Queenstown's centenary project and the sculptures tell the story of the Abt Railway to Strahan and a hundred years of mining. The siding is located where the train station used to be.

## Chairlift

The chairlift beside Penghana Rd rises 369m up the steep side of the valley to a viewing platform from where some short walks lead to an old mine site. It costs $6 for adults, $4

## Spion Kop Lookout

Follow Hunter St uphill, turn left onto Bowes St then sharp left onto Latrobe St to the small car park from where a well-paved, short, steep track leads to the summit of Spion Kop. The track features a rail adit near the car park and the top of the hill has a pithead on it. The panoramic views of the town are excellent, particularly around sunset. If you look at the football oval you'll notice that it is cream instead of green. Queenstown's footy team is tough – it plays on gravel, not grass. (Turf quickly turns to mud underfoot in Queenstown, a result of the exceptionally high rainfall. In fact, the local golf course is said to be so sodden that members sometimes wish they could tee-off in gumboots, or even waders.)

## Iron Blow

On the top of the pass on the Lyell Hwy, just before the final descent into Queenstown, a sealed side road leads to the **Iron Blow**. This is the now deserted open-cut mine where mining for the town began in 1883. A short track leads to a lookout over the flooded open cut.

## Mt Jukes Rd

Continue along Conlan St to Mt Jukes Rd, which will take you to side roads leading to sections of the **Abt Railway** (see the 'Abt Railway' boxed text in this section) and also to **Bradshaws Sawmill**, where you can watch Curly Bradshaw at work at the mill his family has operated since 1937.

Farther along this scenic road is **Newell Creek**, 9km south of Queenstown, where a platform for visitors provides access to a patch of superb King Billy and Huon pine rainforest. The bitumen section of the road ends at **Lake Burbury**, an HEC lake surrounded by mountains that can be seen to magnificent effect from a lookout on the descent to its shores. At the lake itself, there are barbecues and a toilet. All roads past the dam wall are 4WD only and the best way to visit the places farther south is with Lyell Tours (see the Organised Tours entry in this section for details).

## Organised Tours

**Mine Tours** The open-cut section of the Mt Lyell Mine is no longer being worked, but mining is continuing deep beneath the base of the massive West Lyell crater. Lyell Tours (☎ 6471 2388) offers both surface and underground tours (check to see if these are available now that the mine has changed hands). The 1¼ hour surface tour departs from Lyell Tours every day at 9.15 am and 4.30 pm (also 2.30 pm in the high season), and costs $11 (children $6.50). The underground tour takes 3½ hours and isn't open to children under 12 because the mine doesn't stock safety gear in very small sizes. This tour departs from Lyell Tours daily at 8.30 am and 1.30 pm, and costs $48 a person. Bookings are essential and participants must wear long sleeves, long pants and enclosed shoes.

**Wilderness Tours** Lyell Tours also operates 4WD tours to the Bird River rainforest. The half-day tour departs at 8.30 am (also 2 pm in the high season) and costs $60.

**Motorbike Tours** West Coast Harley Tours (☎ 0418 524812) operates from the chairlift site.

## Places to Stay

If you yearn for comfort and pretty scenery, you'll probably prefer to make Strahan your base on the west coast. But if you're made of sterner stuff, consider spending a night or two near Mt Lyell because accommodation here is cheap and abundant, and generally of good quality.

## Places to Stay – Budget

The *Queenstown Cabin & Tourist Park (☎ 6471 1332, 17 Grafton St)* has cheap below-average hostel accommodation for $15 a double plus $5 for each extra person. There are also tent sites for $13 a double, powered sites for $15, on-site vans for $35 a double and cabins for $55 with linen and $50 without; it's about 1km from the town centre, a 10 minute walk south along the Queen River.

A scenic alternative is the *camping ground*, which is 10 minutes or so from Queenstown on the shores of Lake Burbury, on the eastern side of Bradshaw Bridge on the Lyell Hwy (see the following Lake Burbury section).

Just over the bridge on the way to Strahan, the *Mountain View Holiday Lodge* (☎ 6471 1163, 1 Penghana Rd) has very basic backpacker accommodation in two-

bed rooms with shared facilities for $10. It also has small motel units for $55 a double.

The *Empire Hotel* (☎ 6471 1699, 2 Orr St) is a lovely old hotel that dominates the entrance to the town centre. It includes an imposing blackwood staircase classified by the National Trust. It is constructed of timber that was sent to England to be turned then shipped back to Queenstown. Clean and pleasant rooms cost $20/35 a double

## Abt Railway

This is why the company that mined Mt Lyell for so long was called the Mt Lyell Mining *and* Railway Company. If the industrial complex envisaged by its founders was to be a success, a railway line connecting Mt Lyell with the port of Teepookana on the King River, and later with Strahan, was vital. Construction began in 1894, and by the time it was completed the line had cost the company more than half its capital investment in the entire mining enterprise and covered 22 miles of some of the most rugged terrain in Australia.

Opened in 1896 and extended to Strahan in 1899, the line ran along the Queen River and up the one-in-16 Abt section to Rinadeena, before heading down the one-in-20 Abt section through magnificent rainforest to the King River. Here, it crossed a stunning, curved quarter-mile bridge high above the water, before continuing on to Teepookana and Regatta Point.

The Abt system (named after its inventor) was used to cover the section of terrain originally considered too steep for the haulage of huge quantities of ore. In this arrangement, a third toothed rack rail is positioned between the two conventional rails, and locomotives are equipped with geared pinion wheels that lock into the rack rail, thereby making it possible for the trains to climb and descend gradients they would otherwise be unable to negotiate when fully loaded. You can see the pinion wheel and a section of rack rail if you look underneath the locomotive set at a gradient of one-in-16 at the Miner's Siding in Queenstown.

The railway, which was Queenstown's only link with the outside world before the opening of the Lyell Hwy in 1932, was closed in 1963 and soon fell into disrepair, but throughout the 1990s members of the Mt Lyell Abt Railway Society spent incalculable hours clearing vegetation, fixing drainage and mending bridges in the hope that one day they might be able to secure enough funding to reconstruct the railway. In July 1998 their dreams were realised, when federal Cabinet approved the allocation of $20.45 million of Federation Funding to cover the full cost of restoring the line.

Today, the whole of the west coast, but particularly Queenstown, is pinning many of its hopes for prosperity on the drawing potential of this scenic and historic railway. All attempts will be made to have the first train running on the reconstructed line by the first week in January 2001, and it's expected that the journey will take between 1½ and 1¾ hours. While work is in progress, it may no longer be possible to walk the line, but it is expected that afterwards walking or riding a bicycle its entire length will be a popular alternative to taking the train – check with the Mt Lyell Museum, or with Norm Bradshaw on ☎ 6471 1411, for more details.

**Lyn McGaurr**

with shared facilities and $45 a double with *en suite*.

At the time of writing, Hunters Hotel on Orr St had closed down.

## Places to Stay – Mid-Range

The *Mt Lyell Motor Inn* (☎ *6471 1888, 1 Orr St)* is centrally placed and has basic motel suites for $35/45. At the other end of Orr St, the *Queenstown Motor Lodge* (☎ *6471 1866)* on the corner of Bowes St has small rooms for $55/65. The *Commercial Hotel* (☎ *6471 1511)* on Driffield St provides B&B in basic units for $35/60.

The *Silver Hills Motor Inn* (☎ *6471 1755)* on Penghana Rd has a large number of traditional units for $70/80. The décor is dated but the views are great, especially from the top floors of the brick units at the back. *Westcoaster Motor Inn* (☎ *6471 1033)* has pleasant motel rooms fairly close to town for $75 a double, and the nearby *Pioneer's Retreat* has spacious self-contained two-bedroom units in what was previously a block of flats for $110 a double.

Out beside the Lyell Hwy, the *Gold Rush Motor Inn* (☎ *6471 1005)* has very nice self-contained units for $80 a single or double.

## Places to Stay – Top End

*Penghana Guesthouse* (☎ *6471 2560, fax 6471 1535)* is the former residence of the general manager of the Mt Lyell Mining and Railway Company, and stands very grandly above the town amid a surprising number of trees (surprising, given that this is Queenstown). B&B is $90 to $150 a double or twin. The guesthouse itself is a little difficult to find: travelling south down Driffield St, take the first left past Lyell Tours (King St), cross the river and take the second left (Preston St) up to a sign on your left indicating the turn-off.

## Places to Eat

For good cakes and light snacks, such as its justly famous monster burgers, try *Axel's Takeaway* on Orr St. Across the road, *Chester the Chick* has barbecued chicken, hamburgers, pastries and fish and chips. On the way into town from the Lyell Hwy is a *bakery*, open from 8 am to 4 pm Monday to Friday and from 10 am to 4 pm on weekends. The baker here loves a yarn and is a good source of tourist information on the area.

Around the corner, in the BP service station, *The Asian Eating House* has lunch box specials for $6 and dinner specials for $8.50. It's open for lunch Tuesday to Saturday from 11.30 am to 2 pm, and for dinner Tuesday to Thursday and Saturday from 5 to 9 pm and Friday from 5 to 10 pm. You can eat in or take away.

There are plenty of places around town that serve meals and they are all pretty good value. The *Mt Lyell Motor Inn* and the *Empire Hotel* both serve counter meals. The meals at the former are a little cheaper (around $10), but the dining room at the latter has an open fire and, overall, is much more inviting. Of similar standard and price, is the *Commercial Hotel* on Driffield St and *Vics Bistro* at the Mountain View Holiday Lodge on Penghana Rd.

*Maloney's Restaurant* in the Queenstown Motor Lodge has an à la carte menu that is slightly more expensive. *The Old Prospector Restaurant* at the Westcoaster Motor Inn has mains for $13 to $18 and also serves counter dinners in its tavern bar daily for around $10 to $12. The most expensive place in town is *Smelters Restaurant* at the Silver Hills Motor Inn, where mains are around $17 from the à la carte menu.

## Getting There & Away

**Bus** See the Getting There & Around section at the start of this chapter. Buses arrive at and depart from the chairlift office (see the Chairlift entry earlier in this section).

## LAKE BURBURY

This is a large dam created for hydro-electricity production, and its construction flooded 6km of the old Lyell Hwy. The scenery around the lake is magnificent, especially when there is snow on the nearby peaks, and there is an attractive *camping ground* on its shores just east of Bradshaw Bridge where you can camp for $5 a night.

THE WEST

This is also a public picnic area, with covered electric barbecues ($1 coins accepted) and a good children's playground.

## FRANKLIN-GORDON WILD RIVERS NATIONAL PARK

This park is part of the Western Tasmania World Heritage Area and includes the catchments of the Franklin, Olga and Gordon rivers. The most significant peak in the park is Frenchmans Cap, which can be seen from the west coast as well as from many places along the Lyell Hwy. This mountain was formed by glacial action and has Tasmania's tallest cliff face.

The park contains a number of unique plant species and a series of major Aboriginal sites at caves in the Franklin River valley. The most significant is **Kutikina Cave**, where 50,000 artefacts have been found from the Aboriginal occupation of 15,000 to 20,000 years ago.

Much of the park consists of deep river gorges and impenetrable rainforest, but the Lyell Hwy traverses its northern end, where there are a number of signposted features of note, including a few signposted short walks that you can take from the road to see what this park contains:

**Nelson River** Just west of Lake Burbury, at the bottom of Victoria Pass, an easy 20 minute return walk through rainforest leads to Nelson Falls. Signs beside the track highlight the common plants of the area, and the 35m-high falls are excellent.

**Collingwood River** This is the usual starting point for rafting the Franklin River, of which it is a tributary.

**Donaghys Hill** Four kilometres east of the bridge over the Collingwood River, this 40 minute return walk leads to the top of the hill above the junction of the Collingwood and Franklin rivers. This has spectacular views of the Franklin River and Frenchmans Cap.

**Frenchmans Cap** Six kilometres farther east is the start of the three to five day walk to Frenchmans Cap, the park's best known bushwalk, undertaken by up to 900 people each year. It has two shelter huts along the way and lots of lovely, deep mud; you'll find full track notes in Lonely Planet's *Bushwalking In Australia* by John & Monica Chapman. Even if

you are not intending to embark on the bushwalk, you may enjoy a 15 minute walk along the first part of the track to the banks of the Franklin River. You can take a TWT scheduled service to the beginning of this walk – see the Getting There & Around section at the start of this chapter for details. The return fare from Hobart is $50.

**Franklin River Nature Walk** From the picnic ground where the highway crosses the river, a 25 minute return nature trail has been marked through the forest.

For a history of the campaign that saved the Franklin River from being flooded for hydroelectricity production, see the boxed text in the South-West chapter.

### Rafting the Franklin

The best way of all to see this park is to raft down its largest and most sensational river, the Franklin. It is truly wild, and rafting it can be hazardous. Experienced rafters can tackle it if they are fully equipped and prepared, or there are tour companies offering complete rafting packages. About 90% of all rafters who tackle the river go with tour companies. Whether you go with an independent group or a tour operator, you should contact the PWS (☎ 6233 6191) for the latest information on permits, current regulations and environmental considerations.

All expeditions should register at the booth at the junction between the Lyell Hwy and the Collingwood River, 49km west of Derwent Bridge. The trip down the Franklin River, starting at Collingwood River and ending at Sir John Falls, takes about 14 days. From the exit point, you can be picked up by a Wilderness Air seaplane or paddle a farther 22km downriver to a Gordon River cruise boat. It's possible to do just one half of the river. The Upper Franklin takes around eight days from the Collingwood River to the Fincham Track, it passes through the Irenabyss Gorge and you can climb Frenchmans Cap as a side trip. The Lower Franklin takes about seven days from the Fincham Track to Sir John Falls and passes through the Great Ravine. The shorter trips are really only practical for tour groups, as the Fincham Track is for

4WD vehicles only and is a long way from the main highways.

Three of the many tour companies that arrange complete rafting packages from Hobart are: Rafting Tasmania (☎ 6239 1080, PO Box 403, Sandy Bay 2006), which has a five day package for $1150, a seven day package for $1250 and an 11 day package for $1700; Tasmanian Expeditions (☎ toll-free 1800 030 230, 110 George St, Launceston 7250), which has a seven day package for $1200, a nine day package for $1490 and an 11 day package for $1650; and Tasmanian Wild River Adventures (☎ 0409 977 506), which has a five day package for $1150, a seven day package for $1250 and an 11 day package for $1650. Tours operate from November or December to March or April.

If you are organising a rafting trip down the Franklin, check out the Franklin River page on the PWS Web site at www.parks .tas.gov.au.

**Maps** You will need Tasmap's 1:100,000 *Olga and Franklin* and 1:25,000 *Loddon* maps, available from the Tasmanian Map Centre and Service Tasmania in Hobart. A laminated Wilderness Guides map may also be available from outdoor equipment shops.

# Cradle Mountain-Lake St Clair National Park

Tasmania's best known national park is the superb 1262 sq km Cradle Mountain-Lake St Clair, which is part of the World Heritage Area. The spectacular mountain peaks, deep gorges, lakes, tarns and wild open moorlands extend from the Great Western Tiers in the north to Derwent Bridge, on the Lyell Hwy in the south. It was one of the most glaciated areas in Australia and includes Mt Ossa (1617m), Tasmania's highest mountain, and Lake St Clair, Australia's deepest natural freshwater lake.

The preservation of this region as a national park was due, in part, to the Austrian Gustav Weindorfer, who fell in love with the area and claimed: 'This must be a national park for all time. It is magnificent. Everyone should know about it, and come and enjoy it'. In 1912 he built a chalet out of King Billy pine called Waldheim ('Forest Home' in German), and from 1916 he lived there permanently. Today, eight huts for bushwalkers have been constructed near his original chalet at the northern end of the park, and the area is named Waldheim, after his chalet.

There are plenty of day walks in both the Cradle Valley and Cynthia Bay (Lake St Clair) regions, but it is the spectacular 80km Overland Track between the two that has turned this park into a bushwalkers' mecca. The Overland Track is one of the finest bushwalks in Australia, and in summer up to 100 people a day start it. The track can be walked in either direction, but most people walk from north to south (Cradle Valley to Cynthia Bay).

## Information
All walking tracks in this park are signposted and well defined. They are easy to follow but it is still advisable to carry a map, which can be purchased at the visitors' centres.

**Cradle Valley** At the northern park boundary, and built on the verge of an amazing rainforest, the visitors' centre and ranger station (☎ 6492 1133) is open year-round from 8 am to 7 pm in summer and until 5 pm the rest of the year. The centre is staffed by rangers who can advise you about weather conditions, walking gear, bush safety and bush etiquette. Both the static and audio-visual displays are well worth seeing. In summer, the rangers run many free activities, which are advertised on the board at the centre. Participating in some of these activities is a good way to learn what is so special about this area, the problems people have caused and how these problems are being solved.

The centre has a public telephone, clean public toilets, drinking water and EFTPOS (maximum withdrawal $50). It's wheelchair accessible and accepts major credit cards. Dove Lake has flushing toilets but no drinking water, while Waldheim has composting toilets, drinking water and a very good day-use hut with gas heaters.

The visitors' centre also features an easy – but quite spectacular – 500m circular boardwalk through the adjacent rainforest

## Franklin's Overland Journey

In 1842 the Governor of Van Diemen's Land, Sir John Franklin, decided that, with his wife Lady Jane Franklin, he should travel overland from Hobart to Macquarie Harbour on the west coast. At that time over half of the island was still unexplored by Europeans and such a journey was a considerable risk.

The trip started in grand style with Lady Franklin being carried in a palanquin and attended to by a servant. Within three days the entourage had completed 80% of the distance and reached Lake St Clair.

The whole journey was planned to take six or seven days but, as modern bushwalkers know, the country of the Franklin River consists of deep gorges and impenetrable scrub. Heavy rains and the difficult terrain took its toll and the group took 22 days to reach Macquarie Harbour and meet their ship. The troubles were not yet over as winds were unfavourable and the small ship spent a further three weeks trapped in Macquarie Harbour. The group almost starved to death but eventually were able to escape from the harbour and return to Hobart.

A detailed diary was kept of the entire journey and today it makes fascinating reading. The *Narrative of the Overland Journey* by David Burns has been reprinted and is available in many libraries and bookshops at the major museums.

called the **Rainforest-Pencil Pine Falls Walking Track**. This is particularly good for visitors in wheelchairs and for those with youngsters in prams.

Whatever time of the year you visit, be prepared for cold, wet weather in the Cradle Valley area: it rains on seven days out of 10, is cloudy on eight days out of 10, the sun shines all day only one day in 10 and it snows on 54 days each year.

**Cynthia Bay** Cynthia Bay, near the southern park boundary, also has an informative ranger station (☎ 6289 1115) where you register to walk the Overland Track in the opposite direction. At the nearby kiosk (☎ 6289 1137) you can book a seat on the small MV *Idaclair* ferry. See the Getting Around entry in this section for ferry details. From the kiosk you can also hire dinghies for a spot of fishing or relaxing on the lake, but make sure you don't fall in – it's freezing!

### The Overland Track

**Information** The Cradle Mountain visitors' centre (☎ 6492 1133) has an Overland Track Information Kit that staff will send anywhere in the world for $25. The best time to walk the Overland Track is during summer, when the flowering plants are most prolific, although spring and autumn also have their attractions. You can walk the track in winter, but only if you're very experienced.

**The Track** Walkers sometimes start the Overland Track at Dove Lake, but the recommended route actually begins at Waldheim, from where the ascent to Marions Lookout is much easier (provided, of course, that you don't branch off down to Dove Lake along the way). The trail is well marked for its entire length and, at an easy pace, takes around five or six days to complete. Along the track, there are many secondary paths leading up to mountains like **Mt Ossa** or other natural features, making it a great temptation to take a few more days to explore the region fully. In fact, the length of time you take is limited only by the amount of supplies you can carry, and eight to 10 days is ideal.

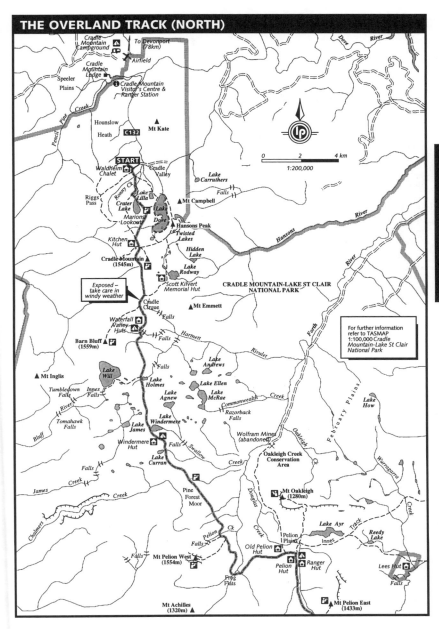

# THE OVERLAND TRACK (NORTH)

Cradle Mountain Campground
To Devonport (78km)
Airfield
Cradle Mountain Lodge
Speeler Plains
Pencil Pine Creek
Cradle Mountain Visitor's Centre & Ranger Station
Hounslow Heath
C132
Mt Kate

0    2    4 km
1:200,000

START
Waldheim Chalet
Cradle Valley
Lake Carruthers
Falls
Riggs Pass
Crater Lake
Lake Lilla
Ronny Ck
Lake Dove
Mt Campbell
Marions Lookout
Hansons Peak
Twisted Lakes
Hidden Lake
Kitchen Hut
Cradle Mountain (1545m)
Lake Rodway
Scott Kilvert Memorial Hut
Hansons River
CRADLE MOUNTAIN-LAKE ST CLAIR NATIONAL PARK
Exposed – take care in windy weather
Cradle Cirque
Mt Emmett
Waterfall Valley Huts
Falls
Barn Bluff (1559m)
Falls
Hartnett
Forth River
Rivulet
For further information refer to TASMAP 1:100,000 Cradle Mountain-Lake St Clair National Park
Falls
Lake Andrews
Mt Inglis
Lake Will
Lake Holmes
Lake Ellen
Tumbledown Falls
Innes Falls
Lake Agnew
Lake McRae
Commonwealth Creek
February Plains
Lake How
Razorback Falls
River
Tomahawk Falls
Lake James
Lake Windermere
Wolfram Mines (abandoned)
Oakleigh Ck
Windermere Hut
Falls
Lake Curran
Swallow Creek
Oakleigh Creek Conservation Area
Bluff
Falls
Creek
James Creek
Chalmers
Falls
Pine Forest Moor
Mt Oakleigh (1280m)
Douglas Creek
Warragarra Creek
Reedy Lake
Pelion Ck
Falls
Lake Ayr
Pelion Plains
Innes Track
Lees Hut
Falls
Mt Pelion West (1554m)
Old Pelion Hut
Pelion Hut
Ranger Hut
Falls
Frog Flats
Mt Achilles (1320m)
Mt Pelion East (1433m)

Dove River

Although the walk takes you through wilderness, the track is well used and you must expect to meet many walkers each day. Most walk from north to south and this is the recommended direction as you will meet fewer travellers coming the other way. Each year approximately 6000 to 7000 people walk the track, and around 100 people embark on the walk daily in the high season.

There are unattended huts along the track, which you can use for overnight accommodation, but you can't rely on them being available. In summer they are usually full, so make sure you carry a tent. Camp fires are banned, so you must also carry a fuel stove. You also need a park pass to enter the park (see the National Parks section of the Facts about Tasmania chapter).

The walk itself is extremely varied, crossing high alpine moors and rocky screes, passing gorges and travelling through tall forest. A detailed description of the walk and major side trips is given in Lonely Planet's *Bushwalking in Australia* by John & Monica Chapman. For detailed notes of all the tracks in the park, read *Cradle Mountain – Lake St Clair and Walls of Jerusalem National Parks* by John Chapman & John Siseman.

### Cradle Valley to Waterfall Valley (3½ to 5 hours)

The Overland Track starts at Waldheim, to the left of the chalet. Follow the signs indicating the Overland Track to Marions Lookout past Crater Falls and Crater Lake. Avoid taking the track to Lake Lilla and Dove Lake (to the left of the Overland Track) and the 'horse track' (to the right of the Overland Track). Continue on the Overland Track past Marions Lookout to Kitchen Hut, a tiny shelter in which you are not permitted to camp except in emergencies. Follow the track to the west of Cradle Mountain to Cradle Cirque, from where there are good views of Waterfall Valley. Follow the track down into the valley and take the signposted track on your right to the two huts, which sleep 28 people in all. Tent sites are in the forest a short distance upstream of the original hut.

### Waterfall Valley Huts to Windermere Hut (2½ to 3½ hours)

Walk back to the Overland Track and follow it over an exposed ridge and down to Lake Windermere. Follow the shore to some tent sites before turning south-east to the hut, which sleeps 40 people.

### Windermere Hut to Pelion Hut (4½ to 6 hours)

Follow the track across a creek to Lake Curran and continue on through Pine Forest Moor, where there are some dry tent sites. Follow the main track to Frog Flats (where there are damp camp sites), across the Forth River and on to Pelion Plains, where a muddy side track leads to Old Pelion Hut. New Pelion Hut, which sleeps 16, is a little farther along the main track.

Large sections of the track before and after Pelion Hut can be heavy going following rain, when less experienced walkers may find the combination of mud, leeches and exposed roots disheartening. At such times, sections of the track between Pelion and the turn-off to Mt Ossa can be especially muddy, and tent sites at Frog Flats are subject to flooding.

### Pelion Hut to Kia Ora Hut (3 to 5 hours)

Follow the track south to Pelion Gap, from where you can take a side trip to Mt Ossa (three hours return), the highest point in Tasmania, and Mt Pelion East (1½ hours return). From Pelion Gap, follow the track into Pinestone Valley, where you will cross Pinestone Creek. Continue on to Kia Ora Hut, which sleeps 24 people. Tent sites are nearby.

### Kia Ora Hut to Windy Ridge Hut (3 to 4½ hours)

Follow the track across Kia Ora Creek and on to Du Cane Hut, which is registered with the National Trust and no longer in use. Good camp sites are available in the vicinity of Du Cane Hut. Continue about 2.5km to the signposted turn-off to Hartnett Falls, an excellent side trip that takes only about one hour return. If you do take this track, make sure you continue from the top of the falls (where there are tent sites) down to the river and upstream to the gorge at the falls' base.

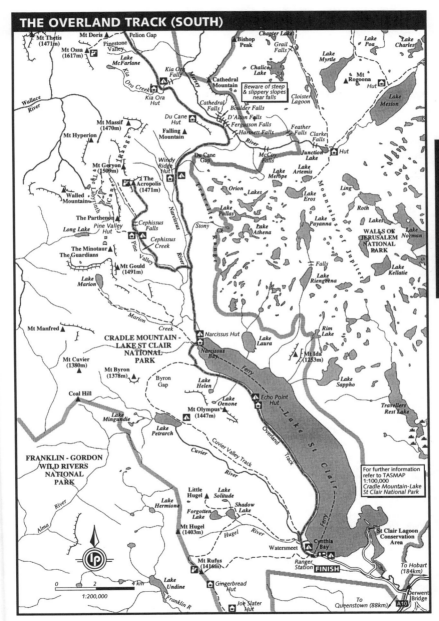

THE OVERLAND TRACK (SOUTH)

Return to the Overland Track and climb to Du Cane Gap, before descending to Windy Ridge Hut, which sleeps 24. Poor camp sites are available a little to the north, near what is left of an earlier hut.

**Windy Ridge Hut to Narcissus Hut (2½ to 3½ hours)** Follow the track across substantial sections of boardwalk and a bridge to Narcissus Hut. About halfway along, there is a side track on the right to Pine Valley and the Acropolis (1471m), which is a highly recommended side trip taking about five hours return. Some climbing is required to reach the peak, but the views on a clear day are magnificent.

From Narcissus Hut, you can radio the MV *Idaclair* ferry to come and pick you up; this will save you a 5½ hour walk. In summer, the ferry runs at regular times every day for $15 a person (or $60 a trip if there are fewer than four people on board). In other seasons, it only operates intermittently – ring for details before setting out on the walk.

It can occasionally be something of an ordeal to find a seat on the ferry: bookings are unreliable (*always* reconfirm by radio when you arrive at the hut); seats on the ferry are limited (if you miss out on a seat, you will have to wait for the next scheduled service); and the batteries in the radio may be flat (not unheard of), in which case you may be stuck at Narcissus until a boat turns up of its own accord. If you wish to avoid using the ferry, simply complete the track on foot, which will take you a minimum of five hours if you stick to the Overland Track. A longer and more scenic route is the Cuvier Valley Track, which branches off to the right of the main track 1km from the raised bridge at Hamilton Creek. This takes seven to nine hours, but should only be walked in very dry conditions.

**Warning** In summer the weather is often fine, but snowfalls and severe storms are also regular features. You must be prepared to camp in snow and walk in cold, wet conditions. A significant number of those who

are walking the track for the first time have inadequate equipment, and when cold weather occurs the walk becomes a struggle for survival rather than an adventure. One year, just before Christmas, an experienced Canadian trekker walking this track alone failed to pack appropriate clothing. When the weather became bitterly cold, he had no option but to continue walking until he reached a hut. By the time he arrived, he was drenched and incapable of moving his fingers. As there was no-one else in the hut, all he could do was stand shivering in his wet clothes until at last his hands regained enough mobility for him to be able to undress himself and build a fire. To this day, he believes he was lucky to survive.

The most dangerous part of the walk is the exposed high plateau between Waldheim and Pelion Creek, near Mt Pelion West. The south-west wind that blows across here can be dangerously cold and sometimes strong enough to knock you off your feet.

## Other Bushwalks
**Cradle Valley** From the visitors' centre there is an excellent circuit walk following **Pencil Pine Creek** and returning via the **Dove River Gorge**, which takes two hours return. There are also short nature walks and loops around the centre itself.

From Waldheim Chalet, **Crater Lake** is a popular two hour return walk. You can also climb Cradle Mountain, but this takes a full day to complete: allow seven hours return. The other place from which walks commence is **Dove Lake**. The best walk there is the circuit of Dove Lake itself, which takes two to three hours to complete. All other walks involve steep climbs, and the walk to **Mt Campbell** and the **Twisted Lakes** provides great views of Cradle Mountain and the nearby lakes for a four hour return walk.

**Cynthia Bay Region** You can follow the management road to **Watersmeet**, then follow the nature trail back to Cynthia Bay; allow one hour return. Most other walks are fairly long: the walk to **Shadow Lake** takes four hours return, while the circuit over **Mt Rufus** is seven hours return.

One way to do some good walking is to use the MV *Idaclair* ferry to drop you at Echo Point or Narcissus Hut. The walk back along the lake shore is interesting. From Echo Point it is about three hours and from Narcissus Hut about five to six hours back to Cynthia Bay.

## Organised Tours

**Bushwalking** The company most experienced at running guided bushwalking tours in this national park is Craclair Tours (☎ 6424 7833, PO Box 516, Devonport), which runs eight-day tours along the Overland Track for $1085 per person. This is a good way to walk the track because all packs, sleeping bags, tents, jackets and overtrousers are supplied. The company also runs a wide variety of shorter trips, such as four days around Cradle Mountain for $620 per person and seven days around Pine Valley for $1195 per person. Three-day tours in which you stay in commercial cabins in the area rather than in tents are $440 all inclusive.

There are several other companies that run similar trips. Tasmanian Expeditions (☎ toll-free 1800 030 230) does an eight day trip for $940 and a three day trip for $395 per person.

Tasman Bush Tours (☎ 6423 4965) operating out of Tasman House Backpackers in Devonport offers a seven day package for $480. This includes camping gear, park pass, ferry tickets to Lake St Clair and transport to/from Devonport, but not food, backpacks or clothing.

If camping is not for you, Cradle Huts P/L (☎ 6331 2006) has private huts along the Overland Track. A six day walk with all meals and sleeping in the huts each night costs $1450 per person, including transport to/from Launceston.

For the much less energetic, TWT offers a $55 day tour to Cradle Mountain from Launceston on Sunday, Monday, Wednesday and Friday that includes three short guided walks.

**Scenic Flights** A less energetic way to see the sights is to go out with Seair Adventure Charters (☎ 6492 1132), on Cradle Mountain Rd, which operates from an airstrip next to the Cradle View Restaurant, about 1.5km from Cradle Mountain Lodge. It offers flights of 25 minutes over Cradle Mountain, 50 minutes over Cradle Mountain, Lake St Clair and the World Heritage Area, and 60 minutes over Frenchmans Cap and the Wild Rivers National Park.

## Places to Stay & Eat

**Cradle Valley Region** The cheapest place in this area is the *Cosy Cabins Cradle Mountain (☎ 6492 1395)*, 2.5km outside the national park; it costs $16 a double to camp. It also provides bunkhouse accommodation for $20 per person. Self-contained cabins with *en suite* and TV are $80 a double. Linen is $4 extra. The camping sites are separated from each other by bush, and the excellent amenities have wheelchair access. The kiosk is open every day from 8 am to 8 pm.

At *Waldheim*, 5km into the national park, there are eight basic huts, all containing gas stoves, cooking utensils and wood heaters but no bedding. The minimum fee for these cabins is between $55 and $75. Check-in and bookings for the huts are handled by the visitors' centre. The four-bunk cabins have recently been refurbished. Only cold water is available in the cabins, but there is hot water in the amenities block.

Between Cosy Cabins and the lodge, *Highlanders Cabins (☎ 6492 1116)* offers attractive, rustic, self-contained timber cottages in a bush setting for between $88 and $160 a double.

Just on the national park boundary, *Cradle Mountain Lodge (☎ 6492 1303)* has pleasant self-contained cabins for $166 to $216 a double. The lodge has good facilities for its guests and anyone is welcome to eat at the *Highland Restaurant*, where most mains are more than $20 and there is a good selection of Tasmanian wines. It's open daily for dinner from 6 pm. Unimaginative lunches and dinners at the public *Tavern*

THE WEST

*Bar* are more reasonably priced. It's open daily from 10 am until late, and also serves tea, coffee and afternoon tea. Basic groceries can be purchased at the *general store*, which also serves tea, coffee and snacks. To buy unleaded petrol, ask at reception. The lodge runs activities including guided walks and trout fishing in the private lake. Some of the activities are free to guests, while others are extra.

The licensed *Cradle View Restaurant*, opposite Cosy Cabins, serves home-style meals; you can also buy takeaway, leaded and unleaded petrol and diesel. It's open from 8.30 am to 8 pm daily, and serves evening meals from 5.30 to 7.30 pm.

**Road to Cradle Mountain** The *High Country – Green Gable* (☎ 6492 1318) at Moina provides B&B in motel-style units for $105 a double. Opposite is *Cradle Country Chalet* (☎ 6492 1401), which has self-catering units with continental breakfast for $95 a double.

A bit farther up Cradle Mountain Rd and along a gravel road, *Lemonthyme Lodge* (☎ 6492 1112) is set among tall trees and rivals Cradle Mountain Lodge. It has rooms with shared facilities in the main lodge for $95 a double with a continental breakfast, or you can rent tasteful chalet-style cabins for $195 to $220 a double. Meals are available every day at the lodge. TWT can drop you off at the turn-off to the lodge; if you give the lodge one day's notice, it will arrange for you to be picked up there, for a fee.

**Cynthia Bay** At the southern end of Lake St Clair, *Lakeside St Clair* (☎ 6289 1137) has several huts, plenty of tent sites and a kiosk that sells basic food supplies and takeaway. Tent sites are $5 a person, which includes the use of the toilets and showers. (If you want to use the campers' kitchen, you must pay extra.) Bunks in the backpackers' accommodation are $20, as are beds in a separate cabin (minimum charge $50) that has its own kitchen but shares all other facilities. The other huts are self-contained and cost $165 a double.

If you wish to *camp* free of charge, walk back along the start of the Overland Track for about 10 minutes to Fergy's Paddock, where there are tent sites.

**Derwent Bridge & Bronte Park** If you've got any sense, the moment you step off the Overland Track or the MV *Idaclair*, you'll step straight into a Maxwells or TWT coach and head for the *Derwent Bridge Wilderness Hotel* (☎ 6289 1144) for a beer, steak and some big talk about your big walk. It's 5km south of Lake St Clair, and you can stay overnight in hostel-standard individual rooms in transportable huts for $20 a person. B&B is also available: it's $75 a double with shared facilities and $85 a double with an *en suite*. While the accommodation is nothing special, the lounge bar is much more impressive than it looks from the outside – a massive, high-roofed structure featuring lots of exposed wood. Good, hearty meals, including breakfast (available from 8 to 9.30 am), are served daily. The soup, which is usually great, is $4.50, roasts are $10.50, snacks are $4.50 to $6, and wallaby pies are $6 to $9.50. It also has a huge open fire, where you can sit and have a cup of coffee.

Next to the garage, the *Derwent Bridge Chalets* (☎ 6289 1000) has four units of a higher standard, but they are $128 a double, with continental breakfast.

*Bronte Park Highland Village* (☎ 6289 1126) is just off the highway, 26km east of Derwent Bridge. It has backpacker accommodation for $15, plain but large and comfortable houses for $85 a double, and rooms with *en suite* in the chalet for $66 and $75 a double. You can also camp for a minimal fee. This accommodation is favoured by fishers trying their luck in Bronte Lagoon. Good food is available in the chalet, and you can arrange transport from Lake St Clair with Maxwells (☎ 6492 1431).

## Getting There & Away

See the Getting There & Around section at the start of this chapter. In summer TWT runs additional services to Cradle Mountain

(Dove Lake) and Lake St Clair from Launceston and Hobart that it calls Wilderness services, but TWT pass-holders should note that these only run if there are at least four full-fare-paying passengers. Bookings are essential, and it's best to contact TWT directly for details.

TWT can drop you off at one end of the Overland Track and pick you up at the other for $69 (Launceston to Cradle Mountain then Lake St Clair to Hobart or Launceston; or Hobart to Lake St Clair then Cradle Mountain to Launceston) or $75 (Hobart to Cradle Mountain then Lake St Clair to Hobart or Launceston). While you don't have to pay to have your luggage transported from one end of the walk to the other, you do have to pay $5 per bag for it to be stored until you are ready to collect it.

Maxwells (☎ 6492 1431) has services from Devonport to Cradle Mountain ($30), Launceston to Cradle Mountain ($40), Devonport and Launceston to Lake St Clair ($50), Lake St Clair to Bronte and Frenchmans Cap ($10), and Cradle Valley to Lake St Clair ($75).

It's possible that you might be able to find a more convenient or cheaper transport option by talking to staff at bushwalking shops or hostels. At the time of writing, the Backpackers Barn (☎ 6424 3628) in Devonport, for example, had information about an unusual taxi service to Cradle Mountain – ring the Barn directly for details.

## Getting Around

**Cradle Valley** TWT buses can be used to get from Cradle Mountain Lodge to Dove Lake for $7. Additionally, Maxwells (☎ 6492 1431) runs a shuttle bus on demand for $5 per person.

**Cynthia Bay** Maxwells also runs an informal taxi to/from Cynthia Bay and Derwent Bridge for $5 (minimum two people), which operates daily on demand. The TWT bus will also transport you between Derwent Bridge and Cynthia Bay for $5.

The MV *Idaclair* runs up to five times daily during summer from Cynthia Bay across Lake St Clair to Narcissus Hut at the northern end of the lake. The timetable changes according to the season, but at the busiest times services run at 9 and 11 am and 12.30, 2 and 3 pm. The ferry returns from Narcissus Hut 30 minutes later. The fare one way is $15 for adults and $8 for children, or $20 for adults and $12 for children return if you go up and back in the one day. Times are posted at the kiosk, where bookings can be made. Minimum fees apply at all times of year: it will always cost at least $60 one way, even if there are fewer than four passengers.

THE WEST

# Mt Field & The South-West

## MT FIELD NATIONAL PARK

Mt Field, only 80km from Hobart, is a favourite place for both locals and visitors. The park is well known for its spectacular mountain scenery, alpine moorlands, dense rainforest, lakes, abundant wildlife and spectacular waterfalls. The area around Russell Falls was made a reserve in 1885, and by 1916 it had became one of the first national parks in Australia. To many locals it's simply known as National Park, and this title has been given to the small town at its entrance. The abundance of wildlife that can be viewed at dusk makes this a great place to stay overnight with children.

### Information

Informative brochures are available from the Parks and Wildlife Service (PWS) office near the Russel Falls car park. The history of the park is enchanting, and the brochure *Mount Field National Park: A History of Tasmania's First Nature Reserve* enlivens its information with charming historical photographs. There are also brochures to some of the more accessible nature walks, and these may be of particular interest to those travelling with children.

**Warning** If you're staying in the huts at Lake Dobson, skiing on Mt Mawson or taking the Pandani Grove Nature Walk or any of the high country walks, you will have to drive along the 15km Lake Dobson Rd. If you are using this road in winter, you will need chains and antifreeze, and should not travel uphill after 3 pm.

### Russell Falls

The major attraction of the park for most people is the magnificent 40m Russell Falls, which is in the valley close to the park entrance. It's an easy 15 minute walk from the car park along a path suitable for wheelchairs. From Russell Falls, continue along the **Tall Trees Circuit** to **Lady Barron**

## HIGHLIGHTS

- Standing at the base of the 40m Russell Falls
- Walking along the Tarn Shelf in Mt Field National Park
- Abseiling on the massive Gordon Dam wall
- Driving beside the shores of Lake Pedder
- Camping and birdwatching at tiny, remote Melaleuca

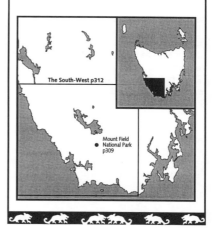

The South-West p312

Mount Field
National Park
p309

**Falls**, a walk of two hours return past swamp gums, which are the world's tallest flowering plants.

### Nature Walks

The 15 minute **Lyrebird Nature Walk** starts 7km up Lake Dobson Rd and is an excellent introduction to the flora and fauna of the park. It's particularly suitable for children: there are numbers along the track that correspond to information provided in a brochure available at the PWS office.

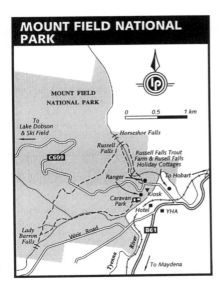

**MOUNT FIELD NATIONAL PARK**

## Tarn Shelf

From the Lake Dobson car park, take the Urquhart Track to its junction with the gravel road. Both the track and the road are steep. Continue along the road to the ski fields, at the top of which is the start of the Tarn Shelf Track. At this point the track is fairly level, and the boardwalk has been laid across large sections to protect the delicate vegetation and keep walkers out of the mud. Either continue as far as you like along the track and then return by the same route, or take one of two routes that branch off at Lake Newdegate and circle back to the ski fields: if you travel east past Twisted Tarn, Twilight Tarn and Lake Webster, the walk takes five hours return from the car park, while the wonderful Rodway Range circuit to the west takes six hours return from the car park.

The Tarn Shelf can be an enjoyable walk at any time of year if the weather is clear. In summer the temperature is pleasant, in autumn the leaves of the deciduous beeches along the way are golden, in winter you may need skis or snowshoes, while in spring the sound of melting snow trickling beneath the boardwalk actually seems to enhance the silence.

## Other Walks

The brochure you receive as you enter the park outlines many other walks in the high country. A walk of four to five hours return to **Lakes Belton and Belcher** passes some attractive scenery. It can be muddy, but on the other hand, it gives you the opportunity to combine a bit of trout fishing with your walking, if you're so inclined.

## Skiing

Skiing was first attempted here in 1922 on **Mt Mawson**. A low-key resort of club huts and rope tows has developed and is a refreshing change from the highly commercial developments in the ski fields of mainland Australia. Snow cover is unreliable and often patchy and current reports are available on a recorded message service (☎ 6288 1319).

Even better for young children who don't mind a longer walk is the **Pandani Grove Nature Walk**, which follows the edge of Lake Dobson and passes through some magical stands of pandani – heaths that resemble pandanus palms and grow up to 12m in height before falling over. This walk takes about 40 minutes; park at the Lake Dobson car park, which is 15km from the park entrance.

## High Country Walks

There are several magnificent walks at the top of the range, where glaciation has cut steep cliffs and deep valleys into what was once one continuous plateau. There are a number of attractive lakes on the floor of these valleys, but possibly even more beautiful are the many tarns that adorn the tops of the ridges.

If you intend to go walking here, take wet-weather gear and warm clothing at any time of year because the weather can be volatile year-round. There is a good gravel road from Lake Dobson to the ski fields, but this is only open to authorised vehicles.

**MT FIELD & THE SOUTH-WEST**

## Other Activities

In high-season holiday periods the rangers organise many free activities. The slide show is informative, and even better is the after-dark walk to Russell Falls, where you can see glow worms.

## Places to Stay

*Mt Field Caravan Park (☎ 6288 1149)* is just inside the national park. Tent sites are $5 per person, powered sites $7 per person; it's usually booked out in high-season holiday periods. A park entry permit is needed for your stay. The nightly parade of animals here is a bonus, but the price is that all food must be securely locked away.

*Lake Dobson Cabins (☎ 6288 1149)* are three very basic six-bunk cabins 15km inside the park. They cost $20 a night per double, plus $10 for each extra adult. The huts are equipped with mattresses, cold water, wood heaters and firewood, and there is a communal toilet block, but there is no electricity or gas.

Outside the park, the *National Park Youth Hostel (☎ 6288 1369)* is 200m past the turn-off to the park and charges $13 a night. The YHA office, on Criterion St, Hobart, sometimes offers a special deal on weekdays with two nights at this hostel and a bus to and from Hobart for $69.

The hostel is conveniently close to the *National Park Hotel (☎ 6288 1103)*, which has rooms with shared facilities and a cooked breakfast for $55 a double and also serves counter meals nightly. The nearby *Russell Falls Holiday Cottages (☎ 6288 1198)* consists of four one or two-bedroom fully equipped cottages, which cost $50 a double, plus $5 for each extra person.

## Getting There & Away

During summer, Tasmanian Wilderness Transport (TWT, ☎ 6334 4442) runs one daily service. The same service operates a one day tour, which is $49 and includes your park pass. If you are going up and back in a day, take this option, as the regular price is $25 each way, and doesn't include park entry.

# THE SOUTH-WEST

Covering almost one quarter of Tasmania, the south-west is basically a large wilderness area with very few tracks or roads. One road penetrates the region to service the hydro-electricity power scheme that was built in the 1970s. At that stage, very little of the region was known to anyone except hardy bushwalkers, and there were only two national parks: Frenchmans Cap and Lake Pedder. Ironically, the power scheme flooded one of the two original parks – Lake Pedder.

Since Lake Pedder was destroyed, the map has changed drastically. Almost the entire region is now contained within national parks, and every summer thousands of bushwalkers follow the better known tracks across the wilderness. While some short walks can be done from the access road, most walks require you to carry all gear for at least a week. There are no huts and only one marked track across the entire region. In spite of developments such as the dams, most of the area can still be called wilderness. It's something special to be able to visit one of the few regions of the world where people have not yet had a dramatic impact.

The only road into the region starts from Westerway, which is west of New Norfolk. It passes the entrance to the Mt Field National Park then continues to Maydena, the last town on the road. Just past the town is the entrance gate, where park admission fees can be paid. From here the road becomes narrow and winding. At first it passes through tall forests, then traverses open country for 100km to Strathgordon. The final part of the road has wonderful views of rugged mountain ranges. The road continues a short way past the town to the dam walls, which hold back the water for Lakes Pedder and Gordon. The Serpentine Dam on Lake Pedder is very ordinary, while the curved concrete wall of the Gordon Dam is quite spectacular.

About halfway to Strathgordon, a single side road leads south for 40km to Scotts Peak and this is well worth driving along.

The gravel road is in good condition and at the end there are excellent views of the major mountains of the South-West National Park.

## Early History

The south-west has not always been wilderness. The original inhabitants were the Tasmanian Aboriginal people, who arrived about 40,000 years ago. At that stage, the world was in the middle of an ice age and the south-west was covered with open grasslands that were ideal for hunting animals. Evidence of Aboriginal occupation has been found in many of the caves. About 10,000 years ago the ice ages ended and, with the warmer climate, thick forests began growing across the south-west. The Aboriginal people slowed the growth of the forests with regular burning of the grassy plains, but slowly the forest advanced and by the time the Europeans arrived the only Aboriginal people left in the area lived around the coastline.

The European explorers were, at first, appalled by the landscape. Matthew Flinders, the first to circumnavigate Tasmania, described the south-west with the comment: 'The mountains are the most dismal that can be imagined. The eye ranges over these peaks with astonishment and horror.' Other reports from those who climbed the peaks described the interior as a series of rugged ranges that extended to the horizon – an apt description still applicable today.

Most of the early explorers were surveyors who measured the land and, under great hardships, cut tracks across the area. The tracks were cut to provide access to the west coast, and to open the region for development. A road was built into the area from the north to Gordon Bend, and in the 1880s the government seriously considered building a railway tunnel underneath Mt Anne to Port Davey. However, the expected mineral deposits and good farming lands were few and far between. Huon pine was logged around Port Davey, osmiridium was mined at Adamsfield, tin was mined at Melaleuca and a tiny farm existed at Gordonvale, but over-all there was little exploitation and the tracks vanished under the encroaching scrub and forest. So the south-west was left pretty much alone; most Tasmanians regarded it as uninhabitable and dubbed it 'Transylvania'. There is some interesting reading about the early explorers in *Trampled Wilderness – The History of South-West Tasmania* by Ralph and Kathleen Gowlland.

Of all the early developments, all that remains is the tin mine at Melaleuca, a tiny settlement near Port Davey. This is a small-scale operation mining alluvial tin and, for visitors, Melaleuca's most important feature is the small gravel airstrip, which provides access to the area. Melaleuca is an interesting place that can be visited on scenic flights, and is also a good starting point for some of the longer bushwalks.

For details of the area's more recent history, see the boxed text in this chapter.

## MAYDENA

Maydena is along the road between National Park and Strathgordon and *Tyenna Valley Lodge (☎ 6288 2293)* is a good place to stay if you intend visiting the World Heritage Area. B&B in the lodge is $55 a double with shared facilities, while accommodation in the cottage is $85 a double. The hosts will provide transport to and around the World Heritage Area for $20 an hour for two people.

## LAKE PEDDER

At the edge of the south-west wilderness lies Lake Pedder, once a spectacularly beautiful natural lake considered the crown jewel of the region. The largest glacial outwash lake in the world, it was 3 sq km and its wide, sandy beach made an ideal light-plane airstrip. The lake was considered so important that it was the first part of the south-west to be protected in its own national park.

In 1972 however, this status did not help, and it was flooded to become part of the Gordon River hydroelectricity development (see the 'Pedder & Franklin Campaigns' boxed text in this chapter).

MT FIELD & THE SOUTH-WEST

Together with nearby Lake Gordon, the Pedder Dam (named Lake Pedder by officials) now holds 27 times the volume of water in the Sydney Harbour and is the largest inland freshwater catchment in Australia. The underground Gordon Power Station is the largest hydroelectric power station in Tasmania.

Trout fishing is popular and boats are allowed on Lake Pedder. While there are fewer trout than in the boom period of the dam's first 10 years, the fish caught range from one to 20kg in size. Tiny boats like dinghies are discouraged because the lake is 55km long and the frequent storms generate sizeable waves, making it potentially dangerous. Boat ramps exist at the Scotts Peak Dam in the south and near Strathgordon in the north. Given the scale of the controversy surrounding the inundation of Lake Pedder, you will surprised at just how puny the dams on this lake appear, especially when compared with the massive Gordon Dam.

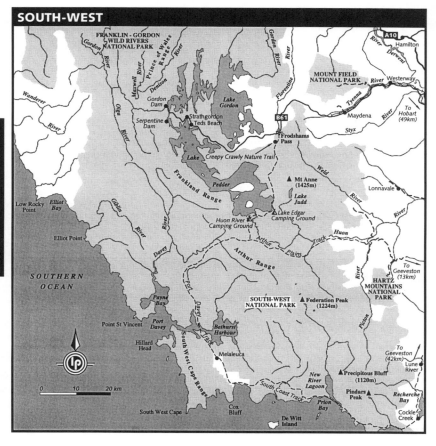

## Places to Stay

There are two free camping grounds near the southern end of the lake. The *Lake Edgar Camping Ground* has pit toilets and water and fine views of the area. In wet weather it is less attractive as it's exposed to the cold winds. A better place to camp is the nearby *Huon River Camping Ground*, which is hidden in tall forest near Scotts Peak Dam. This has pit toilets, a shelter shed and fresh water.

## STRATHGORDON

Built to service Hydro Electric Commission (HEC) employees during the construction of the Gordon River Power Scheme, the township of Strathgordon is the base from which to visit Lakes Pedder and Gordon, the Gordon Dam and the power station. Strathgordon is also becoming a popular bushwalking, trout fishing, boating and water-skiing location. Boats are not allowed on Lake Gordon.

Tours of the **Gordon Power Station** (☎ 6280 1166) run daily at 10 am and 2 pm and entry is $5 for adults or $15 for a family. A maximum of 48 people are allowed on any one tour and booking is suggested. The visitors' centre at the Gordon Dam site has plenty of information about the scheme, but it neglects to tell you that the scheme was never really necessary.

A Hobart company actually organises abseiling on the dam wall – see the Rock Climbing & Abseiling section of the Activities chapter for details.

## Places to Stay & Eat

There's a basic free *camping ground* with few facilities at the place once used as the construction workers' quarters. Better places can be found beside Lake Pedder, such as the *picnic ground* near the Serpentine Dam and at Teds Beach. Rooms with *en suite* are available at the *Lake Pedder Chalet* (☎ 6280 1166), where singles/doubles cost from $55/65 to $80/90. Meals are also available from the restaurant and cost between $14 and $17. Breakfast, lunch and takeaway are also available.

## SOUTH-WEST NATIONAL PARK

There are few places left in the world as isolated and untouched as Tasmania's south-west wilderness, the state's largest national park. It is the home of some of the world's last tracts of virgin temperate rainforest, and these contribute much to the grandeur and extraordinary diversity of this ancient area.

The south-west is the habitat of the endemic Huon pine, which lives for more than 3000 years and of the swamp gum, the world's tallest hardwood and flowering plant. About 300 species of lichen, moss and fern, some rare and endangered, festoon the dense rainforest; superb glacial tarns decorate the jagged mountains, and in summer, the delicate alpine meadows are ablaze with wildflowers and flowering shrubs. Through it all are the wild rivers, with rapids tearing through deep gorges and waterfalls plunging over cliffs. Each year more and more people venture into the heart of this incredible part of Tasmania's World Heritage Area, in search of the peace, isolation and challenge of a region virtually untouched since the last ice age.

The only way to really see the park is to walk across it, something that is only suggested for fit, experienced bushwalkers. You can see a small part of it by following the gravel road from Frodshams Pass on the Strathgordon Rd to Scotts Peak. Not far from the pass the **Creepy Crawly Nature Trail** passes through rainforest beside a creek and is well worth visiting. Farther south, the road leaves the forest near the base of Mt Anne, and wonderful views of many of the mountains in the south-west are obtained in fine weather. Mt Anne towers over the road. To the west lie the Frankland Ranges, while to the south is the jagged crest of the Western Arthur Range. The road ends at the Scotts Peak Dam and nearby in the forest, down a side road, is a good (free) sheltered camping area beside the Huon River. There is also another free camping area with very basic amenities at Lake Edgar.

A whole range of escorted wilderness adventures are possible, including flying, hiking, rafting, canoeing, mountaineering,

MT FIELD & THE SOUTH-WEST

MT FIELD & THE SOUTH-WEST

## Pedder & Franklin Campaigns

Tasmania produces its electricity by harnessing one of its most generous resources, water. In the early stages of what came to be known as 'hydro-industrialisation', the large government body responsible for electricity production in the state, the Hydro Electric Commission (HEC), built dams, power stations and pipelines on the Central Plateau and Derwent River. So successful was the HEC that its dam-building activities went largely unchallenged until the 1960s, when it proposed flooding Lake Pedder, then the only national park in the undeveloped south-west of the state, to create a much larger lake for electricity generation.

By this stage, a small number of people – mainly bushwalkers – had begun to realise that much of Tasmania's natural environment was being altered and that the remaining wilderness should be kept as it was for future generations to see. A bitter fight developed over the proposal to flood Lake Pedder, a move that, it soon became apparent, was not even necessary for the viability of the larger scheme of which it was a part.

Lake Pedder was flooded in 1972, and the HEC soon began working on its next grand power scheme, even though there was no real demand for more electricity. When it began paying particular attention to the lower Gordon and Franklin rivers, the public became uneasy, despite protests by the HEC that it had no plans for the region.

The failure of the Lake Pedder campaign had persuaded conservationists that they would only succeed in halting further dams on the Gordon River if they were extremely well organised. To this end, they formed the Tasmanian Wilderness Society (TWS), which succeeded in having the Wild Rivers National Park declared in 1980. The TWS then lobbied the premier of the state to nominate the area for World Heritage listing. The premier agreed, apparently unaware that such a listing might ultimately be sufficient to prevent the construction of dams in the area, and in 1981 the federal government announced that the entire region had been officially nominated for World Heritage listing.

Also in 1981, the state government attempted to resolve the conflict between the HEC and the TWS by holding a referendum asking the public to choose between two different dam schemes. Despite being told that writing 'No Dams' on their ballot papers would render their votes informal, 46% of voters did just that; it was clear that public opposition was very strong.

While this referendum was being conducted, parliament was in turmoil. Both the premier and the opposition leader were dumped over the issue, and some leaders ended up sitting on the cross benches. The issue forced a state election resulting in a change of government, but once elected, the former opposition party also supported the HEC dam project on the Gordon and Franklin rivers. When the World Heritage Committee eventually announced the World Heritage listing for the area and expressed concern over the proposed dam construction, the new premier attempted to have the listing withdrawn.

Realising that resolving the issue by democratic means was impossible, the TWS and other conservation groups switched attention to federal politics. In May 1982, at a by-election in Canberra, 41% of voters wrote 'no dams' on their ballot papers and politicians began to take

caving and camping. More information can be obtained from the National Park Service (☎ 6233 6191). The standard national park entry fee applies even if you're just driving on the road through the park.

## Day Walks

From the Scotts Peak Rd you can climb to **Mt Eliza**, a steep, five hour return walk. Using the same track, you can walk farther to climb **Mt Anne**, about eight to ten hours

## Pedder & Franklin Campaigns

the issue seriously. Later that year at another by-election, 40% of voters again declared 'no dams' on their ballot papers, but still the federal government refused to intervene.

Construction work began in 1982, and almost immediately, protesters set off from Strahan in what became known as the 'Franklin River Blockade'. They protested peacefully, realising they could only hinder work, not prevent it, but even so, the Tasmanian government passed special laws allowing protesters to be arrested, fined and jailed: in the summer of 1982-83, 1400 people were arrested in a confrontation so intense it received international news coverage.

The Franklin River became a major issue in the federal election of 1983, in which the Labor Party defeated the ruling Liberal-National Party coalition. As promised, Prime Minister Bob Hawke acted promptly to protect the World Heritage status of the Franklin River region and stop the dams. However, the Liberal Tasmanian premier refused to cooperate, and it was left to the High Court (the body responsible for interpreting the Australian constitution) to resolve the matter. The court ruled that the federal government did have the power to stop construction of dams in the area as part of its responsibility for implementing international treaties, of which the World Heritage agreement was one.

After its victory, the TWS changed its name to the Wilderness Society and became involved in conservation issues throughout Australia.

**John & Monica Chapman**

### Vigil for Pedder

At the beginning of the 1970s, south-west Tasmania was a true wilderness. For bushwalkers, Lake Pedder was the highly prized goal at its heart: you weren't really a *bushwalker* until you'd been to *the south-west*, and especially to Pedder. It was a place of matchless, pristine beauty in all its varied moods – a living entity – it was beyond our comprehension that anyone, even the Tasmanian government, could flood the lake to feed a new hydroelectricity scheme.

However, the threat to Pedder became undeniable and the Lake Pedder Action Committee launched a national campaign to save the lake. During the early months of 1972, a continuous vigil was kept there by committee members and supporters. Some walked in across the buttongrass plains, some flew in, the famous white sand on the shore serving as a landing strip for light aircraft. By day we accepted the intrusive noise of small planes, bringing new visitors and curious journalists, but in the evenings and early mornings we could savour Pedder's incomparable peace and tranquillity. My part in the vigil was inspired by a bushwalking trip along the Frankland Range, from where we enjoyed uninterrupted views of Pedder – supremely beautiful but somehow very vulnerable.

The vigil was disbanded, the flood waters inevitably rose, but the images of the white sands, the waters shading from peaty brown on the shore to blues, greens and purples at depth, the surrounding mountains, cloud-capped or sun-drenched, are indelible.

**Sandra Bardwell**

MT FIELD & THE SOUTH-WEST

return. A better walk for most around Mt Anne is to follow the recently upgraded track to **Lake Judd**, about four hours return. This provides some fine views of cliffs and mountains without a long steep climb. This

track starts 9km south of the car park for Mt Anne and is easily missed as there is no large car park and only a small signpost.

From Scotts Peak the best short walk follows the start of the **Port Davey Track** as it passes through a forest and across the buttongrass plain. You can go as far as **Junction Creek**, which takes five hours return, but the first 20 to 30 minutes is the best part. Another short walk nearby is to climb **Red Knoll Hill** by following the road to the top; this provides fine views of the area and takes one hour return.

The road to Strathgordon also provides access to some good walks although none of them are signposted. You should purchase maps and guide books for these walks. **Mt Wedge** is a very popular four hour return walk and, being located between Lake Pedder and Lake Gordon, provides sweeping views. Past Strathgordon, the Serpentine Dam provides the starting point for a long, steep climb on a poorly marked and muddy track to Mt Sprent, seven hours return. From the Gordon Dam it is possible to follow rough tracks to the **Gordon Splits** and the **Truchanas Pine Reserve**. These walks are only suitable for experienced bushwalkers because the tracks are difficult to follow.

### Long Bushwalks

The best-known walk in the park is the **South Coast Track** between Port Davey and Cockle Creek, near Recherche Bay. This takes about 10 or 12 days and should only be tackled by experienced hikers who are well prepared for the often vicious weather conditions. Light planes are used to airlift bushwalkers into the south-west and there is vehicle access to Cockle Creek at the south-eastern edge of the park. Detailed notes to the South Coast and Port Davey tracks are available in Lonely Planet's *Bushwalking in Australia* by John & Monica Chapman.

There are many other walks that can be done in the park, but you should first complete one of the better known walks. Contrary to what you might think, the South Coast Track is not all that hard and is good preparation for the more difficult trips. Most of the other walks are difficult, without marked tracks, and require a high degree of bushwalking skill in order to be completed safely

and enjoyed. The shortest of these is the four day circuit of the Mt Anne Range. You will need at least seven days to visit Federation Peak and nine to 12 days are recommended for a traverse of the Western Arthur Range. For detailed notes of these routes and other major walks in the south-west, refer to *South West Tasmania* by John Chapman.

### Getting There & Away

TWT operates a service to Scotts Peak Dam at the start of the walking tracks on Tuesday and Thursday in November and on Tuesday, Thursday, Saturday and Sunday from December until early April. This costs $79 return from Hobart, but it is a Wilderness service, which means it will only operate if there are four full-fare-paying passengers on board. You can also arrange to be dropped off at Scotts Peak Dam and picked up at Cockle Creek or vice versa, for the same price. While your luggage is carried free on the bus, a fee is charged for it to be stored while you are on your walk.

### MELALEUCA

This is a tiny location deep in the south-west near Port Davey. The only access to it is by sea, light plane or by following walking tracks for at least five days. The settlement contains two families who mine alluvial tin on the buttongrass plain, along with a semi-resident team of national park staff. There are no shops or any facilities apart from two simple huts for bushwalkers. The major attraction for visitors is the excellent bird-hide – quite a substantial building from where you can often see the rare orange-bellied parrot. You can camp at Melaleuca if you bring all your own food and have good bushwalking equipment.

The airstrip is of gravel and is suitable for planes with a maximum of six people. Flights operate on demand from the small airports around the state, with Cambridge airport at Hobart providing the main service. See the Scenic Flights section of the Activities chapter for details.

# The Islands

In Bass Strait there are two groups of islands, the Hunter and Furneaux, which guard the western and eastern entrances to the strait. The largest island in the Hunter Group is King Island; and in the Furneaux Group it is Flinders Island. These were once the transient homes of prospectors, sealers, sailors and resettled Aborigines from the mainland. Today, these two islands are mainly rural communities offering tourist retreats in natural coastal beauty, rich in marine and other wildlife.

Tasmania also has several other islands although they are all difficult to reach unless you have your own boat. Macquarie Island, 1500km to the south-east, is the largest and, being close to Antarctica, has an extremely cold climate. Off the southern coastline of Tasmania are a string of islands that are clearly seen from the South Coast Track. The largest are De Witt Island and Maatsuyker Island, with its lighthouse.

## KING ISLAND
* **pop 1762**

At the western end of Bass Strait, this small island surrounded by rugged coastline is 64km long and only 25km across at its widest point, but its beautiful beaches, rocky coastline and country town atmosphere more than compensate for its size.

The Europeans discovered the island in 1798, and named King Island after Governor King of New South Wales (NSW), King Island quickly gained a reputation as a home and breeding ground for seals and sea elephants. Just as quickly, however, these animals were hunted close to extinction by sealers and sailors known as the Straitsmen.

Over the years, the stormy seas of Bass Strait have claimed many ships, and there are at least 57 **shipwrecks** in the coastal waters around King Island. The island's worst shipwreck occurred in 1845 when the *Cataraqui*, an immigrant ship, went down with 399 people aboard. All lives were lost.

### HIGHLIGHTS

* Indulging in the rich cheeses and cream at the King Island Dairy
* Enjoying the views from Mt Strzelecki
* Diving for 'diamonds' in Killiecrankie Bay
* Immersing yourself in the Aboriginal history of Flinders Island

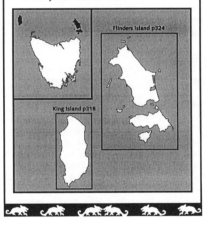

King Island is probably best known for its dairy produce (particularly its rich Brie cheese and cream), although kelp and large crayfish are other valuable exports. Its other main industry was the production of scheelite (used in the manufacture of armaments) until the mine and factory at Grassy closed in December 1990. After several years as a bit of a ghost town, Grassy now has tourist accommodation.

There are many sights to see and things to do on the island. Short walks along beaches, around lakes and through forest will ensure that you will see some of the plentiful wildlife. The calcified forest, kelp industries and rocky coastline are just some of the

THE ISLANDS

diverse features of this delightful island. A weekend visit is just not quite enough time to truly experience all the island has to offer.

The main township is Currie, which is also the main harbour for the island. It's close to the airport and most of the facilities are located here. The other notable settlements are Naracoopa on the east coast and Grassy to the south-east, which has the only other harbour on the island.

There is something to do on King Island nearly all year-round and it does not have the extremes of temperature change that occur in other parts of the country. However, summer is the ideal time if you are keen on water sports, while spring and autumn have many pleasant days.

## Information

For tourist information, ring ☎ 6462 1809 or Top Tours (☎ 6462 1245) on Main St.

## Lighthouses

King Island has four lighthouses to guard its treacherous seas. The one at Currie was built in 1880, while the one at Cape Wickham was built in 1861 and is the tallest in the southern hemisphere. Neither are open, but the latter is surrounded by attractive coastal scenery, and there is a cairn there to commemorate the lighthouse keepers. There is another lighthouse at Stokes Point, the most southern point of the island, while Cumberland lighthouse is south of Naracoopa on the eastern side of the island.

## Currie Museum

Currie Museum, on Lighthouse St, was originally the lighthouse keeper's cottage and is open daily from 2 to 4 pm except from July to mid-September. Entry is $2 for adults. The museum features extensive displays recalling maritime and other local history.

## Kelp Industry

Kelp Industries Pty Ltd, on Netherby Rd, was established in 1975. The factory is the only kelp processing plant in Australia and receives, dries and processes storm-cast bull kelp gathered from the rocks and

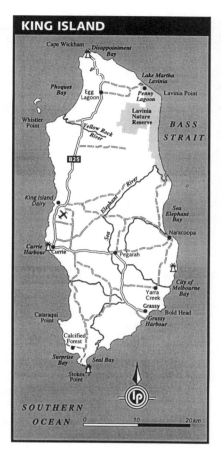

**KING ISLAND**

beaches around the island. From the road, you can see the kelp being air dried on racks. It is left on the racks for about two weeks, then kiln-dried and crushed. It is then shipped to Scotland where it is mixed with kelp from other countries to manufacture a variety of products including sauces, lotions and detergents.

## Calcified Forest

The Calcified Forest is in the south-western part of the island. A walk of 1km from the car park leads to a viewing platform from where the ancient petrified tree trunks can be seen. Some experts believe them to be up to 30 million years old.

## King Island Dairy
You must not go to King Island without visiting the King Island Dairy and sampling some of its products. The dairy is 8km north of Currie and just north of the airport, and is open weekdays from 9 am to 5 pm and Sunday and public holidays from 12.30 to 4 pm. The Brie, Cheddar and very thick cream are all available at discounted prices.

## Water Sports
Surf and freshwater fishing are popular, as is surfing. You can swim at many of the island's long, deserted beaches and freshwater lakes, or scuba dive among exotic marine life and accessible shipwrecks. King Island Dive Charters (☎ toll-free 1800 030 330 or 6461 1133) provides single dives for $72 and full-day diving trips for $129. Dive prices include tank, weight-belt, air per dive or, on the full-day trips, unlimited dives and lunch. The company also offers three, four and five-day packages.

## Horse Riding
King Island Trail Rides (☎ 6463 1147) offers guided horse rides daily for groups of up to four people. A half-day ride to the beach costs $30 per person, and novice and experienced riders are catered for.

## Cycling
If you're into cycling, hire a mountain bike from The Trend (☎ 6462 1360, 26 Edward St, Currie). Cycling is an excellent way to get around, as you can ride all the bush tracks.

## Other Activities
Playing golf and bushwalking are popular pastimes on the island. There is plenty of wildlife to observe, such as duck, quail, wallaby, platypus and seal. Tiger and brown snakes also inhabit the island, and you will see feral pheasant and flocks of wild turkey. What you won't see are rabbits and foxes.

In the summer months, a small colony of fairy penguins comes ashore at dusk at the end of the breakwater at Grassy. Care should be taken not to disturb them or dazzle them with bright lights.

## Organised Tours
King Island Bushwalks (☎ 6461 1276) runs a short, guided walk along the Yarra Creek Gorge on demand, which includes afternoon tea for $20.

Top Tours runs guided full-day tours, including lunch, to the northern or southern part of the island for $55 per person. It does pick-ups from accommodation places in and around Currie. It also offers a half-day tour departing at 2 pm, which includes afternoon tea, viewing the penguins at Grassy and a three course dinner.

King Island Coaches (☎ 6462 1138) runs full-day tours for $55 per person to Whickam and another around the south of the island. It also has a half-day tour of Currie for $25 per person including afternoon tea, and an evening penguin tour that departs half an hour before dusk for $25 including port and nibbles.

Driftwood 4WD Tours (☎ 6462 1180) offers guided day trips and shorter tours around the island that include morning and afternoon tea and lunch. Ring for prices.

## Special Events
The Festival of King Island is held annually in early March. It includes The Imperial 20 Foot Race, an art and craft competition/exhibition, the surfing carnival and the Queenscliff to Grassy Yacht Race. Following on from this is the King Island Show.

## Places to Stay
**Currie** Close to Currie, the *Bass Caravan Park (☎ 6462 1260)*, on North Rd, has onsite vans for $45 a double. Remember, you can't tow your own van over!

In Currie, *Gulhaven Holiday Homes (☎ 6462 1560, 11 Huxley St)* is a four bedroom, self-contained unit that sleeps up to eight people. The daily rate is $60 a double and $25 for each extra person. The *King*

*Island Colonial Lodge* (☎ *6462 1066, 13 Main St*) offers B&B with shared facilities for $57/67 a single/double.

*Boomerang by the Sea* (☎ *6462 1288*), high on a bluff overlooking the nine hole Currie Golf Course, has motel rooms at $80/100, which includes a continental breakfast. It has superb ocean views from all rooms and it's only a short walk from town.

*King Island A-Frame Holiday Homes* (☎ *6462 1260, 95 North Rd*) is 2km north of Currie. It offers self-contained units with great sea views; each unit sleeps six people and the cost is $96 a single or double with $18 for each extra person. The *King Island Gem Motel* (☎ *6462 1260*) has rooms for $90/100, including continental breakfast.

*Parers Hotel* (☎ *6462 1633*), in the centre of Currie, provides good suites for $65/95 and the main bar has a large open fireplace. The hotel provides easy access to shops, the harbour and golf course.

One kilometre west of Currie is *Devil's Gap Retreat* (☎ *6462 1180*), on Charles St, right on the foreshore. The self-contained units have sweeping ocean views and direct access to the beach north of Currie Harbour, but will set you back $126 a double with breakfast.

*St Andrews-King Island* (☎ *6462 1490*), on Netherby Rd, is a three bedroom house available for $100 a double.

*Wavewatcher Holiday Villas* (☎ *6462 1517, 18 Beach Rd*) overlooks the golf course and ocean. The two storey, self-contained units are $140 a double.

**Naracoopa** The *Naracoopa Holiday Units* (☎ *6461 1326*), on Beach Rd, has a seafront location close to the fishing jetty. The self-contained units are $80 a double and are nestled in their own private gardens on Sea Elephant Bay.

*Baudins* (☎ *6461 1110*), on The Esplanade, has self-contained units for up to $124 a double.

**Grassy** Grassy has slowly been redeveloping since the mine closed, and today *King Island Holiday Village* (☎ *6461 1177*) has a number of houses and units in the town for rent. Houses with spas and water views are $150, while self-contained units are $110; both prices include breakfast.

**Other Places to Stay** The *Yarra Creek Host Farm* (☎ *6461 1276*), on Yarra Creek Rd, 27km east of Currie, adjoins a nature reserve and caters for families or groups of up to five people for $80 a double. The price includes breakfast.

Another option is to camp in the bush; however this is only permitted at Penny Lagoon and Lake Martha Lavinia, the two large freshwater lakes at the northern end of the island. Access is by a sandy track off Haines Rd and the only facilities are bush toilets. The lakes are a favourite water-sport location with the locals and are large enough for sailing dinghies, windsurfers and water-skiing. It is advisable to carry in your own fresh water and a stove. Remember to carry out all your rubbish.

## Places to Eat

**Currie** There are many fine eating places in Currie within walking distance of most of the accommodation. The *Coffee Shop* serves a selection of light meals and sandwiches and is open daily, while the *King Island Bakery* serves home-made gourmet pies, which are an ideal snack on a cold day.

The *Jade Kingdom Chinese Restaurant* is fully licensed and serves eat-in or takeaway Chinese and Malaysian meals. The King Island Club has *Hoopers Restaurant* (and a bistro) and is a favourite with the local fishermen, with reasonably priced meals. The bistro at *Parers Hotel* also offers a fine selection of King Island fare.

A little more upmarket is the *Cataraqui Restaurant*, at Parers Hotel. Its à la carte menu offers a wide selection of the island's local produce. Likewise, the restaurant at *Boomerang by the Sea* (☎ *6462 1288*) is also à la carte and attracts locals and visitors alike with its spectacular ocean views. The restaurant features local seafood and beef, and bookings for nonresidents of the motel are essential.

Lake Pedder from White Bluff

The Tarkine Coast

Cradle Mountain and Lake Dove

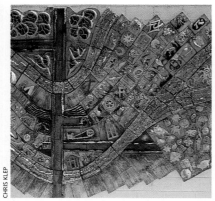

'Layers of Discovery' by Peter Alting, Beaconsfield

The Gordon Dam

Winter in the South-West of Tasmania

Crayfish are a popular item for the live export market.

*Nautilus Coffee Lounge* is open daily and specialises in crayfish rolls. The *Harbour Road Coffee Shop* is also open daily and serves local produce.

For cheap meals and snacks on Friday and Saturday nights, try the *golf club*. It has great views, and you don't need to be a member to visit.

**Naracoopa** For wonderful views over Naracoopa Bay, try *Baudins (☎ 6461 1110)*, which is an à la carte licensed restaurant. Bookings are essential. *Seashells Café* has light snacks and lunches.

**Grassy** There's a supermarket in the town, and the *Grassy Club* has a bar and bistro. At the time of writing, a restaurant and coffee shop were planned.

## Getting There & Away

Aus-Air (☎ toll-free 1800 331 256), Kendell (☎ toll-free 1800 338 894), King Island Airlines (☎ 9580 3777) and Tasair Regional Airlines (☎ toll-free 1800 062 900) have regular flights to the island. From Melbourne the standard economy rate with Aus-Air is $121, from Launceston $149. If you fly with Tasair, the fare from Burnie/Wynyard is $95, from Devonport $95, and from Hobart $175.

Most airlines offer package deals to the island, which vary depending on the season. High-season twin share packages from Melbourne to King Island with two nights accommodation and car hire start at around $400 a person. Brochures are available from the airlines or most travel agents. Due to the competitiveness of the airlines, prepaid package deals definitely offer the best value.

Kendall Airlines has daily flights from Tullamarine airport (Melbourne). On weekends a combination of the 7 am Saturday flight and the 3.40 pm flight on Sunday allows you to spend the best part of two full days on the island.

Aus-Air runs two or three flights a day from Moorabbin airport (Melbourne). You can also fly at 7.45 am on Saturday and return at 4.50 pm on Sunday for a weekend trip. The cheapest way to get to Moorabbin is by train to Cheltenham train station and then a taxi to the airport.

Aus-Air has packages from Melbourne that include air fares, accommodation and car hire on Flinders and King islands and in Launceston, and other packages that visit both islands from Melbourne.

## Getting Around

There is no public transport on the island; however the airlines can arrange airport transfers to Currie for around $7 per person each way and to Naracoopa or Grassy for about $29 per person each way. Hire car companies will meet you at the airport and bookings are highly recommended.

Most of the roads on the island are not sealed and there are no road safety signs. Drive carefully around the more remote areas because the roads can be a bit rough and narrow and there are several blind corners. Unless you have a 4WD, take extra care choosing which roads or tracks you take, or be prepared to dig yourself out of some sandy and muddy situations.

In Currie, you can rent cars from Cheaper Island Rentals (☎ 6462 1603) from around $60 a day with a $700 excess, or $65 a day with a $200 excess. Howell's Auto Rent (☎ 6462 1282) has cars for around $67 a day with a $750 excess.

## FLINDERS ISLAND

- **pop 1130**

Flinders Island is the largest of the 52 islands that comprise the Furneaux Group. It is approximately 60km long and 20km wide and is followed in size by Cape Barren and Clarke islands.

First charted in 1798 by the navigator Matthew Flinders, the Furneaux Group became a base for the Straitsmen, who not only slaughtered seals in their tens of thousands, but also indulged in a little piracy. Of the 120 or so ships wrecked on the islands' rocks, it is thought that quite a number were purposely lured there by sealers displaying false lights.

The most tragic part of Flinders Island's history, however, was its role in the virtual

The Cape Barren goose is no longer close to extinction thanks to its protected habitat.

annihilation of Tasmania's Aboriginal people. Between 1829 and 1834, those who had survived the state's martial law (which gave soldiers the right to arrest or shoot any Aboriginal person found in a settled area) were brought to the island to be resettled. Of the 135 survivors who were transported to Wybalenna (an Aboriginal word that means 'black man's house') to be 'civilised and educated', only 47 survived to make their final journey to Oyster Cove, near Hobart, in 1847.

Flinders Island has many attractions for the visitor. Its beaches, especially on the western side, are beautiful, and the fishing and scuba diving are good. There is no shortage of shipwrecks around the islands, some of which are clearly visible from the shore.

A more unusual pastime is fossicking for 'diamonds' (which are actually fragments of topaz) on the beach and creek at Killiecrankie Bay. At one time there were plenty of stones to be found, but there are fewer now, and the locals dive for them using special equipment.

Flinders Island has some great bushwalks, the most popular being the walk to the granite peaks of Mt Strzelecki, which affords some great views of the surrounding area. There are also a number of lookouts on the island, including Furneaux and Walkers Lookouts, almost in the centre of the island, plus Vinegar Hill in the south and Mt Tanner in the north.

The island's abundant vegetation supports a wide variety of wildlife, including more than 150 species of bird. One of the most well known is the Cape Barren goose. Its protected habitat and increasing numbers mean that it is no longer close to extinction. The other well-known species is the mutton bird, which was once hunted in large numbers. Drive slowly on the roads at night to avoid running over wallabies and other nocturnal wildlife.

Whitemark is the main administrative centre for the island and Lady Barron, in the south, is the main fishing area and deep water port. The main industries on Flinders Island are farming, fishing and seasonal mutton-birding.

Summer, spring and autumn are all good times to visit; however a sunny, winter weekend can also be very enjoyable.

## Information

Contact Thelma Shank at The Gem Shop (☎ 6359 2160) in Killiecrankie for any information and brochures about the island.

There are only four public telephones on the island. They are in Whitemark opposite the Interstate Hotel, near the wharf in Lady Barron, in the foyer of the Flinders Island Lodge and at Killiecrankie outside the general store. Petrol can be purchased in Whitemark and Lady Barron.

## Wybalenna Historic Site

The Wybalenna Historic Site is all that remains of this unfortunate settlement set up to 'care for' the Aboriginal people removed from mainland Tasmania. In truth, it was the scene of genocide, with most of those sent dying of disease. Because of its historical significance, this site is rated as the third most important historic site in the state. Close by are the cemetery and memorial chapel. In 1999 the site was returned to the descendants of those that had lived there.

THE ISLANDS

## Emita Museum

The Emita Museum, housed in what was the first government school on the island, displays a variety of Aboriginal artefacts as well as old sealing and sailing relics. It also has a large display on the mutton bird industry and is open on weekends from 2 to 5 pm; during summer it's also open from 2 to 5 pm on weekdays. The museum is staffed by volunteers and entry is by donation.

## Trousers Point

This is definitely worth a visit to explore the rocks and beaches. There are picnic tables, barbecues and toilets in the camping ground under the drooping sheoaks. The colourful rocks surrounding Trousers Point are easily accessible and offer great views of the Strzelecki peaks. It is a beautiful spot from which to watch the sunset.

## Bushwalking

Bushwalking is a popular activity for visitors to the island. *The Walks of Flinders Island* ($5.50, available from various shops on the island, including the general store and newsagents at Whitemark) gives information on a number of walks of varying lengths and difficulty. Walks along beach and coastal heath trails can be linked with hinterland and mountain tracks throughout the island.

The **Strzelecki Track** starts about 10km south of Whitemark and is approximately 4km long. The well signposted track ascends Mt Strzelecki to a height of 756m and, as you can imagine, in good weather the view from the summit over the Furneaux Group islands is spectacular. It is about a three to five hour return walk, and it is essential that you carry warm clothing, wet-weather gear, food and water at any time of the year.

## Rock Climbing

Rock climbers can find challenging rock stacks or granite walls. Mt Killiecrankie has some very steep granite faces rising from sea level. Although there is a soak at the camp site, you will need to take all your drinking water. The rock climbs within Strzelecki National Park and the ridge walk should only be attempted by experienced walkers and climbers.

## Fossicking

Rock hounds of another variety can find various localities in which to fossick for the elusive Killiecrankie diamond. The Gem Shop in Whitemark and Killiecrankie Enterprises (the general store) can advise lapidaries where to spend some time. The Gem Shop also conducts special fossicking tours.

## Scuba Diving

Scuba divers are also catered for on Flinders Island. There are several good locations on

### Mutton Birds

Each September, the mutton birds return to Flinders and other Bass Strait islands after a summer in the northern hemisphere, to clean out and repair their burrows from the previous year. They then head out to sea again before returning in November for the breeding season, which lasts until April. Eggs are then laid in a three day period, and the parents take it in turns, two weeks at a time, to incubate them.

Once their single chick has hatched, both parents feed the fledgling until mid-April, when all the adult birds depart, leaving the young to fend for themselves and hopefully to follow their parents north.

Unfortunately for the well fed little mutton birds, they make good eating, and once the adult birds leave their nests the 'birders', or mutton-bird hunters, move in.

THE ISLANDS

# FLINDERS ISLAND

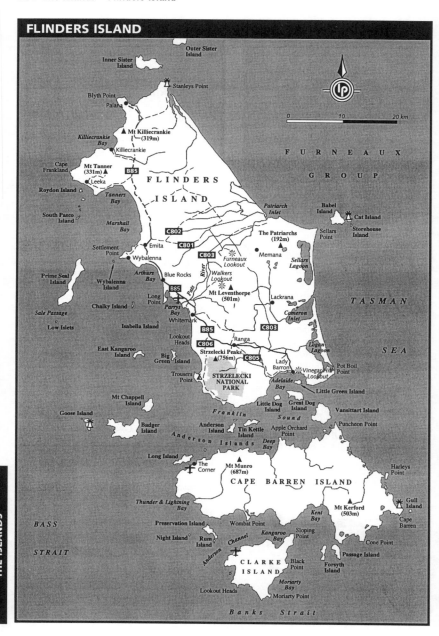

Outer Sister Island

Inner Sister Island

Stanleys Point

Blyth Point
Palana

0        10        20 km

Mt Killiecrankie
(319m)

*Killiecrankie Bay*

Killiecrankie

F  U  R  N  E  A  U  X

Cape Frankland

Mt Tanner
(331m)  B85

G  R  O  U  P

Leeka

F  L  I  N  D  E  R  S

Roydon Island

*Tanners Bay*

Babel Island

Cat Island

I  S  L  A  N  D

South Pasco Island

*Marshall Bay*

*Patriarch Inlet*

Storehouse Island

Sellars Point

C802

C801

The Patriarchs
(192m)

Settlement Point

Emita

Wybalenna

C803

*Furneaux Lookout*

Memana

*Sellars Lagoon*

Prime Seal Island

Wybalenna Island

*Arthurs Bay*

Blue Rocks

*Walkers Lookout*

T  A  S  M  A  N

Long Point  B85

*Parrys Bay*

Mt Leventhorpe
(501m)

Lackrana

Chalky Island

Whitemark

*Cameron Inlet*

Sale Passage

Low Islets

Isabella Island

B85

Ranga

C803

Lookout Heads

C806

*Logan Lagoon*

East Kangaroo Island

C805

Big Green Island

Strzelecki Peaks
(756m)

S  E  A

Lady Barron

Pot Boil Point

Trousers Point

STRZELECKI NATIONAL PARK

Vinegar Hill Lookout

*Adelaide Bay*

Little Green Island

Mt Chappell Island

*Franklin  Sound*

Little Dog Island

Great Dog Island

Vansittart Island

Goose Island

Badger Island

Anderson Island

Tin Kettle Island

Apple Orchard Point

Puncheon Point

*Anderson  Islands*

*Deep Bay*

Long Island

The Corner

Mt Munro
(687m)

Harleys Point

C  A  P  E    B  A  R  R  E  N    I  S  L  A  N  D

*Thunder & Lightning Bay*

*Kent Bay*

Mt Kerford
(503m)

Gull Island

B  A  S  S

Preservation Island

Wombat Point

*Kangaroo Bay*

Sloping Point

Cape Barren

S  T  R  A  I  T

Night Island

Rum Island

*Anderson  Channel*

Black Point

Cone Point

Passage Island

C  L  A  R  K  E
I  S  L  A  N  D

Forsyth Island

*Moriarty Bay*

Lookout Heads

Moriarty Point

B  a  n  k  s    S  t  r  a  i  t

the northern and western coasts. In many places you can enter from the beach or shelving rocks. The water is warmest between January and April and coldest between June and September. Non-commercial diving licences for abalone, crayfish and scallops can be obtained from police stations at Whitemark and Lady Barron. Flinders Island Dive (☎ 6359 8429), at Emita, hires out tanks and weight-belts. It also offers boat charter: a half-day charter with tanks, air, weight-belts and a dive is $60 a person.

## Fishing
Rock fishing along the southern, northern and north-western coasts is good all year. Bait is easily obtained from the rocks and fishing tackle can be purchased from many stores; however, you need to bring your own rod. Beach fishing is popular on the eastern coast and from Red Bluff. The North-East River also has good fishing.

Corporate Fishing Tours (☎ 9654 2022) offers fishing charters of various lengths and prices. It costs $750 to charter a boat for a day's fishing. Alternatively, for $60 a day the company will take you surf fishing.

Flinders Island Adventures (☎ 6359 4507), in Whitemark, charters Powercats for fishing. It costs between $650 and $750 to charter a boat for a day, and bookings are essential.

Killiecrankie Enterprises (☎ 6359 8560) charters its boat, *Maximum*, for fishing or sightseeing for $65 an hour, $250 a half-day or $500 a full day for up to five people.

## Cycling
Mountain bikes are available for hire from Flinders Island Bike Hire (☎ 6359 2000) for $10 per day. You can arrange to collect the bikes from the airport on arrival. Most of the island's roads are fairly level or gently undulating, with good grades, although many are gravel.

## Organised Tours
Flinders Island Adventures (☎ 6359 4507, Whitemark) has full and half-day 4WD tours of the island for $82 and $55 per person, respectively.

Jimmy's Island Tours (☎ 6359 2112, Whitemark) runs full-day coach tours for around $70 per person as well.

Leafmoor Four Wheeler Tours (☎ 6359 3517) takes four wheel motor bike tours of one to three hours through the hills on the eastern side of Mt Strzelecki down to a beach for $30 an hour.

Mutton birds, or short-tailed shearwaters, whose migratory path from Japan to Australia covers some 15,000km, can be found on Flinders Island. Flinders Island Adventures runs evening tours for $25 a head aboard the *Strait Lady*, from December to March from Lady Barron, to see these birds on the small islands in Adelaide Bay.

## Places to Stay
**Whitemark** The *Flinders Park Units* (☎ 6359 2188, Bluff Rd) is 5km north of Whitemark, right next to the airport. It has three *en suite* cabins as well as cabins with communal amenities at $55 a double.

Built in 1911, the *Flinders Island Interstate Hotel* (☎ 6359 2114) is in the centre of Whitemark and has rooms for $48/75. Renovated in heritage style, it's a comfortable hotel within easy walking distance of shops and other facilities.

Other accommodation in and around Whitemark is mainly holiday units and cottages. *Bulloke Holiday Units* (☎ 6359 9709), on Butter Factory Rd, is a three bedroom unit costing $75 a double. *Seaview Cottage* (☎ 6359 2011), 5km south of Whitemark, is a small unit on a farm property that sleeps up to four people. You can rent it for $65 a double plus $10 for each extra adult.

Farther afield is the *Boat Harbour Beach House* (☎ 6359 6510), 45km north-west of Whitemark, which is a three bedroom unit overlooking the beach for $75 double plus $10 for each extra adult.

**Lady Barron** The *Nunamina Hostel* (☎ 6359 3617), on Franklin Parade, provides budget accommodation in separate rooms with shared facilities and linen provided for $20 a night.

*Lady Barron Holiday House* (☎ *6359 3555)*, on Franklin Parade, is a three bedroom unit that costs $70 a double; *Bucks at Lady Barron* (☎ *6233 3055)*, on Franklin Parade, is another three bedroom unit on the same street for $70/90.

*Yaringa Holiday Units* (☎ *6359 4522)*, on Holloway St, has three units at $75/95. For $80 a single or double, you can also stay at *Felicity's Cottage* (☎ *6359 3641)* on the same street.

Overlooking the picturesque Franklin Sound, rooms at the *Flinders Island Lodge* (☎ *6359 3521)* cost $90 to $148 a double including a continental breakfast. Rooms are spacious and the service is friendly.

**Lackrana** The *Echo Hills Holiday Units* (☎ *6359 6509, Madeleys Rd)* is 25km from Whitemark on the east coast of the island, at the foot of the Darling Ranges; the cottages cost $75 a double.

**Memana** The *Carnsdale Holiday Home* (☎ *6359 9718)* is 28km east of Whitemark. This four bedroom unit costs $80 a double and is in a quiet farm setting. *Lisa's Cottage* (☎ *6359 6530)* is a self-contained home for $66 a double.

**Killiecrankie** The *Oakridge Holiday Home* (☎ *6359 2160)*, in Killiecrankie Bay, is a three bedroom home for $45 a double.

*Killiecrankie Holiday House* (☎ *6359 8560, or check at Killiecrankie Enterprises)* has self-contained accommodation for up to 10 people for $35 a person twin share plus $10 for each extra person.

Killiecrankie also has a very basic free camping and picnic area with barbecues, toilets and cold showers.

### Places to Eat

**Whitemark** At the *Bakery* in Whitemark you can buy pies, bread and cold drinks on the weekdays, while *Sweet Surprises Coffee Shop* is a popular café open daily except Sunday.

The *Interstate Hotel* (☎ *6359 2114)*, in the centre of Whitemark, serves a range of moderately priced counter lunches and dinners from Monday to Friday and dinner on Saturday night in the dining room and public bar. Another place for dinner is the *Whitemark Sports Club* (☎ *6359 2220)*, which has a cosy restaurant with a quality menu. Meals are also available in the bistro throughout the week in summer. The Club has its own bottle shop and bookings for the restaurant are necessary.

**Lady Barron** Patterson's Store is open daily and sells basic supplies. It's also a post office and Commonwealth Bank agency and sells fuel.

The restaurant at the *Flinders Island Lodge* (☎ *6359 3521)* has a good selection of bistro meals every day. It also has a lovely outlook over Franklin Sound to the distant peaks on Cape Barron Island.

**Killiecrankie** The only place to buy food is at *Killiecrankie Enterprises*, which is the general store, which has snacks and hot and cold drinks.

### Shopping

Flinders Island fleece products are available from Killarney (☎ 6359 6509) at Lackrana. You can purchase fine quality yarns and knitwear, some of which is locally spun and dyed. Look for the 'Open' sign on weekdays and most Saturday mornings or phone for an appointment.

Killiecrankie 'diamonds' are actually a semi-precious stone called topaz. Usually they are clear; however some can be purchased with a pale blue or pink colouring. The Gem Shop in Whitemark and Killiecrankie Enterprises sells cut stones for around $40 a carat. Uncut stones can also be bought. Both shops offer friendly service and fossick for their own stones.

### Getting There & Away

**Air** Aus-Air (☎ toll-free 1800 331 256) flies from Melbourne for $153, from Traralgon (also in Victoria) for $129 and from Launceston for $113; Island Airlines (☎ toll-free 1800 818 455) flies the same routes for similar prices.

By far the best way to see the island is by using one of the many package deals available. These provide return air fares, accommodation and car hire with unlimited kilometres. On a package deal, for two or more nights, the cost savings mean the car hire is almost free compared with paying separately for these services. High-season twin share packages from Melbourne to Flinders Island with two nights accommodation and car hire start at around $450.

Island Airlines (☎ toll-free 1800 818 826) has air fare, accommodation and car hire high-season packages from Melbourne for $803 for five nights. Aus-Air has packages from Melbourne that include air fares, accommodation and car hire on Flinders and King islands, and in Launceston, and other packages that visit both islands from Melbourne.

Corporate Fishing Tours (☎ 9654 2022) has a $650 package from Melbourne that includes air fares, two days fishing, accommodation, gear and bait.

**Ferry** The Southern Shipping Company (☎ 6356 1753) runs a ferry from Bridport on the north-east coast of Tasmania to Flinders Island and return once a week on Monday night or Tuesday morning. The return fare for a driver and one car can be anything from $340 to $595, depending on the season and size of the vehicle. The single passenger fare is $70 return and the trip takes seven to eight hours one way. Once a month this ferry continues on to Port Welshpool in Victoria. Try to book at the beginning of the month for the Port Welshpool service, as it runs intermittently, usually around the end of the month. The return fare from Bridport for a car and driver on this service is actually between $100 and $500, depending on the season and size of the vehicle (because the government subsidises interstate ferry travel), and you can stay on Flinders Island for up to two weeks.

## Getting Around
There is no public transport on the island. Aus-Air provides airport transfers to Whitemark for a fee. Hire car companies will meet you at the airport and bookings are highly recommended.

There are many unsealed roads on the island, so you'll need to drive carefully, particularly around the more remote areas. Unless you have a 4WD, take extra care choosing which roads or tracks you take. You may find yourself in some sandy or slippery places.

Bowman-Lees Car & Mini Bus Hire (☎ 6359 2388) rents late-model vehicles for $60 a day with a $600 insurance excess and earlier model cars for $50 a day.

## OTHER ISLANDS
## Cape Barren Island
Cape Barren Island is to the south of Flinders Island and is the only other island in the Furneaux Group to have a permanent settlement. Kent Bay on the southern side was the first settlement south of Sydney.

The main settlement on Cape Barren Island, known as **The Corner**, has a small school, church and medical centre. This was the area given over for the resettlement of the Straitsmen from Flinders Island in 1881. Fishing is the main industry, although there are several cattle farms.

**Things to Do** For experienced bushwalkers, the circuit walk of the shoreline offers great coastal views, including the wreck of the *Farsund*, lovely beaches and interesting rock formations. Mt Kerford, at 503m, offers quite a challenge, while Mt Munro, at 687m, can be tackled from the north. Water is less of a problem here than on Flinders Island, with many fresh water sources available.

For those with a reasonable level of fitness, a day walk to the summit of Mt Munro on a clear day provides spectacular views of the surrounding area. Access is from The Corner, up to Big Grassy Hill and along the ridge to the summit.

**Getting There & Away** Flights to Cape Barren Island are infrequent and it would be better to arrange a charter flight from Melbourne or Launceston if you have the

THE ISLANDS

numbers. Alternatively you can fly to Flinders Island and then arrange a boat charter to take you across allowing you to cache supplies on the way to your drop-off point. You can arrange to charter the *Strait Lady* from Flinders Island Adventures (☎ 6359 4507) on Flinders Island for this purpose.

## Swan Island

There are not many islands that you can rent and be the only guests on at reasonably low prices. Swan Island is one of the exceptions. The owners live here and the other house on the island can be rented.

Just 3km off the north-east coast of Tasmania, this small island is 3km long and is dominated by its lighthouse. The lighthouse was built in 1845 and automated in 1986 when the government sold the island. The main attraction of coming here is a get-away-from-it-all experience. Many sea birds nest here, and you can watch the shearwaters and penguins returning to their nests around sunset. The island has several beaches, and fishing and scuba diving are popular.

**Places to Stay** You can stay at the *Swan Island Guesthouse (☎ 6357 2211)*, which is the old lighthouse keeper's quarters. It costs $50 a person and sleeps up to six.

**Getting There & Away** There is an airstrip for light planes, and flights can be arranged from Bridport, Launceston or Flinders Island. Discuss flights with the owners when making your booking.

## Macquarie Island

Discovered in 1820, this isolated island in the Southern Ocean is part of Tasmania. It's 1500km to the south-east of Hobart and is classified as a sub-Antarctic island. For a long time the only visitors to its rocky shores were there for the purposes of harvesting its abundant wildlife. In 1933, after pressure from Antarctic explorers, the island was declared a wildlife reserve, and it contains some important breeding sites for four species of penguin (including the king penguin) and elephant seals. It has been nominated for World Heritage listing. Currently it is managed by the Department of Parks Wildlife and Heritage. There is a permanent scientific base on the northern end of the island.

Most visitors to the island are scientists undertaking research. Ordinary visitors are allowed and they mostly come from cruise ships, the only way to get here is by ship. To protect the wildlife and environment, access is only allowed to specified areas.

Cruises to Macquarie Island are usually part of a general Antarctic tour, which costs about $400 a day. If you have the chance to visit Macquarie Island, then do so, as it is a unique place. Contact Adventure Associates (☎ 02 9389 7466), the Sydney agents for the British/US operator Super Nova Tours, for details.

# Lonely Planet Guides by Region

onely Planet is known worldwide for publishing practical, reliable and no-nonsense travel information in our guides and on our Web site. The Lonely Planet list covers just about every accessible part of the world. Currently there are 16 series: Travel guides, Shoestring guides, Condensed guides, Phrasebooks, Read This First, Healthy Travel, Walking guides, Cycling guides, Watching Wildlife guides, Pisces Diving & Snorkeling guides, City Maps, Road Atlases, Out to Eat, World Food, Journeys travel literature and Pictorials.

**AFRICA** Africa on a shoestring • Botswana • Cairo • Cairo City Map • Cape Town • Cape Town City Map • East Africa • Egypt • Egyptian Arabic phrasebook • Ethiopia, Eritrea & Djibouti • Ethiopian Amharic phrasebook • The Gambia & Senegal • Healthy Travel Africa • Kenya • Malawi • Morocco • Moroccan Arabic phrasebook • Mozambique • Namibia • Read This First: Africa • South Africa, Lesotho & Swaziland • Southern Africa • Southern Africa Road Atlas • Swahili phrasebook • Tanzania, Zanzibar & Pemba • Trekking in East Africa • Tunisia • Watching Wildlife East Africa • Watching Wildlife Southern Africa • West Africa • World Food Morocco • Zambia • Zimbabwe, Botswana & Namibia
**Travel Literature:** Mali Blues: Traveling to an African Beat • The Rainbird: A Central African Journey • Songs to an African Sunset: A Zimbabwean Story

**AUSTRALIA & THE PACIFIC** Aboriginal Australia & the Torres Strait Islands •Auckland • Australia • Australian phrasebook • Australia Road Atlas • Cycling Australia • Cycling New Zealand • Fiji • Fijian phrasebook • Healthy Travel Australia, NZ & the Pacific • Islands of Australia's Great Barrier Reef • Melbourne • Melbourne City Map • Micronesia • New Caledonia • New South Wales • New Zealand • Northern Territory • Outback Australia • Out to Eat – Melbourne • Out to Eat – Sydney • Papua New Guinea • Pidgin phrasebook • Queensland • Rarotonga & the Cook Islands • Samoa • Solomon Islands • South Australia • South Pacific • South Pacific phrasebook • Sydney • Sydney City Map • Sydney Condensed • Tahiti & French Polynesia • Tasmania • Tonga • Tramping in New Zealand • Vanuatu • Victoria • Walking in Australia • Watching Wildlife Australia • Western Australia
**Travel Literature:** Islands in the Clouds: Travels in the Highlands of New Guinea • Kiwi Tracks: A New Zealand Journey • Sean & David's Long Drive

**CENTRAL AMERICA & THE CARIBBEAN** Bahamas, Turks & Caicos • Baja California • Belize, Guatemala & Yucatán • Bermuda • Central America on a shoestring • Costa Rica • Costa Rica Spanish phrasebook • Cuba • Cycling Cuba • Dominican Republic & Haiti • Eastern Caribbean • Guatemala • Havana • Healthy Travel Central & South America • Jamaica • Mexico • Mexico City • Panama • Puerto Rico • Read This First: Central & South America • Virgin Islands • World Food Caribbean • World Food Mexico • Yucatán
**Travel Literature:** Green Dreams: Travels in Central America

**EUROPE** Amsterdam • Amsterdam City Map • Amsterdam Condensed • Andalucía • Athens • Austria • Baltic States phrasebook • Barcelona • Barcelona City Map • Belgium & Luxembourg • Berlin • Berlin City Map • Britain • British phrasebook • Brussels, Bruges & Antwerp • Brussels City Map • Budapest • Budapest City Map • Canary Islands • Catalunya & the Costa Brava • Central Europe • Central Europe phrasebook • Copenhagen • Corfu & the Ionians • Corsica • Crete • Crete Condensed • Croatia • Cycling Britain • Cycling France • Cyprus • Czech & Slovak Republics • Czech phrasebook • Denmark • Dublin • Dublin City Map • Dublin Condensed • Eastern Europe • Eastern Europe phrasebook • Edinburgh • Edinburgh City Map • England • Estonia, Latvia & Lithuania • Europe on a shoestring • Europe phrasebook • Finland • Florence • Florence City Map • France • Frankfurt City Map • Frankfurt Condensed • French phrasebook • Georgia, Armenia & Azerbaijan • Germany • German phrasebook • Greece • Greek Islands • Greek phrasebook • Hungary • Iceland, Greenland & the Faroe Islands • Ireland • Italian phrasebook • Italy • Kraków • Lisbon • The Loire • London • London City Map • London Condensed • Madrid • Madrid City Map • Malta • Mediterranean Europe • Milan, Turin & Genoa • Moscow • Munich • Netherlands • Normandy • Norway • Out to Eat – London • Out to Eat – Paris • Paris • Paris City Map • Paris Condensed • Poland • Polish phrasebook • Portugal • Portuguese phrasebook • Prague • Prague City Map • Provence & the Côte d'Azur • Read This First: Europe • Rhodes & the Dodecanese • Romania & Moldova • Rome • Rome City Map • Rome Condensed • Russia, Ukraine & Belarus • Russian phrasebook • Scandinavian & Baltic Europe • Scandinavian phrasebook • Scotland • Sicily • Slovenia • South-West France • Spain • Spanish phrasebook • Stockholm • St Petersburg • St Petersburg City Map • Sweden • Switzerland • Tuscany • Ukrainian phrasebook • Venice • Vienna • Wales • Walking in Britain • Walking in France • Walking in Ireland • Walking in Italy • Walking in Scotland • Walking in Spain • Walking in Switzerland • Western Europe • World Food France • World Food Greece • World Food Ireland • World Food Italy • World Food Spain **Travel Literature:** After Yugoslavia • Love and War in the Apennines • The Olive Grove: Travels in Greece • On the Shores of the Mediterranean • Round Ireland in Low Gear • A Small Place in Italy

# Lonely Planet Mail Order

onely Planet products are distributed worldwide. They are also available by mail order from Lonely Planet, so if you have difficulty finding a title please write to us. North and South American residents should write to 150 Linden St, Oakland, CA 94607, USA; European and African residents should write to 10a Spring Place, London NW5 3BH, UK; and residents of other countries to Locked Bag 1, Footscray, Victoria 3011, Australia.

**INDIAN SUBCONTINENT & THE INDIAN OCEAN** Bangladesh • Bengali phrasebook • Bhutan • Delhi • Goa • Healthy Travel Asia & India • Hindi & Urdu phrasebook • India • India & Bangladesh City Map • Indian Himalaya • Karakoram Highway • Kathmandu City Map • Kerala • Madagascar • Maldives • Mauritius, Réunion & Seychelles • Mumbai (Bombay) • Nepal • Nepali phrasebook • North India • Pakistan • Rajasthan • Read This First: Asia & India • South India • Sri Lanka • Sri Lanka phrasebook • Tibet • Tibetan phrasebook • Trekking in the Indian Himalaya • Trekking in the Karakoram & Hindukush • Trekking in the Nepal Himalaya • World Food India **Travel Literature:** The Age of Kali: Indian Travels and Encounters • Hello Goodnight: A Life of Goa • In Rajasthan • Maverick in Madagascar • A Season in Heaven: True Tales from the Road to Kathmandu • Shopping for Buddhas • A Short Walk in the Hindu Kush • Slowly Down the Ganges

**MIDDLE EAST & CENTRAL ASIA** Bahrain, Kuwait & Qatar • Central Asia • Central Asia phrasebook • Dubai • Farsi (Persian) phrasebook • Hebrew phrasebook • Iran • Israel & the Palestinian Territories • Istanbul • Istanbul City Map • Istanbul to Cairo • Istanbul to Kathmandu • Jerusalem • Jerusalem City Map • Jordan • Lebanon • Middle East • Oman & the United Arab Emirates • Syria • Turkey • Turkish phrasebook • World Food Turkey • Yemen **Travel Literature:** Black on Black: Iran Revisited • Breaking Ranks: Turbulent Travels in the Promised Land • The Gates of Damascus • Kingdom of the Film Stars: Journey into Jordan

**NORTH AMERICA** Alaska • Boston • Boston City Map • Boston Condensed • British Columbia • California & Nevada • California Condensed • Canada • Chicago • Chicago City Map • Chicago Condensed • Florida • Georgia & the Carolinas • Great Lakes • Hawaii • Hiking in Alaska • Hiking in the USA • Honolulu & Oahu City Map • Las Vegas • Los Angeles • Los Angeles City Map • Louisiana & the Deep South • Miami • Miami City Map • Montreal • New England • New Orleans • New Orleans City Map • New York City • New York City City Map • New York City Condensed • New York, New Jersey & Pennsylvania • Oahu • Out to Eat – San Francisco • Pacific Northwest • Rocky Mountains • San Diego & Tijuana • San Francisco • San Francisco City Map • Seattle • Seattle City Map • Southwest • Texas • Toronto • USA • USA phrasebook • Vancouver • Vancouver City Map • Virginia & the Capital Region • Washington, DC • Washington, DC City Map • World Food New Orleans **Travel Literature:** Caught Inside: A Surfer's Year on the California Coast • Drive Thru America

**NORTH-EAST ASIA** Beijing • Beijing City Map • Cantonese phrasebook • China • Hiking in Japan • Hong Kong & Macau • Hong Kong City Map • Hong Kong Condensed • Japan • Japanese phrasebook • Korea • Korean phrasebook • Kyoto • Mandarin phrasebook • Mongolia • Mongolian phrasebook • Seoul • Shanghai • South-West China • Taiwan • Tokyo • Tokyo Condensed • World Food Hong Kong • World Food Japan **Travel Literature:** In Xanadu: A Quest • Lost Japan

**SOUTH AMERICA** Argentina, Uruguay & Paraguay • Bolivia • Brazil • Brazilian phrasebook • Buenos Aires • Buenos Aires City Map • Chile & Easter Island • Colombia • Ecuador & the Galapagos Islands • Healthy Travel Central & South America • Latin American Spanish phrasebook • Peru • Quechua phrasebook • Read This First: Central & South America • Rio de Janeiro • Rio de Janeiro City Map • Santiago de Chile • South America on a shoestring • Trekking in the Patagonian Andes • Venezuela **Travel Literature:** Full Circle: A South American Journey

**SOUTH-EAST ASIA** Bali & Lombok • Bangkok • Bangkok City Map • Burmese phrasebook • Cambodia • Cycling Vietnam, Laos & Cambodia • East Timor phrasebook • Hanoi • Healthy Travel Asia & India • Hill Tribes phrasebook • Ho Chi Minh City (Saigon) • Indonesia • Indonesian phrasebook • Indonesia's Eastern Islands • Java • Lao phrasebook • Laos • Malay phrasebook • Malaysia, Singapore & Brunei • Myanmar (Burma) • Philippines • Pilipino (Tagalog) phrasebook • Read This First: Asia & India • Singapore • Singapore City Map • South-East Asia on a shoestring • South-East Asia phrasebook • Thailand • Thailand's Islands & Beaches • Thailand, Vietnam, Laos & Cambodia Road Atlas • Thai phrasebook • Vietnam • Vietnamese phrasebook • World Food Indonesia • World Food Thailand • World Food Vietnam

**ALSO AVAILABLE:** Antarctica • The Arctic • The Blue Man: Tales of Travel, Love and Coffee • Brief Encounters: Stories of Love, Sex & Travel • Buddhist Stupas in Asia: The Shape of Perfection • Chasing Rickshaws • The Last Grain Race • Lonely Planet … On the Edge: Adventurous Escapades from Around the World • Lonely Planet Unpacked • Lonely Planet Unpacked Again • Not the Only Planet: Science Fiction Travel Stories • Ports of Call: A Journey by Sea • Sacred India • Travel Photography: A Guide to Taking Better Pictures • Travel with Children • Tuvalu: Portrait of an Island Nation

# Index

## Text

## Boxed Text

# MAP LEGEND

## BOUNDARIES

▬▪▬▪▬▬▪▬ ..............International
▬▪▬▪▬▪▬ ..................State

## HYDROGRAPHY

.....................Coastline
.................River, Creek
...................River Flow
..............................Lake
..........Intermittent Lake
.......................Salt Lake
◎ ➤➤.............Spring, Rapids
.............................Swamp
➤➤➤.......................Waterfalls

## ROUTES & TRANSPORT

...................Freeway
...................Highway
...................Major Road
...................Minor Road
======..............Unsealed Road
...................City Highway
...................City Road
...................City Street, Lane

..........Pedestrian Mall
....Train Route & Station
....Light Rail Route & Stop
— Ⓜ — Underground & Station
..........................Cable
...................Walking Track
...................Bicycle Track
...................Ferry Route

## AREA FEATURES

.....................Beach
.....................Building
.....................Market
✿ ............Park, Gardens
............Rocks
............Urban Area

## MAP SYMBOLS

✈ .....................Airport
✚ .....................Airfield
Θ .....................Bank
⌒ .....................Cave
⊞ ⓗ .....................Church
.....................Cliff
ſ .....................Golf Course
⊕ .....................Hospital
⛩ .....................Lighthouse
✳ .....................Lookout
✕ .....................Mine
⚊ .....................Monument
▲ .....................Mountain
🏛 .....................Museum, Art Gallery
♣ .....................National, State Park

■ .....................Place to Stay
Å .....................Camping Ground
🚐 .....................Caravan Park

▼ .....................Place to Eat
🍴 .....................Pub, Entertainment
📷 .....................Picnic Area

⊙ CAPITAL..........National Capital
◎ CAPITAL ..............State Capital
● CITY ...........................City
● Town ...........................Town
● Town ...................Small Town

← .....................One Way Street
🅿 .....................Parking
★ .....................Police Station
✉ .....................Post Office
❖ .....................Shopping Centre
⚡ .....................Skiing, Downhill
🏛 .....................Stately Building
▭ .....................Swimming Pool
🚻 .....................Toilet
ℹ .....................Tourist Information
⊖ .....................Transport
🔺 .....................Trekking Camp
🔲 .....................Trekking Hut
🔳 .....................Trekking Lookout
⚘ .....................Winery

*Note: not all symbols displayed above appear in this book*

---

# LONELY PLANET OFFICES

**Australia**
Locked Bag 1, Footscray, Victoria 3011
☎ 03 8379 8000  fax 03 8379 8111
email: talk2us@lonelyplanet.com.au

**USA**
150 Linden St, Oakland, CA 94607
☎ 510 893 8555  TOLL FREE: 800 275 8555
fax 510 893 8572
email: info@lonelyplanet.com

**UK**
10a Spring Place, London NW5 3BH
☎ 020 7428 4800  fax 020 7428 4828
email: go@lonelyplanet.co.uk

**France**
1 rue du Dahomey, 75011 Paris
☎ 01 55 25 33 00  fax 01 55 25 33 01
email: bip@lonelyplanet.fr
www.lonelyplanet.fr

**World Wide Web: www.lonelyplanet.com *or* AOL keyword: lp**
**Lonely Planet Images: lpi@lonelyplanet.com.au**